*Everyman, I will go with thee,*
*and be thy guide*

THE EVERYMAN
LIBRARY

*The Everyman Library was founded by J. M. Dent
in 1906. He chose the name Everyman because he wanted
to make available the best books ever written in every
field to the greatest number of people at the cheapest possible
price. He began with Boswell's 'Life of Johnson';
his one thousandth title was Aristotle's 'Metaphysics',
by which time sales exceeded forty million.*

*Today Everyman paperbacks remain true to
J. M. Dent's aims and high standards, with a wide range
of titles at affordable prices in editions which address
the needs of today's readers. Each new text is reset to give
a clear, elegant page and to incorporate the latest thinking
and scholarship. Each book carries the pilgrim logo,
the character in 'Everyman', a medieval morality play,
a proud link between Everyman
past and present.*

# SHAKESPEARE
# MADE FIT
## Restoration Adaptations of Shakespeare

*Selected and edited by*
### SANDRA CLARK

*Birkbeck College, University of London*

**EVERYMAN**
J. M. DENT · LONDON
CHARLES E. TUTTLE
VERMONT

J. M. Dent
Orion Publishing Group
Orion House
5 Upper St Martin's Lane, London WC2H 9EA
and
Charles E. Tuttle Co., Inc.
28 South Main Street,
Rutland, Vermont 05701, USA

Photoset by Deltatype Ltd, Birkenhead, Merseyside
Printed in Great Britain by
The Guernsey Press Co. Ltd, Guernsey, C.I.

British Library Cataloguing-in-Publication Data is available
upon request

ISBN 0 460 87746 1

# CONTENTS

# ILLUSTRATIONS

—

# NOTE ON THE DRAMATISTS AND EDITOR

Details of the lives of JOHN LACY, JOHN DRYDEN, WILLIAM DAVENANT, NAHUM TATE and COLLEY CIBBER can be found in the Chronology of the Dramatists' Lives and Times, pp. viii–xxxix.

SANDRA CLARK is Reader in Renaissance Literature at Birkbeck College, University of London. She has published books and articles on Elizabethan and Jacobean literature, particularly popular prose and drama. Her most recent book is *The Plays of Beaumont and Fletcher: Sexual Themes and Dramatic Representation* (Hemel Hempstead, 1994), and she has edited *Amorous Rites: Elizabethan Erotic Verse* (1994) for Everyman Paperbacks.

# CHRONOLOGY OF THE DRAMATISTS' LIVES

| Year | Life |
|------|------|
| 1606 | William Davenant born, second son of John Davenant, an Oxford tavern keeper and graduate of Emmanuel College, Cambridge, and Jane, née Shepherd, possibly with Shakespeare as his godfather |

# CHRONOLOGY OF THEIR TIMES

| Year | Artistic Events | Historical Events |
|------|-----------------|-------------------|
| 1606 | Birth of Killigrew; Shakespeare, *Macbeth*; Jonson, *Volpone*; Middleton (?) *The Revenger's Tragedy* | |
| 1607 | Birth of Milton; Shakespeare, *Antony and Cleopatra*; Beaumont, *The Knight of the Burning Pestle* | English settlement in Virginia; land in Ulster given to English and Scottish settlers |
| 1609 | Spenser, *The Faerie Queene*, published with the *Cantos of Mutabilitie*; Shakespeare, *Sonnets*; Beaumont and Fletcher, *Philaster* | |
| 1611 | Shakespeare, *The Winter's Tale*, *The Tempest*; Spenser's *Works* published in folio; Authorised version of the Bible; Chapman completes translation of the *Iliad*; Beaumont and Fletcher, *The Maid's Tragedy* | |
| 1612 | Webster, *The White Devil* | Death of Prince Henry, King James's heir |
| 1613 | The Globe theatre burns down; Webster, *The Duchess of Malfi*; Shakespeare and Fletcher, *The Two Noble Kinsmen*; Shakespeare retires to Stratford around this time | Marriage of James's daughter, Princess Elizabeth, to Frederick, Elector of Palatine; Essex divorce case |

*Year*      *Life*

1615      John Lacy born near Doncaster

1624      Davenant marries Mary (surname unknown) and joins
          the household of Fulke Greville where he lives
          intermittently until 1628 when Greville is murdered

1626      Davenant's military career begins; he writes *The Tragedy
          of Albovine, King of the Lombards*, a revenge play,
          published in 1629 but never performed

| Year | Artistic Events | Historical Events |
| --- | --- | --- |
| 1614 | Chapman, translation of the Odyssey, Books 1–12; Ralegh, The History of the World; Globe theatre rebuilt | Napier invents logarithms |
| 1615 | Chapman, translation of the Odyssey, Books 13–24 | |
| 1616 | Death of Shakespeare; Jonson's Works published in folio; James I, Works | Trial of Earl and Countess of Somerset for the murder of Sir Thomas Overbury; Harvey lectures on his discovery of the circulation of the blood |
| 1618 | | Beginning of the Thirty Years' War; execution of Ralegh |
| 1620 | Bacon, Novum Organum | Voyage of the Pilgrim Fathers in the Mayflower to America; first African slaves imported to America |
| 1621 | Burton, The Anatomy of Melancholy | First Parliament since 1614; impeachment of Bacon |
| 1622 | Completion of Inigo Jones's Banqueting House at Whitehall; Middleton and Rowley, The Changeling; Fletcher and Massinger, The Sea Voyage | James dissolves Parliament |
| 1623 | Shakespeare, First Folio | Prince Charles and the Duke of Buckingham in Madrid, negotiating a Spanish marriage for the prince |
| 1624 | Donne, Devotions upon Emergent Occasions | Virginia becomes a Crown colony |
| 1625 | | Death of James I; succession of Charles I, who marries the French Catholic Henrietta Maria; war with Spain |
| 1626 | Death of Bacon; Sandys's translation of Ovid's Metamorphoses | Impeachment of Buckingham, assassinated two years later |

*Year*     *Life*

1627      Davenant's theatrical career begins with his tragedy, *The Cruel Brother*, acted by the King's Men, published in 1630

1629      Davenant writes *The Collonell*, a tragicomedy, never performed but published in 1673 as *The Siege*; and *The Just Italian*, performed at the Blackfriars theatre and published in 1630

1631      John Dryden born, son of a Northampton gentleman; Lacy comes up to London as apprentice to John Ogilvy, then a dancing master

1634      Davenant's comedy, *The Witts*, staged at the Blackfriars after censorship, and published in 1636

1635      Davenant's comedy of English life, *News from Plymouth*, performed at the Globe; his masque, *The Temple of Love*, performed for the Queen's Shrovetide celebration, and his tragi-comedy, The *Platonic Lovers*, performed at the Blackfriars

1636      Davenant's masque, *Triumphs of the Prince D'Amour*, performed at the Middle Temple

1638      Davenant's masque, *Brittania Triumphans*, the first of his three collaborations with Inigo Jones, performed at Whitehall as Charles I's Twelfth Night present to Queen Henrietta Maria, who responds soon after by presenting him with Davenant's next masque, *Luminalia*; he also publishes *Madagascar, With Other Poems*, has two further plays performed, and becomes Poet Laureate

1639      Davenant writes *The Distresses*, published as *The Spanish Lovers* in 1673, but probably never performed

| Year | Artistic Events | Historical Events |
|------|-----------------|-------------------|
| 1627 | Ford, 'Tis Pity She's a Whore; Bacon, The New Atlantis | |
| 1628 | Harvey, Exercitatio Anatomica de Motu Cordis et Sanguinis in Animabilibus (translated 1653 as Anatomical Exercises) | |
| 1629 | | Charles dissolves Parliament; English settle Massachusetts; birth of the future Charles II; peace with Spain |
| 1631 | Death of Donne | |
| 1632 | Van Dyke settles in England | |
| 1633 | Birth of Pepys; Donne's Poems published; death of Herbert and posthumous publication of The Temple | Charles I crowned King of Scotland |
| 1634 | Milton, A Masque (Comus) | Witch trials in Lancashire |
| 1637 | Death of Jonson | |
| 1639 | | War with Scotland (first Bishops' War) |

| Year | Life |
|------|------|
| 1640 | Davenant's last masque, and the last of all court masques, *Salmacida Spolia*, performed at Whitehall |
| 1641 | Davenant serves in the ordnance department and becomes involved in the Army Plot; during the Civil War Lacy serves as lieutenant and quartermaster under Colonel Lord Gerard, later the Earl of Macclesfield |
| 1643 | Davenant knighted |
| 1646–50 | Davenant mostly in Paris with Hobbes and other royalist exiles; in 1650 he sailed for Maryland, of which the future Charles II had made him governor, but was captured by John Green, a former pirate, and imprisoned, first on the Isle of Wight, then in the Tower of London |
| 1649 | Dryden's earliest surviving poem, 'Upon the Death of Lord Hastings' appears in *Lachrimae Musarum*, while he is still a schoolboy at Winchester |

| Year | Artistic Events | Historical Events |
|---|---|---|
| 1640 | Aphra Behn born; Jonson's *Works* published, including later plays, masques, verse and prose | Long Parliament summoned; second Bishops' War |
| 1641 | Several of Milton's pamphlets published, including *Reformation Touching Church Discipline* | The Army Plot; execution of Strafford |
| 1642 | Theatres closed by order of Parliament; Isaac Newton born; unauthorised edition of Browne's *Religio Medici* | Outbreak of Civil War |
| 1643 | Milton, *The Doctrine and Discipline of Divorce* | Many Royalist victories |
| 1644 | Milton, *Areopagitica* | First decisive Parliamentary victory at Marston Moor |
| 1645 | Milton, *Poems* | Abolition of Book of Common Prayer; execution of Laud; Battle of Naseby and many Parliamentary victories |
| 1647 | John Wilmot, Earl of Rochester born; First Folio of Beaumont and Fletcher, *Comedies and Tragedies*; parliamentary ordinances for the suppression of plays | Parliamentary army occupies London and seizes the King, but he escapes to the Isle of Wight |
| 1648 | Herrick, *Hesperides* | Second Civil War; King is again seized and Parliamentary army enters London; end of Thirty Years' War |
| 1649 | Lovelace, *Lucasta* | Trial and execution of the King; Charles II proclaimed King in Scotland; abolition of the House of Lords and the monarchy; proclamation |

*Year*     *Life*

1650     Dryden enters Trinity College, Cambridge

1650–1   Davenant's *Gondibert* published while he is in prison
         awaiting trial; some months before, his *Discourse upon
         Gondibert* was published with Hobbes's *Answer*

1652     Davenant released from prison; Nahum Tate born in
         Ireland

1654     Davenant pardoned; Dryden graduates with a BA, and
         the next year becomes a civil servant in the government
         of the Protectorate

1655     Davenant's first wife dies and he is married for the
         second time, to Henrietta-Maria du Tremblay, in France

1656     Davenant returns to London and begins to re-establish
         the theatrical scene with *The First Day's Entertainment
         at Rutland House*, a philosophical debate with music,
         and then with his opera, *The Siege of Rhodes*, also
         presented at Rutland House

1658     Davenant presents *The Cruelty of the Spaniards in Peru*,
         a musical entertainment in six scenes

1659     Davenant's *The History of Sir Francis Drake* published
         soon after performance; Dryden, with Waller and Sprat,
         publishes a poem on the death of Cromwell, his first
         significant poem

| Year | Artistic Events | Historical Events |
|------|-----------------|-------------------|
| | | of the Commonwealth; Cromwell's campaigns in Ireland and Scotland |
| 1650 | Marvell, 'Horatian Ode'; Jeremy Taylor, *Holy Living*; Vaughan, *Silex Scintillans* | Trade with Royalist colonies forbidden |
| 1651 | Hobbes, *Leviathan*; Milton, *Pro Populo Anglicano*; Jeremy Taylor, *Holy Dying* | Charles II crowned at Scone, but becomes a fugitive after the Battle of Worcester |
| 1652 | | Royalist colonies submit; end of twelve years' war in Ireland; Dutch war |
| 1653 | Margaret Cavendish, Duchess of Newcastle, *Poems and Fancies* | Army seeks toleration, parliamentary and legal reforms; Protectorate established |
| 1654 | Milton, *Defensio Secunda* | Royalist and Leveller plots; peace with Holland; treaties with several other European countries |
| 1655 | | Proclamation on religious liberty; war with Spain |
| 1657 | | Alliance with France against Spain; Cromwell declines kingship, becomes Protector |
| 1658 | Browne, *Hydriotaphia* and *The Garden of Cyrus* | Republican opposition to Cromwell; dissolution of parliament; death of Cromwell; his son Richard becomes Protector |
| 1659 | | Army officers force dissolution of parliament; end of Protectorate |

| Year | Life |
|------|------|
| 1660 | Davenant granted a theatrical patent on 21 August, together with Thomas Killigrew, to erect, purchase or hire a playhouse and to organise a troupe of actors; his company becomes known as the Duke's Company; Dryden publishes *Astraea Redux*, in celebration of the Restoration of the monarchy, and is elected to the Royal Society, but dropped for non-payment of dues six years later |
| 1661 | Davenant's version of *Hamlet* presented at a new theatre, formerly Lisle's Tennis Court, now the Duke's Playhouse, where over the next seven years his company performs nearly fifty plays by a wide range of playwrights, including himself |
| 1662 | Davenant's *The Law Against Lovers*, a combination of *Measure for Measure* and *Much Ado About Nothing*, performed; Lacy plays his first part for the King's Company as Scruple in John Wilson's comedy, *The Cheats*, and later in the same year is seen by Pepys in *The Gentleman Dancing Master* and *Love in a Maze* |
| 1663 | Dryden marries Elizabeth Howard, eldest daughter of the Earl of Berkshire, possibly a Catholic; his first play, *The Wild Gallant*, appears, and is so admired by Lady Castlemaine, the King's mistress, that it is acted at court |
| 1664 | Davenant's *Macbeth* performed; around this time Lacy's first play, the comedy, *The Old Troop, or Monsieur Ragoû*, is performed, with Lacy as the French servant, Monsieur Ragoû |
| 1667 | Davenant and Dryden's collaboration, *The Tempest or The Enchanted Island* performed, and published three years later; Dryden's comedies *Secret Love* and *Sir Martin Mar-All* performed. Dryden publishes *Annus Mirabilis: The Year of Wonders, 1666*, and is now so wealthy that he makes a loan of £500 to Charles II, renewed the following year; Lacy's *Sauny the Scot* performed at the Theatre Royal, and he acts in Edward Howard's *The Change of Crownes*, a satire on court corruption, which offends Charles II |

| Year | Artistic Events | Historical Events |
|---|---|---|
| 1660 | Patents granted to Davenant and Killigrew to erect two playhouses and form two companies of actors; Defoe born; Pepys begins Diary; Milton, *The Ready and Easy Way to Establish a Free Commonwealth* | New parliament recalls Charles II, and he enters London; legislation of Cromwell and Long Parliament regarded as null and void; foundation of the Royal Society |
| 1661 | Bunyan imprisoned, with one small break, until 1672 | Coronation of Charles II |
| 1662 | Butler, *Hudibras*, part 1; Hooker, *Works*; Fuller, *Worthies of England* | Marriage of Charles II to Catherine of Braganza; restoration of the Church of England; Book of Common Prayer restored to use |
| 1663 | Opening of newly built theatre, Bridges Street, in Drury Lane; Butler, *Hudibras*, Part 2 | |
| 1664 | Vanbrugh born; Etherege, *The Comical Revenge* | |
| 1665 | | War declared against the Dutch; plague in London |
| 1666 | Royal Society begins publication of *Philosophical Transactions*; Boileau, *Satires*; Molière, *Le Misanthrope* | French ally with Dutch in the war; great fire of London |
| 1667 | Swift born; Bunyan, *Grace Abounding*; Sprat, *The History of the Royal Society*; Molière, *Tartuffe*; Racine, *Andromaque* | Peace made with French and Dutch |

Year     Life

1668     Davenant dies; Dryden succeeds him as Poet Laureate, and publishes the *Essay of Dramatic Poesy*; his comedy *An Evening's Love* performed; Tate enters Trinity College, Dublin

1669     Dryden's heroic play, *Tyrannick Love*, performed

1670–1   Dryden's two-part heroic play, *The Conquest of Granada*, performed; Buckingham satirises heroic drama in *The Rehearsal*, in which Dryden is represented as Mr Bayes, the role being played by Lacy; in 1670 Dryden is appointed Historiographer Royal with an annual pension of £200

1671     Colley Cibber born, son of Caius Gabriel Cibber, a Danish sculptor settled in England; Dryden's best-known comedy, *Marriage à la Mode,* performed

1672     Tate graduates from Trinity College, Dublin; Lacy's *The Dumb Lady, or The Farrier Made Physician* performed and published the same year

1673–4   Dryden writes *The State of Innocence*, an opera based on *Paradise Lost*

1676     Dryden's *Aureng-Zebe*, his last rhymed heroic tragedy, performed; his poetic satire, *Mac Flecknoe*, against Thomas Shadwell, circulates in manuscript, published in 1682; Lacy's *The Old Troop, or Monsieur Ragoû* published

| Year | Artistic Events | Historical Events |
|------|-----------------|-------------------|
| 1668 | Etherege, *She Wou'd If She Cou'd*; *Mercurius Librarius: or a Catalogue of Books* (the *Term Catalogues*) begins | |
| 1670 | Congreve born; Walton's *Lives*; Aphra Behn, *The Forced Marriage*; Milton, *The History of Britain*; Pascal, *Pensées* | |
| 1671 | Opening of newly built Dorset Garden theatre; Milton, *Paradise Regained* and *Samson Agonistes*; Wycherley, *Love in a Wood* | |
| 1672 | Milton, *Paradise Lost*; Bunyan freed by Declaration of Indulgence, and resumes preaching; Wycherley, *The Gentleman Dancing Master* | Third Dutch war declared; Shaftesbury becomes Lord Chancellor |
| 1673 | | Declaration of Indulgence revoked; Shaftesbury dismissed from the Chancellorship; he joins the opposition |
| 1674 | Opening of Theatre Royal, Drury Lane, after destruction of Bridges Street theatre by fire; death of Milton; Duffett, *The Mock-Tempest*; Shadwell, the operatic *Tempest*; Boileau, *L'Art Poetique* | |
| 1675 | Wycherley, *The Country Wife* | |
| 1676 | Etherege, *The Man of Mode*; Shadwell, *The Virtuoso*; Wycherley, *The Plain Dealer* | |

| Year | Life |
|------|------|
| 1677 | Dryden's *All for Love* performed; his annual pension increased to £300; Tate publishes *Poems* |
| 1678 | Tate's *Brutus of Alba*, a tragedy based on *Aeneid IV*, performed at Dorset Garden theatre; Dryden's comedy, *Mr Limberham*, banned, whether for moral or political reasons is unclear; Dryden's *Oedipus*, a version based on Corneille as well as Classical tragedy, and partly written with Nathaniel Lee, appears |
| 1679 | Dryden beaten up by hired thugs in Rose Alley, Covent Garden, perhaps because he was suspected (probably wrongly) of having written *An Essay on Satire*, which attacks the Earl of Rochester; his version of *Troilus and Cressida*, rewritten as a tragedy, is performed; Tate's *The Loyal General*, a tragedy, to which Dryden contributes a preface, is performed at Dorset Garden theatre |
| 1680 | Dryden's *The Spanish Fryer*, a tragi-comedy, performed; Tate's adaptation of *Richard II*, reset in Italy with the title *The Sicilian Usurper*, performed at Drury Lane theatre, but banned as politically subversive after two performances; Tate contributes, with Dryden and others, to *Ovid's Epistles, Translated by Several Hands* |
| 1681 | Dryden's *Absalom and Achitophel*, his most famous non-dramatic work – a political satire against the Whig Earl of Shaftesbury, then in prison following the Exclusion Crisis – is published; Tate's versions of *The History of King Lear* and *Coriolanus (The Ingratitude of a Commonwealth)* performed at Dorset Garden and Drury Lane theatres respectively; Lacy dies |
| 1682 | Lacy's *Sir Hercules Buffoon, or the Poetical Squire* performed, and published two years later; Dryden's poem *The Medal*, an even more direct attack on Shaftesbury, is published; he also publishes *Religio Laici, or A Layman's Faith: A Poem*, his first major religious work, which appears a fortnight after *The Second Part of Absalom and Achitophel*, largely by Tate; the first, unauthorised, edition of Dryden's *Mac Flecknoe* appears this year; Cibber begins schooling at the Free School, Grantham, Lincolnshire |

| Year | Artistic Events | Historical Events |
|------|-----------------|-------------------|
| 1677 | Aphra Behn, *The Rover* | |
| 1678 | Wren begins work on St Paul's Cathedral; death of Marvell; Farquhar born; Butler, *Hudibras*, part 3; Bunyan *The Pilgrim's Progress*, part 1; Shadwell's adaptation, *The History of Timon of Athens* | Titus Oates and Israel Tonge give evidence of a Popish plot; five Catholic lords sent to the Tower |
| 1679 | Beaumont and Fletcher, the Second Folio; Burnet, *The History of the Reformation*, vol. 1 (vol. 2 in 1681, vol. 3 in 1714) | Duke of York sent abroad; the Duke of Monmouth (Charles's illegitimate son) active against the Covenanters in Scotland |
| 1680 | Otway, *The History and Fall of Caius Marius* (adaptation of *Romeo and Juliet*); Crowne, *The Misery of Civil War* (adaptation of *Henry VI, Parts 2 and 3*) | Shaftesbury and the Whigs indict the Duke of York as a Popish recusant; Monmouth makes quasi-royal progress through the West Country |
| 1681 | Crowne, *Henry the Sixth, The First Part* (adaptation of Shakespeare's *Henry VI, Part 1*) | Shaftesbury proposes that Monmouth be named heir to the throne to secure the Protestant succession; new Exclusion Bill brought in; Shaftesbury committed for treason |
| 1682 | King's Company approaches Duke's Company to form a united enterprise, and they play as one until 1695; Durfey, *The Injured Princess* (adaptation of *Cymbeline*) | Duke of York returns to London; Monmouth arrested; Shaftesbury attempts to raise a rebellion, then flees to Scotland |

*Year*    *Life*

1684    Dryden publishes *Miscellany Poems*, and the next year *Sylvae, or the Second Part of Poetical Miscellanies*; Tate's *A Duke and No Duke*, adapted from Aston Cockaigne's *Trappolin Supposed a Prince*, performed at Drury Lane theatre

1685    Dryden becomes a Roman Catholic on the accession of James II; Tate's *Cuckolds-Haven*, adapted from *Eastward Ho* by Chapman and Marston, performed at Dorset Garden theatre, and an enlarged edition of his *Poems* is published

1687    Dryden writes *The Hind and the Panther* in defence of his new faith; Tate's *The Island Princess*, adapted from the play by Fletcher and Massinger, performed at Drury Lane theatre; Cibber leaves school having failed to get into Winchester, and goes to London, where he supports William of Orange in the Glorious Revolution

1688    Cibber leaves the army without a commission

1689    Purcell's *Dido and Aeneas* performed, with a libretto by Tate

1690    Cibber becomes an actor under Betterton at Drury Lane

1692    Dryden's translations of the *Satires* of Juvenal and Persius published with contributions by Tate; Tate appointed Poet Laureate

| Year | Artistic Events | Historical Events |
|------|-----------------|-------------------|
| 1683 | | Death of Shaftesbury; Rye House Plot; increased severity in treatment of Dissenters |
| 1684 | Bunyan, *The Pilgrim's Progress*, part 2 | |
| 1685 | | Death of Charles II and accession of James II; Scottish uprising in favour of Monmouth suppressed; Monmouth defeated in the Battle of Sedgmore and executed; Louis XIV revokes the Edict of Nantes, causing mass Huguenot flight to England |
| 1687 | Ravenscroft, *Titus Andronicus, or the Rape of Lavinia* (adaptation of Shakespeare) | Declaration of Indulgence; birth of James II's son (the Old Pretender); landing of William of Orange, and flight of James to France |
| 1688 | Pope born; death of Bunyan | Coronation of William and Mary; war declared on France |
| 1689 | | James defeated by William at the Battle of the Boyne |
| 1691 | Death of Etherege; Rochester, *Poems on Several Occasions*; Congreve, *Incognita*; Langbaine, *An Account of the English Poets* | |
| 1692 | Motteux, *The Gentleman's Journal*, the first English literary magazine, which lasted till November 1694; Settle and Purcell, *The Fairy Queen* | |

| Year | Life |
|---|---|
| 1693 | Cibber marries Katherine Shore, an actress, and the next year the first of their ten children is born; Dryden's last play, *Love Triumphant*, performed; Tate's *Essay on Farce* (the preface to the second edition of *A Duke and No Duke*) published |
| 1696 | Tate's *A New Version of the Psalms of David* (with Nicholas Brady) published, with a revised edition in 1698; Cibber's *Love's Last Shift* performed, with Cibber in the role of Sir Novelty Fashion |
| 1697 | Dryden's translation of *The Works of Virgil* published; Cibber's *Woman's Wit* performed |
| 1698 | Lacy's *Sauny the Scot* published |
| 1699 | Cibber's *Xerxes* performed; he plays Lord Foppington in Vanbrugh's *The Relapse*, a riposte to *Love's Last Shift* |
| 1700 | Dryden's *Fables*, translations from Ovid, Boccaccio and Chaucer, published; Dryden dies on 1 May, and is buried in Westminster Abbey; Tate publishes a supplement to *A New Version* and *Panacea: A Poem Upon Tea*; Cibber's *The History of King Richard III* performed, and also *Love Makes a Man*, a combination of Fletcher's two plays, *The Elder Brother* and *The Custom of the Country* |

| Year | Artistic Events | Historical Events |
|------|-----------------|-------------------|
| 1693 | Congreve, *The Old Bachelor*, *The Double Dealer*; Rymer, *A Short View of Tragedy* | Founding of the Bank of England |
| 1694 | Betterton leads breakaway group of actors to open in the remodelled theatre at Lincoln's Inn Fields; Voltaire born | Beginning of Whig Junto and of party government |
| 1695 | Congreve, *Love for Love* | |
| 1696 | Vanbrugh, *The Relapse* | |
| 1697 | Congreve, *The Mourning Bride*; Vanbrugh, *The Provoked Wife* | |
| 1698 | Collier, *A Short View of the Immorality and Profaneness of the English Stage* | |
| 1700 | Birth of James Thomson; Congreve, *The Way of the World*; Defoe, *The Shortest Way with Dissenters*; Gildon, *Measure for Measure* (adaptation of Shakespeare); Betterton, *King Henry IV, With the Humours of Sir John Falstaff* (adaptation of Shakespeare) | Last statute against Papists |
| 1701 | Nicholas Rowe, *Tamerlane*; Granville, *The Jew of Venice* (adaptation of *The Merchant of Venice*) | General election won by Tories; death of James II in France and his son recognised by Louis XIV; second general election with Whig recovery |

| Year | Life |
|---|---|
| 1702 | Tate appointed Historiographer Royal; Cibber's *She Wou'd and She Wou'd Not* performed |
| 1703 | Cibber's *The Rival Queens*, a mock-heroic parody of Nathaniel Lee's *The Rival Queens*, is performed |
| 1704 | Cibber becomes actor-manager at the Theatre Royal, Drury Lane; his *The Careless Husband*, one of his major comedies, is performed |
| 1705 | Cibber's tragedy *Perolla and Izadora* performed |
| 1706 | Cibber deserts the Theatre Royal for the Haymarket theatre |
| 1707 | Tate's last play, *Injured Love*, adapted from Webster's *The White Devil*, is written but never performed; Cibber's comedy *The Double Gallant*, *The Comical Lovers* and *The Lady's Last Stake* performed |
| 1709 | Cibber's *The Rival Fools* performed |
| 1710 | Tate publishes *An Essay for Promoting Psalmody* in answer to criticism of *A New Version*; Cibber becomes a part-sharer in the Theatre Royal, Drury Lane |

| Year | Artistic Events | Historical Events |
|------|-----------------|-------------------|
| 1702 | Susanna Centlivre, *The Stolen Heiress*; Farquhar, *The Inconstant*, *The Twin Rivals*; the *Daily Courant* begins (to 1735); the *Observer* begins (to 1712); Dennis, *The Comical Gallant: or the Amours of Sir John Falstaffe* (adaptation of *The Merry Wives of Windsor*) | Death of King William; Queen Anne becomes sole ruler; war declared on France; War of Spanish Succession |
| 1703 | Death of Pepys; Wesley born; Burnaby, *Love Betray'd: or, The Agreeable Disappointment* (adaptation of *Twelfth Night*) | |
| 1704 | Death of Sir Thomas Browne; opening of Haymarket theatre, designed by Vanbrugh; Swift, *Tale of a Tub*, *The Battle of the Books*; Dennis, *The Grounds of Criticism in Tragedy* | |
| 1706 | Farquhar, *The Recruiting Officer*; Benjamin Franklin born | |
| 1707 | Farquhar, *The Beaux' Stratagem*; Farquhar dies; union of the two theatre companies until 1710 | Union with Scotland ratified |
| 1708 | Downes, *Roscius Anglicanus* | |
| 1709 | Samuel Johnson born; Steele, *The Tatler*; Rowe's edition of *The Works of Shakespeare* | |
| 1710 | Berkeley, *The Principles of Human Knowledge*; first Copyright Act; Addison, *The Spectator*; death of Betterton | |

*Year*     *Life*

1715     Tate dies, and is buried in St George's Church, Southwark

1717–30   Cibber becomes increasingly unpopular with fellow writers, and quarrels with Pope, Fielding and Dennis, among others; during this time several of his plays fail, though *The Non-Juror* (1717) – an adaptation of Moliere's *Tartuffe*, directed against the Tories – is a success

| Year | Artistic Events | Historical Events |
|------|-----------------|-------------------|
| 1711 | David Hume born; Dennis, *An Essay upon the Writings and Genius of Shakespeare* | |
| 1712 | Pope, *The Rape of the Lock* (final form in 1714); Scriblerus Club formed; Rousseau born | |
| 1713 | Anne, Countess of Winchelsea, *Miscellany Poems*; Steele becomes a partner at Drury Lane theatre, with Cibber and other actor-managers | Treaty of Utrecht |
| 1714 | Pope, *The Rape of the Lock* (five cantos) | Death of Queen Anne, and accession of George I; Whigs in office |
| 1715 | Pope, translation of *The Iliad*, vol. 1 (completed 1720) | First Jacobite rebellion; death of Louis XIV |
| 1716 | Death of Wycherley; adaptations of *The Taming of The Shrew* by Christopher Bullock and Charles Johnson (both plays called *The Cobler of Preston*) performed; John Sheffield, *The Tragedy of Julius Caesar, altered*, and *The Tragedy of Marcus Brutus* (adaptation of *Julius Caesar*); Richard Leveridge, *Pyramus and Thisbe. A Comic Masque* (adaptation of *A Midsummer Night's Dream*) | |
| 1717 | Birth of Garrick, and Horace Walpole; Gay's *Three Hours after Marriage*, in which Cibber, among others, is satirised; Pope, *Collected Works* | |
| 1718 | | England and France declare war on Spain |

Year      Life

1719      Cibber's *Ximena*, adapted from Corneille's *Le Cid*, is
          published, after failure on the stage in 1712

1721      Cibber's *The Refusal* performed; he produces a two-
          volume edition of his plays, with the less successful
          omitted

| Year | Artistic Events | Historical Events |
|------|----------------|-------------------|
| 1719 | Defoe, *Robinson Crusoe* | |
| 1720 | Theobald, *The Tragedy of King Richard II* (adaptation of Shakespeare); Dennis, *The Invader of his Country* (adaptation of *Coriolanus*); Steele starts *The Theatre*, a new periodical, and quarrels with Cibber; Charles Molloy, *The Half-Pay Officers* (adaptation of *Henry V* with scenes from *Twelfth Night*) | South Sea Bubble and bill |
| 1722 | | Young Pretender born; taxes imposed on Roman Catholics; oath of allegiance made compulsory |
| 1723 | Aaron Hill, *King Henry the Fifth*; Charles Johnson, *Love in a Forest* (combination of *As You Like It* with the Pyramus and Thisbe plot from *A Midsummer Night's Dream*); William Taverner and Dr Brown, *Every Body Mistaken* (adaptation of *The Comedy of Errors*); Ambrose Phillips, *Humfrey, Duke of Gloucester* (adaptation of *Henry VI*, Part 1); Theophilus Cibber, *An Historical Tragedy of the Civil Wars in the Reign of King Henry VI* (adaptation of *Henry VI*) | |

*Year*      *Life*

1724      Cibber's *Caesar in Egypt*, a version of Fletcher and
          Massinger's *The False One*, is performed

1728      Cibber's *The Provoked Husband*, a response to
          Vanbrugh's *The Provoked Wife*, his most popular
          comedy, is performed
1729      Cibber's ballad-opera *Love in a Riddle* performed; it
          fails, but Cibber salvages its subplot and presents it
          anonymously as *Damon and Phillida*
1730      Cibber becomes Poet Laureate
1731      Cibber writes several laureate poems, including the *Ode
          . . . for the New Year* and *Ode for his Majesty's Birthday*
1733      Cibber retires from theatrical management at Drury Lane,
          though he continues to do special benefit performances;
          after retirement he is frequently attacked in print by
          Fielding

1737      Cibber begins to write *An Apology for the Life of Colley
          Cibber*; it is published in 1740, and immediately causes
          controversy; a revised and abbreviated version appears in
          1742 in the collection *A History of the Stage*

| Year | Artistic Events | Historical Events |
|------|-----------------|-------------------|
| | Parts 2 and 3); John Sheffield, Duke of Buckingham, *The Tragedy of Julius Caesar* (adaptation of Shakespeare) | |
| 1724 | Defoe, *Roxana* | |
| 1725 | Pope's edition of Shakespeare | Treaty of Vienna (Empire and Spain); Treaty of Hanover (between England, France and Prussia) |
| 1726 | Swift, *Gulliver's Travels* | |
| 1727 | First known production of a Shakespeare play by secondary school boys (*Julius Caesar* at Westminster School) | Death of Newton; George I dies and is succeeded by George II |
| 1728 | First edition of Pope's *Dunciad*, attacking Cibber among others | |
| 1729 | Deaths of Steele and Congreve | Treaty of Seville |
| 1731 | Death of Defoe | |
| 1735 | Pope's *Epistle to Dr Arbuthnot*, attacking Cibber; Richard Worsdale, *A Cure for a Scold* (version of *The Taming of the Shrew*) | |
| 1736 | The Licensing Act | Dissenters attempt to repeal the Test Act; Gin Act; Porteous Riots |
| 1737 | James Miller, *The Universal Passion* (adaptation of *Much Ado About Nothing*) | Frederick Prince of Wales heads opposition; Queen Caroline dies |

*Year*      *Life*

1743    Pope revises *The Dunciad*, so as to make Cibber the hero
        instead of Theobald, and their war of words continues
        till Pope's death later that year

1745    Cibber's last appearance on stage, in his play *Papal
        Tyranny in the Reign of King John*
1747    Cibber writes *The Character and Conduct of Cicero*

1750    Cibber seriously ill, but recovers

| Year | Artistic Events | Historical Events |
|---|---|---|
| 1738 | John (or James) Carrington, *The Modern Receipt: or, A Cure for Love* (adaptation of *As You Like It*); George Lillo, *Marina* (adaptation of *Pericles*) | Treaty of Vienna (Polish succession) |
| 1739 | | War with Spain |
| 1740 | Richardson, *Pamela*; Schneemaker's statue of Shakespeare at Poets' Corner, Westminster Abbey, unveiled; Charlotte Charke, Cibber's daughter, puts on versions of *Richard III*, *Henry VIII* and *Henry IV* played by puppets | |
| 1741 | Garrick's premiere at Drury Lane as Hamlet | |
| 1744 | Pope dies | |
| 1747–9 | Richardson, *Clarissa* | |
| 1748 | Theophilus Cibber, *Romeo and Juliet* (adaptation of Shakespeare) | |
| 1749 | Fielding, *Tom Jones* | |
| 1750 | Garrick, *Romeo and Juliet* (adaptation of Shakespeare); Johnson, *The Rambler* (to 1752) | |
| 1751 | Sheridan born; Gray, *Elegy* | |
| 1752 | Chatterton born; Fielding, *Amelia* | |
| 1754 | Richardson, *Sir Charles Grandison*; Garrick, *Catharine and Petruchio* (adaptation of *The Taming of the Shrew*) | |

*Year*      *Life*

1757      Cibber dies

| Year | Artistic Events | Historical Events |
|------|-----------------|-------------------|
| 1755 | Johnson, *Dictionary*; Macnamara Morgan, *The Sheep-Shearing: or, Florizel and Perdita* (adaptation of *A Winter's Tale*); Thomas Sheridan, *Coriolanus: or, The Roman Matron* (adaptation of Shakespeare); *Garrick, The Fairies. An Opera* (adaptation of *A Midsummer Night's Dream*); Francis Gentleman, *King Richard II* (adaptation of Shakespeare) | |
| 1756 | Garrick, *Florizel and Perdita; The Tempest. An Opera*; Charles Marsh, *The Winter's Tale* (adaptation of Shakespeare) | Beginning of the Seven Years War |
| 1757 | | Conquest of India begins under General Clive |

# INTRODUCTION

When the London theatres reopened in 1660 after a prolonged period of enforced closure during the years of the Civil War and Commonwealth, there was a frantic hunt to find plays to put on. While dramatists set to work to write new ones, the staples of the pre-war theatre filled the gap, and naturally enough Shakespeare was conspicuous among them. Yet, with few exceptions, his plays were rarely produced in anything like their original form, and many of them were drastically revised. *King Lear* was given a happy ending, and *Troilus and Cressida* turned into a tragedy; *Romeo and Juliet* was reset in the times of the Roman republic, and *Richard II* became *The Sicilian Usurper*; *Measure for Measure* and *Much Ado About Nothing* were conflated into a single play; a *Henry V* was written in which the king was followed to France by a spurned mistress, dressed as a page; and *Macbeth* was done as a semi-opera with witches in flying machines. The list could be extended almost indefinitely.

Why did playwrights of the new theatre feel the need to adapt the plays in this way? Are we right to dismiss them, as has so often happened, as irresponsible perversions? Are there other ways in which to explore them more profitably? I should like to suggest that there are, in fact, a variety of ways in which the adaptations, represented by five selected examples in this volume, can be seen to have meaning and interest for us at a time when the cultural status of Shakespeare himself is very much up for review.

The process of adapting Shakespeare's plays for the new theatrical conditions, which went on so vigorously at this time, constitutes a small but significant chapter in our cultural history. Initially it was connected with matters of legislation. Patents were issued in 1660 giving Sir William Davenant and Thomas Killigrew, two royalist men of the theatre who had been active as playwrights in pre-Civil War times, rights each to erect or hire a playhouse and organise a troop of actors. Many of the actors in Killigrew's company were experienced professionals from the King's Company of the Caroline era, who had brought with them the rights to perform the old King's Company plays. Davenant's company, on the other hand, was composed of inexperienced actors, and had permanent rights to only two of the old plays, *The Changeling* and *The Bondman*.[1] In order to match the competition from Killigrew's ready-made repertoire Davenant presented the Lord Chamberlain with a 'proposition of reformeing some of the most ancient Playes that were playd at Blackfriers and makeinge them, fitt, for the Company of Actors'.[2] Amongst those he asked for, and was given, were *The Tempest* and *King Lear*. As has been pointed out,[3] Davenant was obliged by law to revise Shakespeare's original, whether he wanted to or not. But in any case after 1660 Shakespeare's plays were preferred in adapted versions; only a handful (*Hamlet*, *Othello*, *The Merry Wives of Windor* and *King Henry IV*, Part 1) were commercially successful in their original form, whereas such plays as the Dryden/Davenant *Tempest*, Tate's *King Lear* and Cibber's *Richard III* were not only highly popular in their own time but held the stage for many years afterwards.

Partly, of course, it was a question of language; by 1660 Shakespeare had begun to sound archaic. Dryden in his preface to *All for Love* acknowledged that 'Words and Phrases must of necessity receive a change in succeeding Ages'; and later, more outspokenly, in his preface to his adaptation of Shakespeare's *Troilus and Cressida*, he referred to the play as 'that heap of Rubbish, under which many excellent thoughts lay wholly bury'd'. But, as has been shown,[4] from the Second Folio (1632) of Shakespeare's plays onwards a process of tacit refinement and correction had been taking place, without any large-scale adaptation in the theatre. However the theatre in 1660 was very different in a number of ways from that of 1642, and it was not only words and phrases that need changing for Shakespeare's texts to satisfy the cultural needs of a new age. Adaptors such as Dryden, Tate and Cibber were brilliantly successful in meeting these needs; their versions revitalised plays that might have suffered theatrical eclipse in a new milieu that regarded itself as infinitely more sophisticated than that of Shakespeare's own time. The diarist John Evelyn was not alone in the disdain he expressed after seeing *Hamlet* done with the minimum of adaptation: 'Now the old playe began to disgust this refined age; since his Majestie being so long abroad.'[5]

Over the centuries the status of these adaptations has changed, along with attitudes to questions of literary property and to the canonisation of Shakespeare. Shakespeare himself seems to have shown little interest in laying claim to the ownership of his plays but with the copyright act of 1710 the early eighteenth century saw the development of the concept of the author as owner of his works, and the status of Shakespeare changed accordingly. Michael Dobson in *The Making of the National Poet*[6] shows how the wholesale rewriting of Shakespeare – along with the late seventeenth-century ransacking of his plays for materials to create new ones – was replaced by a process regarded as essentially corrective. In the editions of Nicholas Rowe (1709), and still more Alexander Pope (1723–5) elements regarded as 'low' or 'corrupt' (either in a moral or a textual sense) were separated from the body of the text, and 'Shakespeare is constructed as a fully decorous Enlightenment author.'[7]

It took a few years after 1660 for a new body of plays to develop, and at first the old ones dominated the stage. Playwrights rose to the challenge presented by texts that were half a century old, and made revisions that shaped the tastes of many generations of theatre-goers to come. Adaptation can be regarded as a creative process, as well as a matter of expediency.

The history of Shakespearean adaptation is complex and chequered. The post-Restoration period with its new emphasis on print rather than oral culture saw a growing separation between page and stage. While Shakespeare's plays appeared in printed editions whose editors claimed to restore his text to the most correct and authentic forms they could – supplying an ever-growing body of emendations and annotations – the most popular of the adapted versions held the stage to the exclusion of the originals. These, in fact, also continued to be printed in popular acting editions until Shakespeare's own versions were restored in the nineteenth century. There is a paradox whereby Shakespeare's works achieved the status of 'classics' in the study while for a long period on the stage the divine Bard (as he came to be called) was often represented by plays only a small proportion of which he actually wrote.

During the eighteenth century the more long-lasting adaptations were subjected to increasing criticism. Not long after Tate's *King Lear* had been replaced on the London stage by a version substantially Shakespeare's, presented by Macready in 1834, vilification of Tate in particular set in: H. N. Hudson coined the term 'tatification' in 1848 and referred to his play as 'this shameless, this execrable piece of dementation'.[8] Twentieth-century critics have until recently often been very hard on the adaptations, implicitly assuming that Shakespeare's text is sacrosanct and any modification of it an act of sacrilege. Odell in his standard account *Shakespeare from Betterton to Irving* refers to the Dryden/Davenant *Tempest* as 'the worst perversion of Shakespeare in the two-century history of such atrocities', and Furness says of it that 'to be fully hated it must be fully seen'. Moelwyn Merchant in 'Shakespeare Made Fit' uses words such as 'vandalism', 'dismemberment' and 'hacked out' in what is otherwise a very fair account of Restoration adaptation.[9] To Hazelton Spencer in his still much-cited account of the adaptations, *Shakespeare Improved*, they were pernicious aberrations, whose contaminating influence needed to be decisively rejected. Davenant in particular was reproved for his part in initiating the 'popular lust for spectacle' to which so many Restoration adaptations seemed to pander. Spencer wrote in his conclusion that despite all modern efforts to 'set forth the actual, the historical, play ... not yet ... have we got wholly free of the Restoration attitude towards revision, or indeed of the Restoration versions themselves'.[10] So intemperately hostile has been the attitude taken towards these versions that, as the editors of the Dryden/Davenant *Tempest* remark, 'from the comments of numerous critics ... one might think that the collaborators had deliberately set out to destroy and ruin Shakespeare's reputation'.[11]

Whatever the motives of the adaptors – who included in their number men of considerable standing and reputation in the literary and cultural worlds of their day[12] – their work is significant to us now as, amongst other things, an important staging-point in the history of Shakespeare's cultural appropriation. Also these adaptations have much light to throw on the place and meaning of theatre in the later seventeenth century, and on ways in which these had changed since Shakespeare's own time. It was a narrower theatrical scene in many ways, with fewer companies, fewer performing spaces, and a more socially selective audience; there was also a more direct input from royal taste and aristocratic patronage than before the war. The physical nature of the performance space had also changed; the plays took place indoors, by artificial lighting, and in a comparatively intimate area where the identity of individual members of the audience could become public knowledge and as such be incorporated into the performance, or, at any rate, form a significant element in the dynamic between actors and audience. There was an increasingly lavish use of scenery – sometimes with illusionistic effects – and also of music and spectacle. The constitution of theatrical companies was vitally different; women's parts were no longer played by boys but by women, and the personalities of the leading actors and actresses, often familiar in London society, might relate closely to the roles they played.

These altered circumstances are reflected in varying degrees in the five texts selected for this edition, although this is not a principal reason for their selection. They cover a generic range – comedy, tragedy, history, romance; they are all versions of familiar and popular plays. Some of them have had considerable influence on the history of Shakespearean production, particularly *The Tempest*, *King Lear* and *Richard III*. Though the plays were written over a period of thirty-three years, the total lifespan of their authors extended much longer; Davenant and Lacy were men whose first experience of theatre was in the times of Charles I, whereas Cibber's started in the reign of Charles II and lasted until the end of George II's. (Cibber was actually born only a year before Davenant died.) The earliest and latest of these plays, Lacy's *Sauny the Scot* and Cibber's *Richard III*, stand in a rather different relation to the theatre from the others in that they were written by actors who played the title roles in the original productions.

The plays exemplify a wide range of attitudes towards the process of revising Shakespeare for a new era, and extremely different ways of handling the Shakespearean text. Dryden's *All for Love* is out on its own here, in that it uses none of Shakespeare's lines directly. It rewrites Shakespeare's extravagant and loosely structured *Antony and Cleopatra* completely, turning it into a neat neo-classical tragedy on modern, French-influenced lines. Cibber in *Richard III*, on the other hand, not only quotes directly and extensively from Shakespeare's play –

following the same sequence of events and incorporating all the major scenes and incidents – but imports textual material from a number of Shakespeare's other history plays in addition. Lacy in *Sauny the Scot* turns a largely verse play, *The Taming of the Shrew*, into contemporary prose, staying generally very close to Shakespeare's plot-line and introducing little new material before the last act. *The Tempest* and *King Lear* are perhaps the plays with the most to tell us about the variety of uses to which Restoration writers could put Shakespeare's text, both incorporating substantial portions of the original but also rewriting, reordering scenes, cutting whole characters and episodes, and adding entirely new ones. In each case political as well as aesthetic considerations determine the direction of the restructuring; but, whereas Tate's *King Lear* has often been related to the specific political conditions of the crisis years 1678–82, it is only recently that the Dryden/Davenant *Tempest* has been discussed in terms of its contribution to contemporary political debate. But all these adaptations participate in the new cultural conditions of their times, revealing, for instance, changed attitudes to domestic life, marriage, and gender roles, as well as new concepts of literary and dramatic decorum. Their contemporary appeal was various; they offered political and social comment, but also spectacle, song and dance, and fine parts for the star performers. They afforded audiences the chance to see Shakespeare in a form specifically designed to appeal to their own times. Few readers of the plays in this edition will have had the opportunity to see any of them professionally staged, though *All for Love* enjoys revivals from time to time, and some of Cibber's *Richard III* lives on – in lines as well as spirit – in the still-available video of Olivier's film of the 1940s. For many readers, their main interest may be their bearing on the issues surrounding the cultural appropriation of Shakespeare. It is none the less worth bearing in mind not only that some of them have had as long a stage history as their originals, but that, with every production in the theatre or, of course, in the cinema or on television, the adaptation and redefinition of Shakespeare's text takes place anew.

## Lacy, Sauny the Scot

John Lacy's *Sauny the Scot* was written for production by the

King's Company – in which Lacy was himself one of the original shareholders ('sharers' was the contemporary term) – and first put on at the Theatre Royal, Drury Lane, in April 1667, with the author in the title role. Though Pepys thought it 'but a mean play' it enjoyed several revivals and was sufficiently well known forty years later for the publisher of the 1708 edition to describe it as 'a still darling entertainment'.[13] Lacy wrote in all four plays, all comedies, of which *Sauny the Scot* was the second, but his main occupation was as an actor. He trained as a dancer before the war, but little is known of his work in those times. During his twenty-year career in the Restoration theatre he was extremely famous for his comic performances and much admired by Pepys. He was also a particular favourite of Charles II, who commissioned a triple portrait of him in three of his best-known roles. This popularity survived an incident when Lacy aroused the royal wrath by his satiric performance in Edward Howard's *The Change of Crownes* (1667) as a country gentleman who, in Pepys's words 'doth abuse the Court with all the imaginable wit and plainness, about selling of places and doing everything for money'. He was arrested and briefly detained as a result, but within two weeks Pepys was 'glad to find the rogue at liberty again'.[14] From what we know of him, Lacy seems to have lived the rakish life of an actor; this brush with the law was not the only one, and a few months after it Pepys records the rumour, false as it turned out, that he was dying of the pox with his whore at his side. He was a handsome man, rumoured to have been Nell Gwyn's lover and certainly her acting teacher, and well-known both for his dancing skills and his character acting, in roles such as Falstaff, Sir Politic Would-Be in *Volpone*, and Mr Bayes in Buckingham's *The Rehearsal*.[15]

These personal facts are of some relevance to *Sauny the Scot*, which is first and foremost the adaptation of *The Taming of the Shrew* with a character role specifically written to be played by Lacy himself. It is worth noting that, unlike Davenant's company, the King's Company could have put on *The Taming of the Shrew* without alteration, since they owned the rights to it, and indeed had done so already in 1663. But obviously Lacy felt that there was room for a new version, and adapted the play with his own needs as a comic actor foremost in his mind. The role of Sauny is that of Petruchio's servant (Grumio in

Shakespeare), who becomes an intrusive, foul-mouthed and outspoken comic character, always ready with a scurrilous or irreverent aside. The foundations are there in Shakespeare, especially for the knockabout routines between Petruchio and his man, but Lacy enlarges the part and redefines it through the new characteristic of Sauny's nationality. His Scottishness explains his outlandish manners, his constant 'scratten and scrubben' at his body, his refusal to doff his cap to his betters more than once a day ('Marry, we say in Scotland Gead Mourn [good morning] til ye for aw [all] the day, and sea [so] put on our bonnets again') [II.ii.61–2], and his preoccupation with food and drink. The language was probably not intended to be any more authentic than stage Scottish usually is. In fact, it resembles the dialect given to a Yorkshire heiress in Lacy's later play *Sir Hercules Buffoon* and is said by Lacy's Victorian editors to 'savour strongly of the meridian of Doncaster, Lacy's birthplace'.

Much of Sauny's dialogue takes the form of subversive commentary and asides to the audience, undercutting the speech and action of the main characters. When in the last act Margaret (Katherine), who has tried Petruchio in many ways, including pretending to be dead, is finally ready to submit to her husband, he asks her, 'Art thou in earnest, Peg? May I believe thee?'. Sauny follows this up with typical cynicism: 'You ken very well she was awway's a lying Quean when she was living, and wull ye believe her now she's Dead?' (V.i.251–3). He is the eternal underdog, regularly beaten by Petruchio and sometimes by Margaret, of whom he remains comically fearful to the end of the play, yet he is always clownishly resilient. He is crude, buffoonish, carnivalesque, sometimes exaggeratedly servile, at others boldly insolent, mocking conventional distinctions of rank and status. An eighteenth-century cleric, Arthur Bedford, who joined Jeremy Collier in fulminating against the stage, was shocked by Sauny's language and insubordinate behaviour:

> [He] is rude and impertinent to both Master and Mistress, and indeed upon all occasions . . . He swears, he curses, he adjures in the Devil's Name, and ridicules the Name of GOD; he prays to the Devil, and is continually talking of him.[16]

But the robust vulgarity of Sauny's language and manners would not have been out of place in the age of Wycherley, nor would his underlying misogyny, less open and perhaps more threatening than in Shakespeare's play. Sauny was a role that offered a comedian plenty of opportunity for physical expression, as well as for establishing a rapport with the audience. Though Lacy, who made something of a speciality of dialect roles,[17] obviously designed it exploit his own theatrical persona, it was taken with success by at least one other well-known comic actor, William Bullock, who is listed in the cast for 1698, when the play was first published.

The role of Sauny is obviously Lacy's most striking change to his source, but he made other fundamental alterations. First, he brought the play up to date by rewriting it in prose, the language of comedy in this period, and turning the characters into the inhabitants of Restoration London. Second, he radically revised the last act so as to allow Margaret a more prolonged period of rebellion against Petruchio, thus giving a rather different account of marriage and sexual politics from Shakespeare. He also omitted the Christopher Sly scenes entirely, a practice that is commonly followed in present-day productions of *The Taming of the Shrew*. The updating of the characters and setting to Restoration London seems firmly established in the opening scene where Winlove (Lucentio), newly graduated from Oxford, and weary, like any gentleman in a Restoration comedy, of country life, has come up to London to enjoy the sophistication of the city: 'London is the Choisest Academy, 'tis that must Polish us, and put a Gloss upon our Country-Studies; Hither I'm come at last, and do resolve to Glean many Vices' (I.i.17–19). The town–country opposition, so familiar in Restoration comedy, is a background against which the play's theme of domestic rebellion is played out.

But the elegant idiom of the opening exchanges between Winlove and his man is not long sustained; the very fact that the man is called Tranio represents the piecemeal nature of the updating, so that Baptista turns into Beaufoy and his elder daughter Margaret, but the younger remains 'Biancha'. Petruchio retains his name, although his chief servant becomes a Scot. However this perfunctoriness is not out of keeping with Shakespeare's 'Italian' setting for *The Taming of the Shrew*, which is largely a matter of throwaway references to Padua, Verona and so forth, but set within an English context of Christopher Sly's Warwickshire and Petruchio's English-sounding country house. Lacy gives his characters a number of English (or, in Sauny's case, Scottish) allusions to establish the play's relocation: for example, Woodall (Gremio) would as gladly marry Margaret as 'be whipt at Chairing-Cross every morning' (I.i.58); Tranio pretends to be 'a Worcestershire gentleman' (II.i.157); and Snatchpenny (the Pedant) claims an estate 'in the Vale of Evesham' (IV.iv.96). But this is all really window-dressing, and *Sauny the Scot*'s main change in idiom comes about through Lacy's switch to prose for the entire play. Again, this modification is not carried through wholeheartedly, and there are patches of dialogue where Shakespeare's verse-rhythms reassert themselves, so little has Lacy changed his original. Petruchio stakes his claim to be Margaret's wooer much as he does in Shakespeare: 'I'm as Peremptory as she's Proud-minded: and where two Rageing fires meet together they do consume the thing that feeds their fury' (II.ii.87–9). Such closeness to Shakespeare is not uncommon. But at other points Lacy's colloquial prose gives the characters an increased vitality. Thus Margaret roundly abuses her sister:

> Marry, come up, Proud Slut. Must you be making yourself Fine before your Elder Sister? You are the Favourite, you are, but I shall make you know your Distance; Give me that Necklace, and those Pendants. I'll have what Whisk too, there's an old Handkercheif good enough for you ... You Flattering Gypsie, I cou'd find it in my Heart to Slit your Dissembling Tongue; Come, tell me, and without Lying, which of your Sutors you love best. Tell me, or I'll beat you to Clouts, and Pinch thee like a Fairy. (II.ii.1–10)

She has a more vivid and earthy idiom than her predecessor, and is more forceful in her exchanges with Petruchio:

> PETRUCHIO: Where did'st thou Learn the grand Paw, Peg? It becomes thee rarely.
>
> MARGARET: Doe's it so, Saucebox? How will a halter become you with a running knot under one Ear?
>
> PETRUCHIO: Nay, no knot, Peg, but the knot of Matrimony 'twixt thee and me; we shall be an Excellent *Mad Couple well match'd*.
>
> MARGARET: *I* match'd to thee? What, to such a fellow with such a Gridiron face, with a Nose set on like a Candels end stuck against a Mud wall, and a Mouth to eat Milk Porridge

with Ladles? Foh, it almost turns my Stomach to look at it.
(II.ii.142–51)

Margaret's greater forcefulness is reflected in the changes which
Lacy makes to the structure. Overall, these are few, and their
main effect is to marginalise the Biancha-Winlove subplot and to
highlight the sex-war theme in the main plot. At an early stage
Lacy hints at Margaret's motivation, in a way that Shakespeare
never does for Katherine, giving her an aside near the end of II.ii,
the first big taming scene, to indicate her future intentions: 'The
Devil's in this fellow, he has beat me at my own Weapon. I have
a good mind to marry him to try if he can Tame me'
(II.ii.202–3). In the new Act V Margaret tells Biancha of her
plans to turn the tables on her husband:

> I am resolv'd now I'm got home again I'll be reveng'd. I'll muster
> up the spight of all the Curs'd Women since *Noahs* flood to do
> him Mischeif, and add new vigour to my Tongue. I have not par'd
> my Nails this fortnight; they are long enough to do him some
> Execution, that's my Comfort ... I'll make *Petruchio* glad to
> wipe my Shoes, or walk my Horse, ere I have done with him.'
> (V.i.3–7, 21–2)

Petruchio, however, is still back in Shakespeare's play, and
jovially invites his wife to pick up his glove; when she refuses he
threatens to remove her from London and take her back to his
house in the country, but Margaret has no intention of giving in:
'No, Sir, I won't say, "Pray let me go"; but boldly, I won't go.
You force me, if you can or dare. You see I am not Tongue-ty'd,
as silent as you thought you made me.' (V.i.91–4) Newly
empowered as a wife, she has found her voice, and it is her turn
to put Petruchio through a series of humiliating tests. 'You shall
know me to be the Master', she asserts (V.i.119), and there may
even be the implication that it is Petruchio himself who has
taught her by example how to flout the conventional expecta-
tions of gender roles. 'You cannot raise the Spirit you have laid,
with all your Arts', as Winlove tells Petruchio (V.i.180–1).

In the end it seems as if the two reach a compromise.
Petruchio calls Margaret's final bluff, when she pretends to be
dead, by summoning bearers and making preparations for the
funeral. She is forced to end her silence, and Petruchio cries out,
'A Miracle! a Miracle! She lives' (V.i.240). They agree that they
will 'change kindness and be each others Servant', and the

compact seems sealed when Margaret responds positively, as in Shakespeare, to the wager on the obedience of the three wives, and concludes with a two-line summary of Katherine's address in wifely duty.

It is likely that Lacy's changed last act was influenced by Fletcher's version of *The Taming of the Shrew*, *The Woman's Prize, or, The Tamer Tamed* (*c.*1611), which was popular in the Restoration, and sometimes performed in tandem with *Sauny the Scot*, as Lacy's brief epilogue implies. In this play – which Fletcher clearly conceived as an answer to Shakespeare's – Petruchio struggles against the efforts of his second wife, Maria, who takes steps, with the support of a band of women friends, to educate her husband into a right view of marriage. The device of the fake death is Petruchio's; the ostensible message[18] of the play seems to be the desirability of partnership in marriage: 'To teach both sexes due equality / And, as they stand bound, to love mutually' (Epilogue to *The Woman's Prize*).

Although Lacy's play ends, like Shakespeare's, with a triple wedding feast, Margaret's behaviour in the obedience test, and subsequently, does not suggest the total submission that some critics (though by no means all) have seen in Katherine; neither does the play afford any strong justification for patriarchy. Rather, it reinforces the sense of a 'loss of belief in the traditional underpinnings of a husband's claim to authority'[19] that seems widespread in drama after 1660.

*Sauny the Scot*, the most unpretentious of the adaptations in this volume, exemplifies in a very basic form some of the ways in which a Shakespeare play could be adapted for a new age and the new theatre. Lacy's agenda is clear enough: he wanted a play that would function as a good vehicle for his own theatrical talents and one whose concerns could easily be made to address what was current on the comic stage. *The Taming of the Shrew* was later adapted to suit topical political concerns,[20] but there is no implication here, nor, in the context of its time, that its view of marriage was a radical one.

## Dryden and Davenant, The Tempest

Unusually for a Shakespeare comedy in this period, *The Tempest, or The Enchanted Island* was highly successful. The fourth of Davenant's adaptations from Shakespeare, and the only one co-written with the young John Dryden, it was first produced in November 1667 to great enthusiasm which was shared by Pepys, who saw it seven more times before February 1669. It was published in 1670, two years after Davenant's death, and then revised in 1674 (probably by Shadwell) into an opera, on which most eighteenth-century productions of the play were based. In 1695 there was a sumptuous new production with a score by Purcell. Between 1660 and 1700 *The Tempest* was the most performed revival of a Shakespeare play, and it held the stage for some time, until Shakespeare's original began to take over midway through the eighteenth century. By the end of this century eight different versions of the play, none of them entirely by Shakespeare, had been performed.[21] Hippolyto and Dorinda, the latter regarded by Dryden as one of Davenant's happiest inventions, did not finally quit the stage until Macready's production in 1838.

The plot involving Miranda and Dorinda, and their suitors Ferdinand and Hippolyto, is the most prominent of the changes made in the play to fit it for a new cultural climate. The provision of a female companion for Miranda enables an exploration of female sexuality in scenes which exploit the characters' naivety to the full for its comic potential. The two young women know nothing of men except what Prospero has taught them, but their instinctive curiosity about the opposite sex is so powerful that they are prepared to disobey their father's orders for a glimpse of Hippolyto.

MIRANDA: We'll find him sitting like a Hare in's Form,
  And he shall not see us.
DORINDA: I, but you know my Father charg'd us both.
MIRANDA: But who shall tell him on't? we'll keep each
  Others Counsel.
DORINDA: I dare not for the world.
MIRANDA: But how shall we hereafter shun him, if we do not
  Know him first?
DORINDA: Nay I confess I would fain see him too. I find it in my
  Nature, because my Father has forbidden me.
MIRANDA: I, there's it, Sister; if he had said nothing I had been quiet.
  (II.iv.124–35)

What is actually a culturally constructed stereotype of femininity is seen here as inherent and natural. Without any apparent prompting from society Miranda and Dorinda are already disobedient, perverse, and in need of control. They are also spontaneously drawn to the prospect of motherhood as their destiny, and readily accept patriarchal authority as necessary:

MIRANDA: Sister, I have stranger news to tell you
 ... Shortly we may chance to see that thing,
 Which you have heard my Father call, a Man.
DORINDA: But what is that? for yet he never told me.
MIRANDA: I know no more than you: but I have heard
 My Father say we Women were made for him. (I.ii.314–20)

Davenant's invention of Hippolyto, the 'man who had never seen a woman', while completing the neo-classical symmetry of the youthful quartet, similarly enables his relationship with Ferdinand to explore the masculine sexual nature, and to show it as differentiated from the feminine. Whatever questions the play raises about social and political institutions, it is assumed that gender roles as enacted in Restoration society take their origins from inherent human nature. In addition, Hippolyto is a version of the 'natural' man, brought up in the wild in isolation from society and its conditioning, a figure which Dryden was to develop in plays of his own like *The Indian Queen* and *The Conquest of Granada*. This Restoration noble savage, who subsumes something of Caliban's original role in Shakespeare, was an important figure in a period much concerned with libertine philosophies and the relation between culture and nature. Like Miranda and Dorinda, Hippolyto is delighted by the discovery of the opposite sex, but unlike them his instinctive response is a promiscuous desire for possession. When he hears from Ferdinand – who represents socialised man instructing the spirited but ignorant Hippolyto in culturally acceptable behaviour – that there are women in the world other than Dorinda, the following exchange takes place:

HIPPOLYTO: I will have all of that kind, if there be a hundred of 'em.
FERDINAND: But noble youth, you know not what you say.
HIPPOLYTO: Sir, they are the things I love, I cannot be without 'em:
 O, how I rejoyce! more women!
FERDINAND: Sir, if you love you must be ty'd to one.
HIPPOLYTO: Ty'd! how ty'd to her?
FERDINAND: To love none but her.
HIPPOLYTO: But, Sir, I find it is against my Nature.

I must love where I like, and I believe I may like all,
All that are fair: come! bring me to this Woman,
For I must have her. (III.vi.53–63)

The satisfaction of the 'natural' masculine sexual appetite poses a problem: in Hippolyto's horoscope Prospero has read that Hippolyto will die if he sees a woman when young, and this fate appears to be fulfilled when Hippolyto is mortally wounded in a duel with Ferdinand over Miranda. This duel, interestingly, shows the natural man to be no match for the socialised man in a fight: Hippolyto has neither sense of danger nor any skill with a weapon. Ariel saves the day by producing a magical panacea; Hippolyto, weakened by loss of blood, and newly instructed in the sensation of jealousy when he sees Ferdinand with Dorinda, agrees to confine himself to a single woman. The two pairs of lovers are then married by Prospero. The naive responses of Hippolyto and Dorinda to the concept of marriage slyly demystify its ceremony, and by implication define it as a social agreement:

PROSPERO: And that your happiness may be compleat,
   I give you my Dorinda for your Wife, she shall
   Be yours for ever, when the Priest has made you one.
HIPPOLYTO: How can he make us one, shall I grow to her?
PROSPERO: By saying holy words you shall be joyn'd in marriage
   To each other.
DORINDA: I warrant those holy words are charms.
   My Father means to conjure us together. (V.ii.165–71)

The secularity of this *Tempest* is evident in Prospero: he wears no magic garment, conjures no betrothal masque for the lovers, and has no need to break his staff and drown his book. His magic has not the potency of the original Prospero, and at times brings about more harm than good: 'I am curs'd because I us'd it' (IV.iii.160), he says at the apparent death of Hippolyto in the duel with Ferdinand. Though less powerful than Shakespeare's character he appears more repressive, in that he has to spend so much of his time in the role of an anxious father trying, unsuccessfully, to control the sexual behaviour of his daughters and his ward, and feeding them misinformation. By contrast, he has less to do to bring about the punishment of his political enemies, for Alonso and Antonio (Sebastian does not appear) are repentant as early as the second act. Political themes take a different form in this play, and are largely displaced onto the comic subplot. Here Stephano and Trincalo (*sic*) are sailors, Master and Boatswain, not servants from a royal household, and accompanied by two other sailors, Mustacho and Ventoso. Their drunken arguments over the establishment of order on the island specifically mock social contract theories of popular sovereignty from the Interregnum period.[22] Echoes of Hobbes's *Leviathan* have been found in this part of the play.[23]

> MUSTACHO: Our ship is sunk, and we can never get home agen: we must e'en turn Salvages, and the next that catches his fellow may eat him.
>
> VENTOSO: No, no, let us have a Government; for if we live well and orderly, Heav'n will drive the Shipwracks ashore to make us all rich, there let us carry good Consciences, and not eat one another.
>
> STEPHANO: Whoever eats any of my subjects, I'le break out his Teeth with my Scepter: for I was Master at Sea, and will be Duke on Land: you *Mustacho* have been my Mate, and shall be my Vice-Roy.
>
> VENTOSO: When you are Duke you may chuse your Vice-Roy; but I am a free subject in a new Plantation, and will have no Duke without my voice. And so fill me the other soop.
>
> STEPHANO: (*whispering*) *Ventoso*, dost thou hear? I will advance thee, prithee give me thy voice.
>
> VENTOSO: I'le have no whisperings to corrupt the Election; and to show that I have no private ends, I declare aloud that I will be Vice-Roy, or I'le keep my voice for myself. (II.iii.48–65)

Whereas all would-be usurpers in Shakespeare's *Tempest* seek to establish themselves as kings, there are no kings at all in this play, and the low characters aim to constitute state authority on a different basis. As has been pointed out,[24] Ventoso's use of the word 'plantation' here has specific colonial connotations, and the playwrights may be satirising the political intentions of colonists, and alluding to the conflicting claims of authority over the colonies during the Interregnum period, of which Davenant had personal experience.

The mutinous sailors constantly fear the outbreak of civil war, but cannot agree on a power structure. Stephano proclaims himself Duke, and Mustacho and Ventoso his viceroys, but Trincalo is equally determined to be Duke; he consolidates his

power by alliance with Caliban, and subsequently marriage to
the gross Sycorax, Caliban's sister, thus claiming the right to the
island by inheritance, as well as by popular vote (III.iii.118–22).
Since Trincalo has access to the only remaining supply of liquor
there is no contest, but when Stephano and his supporters come
to make peace the harmony is undermined by a new alliance
forged between Stephano and Sycorax, already discontented
with her first husband and on the lookout for another. Trincalo
determines to take the first step in ending the marriage: 'She will
be in the fashion else; first Cuckold her Husband, and then sue
for a separation, to get Alimony' (IV.ii.164–6).

Sycorax, whose part was played by a man, adds a further
perspective to the gender politics of the play. In one sense she is
the inverse of Hippolyto (played by a woman), but she is also a
version of the natural, or wild, man. Whereas in Hippolyto, who
is the long-lost Duke of Mantua, untaught impulses have the
potential for noble development into expressions of love and
honour, in Sycorax, who is a type of the native black woman
imagined by European colonists, there is only uncontrolled,
unashamed, sexuality.[25] Where promiscuous appetite is a natural expression of Hippolyto's masculine sexuality, and represented as comically innocent, in Sycorax it is gross and
repulsive.

It has been suggested that the play responds to topical foreign
events as well as to domestic politics. Alonso is Duke of Savoy
here, instead of King of Naples, and the relations between the
dukedoms of Savoy, Milan and Mantua may mirror those
between France, Spain and England (there was much anti-
French feeling at the time, and France had declared war on
England in 1666). In July 1667 the Duke of Savoy was thought
in England to have formed an alliance with the King of France.[26]
At home, of course, 'restoration' themes were popular, and the
play shows the restoration of two rightful dukes, Prospero and
Hippolyto. But it is less certain whether the play takes a Whig or
a Tory direction in its treatment of the relations between ruler
and subject. On one hand, the failure of Prospero to control
things better on the island – which Ariel points out in his
soliloquy at the end of Act IV, 'Harsh discord reigns throughout
this fatal Isle' – and the need for Ariel to intervene in saving
Hippolyto's life, have been thought to show a Whiggish
tendency: 'The potential for a creative political order resides not

with the benevolent monarch but with the loyal, resourceful subject.'[27] On the other hand, the impotence of the ducal figures along with the stress on divine will suggested in the mysterious 'purple Panacea' which Ariel travels so far to find, might imply a more Tory view that royal authority is what is really needed.[28] In truth, the play cannot be said to take a clear position, although it does engage with contemporary debates on the nature of government in both main and subplots. The support for divine-right absolutism that has been seen in Shakespeare's *Tempest*[29] is not evident here. At one point Prospero is quite explicit as to the limited nature of his own secular power, and its distinction from absolutism:

> The Powers above may pardon or reprieve,
> As Sovereign Princes may dispense with Laws,
> Which we, as Officers, must execute. Our Acts of grace
> To Criminals are Treason to Heavens prerogative. (V.i.10–13)

It is not difficult to see the attraction of Dryden's and Davenant's reshaping: the additional characters allow for enhanced effects of parallelism and contrast already potentially available in Shakespeare; the moral values are more clearly delineated in the interests of social decorum, in that the noble characters are more noble, the lower more low; and there is a satisfyingly clear hierarchical ordering of the several sets of lovers, from the platonic pair, Ariel and Milcha, to the sensual Caliban and Sycorax. The transvestism in the roles of Hippolyto and Sycorax, along with the spectacular elements and the large amounts of song and dance, foreshadow the genre of the popular pantomime. In the passages adapted from Shakespeare's text the language is modernised and clarified, and word order regularised; oaths are omitted, and vocabulary often made more decorous. The invented scenes between Miranda, Dorinda, Ferdinand and Hippolyto move easily between rhythmic prose and verse, the transparency of the language rendering the innocent responses of the characters:

DORINDA: I much wonder what it is to dye.
HIPPOLYTO: Sure 'tis to dream, a kind of breathless sleep
   When once the Soul's gone out.
DORINDA: What is the Soul?
HIPPOLYTO: A small blew thing that runs about within us.

DORINDA: Then I have seen it in a frosty morning run
        Smoking from my mouth. (V.ii.16–22)

Critics in the earlier part of this century were censorious in their
attitude towards the 'vulgar wit and suggestiveness . . . coarse-
ness . . . innuendoes',[30] but a change in the moral climate of the
late twentieth century enables us to respond more sympatheti-
cally to Restoration manners and their expression.

## Dryden, All for Love

*All for Love*, which Dryden regarded as his masterpiece, and
was, he said, the only one of his plays he wrote to please himself,
is an adaptation of Shakespeare only in a special sense. Unlike
Dryden's earlier collaboration with Davenant on *The Tempest*,
or his own version of *Troilus and Cressida*, it neither borrows
Shakespeare's lines nor follows his original in structure or
content. In comparison with *Antony and Cleopatra*, whose
action moves between continents and takes place over a long
span of time, *All for Love* is a taut neo-classical tragedy with a
small cast of characters, confined, with some contrivance, to a
single location and to the last hours in the lives of its
protagonists. Dryden in his preface draws attention to his
meticulous observance of the Aristotelian unities, and especially
to the fact that the structure is 'without Episode, or Underplot'.
Although he had a life-long involvement with the work of
Shakespeare, the immediate impetus to write *All for Love* could
have come from elsewhere; his friend Charles Sedley had a play
on the same subject successfully performed in February 1677 by
the Duke's Company, and this is closer to Dryden in structure
and tragic conception than is Shakespeare's play. Dryden's *All
for Love*, 'by Envy fir'd', as a contemporary has it, might well
have been a venture by the commercially less successful King's
Company – which he was anyway soon to desert – to keep up
with its rival. Presumably Killigrew felt that a new *Antony and
Cleopatra* would work better to this end than a revival of the
original which he could, had he wished, have put on, since it
was among the plays allocated to his company. Dryden's play
was first performed in December 1677 and published soon
afterwards.

There had been a number of earlier plays on the story of
Antony and Cleopatra, as Dryden mentions in his preface, and
there is evidence in his text that he knew Samuel Daniel's *The

*Tragedie of Cleopatra* (1594), but he certainly wrote with a close eye on 'the divine Shakespeare', whose style he professed to imitate. Since Walter Scott's edition of Dryden's works in 1808 it has become standard to compare *All for Love* with *Antony and Cleopatra*; but in fact Shakespeare's play was probably not acted in the Restoration theatre, and not popular on stage before the twentieth century. *All for Love*, a 'moderately popular success' in its own day, according to modern editors, kept it off the stage till 1849.[31] Dryden may have written his play consciously to rival Shakespeare's, something which could not be said of any of the other adaptations in this edition. Ironically, it seems to be the sort of imitation of which Dryden claimed to disapprove, although it became a genre of its own in the eighteenth century, 'when neither the thought nor words are drawn from the original: but instead of them there is something new produced'.[32]

*All for Love* begins with the battle of Actium already lost, the protagonists separated, and their individual supporters, who function like confidants in Racine (Alexas for Cleopatra, Ventidius for Antony), eager to keep them at odds. The focus is on Antony's commitment. Will he return to military duty, to life as a Roman general, and to his wife and children, or will he reject all this for Cleopatra's love? As in a classical tragedy, we already know the outcome, and the interest lies in the way the choice is made. After the first act, in which Cleopatra does not appear, the balance is evenly distributed. Ventidius and Alexas play parallel roles, and where the unexpected appearance of Octavia (who has travelled to Egypt specially for the purpose) creates a dilemma for Antony in Act 3, Dollabella in turn creates a different sort of dilemma for Cleopatra in Act 4. Antony fatally wounds himself in a suicide pact with Ventidius when all seems lost to him, both personally and politically, but survives to be reconciled with Cleopatra, who then kills herself only a hundred lines later. The action consists largely of a series of encounters, of which the confrontation between Cleopatra and Octavia when 'their trains come up on either side' (III.415) is the most formal. As Moelwyn Merchant puts it, 'For the cinematic *montage* of Shakespeare's brief scenes Dryden substitutes tableaux, the nearest approach of English drama to the statuesque of Racine.'[33]

Neo-classical though the form of the play may be, the

language is not Racinian. Dryden had decided to abandon the rhymed heroic couplets he had previously thought proper to heroic drama for the greater freedom of Shakespearean blank verse, which allowed him not only grandly emotional effects but also a rhythmic delicacy:

> How I lov'd
> Witness ye Dayes and Nights, and all your hours,
> That danc'd away with Down upon your Feet,
> As all your bus'nes were to count my passion.
> One day past by, and nothing saw but Love;
> Another came, and still 'twas only Love:
> The Suns were weary'd out with looking on,
> And I untyr'd with loving. (II.281–8)

But although *Antony and Cleopatra* is usually supposed to be the primary text behind this play, Dryden is often at his best when least Shakespearean, expanding imaginatively into similes where Shakespeare is more typically metaphorical and compressed. Dollabella's perceptive soliloquy on Antony's blindness to his own feelings is a good example:

> Men are but Children of a larger growth,
> Our appetites as apt to change as theirs,
> And full as craving too, and full as vain:
> And yet the Soul, shut up in her dark room,
> Viewing so clear abroad, at home sees nothing;
> But, like a Mole in Earth, busie and blind,
> Works all her folly up, and casts it outward
> To the World's open view. (IV.43–50)

Antony's lines where he is reconciled with Cleopatra in the last moments of their lives are appropriately simple and tender:

> CLEOPATRA: How is it with you?
> ANTONY:     'Tis as with a man
>   Removing in a hurry; all pack'd up,
>   But one dear Jewel that his haste forgot;
>   And he, for that, returns upon the spur:
>   So I come back, for thee. (V.365–9)

*All for Love*, critically highly regarded in the later seventeenth and eighteenth centuries, was an example of what came to be known as 'affective tragedy', that is, tragedy defined in terms of the emotional effects it produces upon its audiences, rather than more formally in terms of structure dependent upon plotting towards a catastrophe. The rather pat statement of didactic purpose in the preface, that 'the chief persons represented, were famous patterns of unlawful love; and their end accordingly was unfortunate', does not do justice to Dryden's handling of erotic passion. His Antony is a man obsessed, who, in Ventidius's words, 'runs to meet his ruine' (III.47). Although when absent from Cleopatra he can recognise the anti-social nature of their mutual self-absorption, in her company nothing else matters. Meaningless, the world is an empty circle, a toy, a rattle to 'give to your Boy, your Caesar', and their mutual passion is endlessly fulfilling:

> There's no satiety of Love, in thee;
> Enjoy'd, thou art still new; perpetual Spring
> Is in thy armes; the ripen'd fruit but falls,
> And blossoms rise to fill its empty place;
> And I grow rich by giving. (III.24–9)

The social responsibilities that Antony abandons for love are not passed over lightly: Octavia, a more forceful figure than Shakespeare's feather on the water, is also a mother, while Cleopatra seems (unhistorically) to have borne no children. Antony gives up the family and the civic duty and public service represented by his role as a soldier, and allows himself to become progressively more diminished: 'shrunk from the vast extent of all his honors, / And crampt within a corner of the World' (I.178–9). Dryden's tightly structured play helps create a sense of confinement, and the singlemindedness of his Cleopatra enhances it. There is no ambivalence about her fidelity or devotion: she has been genuinely high-minded, not calculating, in refusing Caesar's offer of terms, she pretends to flirt with Dollabella only on Alexas's persuasions, and her posing is exposed when she faints (always a revelation of true feeling) at being told Antony hates her. It is Alexas, not she, who in a last-ditch attempt to save himself, devises the plan to win back Antony by a false report of her death.

The changed representation of Cleopatra is, as Catherine Belsey has said, 'a measure of the transformation of love in the course of the seventeenth century'[34], and a revaluing of the conjugal. Dryden's Cleopatra is a virtuous mistress who longs for nothing more than to be a wife. The alluring and alternative values of Shakespeare's 'serpent of old Nile' are largely absent from this play, in which Cleopatra's wiles and contrivances are displaced onto Alexas. Her relationship with Antony is domesticated, as is her sexuality. Dryden tries to convey the idea of her dangerously irresistible beauty through Ventidius, who is forced to admit to desiring her against his will (IV.233–43), but her own exhibitions of power-play reveal a more conventional feminity:

> Go; leave me, Soldier;
> (For you're no more a Lover:) leave me dying:
> Push me all pale and panting from your bosome,
> And, when your March begins, let one run after,
> Breathless almost for joy, and cry, *She's dead*! (II.410–15)

Although Belsey, in stressing the play's demonstration of how 'women have become identified as the agents of conjugal love' rather than disruptive and unruly, overstates her case, undoubtedly there is a new conception of gender roles in Dryden's play. Antony is now a fanciful, gentlemanly character, given to self-indulgent displays of nostalgia and despair. Like Orsino, he invokes music to feed his melancholy. He overflows with sensibility. He and Ventidius weep together (in a scene that Dryden confesses to admiring particularly) over one another's unhappiness, and he is ready to burst into tears at the thought of Cleopatra's misery should he leave her. He recalls his affection for Dollabella with intensity:

> I was his Soul; he liv'd not but in me:
> We were so clos'd within each others brests,
> The rivets were not found that join'd us first.
> That does not reach us yet: we were so mixt,
> As meeting streams, both to ourselves were lost;
> We were one mass. (III.91–6)

The polarised view of sexual differentiation that creates the frisson in Antony and Cleopatra's tales of cross-dressing in Shakespeare is absent here. Nor are Dryden's characters looking to push back boundaries or to demonstrate their disregard for conventional morality by flouting the rules of sexual behaviour. There are new stereotypes for defining men's and women's social and sexual roles with a greater degree of flexibility; virtuous soldiers can throw themselves to the ground in sorrow and weep without apology or loss of masculinity, and women can be honourable as well as desirable.

Both Antony and Cleopatra are more unambiguously honourable and heroic than their Shakespearean counterparts. Serapion's epitaph, 'No lovers liv'd so great, or dy'd so well', comes across as a moral as well as an aesthetic verdict. Written at a time when many people were outraged by the power and importance attained at court by Charles II's French mistress, Louise de Kerouille, Duchess of Portsmouth, a play celebrating the love between a ruler and his mistress might seem to carry a political message. Certainly it was seen that way some forty years later by the critic John Dennis who was enraged by the play's last lines which he read as an 'Encomium of the Conduct and Death of *Anthony* and *Cleopatra*, a Conduct so immoral, and a Self-murder so criminal . . . put into the mouth of the High-Priest of *Isis*'. He saw the play as an endorsement of the libertine behaviour and political absolutism of the king: 'Certainly never could the design of an Author square more exactly with the design of White-hall, at the time when it was written, which was by debauching the People so absolutely to enslave them.'[35] A contemporary poem, 'On the Dutchess of Portsmouth's Picture', not only makes a complimentary analogy between the effect of Portsmouth's beauty on rulers and that of Cleopatra, but also seems to play on Dryden's title. Dryden, who was a royalist, and attacks certain important opposition leaders (such as Buckingham) in his preface, may well have intended his play about a ruler's passion broadly to reflect a sympathetic view of the monarch's amours and to offer support to an embattled regime. Sedley's more overtly political play, after all, has been seen as offering a criticism of Charles II through an analogy with Antony and the tyrannical misgovernment caused by his passion for Cleopatra.[36] There has also been the suggestion that the casting of the female roles, with the small and innocent-looking Betty Boutell as a sympathetic Cleopatra, and the larger, more forceful, Elizabeth Corey as a challenging Octavia, supports this view. Dryden's dedication to Danby, Charles II's chief minister at the time (though soon to fall) also lends it weight.

## *Tate,* King Lear

Nahum Tate's much maligned *The History of King Lear* (1681) is the most notorious of those plays on which critical and popular opinion have markedly diverged. Shakespeare's own *King Lear* had been produced in the Restoration, in 1674 and 1675, but after Tate's appeared Shakespeare's was ousted from the stage until Garrick's version in 1756. Even then, Tate's controversial innovations, such as the introduction of a love affair between Edgar and Cordelia and the expunging of the Fool, were retained into the nineteenth century.[37] But despite twentieth-century academic revulsion against Tate, his decision, motivated both by political and aesthetic considerations, to reorganise the play so as to produce a happy ending had respectable supporters early on. Critics like John Dennis and Dr Johnson, who found Shakespeare's indifference to poetic justice (a term coined by Thomas Rymer in 1678) hard to accept, were happier with a play in which Lear, Cordelia, Gloucester and Kent all survived to see happier times: 'In the present case the publick has decided', pronounced Johnson. Tragedy with a happy ending, though regarded by Aristotle as generically imperfect, came into its own in various ways in the seventeenth century, but Tate felt the need to justify it by quoting Dryden in support in his dedicatory epistle: "Tis more difficult to Save than 'tis to Kill: The Dagger and Cup of Poyson are alwaies in Readiness; but to bring the Action to the last Extremity, and then by probable Means to recover All, will require the Art and Judgment of a Writer.'

The play ends with Edgar, in distinctly more upbeat mood than his Shakespearean predecessor, looking forward to the restoration of the monarchy after the defeat of oppressive tyrants (Goneril and Regan), and the suppression of the threat to the legitimate line from a strong and ambitious bastard (Edmund): 'Our drooping Country now erects her Head, / Peace spread her balmy Wings, and Plenty blooms' (V.vi.155–6). The play, particularly when considered in the context of the political upheaval during the period of its composition – centring on the Exclusion Crisis – makes a very strong political statement, and its initial popularity is likely to have stemmed from topical appeal. After the exposure of the Popish Plot by Titus Oates in 1678, a period of crisis ensued, lasting some five years, and during this time a spate of Shakespearean adaptations, including

two others by Tate, appeared in response to it. Most of them
supported Charles II and the right of his brother, the Catholic
James, Duke of York, to succeed him. Tate's prologue, referring
to the intrigues of churchmen, explicitly alludes to the Popish
Plot and implies the play's involvement in political discourse.
Like Tate's other Shakespearean adaptations, *The Sicilian
Usurper* (*Richard II*) and *The Ingratitude of a Commonwealth*
(*Coriolanus*), *King Lear* takes a conservative line on issues
raised by the Exclusion Crisis, namely 'insurrection, abdication,
succession, and the dangers of mob rule'.[38]

In the latter part of 1680, when Tate's *King Lear* was first
staged, the House of Commons was making strenuous efforts to
pass an Exclusion Bill which would prevent James ever becoming king. The Whigs, who supported the bill in parliamentary
opposition to Charles, had as their candidate for succession the
Protestant Duke of Monmouth, Charles's illegitimate eldest son.
The problem of succession was of course exacerbated by the fact
that Charles had no legitimate offspring, and the fear of a
Catholic conspiracy to take over the monarchy was widespread
in the country, as the Oates affair demonstrated. Tate's play,
with its strong focus on the Bastard Edmund, who, unlike
Shakespeare's character, has ruling ambitions and even, at one
point, imagines himself the secret son of a king, clearly relates to
the controversy over Monmouth's position. This Bastard (as he
is known in the Dramatis Personae) wants not just to cheat his
brother of Gloster's 'vast revenues' (III.ii.59) but to achieve
royal power. He envies the despotic behaviour of Gonerill (*sic*)
and Regan, who have lost no time in assuming royal preroga-
tives and provoking the peasants to rebellion by the imposition
of harsh taxes. These features, absent in Shakespeare, reinforce
Tate's theme of the need for just, but legitimate, rule. Political
opposition to the Bastard develops from the unlikely direction of
the blinded Gloster, who astutely sees his affliction as a means
of enlisting support for the restoration of Lear:

> with these bleeding Rings
> I will present me to the pittying Crowd,
> And with the Rhetorick of these dropping Veins
> Enflame 'em to Revenge their King and me. (III.v.84–7)

Reunited with the banished Kent (perhaps a figure for the Duke

of York, who had for a time lived in exile in France), Gloster
urges him to cast off his disguise and assert himself as a leader:

> Our injur'd Country is at length in arms,
> Urg'd by the King's inhumane wrongs and Mine,
> And only want a Chief to lead 'em on.
> That Task be Thine. (IV.ii.102–5)

Cordelia too enlists in the cause of her father's restoration,
though as a woman she can only support it 'with women's
weapons, piety and prayers' (IV.v.66). She calls for help from
the 'never-erring gods': 'Your image suffers when a monarch
bleeds' (IV.v.70). The last two acts of the play concentrate on
the theme of 'the King's blest restoration' (V.vi.117). Lear
himself briefly entertains the idea of resuming authority, but
decides instead that Cordelia, 'th'imperial grace fresh blooming
on her brow' shall rule, married to Edgar. The promise of their
joint authority curiously foreshadows the reign of William and
Mary, daughter of James II, to follow not long after in 1688.

The political relevance of Tate's play did not, of course,
account for its lasting popularity. In his dedicatory epistle he
describes Shakespeare's play as 'a heap of jewels, unstrung and
unpolished . . . dazzling in their disorder'. In order to provide
these rough diamonds with the necessary polish and setting he
found a single expedient, 'which was to run through the whole a
love between Edgar and Cordelia, that never chang'd word with
each other in the original'. This invention, as Tate goes on to
point out, helps to streamline Shakespeare's play in a number of
ways, clarifying motivation, erasing various improbabilities,
heightening what he calls 'the distress of the story', and,
especially, providing for an ending without a stage 'incumbered
. . . with dead bodies', but with 'success to the innocent
distressed persons'. The characterisation of Edgar and Cordelia
is distinctly changed: Edgar's disguise as Poor Tom now
becomes 'a generous design' in that he assumes it in order to be
able to watch over and protect Cordelia rather than as 'a poor
shift to save his life'; while Cordelia, a romantic ingenue instead
of a tragic heroine, speaks coldly to her father in the first scene
not to make any kind of moral point about the nature of family
bonds and honesty of expression but in order to get herself out
of marrying the Duke of Burgundy.

As has been mentioned, the significance of Gloster's role has also been radically altered. Given his desire to enhance the villainy of Lear's and Gloster's opponents, Tate could hardly avoid having Gloster blinded; but in the light of Gloster's subsequent political manipulation of his impairment the act is no longer to be perceived as one of meaningless savagery, emblematic of a morally baffling world in which gods can seem to behave 'like wanton boys'. The philosophical tone of Gloster's soliloquy on his blindness at the end of act III, influenced, no doubt, by Milton's *Paradise Lost*, captures the 'distress' that Tate sought for while softening the pain and cruelty of Shakespeare.

These kinds of changes are representative of the whole nature of Tate's transformation; where Shakespeare's play is open, ambiguous, multi-faceted, Tate's operates to restrict meanings and render the rough places plain. The complete omission of the Fool, with his cryptic mockery and indecorous rhymes, contributes to this drive for clarification. He had no contribution to make to the plot, and since the behaviour of Tate's King Lear, initially at least, is explained by his choleric disposition – and therefore his wilful folly is played down rather than illuminated – the Fool was not missed. His part was not reinstated till 1838, and then played by a pretty young woman.

Tate's changes respond in various ways to the cultural demands of his time. Edmund is a Hobbesian-style 'natural man', self-confessedly 'born a libertine', concerned only with the pursuit of power and pleasure. He dies unrepentant, acknowledging his brother's success in the fight – 'Legitimacy at last has got it' – and quitting the play with a characteristically boastful couplet: 'Who wou'd not choose, like me, to yield his Breath / T'have Rival queens contend for him in Death?' (V.v.114–15). Lust is a more important component of his nature than in Shakespeare. Regan, whose part is the larger of those belonging to the sisters, notices him with interest as early as II.iii ('A charming youth, and worth my further thought'), and by III.ii both sisters have sent him amorous letters. Not content with their attentions, he also plans to kidnap and rape Cordelia during the storm, but, in a completely new scene, she and her companion are saved by the timely arrival of Edgar. Act IV opens with another new scene, set in a grotto, where Edmund and Regan are discovered 'amorously seated, listening to music'. It has been suggested that this grotto setting was devised to employ the stage facilities available at the well-equipped Dorset Garden theatre, where the Duke's Company would have given the play its premiere.[39] Perhaps the enlargement of all three female roles was also carried out with the company's resources in mind, since it had several accomplished actresses available, including Elizabeth Barry, once mistress to the Earl of Rochester, who played Cordelia, and Mary Lee, who played Regan; but the play's enhanced love-interest would, in any case, have been in line with the tastes of Restoration audiences. Shakespeare's perfunctory account of the triangular intrigue between Edmund, Goneril and Regan provided Tate with the raw material for developing the play in the direction of romantic melodrama.

Yet, despite Tate's radical alterations, considerable portions of Shakespeare's original survive, particularly in the more linguistically challenging and imaginatively original parts such as Lear's mad scenes and Gloster's Dover cliff adventure. Tate abridged and telescoped these scenes but retained, without serious dilution, many of the important speeches. He tended not to tamper with Shakespeare's language: either he changed it completely, or he stayed close to the original.[40] Edgar's Poor Tom idiom, for example, appears almost unchanged in III.iii, and Lear in IV.iv retains much of his dialogue from Shakespeare's IV.vi., especially on adultery and injustice. Tate in his preface apologises for a certain lack of stylistic elegance in his adaptation ('less quaintness of expression'), claiming that he had intentionally modified his style in the interests of decorum and consistency. But it is difficult to avoid the feeling, particularly in acts III and IV of *King Lear*, of there being two different plays uneasily combined, which is exacerbated by the inclusion of large chunks of Shakespeare's text. Perhaps this is also in part the effect of the transition taking place in Act IV from tragedy to romance. It is most evident in the handling of Gloster, who alternates after his blinding between political opportunist and ruined pathetic old man. At the end of Act III he is devising ways to use his blindness for the advantage of Lear's cause, and in IV.ii he is urging Kent to take the role of leader of the uprising against Gonerill and Regan. Yet shortly afterwards he attempts suicide in a version of Shakespeare's Dover cliff scene, and, encountering mad Lear garlanded with flowers, responds with pity (as in Shakespeare's IV.vi), without mention of any political rebellion.

In Act V Tate appears more in control of his materials, perhaps because he is freer of the need to do obeisance to his original, and the shaping of events to bring about the necessary happy ending is achieved with no loss of dramatic excitement. A productive tension is created by the oscillations in the fortunes of the rebellion, so that Gloster's frustration at being unable to take an active part in battle like the courageous fighter he evidently once was (V.iii.) relates consistently to his despair and desire for death at a moment when it seems as if the outcome of events is still uncertain. The fight between Edmund and Edgar is decisive. Albany, a less compromised and impotent figure than his Shakespearean counterpart, intervenes in time to save Lear from death. Lear in fact takes an active part in his own rescue, killing onstage two of the murderers sent by Edmund. Kent gets due recognition from his king, and Gloster, preserved from suicide, kneels at Lear's feet 'to hail his second birth of empire'. The sequence of misfortune and mistiming which accounts for so much of the random cruelty of Shakespeare's tragic ending is avoided, and Tate arranges events to demonstrate, as Cordelia says, that 'there are Gods, and Virtue is their care'. The sense of contrivance is actually less felt than in Shakespeare's play, where it seems as if the organisation of the play's final scene deliberately foregrounds contingency and bad luck; in Tate, events fall out more probably, given the preparations that have been made through characterisation and motivation. Though the initial impetus for the adaptation may have been political, its long theatrical success is not hard to understand.

## Cibber, Richard III

Colley Cibber's *The Tragical History of King Richard III* was premiered at the Theatre Royal in July 1700 – inaugurating what is sometimes known as the century of the actor[41] – and became theatrically the most popular of all the Shakespeare adaptations. Cibber himself played the role eighty-seven times right up until his retirement in 1733. Garrick created a sensation as Richard at his first stage appearance in 1741, and subsequently actors of such different styles as John Kemble and Edmund Kean enjoyed great success in Cibber's play. Macready attempted a partial reconstruction of the Shakespearean original, but continued to use many of Cibber's innovations, and the dominance of Cibber as *the* acting version lasted until the 1870s. Nor has it entirely disappeared in our own times: Olivier's influential film version of 1944, like Cibber, kept in lines from *Henry VI*, cut Queen Margaret entirely, and also included some of Cibber's most famous additions such as 'Off with his head. So much for Buckingham' (IV.iv.188) and 'Richard's himself again' (V.v.85).

When Cibber wrote the play he was still a young man, not yet thirty, and was enjoying a high reputation as a comic playwright and actor, initiated by his success with *Love's Last Shift* (1696). This was a play so good that the waspish John Dennis thought Cibber – then 'an arrant boy' and not well educated – must have stolen it. He had little experience of tragedy, and had not tried his hand at adapting Shakespeare. The manner in which he imports lines from a number of Shakespeare's other plays (particularly *Henry VI*, Part 3, but also *Henry VI*, Part 2, *Henry V*, *Henry IV*, Part 2, and *Richard II*) suggests a considerable familiarity with these texts, which he cannot have seen on the stage. He might have known of John Caryl's *The English Princess, or the Death of Richard III* (1666), a romantic rhymed play centring on the rivalry of Richard and Richmond for the hand of Princess Elizabeth, and of John Crowne's versions of *Henry VI*, *Parts 2 and 3*, *Henry the Sixth, The First Part* (1681) and *The Misery of Civil War* (1680). There is no evidence that he saw the production of Shakespeare's own *Richard III*, performed by the King's Company, probably in 1689–90 (the inference from his autobiography is that he did not); but nonetheless it had an important imaginative effect on his adaptation through the influence of the actor who played Richard, Samuel Sandford. It seems significant that Thomas Betterton, the company's leading actor, who had been applauded as Richard in Caryl's plays, played Edward IV in this production, leaving the title role to a character actor who specialised in villain parts. Cibber wrote that in his view Sandford was so perfect for the part that Shakespeare himself would have chosen him if he could:

> He had sometimes an uncouth Stateliness in his Motion, a harsh and sullen Pride of Speech, a meditating Brow, a stern Aspect, occasionally changing into an almost ludicrous triumph over all Goodness and Virtue: From thence falling into the most asswasive Gentleness, and soothing candour of a designing Heart.[42]

But since Sandford was contracted to Cibber's rival company, Cibber had to play the title role himself, apparently modelling his performance on his imaginative recreation of Sandford's. The performance seems to have been controversial, and though Steele and (according to Cibber) Vanbrugh much admired it, the approbation was not universal. Genest in *Some Account of the English Stage* quotes *The Laureat* (1740): 'he screamed through 4 acts without Dignity or Decency', and Thomas Davies says that he was only 'endured in this [Richard] and other tragic parts on account of his general merit in comedy'.[43] Though the production was soon taken off and not revived until 1704, Cibber persisted in the part and did the play's reputation no lasting harm; it apparently enjoyed its greatest popularity with audiences in the mid-eighteenth century, once Garrick had taken on the role.

Cibber's *Richard III* as an adaptation of Shakespeare (it was his only attempt) belongs with Lacy's *Sauny the Scot* rather than with *The Tempest*, *All for Love* and *King Lear*, in that it was the work of an actor turned playwright and conceived primarily as a theatrical vehicle. Though Cibber was known in later life to be a staunch Hanoverian, this play sidesteps any involvement with political issues. It is ironic that at the first performance Cibber's first act, which incorporates material from *Henry VI, Part 3*, was dropped by order of the Lord Chamberlain's office on account, he says, of presumed political content:

> [the Lord Chamberlain] had an Objection to the whole Act, and the Reason he gave for it was, that the distresses of King Henry the Sixth, who is kill'd by Richard in the first act, would put weak people too much in mind of King James, then living in France; a notable proof of his Zeal for the Government! Those who have read, either the Play, or the History, I dare say, will think he strain'd hard for the Parallel.[44]

The alterations Cibber makes to Shakespeare in fact eradicate rather than reinforce elements in the earlier play which could contribute to Elizabethan debates about political legitimacy. The removal of a number of characters, particularly Queen Margaret, Clarence, Edward and Hastings, narrows Shakespeare's dynastic focus and his play's historical perspective: there is no longer much sense of Richard's rise to power as the horrendous culmination of a long and bloody period of civil war, of family vendettas and age-old enmities reaching a purgative climax of monstrous bloodshed. Equally, the earlier play's comically shocking disclosure of the strategies by which Richard manipulates the apparatus of both church and state in order to achieve power is largely absent, partly on account of the reduction in Buckingham's political role but also because of the greater clarification of motivation generally. This is a more personal play than its predecessor, in which the part of Richard is rewritten so as to focus interest on his moral life, creating for him a role that lends itself more easily to readings in terms of inwardness and personal development. He is much less the comic Vice of Shakespeare, although some of Cibber's alterations enhance his wit. This can be seen early in the play, in his irreverent comment on the corpse of Henry VI – 'But first I'll turn St Harry to his grave' (II.i.276), for example – and the comic sadism of some of his exchanges with Anne:

RICHARD: Your absence, Madam, will be necessary.
LADY ANNE: Wou'd my death were so.
RICHARD:   It may be shortly. (III.ii.71–3)

More significant is the fact that Cibber writes him seven new soliloquies, and also considerably strengthens his role in the latter part of the play. Several of these soliloquies clarify Richard's motivation, and create for him an inner conflict between the demands of ambition and of conscience. Act III.i, in which he is publicly taunted by the child Duke of York, concludes with a soliloquy in which he begins to plot the murder of the princes; the plan presents itself to him in a moral dimension, albeit briefly:

How many frightful stops wou'd Conscience make
In some heads to undertake like me:
– Come; this Conscience is a convenient Scarecrow,
It guards the fruit which Priests and Wisemen tast,
Who never set it up to fright themselves:
They know 'tis rags. (III.i.157–62)

But he dismisses this idea in the tones of a Restoration libertine:

Why were Laws made, but that we're Rogues by Nature?
Conscience! 'tis our Coin, we live by parting with it,
And he thrives best that has the most to spare. (III.i.165–7)

The pangs of conscience grow even stronger during the soliloquy
he makes immediately before the murder of the princes in the
Tower, and for a moment he feels how 'Nature . . . as if she
knew me Womanish and weak /Tugs at my Heart-strings'
(IV.iii.23). This, and other soliloquies, recall Macbeth, who
might well have been in Cibber's mind. At the end of Act III, left
alone after the staged appearance in front of the Lord Mayor of
London, Richard exclaims

> Why now my golden dream is out –
> Ambition like an early Friend throws back
> My Curtains with an eager Hand, o'rejoy'd
> To tell me what I dreamt is true – A Crown!
> . . .
> Conscience, lie still – more lives must yet be drain'd
> Crowns got with Blood must be with Blood maintain'd.
> (III.ii.270–83)

The development of an inwardness for Richard is accompanied
by an increase in other elements of pathos and private feeling.
Anne's role is enlarged by a completely new scene at the
beginning of III.ii. in which she laments, to musical accompani-
ment, the misery of her marriage, and in lines borrowed from
*Henry IV*, Part 2 her inability to sleep. The Princes also get more
lines, and in another new scene at the beginning of Act IV are
shown with their mother and other women expressing their
fears and foreboding. It ends with their being torn away from
their weeping mother:

> BOTH PRINCES: O Mother! Mother!
> QUEEN:       O my poor Children!
>
> > [*Exeunt parted severally*]
> > (IV.i.124)

In the first quarto text of the play there is even a brief scene
depicting the actual murder: the Princes cannot sleep, the clock
strikes two, Dighton and Forrest enter with lanterns, and,
having urged the children to pray, smother them. This was
omitted from later editions, but even without it there remains a
strong element of the domestic and the pathetic in Cibber's play,
which links it with the kind of sentimental tragedy popularised
by Otway, who adapted *Romeo and Juliet* in this mode.

These new scenes never distract attention from Richard, and

serve further to define his role as a conscienceless monster of evil. In the latter part of the play (where Shakespeare's character, having achieved the crown, begins to falter and lose confidence) Cibber's Richard continues actively aggressive, his part strengthened by extra speeches drawn from other Shakespeare plays, especially soliloquies from *Henry IV*, Part 2 (at the end of Act IV) and from *Henry V* at the beginning of V.v. (the ghost scene). The alteration of this scene clearly indicates Cibber's purpose for the ending of his play: the new speech, borrowing lines from the Chorus before the battle of Agincourt, reinstates Richard as commander in battle; while the much-abridged ghost scene is followed not by a long and fearful soliloquy but a few brief conscience-stricken lines, after which Richard briskly admonishes himself, 'Conscience avant; Richard's himself again' (V.v.85). He challenges Richmond to fight, and dies with lines from *Henry VI*, Part 2, after which Richmond pays tribute to his courage:

'Had thy aspiring Soul but stir'd in Vertue / With half the spirit it has dar'd in Evil, / How might thy Fame have grac'd our *English* Annals' (V.ix.23–5). The reference to history is typical of a certain self-consciousness that informs the play at critical moments. The scene in which Richard wooes Anne, for example, includes commentary by Stanley and Tressell, who are present, unobserved, throughout; at one point Tressell remarks:

'When future Chronicles shall speak of this / They will be thought Romance, not History' (II.i.203–4). In this instance it is as if the device of the commentators, while distancing the scene from the audience, presents it self-consciously as theatre. Cibber is aware of himself rewriting both history and Shakespeare; his play rejoices in its staginess.

Like Tate's *King Lear* and the Dryden/Davenant *Tempest*, Cibber's *Richard III* has come in for its fair share of critical abuse, not least from editors of Shakespeare's play (the moral disapproval of Dover Wilson, who calls it 'a viciously adulterated version of our play', is typical). Yet the theatrical insight behind Cibber's changes reflects not just audience tastes of the late seventeenth century but a more general sense of what is intractable in Shakespeare's play that has been shared by later generations of directors and theatre-goers. Many of his cuts speed up and clarify the lines of action, and one, at least, of his major additions acknowledges audience needs that are by no means culturally specific to seventeenth- and eighteenth-century England. His new first act, with scenes from *Henry VI, Part 3*, helps considerably to fill in the complex historical background of wars and factions; the tediousness of following what Ben Jonson had called 'York and Lancaster's long jars'[45] is acknowledged in modern productions in other ways such as showing family trees onstage or using some other expositionary opening, but it remains an implicit problem. His cutting of the rhetorical lamentations of the women and children is still regularly imitated. Literate modern audiences equipped with detailed programme notes are probably no more aware than Cibber's first audiences were that the lines they are hearing differ in a hundred ways from any printed text. But the publication of Cibber's play in 1700 makes explicit the divide between stage and page, in that, as he specifically points out in his preface, a typographical distinction is made between original and invented lines:

> I have caus'd those that are intirely *Shakespear's* to be Printed in this *Italick Character*; and those lines with this mark (') before 'em, are generally his thoughts, in the best dress I could afford 'em: What is not so mark'd, or in a different Character is intirely my own.

The demarcations were not always entirely accurate, as my notes will illustrate, but the intention behind them, to separate out different literary property, is clear. On the stage, of course, the more successful Cibber's effort to 'imitate [Shakespeare's] Style, and manner of thinking', the less an audience will be aware of two playwrights at work; but for his readers Cibber obviously thought it important to draw attention both to his literary integrity and to his share in creating the text as a whole. His handling of Shakespeare suggests both knowledge of and respect for his predecessor's work; when a scene needed strengthening he would regularly do this with some extra Shakespearean material, and he knew where to look for it. His sense of what would work in the theatre does not run counter to his model, as could sometimes be said for Tate's or Dryden's; of all the adaptations, this is the most faithful.

SANDRA CLARK

## References

1 For documentation on the patents see G. E. Bentley, *The Jacobean and Caroline Stage* (Oxford: Clarendon Press, 1941–68), vol. 6, pp. 304–9; and also G. Sorelius, 'The Rights of the Restoration Theatrical Companies in the Older Drama', *Studia Neophilologica* 37 (1965), 188.

2 Quoted from A. Nicoll, *A History of Restoration Drama 1660–1700* (Cambridge: Cambridge University Press, 1923), p. 314.

3 See J. Freehafer, 'The Formation of the London Patent Companies in the 1660s', *Theatre Notebook* vol. 20 (1965), p. 27; and R. D. Hume, *The Development of English Drama in the Late Seventeenth Century* (Oxford: Clarendon Press, 1976), p. 20. Hume interprets the proposition somewhat differently in 'Securing a Repertory: Plays on the London Stage 1660–5', in *Poetry and Drama 1570–1700: Essays in Honour of Harold Brooks*, eds A. Coleman and A. Hammond (Methuen: London and New York, 1981), p. 159.

4 M. W. Black and M. A. Shaaber, *Shakespeare's Seventeenth Century Editors, 1632–85*, MLA, General Series vol. 6 (New York and London, 1937), p. 95.

5 John Evelyn, *The Diary of John Evelyn*, ed. E. S. de Beer (Oxford, 1955), vol. 3, p. 304.

6 Michael Dobson, *The Making of the National Poet: Shakespeare, Adaptation, and Authorship* (Oxford: Clarendon Press, 1992).

7 Dobson, p. 101.

8 Quoted from *Five Restoration Adaptations of Shakespeare*, ed. C. Spencer (Urbana, Illinois: University of Illinois Press, 1965), p. 8.

9 W. Moelwyn Merchant, 'Shakespeare Made Fit', in *Restoration Theatre*, Stratford-upon-Avon Studies, series 6 (Edward Arnold: London and New York, 1965), pp. 194–219; G. C. Odell, *Shakespeare from Betterton to Irving*, 2 vols (London: Constable, 1920), vol. 1, p. 31; and *The Tempest, A New Variorum*, ed. H. H. Furness (Philadelphia, 1897), p. viii.

10 H. Spencer, *Shakespeare Improved: The Restoration Versions in Quarto and on the Stage* (Cambridge, Mass.: Harvard University Press, 1927), pp. 54, 371.

11 *The Works of John Dryden*, eds M. E. Novak and G. R. Guffey (University of California Press: Berkeley, Los Angeles; and London: University of California Press, 1970), vol. 10, p. 328.

12 Dryden, Tate and Cibber were all at some time Poets Laureate.

13 The publisher's preface is printed in *The Dramatic Works of John Lacy, Comedian*, eds James Maidment and W. H. Logan (Edinburgh: William Paterson, London: H. Sotheran and Co., 1875), p. 316.

14 Diary entries, 15 April, 1667, 1 May 1667.

15 On Lacy's other parts, see Nicholl, *A History of Restoration Drama*, p. 69.

16 Arthur Bedford, *A Serious Remonstrance in behalf of the Christian Religion, against The Horrid Blasphemies and Impieties which are still used in the English Play-Houses* (1719), p. 372.

17 For example, he was famous as the Irish servant Teague in Sir Robert Howard's *The Committee* (1662), and played Ragoû, a Frenchman, in his own comedy, *The Old Troop* (c. 1665).

18 For a view of *The Woman's Prize* as a play whose sexual politics are compromised, see Sandra Clark, *The Plays of Beaumont and Fletcher: Sexual Themes and Dramatic Representation* (Hemel Hempstead: Harvester-Wheatsheaf, 1994), pp. 97–100.

19 Susan Staves, *Players' Sceptres: Fictions of Authority in the Restoration* (Lincoln and London: University of Nebraska Press, 1979), p. 134.

20 For example, by Charles Johnson, in *The Cobler of Preston* (1716), which uses the Christopher Sly scenes as the basis of an anti-Jacobite satire.

21 J. R. Brown, 'Three Adaptations', *Shakespeare Survey* 13 (1960), p. 137.

22 See Dobson, *The Making of the National Poet*, p. 42.

23 Dobson, pp. 44–9, and M. Raddadi, *Davenant's Adaptations of Shakespeare* (Uppsala: Studia anglistica upsallensis. Almqvist and Wiksell International, 1979), p. 145.

24 M. H. Wikander, '"The Duke my Father's Wrack": the Innocence of the Restoration *Tempest*', *Shakespeare Survey* vol. 43 (1991), p.95.

25 As Novak and Guffey, the editors of the play, point out, by 1668 'polygamous, polyandrous, and even incestuous societies had been discovered by voyagers, and the handling of Sycorax's sexuality supports the play's depiction of monogamous marriage as a social and cultural convenience rather than a law of nature' (*The Works of John Dryden*, vol. 10, p. 335).

26 Pepys, in his Diary for 30 September 1661, notes the popular preference for Spain over France.

27 K. A. Maus, 'Arcadia Lost: Politics and Revision in the Restoration *Tempest*', *Restoration Drama*, new series 13 (1982), p. 144.

28 Wikander, pp. 92–3.

29 See, for example, G. Schmidgall, *Shakespeare and the Courtly Aesthetic* (Berkeley: University of California Press, 1981).

30 A. Nicholl, *A History of Restoration Drama*, pp. 165–6.

31 *The Works of John Dryden*, eds E. N. Hooker and H. T. Swedenberg, vol. 13, pp. 363, 365.

32 Dryden, *Of Dramatic Poesy and other Critical Essays*, ed. G. Watson (London: Dent, 1962), vol. 1, p. 271.

33 Moelwyn Merchant, 'Shakespeare Made Fit', p. 206.

34 Catherine Belsey, *The Subject of Tragedy: Identity and Difference in Renaissance Drama* (London: Routledge, 1985), p. 210.

35 *The Critical Works of John Dennis*, ed. E. N. Hooker, 2 vols (Baltimore: The Johns Hopkins Press, 1943), vol. 2, p. 163.

36 *All for Love*, ed. N. J. Andrew, New Mermaids (London and Tonbridge: Ernest Benn, 1975), p. xvi. Andrew's introduction gives some helpful information about Sedley's play.

37 For an account of the adaptations made to Tate's version by Garrick, Kemple and others, see *King Lear*, ed. J. S. Bratton, Plays in Performance (Bristol: Bristol Classical Press, 1987), especially the introduction and Appendix B.

38 M. H. Wikander, 'The Spitted Infant: Scenic Emblem and Exclusionist Politics in Restoration Adaptations of Shakespeare', *Shakespeare Quarterly*, 37 (1986), p. 351.

39 J. Black, 'An Augustan Stage-history: Nahum Tate's *King Lear*', *Restoration and Eighteenth Century Theatre Research*, 6 (May, 1967), p. 44.

40 H. Spencer, *Shakespeare Improved*, makes this point, p. 249.

41 A. P. Wood, *The Stage History of Shakespeare's King Richard the Third* (New York: California University Press, 1909), p. 94.

42 *An Apology for the Life of Colley Cibber*, ed. B. R. S. Fone (Ann Arbor: University of Michigan Press, 1968), p. 81.

43 *Richard III*, ed. J. Hankey, Plays in Performance (London: Junction Books, 1981), p. 31. The introduction and notes in this edition provide much detailed information about Cibber's performance.

44 *An Apology*, p. 152.

45 In the prologue to the 1616 version of *Everyman in his Humour*.

# NOTE ON THE TEXTS

*Sauny the Scot*, by John Lacy, was first published in 1698; the play was edited (and mildly bowdlerised) by James Maidment and W. H. Logan in *The Dramatic Works of John Lacy, Comedian* (Edinburgh and London, 1875). The text of this edition follows the 1698 quarto; punctuation has been modernised only so far as is necessary in the interests of clarity, and the original spelling retained. The 1698 quarto contains no scene divisions; they have been added in this edition. Footnotes relate to lines in Shakespeare's *The Taming of the Shrew*.

*The Tempest, or Enchanted Island*, by John Dryden and William Davenant, was first published in 1670. The text of this edition follows that of M. E. Novak and G. R. Guffey in vol. X of *The Works of John Dryden*, 20 vols, E. N. Hooker and H. T. Swedenberg, general editors (Berkeley, Los Angeles and London: University of California Press, 1956–89). Footnotes relate to lines in Shakespeare's *The Tempest*.

*All for Love; or, The World Well Lost*, by John Dryden, was first published in 1678. The text of this edition follows that of Novak and Guffey in vol. XIII of *The Works of John Dryden* as cited above. Footnotes relate to lines in Shakespeare's *Antony and Cleopatra*.

*The History of King Lear*, by Nahum Tate, was first published in 1681. The text of this edition follows that of Christopher Spencer, *Five Restoration Adaptations of Shakespeare* (Urbana, Illinois: University of Illinois Press, 1965). The scene divisions are those added by Spencer. Footnotes relate to lines in Shakespeare's *King Lear*.

*The Tragical History of King Richard III*, by Colley Cibber, was first published in 1700. The text of this edition follows that of

Christopher Spencer, *Five Restoration Adaptations of Shake-speare*, as cited above. It includes the alternative version of IV.iii. given in Spencer's Textual Variants.

*The History and Fall of Caius Marius* by Thomas Otway, was first published in 1680. The text of this edition follows that of J. C. Ghosh, in vol. 1 of *The Works of Thomas Otway*, 2 vols, (Oxford: Clarendon Press, 1932).

All the plays conform to the Everyman house-style: *Enter* is centred, without brackets; *Exit* is ranged right, in square brackets; stage instructions are generally centred on a new line in round brackets but some do continue in round brackets on the same line of speech; scene setters are centred if two lines or less, but indented if more; instructions following a speaker's name are in round brackets without a capital letter, but elsewhere instructions within brackets do begin with a capital letter, the full point being omitted in either instance; speakers' names are always given in full and are set in small capital letters.

# SHAKESPEARE MADE FIT

# SAUNY THE SCOT

BY JOHN LACY

# PERSONS REPRESENTED

LORD BEAUFOY, father to Margaret and Biancha
WOODALL, a rich old citizen
PETRUCHIO, suitor to Margaret
GERALDO, suitor to Biancha
SIR LYONEL WINLOVE, a country gentleman
WINLOVE, his son
TRANIO, Winlove's servant
SNATCHPENNY, a petty crook
JAMY, Winlove's servant
SAUNY, Petruchio's scottish footman
CURTIS, NICK, PHILIP, and other SERVANTS to Petruchio

MARGARET, Beaufoy's elder daughter
BIANCHA, her sister
A WIDOW

# Sauny the Scott:

## OR, THE

# Taming of the Shrew:

## A

# COMEDY.

---

As it is now *ACTED* at the

# THEATRE-ROYAL.

---

*Written by* J. LACEY, *Servant to*

# His MAJESTY.

---

And Never before Printed.

---

*Then I'll cry out , Swell'd with Poetick Rage,*
*'Tis I , John Lacy , have Reform'd your Stage.*
                              *Prol. to Rehers.*

---

*London*, Printed and Sold by E. Whitlock, near *Stationers-Hall.* 1 6 9 8.

# ACT I

## Scene i

*Enter* WINLOVE, *and his Man* TRANIO

WINLOVE: I am quite weary of the Country Life; there is that Little thing the World calls *Quiet*, but there is nothing else; Clowns live and die in't, whose *Souls* lye hid here, and after Death their *Names*. My Kinder Stars (I thank 'em) have Wing'd my Spirit with an Active Fire, which makes me wish to know what Men are Born for. To Dyet a Running Horse, to give a Hawk casting, to know Dogs Names: These make not Men. No, 'tis Philosophy, 'tis Learning, and Exercise of Reason to know what's Good and Virtuous, and to break our Stubborn and Untemper'd Wills, to Choose it. This makes us Imitate that Great Divinity that Fram'd us.

TRANIO: I thought you had Learn't *Philosophy* enough at *Oxford*. What betwixt *Aristotle* on one side, and *Bottle-Ale* on the other, I am confident you have arriv'd at a Pitch of Learning and Virtue sufficient for any Gentleman to set up with in the Countrey: that is, to be the Prop of the Family.

WINLOVE: My Father's Fondness* has kept me so long in the Country, I've forgot all I'd Learn't at the University. Besides, take that at Best, it but Rough-casts*us; No, *London* is the Choisest Academy, 'tis that must Polish us, and put a Gloss upon our Country-Studies; Hither I'm come at last, and do resolve to Glean many Vices. Thou, *Tranio*, hast been my Companion; still one Bed has held us, one Table fed us; and tho' our Bloods give me Precedency (that I count Chance) My Love has made us Equal, and I have found a frank return in thee.

TRANIO: Such a Discourse commands a Serious Answer.

Know then, your Kindness tells me, I must Love you: The  30
Good you have Taught me Commands me to Honour
you; I have Learnt, with you, to hate Ingratitude. But
setting those aside, for thus I may seem to do it: for my
own sake, be assur'd, I must Love you, though you hate
me; I neither look at Vice nor Virtue in you, but as you
are the Person I dote on.

WINLOVE: No more; I do believe and know thou lov'st me.
I wonder *Jamy* stays so long behind. You must look out
to get me handsome Lodgings, fit to receive such Friends
the Town shall bring me; you must take care of all, for I'm  40
resolv'd to make my Study my sole Business. I'll live
handsomely, not over high, nor yet beneath my Quality.

*Enter* BEAUFOY, MARGARET, BIANCHA, WOODALL, *and*
GERALDO

But stay a little, What Company's this?

BEAUFOY: Gentlemen, Importune no farther, you know my
firm Resolve, not to bestow my *Youngest* Daughter,
before I have a Husband for the *Elder*; if either of you
both Love *Pegg*, because I know you well, and love you
well, You shall have freedom to Court her at your
Pleasure.[1]

WOODALL: That is to say, we shall have leave to have our  50
Heads broken: a prime Kindness, by'ur Lady, she's too
rough for me. There, *Geraldo*, take her for me, if you
have any Mind to a Wife; to her, you are Young, and may
clap Trammel's* on her, and strike her to a Pace in time. I
dare not deal with her, I shall never get her out of her high
Trot.

MARGARET: 'Tis strange, Sir, you should make a Stale* of
me among these Mates* thus.

GERALDO: Mates, Madam? 'Faith, no Mates for you,
unless you were a little Tamer; wo worth him that has the  60
Breaking of you.[2]

MARGARET: Take heed I don't bestow the Breaking of your
Calves Head for you. You Mate? Marry come up. Go, get

---

[1] 35–8. Based on *Shrew*, I.i.48–54: 'Gentlemen, importune me ... at your pleasure.'
[2] 44–7: I.i.58–60: 'To make a stale ... milder mould.'

you a Sempstress, and run in Score with her for Muckinders* to dry your Nose with, and Marry her at last to
pay the Debt. And you there, Goodman Turnep-eater,
with your Neats-Leather* Phisnomy, I'll send your
Kitchen-wench to liquor it this Wet-weather. Whose old
Bootes was it cut out of?

GERALDO: From all such *Petticoate Devils* deliver us, I   70
pray.

TRANIO: Did you ever see the like, Sir? That Wench is
either stark Mad, or wonderful Froward.*

WOODALL: I can't tell, but I had as live* take her Dowry
with this condition, to be whipt at *Chairing-cross* every
morning.

GERALDO: Faith as you say, there's small choice in rotten
*Apples* but since 'tis as 'tis, let us be Friendly Rivals, and
endeavour for a Husband for *Margaret*, that *Biancha* may
be free to have one, and then he that can win her, wear   80
her.*

WOODALL: I would give the best Horse in *Smith-field* to
him that would throughly Woe her, Wed her, and Bed
her,* and rid the House of her, to carry her far enough of.
Well, come, agreed!                                    [*Exit*]

TRANIO: But pray Sir, is't possible that Love should of a
sudden take such hold of you.[3]

WINLOVE: O *Tranio*, till I found it to be true, I never found
it possible; but she has such attractive Charms, he were a
stone that did not Love her. I am all fire, burn, pine,   90
perish, *Tranio*, unless I win her. Counsel me, and Assist
me, Dear *Tranio*.[4]

TRANIO: Are all your Resolutions for Study come to this?
You have got a book will hold your tack;* you are like to
be a fine *Virtuoso*. Now must we to a *Chymist* to set his
Still a going for *Philters*, *Love Powders* and Extracts of
Sigh's and Highoe's.

WINLOVE: Nay *Tranio*, do not make Sport with my
Passion: it is a thing so deeply rooted here, it cannot dye,

---

[3] 66-7: I.i.146-7: 'Is it possible ... sudden hold?'
[4] 69-70. Based on *Shrew*, I.i.155-6: 'I burn, I pine ... modest girl.'

but it must take me with it. Help me, or hope not long to  100
see thy Master.

TRANIO: Nay sir, if you are so far gone there's no remedy,
we must contrive some way; but 'twill be difficult, for you
know her Father has mew'd her up,* and till he has rid
his hands of her Sister there's no coming near her.

WINLOVE: Ah, *Tranio*, what a cruel Father's he; but don't
you remember what care he took to provide Masters for
her.

TRANIO: I, Sir, and what of all that?

WINLOVE: Y' are a Fool. Can't I be perfer'd to her, to teach  110
her *French*? I have a good command of the Language, and
it may be easily done.

TRANIO: I don't apprehend the easiness of it; for who shall
be Sir *Lyonels* Son here in Town, To ply his Studyes, and
wellcome his Friends, visit his Kindred, and entertain
'em?

WINLOVE: Be content, I have a Salve* for that too; we have
not yet been seen in any House, nor can be distinguish'd
by our Faces, for *Man* or *Master*. Then it follows thus,
you *Tranio* must be young *Winlove* in my stead, and bear  120
yourself according to my rank; I'll be an ordinary French
Master about the Town. The time I stay'd in *France*, in
that will help me;[5] it must be so. Come, come, uncase*
and take my Cloath's, and when we're at our Lodgings,
we'll make a full change; when *Jamy* comes he waits on
thee, but first I'll charme his Tongue.

TRANIO: 'Twill be needful. Since this is your Pleasure I'me
ty'd to be Obedient, for so your Father charg'd me at your
Parting, altho I think 'twas in another sence.[6] In short,
I'm ready to serve you, and assist you in your Enterprize.  130

                    *Enter* JAMY

WINLOVE: Here comes the Rogue. Sirrah, Where have you
been?

JAMY: Where have I been? Pray, how now, Master, where

[5] 88–95. Based on *Shrew*, I.i.194–6, 204: 'Who shall bear ... some Florentine.'
[6] 99–101. Based on *Shrew*, I.i.212–15: 'I am tied ... another sense.'

are you, Master? Has *Tranio* Stoln your Cloathes, or you
his, or both?[7]

WINLOVE: Sirrah, come hither: this is not time to Jest.
Some weighty Reason makes me take this Habit. Enquire
not; You shall know e'm time enough. Mean while wait
you on *Tranio* in my stead, I charge you, as becomes you.
You understand me?                                          140

JAMY: I, Sir, ne'r a whit.

WINLOVE: And not of *Tranio* one word in your Mouth;
he's turn'd to *Winlove*.

JAMY: The better for him; would I were so too.

TRANIO: When I am alone with you, why then I am *Tranio*
still; in all places else, your Master *Winlove*.

WINLOVE: *Tranio*, let's go. One thing yet remains, which
you must by no means neglect: that is, to make one
amongst these Wars. Ask me not why, but be satisfy'd my
Reasons are both good and weighty.                          150

TRANIO: I obey, sir.                                  [*Exeunt*]

---

[7] 104-5: I.i.221-3: 'Where have I ... or both?'

## ACT II

## Scene i

*Enter* PETRUCHIO, *and his Man* SAUNY

PETRUCHIO: Sirrah, leave off your *Scotch*, and speak me *English*, or something like it.

SAUNY: Gude, will I, Sir.

PETRUCHIO: I think we have Ridden Twenty Miles in Three houres, *Sawny*. Are the Horses well Rubb'd down and Litter'd?

SAUNY: Deel O my Saul, Sir, I ne'r Scrub'd my sell better than I Scrub'd your Naggs.

PETRUCHIO: And thou need'st Scrubbing, I'll say that for thee, thou Beastly Knave; Why do ye not get your self 10 Cur'd of the Mange?

SAUNY: S'breed, Sir, I w'ud ne'a be cur'd for a Thousand Pund; there's nea a Lad in aw *Scotland* but Loves it. Gude, *Sawny* might hang himsel an it were not for Scratting and Scrubbing.

PETRUCHIO: Why so, Prethee?

SAUNY: When ye gea 'tull a Ladies House ye are Blith and Bonny, Sir, and gat gud Meat, but the Dee'l a bit gat's *Sawndy* meere than Hunger and Cawd, Sir; Ba then, Sir, when aw the Footmen stan still, Sir, and ha nothing to 20 dea, then gees *Saundy* tul his Pastime, Scratten and Scrubben.

PETRUCHIO: Dost call it Pastime?

SAUNY: A my Saul de I, Sir; I take as Muckle* Pleasure, Sir, in Scratten and Scrubben, as ye de in Tiplin' and Mowing.*

PETRUCHIO: Nay, if it be so, keep it, and much good may it d' ye. This is my old Friend *Geraldo*'s Lodgings, for whose sake now I am come to Town. I hope he's at home; there *Sauny*, Knock. 30

SAUNY: Wuns, Sir, I see nean to Knock boe' yer ean sel, Sir.

PETRUCHIO: Sirrah, I say Knock me soundly at this Gate.[8]

SAUNY: Out, out, in the Muccle Dee'ls Name t' ye; you'l gar* me strike ye, and then ye'l put me a-wau, Sir. With ye'r favour Ise ne're do't Sir. Gude, an ye ne ken when ye an a gued Man, S'breed' I wo't when I've a gued Master. Ye's bang yer Sel for *Saundy*.

PETRUCHIO: Rogue, I'll make you understand me.

(*Beats him*)

SAUNY: Gude, an yee'd give *Sawndy* ea bang ar twa mere e that place, for I can ne're come at it to Scrat it my sel, Sir. 40

PETRUCHIO: Yes, thus, Sir.

SAUNY: The Dee'l faw yer Fingers, I may not beat yea o' yee'r e'ne Dunghill,* Sir; bot gin I had yea in *Scotland*, Is'e ne give yea a Bawbee for your Luggs.

*Enter* GERALDO

GERALDO: How now, *Sauny*? What, Crying out? Dear *Petruchio*, most wellcome; When came you to Town? What Quarrel is this 'twixt you and *Sauny*? I pray let me Compose the Difference, and tell me now what happy Gale drove you to Town, and why in this Habbit? Why in Mourning? 50

PETRUCHIO: A common Calamity to us young Men, my Father has been Dead this four Months.

GERALDO: Trust me, I am sorry, a good old Gentleman.

SAUNY: Gee yer gate, Sir, ge yer gate. On ye be fow a grief ye're nea friend, Sir; we are blyth and bonny, Sir; we nere woe for't.

PETRUCHIO: Sirrah, you long to be basted.

SAUNY: Gad, do I not, Sir.

PETRUCHIO: Hether I come to try my Fortunes, to see if good luck and my Friends will help me to a Wife; Will 60 you wish me to one?

GERALDO: What Qualifications do you look for?

---

8 25-7. Based on *Shrew*, I.ii.8-11: 'Villain, I say ... at this gate'.

PETRUCHIO: Why, money, a good Portion.

GERALDO: Is that all?

PETRUCHIO: All, Man? All other things are in my making.

GERALDO: I shall come roundly to you, and wish you to a rich Wife, but her Face—

PETRUCHIO: That shall break no Squares;* a Mask will mend it. Wealth is the burthen of my Wooing Song.[9] If she be rich, I care not if she want a Nose or an Eye; anything with Money. 70

SAUNY: De ye nea gi him Creedit, Sir. I wud a halp't him tul a Highland Lady with Twanty thousand pund; Gude, he wud nea have her, Sir.

PETRUCHIO: Sirrah, your Twenty thousand Pounds *Scotch* will make but a Pittiful *English* portion.

SAUNY: Gude, Sir, Bo a Muckle deal of *Scotch* Punds is as gued as a Little deale of *English* Punds.

GERALDO: She has nothing like this, but a thing worse; she has a *Tongue* that keep's more Noise then all that ever 80 Mov'd at *Billingsgate*.

PETRUCHIO: Pish, a triffle; Where lives she? I long to be Wooing her. Let me alone with her Tongue; I'me in Love with the news of it. Who is't? Who is't? I'm resolv'd for her or Nobody.

GERALDO: But look before you Leap, Sir, and say you were warn'd.

SAUNY: Our, out, he can nea break his Cragg* upon her. Gude, an ye'd venter your bonny Lass, Ise venter my bonna Lad at her, Sir. 90

GERALDO: Her Father is the brave Noble *Beaufoy*, her Name *Margaret*, fam'd about Town for a *Vixen*.

PETRUCHIO: The Town's an Ass. Come, prithee shew me the House; I will not sleep 'till I see her. I know her Father. Nay, I am resolv'd man; come, prithee, come.

SAUNY: Wun's, man, an she be a Scawd, awaw with her, awaw with her, and *Johnee Johnstons* Curse go with Her.

GERALDO: Prethee, what's that?

[9] 56-7: I.ii.67: 'As wealth is burden ... song.'

SAUNY: That is, the Deel creep into her weem t'ith very
bottome on't: that's to the Croone, gued faith, of her 100
head.

GERALDO: Well, Sir, if you are resolv'd, I'll wait on you.
To say the truth, 'twill be my great advantage, for if you
win her, I shall have liberty to see her younger Sister,
sweet *Biancha*, to whose fair Eyes I am a Votary, and
you, in order to my Love, *Petruchio*, must help me. I'll tell
you why, and how you must prefer me as a Musick-
Master to old *Beaufoy*.

PETRUCHIO: I understand you not.

SAUNY: He'd ha ye make him her Piper, Sir. Gued, 'at ye'd 110
make *Sawndy* her Piper, wun's 'Ide sea blea her Pipe.

PETRUCHIO: Sirrah, be quiet. What I can, I'll serve you in.
But who comes here, *Geraldo*?

*Enter* WOODALL *and* WINLOVE *Disguis'd*

GERALDO: 'Tis Mr. *Woodall*, a rich old Citizen, and my
Rival. Hark.

SAUNY: Out, out, What sud an awd Carle do with a young
bonny Lass? Are ye not an Aud theif, Sir?

WOODALL: How!

SAUNY: Are ye not an Aud Man, Sir?

WOODALL: Yes, marry am I, Sir.

SAUNY: And are not ye to Marry a young Maiden? 120

WOODALL: Yes, What then?

SAUNY: And are not ye troubled with a sear griefe, Sir?

WOODALL: A sear grief? What sear grief?

SAUNY: You're troubled with a great weakness i'th' bottome of your Bally. What sid yea dea with a young
Maiden? Out, out, out.

WOODALL: You understand me? Your French Books treat
most of Love; those use her too, and now and then you
may urge something of my Love and Merit. Besides her 130
Father's bounty, you shall find me Liberal.

WINLOVE: Mounsier, me will tell her the very fine ting of
you; me vill make her Love you whether she can or noe.

WOODALL: Enough, Peace, here's *Geraldo*. Your servant,

Sir, I am just going to Sir *Nicholas Beaufoy* to carry him this Gentleman, a *Frenchman*, most Eminent for teaching his Country* Language.

GERALDO: I have a Master for *Biancha* too; but waving that, I have, some news to tell you. I have found out a Friend that will Woo *Margaret*. What will you contribute, for he must be hir'd to't?                    140

WOODALL: Why, I will give him forty Peeces in hand, and when he has don't, I'll double the Sum.

GERALDO: Done, Sir, I'll undertake it.

SAUNY: S'breed, Sir, I'se gat it done muckle* Cheaper; for twenty Punds I'se dea it my Sel.

GERALDO: Come, down with your Money, and the Bargain's made.

WOODALL: But if He shud not do it? I don't care for throwing away so much Money.                    150

GERALDO: If he don't, I'll undertake he shall refund.

WOODALL: Why, then, here's ten Pieces, and that Ring I'll pawn to you for 'nother Forty, 'tis worth a Hundred. But doe's the Gentleman know her Qualities?

PETRUCHIO: I, Sir, and they are such as I am fond on; I wou'd not be hir'd for any thing to Woo a person of another Humour.

*Enter* TRANIO *brave,* and JAMY

TRANIO: Save you, Gentlemen; Pray, which is the way to Sir *Nicholas Beaufoy's* House?

WOODALL: Why, Sir, what's your Business there? You pretend not to be a Servant to either of his Daughters, d' ye?                    160

TRANIO: You are something blunt in your Questions; perhaps I do.

PETRUCHIO: Not her that Chides, on any hand, I pray.[10]

TRANIO: I Love no Chiders; come, *Jamy.*

GERALDO: Pray, stay, Sir; Is it the other?

TRANIO: May be it is; Is it any offence?

---

[10] 135-6. Based on *Shrew*, I.ii.225-6: 'Not her … no chiders'.

WOODALL: Yes, 'tis, Sir; she is my Mistriss.

GERALDO: I must tell you, Sir, she is my Mistriss too.   170

TRANIO: And I must tell you both she is my Mistriss; Will that content you? Nay, never frown for the Matter.

SAUNY: And I mun tell ye all, there's little hopes for *Saundy* then.

WINLOVE: The Rogue does it rarely.

PETRUCHIO: Nay, nay, Gentlemen, no Quarrelling, unless it were to the purpose. Have you seen this young Lady, Sir?

TRANIO: No, Sir, but I'm in Love with her Character. They say she has a Sister moves like a Whirlwind.   180

PETRUCHIO: Pray, spare your Descriptions Sir. That Furious Lady is my Mistriss, and till *I* have Married her, *Biancha* is Invisible, her Father has Sworn it, and, till then, you must all move Forty foot off.

TRANIO: I thank you for your Admonition; I should have lost my Labour else; and since you are to do all of us the Favour, *I* shall be glad to be numbred among your Servants, Sir.

PETRUCHIO: You will honour me to accept of me for yours. But pray, Sir, let me know who obliges me with   190 this Civility.

TRANIO: My Name is *Winlove*, Sir, a *Worstershire* Gentleman, where *I* have something an Old Man's Death will Intitle me to, not inconsiderable. Come, Gentlemen, let's not fall out, at least till the Fair *Biancha*'s at Liberty; Shall we go sit out half an hour at the Tavern, and Drink her Health?[11]

SAUNY: Do, my Bearns; and I'se Drink with ye to Countenance ye.

PETRUCHIO: I, I, agreed; Come, and then I'll to my   200 Mistriss.

SAUNY: Gude, these Lades are o' *Saundyes* Mind, they'l rather take a Drink, nor Fight.   [*Exeunt*]

---

[11] 160-1. Based on *Shrew*, I.ii.274-5: 'Please ye ... our mistress' health.'

# Scene ii

## Enter MARGARET *and* BIANCHA

MARGARET: Marry, come up, Proud Slut. Must you be
making your self Fine before your Elder Sister? You are
the Favourite, you are, but I shall make you know your
Distance; Give me that Necklace, and those Pendants. I'll
have that Whisk* too, there's an old Handkercheif good
enough for you.

BIANCHA: Here, take 'em, Sister, I resign 'em freely. I
wou'd give you all I have to Purchase your Kindness.

MARGARET: You Flattering Gypsie, I cou'd find in my
Heart to slit your Disembling Tongue; Come, tell me, and    10
without Lying, which of your Sutors you Love best. Tell
me, or I'll beat you to Clouts,* and Pinch thee like a
Fairy.

BIANCHA: Believe me, Sister, of all Men alive, I never saw
that Particular Face which I cou'd Fancy more than
another.[12]

MARGARET: Huswife, you Lye; and I could find in my
Heart to Dash thy Teeth down thy Throat; I know thou
Lov'st *Geraldo*.

BIANCHA: If you Affect him, Sister, I Vow to plead for you    20
my self, but you shall have him.[13]

MARGARET: O, then belike you fancy Riches more; you
Love Old *Woodall*.

BIANCHA: That Old Fool: Nay, now I see you but Jested
with me all this while. I know you are not Angry with me.

MARGARET: If this be Jest, then all the rest is so. I'll make
ye tell me e're I have done with you, Gossip.

## Enter BEAUFOY

BEAUFOY: Why, now now, Dame, Whence grows this
Insolence? *Biancha* get thee in. My Poor Girle, she Weeps.
Fye, *Peg*, put off this Devillish Humour. Why dost thou    30
Cross thy Tender Innocent Sister? When did she Cross
thee with a Bitter Word?

---

[12] 8–12. Based on *Shrew*, II.i.8–12: 'Of all thy suitors ... than any other.'

[13] 15–16. Based on *Shrew*, II.i.14–16: 'If you affect him ... keep you fair.'

MARGARET: Her Silence Flouts me, and I'll be Reveng'd.
(Flyes at BIANCHA)

BEAUFOY: What in my sight too? You scurvy Ill-natur'd Thing. Go, poor *Biancha*, get thee out of her way.
(Exit)

MARGARET: What, will you not suffer me? Nay, now I see she is your Treasure; She must have a Husband; and I Dance Bare-foot on her Wedding-Day; And, for your Love to her, lead Apes in Hell.* I see your care of me. I'll go and cry till I can find a way to be quit with her.                    40
[Exit]

BEAUFOY: Was ever poor Man thus plagu'd?

*Enter* WOODALL *with* WINLOVE *Disguis'd, with* JAMY
*carrying a* Lute *and* Books, *and* TRANIO

How now, who'se here?[14]

WOODALL: Sir, your Servant. I am bold to wait on you to present you this Gentleman, an Acute teacher of the *French* Tongue; his Name's *Mounsieur Mawgier*. Pray accept his service.

BEAUFOY: I am your debtor, Sir. *Mounsieur*, you'r well-come.

WINLOVE: Me give you humble thanks, Sir.

BEAUFOY: But what Gentleman is that?                    50

WOODALL: I don't love him so well to tell you his Errant, but he wou'd come along with me. You had best ask him.

TRANIO: I beg your Pardon for my Intrusion. We heard your Fair and Virtuos Daughter *Biancha* prais'd to such a height of Wonder, Fame has already made me her Servant. I've heard your Resolution not to Match her till her Eldest Sister be bestow'd; mean while I beg Admittance like the rest to keep my hopes alive; this *Lute*, Sir, and these few French Romances, I wou'd Dedicate to her Service.                    60

BEAUFOY: Sir, you oblige me, Pray, your Name?

TRANIO: 'Tis *Winlove*, Son and Heir to Sir *Lyonell Winlove*.

---

[14] 22–34. Based on *Shrew*, II.i.23–37: 'Why, how now ... who comes here?'

BEAUFOY: My noble Friend, he has been my School-fellow.
For his sake you are most kindly welcome; you shall have
all the freedome I can give you.[15]

*Enter* SAUNY *and* GERALDO *Disguis'd*

SAUNY: Hand in hand, Sir, I'se go tell him my sel. Whare is
this Laird?

BEAUFOY: Here, Sir. What wou'd you have, what are you?

SAUNY: Marry, I'se ean a bonny *Scot*, Sir.                                70

BEAUFOY: A *Scotchman*. Is that all?

SAUNY: Wun's, wud ye have me a Cherub? I ha brought ye
a small teaken, Sir.

BEAUFOY: But d'ye hear, you Scot, don't you use to put off
your Cap to your betters?

SAUNY: Marry, we say in *Scotland* Gead Mourn til ye for
aw the day, and sea put on our bonnets again, Sir; Bud
Sir, I ha brought ye a Teaken.

BEAUFOY: To me? Where is't? From whence is your
Teaken?                                                                80

SAUNY: Marry, from my good Master *Petruchio*, Sir. He
has sen ye a Piper to teach your Bonny Lasses to Pipe; but
gin yet let *Sauny* teach 'em, I'se pipe 'em sea Whim—
Whum,* their Arses shall nere leave giging and joging
while their's a Tooth in their head.

BEAUFOY: *Petruchio*! I remember him now, How does thy
Master?

SAUNY: Marry, Sir, he means to make one of your Lasses
his Wanch, that is, his love and his Ligby.*

BEAUFOY: You are a Sawcy Rogue.                                       90

SAUNY: Gud wull a' Sir, he'll tak your Lass with a *Long
Tang* that the *Deel* and *Saundy* wun a venter on; but he's
here his aun sel, Sir.

*Enter* PETRUCHIO

PETRUCHIO: Your most humble Servant.

BEAUFOY: Noble *Petruchio*, welcome; I thank you for your
kindness to my Daughters. Within there.

*Enter* Servant

---

[15] 43-52. Based on *Shrew*, II.i.88-101: 'Pardon me, sir ... welcome, sir.'

Conduct these gentlemen to my Daughters. Tell 'em these
are both to be their Masters; bid 'em use 'em Civily. Take
in that Lute, and those Books there. *Petruchio*, I hear you
have lost your Father lately. 100

PETRUCHIO: 'Tis true, but I hope to find another in you; in
short, I hear you have a fair Daughter call'd *Margaret*; the
World says she is a *Shrew*, But I think otherwise. You
know my Fortune; if you like my Person, with your
Consent, I'll be your Son-in-Law.

BEAUFOY: I have such a Daughter, but I so much Love you,
I would not put her into your hands; she'll make you
mad.

SAUNY: Gud, he's as mad as heart can wish, Sir; he need
nea halp, Sir. 110

PETRUCHIO: I'll venture it, Father, so I'll presume to call
ye. I'm as Peremptory as she's Proud-minded: and where
two Rageing fires meet together they do consume the
thing that feed's their fury.[16] My Fathers Estate I have
better'd, not imbezell'd, then tell me, if I can get your
Daughters Love, What Portion* you will give?

BEAUFOY: After my Death the Moiety of my Estate, and on
the Wedding day Three Thousand Pounds.

PETRUCHIO: And I'll assure her Jointure* answerable.[17]
Get Writings drawn; I'll warrant you I'll carry the Wench. 120

BEAUFOY: Fair Luck betide you.

*Enter* GERALDO *Bleeding*

How now, Man, What's the matter? Will my Daughter be
a good *Lutanist*?

GERALDO: She'll prove a better *Cudgel Player*; Lutes* will
not hold her.

BEAUFOY: Why, then, thou canst not break her to thy
Lute?*

GERALDO: No, but she has broke the Lute to me. I did but
tell her she mistook her fretts, and bow'd her head to
teach her Fingrings. 'Fretts call you these', (quoth she) 130
'and I'll frett with you'; so fairly took me o're the Pate

---

[16] 88–9: II.i.130–3: 'for I tell you ... feeds their fury.'
[17] 90–4: II.i.119–23: 'Then tell me ... I'll assure her.'

with the *Lute*, and set me in the Pillory, and follow'd it
with loud Volly's of Rogue, Rascal, Fidler, Jack, Puppy,
and such like.

PETRUCHIO: Now, by the World, *I* Love her ten times
more than er'e *I* did.[18]

SAUNY: Gud, bo the De'll a bit ye's wad her, Sir. Wun's,
I'se nea gi twa Pence for my Luggs* gin you make her yer
Bride.

PETRUCHIO: I'll warrant you, *Sauny*, we'll deal with her   140
well enough.

BEAUFOY: Well Sir, I'll make you Reperation. Proceed still
with my youngest Daughter, she's apt to Learn. *Petruchio*, will you go with us, or shall *I* send my Daughter to
you?

PETRUCHIO: Pray do, Sir, and I'll attend her here.

       [*Exeunt. Manent* PETRUCHIO; SAUNY]

SAUNY: Gud, at ye gi *Saundy* a little Siller to gea to
*Scotland* agen.

PETRUCHIO: Why, *Sauny*, I have not us'd thee so unkindly.

SAUNY: Gud, *I*'se nea tarry with a Scauding Quean, Sir. Yet   150
the Dee'l faw* my Luggs if Ise ken which is worse, to
tarry and venture my Cragg, or gea heam to *Scotland*.

       *Enter* MARGARET

PETRUCHIO: Peace, Sirrah, here she comes; now for a
Rubbers at Cuffs* O' Honey, Pretty *Peg*, how do'st thou
do Wench?

MARGARET: Marry, come up, Ragmanners,* *Plain Peg*?
Where were you bred? *I* am call'd *Mrs. Margaret*.

PETRUCHIO: No, no, thou ly'st *Peg*, thou'rt call'd plain
*Peg*, and Bonny *Peg*, and sometimes *Peg the Curst*; take
this from me. Hearing thy Wildness prais'd in every   160
Town, thy Virtues Sounded and thy Beauty spoke off, my
self am *mov'd* to take thee for my Wife.

MARGARET: I knew at first you were a *Moveable*.*

PETRUCHIO: Why, what's a Moveable.

MARGARET: A Joint Stool.

---

[18]  97-106. Based on *Shrew*, II.i.144-61: 'What, will my Daughter ... e're I did.'

PETRUCHIO: Thou hast hit it *Peg*. Come, sit upon me.

MARGARET: Asses were made to bear, and so were you.[19]

PETRUCHIO: Why, now *I* see the World has much abus'd
thee. 'Twas told me thou wert rough and Coy, and Sullen,
but *I* do find thee pleasant, Mild and Curteous; Thou   170
can'st not frown, nor Pout, nor bite the Lip as angry
wenches do. Thou art all sweetness.[20]

MARGARET: Do not Provoke me; *I* won't stand still and
here my self abus'd.

PETRUCHIO: What a Rogue was that told me thou wert
Lame, thou art as streight as an Osier, and as Plyable; O,
what a rare walk's there! Why, there's a gate puts down
the King of *Frances* best great Horse.

SAUNY: And the King of *Scotland*'s tea.*

PETRUCHIO: Where did'st thou Learn the grand Paw,*  180
*Peg*? It becomes thee rarely.

MARGARET: Doe's it so, sawcebox? How will a halter
become you with a running knot under one Ear?

PETRUCHIO: Nay, no knot, *Peg*, but the knot of Matrimony 'twixt thee and me; we shall be an Excellent *Mad
Couple well match'd.**

MARGARET: *I* match'd to thee? What, to such a fellow with
such a Gridiron face, with a Nose set on like a Candels
end stuck against a Mud wall, and a Mouth to eat Milk
Porridge with Ladles? Foh, it almost turns my Stomach to   190
look on't.

SAUNY: Gud, an your Stomach wamble* to see his *Face*,
What will ye dea when ye see his *Arse*, Madam.

MARGARET: Marry, come up, *Abberdeen*, take that (*Hits
him a box on the Ear*), and speak next when it comes to
your turn.

SAUNY: S'breed, the Deel tak a gripe O yer faw* fingers,
and Driss your Doublat for ye.

PETRUCHIO: Take heed, *Peg*, *Sauny*'s a Desperate Fellow.

MARGARET: You'r a couple of Logger heads,* Master and   200
Man, that *I* can tell you.

---

[19] 120–31. Based on *Shrew*, II.i.182–99: 'Good morrow, Kate ... so are you.'
[20] 132–5. Based on *Shrew*, II.i.237–42: 'I find you ... angry wenches will.'

PETRUCHIO: Nay, nay, Stay, *Peg*; for all this *I* do like thee, and *I* mean to have thee, in truth, *I* am thy Servant.

MARGARET: Are you? Why, then, I'll give you a favour, and thus I'll tye it on; there's for you.          (*Beats him*)

SAUNY: Out, out, *I*'se gea for *Scotland*. Gud, an she beat ye, *Saundy*'s a Dead Man.

PETRUCHIO: *I*'ll swear *I*'ll cuff you, if you Strike agen.[21]

MARGARET: That's the way to loose your Armes.* If you strike a Woman, you are no Gentleman.                                           210

PETRUCHIO: A Herald, *Peg*? Prithee, Blazon* my *Coat*.

MARGARET: *I* know not your *Coat*, but your *Crest* is a *Coxcombe*.                          (*Offers to go away*)

PETRUCHIO: Stop her, Sirrah, stop her.

SAUNY: Let her gea her gate, Sir; an e'en twa Deels and a Scotch wutch* blaw her weeme* full of Wind.

PETRUCHIO: Stay her, Sirrah; stay her, *I* say.

SAUNY: S'breed, Sir, stay her yer sen. But hear ye, Sir, an her tale gea as fast as her tang, Gud, ye ha meet with a Whupster,* Sir.                                                               220

PETRUCHIO: Prethee, *Peg*, stay, and *I*'ll talk to thee in Earnest.

MARGARET: You may pump* long enough er'e you get out a wise word. Get a Night Cap to keep your brains warm.

PETRUCHIO: *I* mean thou shalt keep me warm in thy Bed, *Peg*. What think'st thou of that, *Peg*? In plain terms, without more ado, *I* have your Fathers Consent; your Portions agreed upon, your Joynture settled; and for your own part, be willing or unwilling, all's one, you *I* will marry, *I* am resolv'd on't.

MARGARET: Marry, come up? Jack a Lent,* without my          230
Leave?

PETRUCHIO: A Rush for your Leave. Here's a Clutter* with a troublesom Woman. Rest you contented, I'll have it so.

MARGARET: You shall be bak'd first, you shall. Within there, ha!

---

[21] 167: II.i.218: 'I swear . . . strike again.'

PETRUCHIO: Hold, get me a Stick there, *Sauny*. By this hand, deny to Promise before your Father, I'll not Leave you a whole rib; I'll make you do't and be glad on't.

MARGARET: Why, you will not Murther me Sirrah? You are a couple of Rascals. *I* don't think but you have pickt my Pockets.

SAUNY: I'se sooner pick your tang out O' your head, nor pick your Pocket.

PETRUCHIO: Come, leave your idle prating. Have you *I* will, or no man ever shall. Whoever else attempts it, his throat will *I* Cut before he lyes one night with thee; it may be, thine too for company. *I* am the Man am born to tame thee, *Peg*.[22]

*Enter* BEAUFOY, WOODALL *and* TRANIO

Here comes your Father. Never make denial; if you do, you know what follows.

MARGARET: The Devil's in this fellow, he has beat me at my own Weapon. *I* have a good mind to marry him to try if he can *Tame* me.

BEAUFOY: Now, *Petruchio*, how speed you with my Daughter?

PETRUCHIO: How but well? It were Impossible *I* shou'd speed amiss. 'Tis the best Naturd'st Lady—

BEAUFOY: Why, how now, Daughter, in your Dumps?[23]

MARGARET: You shew a Fathers care indeed to Match me with this mad Hectoring Fellow.

PETRUCHIO: She has been abus'd, Father, most unworthily. She is not Curst unless for Pollicy; for Patience, a second Grizel.* Betwixt us we have so agreed, the Wedding is to be on Thursday next.

SAUNY: Gud, *Saundy*'s gea for *Scotland* a Tuesday then.

WOODALL: Heark, *Petruchio*, shee says shee'll see you hang'd first. Is this your speeding? *I* shall make you refund.

PETRUCHIO: Pish, that's but a way she has gotten. *I* have Wood her, Won her, and shee's my own. We have made a

---

[22] 198–9: II.i.269: 'I am he ... tame you, Kate'.
[23] 204–7: II.i.274–7: 'Now, Signor Petruchio ... in your dumps?'

bargin that before Company she shall maintain a little of her Extravagant Humour, for she must not seem to fall off from't too soon; when we are alone, we are the kindest, Lovingst, tender'st Chickins to one another![24] Pray, Father, provide the Feast, and bid the Guests; I must home to settle some things, and fetch some writings in order to her Joynture.—Farewel Gallants. Give me thy hand, *Peg*.

BEAUFOY: I know not what to say, but give me your hands, 280 send you Joy. *Petruchio*, 'tis a Match.

WOODALL, TRANIO: Amen say we; we all are Witnesses.[25]

MARGARET: Why, Sir, de' ye mean to Match me in spight of my Teeth?

PETRUCHIO: Nay, peace, *Peg*, Peace, thou needst not be pevish before these; 'tis only before strangers according to our bargain. Come *Peg*, thou shalt go see me take horse. Farewel, Father.

MARGARET: As I live, I will not.

PETRUCHIO: By this Light, but you shall; nay, no testy 290 tricks, away.                                    [*Exeunt*]

SAUNY: Gud' I'se be your Lieutenant and bring up your reer, Madam.                                   [*Exit*]

WOODALL: Was ever match clapt up so suddingly?

BEAUFOY: Faith, Gentlemen, I have ventur'd madly on a Desperate Mart.[26]

WOODALL: But now, Sir, as to your younger Daughter, you may remember my long Love and Service.

TRANIO: I hope I may (without Arrogance, Sir,) beg you to look on me as a Person of more Merit.                       300

BEAUFOY: Content ye, Gentlemen, I'll compound this strife; 'tis Deeds not Words must win the Prize. I love you both, but he that can assure my Daughter the Noblest Joynture has her.[27] What say you, Sir?

WOODALL: I'll make it out my Estate is worth, *De clara*,*

---

[24] 217-20: II.i.297-300: 'Tis bargained ... the kindest Kate.'

[25] 224-6: II.i.311-13: 'I know not ... witnesses.'

[26] 234-6. Based on *Shrew*, II.i.318-20: 'Was ever match ... desperate mart.'

[27] 241-3: II.i.334-7: 'Content you ... my Bianca's love.'

full Twenty Thousand Pounds, besides some ventures at
Sea, and all I have at my Discease I give her.

TRANIO: Is that all, Sir? Alas, too Light, Sir. I am my
Fathers Heir, and only Son, and his Estate is worth Three
thousand pound *per Annum*; that will aford a Joynture 310
answerable to her Portion: no Debts, nor incumbrances,
No Portions to be paid— have I nip't* you, Sir?

BEAUFOY: I must confess your offer is the best; and let
your Father make her this assureance, she is your own.
Else you must pardon me, if you should dye before him,
where's her Power?

TRANIO: That's but a Cavel;* hee's old, I young.

WOODALL: And may not young men dye as well as old?
Have I nip't you there again?

BEAUFOY: Well, Gentlemen, *I* am thus resolv'd: on *Thurs-* 320
*day* my Daughter *Peg* is to be Married;[28] the *Thursday*
following *Biancha*'s yours, if you make this Assurance; if
not, Mr. *Woodall* has her. And so *I* take my Leave, and
thank you both.                                    [*Exit*]

WOODALL: Sir, your Servant. Now *I* fear you not: Alas,
Young Man, your Father is not such a Fool, to give you
all, and in his waining Age, set footing* under your
Table. You may go Whistle for your Mistriss, ha, ha, ha.
                                                   [*Exit*]

TRANIO: A Vengance on your Crafty Wither'd Hide. Yet
'tis in my head to do my Master good: *I* see no reason 330
why this suppos'd young *Winlove* should not get a
suppos'd Father, call'd Sir *Lyonell Winlove*. And that's a
wonder: Fathers commonly *get* their Children, but here
the Case must be alter'd.*

> Love Brings such Prodigies as these to Town,
> For that, at Best, turns all things upside Down.
>                                                [*Exit*]

---

[28] 252–9. Based on *Shrew*, II.i.379–403: 'I must confess ... get their children.'

# ACT III

## Scene i

*Enter* WINLOVE, GERALDO, BIANCHA. *Table cover'd with Velvet, Two Chaires and Guitar. A Paper Prickt\* with* SONGS

GERALDO: Pray, Madam, will you take out this Lesson on the Gittar?

WINLOVE: Here be de ver fine Story in de Varle of Mounsieur *Appollo*, And Madamoselle *Daphne*; Me vill Read you dat, Madam.

GERALDO: Good Madam, mind not that Monsieur Shorthose; But Learn this Lesson first.

WINLOVE: Begar, Monsieur Fideler, you be de vera fine troublesome Fellow; me wil make de great hole in your Head wid de Gittar, as *Margaret* did.                              10

GERALDO: This is no Place to Quarrel in; but Remember—

BIANCHA: Why, Gentlemen, you do me double wrong, to strive for that which Resteth in my Bare Choice. To end the Quarrel, sit down and Tune your *Instrument*, and by that time his Lecture will be done.[29]

GERALDO: You'l leave his Lecture, when *I* am in Tune?

BIANCHA: Yes, yes; Pray be satisfied. Come, Monsieur, let's see your Ode.

WINLOVE: *I* do suspect that Fellow. Sure he's no Lute-Master.                                                      20

BIANCHA: Here's the Place. Come, Read.          (*Reads*)
Do not Believe *I* am a *Frenchman*; my Name is *Winlove*. He that bears my Name about the Town, is my Man *Tranio*. *I* am your passionate Servant, and must live by your Smiles. Therefore be so good, to give Life to my hopes.

---

[29] 10–11: III.i.16–17, 21–2: 'Why, gentlemen ... you have tuned.'

GERALDO: Madam, your Gittar is in Tune.

BIANCHA: Let's hear. Fye, there's a String split.

WINLOVE: Make de spit in the Whole, Man, and Tune it
again.[30]

BIANCHA: Now let me see. *I* know not how to believe you.
But if it be true, Noble Mr. *Winlove* deserves to be
belov'd; and, in the mean time, keep your own Councell,
and it is not impossible but your hopes may be Converted
into Certainties.

GERALDO: Madam, now 'tis Perfectly in Tune.

WINLOVE: Fye, fye, Begar, no Tune at all.

BIANCHA: Now, Sir, *I* am for you.

GERALDO: Monsieur, Pray walk now, and give me leave a
while; my Lesson will make no Musick in Three Parts.

WINLOVE: Me vil no trouble you, Mounsieur Fiddeller. *I*
am confident it is so: this must be some Person that has
taken a Disguise, like me, to Court *Biancha*. *I*'ll watch
him.                                                    (*Aside*)

GERALDO: First, Madam, be pleas'd to sing the Last Song
that *I* Taught you, and then we'll proceed.

BIANCHA: I'll try, but I'm afraid I shall be out.

### (SONG)

GERALDO: Madam, before you proceed any farther, there
be some few Rules set down in this Paper, in order to
your Fingering, will be worth your Perusal.

BIANCHA: Let's see.                                    (*Reads*)
*Tho' I appear a Lute-Master, yet know, my fair* Biancha,
*I have but taken this disguise to get Access to you, and tell
you I am your humble Servant and Passionate Admirer,*
Geraldo. Pish, take your Rules again; I like 'em not. The
old way pleases me best, I do not care for changing old
Rules for these Foolish new Inventions.

### Enter Servant

SERVANT: Madam, my Lord calls for you to help dress the
Bride.

---

[30] 23: III.i.39: 'Spit in the hole . . . tune again.'

BIANCHA: Farewell then, Master; I must be gone.                    60

[Exeunt]

GERALDO: I know not what to think of her. This fellow
looks as if he were in Love, and she caresses him. These
damn'd French men have got all the trade in Town; if they
get up all the handsome Women, the *English* must e'en
march into *Wales* for Mistresses. Well, if thy thoughts,
*Biancha*, are grown so low, to cast thy wandring Eyes on
such a kikshaw,* I'me resolv'd to ply my Widow.[*Exit*]

WINLOVE: I am glad I'me rid of him, that I may speak my
mother Tongue agen. *Biancha* has given me hopes; I dare
half believe she Loves me.                                        70

Enter BEAUFOY, WOODALL, TRANIO, MARGARET,<br>BIANCHA, and Attendants.

But here's her Father.

BEAUFOY: Believe me, Gentlemen, 'tis very strange! This
day *Petruchio* appointed, yet he comes not; methinks he
shou'd be more a Gentleman, then to put such a slur upon
my Family.

MARGARET: Nay, you have us'd me finely, and like a
Father: I must be forc'd to give my hand against my will,
to a rude mad brain'd Fellow here, who Woo'd in hast,
and means to Wed at Leisure.[31]* This comes of obeying
you; if I do't again, were you ten thousand Fathers, hang   80
me.

TRANIO: Be Patient, Madam; on my life hee'll come.
Though he be blunt and merry, I'm sure hee's Noble.
Good Madam, go put on your Wedding Cloaths; I know
he'll be with you e're you be Drest.

MARGARET: Wedding Cloaths. I'll see him hang'd before
I'll have him, unless it be to scratch his Eyes out.

[Exit weeping]

BEAUFOY: Poor Girl. I cannot blame thee now to weep, for
such an Injury wou'd vex a saint; Tho I am old, I shall
find some body will call him to a strict Account for this.   90

Enter JAMY

---

[31] 62–4: III.ii.8–11: 'I must forsooth . . . wed at leisure.'

JAMY: O Master, News! News! and such News as you never heard off.

BEAUFOY: Why, what News have you, Sir?

JAMY: Is't not News to hear of *Petruchio*'s Coming?

BEAUFOY: Why, is he come?

JAMY: Why, no, my Lord.

BEAUFOY: What then, Sirrah?

JAMY: He's coming, Sir.

BEAUFOY: When will he be here?

JAMY: When he stands where I am and sees you there.      100

BEAUFOY: Well, sirrah, is this all the News?

JAMY: Why, *Petruchio* is coming in a new Hat, and an old Jerkin, a pair of Britches thrice turn'd, a pair of Boots that have been Candle-cases, an old rusty Sword with a broken hilt and never a Chape,* upon an old Lean, Lame, Spavin'd,[32]* Glander'd,* Broken-winded Jade, with a Womans Crupper of Velvit here and there peec'd with packthreed.

TRANIO: Who comes with him?

JAMY: O, Sir, his man *Sauny*, and in an Equippage very     110 suitable to his Master; he looks no more like a Christian Footman then I look like a Windmill.

WOODALL: This is a most strange Extravagant Humour.

BEAUFOY: I'me glad he comes, however he be!

*Enter* PETRUCHIO *and* SAUNY, *strangely Habbited*

PETRUCHIO: Come, Where be these Gallants? Who's at home?

BEAUFOY: You're Wellcome, Sir. I'm glad you're come at last.

TRANIO: I think I have seen you in better Cloathes.

PETRUCHIO: Never, never, Sir; this is my Wedding Suite.     120 Why, how now, how now, Gentlemen? What d'ye stare at? D'ye take me for a Monster?

WOODALL: Faith, in that Habit you might pass for one in the Fair.

PETRUCHIO: O, you talk merrily; my Taylor tells me it is

[32] 71-87. Based on *Shrew*, III.ii.27-69: 'I cannot blame thee ... gentleman's lackey' (considerably shortened).

the newest Fashion. But where's my *Peg*? I stay too long
from her. The Morning wears; 'tis time we were at
Church.

TRANIO: Why, you won't Visit her thus.

PETRUCHIO: Marry, but I will.                                    130

SAUNY: And sea will *Saundy* tea, Sir.

BEAUFOY: But you will not Marry her so, will you?

SAUNY: A my Saul sal he, Sir.

PETRUCHIO: To me shee's Married, not to my Cloathes.[33]
Will ye along, Father and Gentlemen? I'll to church
imediately, not tarry a minute.

SAUNY: Here ye, Sir, ye sal Marry her after the Scotch
Directory,* then gin ye like her not, ye maw put her
awaw. How say ye now?

                                     [*Exit* PETRUCHIO *and* SAUNY]

TRANIO: He has some meaning in this mad Attire,[34] but  140
you must perswade him to put on a better, e're he goes to
Church.

BEAUFOY: Let's after and see what will become of it.

                                                        [*Exit*]

TRANIO: Well, Sir, you find there's no other way; tis too
short warning to get your Father up. Shou'd you steal the
Match, who knows but both the old Fools wou'd so
deeply resent it to your Prejudice.

WINLOVE: Why, Prethee, this way it will be Stolen, for 'tis
but a Cheat, which will be in a little time Discover'd.

TRANIO: That's all one; it Carries a better face, and we  150
shall have the more sport. Besides, e're it comes out, your
Father may be wrought to like it, and Confirm my
Promises. She is suitable to you every way, and she is rich
enough to do it, and Loves you well enough besides.

WINLOVE: Well, if it must be so, let's contrive it handsomly.

TRANIO: Let me alone, *Jamy* shall do the business. He shall
find out some Knight of the Post,* that shall be old Sir
*Lyonel Winlove* here, and make Assurance of a greater

---

[33] 109: III.ii.115: 'To me she's married ... my clothes.'

[34] 114–15. Based on *Shrew*, III.ii.122–5: 'He hath ... event of this.'

Joynture then I propos'd. Ne're fear it, Sir, I'll so Instruct  160
him, it shall be carryed without the least Suspition.

WINLOVE: Ay, but you know old *Beaufoy* knows my
Father.

TRANIO: That's nothing, 'tis so many years since he saw
him, he will never distinguish him by his face.

WINLOVE: This may be done. But, notwithstanding all did
not my fellow Teacher, that damn'd Lute-master, so
nearly watch us, 'twou'd not be amiss to steal a Marriage,
and that once perform'd, let all the World say no, I'll keep
my own.[35]                                              170

TRANIO: That we may think on too; this same Lute-Master
I more then half suspect.

WINLOVE: And so do I.

TRANIO: I have mist a Gentleman out of the gang a good
while. But let that pass: I have already sent *Jamy* to find a
Man.

#### *Enter* WOODALL

To our postures. Here's Mr. *Woodall*; he must be
Chous'd* too among the rest. Save you, Sir. Came you
from the Church?                                         180

WOODALL: As willingly as e're I came from Schoole.

TRANIO: And is the Bride and Bridegroome coming home?

WOODALL: A Bridegroom? Why, hee's a Bridegroome for
the Devil – a Devil, a very Fiend.

TRANIO: Why, shee's a Devil, an errant Devil; nay, the
Devils Dam.

WOODALL: But shee's a Lamb, a Dove, a Child to him.
When the Priest askt if he would take *Margaret* for his
Wife, 'I, by Gogs wound's' quoth he, and Swore so loud
that, all amaz'd, the Priest lets fall the Book, and as the
Sexton stoop'd to take it up, this mad brain'd Bride-  190
groome took him such a cuff that down fell Sexton, Book
and all again. 'Now take it up', quoth he, 'if any list'.

TRANIO: What said the poor Bride to this?

WOODALL: Trembl'd and shook like an Aspen Leafe. After

---

[35] 134–5: III.ii.138–9: "were gird, methinks ... of all the world.'

this, just as the Parson joyn'd their hands, he call'd to his
Roguy *Scotchman* for a Glass of Muscadine, drank his
Wives Health, and threw the Toast in the Clarks face,
because his Beard grew thin and hungry; then took the
Bride about the Neck and gave her such a Smack the
Church eccho'd again. The sight of this made me run      200
away for shame. I know they are following by this time;
but hark, I hear the Minstrels.                    (*Musick*)

*Enter* WOODALL, PETRUCHIO, MARGARET, BIANCHA,
          GERALDO, SAUNY, *&c.*

PETRUCHIO: Gentleman and Friends, I thank you for your
     Pains. I know you think to Dine with me to day, and have
     prepar'd great store of Wedding Chear; but so it is, grand
     business calls me hence, and I take my leave.

BEAUFOY: Is't Possible you will away to night?

PETRUCHIO: I must immediately. If you knew my business
     you wou'd not wonder. Well, honest Gentlemen, I thank
     you all that have beheld me give away my self to this most   210
     Patient, Sweet and virtuous Wife. Dine with my Father
     here, and drink my health, for I must hence; so farewel to
     you all.

SAUNY: Wun's, will ye nea eat your Wadden Dunner, Sir?

TRANIO: Let us Intreat you to stay till after Dinner.

PETRUCHIO: It must not be.

MARGARET: Let me Intreat you.

PETRUCHIO: That will do much; I am Content.

MARGARET: Are you content to stay?

PETRUCHIO: *I* am content you shou'd Intreat me; but yet *I*    220
     will not stay, intreat me how you can.

MARGARET: Now, if you Love me, stay.

PETRUCHIO: *I* cannot. *Sauny*, the Horses.

SAUNY: They have nea ea't their Wadden Dunner yet.

PETRUCHIO: Sirrah, get the Horses.

MARGARET: Nay, then, do what thou canst, *I* wont go to
     day, nor to morrow, nor till *I* please my self. The door is
     open, Sir, there lyes your way, you may be jogging while
     your boots be green.*

PETRUCHIO: O, *Peg* content thee. Prithee be not angry.    230

MARGARET: *I* will be angry. What hast thou to do? Father, be quiet; he shall stay my Leisure.

WOODALL: *I*, marry, Sir, now it begins to Work.

MARGARET: Gentlemen, forward to the Bridal Dinner. *I* see a Woman may be made a fool off, if she want Spirit to resist.

PETRUCHIO: They shall go forward, *Peg*, at thy Command. Obey the Bride, you that attend on her. Go to the Feast, Revel, Carouse, and Dance, be Mad or Merry, or go hang your selves, but for my *Bonny Peg*, shee must with me. 240 Nay, look not big* upon't, nor stamp, nor stair, nor fret. Come, come, gently, so, so, so, that's my good *Peg*. *I* will be master of my own; She is my proper goods and Chattells, my House, my Ox, my Ass,* my any thing. Look, here she stands, touch her who dare; I'll make him smoak* that offers to stop me in my way. *Sauny*, unsheath thy Dudgeon Dagger,* we are beset with Thieves; rescue thy Mistriss if thou beest a Man. Fear not, sweet Wench, I'll Buckler* thee against a Million; nay, come.[36]                                                          250

MARGARET: Will none of you help me?

SAUNY: The Deel a bit of Dunner ye gat. Gud, at ye woud speak to your Cuke to gi *Saundy* a little Mutton and Porridge to put in his Wallet.

[*Exeunt* PETRUCHIO, MARGARET, SAUNY]

BEAUFOY: Nay, let 'em go, a couple of quiet ones.[37]

TRANIO: Never was so mad a Match.

BEAUFOY: Well, Gentleman, let's in, we have a Dinner, although we want a Bride and Bridegroome to it. *Biancha*, you shall take your Sisters Roome; and Mr. *Winlove*, you may Practise for a Bridegroome. [*Exeunt*] 260

WOODALL: Mounsieur, how do ye find my Mistress inclin'd?

WINLOVE: Me can no tell dat yet, but in time Mounsieur sal inform you.

[36] 143–202. Based on *Shrew*, III.ii.147–237: 'Came you from the church … against a million' (considerably shortened).

[37] 207–8: III.ii.238–40: 'Nay, let them go … was the like.'

WOODALL: Pray, Ply her close; here's something for you.

[*Exit* WOODALL]

WINLOVE: Me tank you, Sir. Ha, ha, ha, I must go tell this
to my *Biancha*.                                    [*Exit* WINLOVE]

TRANIO: Hark ye, sir, you may inform me, Pray, what
think you, does Madam *Biancha* fancy any other but my
self? She bears me fair in hand.* Pray discover, Sir; I shall 270
not be ungrateful.

GERALDO: Troth, Sir, I think shee's as all other Women
are.

TRANIO: How is that, pray?

GERALDO: Why, Fickle and Foolish.

TRANIO: Why d' ye think so of her? Shee was always held
Discreet.

GERALDO: No sober Man will think so. I tell you, Sir, shee
cares neither for you nor any Man that's worth careing
for; shee's falne in love with a Mounsier Jack-daw, a 280
fellow that teaches bad *French*, in worse *English*.

TRANIO: That fellow, why, 'tis impossible.

GERALDO: 'Tis true, tho.

TRANIO: Why, I am confident he was employ'd by old
*Woodall* as his instrument to Court her for him.

GERALDO: If he were, he has spoken one word for him and
two for himself.

*Enter* WINLOVE *leading* BIANCHA

See, here they come hand in hand; stand close, perhaps
your Eyes may convince you.

WINLOVE: Madam, you need not doubt my Passion; by 290
those fair Eyes I swear (an Oath inviolable) you have
made a Conquest over me so absolute that I must dye
your Captive.

TRANIO: What does he say? What does he say?

GERALDO: I cannot hear. Listen.

BIANCHA: I must believe you, Sir; there's some strange
power attends your Words, your Attractive* Actions and
your Person, which is too strong for my weak resistance.
You have won, but do not boast your Victory.

TRANIO: Nay, then, I see 'tis so. I cannot hold! Madam, 300

you must forgive my interruption: you have us'd me
kindly, fool'd me with fine hopes; your Mounsieur there
has read Excellent Lessons to you.

BIANCHA: Sir, I understand you not.

GERALDO: That is, you won't.

WINLOVE: What be de matter, Mounsieur Fiddeler?

GERALDO: No fiddler, nor no Lutanist, *Mounsieur No
point*,* but one that scorns to live in a Disguise for such a
one as leaves a Gentleman to doat upon a *Pardon a moy*
Jack-pudding;* know, I am a Gentleman, my name  310
*Geraldo*.

BIANCHA: Alas, Sir, And have you been my Master all this
while, and I never knew it?

GERALDO: Yes, Sweet Lady, you did know it; I see you
have a Little Spice of *Peg* in you. But I have done with
you. Mr. *Winlove*, Pray tell me, Don't you hate this
Gentlewoman now?

TRANIO: I cannot say I Hate her, but I'm sure I don't Love
her for this days Work; Wou'd she Court me, I Swear I
wou'd not have her.                                      320

GERALDO: Nor *I*, by Heavens; *I* have Sworn, and will keep
my Oath.

BIANCHA: Why, Gentlemen, *I* hope you will not both give
the Willow Garland.*

GERALDO: Go, go; you are a Scurvy Woman. *I* have a
Widdow that has Lov'd me as Long as *I* have Lov'd you.
Sweet Lady, *I* am not Bankrupt for a Mistriss. 'Tis true,
she's something of your Sisters Humour, a Little *Way-
ward*; but one Three Dayes time at the *Taming-Schoole*
will make her Vye with any Wife in *England*. And then *I*  330
can pass by you unconcern'd.

BIANCHA: The *Taming-School*? For Heavens-sake, where is
that Sir?

GERALDO: Why, your Brother *Petruchio's* House.[38] *I*
doubt you must there too, e're you'll be good for any
thing. I'll to him immediately. Farewell, thou Vile
Woman.                                              [*Exit*]

---

[38] 265-9: IV.ii.54-6: 'Faith, he is gone ... Petruchio is the master'.

BIANCHA: Ha, ha, ha, this is Excellent.

TRANIO: Madam, I beg your Pardon, but I hope my boldness with you has done my Master some Service.

WINLOVE: Believe me, has it, *Tranio*, and I must thank 340 thee.

*Enter* JAMY

Now, Sirrah, Whither away in such hast?

JAMY: O, Master, I have found him.

WINLOVE: What? Who hast thou found?

JAMY: A rare old Sinner in the *Temple Cloysters* will do the Feat to a hair.*

BIANCHA: What feat? What's to be done?

WINLOVE: That which I told you of my Fairest. Where is he?

JAMY: Here, here, he Walks in the Court.      [*Exit*] 350

BIANCHA: Well, I must in, or I shall be mist. Carry the Matter handsomly, and let me not suffer.

[*Exit*]

WINLOVE: Fear not, Madam. Call him in, *Tranio*. You must instruct him; I'll not be seen in't.      [*Exit*]

*Enter* JAMY *and* SNATCHPENNY

TRANIO: Now, Friend, What are you?

SNATCHPENNY: Any thing that you please, Sir.

TRANIO: Any thing? Why, what can you do?

SNATCHPENNY: Any thing. For so much as Concerns *Swearing* and *Lying*, to your Worships Service, and to get an *Honest Livelyhood*, So please you to Imploy me.      360

TRANIO: Why, thou may'st serve turn, I think; But I'll put thee to no *Swearing*; *Bare Lying* and *Impudence* will serve for my Occasion. You must bate of the Price for that.

SNATCHPENNY: Faith, Sir, they'r both of a Price; take e'm or leave e'm.

TRANIO: But canst thou Mannage and Carry off a good Well-contriv'd Lye to the best advantage?

SNATCHPENNY: I should be very sorry else; it has been my Trade these Seven and thirty Years. Never fear it, Sir.      370

JAMY: Nay, I pickt him out amongst half a Score;

I fancy'd he had the best Lying Face amongst e'm.

TRANIO: Well, come along with me, and I'll Instruct you;
But if you fail, look to your Eares,* if you have any.

SNATCHPENNY: I'll venture Neck and all to do it, Sir.

[Exit]

## Scene ii

PETRUCHIO's House. Enter SAUNY and CURTIS severally

CURTIS: Honest Sauny, Wellcome, wellcome.

SAUNY: Saundy's Hungry; Can't you get a little Meat, Sir?

CURTIS: Yes, yes, Sawny.

SAUNY: Ye mun gat a gude Fire, Sir. Mrs. Bride has gat a
faw intull a Dike; She's aw wet, Sir; Gud, she has not a
dry thread to her arse.

CURTIS: Is Master and Mistriss coming, Sauny?

SAUNY: Gud, are they, gin they be nea frozen to the grund;
bo whare's you Fire, man?

CURTIS: 'Tis making, 'tis making; all things are ready.    10
Prithee, what News, good Sauny, what kind of Woman is
our Mistriss?

SAUNY: Ken ye twa twenty Deel's, Sir?

CURTIS: Marry, Heaven defend us.

SAUNY: Gud, shee has ean twa twenty Deel's; I'se nea bate
ye ean of 'em.

CURTIS: They say shee's a Cruel Shrew.

SAUNY: O my saul Sir, I'se hau'd a thousand pund, shee's
set up her Tang, and Scaud* fro Edingbrough to London,
and nere draw bit* for 't.                                20

CURTIS: What shall we do, then? There will be no living for
us.

SAUNY: Gud, will there not. Wun's, I think the Deel has
flead off her Skin, and put his Dam intul't. Bo where's
Phillip and George and Gregory?

CURTIS: They'r all ready. What ho, come forth here,
Phillip, George, Joseph, Nick, where are you?

Enter 4 or 5 SERVING MEN

PHILLIP: Honest *Sawny*, Wellcome home.

SAUNY: Gat me some Meat, and I'll believe ye, Sir.

GEORGE: I am glad to see thee, *Sawny*.                        30

SAUNY: Gat me a Drink, and Is'e believe ye tea.

JOSEPH: What, *Sawny*, come to Town again? Wellcome.

SAUNY: Wun's, Walcome, walcome, gar me gude Meat and Drink, that is Walcome, Sir.

NICK: Old Lusty Fellow, *Sawny*, Wellcome.

SAUNY: How d'ye, *Wully*?

NICK: D'ye hear the News, *Sawny*? *Wally Watts* is Dead.

SAUNY: S'breed, nea Man that geas on twa Leggs cou'd slay *Wully Watts*, Sir.

NICK: True; for he was fairly Hang'd.                          40

SAUNY: I was sure nea Man that went on twa Leggs could slay him.

NICK: You are in the right, *Sawny*, for 'twas one with Three Leggs; 'twas Mr. *Tyburne*, for he was fairly Hang'd.

SAUNY: S'breed, ye Lye, Sir, the Gallows might kill him, and break his stout heart, but it cou'd nea hang him. 'Tis hang an *English Man*.

NICK: Well, But what kind of Woman is our Mistriss, *Sawny*?

SAUNY: You'l ken soon enough 'tea your Sorrow and wea,   50 Sir. Ye've awe twa Luggs apeece o'your Head: A my Saul I'se nea gea ye twa Pennys for them by'th Morn. How say ye now?

*Enter* PETRUCHIO *and* MARGARET

PETRUCHIO: Where be these Idle Rogues? What, no more at Door to hold my Stirrip, or take my Horses? Where's *Curtis*, *Phillip*, *Nick* and *Gregory*?

ALL: Here, Here, Here, Sir.

PETRUCHIO: Here, here, here, you Loggerhead Currs. What, no Attendance, no Regard, no Duty? Where's that Foolish Knave I sent before.[39]                              60

SAUNY: Wuns, Sir, Ise be sea hungry, and sea empty, ye

---

[39] 46–50. Based on *Shrew*, IV.i.107–18: 'Where be ... rascal knaves with thee?'

may travell quite through me, and nere faw* your fingers,
Sir.

PETRUCHIO: You Mangy Rogue, Did not I bid you meet
me in the Park, and bring these Rascals with you?

SAUNY: Gud, did ye, Sir; bo Ise sea hungry, Ise ha nea
Memory. Deliver your Message your sel, Sir.

PETRUCHIO: Be gone, you Slaves, and fetch my Supper in.
Rogues do I speak, and don't you fly to make hast?

[Exeunt 2 or 3 Servants]

Sit down, *Peg*, and Wellcome. Why, when, I Pray; nay, 70
good sweet *Peg*, be Merry; These are Country Clownish
Fellows; Prithee be Merry. Off with my Bootes, Sirrah,
you Rogues, ye Villains. When?

(SINGS)

*It was the Orders of the Fryar Gray,*
*As forth he walked on his Way.*

MARGARET: Sure he will run himself out of Breath, and
then it will be my turn.

PETRUCHIO: Out, you Rogue, You pluck my Boot awry;
take that, and mend it in pulling off the other. Be Merry,
*Peg*. Some Water here, ho. Where's my Spaniel, Sirrah?
Make hast and desire my Cousin *Ferdinand* to come
hither, one, *Peg*, you must Kiss, and be Acquainted with. 80
Where are my Slippers? Shall I have some Water? Come,
*Peg*, wash and Welcome Heartily.

SAUNY: Wuns, bo whare is the Meat to mack her Welcome.

MARGARET: We shall fall out if we wash together.

PETRUCHIO: You Whorson Villain, will you let it fall?

MARGARET: Pray, Sir, be Patient, 'twas an unwilling Fault.

*Table Cover'd. Enter Servants with Meat*

PETRUCHIO: An Idle, Careless, Beetle-headed-Slave.
Come, *Peg*, sit down. I know you have a Stomach.
Will you give Thanks, Sweet *Peg*, or shall I?
Or each for our selves? Come, fall too. 90
What's this, Mutton?

SAUNY: Gud, it is, Sir.

PETRUCHIO: Who bought it?

CURTIS: I did, Sir.

PETRUCHIO: You Rascal you, 'tis not Mutton, 'tis the Breast of a Dog. What Currs are these! 'Tis dry'd and burn't to a Coal too. Where is this Rascal Cook? How dare you bring such rotten Meat to my Table? Why, d' ye mean to Poyson me, ye heedless Joltheads, ye ill manner'd Whelps? What, d' ye grumble? I'll be with you straight. 100

MARGARET: Pray, Husband, be content. The Meat is good Meat, and I am very hungry; I must and will eat some of it.

PETRUCHIO: Not for the World, *Peg*; I Love thee better then so. 'Tis burnt and will Ingender Chollar,* a Disease we are both too Subject to.[40] I Love thee too well to give thee any thing to hurt thee. We'll fast to night, to morrow we'll make it up.

MARGARET: Say what you will, Sir, I'll eat some of it; Did you bring me hither to Starve me? 110

PETRUCHIO: Why, ye Rascals, will ye stand Still and see your Mistriss Poyson her self? Take it away out of her sight, quickly.

(*Throws the Meat at 'em,* SAUNY *gets it*)

SAUNY: Gud, *Saundy* will venture, Poyson and 'twill.

PETRUCHIO: Well, *Peg*, this night we'll fast for Company; Come, I'll bring thee to the Bridall Chamber.

MARGARET: I must Eat something, I shall be Sick else; But an Egg.

PETRUCHIO: No, no, Prithee dont talk on't; to Bed upon a full stomach? 120

MARGARET: But a Crust of Bread.

PETRUCHIO: To morrow, to morrow; Come, prithee away.

[*Exeunt*]

GEORGE: Did'st ever see the like?

CURTIS: He kills her in her own Humour.[41]

PHILLIP: Have you said Grace, *Sauny*?

---

[40] 69–92. Based on *Shrew*, IV.i.134–61: 'Out, you rogue ... ourselves are choleric' (shortened).

[41] 106–7: IV.i.166–7: 'Peter, didst ever see ... in her own humour.'

SAUNY: Gud, I was sea hungry, I forgot grace. O thou that hast fill'd our Boyes,* and our blathers,* keep us aw from Whoredome, and Secrisie.

NICK: Secrecy, why, *Sauny*?

SAUNY: Wuns, Man, it is wutchcraft. Peace, you put me out, with the Deel's name to ye: Keep us aw from Whoredome and Secresie, fro the Dinger* o' the swatch* to the gallow Tree, keep us aw we Beseech thee. Tak a Drink man.

PHILLIP: Are ye full now, *Sauny*?

SAUNY: As fow as a Piper. We may put ean finger in at my Mouth, and another in mine Arse and feel beath ends o' my Dinner.                    [*Exeunt*]

## Scene iii

*Enter, as in a Bed-Chamber,* PETRUCHIO, PEG, *and Servants,* SAUNY

PETRUCHIO: Where are you, you Rogues? Some lights there. Come, *Peg*, undress; to bed, to bed.

MARGARET: Pray send your Men away, and call for some of your Maids.

PETRUCHIO: Maids, hang Maids; I have no such vermine about my house. Any of these will do as well. Here, *Sauny*, come hither, Sirrah, and undress your Mistress.

SAUNY: O my Saul, Sir, I'se put on my head-peice.* Now, an ye'll bind her hands behind her, I'se undress her.

                    (*Goes to take up her Coats*)

PETRUCHIO: What dost thou do?

SAUNY: In *Scotland* we aw wayes begin at the nether end of a bonny Lass.

PETRUCHIO: Who made his Bed? What Rascals are these? Foh, these Sheets are Musty as the Devil and what Rags are here upon my Bed? Is this a Counterpain? 'Tis a Dishclout.

MARGARET: Why, the Counterpain is well enough, and

Rich enough, and the Sheet's are as Clean and as Sweet as
may be.

PETRUCHIO: Fye, fye, *Peg*, thou hast got a Cold, and lost    20
thy Smelling. I tell thee they are all Damp and Musty. I
wou'd not have thee to venture to Lye in 'em for the
world; it wou'd be thy Death. Here, take 'em away. We
must ee'n sit up; there's no remedy.

MARGARET: Pray, Sir, talk not of sitting up; I am so sleepy
I cant hold my Eyes open. I must to Bed.

PETRUCHIO: I'll keep thee waking, I warrant thee. Ho,
*Curtis*, bring us a Flaggon of March Beer,* and some
Tobacco, and clean Pipes, we'll be merry.

[Exit CURTIS]

MARGARET: Why, what d' ye mean, are you Mad?    30

PETRUCHIO: Mad? I, what should we do? I mean thou and
I hand to fist will drink a Health to my Father, and my
Sister, and all our good Friends at *London*.

Enter Servant with Beer and Tobacco

MARGARET: Why, you dont take me to be one of your
fellow Tospots?

PETRUCHIO: I mean to Teach thee to Drink; thou must
Learn that, or thou'rt no Wife for me. Here, *Peg*, to thee
with all my Heart, a whole one, and thou art Wellcome;
My Father's good Health, *Peg*, you shall Pledge it.

MARGARET: I can't Drink without Eating; 'twill make me    40
sick.

PETRUCHIO: Pish, Pish, that's but a Fancy; Come, off with
it, or thou shalt neither eat nor drink this Month.

MARGARET: Shall I go to Bed when I have drank it?

SAUNY: Gud, at ye gi *Sawndy* a little Drink, Madam.

PETRUCHIO: Talk of that anon.            (*She Drinks*)
So, here, *Peg*, heres a Pipe I have fill'd for thee my self;
Sit down, and Light it.

MARGARET: D'ye mean to make a meer Hackny Horse* of
me? What d'offer me your nasty Tobacco for?    50

PETRUCHIO: Nay, ne're make so shy; I know thou Lov'st
it. Come, young Ladies are often troubled with the Tooth-
ach, and take it in their Chambers, though they won't

appear Good Fellows amongst us. Take it, or no Sleep nor
Meat, *Peg*, D'ye hear?

MARGARET:  Yes, to my Griefe; I won't be Abus'd thus.

*(Weeps)*

PETRUCHIO:  Nay, nay, Goe where thou wilt, I'll make thee
Smoak before I Sleep.                         [*Exeunt*]

# ACT IV

## Scene i

*Enter* PETRUCHIO *and* SAUNY

PETRUCHIO: Sirrah, wait on your Mistriss. Say what you will to her, and Vex her, but do not touch her; and let her have no Meat, I Charge ye.

SAUNY: S'breed, Sir, send her into the Highlands in *Scotland*; there's Hunger and Caud enough; there she may starve her Bally soo.

PETRUCHIO: Well, Sirrah, Doe as I direct you.  [*Exit*]

SAUNY: O' my Saul, wull I, Sir. Yee'l let me take my Head-piece to defend me, Sir.

*Enter* MARGARET

MARGARET: What, *Gregory, Phillip!* No Body near me?    10
*Sawny,* Where are you?

SAUNY: Is'e een hard at your Arse, Madam.

MARGARET: Where's your Master?

SAUNY: He's gone to the Market himself, and he'l bring ye heam a Braw* Bull's Puzzle* to Swaddle your Weam with.

MARGARET: And in the mean time I am Famisht. Was ever Woman us'd so Damnably? I am Starv'd for Meat, Giddy for want of Sleep; and that which Spites me more then all the rest, is, he pretends 'tis out of Care and Love to me.[42]    20
Prithee, good *Sawny,* give me some Meat.

SAUNY: O my Saul, *Sawndy* wou'd be Hang'd gin I sud bestow an aw'd Liquor'd Bute;* *Sawny* will cut it into Tripes to Stuff your Weam with.

MARGARET: Good *Sawny,* here's Money for thee: but one little bit of any thing to stay my fainting Spirits.

SAUNY: What, will ye eat a Bit of Beefe?

[42] 16–18: IV.iii.9–12: 'Am starved for meat ... name of perfect love.'

MARGARET: I, good *Sawny*.

SAUNY: Will ye eat some Mustard to't?

MARGARET: I, good *Sawny*, quickly.                                        30

SAUNY: Mustard is nea gu'd for your Tang; 'twill make it
tea keen, and ye can Scau'd fast enough without.[43]

MARGARET: Why then, the Beef without Mustard.

SAUNY: Gud Beef is nee gued without Mustard. *Sawny* will
fetch ye some Meal and Water; ye'st make ye a *Scotch*
Pudding;* ye'st Eat of that tull your Weam crack.

MARGARET: You Abusive Rogue, take that.   (*Beats him*)
Must I be Brav'd thus by my own Servant?

SAUNY: The Dee'l wash your Face with a Fou* Clout.

*Enter* GERALDO

GERALDO: Why, how now, Sirrah, Will you strike your        40
Mistriss? You Cowardly Rogue, strike a Woman?

SAUNY: S'breed, Sir, D'ye Caw a *Scotchman* a Coward?
Gin Is'e had ye in *Scotland*, Is'e put my Whinyard* in
your Weam, gin ye were as stout as *Gilderoy*.*

GERALDO: Why, *Gilderoy* was as arrant a Coward as thou
art.

SAUNY: Wuns, yeed be lath* to keep the Grund that
*Gilderoy* quits; yet I must confess he was a little Shame-
fac'd before the Enemy.

MARGARET: O, Mr. *Geraldo*, never was Poor Woman so        50
us'd. For Charity sake, Convey me home to my Father.

*Enter* PETRUCHIO *with a Dish of Meat*

PETRUCHIO: Here, *Peg*, here's Meat for thee; I have Drest
it my self, my Dear. Geraldo, wellcome, this was kindly
done to Visit *Peg* and Me. Come, *Peg*, fall too; here's an
Excellent piece of *Veal*.

MARGARET: Why, 'tis a *Pullet*.

PETRUCHIO: Why, 'tis *Veal*, Art thou Mad?

MARGARET: You won't Perswade me out of my Sences.
'Tis a *Pullet*.                                                        60

SAUNY: A Gud, is it, Sir.

PETRUCHIO: What an unhappy Man am I; my poor Dear
*Peg*'s Distracted. I always fear'd 'twould come to this.

[43] 22–8: IV.iii.23–6: 'What say you ... mustard rest.'

Take the *Meat* away, *Curtis*. Is the Room Ready as I
Order'd? Are the Lights Damn'd up?

CURTIS: Yes, Sir.

MARGARET: Why, what d'ye mean to do with me?

PETRUCHIO: Poor *Peg*, I Pitty thee; but thou shalt want no
Help for thy Cure. You must be kept from the Light; it
troubles the Brain.                                                70

GERALDO: I see I shall Learn, he's an excellent Teacher.

MARGARET: Why, Sir, Pray tell me, Have you a mind to
make me Mad? This is the way indeed. How have I
injur'd you that you use me thus inhumanely? Did you
Marry me to starve me?

SAUNY: He means to bring down your Weam for a Race;*
For we awways Cry, a Nag with a Weam, but a Mare
with Nean.*

PETRUCHIO: No, no; Good *Peg*, thou know'st I have a
Care of thee. Here's a Gown just brought home for thee,  80
*Peg*. Now thou art empty, it will fit Handsomely. Where
is this Taylor? Call him in, *Sawny*. If it fits you, you shall
put it on, and wee'l Gallop o're to *London*, and see your
Father. Your Sisters *Wedding* is at hand, you must help
her.

*Enter* TAYLOR *with a Gown*

MARGARET: If she be Match'd as I am, Heaven help her!
But there's some Comfort in going Home; there's *Meat*
and *Sleeping-room*.

PETRUCHIO: Come, Taylor, lets see the Gowne. How now,
what's here? Bless me, what Masquing Suite is this?       90
What's this? A Sleve? Why, 'tis like a Demmy cannon.[44]*
Why, what a Devil, Taylor, dost thou mean? Is this a
Gown?

TAYLOR: A gown, Sir? Yes, Sir, and a handsome Gown as
any Man in *London* can make; 'tis the newest Fashon
lately come out of *France*.

PETRUCHIO: What a lying knave art thou! My great
Grand-mothers Picture in the Matted Gallery is just such
another.

---

[44] 75–6: IV.iii.87–8: 'O mercy God . . . a demi-cannon.'

SAUNY: It is like the Picture of Queen Margaret* in 100
*Edenbrough* Castle, Sir.

MARGARET: I never saw a better Fashon'd gown in my life,
more quaint nor better shap'd. I like the Gown, and I'll
have this Gown or I'll have none. Say what you will, I like
it; 'tis a handsom Gown.

PETRUCHIO: Why, thou sayst true, *Peg*, 'tis an ugly paltrey
Gown. I am glad to hear thee of my mind; 'tis a beastly
Gown.

MARGARET: Why, I say 'tis a good Gown, a handsome
fashionable Gown. What, d' ye mean to make a Puppet of 110
me?

PETRUCHIO: Ay, this fellow wou'd make a Puppet of thee.

TAYLOR: She says your Worship means to make a Puppet
of her.

PETRUCHIO: Thou Impudent, lying Threed, Bodkin and
Thimble, Flea, thou nit, brave me in my own house? Go,
take it, I'll ha none on't.

TAYLOR: Sir, I made it according to your Directions, and I
cannot take it again.[45]

SAUNY: Tak it awaw, or the Deel O my Luggs, but ye'st tak 120
my Whineyard.

MARGARET: He shall not take it agen. What need you
trouble your self about it, as long as it pleases me. Lay it
down there.

PETRUCHIO: Sirrah, take it away, I say. We shall find more
Taylors. I wont have my wife so Antickly* drest that the
Boys shoud hoot at her.

MARGARET: Come, come, all this is but fooling; you dont
understand what belongs to a Gown. Say what you will,
I'm resolv'd to have it; if it were an ugly one I wou'd wear 130
it, and it were but to Cross you.

SAUNY: Now the Deel's a cruppen* untell her Mouth, Sir.
You may see a little of his Tail hang out; it looks for aw
the world an it were a Sting, Sir.

PETRUCHIO: Why, that's my good *Peg*; I know thou dost

---

[45] 84–95. Based on *Shrew*, IV.iii.101–17: 'I never saw ... master had direction.'

not care for it. Say no more, prithee, thou shalt have
another.

MARGARET: I know not what you mean to do with me, but
methinks I might have leave to speak, and speak I will; I
am no Child, no Baby. Your Betters have endur'd me to 140
speak my mind, and if you cannot you had best stop your
Ears. 'Tis better set my Tongue at Liberty, then let my
Heart break.[46]

PETRUCHIO: Speak, *Peg*, by all means, say what thou wilt.
Sirrah, carry that tawdry thing away. *Geraldo*, tell him
you'll see him paid, (*Aside*) and bid him leave it. Come,
what sayst thou, *Peg*?

GERALDO: Leave the Gown in the next Room, Taylor, and
take no notice of what he says; I'll see you paid for't.[47]

(*Aside*) [*Exit Tailor*]

MARGARET: Why, I say I will have that Gown, and every 150
thing I have a mind for; I did not bring you such a Portion
to be made a Fool of.

PETRUCHIO: Very true; thou'rt in the right, *Peg*. Come, lets
to Horse; these Cloaths will serve turn at present till we
can get better. Go, Sirrah, lead the Horses to the Lands
end;* thether we'll walk a foot. Lets see, I think 'tis about
seven a Clock; we shall reach to my Father in Laws by
Dinner time with Ease.

MARGARET: 'Tis almost Two; you cannot get thether by
Supper time.                                                                        160

PETRUCHIO: It shall be seaven e're I go. Why, what a
Mischief's this; what I say or do, you are still crossing it.
Let the Horses alone; I will not go to day, and e're I do it
shall be what a Clock I please.[48]

MARGARET: Nay, Sir, that shant stop our Journey. 'Tis
seaven, or two or nine, or what a Clock you please; pray,
lets go.

SAUNY: Ye's have it what hour you wull, Sir.

PETRUCHIO: Very well, it is so. Get ready, quickly. Come,

---

[46] 109–12: IV.iii.73–8: 'Why sir, I trust ... it will break.'
[47] 116–17: IV.iii.163–4: 'Tailor, I'll pay ... hasty words.'
[48] 124–7: IV.iii.186–92: 'I dare assure you ... o'clock I say it is.'

*Geraldo*, let's all go; we shall help mend the Mirth at my   170
Sisters Wedding.

GERALDO: I'll wait on you.

PETRUCHIO: Come, *Peg*, get on your things.

MARGARET: Let me but once see *Lincolns-Inn-Fields* agen,
and Yet* thou shalt not Tame me.          [*Exeunt*]


## Scene ii⁴⁹

### *Enter* TRANIO *and* SNATCHPENNY

TRANIO: Now, Sirrah, be but Impudent enough and keep
state like the old Knight, and thou art made for ever.

SNATCHPENNY: I warrant ye, Sir, I know it to a hair. My
Lord *Beaufoy* and I were School fellows together at
*Worster*; my Estate lyes in the Vale of *Evesham*, Three   10
thousand Pound a year, and Fifteen hundred a year I settle
upon you upon the Marriage. Let me alone, *I* am Sir
*Lyonell* himself.

TRANIO: Right, right; Excellent brave, How now?

### *Enter* JAMY

JAMY: To your Postures, old sinner. Be an exquesite
Rascal, and then thou shalt be a Rogue Paramount;* thou
shalt lay the Dragon asleep while my Master steals the
Pippins.*

TRANIO: Well, *Jamy*, What hast thou done?

JAMY: *I* have been with my Lord *Beaufoy*, presented your   20
Fathers and your Service to him, and told him the old
Knight was happily come to Town and hearing of your
Love to *Biancha* was so overjoy'd he would Settle all
upon you.

TRANIO: Well, and what said he?

JAMY: He gave me a Peece* for my News. *I* told him Sir
*Lyonell* desired his Company just now to treat upon the
Match. He's coming in all hast; he longs to be Couzend,
and, *Snatchpenny*, if thou dost not do it—

---

⁴⁹ [Scene ii] Closely based on *Shrew*, IV.iv, up to l. 67.

SNATCHPENNY: Then hang me.                                               30
JAMY: Mum, look to't; he's here.

*Enter* BEAUFOY *and* WINLOVE

BEAUFOY: Mr. *Winlove*, your Man tells me your Father is
just happily come to Town. Where is he?

TRANIO: Here, Sir, this is my Father. Time has been too
Bold to weare ye out of each others Memory.

SNATCHPENNY: Is this my Lord *Beaufoy*, Sir?

TRANIO: Yes, Sir.

SNATCHPENNY: My Lord, your humble Servant; I'm happy
at last to meet a Person I have formerly so much Lov'd.

BEAUFOY: Noble Sir *Lyonell*, I joy to see you.                          40

SNATCHPENNY: O, the merry Days that you and I have
seen, my Lord; Well fare the good old times, I say.

BEAUFOY: I, Sir *Lyonell*, when you and I were acquainted
first.

SNATCHPENNY: I, Marry, there were Golden Days indeed,
no Couzening, no Cheating; the World is alter'd.

BEAUFOY: But we will remember these times, and be
honest still.

SNATCHPENNY: That's een the best way. There's hopes we
may have honest Grand Children too, if all be true as I      50
hear; my Son tells me your Daughter has made a Captive
of him.

BEAUFOY: *I* wou'd she were better for his sake. She's a
good Girle, and a handsome one, though *I* say it; if she
were not, *I* wou'd give her somewhat shou'd make her so.

TRANIO: *It* takes Rarely.

SNATCHPENNY: *I*'m even overjoy'd that you think my Son
worthy your Allyance. *I*'ll give something they shall make
a shift to Live on; in Plain and in breif, if you'll approve   60
of it, *I*'ll settle Fifteen hundred Pound a year upon him at
Present, which shall be her Joynture; after my Death, all *I*
have, with a good will. What say you, my Lord?

BEAUFOY: Sir *Lyonell*, Your Freedome pleas's me; I see
you are an honest meaning Gentleman. The Young Folks
(if I am not mistaken) like one another. Well, I say no
more; it is a *Match*.

TRANIO: You bind me to you Ever. Now I may boldly say, *I* am truly happy. Where will you please to have the business made up?

BEAUFOY: Not in my House, Son; *I* wou'd have it Private. 70 Pitchers have Eares,* and *I* have many Servants.[50] Besides, Old *Woodall* will be hindring of us; He's hearkening still, and will be interrupting.

TRANIO: Then at my Lodging; there my Father Lyes, and there the Business may be all Dispatch'd. Send for your Daughter by this Gentleman; my Boy shall fetch a Scrivener presently. The worst on't is, 'tis too small a Warning. You are like to have but slender entertainment.

BEAUFOY: No matter, no matter; *I* shall like it.

SNATCHPENNY: I wou'd feign see your Daughter, my Lord; 80 *I* have heard great Commendations of her.

BEAUFOY: That you shall presently. *Mounsier*, pray go to *Biancha*, and tell her from me. She must come hither with you immediately; you may tell her too, if you will, what has hapned, and that she must prepare to be *Mr. Winlove's* Bride.

WINLOVE: *My Lord*, me vil fetch her presant.

TRANIO: *My Lord*, Will your Lordship please to walk in with my Father; this is my Lodging.

BEAUFOY: *I*, Sir. Come, Sir *Lyonell*, I'll follow you. 90

SNATCHPENNY: Good my Lord, *I* will wait upon you.

[*Exit.* BEAUFOY, SNATCHPENNY, TRANIO]

WINLOVE: Thus far 'tis well Carry'd on, *Jamy*; But how shall we prosecute it?

JAMY: Why, there is but one way in the World, Sir.

WINLOVE: And what's that?

JAMY: Why, thus: I have got a Parson ready for the Purpose; when you have got *Biancha* abroad, whip her into *Covent-Garden* Church, and there *Marry* her, and your Work's done.

WINLOVE: Troth, thou say'st true. But is the Parson 100 Orthodox and Canonical? I wou'd not have an *Obadiah*\* to make us enter into Covenant of Matrimony.

---

[50] 54-5: IV.iv.51-2: 'Not in my house . . . many servants.'

JAMY: Trust me, Sir, he's as true as Steel. He says all *Matrimony*\* without Book; he can Christen, Wed, and Bury Blindfold.

WINLOVE: Well, I'll take thy Counsel, if I can perswade her to't, as I hope *I* shall, for *I* know she Loves me; fair Luck betides me. But who comes here?

*Enter* WOODALL

JAMY: 'Tis the old Grub\* *Woodall*; What shall we do with him?                                                                        110

WINLOVE: We must contrive some way to get him off.

WOODALL: *I* don't like those shuffling matters; *I* doubt there's some false Play towards me in hand. Here's my *Monsieur*, he may Informe me— *Mounsieur*.

WINLOVE: Che Dict a vouz *Mounsieur*. *Mounsieur*, Your Servant.

WOODALL: *Mounsieur*, Prithee tell me, if thou canst, how Affaires go; things are carry'd very closely. How stands my *Mistriss* affected?

WINLOVE: Moy foy, *Mounsieur*; Me tell you de bad News   120 in the Varle, *Madamoselle Biancha* no stand Affected to you at all. My Lord has sent me to fetch her just now to be *Marry* to *Mounsieur* Vat you call? *Mounsieur Le . . .*

WOODALL: What, not to *Winlove*.

WINLOVE: Yes, to *Mounsieur Winlove*. Begar, me be very sorry, but me canno help dat.

WOODALL: Is Old *Beaufoy* mad to *Match* her to him without his Father's Privity.\*

WINLOVE: Here be de ver Fine Old *Man* new come to Town; me Lord be wid him now.                                              130

WOODALL: Upon my Life, old Sir *Lyonell*. Nay, then, she's lost quite. Hark you, Mounsier, yet 'tis in your Power to make me a happy Man.

WINLOVE: O, Mounsier, me be your humble Servant.

WOODALL: Why, look you, you are to fetch her; here's forty Pound in Gold to buy you a pair of Gloves. Let me take her from you, as you are carrying her thither; I will have two or three with me, and you may safely say she was forc'd from you.

WINLOVE: Mounsier, begarr, me do you all de Service in  140
the Varle, but me sal be the grand Sheat* Knave then.

WOODALL: That's nothing. Here's more Money; I'll save
you harmless.* Come, you shall do it.

WINLOVE: Mounsier, me have no mind to be van Knave;
but to do you Service, if you will meet me upon de Street.

WOODALL: Fear not; *I'*ll secure you. Honest Mounsieur,
farewell; I will be your Friend for Ever.          [*Exit*]

WINLOVE: Ha, ha, ha, this is rare; What an Ass this Fellow
will make himself, do what we can. Here, *Jamy*, thou
shalt share with me.                                      150

JAMY: Thank you, Sir; Wou'd we had such a Windfall
every day. But come, Sir, you must make haste. This is the
Critical Minute; if you miss it, you lose *Biancha*.

WINLOVE: Thy Counsel's good; away. I'll buy a Ring and
Pay the Priest with some of *Woodall's* Money. Ha, ha,
hah.                                              [*Exeunt*]


## Scene iii

*Enter* PETRUCHIO, MARGARET, GERALDO *and* SAWNY


PETRUCHIO: Walk your Horses down the Hill before; we
shall reach *London* time enough. 'Tis a fair Night; How
bright and goodly the *Moon* shines.

MARGARET: The *Moon!* The *Sun*; 'tis not the *Moon-light*
now.

PETRUCHIO: I say 'tis the *Moon* that Shines so Bright.

MARGARET: I say 'tis the *Sun* that shines so Bright.

PETRUCHIO: Now, by my *Mothers Son*, and that's my Self,
it shall be the *Moonlight*, or what *I* please, before you set
Sight of your Father's House. Sirrah, go fetch the Horses  10
back. Evermore Crost, and Crost, and nothing but Crost?

GERALDO: Say as he sayes, or we shall never go.

MARGARET: Forward, *I* Pray, Sir, since we are come so far;
And be it *Sun* or *Moon* or what you please. Nay, if you
call it a Rush-Candle, henceforth it shall be so for me.

PETRUCHIO: *I* say tis the *Moon*.

SAUNY: S'breed, but *I* say nay, Sir. Out, out, a Lies.

MARGARET: *I* know 'tis the *Moon*.

PETRUCHIO: Nay, then, you Lie; 'tis the Blessed *Sun*.

MARGARET: Why, Heaven be Blest for it; 'tis even what      20
you have a mind to. Pray, let us forward.

GERALDO: *Petruchio*, go thy wayes; the Field is Won.

PETRUCHIO: Well, forward, forward; Now the Bowl runs
with a Right Byas.[51]* But soft, here's Company.

*Enter* SIR LYONELL WINLOVE

SIR LYONELL: Boy, Bid the Coachman drive gently down
the Hill. *I* wonder *I* meet nor overtake no Passengers to
day. Stay, *I* think here be some.

PETRUCHIO: I will have one bout more with thee, *Peg*.
Good-morrow, Gentle Lady; Which way Travel you?
Come hither, *Peg*; Didst thou ever behold so Exquisite a     30
Beauty as this Fair Virgin beares about. Go to her, *Peg*,
and Salute her.

MARGARET: Are you Mad? 'Tis an Old Man.

PETRUCHIO: Beat back agen then; still Cross? Will you do
it?

SAUNY: Why, i'th' Deel's Name, What mean ye? It's nea
bonny Lass, Sir; S'breed, it's an aw faw Thefe.

GERALDO: He'll make this old Man Mad.

MARGARET: You Budding Virgin, so fair, so sweet, so
fresh, which way Travel you? How happy shou'd we be in     40
the Enjoyment of so fair a Fellow Traveller.

SAUNY: The Dee'l has built a Bird's Nest in your Head.
Gud, ye'r as mad as he; and he as Mad as gin he were the
son of a March Hare,* Sir.

SIR LYONELL: Why, what do ye mean, Gentlewoman?

PETRUCHIO: Why, now, now, *Peg*, I hope thou art not
Mad. A Virgin Quotha! 'Tis an Old Wrinckled Wither'd
Man.

MARGARET: Reverend sir, Pardon my mistaking eyes, that
have been so dazled with the *Moon* (*Sun, I* mean) I cou'd    50

---

[51] 2-21. Based on *Shrew*, IV.v.2-24: 'Good Lord, how bright ... against the bias.'
(shortened).

not distinguish you. *I* now perceive you are a Grave Old Man; pray excuse me.[52]

SIR LYONELL: Indeed you are a Merry Lady; your encounter has amaz'd me. But *I* like such Chearful Company. *I* am for *London* to see a Son of mine, that went lately from me thither.

PETRUCHIO: We shall be glad of your Company. You must pardon my Wifes Errour; she has not slept well to Night, and *I* cou'd not perswade her but she wou'd come out Fasting, which makes her Fancy a little extravagant.    60

SAUNY: The Dee'l O' my Saul, but you are a false Trundle Taile Tike.* The Dee'l a bit hee'd lat her eat these three days, Sir.

MARGARET: Curse upon your Excuse, and the Cause of it; *I* cou'd have eaten my Shooe-Soules, if *I* might have had 'em Fry'd.

PETRUCHIO: Your name, *I* beseech you, Sir.

SIR LYONELL: I am Call'd Sir *Lyonell Winlove* in the Country.

PETRUCHIO: Father to young Mr. *Winlove*?    70

SIR LYONELL: The same, Sir.

PETRUCHIO: Then *I* am happy indeed to have met you. *I* can tell you some News perhaps may not be Unwelcome to you. Your Son is in a fair probability of Calling me Brother within these Two dayes.

SIR LYONELL: How so, *I* pray, Sir.

PETRUCHIO: Why, he's upon Marrying my Wifes Sister, my Lord *Beaufoyes* youngest Daughter. A brave Match, *I* can assure you, and a Sweet Bedfellow.

SAUNY: Gud, she's tea gued for any man but *Saundy*; Gud,    80
Gin poor *Saundy* had her in *Scotland*, Wun's, I'de sea Swing her about.

SIR LYONELL: You Amaze me! Is this true? Or have you a mind, like a pleasant Traveller, to break a Jest on the company you overtake?[53]

GERALDO: Upon my Word, sir, 'tis very true. 'Twas so

---

[52] 40–4. Based on *Shrew*, IV.v.41–8: 'Why, how now Kate . . . mad mistaking.'
[53] 67–8: IV.v.70–2: 'But is this true . . . you overtake?'

design'd, but *I* don't think he'll Marry her; he's Forsworn
if he do.

SIR LYONELL: You make me Wonder more and more.

PETRUCHIO: Mind him not, he's a Party Concern'd. 'Tis  90
true.

SIR LYONELL: Pray, Gentlemen, let's make haste. *I* must
look after this Business. It soundes strangely; he wou'd
not do't without my Consent. He's my only Son, my Heir,
the Prop of my Family; *I* must be careful.

PETRUCHIO: I see you are Jealous, Sir, but you need not; he
cannot have a better Match.

SIR LYONELL: *I* doubt it not, if all be fair. *I* should be glad
of my Lord *Beaufoyes* allyance; he was my School-fellow,
but Time, *I* doubt, has worn out our Old Acquaintance. 100
Gentlemen, *I* must hasten to prevent the worst.

SAUNY: What mean ye, Sir? Yea will nea bawk the Bonna
Lad, and tak fro his mattle,* Sir.

GERALDO: Well, *Petruchio*, thou hast put me in a Heat.*
Have at my Widdow now.                    [*Exeunt*]


## Scene iv

### *Enter* WINLOVE, BIANCHA, JAMY

WINLOVE: How good you are, my Faire one. *Jamy*, Ar't
sure the Priest is ready for us?

JAMY: I warrant you, Sir. Pray make hast; some Devil or
other may come else and Cross it. Don't stay Thrumming
of Caps.* Here, Body o' me, away. Here's *Woodall*; shift
for your selves, all will be spoyl'd else.

                         [*Exit* WINLOVE *and* BIANCHA]
               *Enter* WOODALL *with* 3 *or* 4 *Fellows*

WOODALL: Be sure you seize on her, and Clap her into a
chair, and one stop her mouth. Fear not, I'll save you
harmless.

1ST FELLOW: I warrant you, Sir.                              10

WOODALL: What a Devil makes this Rogue Poaching here?

JAMY: Tum, te Dum, te Dum; Sing Old Coale of *London*.

[*Sings*]

WOODALL: Now, *Jamy*, What Walk you here for.

JAMY: Why, to look about me; te Dum, te dum, &c,

WOODALL: They say your Master is to be Marry'd to Madam *Biancha* to day.

JAMY: Why, then, we'll be merry at Night; Te Dum, te Dum, &c.

WOODALL: The Rogue won't be gone. What, Hast no Business? Thou look'st as if thou hadst not Drank to day. 20 There's something for thee; go get thy Mornings Draught.

JAMY: I thank your Worship. Will you take part of a Pot of Ale and a Toast?

WOODALL: No, Sirrah, *I* Drank Coffee this morning.

[*Exit* JAMY]

So he's gone; *I* wonder Mounsieur appears not with *Biancha*.

*Enter* PETRUCHIO, MARGARET, SIR LYONELL, GERALDO, *and* SAUNY, *with Attendants*

WOODALL: Ha, Who comes there?

GERALDO: Now you are there, I'll take my Leave. Your Servant. [*Exit*]

PETRUCHIO: Sir *Lyonell*, you are Wellcome to Town. 30 There's your Sons Lodgings. My Father Lives on the other side; thither we must, and therefore here I take my Leave.

SIR LYONELL: Pray, stay a little. May be he's not within; if so, I'll wait upon you to the Lord *Beaufoy*.

SAUNY: O' my Saul, nea ean cou'd have Beg'd. (*Knocks*) Dunner better then this awd Theife has done.

WOODALL: They are all busy within, Sir; you must *Knock* Louder if you mean to be heard.

[SNATCHPENNY *Above*]

SNATCHPENNY: Who is that *Knocks* as if he wou'd Beat down the Gate? 40

SIR LYONELL: Is Mr. *Winlove* within?

SNATCHPENNY: He is within, but not to be spoken with.

SIR LYONELL: What if a Man bring him a Hundred Pounds or Two to make Merry withall.

SNATCHPENNY: Keep your Hundred Pounds for your self;
he shall need none as long as I Live.

PETRUCHIO: Nay, I told you, Sir, Your Son was well
Belov'd in *London*. D'ye hear, sir, leaving your Frivelous
Circumstances,* pray tell him, His Father's just now
come out of the Countrey to see him, and is here at the
Door to speak with him.                                         50

SNATCHPENNY: That is a Lye, Sir; his Father came to
Town yesterday, and is now here Looking out at
Window.

SIR LYONELL: The Devil he is. Are you his Father?

SNATCHPENNY: I, sir; so his Mother says, if I may believe
her.[54]

SAUNY: Can they Hang him for having twa Fathers Sir?
Gud, and 'twas sea, poor *Sawndy* wou'd be Hang'd sure
enough.

PETRUCHIO: Why, Hast thou two Fathers?                          60

SAUNY: Gud, have I, and Twa, and Twa to that, Sir.

PETRUCHIO: Why, how now, Gentlemen; this is flat Knav-
ery, to take another Man's Name upon you.

SNATCHPENNY: Lay hands upon this Villain; I believe he
means to Cheat some body here under my Counter-
Name.*

*Enter* JAMY

JAMY: I have seen the Church on their Back;* send them
Good Speeding. Ha, how now, my Old Master, Sir
*Lyonell*? S'foot, we are all lost, undone. I must Brazen it
out.                                                           70

SIR LYONELL: Come hither, Crack Hemp.*[55]

JAMY: You may save me that Labour, and come to me, if
you have any thing to say to me.

SIR LYONELL: Come hither, you Rogue. What, have you
forgot me?

JAMY: Forgot you, Sir? I cou'd not forget you, for I never
saw you in all my Life before.

---

[54] 33–47. Based on *Shrew*, V.i.14–30: 'What's he that knocks . . . I may believe her.'
[55] 59: V.i.40: 'Come hither, crackhemp.'

SIR LYONELL: You notorious Villain, Didst thou never see thy Master's Father, Sir *Lyonell Winlove?*

JAMY: What, my Worshipfull old Master? Yes, marry, Sir; 80 See where his Worship Looks out of the Window.

SIR LYONELL: Does he so, Sir? I'll make you find him below stayres.*                              (*Beats him*)

JAMY: Help, help, here's a Mad-man will Murder me.[56]

SAUNY: Dea Caw your sel *Jamy*, And wull ye be Beten by an aw faw Theefe? An yea Caw your sel *Jamy* eance meare, I'se bang ye tea Clootes;* breed a Gud, will I, Sir.

SNATCHPENNY: Help, Son, help, Brother *Beaufoy. Jamy* will be kill'd.

PETRUCHIO: Prethee, *Peg*, stand by to see this Contro- 90 versy.

*Enter* SNATCHPENNY *with Servants,*
BEAUFOY *and* TRANIO

TRANIO: 'Sheart, 'tis Sir *Lyonell*; but we must bear it a little time. Sir, What are you that offer to Beat my Servant?

SIR LYONELL: What am *I*, Sir? Nay, What are you, Sir? O Heaven, what do *I* see? O fine Villains, I'me undone; while *I* play the Good Husband* at home in the Countrey, my Son and my Servant spend my Estate lavishly at *London*.

SAUNY: Your son sal allow you Siller to keep an Awd Wutch to rub your Shins; And what to anger* wou'd ye 100 ha meer, Sir?

TRANIO: How now, What's the Matter?

BEAUFOY: Is the Man Frantick?

TRANIO: Sir, You seem a sober Antient Gentleman by your Habit, but your Words shew you a Madman. Why, Sir, What concerns it you what Rich Cloaths *I* wear? *I* thank my good Father *I* am able to maintain it.[57]

SIR LYONELL: Thy Father! O Villain! He's a Hemp-dresser* in *Partha.*

SAUNY: Mara, the Deel stuff his Wem fow* a Hemp, and 110 his Dam Spin it out at his Arse.

---

[56] 70: V.i.51: 'Help . . . murder me.'
[57] 87–8: V.i.56–7: 'What are you . . . what are you, sir?'

BEAUFOY: You mistake, you mistake. What d'ye think his
 Name is?

SIR LYONELL: His Name? As if I knew not his Name; *I*
 have Bred him up e're since he was Three Years old, and
 his Name is *Tranio*.

SNATCHPENNY: Away, away, mad Ass, his Name is *Win-love*, my only Son, and Heir to all my Estate in the Vale of
 *Evesham*.

SIR LYONELL: Heavens! He has murther'd his Master; lay 120
 hold on him, I charge you in the King's Name. O my Son,
 tell me, thou Villain, Where is my Son *Winlove*?

TRANIO: Run for an Officer to carry this mad Knave to the
 Jayle.[58] Lay hold on him, I charge ye, and see him forth-
 coming.*

SAUNY: Awa, awa with the Hampdresser, Sir.

SIR LYONELL: Carry me to the Jayle, ye Villaines!

PETRUCHIO: Hold, Gentlemen. Your Blessing, Father.

BEAUFOY: Son *Petruchio*, Welcome. You have it; and you,
 *Peg*, how d'ye? Know ye any thing of this matter?          130

PETRUCHIO: My Lord, take heed what you do. So much I
 know, I dare Swear this is Sir *Lyonell Winlove*, and that a
 Counterfeit.

SAUNY: Wuns, I think sea tea. Gud'an ye please, I'se take
 the *Covenant** on't.

WOODALL: So durst I Swear too, almost.

SNATCHPENNY: Swear if thou durst.

WOODALL: Sir, I dare not Swear Point Blank.

TRANIO: You had best Swear I am not *Winlove* neither.

WOODALL: Yes, I know you to be Mr. *Winlove*.          140

BEAUFOY: Away with the Doater'd, to the Jayle with
 him.[59]

SIR LYONELL: Are you all setled to do mischief to me?
 Why, my Lord *Beaufoy*, methinks you might know me.

TRANIO: Away with him to my Lodgings for the present,
 'till we can get a Constable to charge him upon. We shall
 have a hubbub in the Streets. Drag him, *I* say.

[58] 86–100. Based on *Shrew*, V.i.57–83: 'Sir, you seem ... call forth an officer.'
[59] 116: V.i.97: 'Away ... the jail with him.'

SIR LYONELL: Rogues, Villains, Murders! I shall have
   Justice.                    [*Exit with* SIR LYONELL]

WOODALL:  These are strange Passages, I know not what to 150
   think, of 'em; but I am glad *Biancha* came not when they
   were here. Sure my Mounsier will not fail me.

          *Enter* WINLOVE *and* BIANCHA

WINLOVE: Now, my *Biancha*, I am truly Happy; our Loves
   shall like the Spring be ever growing.

BIANCHA: But how shall we Escape my Fathers Anger?

WINLOVE: Fear not, I'll warrant thee.

WOODALL:  O here's *Biancha*. How now, Mounsier, brave?
   What fancy's this?

WINLOVE: O, Mounsieur, te Vous la Menes.* How d'ye
   do, good Mr. *Woodall*? How d'ye like my new Bride?  160

WOODALL: How, how, how, Sir, your Bride? Seize on her
   quickly.

WINLOVE: Hands off. She's my Wife, touch her who dares.
   Will you have your Teeth pickt? What d'ye think of
   giving 20 Peeces to teach your Mistriss *French*.

WOODALL: O Rogue, I'll have thee hang'd.

WINLOVE: Or 40 Peeces to buy a Pair of Gloves to let you
   Steal Madam *Biancha*. This Ring was bought with some
   of it, ha, ha, ha.

WOODALL: Down with him, down with him, a damn'd 170
   Rascal.

WINLOVE: I, do. Which of you has a mind to breath a
   Vein?*

2ND FELLOW: Nay, if she be his Wife we dare not touch
   her.

WOODALL: I'll fetch some body that shall. O, Devil.

                              [*Exit*]

WINLOVE: Ay, do. I am your poor Mounsieur, ha, ha ha.
   Fear not, *Biancha*; he'll fetch 'em all, I know. I warrant
   thee we shall appease thy Father Easily.

BIANCHA: Trust me, Sir, I fear the Storm.            180

*Enter* BEAUFOY, TRANIO, PETRUCHIO, MARGARET,
   SAUNY, SNATCHPENNY, JAMY, SIR LYONELL,
          WOODALL, *and Attendants*

WOODALL: That Rogue, that Damn'd Counterfit Frenchman has stolne your Daughter and Marryed her. Here
they are.

WINLOVE: Bless me. What do I see yonder? My Father, in
earnest? Dear Sir, your Blessing, and your Pardon.

SIR LYONELL: My Dear Son, Art thou alive? Then take it.

BIANCHA: I must beg your Pardon too, Sir.

WINLOVE: And I, most Honoured Father.

BEAUFOY: Why, what's the Matter? What hast thou done?
*Woodall* tells me thou hast Married the *Frenchman*.          190

WINLOVE: Me she has Married, but no Frenchman. The
right *Winlove*, Son to the right *Winlove*, is her Husband
and your Son in-Law.

SAUNY: S'breed, Sir, ye act twa parts, ye were but a *Hampdresser* in the last Act, Sir.

SNATCHPENNY: 'Tis time for us to be going; I feel one Ear
going off already.                                        [*Exit*]

BEAUFOY: You amaze me. Are not you the *Frenchman* Mr.
*Woodall* prefer'd to teach my Daughter?

BIANCHA: No, my Lord, he put on that Disguise to Court  200
me. He is the true *Winlove*.

SIR LYONELL: Marry is he my Son, Sir.

WINLOVE: Those were but Counterfits of my making.

WOODALL: Here's Patching with a Mistriss.* I'm sure I am
Gull'd.

BEAUFOY: But d'ye hear, Sir? Have you Married my
Daughter without my Consent?

SIR LYONELL: Come, my Lord, now you must know me. I
will beg both their Pardons, and Secure her a Jointure
worthy her Birth and Fortune.                             210

WINLOVE: You are a Father now Indeed.

BEAUFOY: Sir *Lyonell*, excuse my rashness; I accept your
noble Proffer. You are forgiven.

SAUNY: S'breed, Sir, we sal nere go to Dunner, Sir. The
Deel forgat and forgive* you aw, Sir.

SIR LYONELL: But where is that Rogue that would have
sent me to Jayle? I'll slit his Nose for him.

WINLOVE: I must beg his Pardon, for he did all for my Sake.

SIR LYONELL: Well, Sir, for your Sake I Pardon him. 220

BEAUFOY: Come, Gentlemen, all to my house; we shall there end all our Doubts, and drownd our fears.

WOODALL: Sir, I shall expect my Money back again; 'tis enough to loose my Mistriss.

WINLOVE: No, Faith, 'tis in better hands already. You'll but fool it away, you'll be hireing *Frenchmen* agen.

WOODALL: Well, mock on. I'll in and eat out part of it.

BEAUFOY: Come, Gentlemen.

MARGARET: Husband, will you not go with my Father?

PETRUCHIO: First kiss me, *Peg*, and I will.[60] 230

MARGARET: What, in the middle of the Street.

PETRUCHIO: What, art thou Asham'd of me?

MARGARET: Not so, Sir, but asham'd to kiss so openly.

PETRUCHIO: Why, then, let's home again. *Sauny*, lead the way.

SAUNY: Gud, the Deel a bit will *Saundy* Budge before Dunner, Sir.

MARGARET: Nay, I will give thee a kiss; nay, pray now, stay.

PETRUCHIO: So, is not this well? Come, my sweet *Peg*. 240

BIANCHA: Sister, I hope we shall be friends now.

MARGARET: I was never Foes with you.

WINLOVE: Come, fairest; all the Storms are overblown. Love hath both Wit and Fortune of her own.

[*Exeunt*]

[60] 190-7. Based on *Shrew*, V.i.131-7: 'First kiss me ... my sweet Kate, and we will.'

# ACT V

## Scene i

*Enter* MARGARET *and* BIANCHA

BIANCHA: But is't Possible, Sister, he shu'd have us'd you thus?

MARGARET: Had I serv'd him as bad as *Eve* did *Adam,* he coud not have us'd me worse. But I am resolv'd now I'm got home again I'll be reveng'd. I'll muster up the Spight of all the Curs'd Women since *Noahs* flood to do him Mischeif, and add new Vigour to my Tongue. I have not par'd my Nails this fortnight; they are long enough to do him some Execution, that's my Comfort.

BIANCHA: Bless me, Sister, how you talk.                                 10

MARGARET: Thou art a Fool, *Biancha.* Come, Learn of me. Thou art Married to a Man too; thou dost not know but thou mayst need my Councel, and make good use on't. Thy Husband bares thee fair yet, but take heed of going home with him, for when once he has thee within his verge,* 'tis odds he'll have his freaks* too; there's no trusting these Men. Thy temper is soft and easy; thou must Learn to break him, or he'll break thy Heart.

BIANCHA: I must Confess I shou'd be Loath to be so us'd, but sure Mr. *Winlove* is of a better Disposition.        20

MARGARET: Trust him and hang him;* they'r all alike. Come, thou shalt be my Schollar. Learn to Frown and cry out for unkindness, but brave Anger. Thou hast a tongue; make use on't. Scould, Fight, Scratch, Bite, any thing. Still take Exceptions at all he does, if there be Cause or not; if there be reason for't, he'll Laugh at thee. I'll make *Petruchio* glad to wipe my Shoes, or walk my Horse, ere I have done with him.

*Enter* PETRUCHIO, WINLOVE, SAUNY

BIANCHA: Peace, Sister, our Husbands are both here.

MARGARET: Thou Child, I am glad on't; I'll speak louder. 30

PETRUCHIO: Well, Brother *Winlove*, now we are truly happy; never were Men so blest with two such Wives.

WINLOVE: I am glad to hear you say so, Sir; my own I'm sure I'm blest in.

PETRUCHIO: Yours? Why, *Biancha*'s a Lyon, and *Margaret* a meer Lamb to her. I tell thee, *Winlove*, there's no Man living, tho I say't (but 'tis no matter since she does not hear me), that has a Wife so gentle, and so active* and affable; poor thing, I durst be sworn she wou'd walk barefoot a hundred Miles to do me good. 40

MARGARET: No, but she wou'd not, nor one Mile neither.

SAUNY: Now have at your Luggs, Sir.

PETRUCHIO: O, *Peg*, art thou there? How dost thou do, my Dear?

MARGARET: You may go look; What's that to you?

SAUNY: Stand o' yer guard, Sir. Gud, *Saundy* will put on his head Peice.

PETRUCHIO: I am glad to hear thee say thou'rt well, introth.

MARGARET: Never the better for you, which you shall find. 50

PETRUCHIO: Nay, I know thou lov'st me. Prithee, take up my Glove, *Peg*.

MARGARET: I take up your Glove. Marry, come up, command your Servants. Look you, there it lyes.

PETRUCHIO: I am glad to see thee merry, poor wanton Rogue.

MARGARET: 'Tis very well. You think you are in the Country but you are mistaken; the case is alter'd,* I am at home now, and my own disposer. Go, swagger at your greazy Lubber there, your Patient Wife will make you no 60 more Sport; she has a Father will allow her Meat and Lodging, and another gaits* Chamber-Maid then a *Highlander*.

SAUNY: Gud, an ye were a top of *Grantham Steple** that aw the Toon may hear what a Scauden Queen* ye are. Out, out.

PETRUCHIO: Why, what's the matter *Peg*? I never saw thee in so jolly a Humour. Sure thou hast been Drinking.

SAUNY: Gud, has she. Haud ye tang, ye faw dranken Swine. Out, out, out. Was ye tak a Drink and nere tak *Saundy* to yee? Out, out, out.                        70

MARGARET: 'Tis like I have, I am the fitter to talk to you, for no sober Woman is a Companion for you.

PETRUCHIO: Troth, thou sayst right; we are excellently Matcht.

MARGARET: Well, mark the end on't. *Petruchio*, prithee come hither, I have something to say to you.

SAUNY: De ye nea budge a foot Sir. Deel a my saul, bo she'll Scratch your eyn out.

PETRUCHIO: Well, your Pleasure, Madam.                   80

MARGARET: First, thou art a Pittiful fellow, a thing beneath me, which I scorn and Laugh at, ha, ha, ha.

WINLOVE: She holds her own yet, I see.

MARGARET: I know not what to call thee. Thou art no Man; thou coudst not have a Woman to thy Mother, thou paltry, Scurvy, ill condition'd fellow. Dost thou not tremble to think how thou hast us'd me? What, are you silent, Sir? *Biancha*, see; Looks he not like a Disbanded Officer, with that hanging dog look there? I must eat nothing because your Cook has Roasted the Mutton dry,   90 as you us'd to have it when your Worship was a Batchellor. I must not go to Bed neither, because the Sheets are Damp.

PETRUCHIO: Mark you, *Peg*; What a strange Woman are you to Discourse openly the Fault of your Servants in your own Family.

MARGARET: No, no, Sir, this wont serve your turn; your Old Stock of Impudence won't carry you off so. I'll speak your Fame, and tell what a fine Gentleman you are, how valliantly you and halfe a Douzen of your Men got the  100 better of a Single Woman, and made her lose her Supper.

SAUNY: Gud, she Lyes, Sir; I wou'd a gin her an awd Boot tull a made Tripes on, and it wod a bin bra* Meat with *Mustard*, and she wou'd nea have it.

MARGARET: My Faults? No, good Squire of the country, you thought to have Tam'd me, I warrant, in good time. Why, you see I am even with you: Your Quiet Patient Wife, that will go no more in the Country with you, but will stay in Town, to Laugh at your Wise Worship, and wish you more Wit.                                                           110

PETRUCHIO: I shou'd Laugh at that; why, we are just now a going. *Sauny*, go get the Horses ready quickly.

SAUNY: Gud, will I, Sir; I'se Saddle a Highland-Wutch to Carry your Bride. Gud, she'll mount your Arse for you, Madam.

MARGARET: Sirrah, touch a Horse, and I'll Curry* your Coxcomb for you. No, Sir, I won't say, 'Pray let me not go'; but boldly, I won't go. You force me if you can or dare. You see I am not tongue-ty'd, as silent as you thought you made me.                                               120

PETRUCHIO: Prithee, *Peg*, Peace a little, I know thou canst Speak; leave now, or thoul't have nothing to say to morrow.

MARGARET: Yes, I'll say this over again, and something more if I can think on't, to a poor despised *man of Clouts.** Sister, how he smoakes* now he's off his own Dunghill.*

PETRUCHIO: Prithee, *Peg*, leave making a Noise; I'faith thou'lt make my Head ach.

MARGARET: Noise? Why, this is Silence to what I intend; 130 I'll talk Louder than this every Night in my Sleep.

SAUNY: The Dee'l shall be your Bed fellow for *Sawndy* then.

MARGARET: I will learn to Rail at thee in all Languages; Thunder shall be soft-musick to my Tongue.

SAUNY: The Dee'l a bit Scot's ye gat to brangle* in. Marry, the Dee'l gi ye a Clap wi a *French* Thunder-bolt.

PETRUCHIO: Very pretty; Prithee go on.

MARGARET: I'll have a Collection of all the Ill Names that ever was Invented, and call you over by 'em twice a-day. 140

PETRUCHIO: And have the Catalogue publish'd for the Education of young Scolds. Proceed, *Peg*.

MARGARET: I'll have you Chain'd to a Stake at *Billings-gate*, and Baited by the Fish-wives, while I stand to Hiss 'em on.

PETRUCHIO: Ha, ha, ha. Witty *Peg*, forward.

MARGARET: You shan't dare to Blow your Nose but when I bid you; you shall know me to be the Master.

SAUNY: Wuns, gat her to the Stool of Repantance,* Sir.

PETRUCHIO: Nay, I believe, thou wilt go in Breeches 150 shortly. On, on. What, have you no more on't? Ha, ha, ha.

MARGARET: D'ye Laugh and be Hang'd?* I'll spoil your Sport.                                    (*Flys at him*)

PETRUCHIO: Nay, *Peg*, Hands off; I thought you wou'd not have Disgrac'd your Good Parts to come to Blows so soon. Prithee Chide on; thou can'st not believe what Delight I take to hear thee, It does become thee so well. What, Pumpt dry already? Prithee, talk more and longer, and faster, and sharper; this is nothing.          160

MARGARET: I'll see you in the *Indies* before I'll do any thing to please you. D'ye like it?

PETRUCHIO: Extreamly! On, *Peg*, you'll cooll too fast.

MARGARET: Why, then, Mark me; if it were to save thee from Drowning, or Breaking thy Neck, I won't speak one word more to thee these Two Months.    (*Sits Sullenly*)

SAUNY: Ah, Gud, an ye do nea Ly, Madam.

PETRUCHIO: Nay, Good *Peg*, be not so hard-harted. What, Melancholly all o'th' sudden? Come, get up, we'll send for the Fidlers, and have a Dance; Tho'lt break thy Elbow 170 with Leaning on that hard Table. *Sawny*, go get your Mistriss a Cushion. Alas! I doubt she's not well. Look to her, Sister.

BIANCHA: Are you not well, Sister? What, ail you? Pray speak, Sister. Indeed, Brother, you have so Vext her, she'll be Sick.

PETRUCHIO: Alas, alas! I know what's the matter with her, she has the Tooth Ach. See how she holds her Cheek; the Wind has gotten into her Teeth, by keeping her Mouth open this Cold Weather.          180

BIANCHA: Indeed it may be so, Brother; she used to be troubled with that Pain sometimes.

PETRUCHIO: Without all Question. Poor *Peg*, I pitty thee. Which Tooth is it? Wilt thou have it Drawn, *Peg*? The Tooth-Ach makes Fooles of all the *Physitians*; there is no Cure, but Drawing. What say'st thou? Wilt thou have it pull'd out? Well, thou shalt. *Sauny*, Run, Sirrah, hard by: you know where my Barber Lives that Drew me a Tooth last Week; fetch him quickly. What d'ye stand staring at? Run and fetch him immediately, or I'll cut your Legs off. 190

SAUNY: Gud, I'se fetch ean to pull her head off an ye wull.
[*Exit*]

WINLOVE: This will make her find her Tongue agen, or else for certain she has lost it.

PETRUCHIO: Her Tongue, Brother? Alas! You see her Face is so Swell'd, she cannot speak.

BIANCHA: You Jest, Brother; her Face is not swell'd. Pray let me see, Sister; I can't perceive it.

PETRUCHIO: Not Swell'd? Why, you are blind then. Prithee let her alone; you trouble her.

*Enter* SAUNY *and* BARBER

Here, Honest Barber, have you brought your Instru- 200 ments?

BARBER: Yes, Sir; What must I do?

PETRUCHIO: You must Draw that Gentlewoman a Tooth there. Prithee do it neatly, and as gently as thou can'st; And, de hear me, take care you don't tear her Gums.

BARBER: I warrant you, Sir.

SAUNY: Hear ye, Sir, Cou'd not ye Mistake and pull her Tang out instead of her Teeth?

BIANCHA: I'll be gone; I can't endure to see her put to so much Pain. [*Exit*] 210

BARBER: Pray, Madam, open your Mouth, that I may see which Tooth it is. (*She Strikes him*) Why, Sir, Did you send for me to Abuse me?

SAUNY: Gud, be nea Angry; Ye ha ne aw yer Pay yet, Sir. Cud ye not Mistake, and Draw her Tang instead of her Teeth, Sir.

PETRUCHIO: No, no. But it seems now she wo not have it
Drawn. Go; there's something for your Paines however.
[*Exit* BARBER]

SAUNY: Ye sid ha taken my Counsel, Sir.

WINLOVE: This will not do, Sir. You cannot raise the Spirit 220
you have laid, with all your Arts.

PETRUCHIO: I'll try. Have at her once more. *Winlove*, you
must assist me; I'll make her Stir, if I can't make her
Speak. Look, look! alas! How Pale she is! She's gone o'th'
sudden. Body O' me, she's stiff too. Undone, undone.
What an unfortunate Man am I? She's gone! She's gone!
Never had man so great a Loss as I. O, *Winlove*, pity me,
my poor *Peg* is Dead. Dear *Winlove*, call in my Father
and the Company that they may share in this sad
Spectacle, and help my Sorrows with their joyning Griefs. 230
[*Exit* WINLOVE]

(*Aside*) Speak, or by this hand I'll bury thee alive. *Sauny*,
thou seest in how sad a condition thy poor Master is in;
thy good Mistriss is Dead. Hast to the next Church and
get the Bier and the Bearers hither; I'll have her buried out
of hand. Run, *Sauny*.

SAUNY: An you'll mack her Dead, we'll bury her deep
enough; we'll put her doon intill a Scotch Coalepit,* and
she shall rise at the Deel's arse o' Peake.*

PETRUCHIO: I will see that last Pious act Perform'd, and
then betake my self to a willing Exile; my own Country's 240
Hell, now my dear *Peg* has left it. (*Aside*) Not yet? Upon
my Life I think thou hast a mind to be buried quick; I
hope thou hast.

*Enter* WINLOVE, BEAUFOY, SIR LYONELL, WOODALL,
BIANCHA, TRANIO, JAMY, &c.

BEAUFOY: Bless me, Son *Petruchio*, Is my dear Daughter
Dead?

PETRUCHIO: Alas, alas, 'tis but too true, wou'd I had ta'ne
her roome.

BEAUFOY: Why, methinks she looks brisk, fresh and lively.

PETRUCHIO: So much Beauty as she had must needs leave
some wandring remains to hover still about her face.    250

BEAUFOY: What could her Disease be?

PETRUCHIO: Indeed, I grieve to tell it, but truth must out: she Dyed for spight; she was strangely Infected.

BIANCHA: Fye, Sister, for shame, speak. Will you let him abuse you thus?

PETRUCHIO: Gentleman, you are my loving Friends and knew the Virtues of my matchless Wife; I hope you will accompany her Body to its long home.*

ALL: We'll all wait on you.

BEAUFOY: Thou wilt break her heart indeed. 260

PETRUCHIO: I warrant you, Sir, 'tis tougher then so.

*Enter* SAUNY *and* Bearers *with a* Beir

SAUNY: I bring you here vera gued Men; an she be nea Dead, Sir, for a Croon more they'll bury her quick.

PETRUCHIO: O, honest friends, you'r Wellcome; you must take up that Corps. How! Hard-hearted? Why de ye not weep, the loss of so much Beauty and goodness? Take her up, and lay her upon the Beir.

1ST BEARER: Why, what d'ye mean Sir? She is not Dead.

PETRUCHIO: Rogues, tell me such a Lye to my face? Take 270 her up or I'll swinge ye.

SAUNY: Tak her up, tak her up. We'll mak her Dead, Billy; ye'st a twa Croons mear. Tak her up Man.

1ST BEARER: Dead or alive, all's one to us, let us but have our fees.

PETRUCHIO: There. Nay, she is stiff. However, on with her. (*Aside*) Will you not speak yet? So, here, take these Strings and bind her on the Beir; she had an active stirring body when she Liv'd, she may chance fall off the Hearse now she's Dead. So, now take her up and away. Come, 280 Gentlemen, you'll follow. I mean to carry her through the *Strand* as far as St. *James*'s. People shall see what respect I bore her— She shall have so much Ceremony to attend her now she's Dead. There my Coach shall meet her and carry her into the Country. I'll have her laid in the Vault belonging to my Family; she shall have a Monument. Some of you inquire me out a good Poet to write her Epitaph suitable to her Birth, Quallity and Conditions.

Pitty the remembrance of so many Virtues shou'd be lost. March on; I wou'd say more, but grief Checks my 290 Tongue.

MARGARET: Father, Sister, Husband, Are you all Mad? Will you expose me to open shame? Rogues, set me down, you had best.

PETRUCHIO: A Miracle! a Miracle! She Lives! Heaven make me thankful for't. Set her down. Liv'st thou, my Poor *Peg*?

MARGARET: Yes, that I do, and will to be your Tormentor.

SAUNY: Out, out, gea her nea Credit. Gud, she's as Dead as mine Grannam. Tak her, away with her, Sir. 300

PETRUCHIO: Bless me, my hopes are all vanisht agen; 'tis a Demon speaks within her Body. Take her up again; we'll bury 'em together.

MARGARET: Hold, hold. My dear *Petruchio*, you have overcome me, and I beg your Pardon; henceforth I will not dare to think a thought shall Cross your Pleasure; set me at Liberty, and on my knees I'll make my Recantation.

ALL: Victoria, victoria, the field is won.

PETRUCHIO: Art thou in earnest, *Peg*? May I believe thee?

SAUNY: You ken very well she was awway's a lying Quean 310 when she was Living, and wull ye believe her now she's Dead?

MARGARET: By all that's good, not truth it self truer.

PETRUCHIO: Then thus I free thee, and make thee Mistriss both of my self and all I have.

SAUNY: S'breed, bo ye'l nea gi *Saundy* tull her, Sir?

WOODALL: Take heed of giving away your Power, Sir.

PETRUCHIO: I'll venture it, nor do I fear I shall repent my bargain.

MARGARET: I'm sure *I* will not give you Cause, y've taught 320 me now what 'tis to be a Wife, and I'll still shew my self your humble Handmaid.

PETRUCHIO: My best *Peg*, we will change* kindness and be each others Servant. Gentlemen, why do you not Rejoyce with me?

BEAUFOY: *I* am so full of joy *I* cannot Speak. May you be happy, this is your Wedding day.

SAUNY: Shall *Saundy* get her a Bride-Cake, and Brake o'r her Head, Sir, and wee's gatt us a good Wadding Dunner?

*Enter* GERALDO

GERALDO: Save ye all, Gentlemen; Have ye any Room for more Guests? I am come to make up the *Chorus*. 330

PETRUCHIO: My Noble Friend, Wellcome. Where have you been so long?

GERALDO: *I* have been about a little trivial Business; I am just now come from a Wedding.

PETRUCHIO: What Wedding, I pray, Sir?

GERALDO: Troth, e'en my own; *I* have ventur'd upon't at last. Madam, I hope you'l pardon me.

BIANCHA: Yes, Sir; and so will this Gentleman.

SAUNY: Are not you a Gentleman-Hampdresser? 340

PETRUCHIO: 'Tis e'en so; this proves to be *Winlove* in earnest.

GERALDO: Good Gentlemen, undo this riddle; I'm all in the Dark.

PETRUCHIO: You shall know anon; in the mean time Believe it, Gentlemen. We want another Woman, or we might have a Dance.

GERALDO: My Widdow is within; she'll supply you.

BEAUFOY: Good *Peg*, go and wait on her, and you *Biancha* too. [*Exit* PEG, BIANCHA] 350

PETRUCHIO: I tell thee, *Geraldo*, never had Man so Obedient and Loving a Wife as I have now; *I* defy the World to equal her.

WINLOVE: Nay, Brother, you must except her Sister.

GERALDO: You must except mine too, or I shall have a hard Bargain of it; my *Widdow* is all Obedience.

PETRUCHIO: I'll tell you what I'll do with you, I'll hold you Ten Pieces, to be spent in a Collation on them, That mine has more Obedience than both them; to try which, each send for his Wife, and if mine come not first I'll lose my 360 Bett.

GERALDO: Gud, yeel lose your Siller sure enough, Sir.

BOTH: A Match.

WOODALL: I'll be your halves,* *Geraldo*, and yours, Mr.
    *Winlove*, too.

WINLOVE: *Jamy*, Go tell your *Mistress*, I desire her to come
    hither to me presently.                  [*Exit* JAMY]

PETRUCHIO: A Piece more she does not come.

BEAUFOY: You'll lose, Son, you'l lose; I know she'll come.

PETRUCHIO: I know she won't; I find by Instinct I shall 370
    Win my Wager.

*Enter* JAMY

JAMY: Sir, she says she's busie, and she can't leave Mr.
    *Geraldo's* Lady.

PETRUCHIO: Look ye there now. Come, your Money.

GERALDO: Prithee go again and tell my wife I must needs
    speak with her immediately.         [*Exit* JAMY]

PETRUCHIO: I shall win yours too, as sure as in my Pocket.

GERALDO: I warrant you no such matter. What will you
    give to be off your Bett?

PETRUCHIO: I won't take forty Shillings.              380

*Enter* JAMY

How now?

JAMY: Sir, she says you have no Business with her; if you
    have you may come to her.

PETRUCHIO: Come, produce, I knew 'twould be so. *Sauny*,
    go and tell *Peg* from me, I command her to come to me
    instantly.

SAUNY: I'se gar her gea wuth me, Sir, or I'se put my
    Durke* to the hilt in her Weam.

WOODALL: Yet you wont win; I'll hang for't if she'll come.

PETRUCHIO: Yes, but she will; as sure as you gave forty 390
    peices to Court *Biancha*, I'll venture them to twenty more
    upon't with you.

WOODALL: Nay, I have lost enough already.

*Enter* PEG *and* SAUNY

PETRUCHIO: Look ye here, Gentlemen.

SAUNY: O my Saul, she's ean a daft* gued Lass; she's at
    your Beck, steake* her and kiss her Man.

MARGARET: I come to receive your Commands, Sir.

PETRUCHIO: All I have to say to thee, *Peg*, is to bid thee
  demand ten pound of these two Gentlemen; thou hast
  Won it.                                                          400

MARGARET: *I*, Sir, for what?

PETRUCHIO: Only for being so good natur'd to come when
  *I* send for you.

MARGARET: *It* was my duty, Sir.

PETRUCHIO: Come, pay, pay, give it her; *I*'ll not bate ye
  two pence.

GERALDO: There's mine.

WINLOVE: And mine, Sister, much good may it do ye.

BEAUFOY: Well, *Peg*, *I*'ll find thee one Thousand Pound the
  more for this.                                                  410

SAUNY: Bo what wull ye gi *Saundy* that halpt to make her
  gued and tame? Wuns, she was as Wild as a Galloway
  Coalt.

*Enter* BIANCHA *and* WIDDOW

WINLOVE: Look, here they come at last.

BIANCHA: What did you send for me for?

WINLOVE: Why, to win me five Pound, if you had been as
  obedient as you should a been.

BIANCHA: You have not known me long enough to venture
  so much upon my Duty; *I* have been my Sisters Schollar a
  little.                                                         420

SAUNY: Bo put her to *Saundy* to teach, Gud, *I*'se mak her
  sea gentle ye may streake* her and handle her all o're, Sir.

GERALDO: You might have got me five Pound if you had
  done as you should do.

WIDDOW: Were it to do again, you should be sure to loose.

MARGARET: Fy, Ladys, for shame. How dare you infringe
  that Duty which you justly owe your Husbands; they are
  our Lords and we must pay 'em Service.

BEAUFOY: Well said, *Peg*; you must be their Tutor. Come,
  Son, if you'll have a Dance, dispatch it quickly, the  430
  Musick's ready, and the Meat will be spoil'd.

PETRUCHIO: Come, then, play, play.

(DANCE)

Now let us in, and Eate, the Work is done,
Which neither Time nor Age can wear from Memory;
I've *Tam'd the Shrew*, but will not be asham'd,
If next you see the very *Tamer Tam'd*.*

FINIS

# THE TEMPEST

---

## BY JOHN DRYDEN
## AND
## WILLIAM DAVENANT

# THE
# TEMPEST,
## OR THE
# Enchanted Island.
## A
# COMEDY.

As it is now Acted at his Highness the Duke of *York's*
THEATRE.

---

*LONDON,*

Printed by *J. M.* for *Henry Herringman* at the *Blew*
*Anchor* in the *Lower-walk* of the *New-Exchange.*
MDCLXX.

# PREFACE
## TO THE
## *ENCHANTED ISLAND*

*The writing of Prefaces to Plays was probably invented by some very ambitious Poet, who never thought he had done enough: Perhaps by some Ape of the* French *Eloquence, who uses to make a business of a Letter of gallantry, an examen of a Farce; and in short, a great pomp and ostentation of words on every trifle. This is certainly the talent of that Nation, and ought not to be invaded by any other. They do that out of gayety which would be an imposition upon us.*

*We may satisfie our selves with surmounting them in the Scene, and safely leave them those trappings of writing, and flourishes of the Pen, with which they adorn the borders of their Plays, and which are indeed no more than good Landskips to a very indifferent Picture. I must proceed no farther in this argument, lest I run my self beyond my excuse for writing this. Give me leave therefore to tell you, Reader, that I do it not to set a value on any thing I have written in this Play, but out of gratitude to the memory of Sir* William D'avenant, *who did me the honour to joyn me with him in the alteration of it.\**

*It was originally* Shakespear's: *a Poet for whom he had particularly a high veneration, and whom he first taught me to admire. The Play it self had formerly been acted with success in the* Black-Fryers: *and our excellent* Fletcher *had so great a value for it, that he thought fit to make use of the same Design, not much varied, a second time. Those who have seen his Sea-Voyage, may easily discern that it was a Copy of* Shakespear's *Tempest:\* the Storm, the desart Island, and the Woman who had never seen a Man, are all sufficient testimonies of it. But* Fletcher *was not the only Poet who made use of* Shakespear's *Plot: Sir* John Suckling, *a profess'd admirer of our Author, has follow'd his* *footsteps in his* Goblins; *his* Regmella *being an open imitation of* Shakespear's Miranda; *and his Spirits, though counterfeit, yet are copied from* Ariel.* *But Sir* William D'avenant, *as he was a man of quick and piercing imagination, soon found that somewhat might be added to the Design of* Shakespear, *of which neither* Fletcher *nor* Suckling *had ever thought: and therefore to put the last hand to it, he design'd the Counterpart to* Shakespear's *Plot, namely that of a Man who had never seen a Woman,* *that by this means those two Characters of Innocence and Love might the more illustrate and commend each other. This excellent contrivance he was pleas'd to communicate to me, and to desire my assistance in it. I confess that from the very first moment it so pleas'd me, that I never writ any thing with more delight. I must likewise do him that justice to acknowledge, that my writing received daily his amendments, and that is the reason why it is not so faulty, as the rest which I have done without the help or correction of so judicious a friend. The Comical parts of the Saylors were also his invention, and for the most part his writing, as you will easily discover by the style. In the time I writ with him I had the opportunity to observe somewhat more neerly of him than I had formerly done, when I had only a bare acquaintance with him: I found him then of so quick a fancy, that nothing was propos'd to him, on which he could not suddenly produce a thought extreamly pleasant and surprizing: and those first thoughts of his, contrary to the old* Latine *Proverb,* *were not alwaies the least happy. And as his fancy was quick, so likewise were the products of it remote and new. He borrowed not of any other; and his imaginations were such as could not easily enter into any other man. His corrections were sober and judicious: and he corrected his own writings much more severely than those of another man, bestowing twice the time and labour in polishing which he us'd in invention. It had perhaps been easie enough for me to have arrogated more to my self than was my due in the writing of this Play, and to have pass'd by his name with silence in the publication of it, with the* *same ingratitude which others have us'd to him, whose Writings he hath not only corrected, as he has done this, but has had a greater inspection over them, and sometimes added whole Scenes together, which may as easily be distinguish'd from the rest, as true Gold from counterfeit by the weight. But besides the unworthiness of the action which deterred me from it (there being nothing so base as to rob the dead of his reputation) I am satisf'd I could never have receiv'd so much honour in being thought the Author of any Poem how excellent soever, as I shall from the joining my imperfections with the merit and name of* Shakespear *and Sir* William D'avenant.

Decemb. 1. 1669.                               JOHN DRYDEN

# Prologue to the *Tempest*, or the *Enchanted Island*

As when a Tree's cut down the secret root
Lives under ground, and thence new Branches shoot;
So, from old Shakespear's honour'd dust, this day
Springs up and buds a new reviving Play:
Shakespear, *who (taught by none)** did first impart
To Fletcher *Wit*, to labouring Johnson *Art*.
He Monarch-like gave those his subjects law,
And is that Nature which they paint and draw.
Fletcher *reach'd that which on his heights did grow*,
Whilst Johnson *crept and gather'd all below*.          10
This did his *Love*, and this his *Mirth* digest:
One imitates him most, the other best.
If they have since out-writ all other men,
'Tis with the drops which fell from Shakespear's Pen.
The Storm which vanish'd on the Neighb'ring shore,
Was taught by Shakespear's Tempest first to roar.
That innocence and beauty which did smile
In Fletcher, grew on this Enchanted Isle.
But Shakespear's Magick could not copy'd be,
Within that Circle none durst walk but he.              20
I must confess 'twas bold, nor would you now,
That liberty to vulgar Wits allow,
Which works by Magick supernatural things:
But Shakespear's pow'r is sacred as a King's.
Those Legends from old Priest-hood were receiv'd,
And he then writ, as people then believ'd.
But, if for Shakespear we your grace implore,
We for our Theatre shall want it more:
Who by our dearth of Youths are forc'd t'employ
One of our Women to present a Boy*                       30
And that's a transformation you will say
Exceeding all the Magick in the Play.
Let none expect in the last Act to find,
Her Sex transform'd from man to Woman-kind.

*What e're she was before the Play began,*
*All you shall see of her is perfect man.*
*Or if your fancy will be farther led,*
*To find her Woman, it must be abed.*

# DRAMATIS PERSONAE

Alonzo Duke of Savoy, and Usurper of the Dukedom of Mantua.

Ferdinand his Son.

Prospero right Duke of Millain.

Antonio his Brother, Usurper of the Dukedom.

Gonzalo a Nobleman of Savoy.

Hippolito, one that never saw Woman, right Heir of the Dukedom of Mantua.

Stephano Master of the Ship.

Mustacho his Mate.

Trincalo Boatswain.

Ventoso a Mariner.

Several Mariners.

A Cabbin-Boy.

Miranda and
Dorinda } (Daughters to Prospero) that never saw man.

Ariel an aiery Spirit, attendant on Prospero.

Several Spirits, Guards to Prospero.

Caliban and
Sycorax his Sister } Two Monsters of the Isle

# ACT I

# Scene i

*Enter* MUSTACHO *and* VENTOSO

VENTOSO: What, a Sea comes in?

MUSTACHO: A hoaming* Sea! we shall have foul weather.

*Enter* TRINCALO

TRINCALO: The Scud* comes against the Wind, 'twill blow
hard.

*Enter* STEPHANO

STEPHANO: Bosen!

TRINCALO: Here, Master what cheer?

STEPHANO: Ill weather! let's off to Sea.

MUSTACHO: Let's have Sea-room enough, and then let it
blow the Devil's head off.

STEPHANO: Boy!

*Enter* CABIN-BOY

BOY: Yaw, yaw, here Master.                                   10

STEPHANO: Give the Pilot a dram of the Bottle.

*[Exeunt* STEPHANO *and* BOY]

*Enter Mariners and pass over the Stage*

TRINCALO: Heigh, my hearts, chearly, chearly, my hearts,
yare,[1] yare.

*Enter* ALONZO, ANTONIO, GONZALO

ALONZO: Good Bosen have a care; where's the Master?
Play the men.

TRINCALO: Pray keep below.

ANTONIO: Where's the Master, Bosen?

TRINCALO: Do you not hear him? you mar our labour:
keep your Cabins, you help the storm.

GONZALO: Nay, good friend be patient.                        20

TRINCALO: I, when the Sea is: hence; what care these

---

[1] 12: I.i.5: 'Heigh ... yare.'

roarers for the name of Duke? to Cabin; silence; trouble us not.

GONZALO: Good friend, remember whom thou hast aboard.

TRINCALO: None that I love more than my self: you are a Counsellour, if you can advise these Elements to silence: use your wisdom: if you cannot, make your self ready in the Cabin for the ill hour. Cheerly good hearts! out of our way, Sirs.

*[Exeunt* TRINCALO *and Mariners]*

GONZALO: I have great comfort from this Fellow; methinks his complexion is perfect Gallows; stand fast, good fate, to his hanging; make the Rope of his destiny our Cable,    30 for our own does little advantage us; if he be not born to be hang'd we shall be drown'd.[2]

*[Exeunt* ALONZO, ANTONIO, *and* GONZALO]
*Enter* TRINCALO *and* STEPHANO

TRINCALO: Up aloft Lads. Come, reef* both Top-sails.

STEPHANO: Let's weigh, Let's weigh, and off to sea.

*[Exit* STEPHANO]
*Enter two Mariners and pass over the Stage*

TRINCALO: Hands down! man your main-Capstorm.

*[Exeunt two Mariners]*
*Enter* MUSTACHO *and* VENTOSO *at the other door*

MUSTACHO: Up aloft! and man your jeere-Capstorm.

VENTOSO: My Lads, my hearts of Gold, get in your Capstorm-Bar. Hoa up, hoa up, *&c.*

*[Exeunt* MUSTACHO *and* VENTOSO]
*Enter* STEPHANO

STEPHANO: Hold on well! hold on well! nip well there; Quarter-master, get's more Nippers.    40

*[Exit* STEPHANO]
*Enter two Mariners and pass over again*

TRINCALO: Turn out, turn out all hands to Capstorm! You dogs, is this a time to sleep?
Heave together Lads.    (TRINCALO *whistles*)
*[Exeunt two Mariners]*

---

[2] 13-32: I.i.9-33: 'Good boatswain . . . is miserable.'

MUSTACHO: (*within*) Our Viall's broke.

VENTOSO: (*within*) 'Tis but our Vial-block has given way. Come heave Lads! We are fix'd again. Heave together Bullyes.

#### Enter STEPHANO

STEPHANO: Cut off the Hamocks! cut off the Hamocks, come my Lads: Come Bullys, chear up! heave lustily. The Anchor's a peek.

TRINCALO: Is the Anchor a peek? 50

STEPHANO: Is a weigh! Is a weigh!

TRINCALO: Up aloft my Lads upon the Fore-Castle! Cat the Anchor, cat him.

ALL: (*within*) Haul Catt, Haul Catt, &c. Haul Catt, haul: haul, Catt, haul. Below.

STEPHANO: Aft, Aft! and loose the Misen!

TRINCALO: Get the Misen-tack aboard. Haul Aft Misen-sheat!

#### Enter MUSTACHO

MUSTACHO: Loose the main Top-sail!

STEPHANO: Furle him again, there's too much Wind.

TRINCALO: Loose Fore-sail! Haul Aft both sheats! trim her 60 right afore the Wind. Aft! Lads, and hale up the Misen here.

MUSTACHO: A Mackrel-Gale, Master.

STEPHANO: Port hard, port! the Wind grows scant, bring the Tack aboard Port is. Star-board, star-board, a little steady; now steady, keep her thus, no neerer you cannot come.

#### Enter VENTOSO

VENTOSO: Some hands down: the Guns are loose.

[*Exit* MUSTACHO]

TRINCALO: Try the Pump, try the Pump!

[*Exit* VENTOSO]

#### Enter MUSTACHO at the other door

MUSTACHO: O Master! six foot Water in Hold.

STEPHANO: Clap the Helm hard aboard! Flat, flat, flat in the Foresheat there. [*Exit* MUSTACHO] 70

TRINCALO: Over-haul your fore-boiling.

STEPHANO: Brace in the Lar-board. [*Exit*]

TRINCALO: A curse upon this howling,    (*A great cry within*)
They are louder than the weather.

*Enter* ANTONIO *and* GONZALO

Yet again, what do you here! shall we give o're, and
drown? ha' you a mind to sink?

GONZALO: A pox o' your throat, you bawling, blasphe-
mous, uncharitable dog.

TRINCALO: Work you then.

ANTONIO: Hang, Cur, hang, you whorson insolent noise-    80
maker, we are less afraid to be drown'd than thou art.[3]

TRINCALO: Brace off the Fore-yard.                [*Exit*]

GONZALO: I'le warrant him for drowning, though the Ship
were no stronger than a Nut-shell, and as leaky as an
unstanch'd Wench.

*Enter* ALONZO *and* FERDINAND

FERDINAND: For my self I care not, but your loss brings a
thousand Deaths to me.

ALONZO: O name not me, I am grown old, my Son; I now
am tedious to the world, and that, by use, is so to me: but,
*Ferdinand*, I grieve my subjects loss in thee: Alas! I suffer    90
justly for my crimes, but why thou shouldest—O Heaven!
                              (*A cry within*)
Heark, farewel my Son! a long farewel!

FERDINAND: Some lucky Plank, when we are lost by
shipwrack, waft hither, and submit it self beneath you.
Your blessing, and I dye contented.

                              [*Embrace and Exeunt*]

*Enter* TRINCALO, MUSTACHO, *and* VENTOSO

TRINCALO: What, must our mouths be cold then?

VENTOSO: All's lost. To prayers, to prayers.

GONZALO: The Duke and Prince are gone within to
prayers. Let's assist them.

MUSTACHO: Nay, we may e'ne pray too; our case is now
alike.                                              100

ANTONIO: We are meerly cheated of our lives by
Drunkards.
This wide-chopt Rascal: would thou might'st lye drowing

---

[3]  75-81: I.i.38-42: 'Yet again ... Thou art.'

The long washing of ten Tides.

        [*Exeunt* TRINCALO, MUSTACHO *and* VENTOSO]

GONZALO: He'll be hang'd yet, though every drop of water swears against it; now would I give ten thousand Furlongs of Sea for one Acre of barren ground, Long-heath, Broom-furs, or any thing. The wills above be done, but I would fain dye a dry death.[4]

                    (*A confused noise within*)

ANTONIO: Mercy upon us! we split, we split.

GONZALO: Let's all sink with the Duke, and the young Prince.                [*Exeunt*] 110

        *Enter* STEPHANO, TRINCALO

TRINCALO: The Ship is sinking.    (*A new cry within*)

STEPHANO: Run her ashore!

TRINCALO: Luffe! luffe! or we are all lost! there's a Rock upon the Star-board Bow.

STEPHANO: She strikes, she strikes! All shift for themselves.

                        [*Exeunt*]

# Scene ii

### *Enter* PROSPERO *and* MIRANDA

PROSPERO: *Miranda!* where's your Sister?

MIRANDA: I left her looking from the pointed Rock, at the walks end, on the huge beat of Waters.

PROSPERO: It is a dreadful object.

MIRANDA: If by your Art, my dearest Father, you have put them in this roar, allay 'em quickly.

Had I been any God of power, I would have sunk the Sea into the Earth, before it should the vessel so have swallowed.

PROSPERO: Collect your self, and tell your piteous heart, There's no harm done.                    10

MIRANDA: O woe the day!

PROSPERO: There is no harm:

I have done nothing but in care of thee,

---

[4] 96–108: I.i.51–67: 'All lost . . . dry death.'

My Daughter, and thy pretty Sister:
You both are ignorant of what you are,
Not knowing whence I am, nor that I'm more
Than *Prospero*, Master of a narrow Cell,
And thy unhappy Father.

MIRANDA: I ne're indeavour'd to know more than you
were pleas'd to tell me.                                    20

PROSPERO: I should inform thee farther: wipe thou thine
Eyes, have comfort; the direful spectacle of the wrack,
which touch'd the very virtue of compassion in thee, I
have with such a pity safely order'd, that not one creature
in the Ship is lost.

MIRANDA: You often, Sir, began to tell me what I am,
But then you stopt.

PROSPERO: The hour's now come;
Obey, and be attentive. Canst thou remember a time
before we came into this Cell? I do not think thou canst,
for then thou were not full three years old.               30

MIRANDA: Certainly I can, Sir.

PROSPERO: Tell me the image then of any thing which thou
dost keep in thy remembrance still.

MIRANDA: Sir, had I not four or five Women once that
tended me?

PROSPERO: Thou hadst, and more, *Miranda*: what see'st
thou else in the dark back-ward, and abyss of Time?
If thou rememberest ought e're thou cam'st here, then,
how thou cam'st thou may'st remember too.

MIRANDA: Sir, that I do not.

PROSPERO: Fifteen Years since,* *Miranda*, thy Father was    40
the Duke of *Millain*, and a Prince of power.

MIRANDA: Sir, are not you my Father?

PROSPERO: Thy Mother was all virtue, and she said, thou
wast my Daughter, and thy Sister too.

MIRANDA: O Heavens! what foul play had we, that we
hither came, or was't a blessing that we did?

PROSPERO: Both, both, my Girl.

MIRANDA: How my heart bleeds to think what you have
suffer'd. But, Sir, I pray proceed.

PROSPERO: My Brother, and thy Uncle, call'd *Antonio*, to 50
whom I trusted then the manage of my State, while I was
wrap'd with secret Studies: That false Uncle—Do'st thou
attend me Child?

MIRANDA: Sir, most heedfully.

PROSPERO: Having attain'd the craft of granting suits, and
of denying them; whom to advance, or lop, for over-
toping,* soon was grown the Ivy which did hide my
princely Trunck, and suckt my verdure out: thou attend'st
not.

MIRANDA: O good Sir, I do.

PROSPERO: I thus neglecting worldly ends, and bent to 60
closeness, and the bettering of my mind, wak'd in my
false Brother an evil Nature:
He did believe
He was indeed the Duke, because he then did execute the
outward face of Soveraignty. Do'st thou still mark me?

MIRANDA: Your story would cure deafness.

PROSPERO: To have no screen between the part he plaid,
and whom he plaid it for; he needs would be Absolute
*Millain*, and Confederates (so dry he was for Sway) with
*Savoy*'s* Duke, to give him Tribute, and to do him
homage. 70

MIRANDA: False man!

PROSPERO: This Duke of *Savoy* being an Enemy,
To me inveterate, strait grants my Brother's suit,
And on a night
Mated to his design, *Antonio* opened the Gates of *Millain*,
and i'th' dead of darkness, hurri'd me thence with thy
young Sister, and thy crying self.

MIRANDA: But wherefore did they not that hour destroy
us?

PROSPERO: They durst not, Girl, in *Millain*, for the love
my people bore me; in short, they hurri'd us away to 80
*Savoy*, and thence aboard a Bark at *Nissa*'s* Port: bore us
some Leagues to Sea, where they prepare'd a rotten
Carkass of a Boat, not rigg'd, no Tackle, Sail, nor Mast;

the very Rats instinctively had quit it: they hoisted us, to cry to Seas which roar'd to us; to sigh to Winds, whose pity sighing back again, did seem to do us loving wrong.

MIRANDA: Alack! what trouble was I then to you?

PROSPERO: Thou and thy sister were two Cherubins, which did preserve me: you both did smile, infus'd with fortitude from Heaven.

MIRANDA: How came we ashore?

PROSPERO: By Providence Divine,
Some food we had, and some fresh Water, which a Nobleman of *Savoy*, called *Gonzalo*, appointed Master of that black design, gave us; with rich Garments, and all necessaries, which since have steaded much: and of his gentleness (knowing I lov'd my Books) he furnisht me from mine own Library, with Volumes which I prize above my Dukedom.

MIRANDA: Would I might see that man.

PROSPERO: Here in this Island we arriv'd, and here have I your Tutor been. But by my skill I find that my mid-Heaven doth depend on a most happy Star, whose influence if I now court not, but omit, my Fortunes will ever after droop: here cease more question, thou art inclin'd to sleep: 'tis a good dulness, and give it way; I know thou canst not chuse.          (*She falls asleep*)
Come away my Spirit: I am ready now, approach,
My *Ariel*, Come.

*Enter* ARIEL

ARIEL: All hail, great Master, grave Sir, hail; I come to answer thy best pleasure, be it to fly, to swim, to shoot into the fire, to ride on the curl'd Clouds: to thy strong bidding, task *Ariel* and all his qualities.

PROSPERO: Hast thou, Spirit, perform'd to point the Tempest that I bad thee?

ARIEL: To every Article.
I boarded the Duke's Ship, now on the Beak, now in the Waste, the Deck, in every Cabin; I flam'd amazement, and sometimes I seem'd to burn in many places on the Top-Mast, the Yards and Bore-sprit; I did flame distinctly.

PROSPERO: My brave Spirit!

   Who was so firm, so constant, that this coil* did not   70
infect his Reason?

ARIEL: Not a soul

   But felt a Feaver of the mind, and play'd some tricks of
desperation; all, but Mariners, plung'd in the foaming
brine, and quit the Vessel: the Duke's Son, *Ferdinand*,
with hair upstairing (more like Reeds than Hair) was the
first man that leap'd; cry'd, *Hell is empty, and all the
Devils are here.*

PROSPERO: Why that's my Spirit;

   But was not this nigh Shore?

ARIEL: Close by, my Master.                130

PROSPERO: But, *Ariel*, are they safe?

ARIEL: Not a hair perisht.

   In Troops I have dispers'd them round this Isle.

   The Duke's Son I have landed by himself, whom I have
left warming the air with sighs, in an odde angle of the
Isle, and sitting, his arms he folded in this sad knot.

PROSPERO: Say how thou hast dispos'd the Mariners of the
Duke's Ship, and all the rest of the Fleet.

ARIEL: Safely in Harbour

   Is the Duke's Ship; in the deep Nook, where once thou
     call'dst                        140

   Me up at midnight to fetch Dew from the

   Still vext *Bermoothes*, there she's hid;

   The Mariners all under hatches stow'd;

   Whom, with a charm, join'd to their suffer'd labour,

   I have left asleep: and for the rest o'th' Fleet

   (Which I disperst) they all have met again,

   And are upon the *Mediterranean* Float,

   Bound sadly home for *Italy*;

   Supposing that they saw the Duke's Ship wrackt,

   And his great person perish.           150

PROSPERO: *Ariel*, thy charge

   Exactly is perform'd, but there's more work:

   What is the time o'th' day?

ARIEL: Past the mid-season.

PROSPERO: At least two Glasses:* the time 'tween six and now must by us both be spent most preciously.

ARIEL: Is there more toyl? since thou dost give me pains, let me remember thee what thou hast promis'd, which is not yet perform'd me.

PROSPERO: How now, *Moodie*?                                                    160
  What is't thou canst demand?

ARIEL: My liberty.

PROSPERO: Before the time be out? no more.

ARIEL: I prethee!
  Remember I have done thee faithful service,
  Told thee no lyes, made thee no mistakings,
  Serv'd without or grudge, or grumblings:
  Thou didst promise to bate me a full year.

PROSPERO: Dost thou forget
  From what a torment I did free thee?                                          170

ARIEL: No.

PROSPERO: Thou dost, and think'st it much to tread the Ooze
  Of the salt deep:
  To run against the sharp wind of the North,
  To do my business in the Veins of the Earth,
  When it is bak'd with Frost.

ARIEL: I do not, Sir.

PROSPERO: Thou ly'st, malignant thing! has thou forgot the foul Witch *Sycorax*, who with age and envy was grown into a Hoop? hast thou forgot her?                          180

ARIEL: No Sir!

PROSPERO: Thou hast; where was she born? speak, tell me.

ARIEL: Sir, in *Argier*.*

PROSPERO: Oh, was she so! I must
  Once every Month recount what thou hast been, which thou forgettest. This damn'd Witch *Sycorax* for mischiefs manifold, and sorceries too terrible to enter humane hearing, from *Argier* thou knowst was banisht: but for one thing she did, they would not take her life: is not this true?

ARIEL: I, Sir. 190

PROSPERO: This blew-ey'd Hag was hither brought with
  child,
  And here was left by th' Saylors: thou, my slave,
  As thou report'st thy self, wast then her servant;
  And 'cause thou wast a spirit too delicate
  To act her earthy and abhorr'd commands,
  Refusing her grand Hests, she did confine thee,
  By help of her more potent Ministers,
  (In her unmitigable rage) into a cloven Pine;
  Within whose rift imprison'd, thou didst painfully
  Remain a dozen years; within which space she dy'd, 200
  And left thee there; where thou didst vent thy
  Groans, as fast as Mill-wheels strike.
  Then was this Isle (save for two Brats, which she did
  Litter here, the brutish *Caliban*, and his twin Sister,
  Two freckel'd-hag-born Whelps) not honour'd with
  A humane shape.

ARIEL: Yes! *Caliban* her Son, and *Sycorax* his Sister.

PROSPERO: Dull thing, I say so; he, that *Caliban*, and she
  that *Sycorax*, whom I now keep in service. Thou best
  knowst what torment I did find thee in; thy groans did 210
  make Wolves howl, and penetrate the breasts of ever
  angry Bears: it was a torment to lay upon the damn'd,
  which *Sycorax* could ne're again undo: It was my Art,
  when I arriv'd, and heard thee, that made the Pine to gape
  and let thee out.

ARIEL: I thank thee, Master.

PROSPERO: If thou more murmurest, I will rend an Oak,
  And peg thee in his knotty Entrails, till thou
  Has howled away twelve Winters more.

ARIEL: Pardon, Master,
  I will be correspondent to command, and be 220
  A gentle spirit.

PROSPERO: Do so, and after two days I'le discharge thee.

ARIEL: That's my noble Master.
  What shall I do? say? what? what shall I do?

PROSPERO: Be subject to no sight but mine; invisible to

Every eye-ball else: hence with diligence.
My daughter wakes. Anon thou shalt know more.

[*Exit* ARIEL]

Thou hast slept well my child.

MIRANDA: The sadness of your story put heaviness in me.

PROSPERO: Shake it off; come on, I'le now call *Caliban*,
my slave,                                                            230
Who never yields us a kind answer.

MIRANDA: 'Tis a creature, Sir, I do not love to look on.

PROSPERO: But as 'tis, we cannot miss him; he does make
our Fire, fetch in our Wood, and serve in Offices that
profit us. What hoa! Slave! *Caliban*! thou Earth thou,
speak.

CALIBAN: (*within*) There's Wood enough within.

PROSPERO: Come forth, I say, there's other business for
thee.
Come thou Tortoise, when?

*Enter* ARIEL

Fine apparition, my quaint *Ariel*,
Hark in thy ear.                                                    240

ARIEL: My Lord it shall be done.                    [*Exit*]

PROSPERO: Thou poisonous Slave, got by the Devil himself
upon thy wicked Dam, come forth.

*Enter* CALIBAN

CALIBAN: As wicked Dew, as e're my Mother brush'd with
Raven's Feather from unwholsome Fens, drop on you
both: A South-west blow on you, and blister you all o're.

PROSPERO: For this besure, to night thou shalt have
Cramps, sidestitches, that shall pen thy breath up;
Urchins shall prick thee till thou bleed'st: thou shalt be
pinch'd as thick as HoneyCombs, each pinch more         250
stinging than the Bees which made 'em.

CALIBAN: I must eat my dinner: this Island's mine by
*Sycorax* my Mother, which thou took'st from me. When
thou cam'st first, thou stroak'st me, and mad'st much of
me, would'st give me Water with Berries in't, and teach
me how to name the bigger Light, and how the less, that
burn by day and night; and then I lov'd thee, and shew'd

thee all the qualities of the Isle, the fresh Springs, brine-
Pits, barren places, and fertil. Curs'd be I, that I did so:
All the Charms of *Sycorax*, Toads, Beetles, Batts, light on 260
thee, for I am all the Subjects that thou hast. I first was
mine own Lord; and here thou stay'st me in this hard
Rock, whiles thou dost keep from me the rest o'th' Island.

PROSPERO: Thou most lying Slave, whom stripes may
move, not kindness: I have us'd thee (filth that thou art)
with humane care, and lodg'd thee in mine own Cell, till
thou didst seek to violate the honour of my Children.

CALIBAN: Oh ho, Oh ho, would't had been done: thou
did'st prevent me, I had peopl'd else this Isle with
*Calibans*.

PROSPERO: Abhor'd Slave!*
Who ne're would any print of goodness take, being
    capable of all ill: I pity'd thee, took pains to make thee 270
speak, taught thee each hour one thing or other; when
thou didst not (Savage) know thy own meaning, but
would'st gabble, like a thing most brutish, I endow'd thy
purposes with words which made them known: But thy
wild race (though thou did'st learn) had that in't, which
good Natures could not abide to be with: therefore wast
thou deservedly pent up into this Rock.

CALIBAN: You taught me language, and my profit by it is,
that I know to curse: the red botch rid you for learning
me your language. 280

PROSPERO: Hag-seed hence!
Fetch us in fewel, and be quick
To answer other business: shrugst thou (malice)?
If thou neglectest or dost unwillingly what I command,
I'le wrack thee with old Cramps, fill all thy bones with
Aches, make thee roar, that Beasts shall tremble
At thy Din.

CALIBAN: No prethee!
(*Aside*) I must obey. His Art is of such power,
It would controul my Dam's God, *Setebos*, 290
And make a Vassal of him.

PROSPERO: So Slave, hence.[5]

[*Exeunt* PROSPERO *and* CALIBAN *severally*]

*Enter* DORINDA

DORINDA: Oh Sister! what have I beheld?

MIRANDA: What is it moves you so?

DORINDA: From yonder Rock,
  As I my Eyes cast down upon the Seas,
  The whistling winds blew rudely on my face,
  And the waves roar'd; at first I thought the War
  Had bin between themselves, but strait I spy'd
  A huge great Creature.                                    300

MIRANDA: O you mean the Ship.

DORINDA: Is't not a Creature then? it seem'd alive.

MIRANDA: But what of it?

DORINDA: This floating Ram did bear his Horns above;
  All ty'd with Ribbands, ruffling in the wind,
  Sometimes he nodded down his head a while,
  And then the Waves did heave him to the moon;
  He clamb'ring to the top of all the Billows,
  And then again he curtsy'd down so low,
  I could not see him: till, at last, all side-long         310
  With a great crack his belly burst in pieces.

MIRANDA: There all had perisht
  Had not my Father's magick Art reliev'd them.
  But, Sister, I have stranger news to tell you;
  In this great Creature there were other Creatures,
  And shortly we may chance to see that thing,
  Which you have heard my Father call, a Man.

DORINDA: But what is that? for yet he never told me.

MIRANDA: I know no more than you: but I have heard
  My Father say we Women were made for him.                 320

DORINDA: What, that he should eat us, Sister?

MIRANDA: No sure, you see my Father is a man, and yet
  He does us good. I would he were not old.

DORINDA: Methinks indeed it would be finer, if we two
  Had two young Fathers.

---

[5] 5-292. Closely based on *Tempest*, I.ii.1-376, but with cuts in the Prospero/Miranda section.

MIRANDA: No Sister, no, if they were young, my Father
    Said that we must call them Brothers.

DORINDA: But pray how does it come that we two are not
    Brothers then, and have not Beards like him?

MIRANDA: Now I confess you pose me.                        330

DORINDA: How did he come to be our Father too?

MIRANDA: I think he found us when we both were little,
    and grew within the ground.

DORINDA: Why could he not find more of us? pray sister,
    let you and I look up and down one day, to find some
    little ones for us to play with.

MIRANDA: Agreed; but now we must go in. This is the hour
    Wherein my Father's Charm will work,
    Which seizes all who are in open Air:
    Th' effect of his great Art I long to see,            340
    Which will perform as much as Magick can.

DORINDA: And I, methinks, more long to see a Man.

                                *[Exeunt]*

# ACT II

## Scene i

*Enter* ALONZO, ANTONIO, GONZALO, *Attendants*

GONZALO: Beseech your Grace be merry; you have cause,
so have we all, of joy for our strange scape: then wisely,
good Sir, weigh our sorrow with our comfort.[6]

ALONZO: Prithee peace! you cram these words into my
Ears against my stomack.[7] How can I rejoyce, when my
dear Son, perhaps this very moment, is made a meal to
some strange Fish?

ANTONIO: Sir, he may live,
I saw him beat the billows under him, and ride upon their
backs; he trod the Water, whose enmity he flung aside,
and breasted the most swoln surge that met him; his bold    10
head 'bove the contentious waves he kept, and oar'd
himself with his strong arms to shore: I do not doubt he
came alive to land.

ALONZO: No, no, he's gone,[8] and you and I, *Antonio*, were
those who caus'd his death.

ANTONIO: How could we help it?

ALONZO: Then, then, we should have helpt it, when thou
betrayedst thy Brother *Prospero*, and *Mantua*'s Infant,
Sovereign to my power: And when I, too ambitious, took
by force anothers right; then lost we *Ferdinand*, then
forfeited our Navy to this Tempest.    20

ANTONIO: Indeed we first broke truce with Heav'n;
You to the waves an Infant Prince expos'd,
And on the waves have lost an only Son;
I did usurp my Brother's fertile lands, and now

---

[6] 1–3: II.i.1–2, 8–9: 'Beseech you . . . our escape . . . then wisely . . . comfort.'

[7] 4–5: II.i.102–3: 'You cram . . . stomach of my sense.'

[8] 7–13: II.i.110–18: 'Sir, he may . . . he's gone.'

Am cast upon this desert Isle.

GONZALO: These, Sir, 'tis true, were crimes of a black Dye,
But both of you have made amends to Heav'n,
By your late Voyage into *Portugal*,*
Where, in defence of Christianity,
Your valour has repuls'd the *Moors* of *Spain*.                    30

ALONZO: O name it not, *Gonzalo*.
No act but penitence can expiate guilt.
Must we teach Heaven what price to set on Murthers?
What rate on lawless power, and wild ambition?
Or dare we traffic with the Powers above,
And sell by weight a good deed for a bad?

*(Musick within)*

GONZALO: Musick! and in the air! sure we are shipwrackt
on the Dominions of some merry Devil.

ANTONIO: This Isle's inchanted ground, for I have heard
Swift voices flying by my Ear, and groans                    40
Of lamenting Ghosts.

ALONZO: I pull'd a Tree, and Blood pursu'd my hand.* O
Heaven! deliver me from this dire place, and all the after
actions of my life shall mark my penitence and my
bounty.
Heark!                    *(A Dialogue within sung in parts)*
The sounds approach us.

1. D.        *Where does proud* Ambition *dwell?**
2.           *In the lowest Rooms of Hell.*
1.           *Of the damn'd who leads the Host?*
2.           *He who did oppress the most.*                    50
1.           *Who such Troops of damned brings?*
2.           *Most are led by fighting Kings.*
             *Kings who did Crowns unjustly get,*
             *Here on burning Thrones are set.*

CHORUS: *Kings who did Crowns,* &c.

ANTONIO: Do you hear, Sir, how they lay our Crimes
before us?

GONZALO: Do evil Spirits imitate the good,
In shewing men their sins?

ALONZO: But in a different way,
Those warn from doing, these upbraid 'em done.    60

1. D.        *Who are the Pillars of Ambitions Court?*
2.           *Grim Deaths and Scarlet Murthers it support.*
1.           *What lyes beneath her feet?*
2.                                    *Her footsteps tread,*
             *On Orphans tender breasts, and Brothers dead.*
1.           *Can Heaven permit such Crimes should be*
             *Rewarded with felicity?*
2.           *Oh no! uneasily their Crowns they wear,*
             *And their own guilt amidst their Guards they*
                 *fear.*
             *Cares when they wake their minds unquiet keep,*
             *And we in visions lord it o're their sleep.*    70
CHORUS: *Oh no! uneasily their Crowns, &c.*

ALONZO: See where they come in horrid shapes!
*Enter the two that sung, in the shape of Devils, placing*
             *themselves at two corners of the Stage*
ANTONIO: Sure Hell is open'd to devour us quick.

1. D.        Say Brother, shall we bear these mortals hence?
2.           First let us shew the shapes of their offence.
1.           We'll muster then their crimes on either side.
         Appear! appear! their first begotten, *Pride.*
                    *Enter* PRIDE
PRIDE: Lo! I am here, who led their hears astray,
    And to *Ambition* did their minds betray.
                    *Enter* FRAUD
FRAUD: And guileful *Fraud* does next appear,    80
    Their wandring steps who led,
    When they from virtue fled,
    And in my crooked paths their course did steer.
                    *Enter* RAPINE
RAPINE: From *Fraud* to *Force* they soon arrive,
    Where *Rapine* did their actions drive.
                    *Enter* MURTHER
MURTHER: There long they cannot stay,

Down the deep precipice they run,
And to secure what they have done,
To murder bend their way.
(*After which they fall into a round encompassing the
                    Duke, &c. Singing*)

> *Around, around, we pace*                    90
> *About this cursed place,*
> *Whilst thus we compass in*
> *These mortals and their sin.*        (*Dance*)

                                (*All the spirits vanish*)

ANTONIO: Heav'n has heard me! they are vanish'd.
ALONZO: But they have left me all unmann'd;
  I feel my sinews slacken'd with the fright,
  And a cold sweat trills down o're all my limbs,
  As if I were dissolving into Water.
  *O Prospero!* my crimes 'gainst thee sit heavy on my heart.
ANTONIO: And mine, 'gainst him and young *Hippolito*.   100
GONZALO: Heav'n have mercy on the penitent!
ALONZO: Lead from this cursed ground;
  The Seas, in all their rage, are not so dreadful.
  This is the Region of despair and death.
GONZALO: Shall we not seek some food?
ALONZO: Beware all fruit but what the birds have peid,*
  The shadows of the Trees are poisonous too:
  A secret venom slides from every branch.
  My conscience doth distract me, O my Son!
  Why do I speak of eating or repose,                    110
  Before I know thy fortune?                    [*Exeunt*]

## Scene ii

*Enter* FERDINAND *and* ARIEL, *invisible, playing and singing*

### ARIEL's *Song*

*Come unto these yellow sands*
  *And then take hands.*

> *Curtsy'd when you have and kiss'd,*
>    *The wild waves whist.*
> *Foot it featly here and there, and sweet sprights bear*
>    *the Burthen*                    (Burthen* dispersedly)
> *Hark! hark!* Bow-waugh; *the watch-dogs bark,*
>    Bow-waugh.

ARIEL: *Hark! hark! I hear the strain of strutting* Chanti-
cleer
   *Cry* Cock a doodle do.                                    10

FERDINAND: Where should this Musick be? i'th' Air, or
   th' Earth?
   It sounds no more, and sure it waits upon some God
   O'th' Island, sitting on a bank weeping against the
   Duke
   My Father's wrack. This musick hover'd o're me
   On the waters, allaying both their fury and my passion
   With charming Airs; thence I have follow'd it (or it
   Hath drawn me rather) but 'tis gone;
   No, it begins again.

### ARIEL's *Song*

> *Full Fathoms five thy Father lyes,*
>    *Of his bones is Coral made:*                          20
> *Those are Pearls that were his eyes;*
>    *Nothing of him that does fade,*
> *But does suffer a Sea-change*
> *Into something rich and strange:*
> *Sea-Nymphs hourly ring his knell,*
> *Heark now I hear 'em,* Ding dong Bell.
>                                    (Burthen, *Ding dong*)

FERDINAND: The mournful Ditty mentions my drown'd
   Father,
   This is no mortal business, nor a sound which the
   Earth owns: I hear it now before me,[9]
   However I will on and follow it.                          30
                        [*Exit* FERDINAND *and* ARIEL]

---

[9] 1–29: I.ii.377–410: 'Come unto ... the earth owes.'

## Scene iii

*Enter* STEPHANO, MUSTACHO, VENTOSO

VENTOSO: The Runlet* of Brandy was a loving Runlet, and
floated after us out of pure pity.

MUSTACHO: This kind Bottle, like an old acquaintance,
swam after it. And this Scollop-shell is all our Plate now.

VENTOSO: 'Tis well we have found something since we
landed.

I prethee fill a soop,* and let it go round.
Where hast thou laid the Runlet?

MUSTACHO: I'th' hollow of an old Tree.

VENTOSO: Fill apace,
We cannot live long in this barren Island, and we may      10
Take a soop before death, as well as others drink
At our Funerals.

MUSTACHO: This is prize-Brandy, we steal Custom,* and it
costs nothing. Let's have two rounds more.

VENTOSO: Master, what have you sav'd?

STEPHANO: Just nothing but my self.

VENTOSO: This works comfortably on a cold stomach.

STEPHANO: Fill's another round.

VENTOSO: Look! *Mustacho* weeps. Hang losses as long as
we have Brandy left. Prithee leave weeping.      20

STEPHANO: He sheds his Brandy out of his eyes: he shall
drink no more.

MUSTACHO: This will be a doleful day with old *Bess*. She
gave me a gilt Nutmeg at parting. That's lost too. But as
you say, hang losses. Prithee fill agen.

VENTOSO: Beshrew thy heart for putting me in mind of thy
Wife,
I had not thought of mine else, Nature will shew it self,
I must melt. I prithee fill agen, my Wife's a good old jade,
And has but one eye left: but she'll weep out that too,
When she hears that I am dead.      30

STEPHANO: Would you were both hang'd for putting me in

thought of mine. But well, If I return not in seven years to my own Country, she may marry agen* and 'tis from this Island thither at least seven years swimming.

MUSTACHO: O at least, having no help of Boat nor Bladders.

STEPHANO: Whoe're she marries, poor soul, she'll weep a nights when she thinks of *Stephano*.

VENTOSO: But Master, sorrow is dry!* there's for you agen.

STEPHANO: A Mariner had e'en as good be a Fish as a Man, but for the comfort we get ashore: O for any old dry Wench now I am wet.

MUSTACHO: Poor heart! that would soon make you dry agen: but all is barren in this Isle: here we may lye at Hull till the Wind blow Nore and by South, e're we can cry *a Sail, a Sail* at sight of a white Apron. And therefore here's another soop to comfort us.

VENTOSO: This Isle's our own, that's our comfort, for the Duke, the Prince, and all their train are perished.

MUSTACHO: Our Ship is sunk, and we can never get home agen: we must e'en turn Salvages, and the next that catches his fellow may eat him.*

VENTOSO: No, no, let us have a Government; for if we live well and orderly, Heav'n will drive the Shipwracks ashore to make us all rich, therefore let us carry good Consciences, and not eat one another.

STEPHANO: Whoever eats any of my subjects, I'le break out his Teeth with my Scepter: for I was Master at Sea, and will be Duke on Land: you *Mustacho* have been my Mate, and shall be my Vice-Roy.

VENTOSO: When you are Duke you may chuse your Vice-Roy; but I am a free Subject in a new Plantation, and will have no Duke without my voice. And so fill me the other soop.

STEPHANO: (*whispering*) *Ventoso*, dost thou hear? I will advance thee, prithee give me thy voice.

VENTOSO: I'le have no whisperings to corrupt the Election;

and to show that I have no private ends, I declare aloud
that I will be Vice-Roy, or I'le keep my voice for my self.

MUSTACHO: *Stephano*, hear me, I will speak for the people,
because there are few, or rather none in the Isle to speak
for themselves. Know then, that to prevent the farther
shedding of Christian blood, we are all content *Ventoso*    70
shall be Vice-Roy, upon condition I may be Vice-Roy over
him. Speak good people, are you well agreed? what, no
man answer? well, you may take their silence for consent.

VENTOSO: You speak for the people, *Mustacho*? I'le speak
for 'em, and declare generally with one voice, one word
and all; that there shall be no Vice-Roy but the Duke,
unless I be he.

MUSTACHO: You declare for the people, who never saw
your face! Cold Iron shall decide it.          (*Both draw*)

STEPHANO: Hold, loving Subjects: we will have no Civil
war during our Reign: I do hereby appoint you both to be   80
my Vice-Roys over the whole Island.

BOTH: Agreed! agreed!

     *Enter* TRINCALO *with a great bottle, half drunk*

VENTOSO: How! *Trincalo* our brave Bosen!

MUSTACHO: He reels: can he be drunk with Sea-water?

TRINCALO: (*sings*) *I shall no more to Sea, to Sea,*
     *Here I shall dye ashore.*
This is a very scurvy tune to sing at a man's funeral,
But here's my comfort.                         (*Drinks*)
(*sings*) *The Master, the Swabber, the Gunner, and I,*
          *The Surgeon, and his Mate,*                   90
               *Lov'd Mall, Meg, and Marrian, and Margery,*
               *But none of us car'd for* Kate.
          *For she had a tongue with a tang,*
          *Wou'd cry to a Saylor,* go hang:
          *She lov'd not the savour of Tar nor of Pitch,*
          *Yet a Taylor might scratch her where e're she did*
               *itch.*
This is a scurvy Tune too, but here's my comfort agen.[10]
                                               (*Drinks*)

---

[10]  85-97: II.ii.43-56: 'I shall no more ... my comfort.'

STEPHANO: We have got another subject now; welcome,
Welcome into our Dominions!

TRINCALO: What Subject, or what Dominions? here's old 100
Sack

Boys: the King of good fellows can be no subject.
I will be Old *Simon* the King.*

MUSTACHO: Hah, old Boy! how didst thou scape?

TRINCALO: Upon a Butt of Sack, Boys, which the Saylors
Threw overboard: but are you alive, hoa! for I will
Tipple with no Ghosts till I'm dead: thy hand *Mustacho*,
And thine *Ventoso*; the storm has done its worst:
*Stephano* alive too! give thy Bosen thy hand, Master.

VENTOSO: You must kiss it then, for, I must tell you, we
have chosen him Duke in a full Assembly.    110

TRINCALO: A Duke! where? what's he Duke of?

MUSTACHO: Of this Island, man. Oh *Trincalo* we are all
made, the Island's empty; all's our own, Boy; and we will
speak to his Grace for thee, that thou may'st be as great
as we are.

TRINCALO: You great? what the Devil are you?

VENTOSO: We two are Vice-Roys over all the island; and
when we are weary of Governing thou shalt succeed us.

TRINCALO: Do you hear, *Ventoso*, I will succeed you in
both your places before you enter into 'em.

STEPHANO: *Trincalo*, sleep and be sober; and make no 120
more uproars in my Country.

TRINCALO: Why, what are you, Sir, what are you?

STEPHANO: What I am, I am by free election, and you
*Trincalo* are not your self; but we pardon your first fault,
Because it is the first day of our Reign.

TRINCALO: Umph, were matters carried so swimmingly
against me, whilst I was swimming, and saving my self for
the good of the people of this Island?

MUSTACHO: Art thou mad *Trincalo*, wilt thou disturb a
settled Government?    130

TRINCALO: I say this Island shall be under *Trincalo*, or it
shall be a Common-wealth; and so my Bottle is my
Buckler, and so I draw my Sword.    (*Draws*)

VENTOSO: Ah *Trincalo*, I thought thou hadst had more
　　grace,
Than to rebel against thy old Master,
And thy two lawful Vice-Roys.

MUSTACHO: Wilt not thou take advice of two that stand
For old Counsellors here, where thou art a meer stranger
To the Laws of the Country.

TRINCALO: I'll have no Laws.                               140

VENTOSO: Then Civil-War begins.

　　　　　　　　　(VENTOSO, MUSTACHO *draw*)

STEPHANO: Hold, hold, I'le have no blood shed,
My Subjects are but few: let him make a rebellion
By himself; and a Rebel, I Duke *Stephano* declare him:
Vice-Roys, come away.

TRINCALO: And Duke *Trincalo* declares, that he will make
open war wherever he meets thee or thy Vice-Roys.

　　　　　　[*Exeunt* STEPHANO, MUSTACHO, VENTOSO]
　　　　　*Enter* CALIBAN *with wood upon his back*

TRINCALO: Hah! who have we here?

CALIBAN: All the infections that the Sun sucks up from
Fogs, Fens, Flats, on *Prospero* fall; and make him by inch-  150
meal a Disease: his spirits hear me, and yet I needs must
curse; but they'l not pinch, fright me with Urchin shows,*
pitch me i'th' mire, nor lead me in the dark out of my
way, unless he bid 'em: but for every trifle he sets them on
me; sometimes like Baboons they mow and chatter at me,
and often bite me; like Hedge-hogs then they mount their
prickles at me, tumbling before me in my barefoot way.
Sometimes I am all wound about with Adders, who with
their cloven tongues hiss me to madness. Hah! yonder
stands one of his spirits sent to torment me.[11]

TRINCALO: What have we here, a man, or a fish?          160
This is some Monster of the Isle; were I in *England*,
As once I was, and had him painted,
Not a Holy-day fool there but would give me
Six-pence for the sight of him;[12] well, if I could make

---

[11] 149–59: II.ii.1–14: 'All the infections . . . into madness.'
[12] 160–5: II.ii.24–30: 'What have we . . . a piece of silver.'

Him tame, he were a present for an Emperour.
Come hither pretty Monster, I'le do thee no harm.
Come hither!

CALIBAN: Torment me not;
I'le bring thee Wood home faster.

TRINCALO: He talks none of the wisest, but I'le give him    170
A dram o'th' Bottle, that will clear his understanding.[13]
Come on your ways Master Monster, open your mouth.
How now, you perverse Moon-calf! what,
I think you cannot tell who is your friend!
Open your chops, I say. (*Pours Wine down his throat*)

CALIBAN: This is a brave God, and bears cœlestial
    Liquor,[14]
I'le kneel to him.

TRINCALO: He is a very hopeful monster.[15] Monster, what
say'st thou, art thou content to turn civil and sober, as I
am? for then thou shalt be my subject.    180

CALIBAN: I'le swear upon the Bottle to be true; for the
liquor is not Earthly: did'st thou not drop from Heaven?[16]

TRINCALO: Only out of the Moon, I was the man in her
when time was.—(*Aside*) By this light, a very shallow
Monster.[17]

CALIBAN: I'le shew thee every fertile inch i'th' Isle,[18] and
kiss thy foot: I prithee be my God, and let me drink.
                                    (*Drinks agen*)

TRINCALO: Well drawn, Monster, in good faith.

CALIBAN: I'le shew thee the best Springs, I'le pluck thee
    Berries,
I'le fish for thee, and get thee wood enough:
A curse upon the Tyrant whom I serve, I'le bear him    190
No more sticks, but follow thee.

TRINCALO: The poor Monster is loving in his drink.
                                    (*Aside*)

[13] 165-71: II.ii.70-5: 'If I can ... after the wisest.'
[14] 172-6: II.ii.84-7: 'Come your ways ... your chaps again.'
[15] 177-8: II.ii.117-18: 'That's a brave ... kneel to him.'
[16] 181-2: II.ii.126-7: 'I'll swear ... not earthly.'
[17] 182-4: II.ii.136-40: 'Hast Thou not ... when time was.'
[18] 185: II.ii.160: 'I'll show thee ... berries.'

CALIBAN: I prithee let me bring thee where Crabs grow,
    And I with my long Nails, will dig thee Pig-nuts,
    Shew thee a Jay's Nest, and instruct thee how to snare
    The Marmazet; I'le bring thee to cluster'd Filberds;
    Wilt thou go with me?[19]

TRINCALO: This Monster comes of a good natur'd race.
                                        (*Aside*)

Is there no more of thy kin in this Island?

CALIBAN: Divine, here is but one besides my self;        200
    My lovely Sister, beautiful and bright as the full Moon.

TRINCALO: Where is she?

CALIBAN: I left her clambring up a hollow Oak,
    And plucking thence the dropping Honey-Combs.
    Say my King, shall I call her to thee?

TRINCALO: She shall swear upon the Bottle too.
    If she proves handsom she is mine: here Monster,
    Drink agen for thy good news; thou shalt speak
    A good word for me.            (*Gives him the Bottle*)

CALIBAN: Farewel, old Master, farewel, farewel.        210
    (*Sings*) *No more Dams I'le make for Fish,*
            *Nor fetch in firing at requiring,*
            *Nor scrape Trencher, nor wash Dish;*
            *Ban, Ban, Cackaliban*
            *Has a new Master, get a new man.*
    Heigh-day, Freedom, freedom!

TRINCALO: Here's two subjects got already, the Monster,
    And his Sister: well, Duke *Stephano*, I say, and say agen,
    Wars will ensue, and so I drink.            (*Drinks*)
    From this worshipful Monster, and Mistress        220
    Monster, his Sister,
    I'le lay claim to this Island by Alliance.
    Monster, I say thy Sister shall be my Spouse:
    Come away Brother Monster, I'le lead thee to my Butt
    And drink her health.            [*Exeunt*]

---

[19] 188–97: II.ii.160–72: 'I'll show thee ... go with me?'

## Scene iv

*Enter* PROSPERO *alone*

PROSPERO: 'Tis not yet fit to let my Daughters know I kept
  The infant Duke of *Mantua* so near them in this Isle,
  Whose Father dying bequeath'd him to my care,
  Till my false Brother (when he design'd t'usurp
  My Dukedom from me) expos'd him to that fate
  He meant for me. By calculation of his birth
  I saw death threat'ning him, if, till some time were
  Past, he should behold the face of any Woman:
  And now the danger's nigh.—*Hippolito!*

*Enter* HIPPOLITO

HIPPOLITO: Sir, I attend your pleasure.          10

PROSPERO: How I have lov'd thee from thy infancy,
  Heav'n knows, and thou thy self canst bear me witness,
  Therefore accuse not me for thy restraint.

HIPPOLITO: Since I knew life, you've kept me in a Rock,
  And you this day have hurry'd me from thence,
  Only to change my Prison, not to free me.
  I murmur not, but I may wonder at it.

PROSPERO: O gentle Youth, Fate waits for thee abroad,
  A black Star threatens thee, and death unseen
  Stands ready to devour thee.          20

HIPPOLITO: You taught me not to fear him in any of his
    shapes:
  Let me meet death rather than be a Prisoner.

PROSPERO: 'Tis pity he should seize thy tender youth.

HIPPOLITO: Sir, I have often heard you say, no creature
    liv'd
  Within this Isle, but those which Man was Lord of;
  Why then should I fear?

PROSPERO: But there are creatures which I nam'd not to
    thee,
  Who share man's soveraignty by Nature's Laws,
  And oft depose him from it.

HIPPOLITO: What are those Creatures, Sir?         30

PROSPERO: Those dangerous enemies of men call'd
women.

HIPPOLITO: Women! I never heard of them before.
But have I Enemies within this Isle, and do you
Keep me from them? do you think that I want
Courage to encounter 'em?

PROSPERO: No courage can resist 'em.

HIPPOLITO: How then have you, Sir,
Liv'd so long unharm'd among them?

PROSPERO: O they despise old age, and spare it for that
reason:
It is below their conquest, their fury falls          40
Alone upon the young.

HIPPOLITO: Why then the fury of the young should fall on
them again.
Pray turn me loose upon 'em: but, good Sir,
What are women like?

PROSPERO: Imagine something between young men and
Angels:
Fatally beauteous, and have killing Eyes;
Their voices charm beyond the Nightingales;
They are all enchantment; those who once behold 'em,
Are made their slaves for ever.

HIPPOLITO: Then I will wink and fight with 'em.          50

PROSPERO: 'Tis but in vain, for when your eyes are shut,
They through the lids will shine, and pierce your soul;
Absent, they will be present to you.
They'l haunt you in your very sleep.

HIPPOLITO: Then I'le revenge it on 'em when I wake.

PROSPERO: You are without all possibility of revenge;
They are so beautiful that you can ne're attempt,
Nor wish to hurt them.

HIPPOLITO: Are they so beautiful?

PROSPERO: Calm sleep is not so soft, nor Winter Suns,          60
Nor Summer Shades so pleasant.

HIPPOLITO: Can they be fairer than the Plumes of Swans?
Or more delightful than the Peacocks Feathers?
Or than the gloss upon the necks of Doves?

Or have more various beauty than the Rain-bow?
These I have seen, and without danger wondred at.
PROSPERO: All these are far below 'em: Nature made
Nothing but Woman dangerous and fair:
There if you should chance to see 'em,
Avoid 'em streight, I charge you.                    70
HIPPOLITO: Well, since you say they are so dangerous,
I'le so far shun 'em as I may with safety of the
Unblemish'd honour which you taught me.
But let 'em not provoke me, for I'm sure I shall
Not then forbear them.
PROSPERO: Go in and read the Book I gave you last.
To-morrow I may bring you better news.
HIPPOLITO: I shall obey you, Sir.       [Exit HIPPOLITO]
PROSPERO: So, so; I hope this lesson has secur'd him,
For I have been constrain'd to change his Lodging    80
From yonder Rock where first I bred him up.
And here have brought him home to my own Cell,
Because the Shipwrack happen'd near his Mansion.
I hope he will not stir beyond his limits,
For hitherto he hath been all obedience:
The Planets seem to smile on my designs,
And yet there is one sullen cloud behind;
I would it were disperst.
             Enter MIRANDA and DORINDA
How, my daughters! I thought I had instructed
Them enough—Children! retire;                        90
Why do you walk this way?
MIRANDA: It is within our bounds, Sir.
PROSPERO: But both take heed, that path is very danger-
ous.
Remember what I told you.
DORINDA: Is the man that way, Sir?
PROSPERO: All that you can imagine ill is there,
The curled Lyon, and the rugged Bear
Are not so dreadful as that man.
MIRANDA: Oh me, why stay we here then?

DORINDA: I'le keep far enough from his Den, I warrant
him.                                                              100

MIRANDA: But you have told me, Sir, you are a man;
And yet you are not dreadful.

PROSPERO: I child! but I am a tame man; old men are tame
By Nature, but all the danger lies in a wild
Young man.

DORINDA: Do they run wild about the Woods?

PROSPERO: No, they are wild within Doors, in Chambers,
And in Closets.

DORINDA: But Father, I would stroak 'em and make 'em
gentle,
Then sure they would not hurt me.                               110

PROSPERO: You must not trust them, Child: no woman
can come
Neer 'em but she feels a pain full nine Months:
Well I must in; for new affairs require my
Presence: be you, *Miranda*, your Sister's Guardian.

[*Exit* PROSPERO]

DORINDA: Come, Sister, shall we walk the other way?
The man will catch us else, we have but two legs,
And he perhaps has four.

MIRANDA: Well, Sister, though he have; yet look about you
And we shall spy him e're he comes too near us.

DORINDA: Come back, that way is towards his Den.        120

MIRANDA: Let me alone; I'le venture first, for sure he can
Devour but one of us at once.

DORINDA: How dare you venture?

MIRANDA: We'll find him sitting like a Hare in's Form,*
And he shall not see us.

DORINDA: I, but you know my Father charg'd us both.

MIRANDA: But who shall tell him on't? we'll keep each
Others Counsel.

DORINDA: I dare not for the world.

MIRANDA: But how shall we hereafter shun him, if we do
not                                                              130
Know him first?

DORINDA: Nay I confess I would fain see him too. I find it
    in my Nature, because my Father has forbidden me.

MIRANDA: I, there's it, Sister; if he had said nothing I had
    been quiet. Go softly, and if you see him first, be quick
    and becken me away.

DORINDA: Well, if he does catch me, I'le humble my self to
    him,
    And ask him pardon, as I do my Father,
    When I have done a fault.

MIRANDA: And if I can but scape with life, I had rather be
    in pain nine Months, as my Father threatn'd, than lose my
    longing.

[Exeunt]

## Scene v

*The Scene changes, and discovers* HIPPOLITO *in a Cave
walking, his face from the Audience*

HIPPOLITO: *Prospero* has often said that Nature makes
    Nothing in vain: why then are women made?
    Are they to suck the poyson of the Earth,
    As gaudy colour'd Serpents are? I'le ask that
    Question, when next I see him here.
        *Enter* MIRANDA *and* DORINDA *peeping*

DORINDA: O Sister, there it is, it walks about like one of
    us.

MIRANDA: I, just so, and has legs as we have too.

HIPPOLITO: It strangely puzzles me: yet 'tis most likely
    Women are somewhat between men and spirits.

DORINDA: Heark! it talks, sure this is not it my Father
    meant,                                                    10
    For this is just like one of us: methinks I am not half
    So much afraid on't as I was; see, now it turns this way.

MIRANDA: Heaven! what a goodly thing it is!

DORINDA: I'le go nearer it.

MIRANDA: O no, 'tis dangerous, Sister! I'le go to it.

I would not for the world that you should venture.
My Father charg'd me to secure you from it.

DORINDA: I warrant you this is a tame man, dear Sister,
He'll not hurt me, I see it by his looks.

MIRANDA: Indeed he will! but go back, and he shall eat me
first:                                                          20
Fye, are you not asham'd to be so much inquisitive?

DORINDA: You chide me for't, and wou'd give your self.

MIRANDA: Come back, or I will tell my Father.
Observe how he begins to stare already.
I'le meet the danger first, and then call you.

DORINDA: Nay, Sister, you shall never vanquish me in
kindness.
I'le venture you, no more than you will me.

PROSPERO: (within) Miranda, Child, where are you?

MIRANDA: Do you not hear my Father call? go in.

DORINDA: 'Twas you he nam'd, not me; I will but say my
Prayers,                                                        30
And follow you immediately.

MIRANDA: Well, Sister, you'l repent it. [Exit MIRANDA]

DORINDA: Though I dye for't, I must have th'other peep.

HIPPOLITO: (seeing her) What thing is that? sure 'tis some
Infant of the Sun, dress'd in his Fathers gayest Beams, and
comes to play with Birds: my sight is dazl'd, and yet I find
I'm loth to shut my Eyes.
I must go nearer it—but stay a while;
May it not be that beauteous murderer, Woman,
Which I was charg'd to shun? Speak, what art thou?             40
Thou shining Vision!

DORINDA: Alas I know not; but I'm told I am a Woman;
Do not hurt me, pray, fair thing.

HIPPOLITO: I'd sooner tear my eyes out, than consent to
do you any harm; though I was told a Woman was my
Enemy.

DORINDA: I never knew what 'twas to be an Enemy, nor
can I e're prove so to that which looks like you: for
though I have been charg'd by him (whom yet I never
disobey'd) to shun your presence, yet I'd rather dye than

lose it; therefore I hope you will not have the heart to hurt    50
me: though I fear you are a man, that dangerous thing of
which I have been warn'd; pray tell me what you are.

HIPPOLITO: I must confess, I was inform'd I am a man,
But if I fright you, I shall wish I were some other
Creature. I was bid to fear you too.

DORINDA: Ay me! Heav'n grant we be not poyson to each
other!
Alas, can we not meet but we must die?

HIPPOLITO: I hope not so! for when two poysonous
Creatures,
Both of the same kind, meet, yet neither dies.
I've seen two serpents harmless to each other,    60
Though they have twin'd into a mutual Knot:
If we have any venome in us, sure, we cannot be more
Poysonous, when we meet, than Serpents are.
You have a hand like mine, may I not gently touch it?
(*Takes her hand*)

DORINDA: I've touch'd my Father's and my Sister's hands
And felt no pain; but now, alas! there's something,
When I touch yours, which makes me sigh: just so
I've seen two Turtles mourning when they met;
Yet mine's a pleasing grief; and so methought was theirs;
For still they mourn'd, and still they seem'd to murmur
too,    70
And yet they often met.

HIPPOLITO: Oh Heavens! I have the same sense too; your
hand
Methinks goes through me; I feel at my heart,
And find it pleases, though it pains me.

PROSPERO: (*within*) Dorinda!

DORINDA: My Father calls agen, ah, I must leave you.

HIPPOLITO: Alas, I'm subject to the same command.

DORINDA: This is my first offence against my Father,
Which he, by severing us, too cruelly does punish.

HIPPOLITO: And this is my first trespass too: but he hath
more    80
Offended truth than we have him:

He said our meeting would destructive be,
But I no death but in our parting see.

[*Exeunt several ways*]

# ACT III

## Scene i

*Enter* PROSPERO *and* MIRANDA

PROSPERO: Excuse it not, *Miranda*, for to you (the elder, and, I thought the more discreet) I gave the conduct of your Sister's actions.

MIRANDA: Sir, when you call'd me thence, I did not fail to mind her of her duty to depart.

PROSPERO: How can I think you did remember hers, when you forgot your own? did you not see the man whom I commanded you to shun?

MIRANDA: I must confess I saw him at a distance.

PROSPERO: Did not his Eyes infect and poyson you? What alteration found you in your self? 10

MIRANDA: I only wondered at a sight so new.

PROSPERO: But have you no desire once more to see him? Come, tell me truly what you think of him.

MIRANDA: As of the gayest thing I ever saw, so fine that it appear'd more fit to be belov'd than fear'd, and seem'd so near my kind, that I did think I might have call'd it Sister.

PROSPERO: You do not love it?

MIRANDA: How is it likely that I should, except the thing had first lov'd me? 20

PROSPERO: Cherish those thoughts: you have a gen'rous soul;
And since I see your mind not apt to take the light
Impressions of a sudden love, I will unfold
A secret to your knowledge.
That Creature which you saw, is of a kind which
Nature made a prop and guide to yours.

MIRANDA: Why did you then propose him as an object of terrour to my mind? you never us'd to teach me any thing

but God-like truths, and what you said I did believe as
sacred.

PROSPERO: I fear'd the pleasing form of this young man 30
Might unawares possess your tender breast,
Which for a nobler Guest I had design'd;
For shortly, my *Miranda*, you shall see another of his
kind,
The full blown-flower, of which this youth was but the
Op'ning-bud. Go in, and send your sister to me.

MIRANDA: Heav'n still preserve you, Sir. [*Exit* MIRANDA]

PROSPERO: And make thee fortunate.
*Dorinda* now must be examin'd too concerning this
Late interview. I'm sure unartful truth lies open
In her mind, as Crystal streams their sandy bottom show. 40
I must take care her love grow not too fast,
For innocence is Love's most fertile soil.
Wherein he soon shoots up and widely spreads;
Nor is that danger which attends *Hippolito* yet overpast.

*Enter* DORINDA

PROSPERO: O, come hither, you have seen a man to day,
Against my strict command.

DORINDA: Who I? indeed I saw him but a little, Sir.

PROSPERO: Come, come, be clear. Your Sister told me all.

DORINDA: Did she? truly she would have seen him more
than I,
But that I would not let her. 50

PROSPERO: Why so?

DORINDA: Because, methought, he would have hurt me
less
Than he would her. But if I knew you'd not be angry
With him, I could tell you, Sir, that he was much to
blame.

PROSPERO: Hah! was he to blame?
Tell me, with that sincerity I taught you, how you became
so bold to see the man.

DORINDA: I hope you will forgive me, Sir, because I did
not see him much till he saw me. Sir, he would needs
come in my way, and star'd, and star'd upon my face; and 60

so I thought I would be reveng'd of him, and therefore I
gaz'd on him as long; but if I e're come neer a man
again—

PROSPERO: I told you he was dangerous; but you would
not be warn'd.

DORINDA: Pray be not angry, Sir, if I tell you, you are
mistaken in him; for he did me no great hurt.

PROSPERO: But he may do you more harm hereafter.

DORINDA: No, Sir, I'm as well as e're I was in all my life,
But that I cannot eat nor drink for thought of him.
That dangerous man runs ever in my mind.                    70

PROSPERO: The way to cure you, is no more to see him.

DORINDA: Nay, pray, Sir, say not so; I promis'd him
To see him once agen; and you know, Sir,
You charg'd me I should never break my promise.

PROSPERO: Wou'd you see him who did you so much
mischief?

DORINDA: I warrant you I did him as much harm as he did
me,
For when I left him, Sir, he sigh'd so as it griev'd
My heart to hear him.

PROSPERO: Those sighs were poysonous, they infected
you:
You say they griev'd you to the heart.                      80

DORINDA: 'Tis true; but yet his looks and words were
gentle.

PROSPERO: These are the Day-dreams of a maid in love,
But still I fear the worst.

DORINDA: O fear not him, Sir,
I know he will not hurt you for my sake;
I'le undertake to tye him to a hair,
And lead him hither as my Pris'ner to you.

PROSPERO: Take heed, Dorinda, you may be deceiv'd;
This Creature is of such a Salvage race,
That no mild usage can reclaim his wildness;
But, like a Lyon's whelp bred up by hand,                   90
When least you look for't, Nature will present
The Image of his Fathers bloody Paws,

Wherewith he purvey'd* for his couching Queen;
And he will leap into his native fury.

DORINDA: He cannot change from what I left him, Sir.

PROSPERO: You speak of him with too much passion; tell
me
(And on your duty tell me true, *Dorinda*)
What past betwixt you and that horrid creature?

DORINDA: How, horrid, Sir? if any else but you should call
it so,                                                             100
Indeed I should be angry.

PROSPERO: Go to! you are a foolish Girl; but answer to
what I ask, what thought you when you saw it?

DORINDA: At first it star'd upon me and seem'd wild,
And then I trembled; yet it look'd so lovely, that when
I would have fled away, my feet seem'd fasten'd to the
ground;
Then it drew near, and with amazement askt
To touch my hand; which, as a ransom for my life,
I gave: but when he had it, with a furious gripe
He put it to his mouth so eagerly, I was afraid he                 110
Would have swallow'd it.

PROSPERO: Well, what was his behaviour afterwards?

DORINDA: He on a sudden grew so tame and gentle,
That he became more kind to me than you are;
Then, Sir, I grew I know not how, and touching his hand
Agen, my heart did beat so strong as I lackt breath
To answer what he ask'd.

PROSPERO: You have been too fond, and I should chide
you for it.

DORINDA: Then send me to that creature to be punisht.

PROSPERO: Poor Child! thy passion like a lazy Ague              120
Has seiz'd thy blood, instead of striving thou humour'st
And feed'st thy languishing disease; thou fight'st
The Battels of thy Enemy, and 'tis one part of what
I threatn'd thee, not to perceive thy danger.

DORINDA: Danger, Sir?
If he would hurt me, yet he knows not how:
He hath no Claws, nor Teeth, nor Horns to hurt me,

But looks about him like a Callow-bird
Just straggl'd from the Nest: pray trust me, Sir,
To go to him agen.                                          130

PROSPERO: Since you will venture,
I charge you bear your self reserv'dly to him,
Let him not dare to touch your naked hand,
But keep at distance from him.

DORINDA: This is hard.

PROSPERO: It is the way to make him love you more;
He will despise you if you grow too kind.

DORINDA: I'le struggle with my heart to follow this,
But if I lose him by it, will you promise
To bring him back agen?                                     140

PROSPERO: Fear not, *Dorinda*;
But use him ill and he'l be yours for ever.

DORINDA: I hope you have not couzen'd me agen.

[*Exit* DORINDA]

PROSPERO: Now my designs are gathering to a head.
My spirits are obedient to my charms.
What, *Ariel*! my servant *Ariel*, where art thou?

*Enter* ARIEL

ARIEL: What wou'd my potent Master? here I am.

PROSPERO: Thou and thy meaner fellows your last service
Did worthily perform, and I must use you in such another
Work: how goes the day?[20]                                 150

ARIEL: On the fourth, my Lord, and on the sixth you said
our work should cease.

PROSPERO: And so it shall;[21]
And thou shalt have the open air at freedom.

ARIEL: Thanks my great Lord.

PROSPERO: But tell me first, my spirit,
How fares the Duke, my Brother, and their followers?

ARIEL: Confin'd together, as you gave me order,
In the Lime-Grove which weather-fends your Cell;
Within that Circuit up and down they wander,                160
But cannot stir one step beyond their compass.

[20] 147–50: IV.i.33–6: 'What, Ariel! . . . such another trick.'
[21] 150–3: V.i.3–4: 'How's the day? . . should cease.'

PROSPERO: How do they bear their sorrows?

ARIEL: The two Dukes appear like men distracted, their
 Attendants brim-full of sorrow mourning over 'em;
 But chiefly, he you term'd *the good Gonzalo*:
 His tears run down his Beard, like Winter-drops
 From Eaves of Reeds; your Vision did so work 'em,
 That if you now beheld 'em, your affections
 Would become tender.

PROSPERO: Dost thou think so, Spirit?                    170

ARIEL: Mine would, Sir, were I humane.

PROSPERO: And mine shall:
 Hast thou, who art but air, a touch, a feeling of their
 Afflictions, and shall not I (a man like them, one
 Who as sharply relish passions as they) be kindlier
 Mov'd than thou art? though they have pierc'd
 Me to the quick with injuries, yet with my nobler
 Reason 'gainst my fury I will take part;
 The rarer action is in virtue than in vengeance.[22]
 Go, my *Ariel*, refresh with needful food their                    180
 Famish'd bodies. With shows and cheerful
 Musick comfort 'em.

ARIEL: Presently, Master.

PROSPERO: With a twinckle, *Ariel*.

ARIEL: Before you can say *come* and *go*,
 And breath twice, and cry *so, so,*
 Each spirit tripping on his toe,
 Shall bring 'em meat with mop and moe;
 Do you love me, Master, I, or no?

PROSPERO: Dearly, my dainty *Ariel*, but stay, spirit;[23]                    190
 What is become of my Slave *Caliban*,
 And *Sycorax* his Sister?

ARIEL: Potent Sir!
 They have cast off your service, and revolted
 To the wrack'd Mariners, who have already
 Parcell'd your Island into Governments.

PROSPERO: No matter, I have now no need of 'em;

[22] 156–79: V.i.6–27: 'Say, my spirit ... than in vengeance.'
[23] 183–190: IV.i.41–49: 'Presently? ... my delicate Ariel.'

But, spirit, now I stay thee on the Wing;
Haste to perform what I have given in charge:
But see they keep within the bounds I set 'em.                    200

ARIEL: I'le keep 'em in with Walls of Adamant,
Invisible as air to mortal Eyes,
But yet unpassable.

PROSPERO: Make hast then.                    [*Exeunt severally*]


## Scene ii

### *Enter* ALONZO, ANTONIO, GONZALO

GONZALO: I am weary, and can go no further, Sir;
My old Bones ake: here's a Maze trod indeed
Through forth-rights and Meanders:* by your patience
I needs must rest.

ALONZO: Old Lord, I cannot blame thee, who am my self
    seiz'd
With a weariness to the dulling of my Spirits:
Sit and rest.                    (*They sit*)
Even here I will put off my hope, and keep it no longer
For my Flatterers: he is drown'd whom thus we
Stray to find, and the Sea mocks our frustrate                    10
Search on Land: well! let him go.

ANTONIO: Do not for one repulse forego the purpose
Which you resolv'd t'effect.[24]

ALONZO: I'm faint with hunger, and must despair
Of food, Heav'n hath incens'd the Seas and
Shores against us for our crimes.                    (*Musick*)
What! Harmony agen, my good friends, heark!

ANTONIO: I fear some other horrid apparition.
Give us kind Keepers, Heaven I beseech thee!

GONZALO: 'Tis chearful Musick, this, unlike the first;                    20
And seems as 'twere meant t'unbend our cares,
And calm your troubled thoughts.

---

[24] 1-13: III.iii.1-11: 'I can go ... resolv'd t'effect.'

ARIEL *invisible Sings*

*Dry those eyes which are o'reflowing,*
*All your storms are over-blowing:*
*While you in this Isle are bideing,*
*You shall feast without providing:*
*Every dainty you can think of,*
*Ev'ry Wine which you would drink of,*
*Shall be yours; all want shall shun you,*
*Ceres blessing so is on you.*                           30

ALONZO: This voice speaks comfort to us.

ANTONIO: Wou'd 'twere come; there is no Musick in a
    Song
To me, my stomack being empty.

GONZALO: O for a heavenly Vision of Boyl'd,
    Bak'd, and Roasted!

*Enter eight fat Spirits,* with Cornu-Copia *in their hands*

ALONZO: Are these plump shapes sent to deride our
    hunger?

GONZALO: No, no; it is a Masque of fatten'd Devils, the
    Burgo-Masters* of the lower Region.(*Dance and vanish*)
    O for a Collop of that large-haunch'd Devil
    Who went out last!                                   40

ANTONIO (*going to the door*): My Lord, the Duke, see
    yonder.
    A Table, as I live, set out and furnisht
    With all varieties of Meats and fruits.

ALONZO: 'Tis so indeed, but who dares tast this feast,
    Which Fiends provide, perhaps, to poyson us?

GONZALO: Why that dare I; if the black Gentleman be so
    ill-natur'd, he may do his pleasure.

ANTONIO: 'Tis certain we must either eat or famish,
    I will encounter it, and feed.

ALONZO: If both resolve, I will adventure too.          50

GONZALO: Then good my Lord, make haste,
    And say no Grace before it, I beseech you,
    Because the meat will vanish strait, if, as I fear,
    An evil Spirit be our Cook.              [*Exeunt*]

## Scene iii

*Enter* TRINCALO *and* CALIBAN

TRINCALO: Brother Monster, welcome to my private Palace.

But where's thy Sister, is she so brave a Lass?

CALIBAN: In all this Isle there are but two more, the Daughters of the Tyrant *Prospero*; and she is bigger than 'em both. O here she comes; now thou may'st judge thy self, my Lord.

*Enter* SYCORAX

TRINCALO: She's monstrous fair indeed. Is this to be my Spouse? well, she's Heir of all this Isle (for I will geld Monster). The *Trincalos*, like other wise men, have anciently us'd to marry for Estate more than for beauty.

*(Aside)*

SYCORAX: I prithee let me have the gay thing about thy neck, and that which dangles at thy wrist.

(SYCORAX *points to his Bosens Whistle, and his Bottle*)

TRINCALO: My dear Blobber-lips; this, observe my Chuck, is a badge of my Sea-Office; my fair Fuss, thou dost not know it.

SYCORAX: No, my dread Lord.

TRINCALO: It shall be a Whistle for our first Babe, and when the next Shipwrack puts me again to swimming, I'le dive to get a Coral to it.

SYCORAX: I'le be thy pretty child, and wear it first.

TRINCALO: I prithee sweet Babby, do not play the wanton, and cry for my goods e're I'm dead. When thou art my Widow, thou shalt have the Devil and all.

SYCORAX: May I not have the other fine thing?

TRINCALO: This is a sucking-Bottle for young *Trincalo*.

CALIBAN: This is a God-a-mighty liquor, I did but drink thrice of it, and it hath made me glad e're since.

SYCORAX: He is the bravest God I ever saw.

CALIBAN: You must be kind to him, and he will love you.

I prithee speak to her, my Lord, and come neerer her.

TRINCALO: By this light, I dare not till I have drank: I must
Fortifie my stomack first.                                    30

SYCORAX: I shall have all his fine things when I'm a
Widow.

           (*Pointing to his Bottle, and Bosens Whistle*)

CALIBAN: I, but you must be kind and kiss him then.

TRINCALO: My Brother Monster is a rare Pimp.  (*Aside*)

SYCORAX: I'le hug thee in my arms, my Brother's God.

TRINCALO: Think o' thy soul *Trincalo*, thou art a dead
man if this kindness continue.

CALIBAN: And he shall get thee a young *Sycorax*. Wilt thou
not, my Lord?

TRINCALO: Indeed I know not how, they do no such thing
in my Country.                                                40

SYCORAX: I'le shew thee how: thou shalt get me twenty
*Sycoraxes*; and I'le get thee twenty *Calibans*.

TRINCALO: Nay, if they are got, she must do't all her self,
that's certain.

SYCORAX: And we will tumble in cool Plashes,* and the
soft Fens,
Where we will make us Pillows of Flags and Bull-rushes.

CALIBAN: My Lord, she would be loving to thee, and thou
wilt not let her.

TRINCALO: Ev'ry thing in its season, Brother Monster; but
you must counsel her; fair Maids must not be too
forward.                                                      50

SYCORAX: My Brother's God, I love thee; prithee let me
come to thee.

TRINCALO: Subject Monster, I charge thee keep the Peace
between us.

CALIBAN: Shall she not taste of that immortal Liquor?

TRINCALO: Umph! that's another question: for if she be
thus flipant* in her Water, what will she be in her
Wine?

*Enter* ARIEL *(invisible) and changes the Bottle which
stands upon the ground*

ARIEL: There's Water for your Wine.          [*Exit* ARIEL]

TRINCALO: Well! since it must be so.

*(Gives her the Bottle)*

How do you like it now, my Queen that                    60
Must be?                                *(She drinks)*

SYCORAX: Is this your heavenly liquor? I'le bring you to a
River of the same.

TRINCALO: Wilt thou so, Madam Monster? what a mighty
Prince shall I be then! I would not change my Dukedom
to be great Turk *Trincalo*.

SYCORAX: This is the drink of Frogs.

TRINCALO: Nay, if the Frogs of this Island drink such, they
are the merryest Frogs in Christendom.

CALIBAN: She does not know the virtue of this liquor:          70
I prithee let me drink for her.

TRINCALO: Well said, Subject Monster. (CALIBAN *drinks*)

CALIBAN: My Lord, this is meer water.

TRINCALO: 'Tis thou hast chang'd the Wine then, and
    drunk it up,
Like a debauch'd Fish as thou art. Let me see't,
I'le taste it my self. Element! meer Element! as I live.
It was a cold gulp such as this which kill'd my famous
Predecessor, old *Simon* the King.*

CALIBAN: How does thy honour? prithee be not angry, and
I will lick thy shoe.                                      80

TRINCALO: I could find in my heart to turn thee out of my
Dominions for a liquorish Monster.

CALIBAN: O my Lord, I have found it out; this must be
done by one of *Prospero*'s spirits.

TRINCALO: There's nothing but malice in these Devils, I
never lov'd 'em from my Childhood. The Devil take 'em, I
would it had bin holy-water for their sakes.

SYCORAX: Will not thy mightiness revenge our wrongs, on
this great Sorcerer? I know thou wilt, for thou art valiant.

TRINCALO: In my Sack, Madam Monster, as any flesh
alive.                                                    90

SYCORAX: Then I will cleave to thee.

TRINCALO: Lovingly said, in troth: now cannot I hold out

against her. This Wife-like virtue of hers, has overcome
me.

SYCORAX: Shall I have thee in my arms?

TRINCALO: Thou shalt have Duke *Trincalo* in thy arms:
But prithee be not too boistrous with me at first;
Do not discourage a young beginner.    (*They embrace*)
Stand to your Arms, my Spouse,
And subject Monster;
     *Enter* STEPHANO, MUSTACHO, *and* VENTOSO
The Enemy is come to surprise us in our Quarters.    100
You shall know, Rebels, that I'm marry'd to a Witch,
And we have a thousand Spirits of our party.

STEPHANO: Hold! I ask a Truce; I and my Vice-Roys
(Finding no food, and but a small remainder of Brandy)
Are come to treat a peace betwixt us,
Which may be for the good of both Armies,
Therefore *Trincalo* disband.

TRINCALO: Plain *Trincalo*, methinks I might have been a
Duke in your mouth, I'le not accept of your Embassy
without my title.

STEPHANO: A title shall break no squares betwixt us.    110
Vice-Roys, give him his stile of Duke, and treat with him,
Whilst I walk by in state.
(Ventoso *and* Mustacho *bow whilst* Trincalo *puts on his Cap*)

MUSTACHO: Our Lord and Master, Duke *Stephano*, has
    sent us
In the first place to demand of you, upon what
Ground you make war against him, having no right
To Govern here, as being elected only by
Your own voice.

TRINCALO: To this I answer, that having in the face of the
    world
Espous'd the lawful Inheritrix of this Island,
Queen *Blouze* the first, and having homage done me,    120
By this hectoring Spark her Brother, from these two
I claim a lawful Title to this Island.

MUSTACHO: Who, that Monster? he a Hector?

CALIBAN: Lo! how he mocks me, wilt thou let him, my Lord?

VENTOSO: *Lord!* quoth he: the Monster's a very natural.

SYCORAX: Lo! lo! agen; bite him to death I prithee.

TRINCALO: Vice-Roys! keep good tongues in your heads I advise you, and proceed to your business, for I have Other affairs to dispatch of more importance betwixt Queen Slobber-Chops and my self.                                130

MUSTACHO: First and foremost, as to your claim that you have answer'd.

VENTOSO: But second and foremost, we demand of you, That if we make a peace, the Butt also may be Comprehended in the Treaty.

MUSTACHO: Is the Butt safe, Duke *Trincalo?*

TRINCALO: The Butt is partly safe: but to comprehend it in the Treaty, or indeed to make any Treaty, I cannot, with my honour, without your submission. These two, and the Spirits under me, stand likewise upon their honours.     140

CALIBAN: Keep the liquor for us, my Lord, and let them drink Brine, for I will not show 'em the quick freshes* of the Island.

STEPHANO: I understand, being present, from my Embassadors what your resolution is, and ask an hours time of deliberation, and so I take our leave; but first I desire to be entertain'd at your Butt, as becomes a Prince, and his Embassadors.

TRINCALO: That I refuse, till acts of Hostility be ceas'd. These Rogues are rather Spies than Embassadors; I must take heed of my Butt. They come to pry Into the secrets of my Dukedom.                                  150

VENTOSO: *Trincalo* you are a barbarous Prince, and so farewel.

[*Exeunt* STEPHANO, MUSTACHO, VENTOSO]

TRINCALO: Subject Monster! stand you Sentry before my Cellar; my Queen and I will enter and feast our selves within.

SYCORAX: May I not marry that other King and his two subjects, to help you anights?

TRINCALO: What a careful Spouse have I! well! if she does
   Cornute* me, the care is taken.
   When underneath my power my foes have truckl'd,
   To be a Prince, who would not be a Cuckold? [*Exeunt*]

## Scene iv

*Enter* FERDINAND, *and* ARIEL *(invisible)*

FERDINAND: How far will this invisible Musician conduct
   My steps? he hovers still about me, whether
   For good or ill I cannot tell, nor care I much;
   For I have been so long a slave to chance, that
   I'm as weary of her flatteries as her frowns:
   But here I am—
ARIEL: Here I am.
FERDINAND: Hah! art thou so? the Spirit's turn'd an
      Eccho:
   This might seem pleasant, could the burthen of my
   Griefs accord with any thing but sighs.                    10
   And my last words, like those of dying men,
   Need no reply. Fain I would go to shades, where
   Few would wish to follow me.
ARIEL: Follow me.
FERDINAND: This evil Spirit grows importunate,
   But I'le not take his counsel.
ARIEL: Take his counsel.
FERDINAND: It may be the Devil's counsel. I'le never take
   it.
ARIEL: Take it.
FERDINAND: I will discourse no more with thee,            20
   Nor follow one step further.
ARIEL: One step further.
FERDINAND: This must have more importance than an
      Eccho.
   Some Spirit tempts to a precipice.
   I'le try if it will answer when I sing

My sorrows to the murmurs of this Brook.
                    (*He Sings*)*
                Go thy way.
ARIEL:          Go thy way.
FERDINAND:      Why should'st thou stay?
ARIEL:          Why should'st thou stay?                    30
FERDINAND: Where the Winds whistle, and where the
    streams creep,
    Under yond Willow-tree, fain would I sleep.
                Then let me alone,
                For 'tis time to be gone.
ARIEL:          For 'tis time to be gone.
FERDINAND: What cares or pleasures can be in this Isle?
    Within this desart place
    There lives no humane race;
Fate cannot frown here, nor kind fortune smile.
ARIEL: Kind Fortune smiles, and she                        40
            Has yet in store for thee
            Some strange felicity.
            Follow me, follow me,
            And thou shalt see.
FERDINAND: I'le take thy word for once;
    Lead on Musician.                    [*Exeunt and return*]


## Scene v

*Scene changes, and discovers* PROSPERO *and* MIRANDA

PROSPERO: Advance the fringed Curtains of thine Eyes,
    and say what thou seest yonder.
MIRANDA: Is it a Spirit?
    Lord! how it looks about! Sir, I confess it carries a brave
    form.
    But 'tis a Spirit.
PROSPERO: No Girl, it eats and sleeps, and has such senses
    as we have. This young Gallant, whom thou see'st, was in
    the wrack; were he not somewhat stain'd with grief

(beauty's worst Cancker) thou might'st call him a goodly
person; he has lost his company, and strays about to find
'em.                                                                              10

MIRANDA: I might call him a thing divine, for nothing
natural I ever saw so noble.

PROSPERO: It goes on as my Soul prompts it.—(*Aside to*
ARIEL) Spirit, fine Spirit, I'le free thee within two days for
this.

FERDINAND: She's sure the Mistress, on whom these airs
attend. Fair Excellence, if, as your form declares, you are
divine, be pleas'd to instruct me how you will be
worship'd; so bright a beauty cannot sure belong to
humane kind.

MIRANDA: I am, like you, a mortal, if such you are.

FERDINAND: My language too! O Heavens! I am the best   20
of them who speak this speech, when I'm in my own
Country.

PROSPERO: How, the best? what wert thou if the Duke of
*Savoy* heard thee?

FERDINAND: As I am now, who wonders to hear thee
speak of *Savoy*: he does hear me, and that he does I weep;
my self am *Savoy*, whose fatal Eyes (e're since at ebbe)
beheld the Duke my Father wrackt.

MIRANDA: Alack! for pity.

PROSPERO: At the first sight they have chang'd Eyes, dear
    *Ariel*,
I'le set thee free for this. (*Aside*)—Young Sir, a word.   30
With hazard of your self you do me wrong.

MIRANDA: Why speaks my Father so urgently?
This is the third man that e're I saw, the first whom
E're I sigh'd for; sweet Heaven move my Father
To be inclin'd my way.

FERDINAND: O! if a Virgin! and your affection not gone
    forth,
I'le make you Mistress of *Savoy*.

PROSPERO: Soft, Sir! one word more.
    (*Aside*) They are in each others powers, but this swift
Bus'ness I must uneasie make, lest too light               40

Winning make the prize light.—One word more.
Thou usurp'st the name not due to thee, and hast
Put thy self upon this Island as a spy to get the
Government from me, the Lord of it.

FERDINAND: No, as I'm a man.

MIRANDA: There's nothing ill can dwell in such a Temple;
If th' Evil Spirit hath so fair a house,
Good things will strive to dwell with it.

PROSPERO: No more. Speak not you for him, he's a
Traytor.

Come! thou art my Pris'ner and shalt be in          50
Bonds. Sea-water shalt thou drink, thy food
Shall be the fresh-Brook-Muscles, wither'd Roots,
And Husks, wherein the Acorn cradl'd; follow.

FERDINAND: No, I will resist such entertainment
Till my Enemy has more power.

*(He draws, and is charm'd from moving)*

MIRANDA: O dear Father! make not too rash a tryal
Of him, for he's gentle and not fearful.

PROSPERO: My child my Tutor! put thy Sword up, Traytor,

Who mak'st a show, but dar'st not strike: thy
Conscience is possest with guilt. Come from          60
Thy Ward, for I can here disarm thee with
This Wand, and make thy Weapon drop.

MIRANDA: 'Beseech you, Father.

PROSPERO: Hence: hang not on my Garment.

MIRANDA: Sir, have pity,
I'le be his Surety.

PROSPERO: Silence! one word more shall make me chide
thee.

If not hate thee: what, an advocate for an
Impostor? sure thou think'st there are no more
Such shapes as his?                                 70
To the most of men this is a *Caliban*,
And they to him are Angels.

MIRANDA: My affections are then most humble,
I have no ambition to see a goodlier man.

PROSPERO: Come on, obey:
  Thy Nerves are in their infancy agen, and have
  No vigour in them.
FERDINAND: So they are:
  My Spirits, as in a Dream, are all bound up:
  My Father's loss, the weakness which I feel,                    80
  The wrack of all my friends, and this man's threats,
  To whom I am subdu'd, would seem light to me,
  Might I but once a day through my Prison behold this
    maid:
  All corners else o'th' Earth let liberty make use of:
  I have space enough in such a Prison.
PROSPERO: (aside) It works.—(To FERDINAND) Come on.
  Thou hast done well, fine Ariel.——(To FERDINAND)
    Follow me.
  Heark what thou shalt more do for me.  (Whispers ARIEL)
MIRANDA: Be of comfort!
  My Father's of a better nature, Sir,                    90
  Than he appears by speech: this is unwonted
  Which now came from him.
PROSPERO: Thou shalt be as free as Mountain Winds:
  But then exactly do all points of my command.
ARIEL: To a Syllable.                    [Exit ARIEL]
PROSPERO (to MIRANDA): Go in that way, speak not a
  word for him:[25]
  I'le separate you.                    [Exit MIRANDA]
FERDINAND: As soon thou may'st divide the waters
  When thou strik'st 'em, which pursue thy bootless blow,
  And meet when 'tis past.                    100
PROSPERO: Go practise your Philosophy within,
  And if you are the same you speak your self,
  Bear your afflictions like a Prince.—That Door
  Shews you your Lodging.
FERDINAND: 'Tis in vain to strive, I must obey.
                    [Exit FERDINAND]
PROSPERO: This goes as I would wish it.

[25] 1–96: I.ii.411–504 (with changes of phrasing).

Now for my second care, *Hippolito*.
I shall not need to chide him for his fault,
His passion is become his punishment.
Come forth, *Hippolito*.                                        110

*Enter* HIPPOLITO

HIPPOLITO (*entring*): 'Tis *Prospero*'s voice.

PROSPERO: *Hippolito!* I know you now expect I should
severely chide you: you have seen a woman in contempt
of my commands.

HIPPOLITO: But, Sir, you see I am come off unharm'd;
I told you, that you need not doubt my courage.

PROSPERO: You think you have receiv'd no hurt.

HIPPOLITO: No, none Sir.
Try me agen, when e're you please I'm ready:
I think I cannot fear an Army of 'em.                           120

PROSPERO: How much in vain it is to bridle Nature! (*Aside*)
Well! what was the success of your encounter?

HIPPOLITO: Sir, we had none, we yielded both at first,
For I took her to mercy, and she me.

PROSPERO: But are you not much chang'd from what you
were?

HIPPOLITO: Methinks I wish and wish! for what I know
not,
But still I wish.—Yet if I had that woman,
She, I believe, could tell me what I wish for.

PROSPERO: What wou'd you do to make that Woman
yours?

HIPPOLITO: I'd quit the rest o'th' world that I might live
alone with
Her, she never should be from me.                              130
We two would sit and look till our eyes ak'd.

PROSPERO: You'd soon be weary of her.

HIPPOLITO: O, Sir, never.

PROSPERO: But you'l grow old and wrinckl'd, as you see
me now,
And then you will not care for her.

HIPPOLITO: You may do what you please, but, Sir we two
can never possibly grow old.

PROSPERO: You must, *Hippolito*.

HIPPOLITO: Whether we will or no, Sir, who shall make
us?                                                                    140

PROSPERO: Nature, which made me so.

HIPPOLITO: But you have told me her works are various;
She made you old, but she has made us young.

PROSPERO: Time will convince you,
Mean while be sure you tread in honours paths,
That you may merit her, and that you may not want
Fit occasions to employ your virtue: in this next
Cave there is a stranger lodg'd, one of your kind,
Young, of a noble presence, and as he says himself,
Of Princely birth; he is my Pris'ner and in deep         150
Affliction: visit, and comfort him; it will become you.

HIPPOLITO: It is my duty, Sir.          [*Exit* HIPPOLITO]

PROSPERO: True, he has seen a woman, yet he lives;
perhaps I took the moment of his birth amiss, perhaps my
Art it self is false: on what strange grounds we build our
hopes and fears; mans life is all a mist, and in the dark,
our fortunes meet us.
If Fate be not, then what can we foresee,
Or how can we avoid it, if it be?
If by free-will in our own paths we move,
How are we bounded by Decrees above?                      160
Whether we drive, or whether we are driven,
If ill 'tis ours, if good the act of Heaven.
                                                          [*Exit* PROSPERO]


# Scene vi

### *Scene, a Cave*

#### Enter HIPPOLITO *and* FERDINAND

FERDINAND: Your pity, noble youth, doth much oblige
me,
Indeed 'twas sad to lose a Father so.

HIPPOLITO: I, and an only Father too, for sure you said

You had but one.

FERDINAND: But one Father! he's wondrous simple!

(*Aside*)

HIPPOLITO: Are such misfortunes frequent in your world,
Where many men live?

FERDINAND: Such we are born to.
But gentle youth, as you have question'd me,
So give me leave to ask you, what you are.     10

HIPPOLITO: Do not you know?

FERDINAND: How should I?

HIPPOLITO: I well hop'd I was a man, but by your ignorance
Of what I am, I fear it is not so.
Well, *Prospero*! this is now the second time     (*Aside*)
You have deceiv'd me.

FERDINAND: Sir, there is no doubt you are a man:
But I would know of whence?

HIPPOLITO: Why, of this world; I never was in yours.

FERDINAND: Have you a Father?     20

HIPPOLITO: I was told I had one, and that he was a man,
yet I have bin so much deceived, I dare not tell't you for a
truth; but I have still been kept a Prisoner for fear of
women.

FERDINAND: They indeed are dangerous, for since I came I
have beheld one here, whose beauty pierc'd my heart.

HIPPOLITO: How did she pierce? you seem not hurt.

FERDINAND: Alas! the wound was made by her bright eyes,
And festers by her absence.
But to speak plainer to you, Sir, I love her.

HIPPOLITO: Now I suspect that love's the very thing, that I     30
feel too! pray tell me truly, Sir, are you not grown unquiet
since you saw her?

FERDINAND: I take no rest.

HIPPOLITO: Just, just my disease.
Do you not wish you do not know for what?

FERDINAND: O no! I know too well for what I wish.

HIPPOLITO: There, I confess, I differ from you, Sir:

But you desire she may be always with you?

FERDINAND: I can have no felicity without her.

HIPPOLITO: Just my condition! alas, gentle Sir, 40
I'le pity you and you shall pity me.

FERDINAND: I love so much, that if I have her not,
I find I cannot live.

HIPPOLITO: How! do you love her?
And would you have her too? that must not be:
For none but I must have her.

FERDINAND: But perhaps, we do not love the same:
All beauties are not pleasing alike to all.

HIPPOLITO: Why, are there more fair Women, Sir,
Besides that one I love? 50

FERDINAND: That's a strange question. There are many
more besides that beauty which you love.

HIPPOLITO: I will have all of that kind, if there be a
hundred of 'em.

FERDINAND: But noble youth, you know not what you say.

HIPPOLITO: Sir, they are things I love, I cannot be without
'em:
O, how I rejoyce! more women!

FERDINAND: Sir, if you love you must be ty'd to one.

HIPPOLITO: Ty'd! how ty'd to her?

FERDINAND: To love none but her.

HIPPOLITO: But, Sir, I find it is against my Nature. 60
I must love where I like, and I believe I may like all,
All that are fair: come! bring me to this Woman,
For I must have her.

FERDINAND: His simplicity
Is such that I can scarce be angry with him. *(Aside)*
Perhaps, sweet youth, when you behold her,
You will find you do not love her.

HIPPOLITO: I find already I love, because she is another
Woman.

FERDINAND: You cannot love two women, both at once.

HIPPOLITO: Sure 'tis my duty to love all who do resemble 70
Her whom I've already seen. I'le have as many as I can,
That are so good, and Angel-like, as she I love.

And will have yours.

FERDINAND: Pretty youth, you cannot.

HIPPOLITO: I can do any thing for that I love.

FERDINAND: I may, perhaps, by force restrain you from it.

HIPPOLITO: Why, do so if you can. But either promise me
To love no Woman, or you must try your force.

FERDINAND: I cannot help it, I must love.

HIPPOLITO: Well, you may love, for *Prospero* taught me     80
friendship too: you shall love me and other men if you can
find 'em, but all the Angel-women shall be mine.

FERDINAND: I must break off this conference, or he will
Urge me else beyond what I can bear.
Sweet youth! some other time we will speak
Further concerning both our loves; at present
I am indispos'd with weariness and grief,
And would, if you are pleas'd, retire a while.

HIPPOLITO: Some other time be it; but, Sir, remember
That I both seek and much intreat your friendship,     90
For next to Women, I find I can love you.

FERDINAND: I thank you, Sir, I will consider of it.

                                        [*Exit* FERDINAND]

HIPPOLITO: This Stranger does insult and comes into my
World to take those heavenly beauties from me,
Which I believe I am inspir'd to love,
And yet he said he did desire but one.
He would be poor in love, but I'le be rich:
I now perceive that *Prospero* was cunning;
For when he frighted me from woman-kind,
Those precious things he for himself design'd.     [*Exit*]  100

# ACT IV

# Scene i

*Enter* PROSPERO, *and* MIRANDA

PROSPERO: Your suit has pity in't, and has prevail'd.
Within this Cave he lies, and you may see him:
But yet take heed; let Prudence be your Guide;
You must not stay, your visit must be short.   (*She's going*)
One thing I had forgot; insinuate into his mind
A kindness to that youth, whom first you saw;
I would have friendship grow betwixt 'em.

MIRANDA: You shall be obey'd in all things.

PROSPERO: Be earnest to unite their very souls.

MIRANDA: I shall endeavour it.                                    10

PROSPERO: This may secure *Hippolito* from that dark
danger which my art forebodes; for friendship does
provide a double strength t'oppose th' assaults of fortune.

[*Exit* PROSPERO]

*Enter* FERDINAND

FERDINAND: To be a Pris'ner where I dearly love, is but a
double tye; a Link of fortune joyn'd to the chain of love;
but not to see her, and yet to be so near her, there's the
hardship; I feel my self as on a Rack, stretch'd out, and
nigh the ground, on which I might have ease, yet cannot
reach it.

MIRANDA: Sir! my Lord? where are you?

FERDINAND: Is it your voice, my Love? or do I dream?           20

MIRANDA: Speak softly, it is I.

FERDINAND: O heavenly Creature! ten times more gentle,
than your Father's cruel, how on a sudden all my griefs
are vanish'd!

MIRANDA: I come to help you to support your griefs.

FERDINAND: While I stand gazing thus, and thus have leave to touch your hand, I do not envy freedom.

MIRANDA: Heark! heark! is't not my Father's voice I hear? I fear he calls me back again too soon.

FERDINAND: Leave fear to guilty minds: 'tis scarce a virtue when it is paid to Heaven.                                                30

MIRANDA: But there 'tis mix'd with love, and so is mine; yet I may fear, for I am guilty when I disobey my Fathers will in loving you too much.

FERDINAND: But you please Heav'n in disobeying him, Heav'n bids you succour Captives in distress.

MIRANDA: How do you bear your Prison?

FERDINAND: 'Tis my Palace while you are here, and love and silence wait upon our wishes; do but think we chuse it, and 'tis what we would chuse.

MIRANDA: I'm sure what I would.                                                40
But how can I be certain that you love me?
Look to't; for I will dye when you are false.
I've heard my Father tell of Maids, who dy'd,
And haunted their false Lovers with their Ghosts.

FERDINAND: Your Ghost must take another form to fright me,
This shape will be too pleasing: do I love you?
O Heav'n! O Earth! bear witness to this sound,
If I prove false—[26]

MIRANDA: Oh hold, you shall not swear;
For Heav'n will hate you if you prove forsworn.                                                50

FERDINAND: Did I not love, I could no more endure this undeserved captivity, than I could wish to gain my freedom with the loss of you.

MIRANDA: I am a fool to weep at what I'm glad of:[27] but I have a suit to you, and that, Sir, shall be now the only tryal of your love.

FERDINAND: Y'ave said enough, never to be deny'd, were it my life; for you have far o'rebid the price of all that humane life is worth.

[26] 47-8: III.i.66-7.
[27] 54: III.i.72-3: 'I am a fool . . . glad of.'

MIRANDA: Sir, 'tis to love one for my sake, who for his 60
own deserves all the respect which you can ever pay him.

FERDINAND: You mean your Father: do not think his
usage can make me hate him; when he gave you being, he
then did that which cancell'd all these wrongs.

MIRANDA: I meant not him, for that was a request which if
you love I should not need to urge.

FERDINAND: Is there another whom I ought to love?
And love him for your sake?

MIRANDA: Yes, such a one, who for his sweetness and his
goodly shape, (if I, who am unskill'd in forms, may judge) 70
I think can scarce be equall'd: 'Tis a youth, a Stranger too
as you are.

FERDINAND: Of such a graceful feature, and must I for
your sake love?

MIRANDA: Yes, Sir, do you scruple to grant the first request
I ever made? he's wholly unacquainted with the world,
and wants your conversation.* You should have compassion on so meer a stranger.

FERDINAND: Those need compassion whom you discom-
mend, not whom you praise.

MIRANDA: I only ask this easie tryal of you. 80

FERDINAND: Perhaps it might have easier bin
If you had never ask'd it.

MIRANDA: I cannot understand you; and methinks am loth
To be more knowing.

FERDINAND: He has his freedom, and may get access,
when my
Confinement makes me want that blessing.
I his compassion need, and not he mine.

MIRANDA: If that be all you doubt, trust me for him.
He has a melting heart, and soft to all the Seals
Of kindness; I will undertake for his compassion. 90

FERDINAND: O Heavens! would I were sure I did not need
it.

MIRANDA: Come, you must love him for my sake: you
shall.

FERDINAND: Must I for yours, and cannot for my own?

Either you do not love, or think that I do not:
But when you bid me love him, I must hate him.

MIRANDA: Have I so far offended you already,
That he offends you only for my sake?
Yet sure you would not hate him, if you saw
Him as I have done, so full of youth and beauty.

FERDINAND: O poyson to my hopes!                                    100
When he did visit me, and I did mention this    (Aside)
Beauteous Creature to him, he did then tell me
He would have her.

MIRANDA: Alas, what mean you?

FERDINAND: (aside) It is too plain: like most of her frail
Sex, she's false,
But has not learnt the art to hide it;
Nature has done her part, she loves variety:
Why did I think that any Woman could be innocent,
Because she's young? No, no, their Nurses teach them
Change, when with two Nipples they divide their        110
Liking.

MIRANDA: I fear I have offended you, and yet I meant no
harm:
But if you please to hear me—        (A noise within)
Heark! Sir! now I am sure my Father comes, I know
His steps; dear Love retire a while, I fear
I've stay'd too long.

FERDINAND: Too long indeed, and yet not long enough: oh
jealousie!
Oh Love! how you distract me!        [Exit FERDINAND]

MIRANDA: He appears displeas'd with that young man, I
know
Not why: but, till I find from whence his hate proceeds, 120
I must conceal it from my Fathers knowledge,
For he will think that guiltless I have caus'd it;
And suffer me no more to see my Love.

                        Enter PROSPERO

PROSPERO: Now I have been indulgent to your wish,
You have seen the Prisoner?

MIRANDA: Yes.

PROSPERO: And he spake to you?

MIRANDA: He spoke; but he receiv'd short answers from me.

PROSPERO: How like you his converse?

MIRANDA: At second sight                    130
A man does not appear so rare a Creature.

PROSPERO: (aside) I find she loves him much because she hides it.

Love teaches cunning even to innocence,
And where he gets possession, his first work is to
Dig deep within a heart, and there lie hid,
And like a Miser in the dark to feast alone.
But tell me, dear *Miranda*, how does he suffer
His imprisonment?

MIRANDA: I think he seems displeas'd.

PROSPERO: O then 'tis plain his temper is not noble,    140
For the brave with equal minds bear good
And evil fortune.

MIRANDA: O, Sir, but he's pleas'd again so soon
That 'tis not worth your noting.

PROSPERO: To be soon displeas'd and pleas'd so suddenly again,
Does shew him of a various froward Nature.

MIRANDA: The truth is, Sir, he was not vex'd at all, but only
Seem'd to be so.

PROSPERO: If he be not and yet seems angry, he is a dissembler,
Which shews the worst of Natures.                    150

MIRANDA: Truly, Sir, the man has faults enough; but in my conscience that's none of 'em. He can be no dissembler.

PROSPERO: (aside) How she excuses him, and yet desires that I should judge her heart indifferent to him!—Well, since his faults are many, I am glad you love him not.

MIRANDA: 'Tis like, Sir, they are many,
But I know none he has, yet let me often see him
And I shall find 'em all in time.

PROSPERO: I'le think on't.

Go in, this is your hour of Orizons.    160

MIRANDA: (aside) Forgive me, truth, for thus disguising
  thee; if I can make him think I do not love the stranger
  much, he'll let me see him oftner.    [Exit MIRANDA]

PROSPERO: Stay! stay—I had forgot to ask her what she
    has said

Of young *Hippolito*: Oh! here he comes! and with him
My *Dorinda*.

    *Enter* HIPPOLITO *and* DORINDA
        I'le not be seen, let

Their loves grow in secret.    [*Exit* PROSPERO]

HIPPOLITO: But why are you so sad?

DORINDA: But why are you so joyful?

HIPPOLITO: I have within me all, all the various Musick of    170
  The Woods. Since last I saw you I have heard brave news!
  I'le tell you, and make you joyful for me.

DORINDA: Sir, when I saw you first, I through my eyes
    drew

Something in, I know not what it is;

But still it entertains me with such thoughts

As makes me doubtful whether joy becomes me.

HIPPOLITO: Pray believe me;

As I'm a man, I'le tell you blessed news.

I have heard there are more Women in the World,

As fair as you are too.    180

DORINDA: Is this your news? you see it moves not me.

HIPPOLITO: And I'le have 'em all.

DORINDA: What will become of me then?

HIPPOLITO: I'le have you too.

But are not you acquainted with these Women?

DORINDA: I never saw but one.

HIPPOLITO: Is there but one here?

This is a base poor world, I'le go to th' other;

I've heard men have abundance of 'em there.

But pray where is that one Woman?    190

DORINDA: Who, my Sister?

HIPPOLITO: Is she your Sister? I'm glad o' that: you shall
  help me to her, and I'le love you for't.

*(Offers to take her hand)*

DORINDA: Away! I will not have you touch my hand.

My Father's counsel which enjoyn'd          *(Aside)*
reservedness,

Was not in vain I see.

HIPPOLITO: What makes you shun me?

DORINDA: You need not care, you'l have my Sisters hand.

HIPPOLITO: Why, must not he who touches hers touch
yours?

DORINDA: You mean to love her too.          200

HIPPOLITO: Do not you love her?

Then why should not I do so?

DORINDA: She is my Sister, and therefore I must love her:

But you cannot love both of us.

HIPPOLITO: I warrant you I can:

Oh that you had more Sisters!

DORINDA: You may love her, but then I'le not love you.

HIPPOLITO: O but you must;

One is enough for you, but not for me.*

DORINDA: My Sister told me she had seen another;          210

A man like you, and she lik'd only him;

Therefore if one must be enough for her,

He is that one, and then you cannot have her.

HIPPOLITO: If she like him, she may like both of us.

DORINDA: But how if I should change and like that man?

Would you be willing to permit that change?

HIPPOLITO: No, for you lik'd me first.

DORINDA: So you did me.

HIPPOLITO: But I would never have you see that man;

I cannot bear it.          220

DORINDA: I'le see neither of you.

HIPPOLITO: Yes, me you may, for we are now acquainted;

But he's the man of whom your Father warn'd you:

O! he's a terrible, huge, monstrous creature,

I am but a Woman to him.

DORINDA: I will see him,

Except you'l promise not to see my Sister.

HIPPOLITO: Yes, for your sake I needs must see your
  Sister.

DORINDA: But she's a terrible, huge Creature too; if I were
  not

Her Sister she would eat me; therefore take heed.          230

HIPPOLITO: I heard that she was fair, and like you.

DORINDA: No, indeed, she's like my Father, with a great
  Beard,

'Twould fright you to look on her,

Therefore that man and she may go together,

They are fit for no body but one another.

HIPPOLITO: (looking in) Yonder he comes with glaring
  eyes, fly! fly!

Before he sees you.

DORINDA: Must we part so soon?

HIPPOLITO: Y'are a lost Woman if you see him.

DORINDA: I would not willingly be lost, for fear you          240
  Should not find me. I'le avoid him.    [Exit DORINDA]

HIPPOLITO: She fain would have deceived me, but I know
  her

Sister must be fair, for she's a Woman;

All of a Kind that I have seen are like to one

Another: all the Creatures of the Rivers and

The Woods are so.

                    Enter FERDINAND

FERDINAND: O! well encounter'd, you are the happy man!
  Y'have got the hearts of both the beauteous Women.

HIPPOLITO: How! Sir? pray, are you sure on't?

FERDINAND: One of 'em charg'd me to love you for her
  sake.                                                        250

HIPPOLITO: Then I must have her.

FERDINAND: No, not till I am dead.

HIPPOLITO: How dead? what's that? but whatsoe're it be
  I long to have her.

FERDINAND: Time and my grief may make me dye.

HIPPOLITO: But for a friend you should make haste; I ne're
  ask'd

Any thing of you before.

FERDINAND: I see your ignorance;
And therefore will instruct you in my meaning.
The Woman, whom I love, saw you and lov'd you.  260
Now, Sir, if you love her you'l cause my death.

HIPPOLITO: Besure I'le do't then.

FERDINAND: But I am your friend;
And I request you that you would not love her.

HIPPOLITO: When friends request unreasonable things,
Sure th'are to be deny'd: you say she's fair,
And I must love all who are fair; for, to tell
You a secret, Sir, which I have lately found
Within my self, they all are made for me.

FERDINAND: That's but a fond conceit: you are made  270
for one, and one for you.

HIPPOLITO: You cannot tell me, Sir.
I know I'm made for twenty hundred Women,
(I mean if there so many be i'th' World)
So that if once I see her I shall love her.

FERDINAND: Then do not see her.

HIPPOLITO: Yes, Sir, I must see her.
For I wou'd fain have my heart beat again,
Just as it did when I first saw her Sister.

FERDINAND: I find I must not let you see her then.  280

HIPPOLITO: How will you hinder me?

FERDINAND: By force of Arms.

HIPPOLITO: By force of Arms?
My Arms perhaps may be as strong as yours.

FERDINAND: He's still so ignorant that I pity him, and fain
Would avoid force. (*Aside*)—Pray, do not see her, she was
Mine first; you have no right to her.

HIPPOLITO: I have not yet consider'd what is right, but,
Sir,
I know my inclinations are to love all Women:
And I have been taught that to disemble what I  290
Think is base. In honour then of truth, I must
Declare that I do love, and I will see your Woman.

FERDINAND: Wou'd you be willing I should see and love
your

Woman, and endeavour to seduce her from that
Affection which she vow'd to you?

HIPPOLITO: I wou'd not you should do it, but if she should
Love you best, I cannot hinder her.
But, Sir, for fear she shou'd, I will provide against
The worst, and try to get your Woman.

FERDINAND: But I pretend no claim at all to yours;    300
Besides you are more beautiful than I,
And fitter to allure unpractis'd hearts.
Therefore I once more beg you will not see her.

HIPPOLITO: I'm glad you let me know I have such beauty.
If that will get me Women, they shall have it
As far as e're 'twill go: I'le never want 'em.

FERDINAND: Then since you have refused this act of
friendship,
Provide your self a Sword; for we must fight.

HIPPOLITO: A Sword, what's that?

FERDINAND: Why such a thing as this.    310

HIPPOLITO: What should I do with it?

FERDINAND: You must stand thus, and push against me,
While I push at you, till one of us fall dead.

HIPPOLITO: This is brave sport,
But we have no Swords growing in our World.

FERDINAND: What shall we do then to decide our quarrel?

HIPPOLITO: We'll take the Sword by turns, and fight with
it.

FERDINAND: Strange ignorance! you must defend your life,
And so must I: but since you have no Sword
Take this; (gives him his sword) for in a corner of my
Cave    320
I found a rusty one, perhaps 'twas his who keeps
Me Pris'ner here: that I will fit:
When next we meet prepare your self to fight.

HIPPOLITO: Make haste then, this shall ne're be yours
agen.
I mean to fight with all the men I meet, and
When they are dead, their Women shall be mine.

FERDINAND: I see you are unskilful; I desire not to take
  Your life, but if you please we'll fight on
  These conditions; He who first draws bloud,
  Or who can take the others Weapon from him,              330
  Shall be acknowledg'd as the Conquerour,
  And both the Women shall be his.
HIPPOLITO: Agreed,
  And ev'ry day I'le fight for two more with you.
FERDINAND: But win these first.
HIPPOLITO: I'le warrant you I'le push you.

                                        [*Exeunt severally*]


## Scene ii

### *Enter* TRINCALO, CALIBAN, SYCORAX

CALIBAN: My Lord, I see 'em coming yonder.
TRINCALO: Who?
CALIBAN: The starv'd Prince, and his two thirsty Subjects,
  That would have our Liquor.
TRINCALO: If thou wert a Monster of parts I would make
    thee
  My Master of Ceremonies, to conduct 'em in.
  The Devil take all Dunces, thou hast lost a brave
  Employment by not being a Linguist, and for want
  Of behaviour.*
SYCORAX: My Lord, shall I go meet 'em? I'le be kind to all    10
    of 'em,
  Just as I am to thee.
TRINCALO: No, that's against the fundamental Laws of my
  Dukedom: you are in a high place, Spouse, and must give
  good Example. Here they come, we'll put on the gravity
  of Statesmen, and be very dull, that we may be held wise.
        *Enter* STEPHANO, VENTOSO, MUSTACHO
VENTOSO: Duke *Trincalo*, we have consider'd.
TRINCALO: Peace, or War?
MUSTACHO: Peace, and the Butt.

STEPHANO: I come now as a private person, and promise
to live peaceably under your Government.                          20

TRINCALO: You shall enjoy the benefits of Peace; and the
first Fruits of it, amongst all civil Nations, is to be drunk
for joy. *Caliban* skink about.*

STEPHANO: I long to have a Rowse to her Graces health,
and to the *Haunse in Kelder*,* or rather Haddock in
*Kelder*, for I guess it will be half Fish.          (*Aside*)

TRINCALO: Subject *Stephano* here's to thee; and let old
quarrels be drown'd in this draught.          (*Drinks*)

STEPHANO: Great Magistrate, here's thy Sisters health to
thee.                                   (*Drinks to* CALIBAN)

SYCORAX: He shall not drink of that immortal liquor,          30
My Lord, let him drink water.

TRINCALO: O sweet heart, you must not shame yourself to
day.
Gentlemen Subjects, pray bear with her good Huswifry:
She wants a little breeding, but she's hearty.

MUSTACHO: *Ventoso* here's to thee. Is it not better to
pierce the Butt, than to quarrel and pierce one anothers
bellies?

VENTOSO: Let it come Boy.

TRINCALO: Now wou'd I lay greatness aside, and shake my
heels, if I had but Musick.

CALIBAN: O my Lord! my Mother left us in her Will a          40
hundred Spirits to attend us, Devils of all sorts, some
great roaring Devils, and some little singing Sprights.

SYCORAX: Shall we call? and thou shalt hear them in the
Air.

TRINCALO: I accept the motion: let us have our Mother-in-
Law's Legacy immediately.

CALIBAN (*sings*):  *We want Musick, we want Mirth,*
                   *Up, Dam, and cleave the Earth,*
                   *We have now no Lords that wrong us,*
                   *Send thy merry Sprights among us.*
                                        (*Musick heard*)

TRINCALO: What a merry Tyrant am I, to have my          50
Musick and pay nothing for't! come, hands, hands,

Let's lose no time while the Devil's in the
Humour.                                    (*A Dance*)

TRINCALO: Enough, enough: now to our Sack agen.

VENTOSO: The Bottle's drunk.

MUSTACHO: Then the Bottle's a weak shallow fellow if it
be drunk first.

TRINCALO: *Caliban*, give Bottle the belly full agen.

                                    [*Exit* CALIBAN]

STEPHANO: May I ask your Grace a question? pray is that
hectoring Spark, ask you call'd him, flesh or fish?          60

TRINCALO: Subject, I know not, but he drinks like a fish.

                    *Enter* CALIBAN

STEPHANO: O here's the Bottle agen; he has made a good
voyage,
Come, who begins a Brindis* to the Duke?

TRINCALO: I'le begin it my self: give me the Bottle; 'tis my
Prerogative to drink first; *Stephano*, give me thy hand,
Thou has been a Rebel, but here's to thee.     (*Drinks*)
Prithee why should we quarrel? shall I swear
Two Oaths? by Bottle, and by Butt I love thee:
In witness whereof I drink soundly.

STEPHANO: Your Grace shall find there's no love lost,        70
For I will pledge you soundly.

TRINCALO: Thou hast been a false Rebel, but that's all one;
Pledge my Grace faithfully.

STEPHANO: I will pledge your Grace *Up se Dutch*.*

TRINCALO: But thou shalt not pledge me before I have
drunk agen; would'st thou take the Liquor of Life out of
my hands? I see thou art a piece of a Rebel still, but here's
to thee. (*Drinks*)—Now thou shalt have it.

                                    (STEPHANO *drinks*)

VENTOSO: We loyal Subjects may be choak'd for any drink
we can get.                                                  80

TRINCALO: Have patience good people, you are unreasonable, you'd be drunk as soon as I. *Ventoso* you shall have
your time, but you must give place to *Stephano*.

MUSTACHO: Brother *Ventoso*, I am afraid we shall lose our

places. The Duke grows fond of *Stephano*, and will
declare him Vice-Roy.

STEPHANO: I ha' done my worst at your Graces Bottle.

TRINCALO: Then the Folks may have it. *Caliban*
Go to the Butt, and tell me how it sounds. [*Exit* CALIBAN]
Peer *Stephano*, dost thou love me?                    90

STEPHANO: I love your Grace and all your Princely Family.

TRINCALO: 'Tis no matter, if thou lov'st me; hang my
Family:
Thou art my Friend, prithee tell me what
Thou think'st of my Princess.

STEPHANO: I look on her as on a very noble Princess.

TRINCALO: Noble? indeed she had a Witch to her Mother,
and the Witches are of great Families in *Lapland*, but the
Devil was her Father, and I have heard of the Mounsor
*De-Viles** in *France*; but look on her beauty, is she a fit
Wife for Duke *Trincalo*? mark her behaviour too, she's  100
tippling yonder with the serving men.

STEPHANO: An please your Grace she's somewhat homely,
but that's no blemish in a Princess. She is virtuous.

TRINCALO: Umph! virtuous! I am loth to disparage her;
But thou art my Friend, canst thou be close?

STEPHANO: As a stopt Bottle, an't please your Grace.

            *Enter* CALIBAN *agen with a Bottle*

TRINCALO: Why then I'le tell thee, I found her an hour ago
under an Elder-tree, upon a sweet Bed of Nettles, singing
Tory, Rory, and Ranthum, Scantum,* with her own
natural Brother.

STEPHANO: O Jew! make love in her own Tribe?*          110

TRINCALO: But 'tis no matter, to tell thee true, I marry'd
her to be a great man and so forth: but make no words
on't, for I care not who knows it, and so here's to thee
agen. Give me the Bottle, *Caliban*! did you knock the
Butt? how does it sound?

CALIBAN: It sounds as though it had a noise within.

TRINCALO: I fear the Butt begins to rattle in the throat and
is departing: give me the Bottle.              (*Drinks*)

MUSTACHO: A short life and a merry I say.

(STEPHANO *whispers* SYCORAX)

SYCORAX: But did he tell you so?

STEPHANO: He said you were as ugly as your Mother, and 120
that he Marry'd you only to get possession of the Island.

SYCORAX: My Mothers Devils fetch him for't.

STEPHANO: And your Fathers too, hem!—(*To* CALIBAN)
Skink about his Graces health agen.—O if you would but
cast an eye of pity upon me—

SYCORAX: I will cast two eyes of pity on thee, I love thee
more than Haws,* or Black-berries; I have a hoard of
Wildings* in the Moss, my Brother knows not of 'em; But
I'le bring thee where they are.

STEPHANO: *Trincalo* was but my man when time was. 130

SYCORAX: Wert thou his God, and didst thou give him
Liquor?

STEPHANO: I gave him Brandy and drunk Sack my self;
wilt thou leave him, and thou shalt be my Princess?

SYCORAX: If thou canst make me glad with this Liquor.

STEPHANO: I warrant thee we'll ride into the Country
where it grows.

SYCORAX: How wilt though carry me thither?

STEPHANO: Upon a Hackney-Devil* of thy Mothers.

TRINCALO: What's that you will do? hah! I hope you have
not betray'd me? How does my Pigs-nye?* 140

(*To* SYCORAX)

SYCORAX: Be gone! thou shalt not be my Lord, thou say'st
I'm ugly.

TRINCALO: Did you tell her so?—Hah! he's a Rogue, do
not believe him chuck.

STEPHANO: The foul words were yours: I will not eat 'em
for you.

TRINCALO: I see if once a Rebel, then ever a Rebel. Did I
receive thee into grace for this? I will correct thee with my
Royal Hand. (*Strikes* STEPHANO)

SYCORAX: Dost thou hurt my love? (*Flies at* TRINCALO)

TRINCALO: Where are our Guards? Treason, Treason!

(VENTOSO, MUSTACHO, CALIBAN, *run betwixt*)

VENTOSO: Who took up Arms first, the Prince or the People?                                                                150

TRINCALO: This false Traytor has corrupted the Wife of my Bosom.—(*Whispers* MUSTACHO *hastily*) *Mustacho*, strike on my side, and thou shalt be my Vice-Roy.

MUSTACHO: I'm against Rebels! *Ventoso*, obey your Vice-Roy.

VENTOSO: You a Vice-Roy?

                              (*They two fight off from the rest*)

STEPHANO: Hah! Hector Monster! do you stand neuter?

CALIBAN: Thou would'st drink my Liquor, I will not help thee.

SYCORAX: 'Twas his doing that I had such a Husband, but I'le claw him.

                    (SYCORAX *and* CALIBAN *fight,* SYCORAX *beating
                                       him off the Stage*)

TRINCALO: The whole Nation is up in Arms, and shall I   160 stand idle?

                    (TRINCALO *beats off* STEPHANO *to the door.*
                                        *Exit* STEPHANO)

I'le not pursue too far.

For fear the Enemy should rally agen and surprise my Butt in the Cittadel; well, I must be rid of my Lady *Trincalo*, she will be in the fashion else; first Cuckold her Husband, and then sue for a separation, to get Alimony.

                                                              [*Exit*]

## Scene iii

*Enter* FERDINAND, HIPPOLITO, (*with their swords drawn*)

FERDINAND: Come, Sir, our Cave affords no choice of place,

But the ground's firm and even: are you ready?

HIPPOLITO: As ready as your self, Sir.

FERDINAND: You remember on what conditions we must fight?

Who first receives a Wound is to submit.

HIPPOLITO: Come, come this loses time, now for the
Women, Sir. (*They fight a little,* FERDINAND *hurts him*)

FERDINAND: Sir, you are wounded.

HIPPOLITO: No.

FERDINAND: Believe your blood. 10

HIPPOLITO: I feel no hurt, no matter for my blood.

FERDINAND: Remember our Conditions.

HIPPOLITO: I'le not leave, till my Sword hits you too.

(HIPPOLITO *presses on,* FERDINAND *retires and wards*)

FERDINAND: I'm loth to kill you, you are unskilful, Sir.

HIPPOLITO: You beat aside my Sword, but let it come as
near
As yours, and you shall see my skill.

FERDINAND: You faint for loss of blood, I see you stagger,
Pray, Sir, retire.

HIPPOLITO: No! I will ne're go back—
Methinks the Cave turns round, I cannot find— 20

FERDINAND: Your eyes begin to dazle.

HIPPOLITO: Why do you swim so, and dance about me?
Stand but still till I have made one thrust.

(HIPPOLITO *thrusts and falls*)

FERDINAND: O help, help, help!
Unhappy man! what have I done?

HIPPOLITO: I'm going to a cold sleep, but when I wake
I'le fight agen. Pray stay for me. (*Swounds*)

FERDINAND: He's gone! he's gone! O stay sweet lovely
Youth!
Help, help!

*Enter* PROSPERO

PROSPERO: What dismal noise is that? 30

FERDINAND: O see, Sir, see!
What mischief my unhappy hand has wrought.

PROSPERO: Alas! how much in vain doth feeble Art
endeavour
To resist the will of Heaven! (*Rubs* HIPPOLITO)
He's gone for ever; O thou cruel Son of an
Inhumane Father! all my designs are ruin'd

And unravell'd by this blow.

No pleasure now is left me but Revenge.

FERDINAND: Sir, if you knew my innocence—

PROSPERO: Peace, peace,                                                        40

Can thy excuses give me back his life?

What *Ariel*! sluggish spirit, where art thou?

*Enter* ARIEL

ARIEL: Here, at thy beck, my Lord.

PROSPERO: I, now thou com'st, when Fate is past and not

to be

Recall'd. Look there, and glut the malice of

Thy Nature, for as thou art thy self, thou

Canst not be but glad to see young Virtue

Nipt i'th' Blossom.

ARIEL: My Lord, the Being high above can witness

I am not glad; we Airy Spirits are not of temper             50

So malicious as the Earthy,

But of a Nature more approaching good:

For which we meet in swarms, and often combat

Betwixt the Confines of the Air and Earth.

PROSPERO: Why did'st thou not prevent, at least foretell,

This fatal action then?

ARIEL: Pardon, great Sir,

I meant to do it, but I was forbidden

By the ill Genius of *Hippolito*,

Who came and threaten'd me if I disclos'd it,             60

To bind me in the bottom of the Sea,

Far from the lightsome Regions of the Air,

(My native fields) above a hundred years.

PROSPERO: I'le chain thee in the North for thy neglect,

Within the burning Bowels of Mount *Hecla*;*

I'le sindge thy airy wings with sulph'rous flames,

And choak thy tender nostrils with blew smoak;

At ev'ry Hick-up of the belching Mountain

Thou shalt be lifted up to taste fresh Air,

And then fall down agen.                                                70

ARIEL: Pardon, dread Lord.

PROSPERO: No more of pardon than just Heav'n intends
    thee
  Shalt thou e're find from me: hence! flye with speed,
  Unbind the Charms which hold this Murtherer's
  Father, and bring him with my Brother streight
  Before me.
ARIEL: Mercy, my potent Lord, and I'le outfly thy thought.
                                  [*Exit* ARIEL]
FERDINAND: O Heavens! what words are those I heard?
  Yet cannot see who spoke 'em: sure the Woman
  Whom I lov'd was like this, some aiery Vision.     80
PROSPERO: No, Murd'rer, she's, like thee, of mortal
    mould,
  But much too pure to mix with thy black Crimes;
  Yet she had faults and must be punish'd for 'em.
  *Miranda* and *Dorinda*! where are ye?
  The will of heaven's accomplish'd: I have
  Now no more to fear, and nothing left to hope;
  Now you may enter.
           *Enter* MIRANDA *and* DORINDA
MIRANDA: My Love! is it permitted me to see you once
  again?
PROSPERO: You come to look your last; I will
  For ever take him from your Eyes.     90
  But, on my blessing, speak not, nor approach him.
DORINDA: Pray, Father, is not this my Sisters man?
  He has a noble form; but yet he's not so excellent
  As my *Hippolito*.
PROSPERO: Alas poor Girl, thou hast no man: look yonder;
  There's all of him that's left.
DORINDA: Why, was there ever any more of him?
  He lies asleep, Sir, shall I waken him?
          (*She kneels by* HIPPOLITO, *and jogs him*)
FERDINAND: Alas! he's never to be wak'd agen.
DORINDA: My Love, my Love! will you not speak to me? 100
  I fear you have displeas'd him, Sir, and now
  He will not answer me; he's dumb and cold too,
  But I'le run streight, and make a fire to warm him.

[*Exit* DORINDA *running*]
*Enter* ALONZO, GONZALO, ANTONIO, *and* ARIEL
(*invisible*)

ALONZO: Never were Beasts so hunted into toyls,
As we have been pursu'd by dreadful shapes.
But is not that my Son? O *Ferdinand*!
If thou art not a Ghost, let me embrace thee.

FERDINAND: My Father! O sinister happiness! Is it
Decreed I should recover you alive, just in that
Fatal hour when this brave Youth is lost in Death,    110
And by my hand?

ANTONIO: Heaven! what new wonder's this?

GONZALO: This Isle is full of nothing else.

ALONZO: I thought to dye, and in the walks above,
Wand'ring by Star-light, to have sought thee out;
But now I should have gone to Heaven in vain,
Whilst thou art here behind.

FERDINAND: You must indeed in vain have gone thither
To look for me. Those who are stain'd with such black
Crimes as mine, come seldom there.    120

PROSPERO: And those who are, like him, all foul with
    guilt,
More seldom upward go. You stare upon me as
You ne're had seen me; have fifteen years
So lost me to your knowledge, that you retain
No memory of *Prospero*?

GONZALO: The good old Duke of *Millain*!

PROSPERO: I wonder less, that thou *Antonio* know'st me
    not,
Because thou did'st long since forget I was thy Brother,
Else I never had bin here.

ANTONIO: Shame choaks my words.    130

ALONZO: And wonder mine.

PROSPERO: For you, usurping Prince,    (*to* ALONZO)
Know, by my Art, you shipwrackt on this Isle,
Where, after I a while had punish'd you, my vengeance
Wou'd have ended; I design'd to match that Son
Of yours with this my Daughter.

ALONZO: Pursue it still, I am most willing to't.

PROSPERO: So am not I. No marriages can prosper
 Which are with Murd'rers made; look on that Corps;
 This, whilst he liv'd, was young *Hippolito*, that   140
 Infant Duke of *Mantua*, Sir, whom you expos'd
 With me; and here I bred him up till that blood-thirsty
 Man, that *Ferdinand*—
 But why do I exclaim on him, when Justice calls
 To unsheath her Sword against his guilt?

ALONZO: What do you mean?

PROSPERO: To execute Heav'ns Laws.
 Here I am plac'd by Heav'n, here I am Prince,
 Though you have dispossess'd me of my *Millain*.
 Blood calls for blood; your *Ferdinand* shall dye,   150
 And I in bitterness have sent for you
 To have the sudden joy of seeing him alive,
 And then the greater grief to see him dye.

ALONZO: And think'st thou I or these will tamely stand
 To view the execution?  (*Lays hand upon his Sword*)

FERDINAND: Hold, dear Father! I cannot suffer you
 T'attempt against his life who gave her being
 Whom I love.

PROSPERO: Nay then, appear my Guards!—(*Aside*) I
 thought no more to
 Use their aids; (I'm curs'd because I us'd it)   160
     (*He stamps, and many Spirits appear*)
 But they are now the Ministers of Heaven,
 Whilst I revenge this murder.

ALONZO: Have I for this found thee my Son, so soon agen
 To lose thee? *Antonio*, *Gonzalo*, speak for pity:
 He may hear you.

ANTONIO: I dare not draw that blood upon my self, by
 Interceding for him.

GONZALO: You drew this judgment down when you
 usurp'd
 That Dukedom which was this dead Prince's right.

ALONZO: Is this a time t'upbraid me with my sins, when 170
 Grief lies heavy on me? y'are no more my friends,

But crueller than he, whose sentence has
Doom'd my Son to death.

ANTONIO: You did unworthily t'upbraid him.

GONZALO: And you do worse t'endure his crimes.

ANTONIO: *Gonzalo* we'll meet no more as friends.

GONZALO: Agreed *Antonio*: and we agree in discord.

FERDINAND: (*to* MIRANDA) Adieu my fairest Mistress.

MIRANDA: Now I can hold no longer; I must speak.

Though I am loth to disobey you, Sir,                                    180
Be not so cruel to the man I love,
Or be so kind to let me suffer with him.

FERDINAND: Recall that Pray'r, or I shall wish to live,
Though death be all the mends that I can make.

PROSPERO: This night I will allow you, *Ferdinand*, to fit
You for your Death, that Cave's your Prison.

ALONZO: Ah, *Prospero!* hear me speak. You are a Father,
Look on my age, and look upon his youth.

PROSPERO: No more! all you can say is urg'd in vain,
I have no room for pity left within me.                                  190
Do you refuse! help, *Ariel*, with your fellows
To drive 'em in; *Alonzo* and his Son bestow in
Yonder Cave, and here *Gonzalo* shall with
*Antonio* lodge. (*Spirits drive 'em in, as they are appointed*)

*Enter* DORINDA

DORINDA: Sir, I have made a fire, shall he be warm'd?

PROSPERO: He's dead, and vital warmth will ne're return.

DORINDA: Dead, Sir, what's that?

PROSPERO: His soul has left his body.

DORINDA: When will it come agen?

PROSPERO: O never, never!                                              200
He must be laid in Earth, and there consume.

DORINDA: He shall not lye in earth, you do not know
How well he loves me: indeed he'l come agen;
He told me he would go a little while,
But promis'd me he would not tarry long.

PROSPERO: He's murder'd by the man who lov'd your
Sister.
Now both of you may see what 'tis to break

A Father's precept; you should needs see men, and by
That sight are made for ever wretched.
*Hippolito* is dead, and *Ferdinand* must dye     210
For murdering him.

MIRANDA: Have you no pity?

PROSPERO: Your disobedience has so much incens'd me, that
I this night can leave no blessing with you.
Help to convey the body to my Couch,
Then leave me to mourn over it alone.

        (*They bear off the body of* HIPPOLITO)

*Enter* MIRANDA, *and* DORINDA *again*, ARIEL *behind 'em*

ARIEL: I've bin so chid for my neglect by *Prospero*,
That I must now watch all and be unseen.

MIRANDA: Sister, I say agen, 'twas long of you*
That all this mischief happen'd.     220

DORINDA: Blame not me for your own fault, your
Curiosity brought me to see the man.

MIRANDA: You safely might have seen him and retir'd, but
You wou'd needs go near him and converse, you may
Remember my Father call'd me thence, and I call'd you.

DORINDA: That was your envy, Sister, not your love;
You call'd me thence, because you could not be
Alone with him your self; but I am sure my
Man had never gone to Heaven so soon, but
That yours made him go.          (*Crying*) 230

MIRANDA: Sister, I could not wish that either of 'em shou'd
Go to Heaven without us, but it was his fortune,
And you must be satisfi'd.

DORINDA: I'le not be satisfi'd: My Father says he'l make
Your man as cold as mine is now, and when he
Is made cold, my Father will not let you strive
To make him warm agen.

MIRANDA: In spight of you mine never shall be cold.

DORINDA: I'm sure 'twas he that made me miserable,
And I will be reveng'd. Perhaps you think 'tis     240
Nothing to lose a man.

MIRANDA: Yes, but there is some difference betwixt

My *Ferdinand*, and your *Hippolito*.

DORINDA: I, there's your judgment. Your's is the oldest
   Man I ever saw except it were my Father.

MIRANDA: Sister, no more. It is not comely in a Daughter,
   When she says her Father's old.

DORINDA: But why do I stay here, whilst my cold Love
   Perhaps may want me?
   I'le pray my Father to make yours cold too.                    250

MIRANDA: Sister, I'le never sleep with you agen.

DORINDA: I'le never more meet in a Bed with you,
   But lodge on the bare ground and watch my Love.

MIRANDA: And at the entrance of that Cave I'le lye,
   And eccho to each blast of wind a sigh.

[*Exeunt severally, looking discontentedly on one another*]

ARIEL: Harsh discord reigns throughout this fatal Isle,
   At which good Angels mourn, ill Spirits smile;
   Old *Prospero*, by his Daughters rob'd of rest,
   Has in displeasure left 'em both unblest.
   Unkindly they abjure each others bed,                          260
   To save the living, and revenge the dead.
   *Alonzo* and his Son are Pris'ners made,
   And good *Gonzalo* does their crimes upbraid.
   *Antonio* and *Gonzalo* disagree,
   And wou'd, though in one Cave, at distance be.
   The Seamen all that cursed Wine have spent,
   Which still renew'd their thirst of Government;
   And, wanting subjects for the food of Pow'r,
   Each wou'd to rule alone the rest devour.
   The Monsters *Sycorax* and *Caliban*                           270
   More monstrous grow by passions learn'd from man.
   Even I not fram'd of warring Elements,
   Partake and suffer in these discontents.
   Why shou'd a mortal by Enchantments hold
   In chains a spirit of ætherial mould?
   Accursed Magick we our selves have taught,
   And our own pow'r has our subjection wrought!

                                                        [*Exit*]

# ACT V

## Scene i

### Enter PROSPERO *and* MIRANDA

PROSPERO: You beg in vain; I cannot pardon him,
He has offended Heaven.

MIRANDA: Then let Heaven punish him.

PROSPERO: It will by me.

MIRANDA: Grant him at least some respite for my sake.

PROSPERO: I by deferring Justice should incense the Deity
Against my self and you.

MIRANDA: Yet I have heard you say, The Powers above are slow
In punishing; and shou'd not you resemble them?

PROSPERO: The Powers above may pardon or reprieve,     10
As Sovereign Princes may dispense with Laws,
Which we, as Officers, must execute. Our Acts of grace
To Criminals are Treason to Heavens prerogative.

MIRANDA: Do you condemn him for shedding blood?

PROSPERO: Why do you ask that question? you know I do.

MIRANDA: Then you must be condemn'd for shedding his,
And he who condemns you, must dye for shedding
Yours, and that's the way at last to leave none living.

PROSPERO: The Argument is weak, but I want time
To let you see your errours; retire, and, if you love him,    20
Pray for him.          *(He's going)*

MIRANDA: O stay, Sir, I have yet more Arguments.

PROSPERO: But none of any weight.

MIRANDA: Have you not said you are his Judge?

PROSPERO: 'Tis true, I am; what then?

MIRANDA: And can you be his Executioner?
If that be so, then all men may declare their
Enemies in fault; and Pow'r without the Sword

Of Justice, will presume to punish what e're
It calls a crime.                                                          30
PROSPERO: I cannot force *Gonzalo* or my Brother, much
Less the Father, to destroy the Son; it must
Be then the Monster *Caliban*, and he's not here;
But *Ariel* strait shall fetch him.

*Enter* ARIEL

ARIEL: My potent Lord, before thou call'st, I come,
To serve thy will.
PROSPERO: Then Spirit fetch me here my salvage Slave.
ARIEL: My Lord, it does not need.
PROSPERO: Art thou then prone to mischief, wilt thou be
thy self the Executioner?                                                  40
ARIEL: Think better of thy aiery Minister, who
For thy sake, unbid, this night has flown
O're almost all the habitable World.
PROSPERO: But to what purpose was all thy diligence?
ARIEL: When I was chidden by my mighty Lord for my
Neglect of young *Hippolito*, I went to view
His body, and soon found his soul was but retir'd,
Not sally'd out, and frighted lay at skulk in
Th' inmost corner of his scarce-beating heart.
PROSPERO: Is he not dead?                                                  50
ARIEL: Hear me my Lord! I prun'd my wings, and, fitted
for a journey, from the next Isles of our *Hesperides*, I
gather'd Moly first, thence shot my self to *Palestine*, and
watch'd the trickling Balm, which caught, I glided to the
*British* Isles, and there the purple Panacea found.*
PROSPERO: All this to night?
ARIEL: All this, my Lord, I did,
Nor was *Hippolito*'s good Angel wanting, who
Climbing up the circle of the Moon,
While I below got Simples* for the Cure, went to           60
Each Planet which o're-rul'd those Herbs,
And drew it's virtue to increase their pow'r:
Long e're this hour had I been back again,
But that a Storm took me returning back
And flag'd my tender Wings.

PROSPERO: Thou shalt have rest my spirit,
But hast thou search'd the wound?
ARIEL: My Lord I have, and 'twas in time I did it; for
The soul stood almost at life's door, all bare
And naked, shivering like Boys upon a Rivers          70
Bank, and loth to tempt the cold air; but I took
Her and stop'd her in; and pour'd into his mouth
The healing juice of vulnerary* Herbs.
PROSPERO: Thou art my faithful servant.
ARIEL: His only danger was his loss of blood, but now
He's wak'd, my Lord, and just this hour
He must be dress'd again, as I have done it.
Anoint the Sword which pierc'd him with this
Weapon-Salve,* and wrap it close from air till
I have time to visit him again.          80
PROSPERO: It shall be done. Be it your task, *Miranda*,
because your
Sister is not present here, while I go visit your
Dear *Ferdinand*, from whom I will a while conceal
This news, that it may be more welcome.
MIRANDA: I obey you, and with a double duty, Sir: for now
You twice have given me life.
PROSPERO: My *Ariel*, follow me.          [*Exeunt severally*]


# Scene ii

HIPPOLITO *discovered on a Couch,* DORINDA *by him*

DORINDA: How do you find your self?
HIPPOLITO: I'm somewhat cold, can you not draw me
nearer
To the Sun? I am too weak to walk.
DORINDA: My Love, I'le try.
                    (*She draws the chair nearer the Audience*)
I thought you never would have walk'd agen,
They told me you were gone away to Heaven;
Have you bin there?
HIPPOLITO: I know not where I was.

DORINDA: I will not leave you till you promise me you
Will not dye agen.                                                    10
HIPPOLITO: Indeed I will not.
DORINDA: You must not go to Heav'n unless we go
together,
For I've heard my Father say that we must strive
To be each others Guide, the way to it will else
Be difficult, especially to those who are so young.
But I much wonder what it is to dye.
HIPPOLITO: Sure 'tis to dream, a kind of breathless sleep
When once the Soul's gone out.
DORINDA: What is the Soul?
HIPPOLITO: A small blew thing that runs about within us.   20
DORINDA: Then I have seen it in a frosty morning run
Smoaking from my mouth.
HIPPOLITO: But if my soul had gone, it should have walk'd
upon
A Cloud just over you, and peep'd, and thence I would
have
Call'd you.
DORINDA: But I should not have heard you, 'tis so far.
HIPPOLITO: Why then I would have rain'd and snow'd
upon you,
And thrown down Hail-stones gently till I hit you,
And made you look at least. But dear *Dorinda*
What is become of him who fought with me?              30
DORINDA: O, I can tell you joyful news of him,
My Father means to make him dye to day,
For what he did to you.
HIPPOLITO: That must not be, my dear *Dorinda*; go and
beg your
Father he may not dye, it was my fault he hurt me,
I urg'd him to it first.
DORINDA: But if he live, he'll never leave killing you.
HIPPOLITO: O no! I just remember when I fell asleep I
heard
Him calling me a great way off, and crying over me as
You wou'd do; besides we have no cause of quarrel now.   40

DORINDA: Pray how began your difference first?

HIPPOLITO: I fought with him for all the Women in the World.

DORINDA: That hurt you had was justly sent from Heaven, For wishing to have any more but me.

HIPPOLITO: Indeed I think it was, but I repent it: the fault Was only in my blood; for now 'tis gone, I find I do not love so many.

DORINDA: In confidence of this, I'le beg my Father, that he May live; I'm glad the naughty blood, that made You love so many, is gone out.                        50

HIPPOLITO: My Dear, go quickly, lest you come too late.

                                        [*Exit* DORINDA]

*Enter* MIRANDA *at the other door, with* HIPPOLITO's
                    *Sword wrapt up*

HIPPOLITO: Who's this who looks so fair and beautiful, as Nothing but *Dorinda* can surpass her? O! I believe it is that Angel, Woman, Whom she calls Sister.

MIRANDA: Sir, I am sent hither to dress your wound, How do you find your strength?

HIPPOLITO: Fair Creature, I am faint with loss of blood.

MIRANDA: I'm sorry for't.

HIPPOLITO: Indeed and so am I, for if I had that blood, I then                                              60
Should find a great delight in loving you.

MIRANDA: But, Sir, I am anothers, and your love is given Already to my Sister.

HIPPOLITO: Yet I find that if you please I can love still a little.

MIRANDA: I cannot be unconstant, nor shou'd you.

HIPPOLITO: O my wound pains me.

MIRANDA: I am come to ease you.

                                (*She unwraps the Sword*)

HIPPOLITO: Alas! I feel the cold air come to me, My wound shoots worse than ever.

                        (*She wipes and anoints the Sword*)

MIRANDA: Does it still grieve you?                       70

HIPPOLITO: Now methinks there's something laid just
  upon it.

MIRANDA: Do you find no ease?

HIPPOLITO: Yes, yes, upon the sudden all the pain
  Is leaving me, sweet Heaven how I am eas'd!

  *Enter* FERDINAND *and* DORINDA *to them*

FERDINAND: (*to* DORINDA) Madam, I must confess my
  life is yours,
  I owe it to your generosity.

DORINDA: I am o'rejoy'd my Father lets you live, and
  proud
  Of my good fortune, that he gave your life to me.

MIRANDA: How? gave his life to her?

HIPPOLITO: Alas! I think she said so, and he said he ow'd    80
  it
  To her generosity.

FERDINAND: But is not that your Sister with *Hippolito*?

DORINDA: So kind already?

FERDINAND: I came to welcome life, and I have met the
  Cruellest of deaths.

HIPPOLITO: My dear *Dorinda* with another man?

DORINDA: Sister, what bus'ness have you here?

MIRANDA: You see I dress *Hippolito*.

DORINDA: Y'are very charitable to a Stranger.

MIRANDA: You are not much behind in charity, to beg a
  pardon                                                    90
  For a man, whom you scarce ever saw before.

DORINDA: Henceforward let your Surgery alone, for I had
  Rather he should dye, than you should cure his wound.

MIRANDA: And I wish *Ferdinand* had dy'd before
  He ow'd his life to your entreaty.

FERDINAND: (*to* HIPPOLITO) Sir, I'm glad you are so well
  recover'd, you
  Keep your humour still to have all Women.

HIPPOLITO: Not all, Sir; you except one of the number,
  Your new Love there, *Dorinda*.

MIRANDA: Ah *Ferdinand*! can you become inconstant?    100
  If I must lose you, I had rather death should take

You from me than you take your self.

FERDINAND: And if I might have chose, I would have wish'd

That death from *Prospero*, and not this from you.

DORINDA: I, now I find why I was sent away,

That you might have my Sisters company.

HIPPOLITO: *Dorinda*, kill me not with your unkindess,

This is too much, first to be false your self,

And then accuse me too.

FERDINAND: We all accuse each other, and each one    110
denys their guilt,

I should be glad it were a mutual errour.

And therefore first to clear my self from fault,

Madam, I beg your pardon, while I say I only love

Your Sister.        (*To* DORINDA)

MIRANDA: O blest word!

I'm sure I love no man but *Ferdinand*.

DORINDA: Nor I, Heav'n knows, but my *Hippolito*.

HIPPOLITO: I never knew I lov'd so much, before I fear'd

*Dorinda*'s constancy; but now I am convinc'd that

I lov'd none but her, because none else can    120

Recompence her loss.

FERDINAND: 'Twas happy then you had this little tryal.

But how we all so much mistook, I know not.

MIRANDA: I have only this to say in my defence: my Father sent

Me hither, to attend the wounded Stranger.

DORINDA: And *Hippolito* sent me to beg the life of *Ferdinand*.

FERDINAND: From such small errours, left at first unheeded,

Have often sprung sad accidents in love:

But see, our Fathers and our friends are come

To mix their joys with ours.    130

   *Enter* PROSPERO, ALONZO, ANTONIO, GONZALO

ALONZO: (*to* PROSPERO) Let it no more be thought of, your purpose

Though it was severe was just. In losing *Ferdinand*

I should have mourn'd, but could not have complain'd.

PROSPERO: Sir, I am glad kind Heaven decreed it otherwise.

DORINDA: O wonder!
How many goodly Creatures are there here!
How beauteous mankind is!

HIPPOLITO: O brave new World that has such people
in't![28]

ALONZO: (to FERDINAND) Now all the blessings of a glad
Father
Compass thee about,[29]                                            140
And make thee happy in thy beauteous choice.

GONZALO: I've inward wept, or should have spoke e're
this.
Look down sweet Heav'n, and on this Couple drop
A blessed Crown, for it is you chalk'd out the
Way which brought us hither.[30]

ANTONIO: Though penitence forc'd by necessity can scarce
Seem real, yet dearest Brother I have hope
My blood may plead for pardon with you, I resign
Dominion, which 'tis true I could not keep,
But Heaven knows too I would not.                                 150

PROSPERO: All past crimes I bury in the joy of this
Blessed day.

ALONZO: And that I may not be behind in justice, to this
Young Prince I render back his Dukedom,
And as the Duke of *Mantua* thus salute him.

HIPPOLITO: What is it that you render back? methinks
You give me nothing.

PROSPERO: You are to be Lord of a great People,
And o're Towns and Cities.

HIPPOLITO: And shall these people be all Men and
Women?                                                            160

GONZALO: Yes, and shall call you Lord.

HIPPOLITO: Why then I'le live no longer in a Prison, but

---

[28] 135-8: V.i.181-4: 'O, wonder ... people in't.'
[29] 139-40: V.i.179-80: 'Now all ... compass thee about!'
[30] 142-5: V.i.200-4: 'I have inly wept ... brought us hither.'

Have a whole Cave to my self hereafter.

PROSPERO: And that your happiness may be compleat,
  I give you my *Dorinda* for your Wife, she shall
  Be yours for ever, when the Priest has made you one.

HIPPOLITO: How can he make us one, shall I grow to her?

PROSPERO: By saying holy words you shall be joyn'd in
    marriage
  To each other.

DORINDA: I warrant you those holy words are charms.      170
  My Father means to conjure us together.

PROSPERO: (*to his daughter*) My *Ariel* told me, when last
  night you quarrel'd,
  You said you would for ever part your beds,
  But what you threaten'd in your anger, Heaven
  Has turn'd to Prophecy;
  For you, *Miranda*, must with *Ferdinand*,
  And you, *Dorinda*, with *Hippolito* lye in
  One Bed hereafter.

ALONZO: And Heaven make those Beds still fruitful in
  Producing Children to bless their Parents            180
  Youth, and Grandsires age.

MIRANDA: (*to* DORINDA) If Children come by lying in a
  Bed, I wonder you
  And I had none between us.

DORINDA: Sister it was our fault, we meant like fools
  To look 'em in the fields, and they it seems
  Are only found in Beds.

HIPPOLITO: I am o'rejoy'd that I shall have *Dorinda* in a
    Bed,
  We'll lye all night and day together there,
  And never rise again.

FERDINAND: (*aside to him*) *Hippolito*! you yet are ignorant
    of your great                                      190
  Happiness, but there is somewhat which for
  Your own and fair *Dorinda*'s sake I must instruct
  You in.

HIPPOLITO: Pray teach me quickly how Men and Women
    in your

World make love, I shall soon learn
I warrant you.

*Enter* ARIEL *driving in* STEPHANO, TRINCALO,
MUSTACHO, VENTOSO, CALIBAN, SYCORAX

PROSPERO: Why that's my dainty *Ariel*, I shall miss thee,
But yet thou shalt have freedom.[31]

GONZALO: O look, Sir, look, the Master and the Saylors—
The Bosen too—my Prophecy is out, that if                   200
A Gallows were on land, that man could ne're
Be drown'd.

ALONZO: (*to* TRINCALO) Now Blasphemy, what not one
Oath ashore?
Hast thou no mouth by land? why star'st thou so?[32]

TRINCALO: What, more Dukes yet, I must resign my
Dukedom,
But 'tis no matter, I was almost starv'd in't.

MUSTACHO: Here's nothing but wild Sallads without Oyl
or Vinegar.

STEPHANO: The Duke and Prince alive! would I had now
our gallant Ship agen, and were her Master, I'd willingly
give all my Island for her.                                 210

VENTOSO: And I my Vice-Roy-ship.

TRINCALO: I shall need no hangman, for I shall e'en hang
My self, now my friend Butt has shed his
Last drop of life. Poor Butt is quite departed.

ANTONIO: They talk like mad men.

PROSPERO: No matter, time will bring 'em to themselves,
and
Now their Wine is gone they will not quarrel.
Your Ship is safe and tight, and bravely rigg'd,
As when you first set Sail.[33]

ALONZO: This news is wonderful.                             220

ARIEL: Was it well done, my Lord?

PROSPERO: Rarely, my diligence.[34]

---

[31]  197–8: V.i.95–6: 'Why, that's my ... have freedom.'
[32]  199–204: V.i.216–20: 'O, look sir ... mouth by land?'
[33]  218–19: V.i.224–5: 'Our ship ... out to sea.'
[34]  221–2: V.i.240–1: 'Was't well done ... my diligence.'

GONZALO: But pray, Sir, what are those mishapen Creatures?

PROSPERO: Their Mother was a Witch, and one so strong
She would controul the Moon, make Flows
And Ebbs, and deal in her command without
Her power.[35]

SYCORAX: O *Setebos*! these be brave Sprights indeed.[36]

PROSPERO: (*to* CALIBAN) Go Sirrah to my Cell, and as you hope for
Pardon, trim it up.                                230

CALIBAN: Most carefully. I will be wise hereafter.
What a dull fool was I to take those Drunkards
For Gods, when such as these were in the world!

PROSPERO: Sir, I invite your Highness and your Train
To my poor Cave this night; a part of which
I will imploy in telling you my story.

ALONZO: No doubt it must be strangely taking, Sir.

PROSPERO: When the morn draws I'le bring you to your Ship,
And promise you calm Seas and happy Gales.
My *Ariel*, that's thy charge: then to the Elements        240
Be free, and fare thee well.

ARIEL: I'le do it Master.[37]
(*Sings*) *Where the Bee sucks there suck I,*
*In a Cowslips Bell, I lye,*
*There I couch when Owls do cry,*
*On the Swallows wing I flye*
*After Summer merrily.*
*Merrily, merrily shall I live now*
*Under the Blossom that hangs on the Bough.*[38]

SYCORAX: I'le to Sea with thee, and keep thee warm in thy   250
Cabin.

TRINCALO: No my dainty Dy-dapper,* you have a tender
constitution, and will be sick a Ship-board. You are partly
Fish and may swim after me. I wish you a good Voyage.

---

[35] 225-7: V.i.268-71: 'His mother was ... without her power.'
[36] 228: V.i.261: 'O Setebos ... indeed.'
[37] 229-42: V.i.290-317 (with changes of phrasing): 'He is as ... fare Thou well!'
[38] 243-9: V.i.88-94: 'Where the bee ... on the bough.'

PROSPERO: Now to this Royal Company, my servant, be
    visible,
And entertain them with a Dance before they part.
ARIEL: I have a gentle Spirit for my Love,
    Who twice seven years hath waited for my Freedom,
    It shall appear and foot it featly with me.
    *Milcha*, my Love, thy *Ariel* calls thee.
                  *Enter* MILCHA
MILCHA: Here!            *(They dance a Saraband)** 260
PROSPERO: Henceforth this Isle to the afflicted be
    A place of Refuge as it was to me;
    The Promises of blooming Spring live here,
    And all the Blessings of the rip'ning year;
    On my retreat let Heaven and Nature smile,
    And ever flourish the *Enchanted Isle*.      [*Exeunt*]

# EPILOGUE

Gallants, by all good signs it does appear,
That Sixty Seven's a very damning year,
For Knaves abroad, and for ill Poets here.

Among the Muses there's a gen'ral rot,
The Rhyming Mounsieur and the Spanish Plot:
Defie or court, all's one, they go to Pot.

The Ghosts of Poets walk within this place,
And haunt us Actors wheresoe're we pass,
In Visions bloodier than King Richard's was.

For this poor wretch he has not much to say,
But quietly brings in his part o'th' Play,
And begs the favour to be damn'd to day.

He sends me only like a Sh'riffs man here
To let you know the Malefactor's neer;
And that he means to dye, en Cavalier.

For if you shou'd be gracious to his Pen,
Th' Example will prove ill to other men,
And you'll be troubled with 'em all agen.

**FINIS**

# ALL FOR LOVE;
# OR, THE
# WORLD WELL LOST

BY JOHN DRYDEN

# ALL FOR LOVE:

## OR, THE

# World well Loſt.

## A

# TRAGEDY,

As it is Acted at the

## *THEATRE-ROYAL;*

And Written in Imitation of *Shakeſpeare's* Stile.

---

By *John Dryden*, Servant to His Majeſty.

---

*Facile eſt verbum aliquod ardens (ut ita dicam) notare : idque re-ſtinctis animorum incendiis irridere.* Cicero.

---

In the SAVOY:

Printed by *Tho. Newcomb*, for *Henry Herringman*, at the Blew An-chor in the Lower Walk of the *New-Exchange*. 1678.

## PREFACE

*The death of Antony* and *Cleopatra*, is a Subject which has been treated by the greatest Wits of our Nation,* after *Shakespeare*; and by all so variously, that their example has given me the confidence to try my self in this Bowe of *Ulysses** amongst the Crowd of Sutors; and, withal, to take my own measures, in aiming at the Mark. I doubt not but the same Motive has prevailed with all of us in this attempt; I mean the excellency of the Moral: for the chief persons represented, were famous patterns of unlawful love; and their end accordingly was unfortunate. All reasonable men have long since concluded, That the Heroe of the Poem, ought not to be a character of perfect Virtue, for, then, he could not, without injustice, be made unhappy; nor yet altogether wicked, because he could not then be pitied: I have therefore steer'd the middle course; and have drawn the character of *Antony* as favourably as *Plutarch*, *Appian*, and *Dion Cassius** wou'd give me leave: the like I have observ'd in *Cleopatra*. That which is wanting to work up the pity to a greater heighth, was not afforded me by the story: for the crimes of love which they both committed, were not occasion'd by any necessity, or fatal ignorance, but were wholly voluntary; since our passions are, or ought to be, within our power. The Fabrick of the Play is regular enough, as to the inferior parts of it; and the Unities of Time, Place and Action, more exactly observ'd, than, perhaps, the *English* Theater requires. Particularly, the Action is so much one, that it is the only of the kind without Episode, or Underplot; every Scene in the Tragedy conducing to the main design, and every Act concluding with a turn* of it. The greatest errour in the contrivance seems to be in the person of *Octavia*: For, though I might use the priviledge of a Poet, to introduce her into *Alexandria*, yet I

had not enough consider'd, that the compassion she mov'd
to her self and children, was destructive to that which I
reserv'd for *Anthony* and *Cleopatra*; whose mutual love
being founded upon vice, must lessen the favour of the
Audience to them, when Virtue and Innocence were
oppress'd by it. And, though I justified *Antony* in some
measure, by making *Octavia*'s departure, to proceed wholly
from her self; yet the force of the first Machine* still
remain'd; and the dividing of pity, like the cutting of a River
into many Channels, abated the strength of the natural
stream. But this is an Objection which none of my Critiques
have urg'd against me; and therefore I might have let it pass,
if I could have resolv'd to have been partial to my self. The
faults my Enemies have found, are rather cavils concerning
little, and not essential Decencies; which a Master of the
Ceremonies may decide betwixt us. The *French* Poets, I
confess, are strict Observers of these Punctilio's: They
would not, for example, have suffer'd *Cleopatra* and
*Octavia* to have met; or if they had met, there must only
have pass'd betwixt them some cold civilities, but no
eagerness of repartée, for fear of offending against the
greatness of their Characters, and the modesty of their Sex.
This Objection I foresaw, and at the same time contemn'd:
for I judg'd it both natural and probable, that *Octavia*,
proud of her new-gain'd Conquest, would search out
*Cleopatra* to triumph over her; and that *Cleopatra*, thus
attacqu'd, was not of a spirit to shun the encounter: and 'tis
not unlikely, that two exasperated Rivals should use such
Satyre as I have put into their mouths; for after all, though
the one were a *Roman*, and the other a Queen, they were
both Women. 'Tis true, some actions, though natural, are
not fit to be represented; and broad obscenities in words,
ought in good manners to be avoided: expressions therefore
are a modest cloathing of our thoughts, as Breeches and
Petticoats are of our bodies. If I have kept my self within the
bounds of modesty, all beyond it is but nicety and
affectation; which is no more but modesty deprav'd into a

vice: they betray themselves who are too quick of apprehension in such cases, and leave all reasonable men to imagine worse of them, than of the Poet.

Honest *Montaigne** goes yet farther. *Nous ne sommes que ceremonie; la ceremonie nous emporte, & laissons la substance des choses: Nous nous tenons aux branches, & abandonnons le tronc & le corps. Nous avons appris aux Dames de rougir, oyans seulement nommer ce qu'elles ni craignent aucunement a faire: Nous n'osons appeller a droict nos membres, & ne craignons pas de les employer a toute sorte de debauche. La ceremonie nous defend d'exprimer par paroles les choses licites & naturelles, & nous l'en croyons; la raison nous defend de n'en faire point d'illicites & mauvaises, & personne ne l'en croid.* My comfort is, that by this opinion my Enemies are but sucking* Critiques, who wou'd fain be nibbling ere their teeth are come.

Yet, in this nicety of manners does the excellency of *French* Poetry consist: their Heroes are the most civil people breathing; but their good breeding seldom extends to a word of sense: All their Wit is in their Ceremony; they want the Genius which animates our Stage; and therefore 'tis but necessary when they cannot please, that they should take care not to offend. But, as the civilest man in the company is commonly the dullest, so these Authors, while they are afraid to make you laugh or cry, out of pure good manners, make you sleep. They are so careful not to exasperate a Critique, that they never leave him any work; so busie with the Broom, and make so clean a riddance, that there is little left either for censure or for praise: for no part of a Poem is worth our discommending, where the whole is insipid; as when we have once tasted of pall'd* Wine, we stay not to examine it Glass by Glass. But while they affect to shine in trifles, they are often careless in essentials. Thus their *Hippolitus** is so scrupulous in point of decency, that he will rather expose himself to death, than accuse his Stepmother to his Father; and my Critiques I am sure will commend him for it: but we of grosser apprehensions, are

apt to think that his excess of generosity, is not practicable
but with Fools and Madmen. This was good manners with a
vengeance; and the Audience is like to be much concern'd at
the misfortunes of this admirable Heroe: but take *Hippolitus* out of his Poetique Fit, and I suppose he would think it a
wiser part, to set the Saddle on the right Horse, and chuse
rather to live with the reputation of a plain-spoken honest
man, than to die with the infamy of an incestuous Villain. In
the mean time we may take notice, that where the Poet
ought to have preserv'd the character as it was deliver'd to
us by Antiquity, when he should have given us the picture of
a rough young man, of the *Amazonian* strain, a jolly
Huntsman, and both by his profession and his early rising a
Mortal Enemy to love, he has chosen to give him the turn of
Gallantry, sent him to travel from *Athens* to *Paris*, taught
him to make love, and transform'd the *Hippolitus* of
*Euripides* into Monsieur *Hippolite*. I should not have
troubled my self thus far with *French* Poets, but that I find
our *Chedreux** Critiques wholly form their judgments by
them. But for my part, I desire to be try'd by the Laws of my
own Country; for it seems unjust to me, that the *French*
should prescribe here, till they have conquer'd. Our little
Sonnettiers who follow them, have too narrow Souls to
judge of Poetry. Poets themselves are the most proper,
though I conclude not the only Critiques. But till some
Genius as Universal, as *Aristotle*, shall arise, one who can
penetrate into all Arts and Sciences, without the practice of
them, I shall think it reasonable, that the Judgement of an
Artificer in his own Art should be preferable to the opinion
of another man; at least where he is not brib'd by interest,
or prejudic'd by malice: and this, I suppose, is manifest by
plain induction: For, first, the Crowd cannot be presum'd to
have more than a gross instinct, of what pleases or
displeases them: every man will grant me this; but then, by a
particular kindness to himself, he draws his own stake*
first, and will be distinguish'd from the multitude, of which
other men may think him one. But, if I come closer to those
who are allow'd for witty men,* either by the advantage of

their quality, or by common fame, and affirm that neither are they qualified to decide Sovereignly, concerning Poetry, I shall yet have a strong party of my opinion; for most of them severally will exclude the rest, either from the number of witty men, or at least of able Judges. But here again they are all indulgent to themselves: and every one who believes himself a Wit, that is, every man, will pretend at the same time to a right of judging. But to press it yet farther, there are many witty men, but few Poets; neither have all Poets a taste of Tragedy. And this is the Rock on which they are daily splitting. Poetry, which is a Picture of Nature, must generally please: but 'tis not to be understood that all parts of it must please every man; therefore is not Tragedy to be judg'd by a witty man, whose taste is only confin'd to Comedy. Nor is every man who loves Tragedy a sufficient Judge of it: he must understand the excellencies of it too, or he will only prove a blind Admirer, not a Critique. From hence it comes that so many Satyrs on Poets, and censures of their Writings, fly abroad. Men of pleasant Conversation, (at least esteem'd so) and indu'd with a triffling kind of Fancy, perhaps help'd out with some smattering of *Latine*, are ambitious to distinguish themselves from the Herd of Gentlemen, by their Poetry;

> *Rarus enim ferme sensus communis in illâ*
> *Fortunâ.* *

And is not this a wretched affectation, not to be contented with what Fortune has done for them, and sit down quietly with their Estates, but they must call their Wits in question, and needlesly expose their nakedness to publick view? Not considering that they are not to expect the same approbation from sober men, which they have found from their flatterers after the third Bottle? If a little glittering in discourse has pass'd them on us for witty men, where was the necessity of undeceiving the World? would a man who has an ill Title to an Estate, but yet is in possession of it, would he bring it of his own accord, to be try'd at *Westminster*? We who write, if we want the Talent, yet have

the excuse that we do it for a poor subsistence; but what can
be urg'd in their defence, who not having the Vocation of
Poverty to scribble, out of meer wantonness take pains to
make themselves ridiculous? *Horace* was certainly in the
right, where he said, That *no man is satisfied with his own
condition*. A Poet is not pleas'd because he is not rich; and
the Rich are discontented, because the Poets will not admit
them of their number. Thus the case is hard with Writers: if
they succeed not, they must starve; and if they do, some
malicious Satyr is prepar'd to level them for daring to please
without their leave. But while they are so eager to destroy
the fame of others, their ambition is manifest in their
concernment: some Poem of their own is to be produc'd,
and the Slaves are to be laid flat with their faces on the
ground, that the Monarch may appear the greater Majesty.

*Dionysius* and *Nero** had the same longings, but with all
their power they cou'd never bring their business well about.
'Tis true, they proclaim'd themselves Poets by sound of
Trumpet; and Poets they were upon pain of death to any
man who durst call them otherwise. The Audience had a
fine time on't, you may imagine; they sate in a bodily fear,
and look'd as demurely as they could: for 'twas a hanging
matter to laugh unseasonably; and the Tyrants were suspicious, as they had reason, that their Subjects had 'em in the
wind: so, every man in his own defence set as good a face
upon the business as he could: 'Twas known beforehand
that the Monarchs were to be Crown'd Laureats; but when
the shew was over, and an honest man was suffer'd to
depart quietly, he took out his laughter which he had
stiffled; with a firm resolution never more to see an
Emperor's Play, though he had been ten years a making it.
In the mean time the true Poets were they who made the best
Markets, for they had Wit enough to yield the Prize with a
good grace, and not contend with him who had thirty
Legions: They were sure to be rewarded if they confess'd
themselves bad Writers, and that was somewhat better than
to be Martyrs for their reputation. *Lucan*'s* example was
enough to teach them manners; and after he was put to

death, for overcoming *Nero*, the Emperor carried it without dispute for the best Poet in his Dominions: No man was ambitious of that grinning honour* for if he heard the malicious Trumpetter proclaiming his name before his betters, he knew there was but one way with him. *Mæcenas** took another course, and we know he was more than a great man, for he was witty too: but finding himself far gone in Poetry, which *Seneca** assures us was not his Talent, he thought it his best way to be well with *Virgil* and with *Horace*,* that at least he might be a Poet at the second hand; and we see how happily it has succeeded with him; for his own bad Poetry is forgotten, and their Panegyricks of him still remain. But they who should be our Patrons, are for no such expensive ways to fame: they have much of the Poetry of *Mæcenas*, but little of his liberality. They are for persecuting *Horace* and *Virgil*, in the persons of their Successors, (for such is every man, who has any part of their Soul and Fire, though in a lesse degree.) Some of their little *Zanies* yet go farther; for they are Persecutors even of *Horace* himself, as far as they are able, by their ignorant and vile imitations of him;* by making an unjust use of his Authority, and turning his Artillery against his Friends. But how would he disdain to be Copyed by such hands! I dare answer for him, he would be more uneasie in their company, than he was with *Crispinus* their Forefather in the *Holy Way** and would no more have allow'd them a place amongst the Critiques, than he would *Demetrius* the Mimique, and *Tigellius* the Buffoon;

> ——*Demetri, teq; Tigelli,*
> *Discipulorum inter jubeo plorare Cathedras.**

With what scorn would he look down on such miserable Translators, who make Doggrel of his *Latine*, mistake his meaning, misapply his censures, and often contradict their own? His is fix'd as a Land-Mark to set out the bounds of Poetry,

> ——*Saxum, antiquum ingens*

*Limes agro positus litem ut discerneret arvis.* *

But other Arms than theirs, and other Sinews are requir'd, to raise the weight of such an Author; and when they would toss him against their Enemies,

*Genua labant, gelidus concrevit frigore sanguis,*
*Tum lapis ipse, viri vacuum per inane volutus*
*Nec spatium evasit totum, nec pertulit ictum.* *

For my part, I would wish no other revenge, either for my self or the rest of the Poets, from this Rhyming Judge of the Twelvepenny Gallery,* this Legitimate Son of *Sternhold,** than that he would subscribe his Name to his censure, or (not to tax him beyond his learning) set his Mark: for shou'd he own himself publickly, and come from behind the Lyons Skin,* they whom he condemns wou'd be thankful to him, they whom he praises wou'd chuse to be condemned; and the Magistrates whom he has elected,* wou'd modestly withdraw from their employment, to avoid the scandal of his nomination. The sharpness of his Satyr, next to himself, falls most heavily on his Friends, and they ought never to forgive him for commending them perpetually the wrong way, and sometimes by contraries. If he have a Friend whose hastiness in writing is his greatest fault, *Horace* wou'd have taught him to have minc'd the matter, and to have call'd it readiness of thought, and a flowing fancy; for friendship will allow a man to Christen an imperfection by the name of some neighbour virtue:

*Vellem in amicitiâ sic erraremus; & isti*
*Errori, nomen virtus posuisset honestum.* *

But he would never have allow'd him to have call'd a slow man hasty, or a hasty Writer a slow Drudge, as *Juvenal* explains it:

——*Canibus pigris, scabieq; vetustâ*
*Levibus, & siccæ lambentibus ora lucernæ*
*Nomen erit, Pardus, Tygris, Leo; si quid adhuc est*
*Quod fremit in terris violentius.* *

Yet *Lucretius* laughs at a foolish Lover, even for excusing the Imperfections of his Mistress:

*Nigra* μελιζχροος *est, immunda & fœtida* ακοσμος,
*Balba loqui non quit,* τραυλιζει; *muta pudens est, &c.* \*

But to drive it, *ad Æthiopem Cygnum*\* is not to be indur'd. I leave him to interpret this by the benefit of his *French* Version on the other side, and without farther considering him, than I have the rest of my illiterate Censors, whom I have disdain'd to answer, because they are not qualified for Judges. It remains that I acquaint the Reader, that I have endeavoured in this Play to follow the practise of the Ancients, who, as Mr *Rymer*\* has judiciously observ'd are and ought to be our Masters. *Horace* likewise gives it for a Rule in his *Art of Poetry*,

> ——*Vos exemplaria Græca*
> *Nocturnâ versate manu, versate diurnâ.* \*

Yet, though their Models are regular, they are too little for *English* Tragedy; which requires to be built in a larger compass. I could give an instance in the *Oedipus Tyrannus*, which was the Masterpiece of *Sophocles*; but I reserve it for a more fit occasion, which I hope to have hereafter.\* In my Stile I have profess'd to imitate the Divine *Shakespeare*; which that I might perform more freely, I have dis-incumber'd my self from Rhyme. Not that I condemn my former way, but that this is more proper to my present purpose. I hope I need not to explain my self, that I have not Copy'd my Author servilely: Words and Phrases must of necessity receive a change in succeeding Ages: but 'tis almost a Miracle that much of his Language remains so pure; and that he who began Dramatique Poetry amongst us, untaught by any, and, as *Ben Johnson* tells us, without Learning,\* should by the force of his own Genius perform so much, that in a manner he has left no praise for any who come after him. The occasion is fair, and the subject would be pleasant to handle the difference of Stiles betwixt him and *Fletcher*, and wherein, and how far they are both to be imitated. But since I must not be over-confident of my own performance after him, it will be prudence in me to be silent. Yet I hope I may affirm, and without vanity, that by imitating him, I have excell'd my self throughout the Play; and particularly, that I prefer the Scene betwixt *Antony* and *Ventidius* in the first Act, to any thing which I have written in this kind.

# PROLOGUE *to* Antony and Cleopatra

What Flocks of Critques hover here to day, ⎫
As Vultures wait on Armies for their Prey, ⎬
All gaping for the Carcass of a Play! ⎭
With Croaking Notes they bode some dire event;
And follow dying Poets by the scent.
Ours gives himself for gone; y'have watch'd your time!
He fights this day unarm'd; without his Rhyme;
And brings a Tale which often has been told;
As sad as Dido's;* and almost as old.
His Heroe, whom you Wits his Bully *call,*          10
Bates of his mettle* and scarce rants at all:
He's somewhat lewd; but a well-meaning mind;
Weeps much; fights little; but is wond'rous kind:
In short, a Pattern, and Companion fit,
For all the keeping Tonyes* of the Pit.
I cou'd name more; A Wife, and Mistress too; ⎫
Both (to be plain) too good for most of you: ⎬
The Wife well-natur'd, and the Mistress true. ⎭
  Now, Poets, if your fame has been his care;
Allow him all the candour you can spare.          20
A brave Man scorns to quarrel once a day;
Like Hectors,* in at every petty fray.
Let those find fault whose Wit's so very small,
They've need to show that they can think at all:
Errours like Straws upon the surface flow;
He who would search for Pearls must dive below.
Fops may have leave to level all they can;
As Pigmies wou'd be glad to lopp a Man.
Half-Wits are Fleas; so little and so light;
We scarce cou'd know they live, but that they bite.      30
But, as the Rich, when tir'd with daily Feasts,
For change, become their next poor Tenants Ghests;
Drink hearty Draughts of Ale, from plain brown Bowls,

*And snatch the homely Rasher\* from the Coals:*
*So you, retiring from much better Cheer,*
*For once, may venture to do penance here.*
*And since that plenteous Autumn now is past,*
*Whose Grapes and Peaches have Indulg'd your taste,*
*Take in good part from our poor Poets boord,*
*Such rivell'd\* Fruits as Winter can afford.*                    40

# PERSONS REPRESENTED

---

MARC ANTONY, Mr *Hart*
VENTIDIUS, his General, Mr *Mohun*
DOLLABELLA, his Friend, Mr *Clarke*
ALEXAS, the Queens Eunuch, Mr *Goodman*
SERAPION, Priest of *Isis*, Mr *Griffin*
Another Priest, Mr *Coysh*
  Servants to *Antony*

CLEOPATRA, Queen of Ægypt, Mrs *Boutell*
OCTAVIA, *Antony's* Wife, Mrs *Corey*
CHARMION, ⎫
        ⎬ *Cleopatra's* Maids
IRAS, ⎭
ANTONY'S two little Daughters.

Scene *Alexandria*.

# ACT I

## Scene i

*Scene, the Temple of Isis*

*Enter* SERAPION, MYRIS, *Priests of* Isis

SERAPION: Portents, and Prodigies, are grown so frequent,
That they have lost their Name. Our fruitful *Nile*
Flow'd ere the wonted Season, with a Torrent
So unexpected, and so wondrous fierce,
That the wild Deluge overtook the haste
Ev'n of the Hinds that watch'd it: Men and Beasts
Were born above the tops of Trees, that grew
On th' utmost Margin of the Water-mark.
Then, with so swift an Ebb, the Floud drove backward,
It split from underneath the Scaly Herd:                    10
Here monstrous *Phocæ** panted on the Shore;
Forsaken *Dolphins* there, with their broad tails,
Lay lashing the departing Waves: Hard by 'em,
Sea-Horses* floundring in the slimy mud,
Toss'd up their heads, and dash'd the ooze about 'em.
           *Enter* ALEXAS *behind them*
MYRIS: Avert these Omens, Heav'n.
SERAPION: Last night, between the hours of Twelve and
     One,
In a lone Isle o'th' Temple while I walk'd,
A Whirl-wind rose, that, with a violent blast,
Shook all the Dome: the Doors around me clapt,          20
The Iron Wicket, that defends the Vault,
Where the long Race of *Ptolemies* is lay'd,
Burst open, and disclos'd the mighty dead.
From out each Monument, in order plac'd,
An Armed Ghost start up: the Boy-King* last

Rear'd his inglorious head. A peal of groans
Then follow'd, and a lamentable voice
Cry'd, Ægypt *is no more*. My blood ran back,
My shaking knees against each other knock'd:
On the cold pavement down I fell intranc'd,*                    30
And so unfinish'd left the horrid Scene.

ALEXAS: (*showing himself*) And, Dream'd you this? or, Did
    invent the Story,
To frighten our *Ægyptian* Boys withal,
And train 'em up betimes in fear of Priesthood?

SERAPION: My Lord, I saw you not,
    Nor meant my words should reach your ears; but what
    I utter'd was most true.

ALEXAS: A foolish Dream,
    Bred from the fumes of indigested Feasts,
    And holy Luxury.

SERAPION:          I know my duty:
    This goes no farther.                                   40

ALEXAS:             'Tis not fit it should.
    Nor would the times now bear it, were it true.
    All Southern, from yon hills, the *Roman* Camp
    Hangs o'er us black and threatning, like a Storm
    Just breaking on our heads.

SERAPION: Our faint *Ægyptians* pray for *Antony*;
    But in their Servile hearts they own *Octavius*.

MYRIS: Why then does *Antony* dream out his hours,
    And tempts not Fortune for a noble Day,
    Which might redeem, what *Actium** lost?

ALEXAS: He thinks 'tis past recovery.                          50

SERAPION:             Yet the Foe
    Seems not to press the Siege.

ALEXAS:             O, there's the wonder.
    *Mæcenas* and *Agrippa*, who can most
    With *Cæsar*, are his Foes. His Wife *Octavia*,
    Driv'n from his House, solicits her revenge;
    And *Dollabella*, who was once his Friend,
    Upon some private grudge, now seeks his ruine:
    Yet still War seems on either side to sleep.

SERAPION: 'Tis strange that *Antony*, for some dayes past,
  Has not beheld the face of *Cleopatra*;
  But here, in *Isis* Temple, lives retir'd,                60
  And makes his heart a prey to black despair.

ALEXAS: 'Tis true; and we much fear he hopes by absence
  To cure his mind of Love.

SERAPION:                      If he be vanquish'd,
  Or make his peace, *Ægypt* is doom'd to be
  A *Roman* Province; and our plenteous Harvests
  Must then redeem the scarceness of their Soil.
  While *Antony* stood firm, our *Alexandria*
  Rival'd proud *Rome* (Dominions other Seat)
  And Fortune striding, like a vast *Colossus*,
  Cou'd fix an equal foot of Empire here.                  70

ALEXAS: Had I my wish, these Tyrants of all Nature
  Who Lord it o'er Mankind, should perish, perish,
  Each by the others Sword; but, since our will
  Is lamely follow'd by our pow'r, we must
  Depend on one; with him to rise or fall.

SERAPION: How stands the Queen affected?

ALEXAS:                              O, she dotes,
  She dotes, *Serapion*, on this vanquish'd Man,
  And winds her self about his mighty ruins;
  Whom would she yet forsake, yet yield him up,
  This hunted prey, to his pursuers hands,                 80
  She might preserve us all; but 'tis in vain—
  This changes my designs, this blasts my Counsels,
  And makes me use all means to keep him here,
  Whom I could wish divided from her Arms
  Far as the Earth's deep Center. Well, you know
  The state of things; no more of your ill Omens,
  And black Prognosticks,* labour to confirm
  The peoples hearts.

*Enter* VENTIDIUS, *talking aside with a Gentleman of*
                    ANTONY'S

SERAPION:     These *Romans* will o'rehear us.
  But, Who's that Stranger? By his Warlike port,
  His fierce demeanor, and erected look,*                  90

He's of no vulgar note.
ALEXAS:      O 'tis *Ventidius*,
Our Emp'rors great Lieutenant in the East,
Who first show'd *Rome* that *Parthia* could be conquer'd.
When *Antony* return'd from *Syria* last,
He left this Man to guard the *Roman* Frontiers.
SERAPION: You seem to know him well.
ALEXAS: Too well. I saw him in *Cilicia* first,
When *Cleopatra* there met *Antony*:
A mortal foe he was to us, and *Ægypt*.
But, let me witness to the worth I hate,                                    100
A braver *Roman* never drew a Sword:
Firm to his Prince; but, as a friend, not slave.
He ne'r was of his pleasures; but presides
O're all his cooler hours and morning counsels:
In short, the plainness, fierceness, rugged virtue
Of an old true-stampt *Roman* lives in him.
His coming bodes I know not what of ill
To our affairs. Withdraw, to mark him better;
And I'll acquaint you why I sought you here,
And what's our present work.                                              110
(*They withdraw to a corner of the Stage; and* VENTIDIUS,
              *with the other, comes forwards to the front.*)
VENTIDIUS:                        Not see him, say you?
I say, I must, and will.
I GENTLEMAN:              He has commanded,
On pain of death, none should approach his presence.
VENTIDIUS: I bring him news will raise his drooping
    Spirits,
Give him new life.
I GENTLEMAN:       He sees not *Cleopatra*.
VENTIDIUS: Would he had never seen her.
I GENTLEMAN: He eats not, drinks not, sleeps not, has no
    use
Of any thing, but thought; or, if he talks,
'Tis to himself, and then 'tis perfect raving:
Then he defies the World, and bids it pass;
Sometimes he gnawes his Lip, and Curses loud                              120

The Boy *Octavius*;\* then he draws his mouth
Into a scornful smile, and cries, *Take all,*
*The World's not worth my care.*
VENTIDIUS:     Just, just his nature.
Virtues his path; but sometimes 'tis too narrow
For his vast Soul; and then he starts out wide,
And bounds into a Vice that bears him far
From his first course, and plunges him in ills:
But, when his danger makes him find his fault,
Quick to observe, and full of sharp remorse,
He censures eagerly his own misdeeds,                        130
Judging himself with malice to himself,
And not forgiving what as Man he did,
Because his other parts are more than Man.
He must not thus be lost.

                    (ALEXAS *and the Priests come forward*)

ALEXAS: You have your full Instructions, now advance;
Proclaim your Orders loudly.
SERAPION: *Romans, Ægyptians,* hear the Queen's Command.
Thus *Cleopatra* bids, Let Labor cease,
To Pomp and Triumphs give this happy day,
That gave the World a Lord; 'tis *Antony*'s.                 140
Live, *Antony*; and *Cleopatra* live.
Be this the general voice sent up to Heav'n,
And every publick place repeat this eccho.
VENTIDIUS: *(aside)* Fine Pageantry!
SERAPION:     Set out before your doors
The Images of all your sleeping Fathers,
With Laurels crown'd; with Laurels wreath your posts,
And strow with Flow'rs the Pavement; Let the Priests
Do present\* Sacrifice; pour out the Wine,
And call the Gods to joyn with you in gladness.
VENTIDIUS: Curse on the tongue that bids this general joy.   150
Can they be friends of *Antony*, who Revel
When *Antony*'s in danger? Hide, for shame,
You *Romans*, your Great grandsires Images,
For fear their Souls should animate their Marbles,

To blush at their degenerate Progeny.

ALEXAS: A love which knows no bounds to *Antony*,
 Would mark the Day with honours; when all Heav'n
 Labor'd for him, when each propitious Star
 Stood wakeful in his Orb, to watch that hour,
 And shed his better influence. Her own Birth-day   160
 Our Queen neglected, like a Vulgar Fate,
 That pass'd obscurely by.

VENTIDIUS:       Would it had slept,
 Divided far from his; till some remote
 And future Age had call'd it out, to ruin
 Some other Prince, not him.

ALEXAS:  Your Emperor,
 Tho grown unkind, would be more gentle, than
 T' upbraid my Queen, for loving him too well.

VENTIDIUS: Does the mute Sacrifice upbraid the Priest?
 He knows him not his Executioner.
 Or, she has deck'd his ruin with her love,    170
 Led him in golden bands to gaudy slaughter,
 And made perdition pleasing: She has left him
 The blank of what he was;
 I tell thee, Eunuch, she has quite unman'd him:
 Can any *Roman* see, and know him now,
 Thus alter'd from the Lord of half Mankind,
 Unbent, unsinew'd, made a Womans Toy,
 Shrunk from the vast extent of all his honors,
 And crampt within a corner of the World?
 O, *Antony*!                180
 Thou bravest Soldier, and thou best of Friends!
 Bounteous as Nature; next to Nature's God!
 Could'st thou but make new Worlds, so wouldst thou
  give 'em,
 As bounty were thy being: Rough in Battel,
 As the first *Romans*, when they went to War;
 Yet, after Victory, more pitiful,
 Than all their Praying Virgins left at home!

ALEXAS: Would you add to those more shining Virtues,
 His truth to her who loves him.

VENTIDIUS:     Would I could not.
  But, Wherefore waste I precious hours with thee?          190
  Thou art her darling mischief, her chief Engin,*
  *Antony*'s other Fate. Go, tell thy Queen,
  *Ventidius* is arriv'd, to end her Charms.
  Let your *Ægyptian* Timbrels* play alone;
  Nor mix Effeminate Sounds with *Roman* Trumpets.
  You dare not fight for *Antony*; go Pray,
  And keep your Cowards-Holy-day in Temples.

                   [*Exeunt* ALEXAS, SERAPION]

    *Enter second Gentleman of* MARK ANTONY

2 GENTLEMAN: The Emperor approaches, and commands,
  On pain of Death, that none presume to stay.
1 GENTLEMAN: I dare not disobey him.          200
                (*Going out with the other*)

VENTIDIUS:     Well, I dare.
  But, I'll observe him first unseen, and find
  Which way his humour drives: the rest I'll venture.
                   (*Withdraws*)

    *Enter* ANTONY, *walking with a disturb'd Motion,*
            *before he speaks*

ANTONY: They tell me, 'tis my Birth-day, and I'll keep it
  With double pomp of sadness.
  'Tis what the day deserves, which gave me breath.
  Why was I rais'd the Meteor of the World,
  Hung in the Skies, and blazing as I travel'd,
  Till all my fires were spent; and then cast downward
  To be trod out by *Caesar*?
VENTIDIUS: (*aside*)  On my Soul,
  'Tis mournful, wondrous mournful!          210
ANTONY:     Count thy gains.
  Now, *Antony*, Wouldst thou be born for this?
  Glutton of Fortune, thy devouring youth
  Has starv'd thy wanting Age.
VENTIDIUS:     How sorrow shakes him!          (*Aside*)
  So, now the Tempest tears him up by th' Roots,
  And on the ground extends the noble ruin.

ANTONY: (*having thrown himself down*) Lye there, thou
    shadow of an Emperor;
  The place thou pressest on thy Mother Earth
  Is all thy Empire now: now it contains thee;
  Some fews dayes hence, and then twill be too large,
  When thou'rt contracted in thy narrow Urn,      220
  Shrunk to a few cold Ashes; then *Octavia*,
  (For *Cleopatra* will not live to see it)
  *Octavia* then will have thee all her own,
  And bear thee in her Widow'd hand to *Cæsar*;
  *Cæsar* will weep, the Crocodile will weep,
  To see his Rival of the Universe
  Lye still and peaceful there. I'll think no more on't.
  Give me some Musick; look that it be sad;
  I'll sooth* my Melancholy, till I swell,
  And burst my self with sighing—    (*Soft Musick*) 230
  'Tis somewhat to my humor. Stay, I fancy
  I'm now turn'd wild, a Commoner* of Nature;
  Of all forsaken, and forsaking all;
  Live in a shady Forrest's Sylvan Scene,
  Stretch'd at my length beneath some blasted Oke;
  I lean my head upon the Mossy Bark,
  And look just of a piece, as I grew from it:
  My uncomb'd Locks, matted like Misletoe,
  Hang o'er my hoary Face; a murm'ring Brook
  Runs at my foot.      240
VENTIDIUS:    Methinks I fancy
  My self there too.
ANTONY:    The Herd come jumping by me,
  And fearless, quench their thirst, while I look on,
  And take me for their fellow-Citizen.
  More of this Image, more; it lulls my thoughts.
                  (*Soft Musick again*)
VENTIDIUS: I must disturb him; I can hold no longer.
                  (*Stands before him*)
ANTONY: (*starting up*) Art thou *Ventidius*?
VENTIDIUS:    Are you *Antony*?
  I'm liker what I was, than you to him

I left you last.

ANTONY:     I'm angry.

VENTIDIUS:          So am I.

ANTONY: I would be private: leave me.

VENTIDIUS:     Sir, I love you,

And therefore will not leave you.                    250

ANTONY:     Will not leave me?

Where have you learnt that Answer? Who am I?

VENTIDIUS: My Emperor; the Man I love next Heav'n:

If I said more, I think 'twere scarce a Sin;

Y'are all that's good, and god-like.

ANTONY:     All that's wretched.

You will not leave me then?

VENTIDIUS:     'Twas too presuming

To say I would not; but I dare not leave you:

And, 'tis unkind in you to chide me hence

So soon, when I so far have come to see you.

ANTONY: Now thou hast seen me, art thou satisfy'd?

For, if a Friend, thou hast beheld enough;         260

And, if a Foe, too much.

VENTIDIUS: (weeping) Look, Emperor, this is no common
    Deaw,

I have not wept this Forty year; but now

My Mother comes afresh into my eyes;

I cannot help her softness.

ANTONY: By Heav'n, he weeps, poor good old Man, he
    weeps!

The big round drops course one another down

The furrows of his cheeks. Stop 'em, *Ventidius*,

Or I shall blush to death: they set my shame,

That caus'd 'em, full before me.                     270

VENTIDIUS:     I'll do my best.

ANTONY: Sure there's contagion in the tears of Friends:

See, I have caught it too. Believe me, 'tis not

For my own griefs, but thine—Nay, Father.

VENTIDIUS:     Emperor! Why, that's the stile of Victory,

The Conqu'ring Soldier, red with unfelt wounds,

Salutes his General so: but never more

Shall that sound reach my ears.

VENTIDIUS:     I warrant you.

ANTONY: *Actium, Actium!* Oh—

VENTIDIUS:     It sits too near you.

ANTONY: Here, here it lies; a lump of Lead by day,
   And, in my short distracted nightly slumbers,                    280
   The Hag that rides my Dreams—*

VENTIDIUS: Out with it; give it vent.

ANTONY:     Urge not my shame.
   I lost a Battel.

VENTIDIUS:     So has *Julius* done.

ANTONY: Thou favour'st me, and speak'st not half thou
      think'st;
   For *Julius* fought it out, and lost it fairly:
   But *Antony*—

VENTIDIUS:     Nay, stop not.

ANTONY:     *Antony*
   (Well, thou wilt have it) like a coward, fled,
   Fled while his Soldiers fought; fled first, *Ventidius*.[1]
   Thou long'st to curse me, and I give thee leave.
   I know thou cam'st prepar'd to rail.                             290

VENTIDIUS:     I did.

ANTONY: I'll help thee.—I have been a Man, *Ventidius*.

VENTIDIUS: Yes, and a brave one; but—

ANTONY:     I know thy meaning.
   But, I have lost my Reason, have disgrac'd
   The name of Soldier, with inglorious ease.
   In the full Vintage of my flowing honors,
   Sate still, and saw it prest by other hands.
   Fortune came smiling to my youth, and woo'd it,
   And purple greatness met my ripen'd years.
   When first I came to Empire, I was born
   On Tides of People, crouding to my Triumphs;                     300
   The wish of Nations; and the willing World
   Receiv'd me as its pledge of future peace;
   I was so great, so happy, so belov'd,

---

[1] 284–8. Based on *Antony and Cleopatra*, I.ii.109–11.

Fate could not ruine me; till I took pains
And work'd against my Fortune, chid her from me,
And turn'd her loose; yet still she came again.
My careless dayes, and my luxurious nights,
At length have weary'd her, and now she's gone,
Gone, gone, divorc'd for ever. Help me, Soldier,
To curse this Mad-man, this industrious Fool,                        310
Who labour'd to be wretched: pr'ythee curse me.

VENTIDIUS: No.

ANTONY:    Why?

VENTIDIUS:        You are too sensible already
Of what y'have done, too conscious of your failings,
And like a Scorpion, whipt by others first
To fury, sting your self in mad revenge.
I would bring Balm, and pour it in your wounds,
Cure your distemper'd mind, and heal your fortunes.

ANTONY: I know thou would'st.

VENTIDIUS:    I will.

ANTONY:        Ha, ha, ha, ha.

VENTIDIUS: You laugh.

ANTONY:    I do, to see officious* love
Give Cordials to the dead.                                          320

VENTIDIUS:        You would be lost then?

ANTONY: I am.

VENTIDIUS:    I say, you are not. Try your fortune.

ANTONY: I have, to th' utmost. Dost thou think me
    desperate,
Without just cause? No, when I found all lost
Beyond repair, I hid me from the World,
And learnt to scorn it here; which now I do
So heartily, I think it is not worth
The cost of keeping.

VENTIDIUS:    Cæsar thinks not so:
He'll thank you for the gift he could not take.
You would be kill'd, like Tully,* would you? do,
Hold our your Throat to Cæsar, and dye tamely.                      330

ANTONY: No, I can kill my self; and so resolve.

VENTIDIUS: I can dy with you too, when time shall serve;

But Fortune calls upon us now to live,
To fight, to Conquer.

ANTONY:    Sure thou Dream'st, *Ventidius*.

VENTIDIUS: No; 'tis you Dream; you sleep away your
   hours
In desperate sloth, miscall'd *Phylosophy*.
Up, up, for Honor's sake; twelve Legions wait you,
And long to call you Chief: by painful journeys,
I led 'em, patient, both of heat and hunger,
Down from the *Parthian* Marches* to the *Nile*.                340
'Twill do you good to see their Sun-burnt faces,
Their skar'd cheeks, and chopt* hands; there's virtue in
   'em,
They'l sell those mangled limbs at dearer rates
Than yon trim Bands* can buy.

ANTONY:    Where left you them?

VENTIDIUS: I said, in lower *Syria*.

ANTONY:    Bring 'em hither;
There may be life in these.

VENTIDIUS:    They will not come.

ANTONY: Why did'st thou mock my hopes with promis'd
   aids
To double my despair? They'r mutinous.

VENTIDIUS: Most firm and loyal.

ANTONY:    Yet they will not march
To succor me. Oh trifler!                                    350

VENTIDIUS:    They petition
You would make hast to head 'em.

ANTONY:    I'm besieg'd.

VENTIDIUS: There's but one way shut up: How came I
   hither?

ANTONY: I will not stir.

VENTIDIUS:    They would perhaps desire
A better reason.

ANTONY:    I have never us'd*
My Soldiers to demand a reason of
My actions. Why did they refuse to March?

VENTIDIUS: They said they would not fight for *Cleopatra*.

ANTONY: What was't they said?

VENTIDIUS: They said, they would not fight for *Cleopatra*.
Why should they fight indeed, to make her Conquer,     360
And make you more a Slave? to gain you Kingdoms,
Which, for a kiss, at your next midnight Feast,
You'l sell to her? then she new-names her Jewels,
And calls this Diamond such or such a Tax,
Each Pendant in her ear shall be a Province.

ANTONY: *Ventidius*, I allow your Tongue free licence
On all my other faults; but, on your life,
No word of *Cleopatra*: She deserves
More World's than I can lose.

VENTIDIUS:      Behold, you Pow'rs,
To whom you have intrusted Humankind;     370
See *Europe*, *Africk*, *Asia* put in ballance,
And all weigh'd down by one light worthless Woman!
I think the gods are *Antony*'s, and give,
Like Prodigals, this neather World away,
To none but wastful hands.

ANTONY:      You grow presumptuous.

VENTIDIUS: I take the priviledge of plain love to speak.

ANTONY: Plain love! plain arrogance, plain insolence.
Thy Men are Cowards; thou, an envious Traitor;
Who, under seeming honesty, hast vented
The burden of thy rank* o'reflowing Gall.     380
O that thou wert my equal; great in Arms
As the first *Cæsar* was, that I might kill thee
Without a Stain to Honor!

VENTIDIUS:      You may kill me;
You have done more already, call'd me Traitor.

ANTONY: Art thou not one?

VENTIDIUS:      For showing you your self,
Which none else durst have done? but had I been
That name, which I disdain to speak again,
I needed not have sought your abject fortunes,
Come to partake your fate, to dye with you.
What hindred me t' have led my Conqu'ring Eagles     390
To fill *Octavius*'s Bands? I could have been

A Traitor then, a glorious happy Traitor,
And not have been so call'd.

ANTONY:      Forgive me, Soldier:
I've been too passionate.

VENTIDIUS:      You thought me false;
Thought my old age betray'd you: kill me, Sir;
Pray kill me; yet you need not, your kindness
Has left your Sword no work.

ANTONY:      I did not think so;
I said it in my rage: pr'ythee forgive me:
Why did'st thou tempt my anger, by discovery
Of what I would not hear?                                    400

VENTIDIUS:      No Prince but you,
Could merit that sincerity I us'd,
Nor durst another Man have ventur'd it;
But you, ere Love misled your wandring eyes,
Were sure the chief and best of Human Race,
Fram'd in the very pride and boast of Nature,
So perfect, that the gods who form'd you wonder'd
At their own skill, and cry'd, *A lucky hit
Has mended our design.* Their envy hindred,*
Else you had been immortal, and a pattern,
When Heav'n would work for ostentation sake,          410
To copy out again.

ANTONY:      But *Cleopatra*—
Go on; for I can bear it now.

VENTIDIUS:      No more.

ANTONY: Thou dar'st not trust my Passion; but thou
      may'st:
Thou only lov'st; the rest have flatter'd me.

VENTIDIUS: Heav'n's blessing on your heart, for that kind
      word.
May I believe you love me? speak again.

ANTONY: Indeed I do. Speak this, and this, and this.
      (*Hugging him*)
Thy praises were unjust; but, I'll deserve 'em,
And yet mend all. Do with me what thou wilt;
Lead me to victory, thou know'st the way.                420

VENTIDIUS: And, Will you leave this—

ANTONY:    Pr'ythee do not curse her,
And I will leave her; though, Heav'n knows, I love
Beyond Life, Conquest, Empire; all, but Honor:
But I will leave her.

VENTIDIUS:    That's my Royal Master.
And, Shall we fight?

ANTONY:    I warrant thee, old Soldier,
Thou shalt behold me once again in Iron,
And at the head of our old Troops, that beat
The *Parthians*, cry alloud, *Come follow me.*

VENTIDIUS: O now I hear my Emperor! in that word
*Octavius* fell. Gods, let me see that day,                    430
And, if I have ten years behind, take all;
I'll thank you for th' exchange.

ANTONY:    Oh *Cleopatra*!

VENTIDIUS: Again?

ANTONY:    I've done: in that last sigh, she went.
*Cæsar* shall know what 'tis to force a Lover,
From all he holds most dear.

VENTIDIUS:    Methinks you breath
Another Soul: Your looks are more Divine;
You speak a Heroe, and you move a God.

ANTONY: O, thou hast fir'd me; my Soul's up in Arms,
And Mans each part about me: once again,
That noble eagerness of fight has seiz'd me;                    440
That eagerness, with which I darted upward
To *Cassius*'s Camp: In vain the steepy Hill,
Oppos'd my way; in vain a War of Speares
Sung round my head; and planted all my shield:
I won the Trenches, while my formost Men
Lag'd on the Plain below.

VENTIDIUS:    Ye Gods, ye Gods,
For such another hour.

ANTONY:    Come on, My Soldier!
Our hearts and armes are still the same: I long
Once more to meet our foes; that Thou and I,
Like Time and Death, marching before our Troops,              450

May taste fate to 'em;* Mowe 'em out a passage,
And, entring where the foremost Squadrons yield,
Begin the noble Harvest of the Field.          [*Exeunt*]

# ACT II

## Scene i

*Enter* CLEOPATRA, IRAS, *and* ALEXAS

CLEOPATRA: What shall I do, or whither shall I turn?
  *Ventidius* has o'rcome, and he will go.
ALEXAS: He goes to fight for you.
CLEOPATRA: Then he wou'd see me, ere he went to fight:
  Flatter me not: if once he goes, he's lost:
  And all my hopes destroy'd.
ALEXAS:     Does this weak passion
  Become a Mighty Queen?
CLEOPATRA:     I am no Queen;
  Is this to be a Queen, to be besieg'd
  By yon insulting *Roman*; and to wait
  Each hour the Victor's Chain? These ills are small;     10
  For *Antony* is lost, and I can mourn
  For nothing else but him. Now come, *Octavius*,
  I have no more to lose; prepare thy Bands;
  I'm fit to be a Captive: *Antony*
  Has taught my mind the fortune of a Slave.
IRAS: Call Reason to assist you.
CLEOPATRA:     I have none,
  And none would have: my Love's a noble madness,
  Which shows the cause deserv'd it. Moderate sorrow
  Fits vulgar Love; and for a vulgar Man:
  But I have lov'd with such transcendent passion,     20
  I soard, at first, quite out of Reasons view,
  And now am lost above it – No, I'm proud
  'Tis thus: would *Antony* could see me now;
  Think you he would not sigh; for he is noble-natur'd,
  And bears a tender heart: I know him well.

Ah, no, I know him not; I knew him once,
But now 'tis past.

IRAS:       Let it be past with you:
Forget him, Madam.

CLEOPATRA:       Never, never, *Iras*.
He once was mine; and once, though now 'tis gone,                   30
Leaves a faint Image of possession still.

ALEXAS: Think him unconstant, cruel, and ungrateful.

CLEOPATRA: I cannot: if I could, those thoughts were vain;
Faithless, ungrateful, cruel, though he be,
I still must love him.

Enter CHARMION

Now, What news my *Charmion*?
Willl he be kind? and, Will he not forsake me?
Am I to live, or dye? nay, Do I live?
Or am I dead? for, when he gave his answer,
Fate took the word, and then I liv'd, or dy'd.

CHARMION: I found him, Madam—                                      40

CLEOPATRA:       A long Speech preparing?
If thou bring'st comfort, hast, and give it me;
For never was more need.

IRAS:       I know he loves you.

CLEOPATRA: Had he been kind, her eyes had told me so,
Before her tongue could speak it: now she studies,
To soften what he said. But give me death,
Just as he sent it, *Charmion*, undisguis'd,
And in the words he spoke.

CHARMION:       I found him then
Incompass'd round, I think, with Iron Statues;
So mute, so motionless his Soldiers stood,
While awfully he cast his eyes about,                              50
And ev'ry Leaders hopes or fears survey'd:
Methought he look'd resolv'd, and yet not pleas'd.
When he beheld me struling in the croud,
He blush'd, and bade, make way.

ALEXAS:       There's comfort yet.

CHARMION: *Ventidius* fixt his eyes upon my passage,
Severely, as he meant to frown me back,

And sullenly gave place: I told my message,
Just as you gave it, broken and disorder'd;
I numbred in it all your sighs and tears;
And while I mov'd your pitiful request,                    60
That you but only beg'd a last farewel,
He fetch'd an inward groan, and ev'ry time
I nam'd you, sigh'd, as if his heart were breaking,
But shun'd my eyes, and guiltily look'd down;
He seem'd not now that awful *Antony*
Who shook an Arm'd Assembly with his Nod,
But making show as he would rub his eyes,
Disguis'd and blotted out a falling tear.

CLEOPATRA: Did he then weep? and, Was I worth a tear?
If what thou hast to say be not as pleasing,                    70
Tell me no more, but let me dye contented.

CHARMION: He bid me say, He knew himself so well,
He could deny you nothing, if he saw you;
And therefore—

CLEOPATRA:     Thou would'st say, he wou'd not see me?

CHARMION: And therefore beg'd you not to use a power,
Which he could ill resist; yet he should ever
Respect you as he ought.

CLEOPATRA:     Is that a word
For *Antony* to use to *Cleopatra*?
Oh that faint word, *Respect*! how I disdain it!
Disdain my self, for loving after it!                    80
He should have kept that word for cold *Octavia*.
Respect is for a Wife: Am I that thing,
That dull insipid lump, without desires,
And without pow'r to give 'em?

ALEXAS:     You misjudge;
You see through Love, and that deludes your sight;
As, what is strait, seems crooked through the Water:
But I, who bear my reason undisturb'd,
Can see this *Antony*, this dreaded Man,
A fearful slave, who fain would run away,
And shuns his Master's eyes: if you pursue him,                    90
My life on't, he still drags a chain along,

That needs must clog his flight.

CLEOPATRA:     Could I believe thee!—

ALEXAS: By ev'ry circumstance I know he Loves.
True, he's hard prest, by Intrest* and by Honor;
Yet he but doubts, and parlyes, and casts out
Many a long look for succor.

CLEOPATRA:     He sends word,
He fears to see my face.

ALEXAS:     And would you more?
He shows his weakness who declines the Combat;
And you must urge your fortune. Could he speak
More plainly? To my ears, the Message sounds                    100
*Come to my rescue,* Cleopatra, *come;*
*Come, free me from* Ventidius; *from my Tyrant:*
*See me, and give me a pretence to leave him.*
I hear his Trumpets. This way he must pass.
Please you, retire a while; I'll work him first,
That he may bend more easie.

CLEOPATRA:     You shall rule me;
But all, I fear, in vain.     [*Exit with* CHARMION, *and* IRAS]

ALEXAS:     I fear so too;
Though I conceal'd my thoughts, to make her bold:
But, 'tis our utmost means, and Fate befriend it.

                                        (*Withdraws*)

*Enter* LICTORS *with* FASCES; *one bearing the Eagle: then*
     *Enter* ANTONY *with* VENTIDIUS, *follow'd by*
                    *other Commanders*

ANTONY: *Octavius* is the Minion of blind Chance,                    110
But holds from Virtue* nothing.

VENTIDIUS:     Has he courage?

ANTONY: But just enough to season him from Coward.
O, 'tis the coldest youth upon a Charge,
The most deliberate* fighter! if he ventures
(As in *Illyria* once they say he did
To storm a Town) 'tis when he cannot chuse,
When all the World have fixt their eyes upon him;
And then he lives on that for seven years after.
But, at a close* revenge he never fails.

VENTIDIUS: I heard, you challeng'd him.                    120

ANTONY:     I did, *Ventidius*.
  What think'st thou was his answer? 'twas so tame,—
  He said he had more wayes than one to dye;[2]
  I had not.

VENTIDIUS:     Poor!

ANTONY:         He has more wayes than one;
  But he would chuse 'em all before that one.

VENTIDIUS: He first would chuse an Ague, or a Fever.

ANTONY: No: it must be an Ague, not a Fever;
  He has no warmth enough to dye by that.

VENTIDIUS: Or old Age, and a Bed.

ANTONY:     I, there's his choice.
  He would live, like a Lamp, to the last wink,
  And crawl upon the utmost verge of life:               130
  O *Hercules*! Why should a Man like this,
  Who dares not trust his fate for one great action,
  Be all the care of Heav'n? Why should he Lord it
  O're Fourscore thousand Men, of whom, each one
  Is braver than himself?

VENTIDIUS:     You conquer'd for him:
  *Philippi* knows it; there you shar'd with him
  That Empire, which your Sword made all your own.

ANTONY: Fool that I was, upon my Eagles Wings
  I bore this Wren,* till I was tir'd with soaring,
  And now he mounts above me.                             140
  Good Heav'ns, Is this, is this the Man who braves me?
  Who bids my age make way? drives me before him,
  To the World's ridge, and sweeps me off like rubbish?

VENTIDIUS: Sir, we lose time; the Troops are mounted all.

ANTONY: Then give the word to March:
  I long to leave this Prison of a Town,
  To joyn thy Legions; and, in open Field,
  Once more to show my face. Lead, my Deliverer.

                    *Enter* ALEXAS

ALEXAS: Great Emperor,

---

[2] 120–3. Based on *Antony and Cleopatra*, IV.i.3–5.

In mighty Arms renown'd above Mankind,                    150
But, in soft pity to th' opprest, a God:
This message sends the mournful *Cleopatra*
To her departing Lord.
VENTIDIUS:      Smooth Sycophant!
ALEXAS: A thousand wishes, and ten thousand Prayers,
Millions of blessings wait you to the Wars,
Millions of sighs and tears she sends you too,
And would have sent
As many dear embraces to your Arms,
As many parting kisses to your Lips;
But those, she fears, have weary'd you already.          160
VENTIDIUS: (*aside*) False Crocodyle!
ALEXAS: And yet she begs not now, you would not leave
    her,
That were a wish too mighty for her hopes,
Too presuming
For her low Fortune, and your ebbing love,
That were a wish for her more prosp'rous dayes,
Her blooming beauty, and your growing kindness.
ANTONY: (*aside*) Well, I must Man it out.— What would
    the Queen?
ALEXAS: First, to these noble Warriors, who attend,
Your daring courage in the Chase of Fame,                170
(Too daring, and too dang'rous for her quiet)
She humbly recommends all she holds dear,
All her own cares and fears, the care of you.
VENTIDIUS: Yes, witness *Actium*.
ANTONY:      Let him speak, *Ventidius*.
ALEXAS: You, when his matchless valor bears him forward,
With ardor too Heroick, on his foes,
Fall down, as she would do, before his feet;
Lye in his way, and stop the paths of Death;
Tell him, this God is not invulnerable,
That absent *Cleopatra* bleeds in him;                   180
And, that you may remember her Petition,
She begs you wear these Trifles, as a pawn,
Which, at your wisht return, she will redeem

                    (*Gives Jewels to the Commanders*)

With all the Wealth of *Ægypt*.
This, to the great *Ventidius* she presents,
Whom she can never count her Enemy.
Because he loves her Lord.

VENTIDIUS:    Tell her I'll none on't;
  I'm not asham'd of honest Poverty:
  Not all the Diamonds of the East can bribe
  *Ventidius* from his faith. I hope to see                    190
  These, and the rest of all her sparkling store,
  Where they shall more deservingly be plac'd.

ANTONY: And who must wear 'em then?

VENTIDIUS:    The wrong'd *Octavia*.

ANTONY: You might have spar'd that word.

VENTIDIUS:    And he that Bribe.

ANTONY: But have I no remembrance?

ALEXAS:    Yes, a dear one:
  Your slave, the Queen—

ANTONY:    My Mistress.

ALEXAS:        Then your Mistress,
  Your Mistress would, she sayes, have sent her Soul,
  But that you had long since; she humbly begs
  This Ruby bracelet, set with bleeding hearts,
  (The emblems of her own) may bind your Arme.        200
                    (*Presenting a Bracelet*)

VENTIDIUS: Now, my best Lord, in Honor's name, I ask
    you,
  For Manhood's sake, and for your own dear safety,
  Touch not these poyson'd gifts,
  Infected by the sender, touch 'em not,
  Miriads of blewest* Plagues lye underneath 'em,
  And more than Aconite* has dipt the Silk.

ANTONY: Nay, now you grow too Cynical, *Ventidius*.
  A Lady's favors may be worn with honor.
  What, to refuse her Bracelet! On my Soul,
  When I lye pensive in my Tent alone,                    210
  'Twill pass the wakeful hours of Winter nights,
  To tell these pretty Beads upon my arm,

To count for every one a soft embrace,
A melting kiss at such and such a time;
And now and then the fury of her love.
When—And what harm's in this?

ALEXAS:     None, none my Lord,
But what's to her, that now 'tis past for ever.

ANTONY: (*going to tye it*) We Soldiers are so aukward—
help me tye it.

ALEXAS: In faith, my Lord, we Courtiers too are aukward
In these affairs: so are all Men indeed;                    220
Ev'n I, who am not one. But shall I speak?

ANTONY: Yes, freely.

ALEXAS:     Then, my Lord, fair hands alone
Are fit to tye it; she, who sent it, can.

VENTIDIUS: Hell, Death; this Eunuch Pandar ruins you.
You will not see her?

              (ALEXAS *whispers an Attendant, who goes out*)

ANTONY:     But to take my leave.

VENTIDIUS: Then I have wash'd an *Æthiope*.\* Y'are
undone;
Y'are in the Toils; y'are taken; y'are destroy'd:
Her eyes do *Cæsar*'s work.

ANTONY:     You fear too soon.
I'm constant to my self: I know my strength;
And yet she shall not think me Barbarous, neither;          230
Born in the depths of *Africk*: I'm a *Roman*,
Bred to the Rules of soft humanity.
A guest, and kindly us'd, should bid farewel.

VENTIDIUS: You do not know.
How weak you are to her, how much an Infant;
You are not proof against a smile, or glance;
A sigh will quite disarm you.

ANTONY:     See, she comes!
Now you shall find your error. Gods, I thank you:
I form'd the danger greater than it was,
And, now 'tis near, 'tis lessen'd.                          240

VENTIDIUS:     Mark the end yet.

              *Enter* CLEOPATRA, CHARMION *and* IRAS

ANTONY: Well, Madam, we are met.

CLEOPATRA:     Is this a Meeting?
Then, we must part?

ANTONY:     We must.

CLEOPATRA:         Who sayes we must?

ANTONY: Our own hard fates.

CLEOPATRA:     We make those Fates our selves.

ANTONY: Yes, we have made 'em; we have lov'd each other
Into our mutual ruin.

CLEOPATRA: The Gods have seen my Joys with envious
eyes;
I have no friends in Heav'n; and all the World,
(As 'twere the bus'ness of Mankind to part us)
Is arm'd against my Love: ev'n you your self
Joyn with the rest; you, you are arm'd against me.     250

ANTONY: I will be justify'd in all I do
To late Posterity, and therefore hear me.
If I mix a lye
With any truth, reproach me freely with it;
Else, favor me with silence.

CLEOPATRA:     You command me,
And I am dumb.

VENTIDIUS: (aside) I like this well: he shows Authority.

ANTONY: That I derive my ruin
From you alone—

CLEOPATRA:     O Heav'ns! I ruin you!

ANTONY: You promis'd me your silence, and you break it     260
Ere I have scarce begun.

CLEOPATRA:     Well, I obey you.

ANTONY: When I beheld you first, it was in Ægypt,
Ere Cæsar* saw your Eyes; you gave me love,
And were too young to know it; that I setled
Your Father in his Throne, was for your sake:
I left th' acknowledgment for time to ripen.
Cæsar stept in, and with a greedy hand
Pluck'd the green fruit, ere the first blush of red,
Yet cleaving to the bough. He was my Lord,
And was, beside, too great for me to rival,     270

But, I deserv'd you first, though he enjoy'd you.
When, after, I beheld you in *Cilicia*,
An Enemy to *Rome*, I pardon'd you.
CLEOPATRA: I clear'd my self—
ANTONY:     Again you break your Promise.
  I lov'd you still, and took your weak excuses,
  Took you into my bosome, stain'd by *Cæsar*,
  And not half mine: I went to *Ægypt* with you
  And hid me from the bus'ness of the World,
  Shut out enquiring Nations from my sight,
  To give whole years to you.                              280
VENTIDIUS: Yes, to your shame be't spoken.     (*Aside*)
ANTONY:     How I lov'd
  Witness ye Dayes and Nights, and all your hours,
  That Danc'd away with Down upon your Feet,
  As all your bus'ness were to count my passion.
  One day past by, and nothing saw but Love;
  Another came, and still 'twas only Love:
  The Suns were weary'd out with looking on,
  And I untyr'd with loving.
  I saw you ev'ry day, and all the day;
  And ev'ry day was still but as the first:                290
  So eager was I still to see you more.
VENTIDIUS: 'Tis all too true.
ANTONY:     *Fulvia*, my Wife, grew jealous,
  As she indeed had reason; rais'd a War
  In *Italy*, to call me back.
VENTIDIUS:     But yet
  You went not.
ANTONY:     While within your arms I lay,
  The World fell mouldring from my hands each hour,
  And left me scarce a grasp (I thank your love for't.)
VENTIDIUS: Well push'd: that last was home.
CLEOPATRA:     Yet may I speak?
ANTONY: If I have urg'd a falshood, yes; else, not.
  Your silence says I have not. *Fulvia* dy'd;                300
  (Pardon, you gods, with my unkindness dy'd.)
  To set the World at Peace, I took *Octavia*,

This *Cæsar*'s Sister; in her pride of youth
And flow'r of Beauty did I wed that Lady,
Whom blushing I must praise, because I left her.
You call'd; my Love obey'd the fatal summons:
This rais'd the *Roman* Arms; the Cause was yours.
I would have fought by Land, where I was stronger;
You hindred it: yet, when I fought at Sea,
Forsook me fighting; and (Oh stain to Honor!                310
Oh lasting shame!) I knew not that I fled;
But fled to follow you.

VENTIDIUS: What haste she made to hoist her purple
        Sails![3] [4]
And, to appear magnificent in flight,
Drew half our strength away.

ANTONY:     All this you caus'd.
And, Would you multiply more ruins on me?
This honest Man, my best, my only friend,
Has gather'd up the Shipwreck of my Fortunes;
Twelve Legions I have left, my last recruits,
And you have watch'd the news, and bring your eyes        320
To seize them too. If you have ought to answer,
Now speak, you have free leave.

ALEXAS: (*aside*)  She stands confounded:
Despair is in her eyes.

VENTIDIUS: Now lay a Sigh i'th' way, to stop his passage:
Prepare a Tear, and bid it for his Legions;
'Tis like they shall be sold.

CLEOPATRA: How shall I plead my cause, when you, my
        Judge
Already have condemn'd me? Shall I bring
The Love you bore me for my Advocate?
That now is turn'd against me, that destroys me;           330
For, love once past, is, at the best, forgotten;
But oftner sours to hate: 'twill please my Lord
To ruine me, and therefore I'll be guilty.
But, could I once have thought it would have pleas'd you,

<hr>

[3] 308–13. Based on *Antony and Cleopatra*, III.x.1–24.
[4] 313. 'Purple sails': See *Antony and Cleopatra*, II.ii.203.

That you would pry, with narrow searching eyes
Into my faults, severe to my destruction,
And watching all advantages with care,
That serve to make me wretched? Speak, my Lord,
For I end here. Though I deserve this usage,
Was it like you to give it?                                    340

ANTONY:      O you wrong me,
To think I sought this parting, or desir'd
To accuse you more than what will clear my self,
And justifie this breach.

CLEOPATRA:      Thus low I thank you.
And, since my innocence will not offend,
I shall not blush to own it.

VENTIDIUS:                          After this
I think she'll blush at nothing.

CLEOPATRA:      You seem griev'd,
(And therein you are kind) that *Cæsar* first
Enjoy'd my love, though you deserv'd it better:
I grieve for that, my Lord, much more than you;
For, had I first been yours, it would have sav'd           350
My second choice: I never had been his,
And ne'r had been but yours. But *Cæsar* first,
You say, possess'd my love. Not so, my Lord:
He first possessed my Person; you my Love:
*Cæsar* lov'd me; but I lov'd *Antony*.
If I endur'd him after, 'twas because
I judg'd it due to the first name of Men;
And, half constrain'd, I gave, as to a Tyrant,
What he would take by force.

VENTIDIUS:      O Syren! Syren!
Yet grant that all the love she boasts were true,          360
Has she not ruin'd you? I still urge that,
The fatal consequence.

CLEOPATRA:      The consequence indeed,
For I dare challenge him, my greatest foe,
To say it was design'd: 'tis true, I lov'd you,
And kept you far from an uneasie Wife,
(Such *Fulvia* was.)

Yes, but he'll say, you left *Octavia* for me;—
And, Can you blame me to receive that love,
Which quitted such desert, for worthless me?
How often have I wish'd some other *Cæsar*,          370
Great as the first, and as the second young,
Would court my Love to be refus'd for you!

VENTIDIUS: Words, words; but *Actium*, Sir, remember
  *Actium*.

CLEOPATRA: Ev'n there, I dare his malice. True, I Coun-
  sel'd
To fight at Sea; but, I betray'd you not.
I fled; but not to th' Enemy. 'Twas fear;
Would I had been a Man, not to have fear'd,
For none would then have envy'd me your friendship,
Who envy me your Love.

ANTONY:   We're both unhappy:
If nothing else, yet our ill fortune parts us.          380
Speak; Would you have me perish, by my stay?

CLEOPATRA: If as a friend you ask my Judgment, go;
If as a Lover, stay. If you must perish:
'Tis a hard word; but stay.

VENTIDIUS: See now th' effects of her so boasted love!
She strives to drag you down to ruine with her:
But, could she scape without you, oh how soon
Would she let go her hold, and haste to shore,
And never look behind!

CLEOPATRA:   Then judge my love by this.
                    (*Giving* ANTONY *a Writing*)
Could I have born          390
A life or death, a happiness or woe
From yours divided, this had giv'n me means.

ANTONY: By *Hercules*, the Writing of *Octavius*!
I know it well; 'tis that Proscribing hand,
Young as it was, that led the way to mine,
And left me but the second place in Murder.*
See, see, *Ventidius*! here he offers *Ægypt*,
And joyns all *Syria* to it, as a present,
So, in requital, she forsake my fortunes,

And joyn her Arms with his.                                    400
CLEOPATRA:   And yet you leave me!
  You leave me, *Antony*; and, yet I love you.
  Indeed I do: I have refus'd a Kingdom,
  That's a Trifle:
  For I could part with life; with any thing,
  But onely you. O let me dye but with you!
  Is that a hard request?
ANTONY:   Next living with you,
  'Tis all that Heav'n can give.
ALEXAS: (*aside*)  He melts; We conquer.
CLEOPATRA: No: you shall go: your Int'rest calls you
     hence;
  Yes, your dear int'rest pulls too strong, for these
  Weak Armes to hold you here.—        (*Takes his hand*) 410
  Go; leave me, Soldier;
  (For you're no more a Lover:) leave me dying:
  Push me all pale and panting from your bosome,
  And, when your March begins, let one run after,
  Breathless almost for Joy, and cry, *She's dead!*
  The Souldiers shout; you then perhaps may sigh,
  And muster all your *Roman* Gravity:
  *Ventidius* chides; and strait your Brow cleares up,
  As I had never been.
ANTONY: Gods, 'tis too much; too much for Man to bear!
CLEOPATRA: What is't for me then,                              420
  A weak forsaken Woman? and a Lover?—
  Here let me breathe my last: envy me not
  This minute in your Armes: I'll dye apace:
  As fast as ere I can; and end your trouble.
ANTONY: Dye! Rather let me perish: looss'nd Nature
  Leap from its hinges, sink the props of Heav'n,
  And fall the Skyes to crush the neather World.
  My Eyes, my Soul; my all!—              (*Embraces her*)
VENTIDIUS:   And what's this Toy
  In ballance with your fortune, Honor, Fame?
ANTONY: What is't, *Ventidius*? it out-weighs 'em all;         430
  Why, we have more than conquer'd *Cæsar* now:

My Queen's not only Innocent, but Loves me.
This, this is she who drags me down to ruin!
But, could she scape without me, with what haste
Would she let slip her hold, and make to shore,
And never look behind!
Down on thy knees, Blasphemer as thou art,
And ask forgiveness of wrong'd Innocence.

VENTIDIUS: I'll rather dye, than take it. Will you go?

ANTONY: Go! Whither? go from all that's excellent!          440
  Faith, Honor, Virtue, all good things forbid,
  That I should go from her, who sets my love
  Above the price of Kingdoms. Give, you Gods,
  Give to your Boy, your *Cæsar*,
  This Rattle of a Globe to play withal,
  This Gu-gau* World, and put him cheaply off:
  I'll not be pleas'd with less than *Cleopatra*.

CLEOPATRA: She's wholly yours. My heart's so full of joy,
  That I shall do some wild extravagance
  Of Love, in publick, and the foolish World,          450
  Which knows not tenderness, will think me Mad.

VENTIDIUS: O Women! Women! Women! all the gods
  Have not such pow'r of doing good to Man,
  As you of doing harm.                    [*Exit*]

ANTONY:    Our Men are Arm'd.
  Unbar the Gate that looks to *Cæsar*'s Camp;
  I would revenge the Treachery he meant me:
  And long security makes Conquest easie.
  I'm eager to return before I go;
  For, all the pleasures I have known, beat thick
  On my remembrance: how I long for night!          460
  That both the sweets of mutual love may try,
  And once Triumph o're *Cæsar* ere we dye.    [*Exeunt*]

# ACT III

## Scene i

*At one door, Enter* CLEOPATRA, CHARMION, *and* ALEXAS, *a Train of* ÆGYPTIANS: *at the other,* ANTONY *and* ROMANS. *The entrance on both sides is prepar'd by Musick; the Trumpets first sounding on* ANTONY's *part: then answer'd by Timbrels, &c. on* CLEOPATRA's. CHARMION *and* IRAS *hold a Laurel Wreath betwixt them. A Dance of* Ægyptians. *After the Ceremony,* CLEOPATRA *Crowns* ANTONY

ANTONY: I thought how those white arms would fold me in,
    And strain me close, and melt me into love;
    So pleas'd with that sweet Image, I sprung forwards,
    And added all my strength to every blow.
CLEOPATRA: Come to me, come, my Soldier, to my Arms,
    You've been too long away from my embraces;
    But, when I have you fast, and all my own,
    With broken murmurs, and with amorous sighs,
    I'll say, you were unkind, and punish you,
    And mark you red with many an eager kiss.     10
ANTONY: My Brighter *Venus*!
CLEOPATRA:     O my greater *Mars*!
ANTONY: Thou joinst us well, my Love!
    Suppose me come from the *Phlegræan*\* Plains,
    Where gasping Gyants lay, cleft by my Sword:
    And Mountain tops par'd off\* each other blow,
    To bury those I slew: receive me, goddess:
    Let *Cæsar* spread his subtile Nets, like *Vulcan*,\*
    In thy embraces I would be beheld
    By Heav'n and Earth at once:
    And make their envy what they meant their sport.     20

Let those who took us blush; I would love on
With awful* State, regardless of their frowns,
As their superior god.
There's no satiety of Love, in thee;
Enjoy'd, thou still art new; perpetual Spring
Is in thy armes; the ripen'd fruit but falls,
And blossoms rise to fill its empty place;
And I grow rich by giving.[5]

       *Enter* VENTIDIUS, *and stands apart*

ALEXAS: O, now the danger's past, your General comes.
He joyns not in your joys, nor minds your Triumphs;    30
But, with contracted brows, looks frowning on,
As envying your Success.

ANTONY: Now, on my Soul, he loves me; truely loves me;
He never flatter'd me in any vice,
But awes me with his virtue: ev'n this minute
Methinks he has a right of chiding me.
Lead to the Temple: I'll avoid his presence;
It checks too strong upon me.      [*Exeunt the rest*]

(*As* ANTONY *is going,* VENTIDIUS *pulls him by the Robe*)

VENTIDIUS:    Emperor.

ANTONY: (*looking back*) 'Tis the old argument; I pr'ythee
    spare me.

VENTIDIUS: But this one hearing, Emperor.    40

ANTONY:    Let go
My Robe; or, by my Father *Hercules*—*

VENTIDIUS: By *Hercules* his Father, that's yet greater,
I bring you somewhat you would wish to know.

ANTONY: Thou see'st we are observ'd; attend me here,
And I'll return.      [*Exit*]

VENTIDIUS: I'm waining in his favor, yet I love him;
I love this Man, who runs to meet his ruine;
And, sure the gods, like me, are fond of him:
His Virtues lye so mingled with his Crimes,
As would confound their choice to punish one,    50
And not reward the other.[6]

---

[5] 24-8. Based on *Antony and Cleopatra*, II.ii.245-8.
[6] 49-51. Based on *Antony and Cleopatra*, V.i.30-1.

*Enter* ANTONY

ANTONY: We can conquer, you see, without your aid.
  We have dislodg'd their Troops,
  They look on us at distance, and, like Curs
  Scap'd from the Lions paws, they bay far off,
  And lick their wounds, and faintly threaten War.
  Five thousand *Romans* with their faces upward,
  Lye breathless on the Plain.

VENTIDIUS:        'Tis well: and he
  Who lost 'em, could have spar'd Ten thousand more.
  Yet if, by this advantage, you could gain                          60
  An easier Peace, while *Cæsar* doubts the Chance
  Of Arms!—

ANTONY:      O think not on't, *Ventidius*;
  The Boy pursues my ruin, he'll no peace:
  His malice is considerate in advantage;
  O, he's the coolest Murderer, so stanch,
  He kills, and keeps his temper.

VENTIDIUS:        Have you no friend
  In all his Army, who has power to move him?
  *Mæcenas*, or *Agrippa* might do much.

ANTONY: They're both too deep in *Cæsar's* interests.
  We'll work it out by dint of Sword, or perish.                    70

VENTIDIUS: Fain I would find some other.

ANTONY:      Thank thy love.
  Some four or five such Victories as this,
  Will save thy farther pains.

VENTIDIUS: Expect no more; *Cæsar* is on his Guard:
  I know, Sir, you have conquer'd against ods;
  But still you draw Supplies from one poor Town,
  And of *Ægyptians*: he has all the World,
  And, at his back, Nations come pouring in,
  To fill the gaps you make. Pray think again.

ANTONY: Why dost thou drive me from my self, to search   80
  For Forreign aids? to hunt my memory,
  And range all o're a waste and barren place
  To find a Friend? The wretched have no Friends—
  Yet I had one, the bravest youth of *Rome*,

Whom *Cæsar* loves beyond the love of Women;
He could resolve his mind, as Fire does Wax,
From that hard rugged Image, melt him down,
And mould him in what softer form he pleas'd.

VENTIDIUS: Him would I see; that man of all the world:
Just such a one we want.                              90

ANTONY:    He lov'd me too,
I was his Soul; he liv'd not but in me:
We were so clos'd within each others brests,
The rivets were not found that join'd us first.
That does not reach us yet: we were so mixt,
As meeting streams, both to our selves were lost;
We were one mass; we could not give or take,
But from the same; for he was I, I he.

VENTIDIUS: (*aside*) He moves as I would wish him.

ANTONY:    After this,
I need not tell his name: 'twas *Dollabella*.

VENTIDIUS: He's now in *Cæsar*'s Camp.            100

ANTONY:    No matter where,
Since he's no longer mine. He took unkindly
That I forbade him *Cleopatra*'s sight;
Because I fear'd he lov'd her: he confest
He had a warmth, which, for my sake, he stifled;
For 'twere impossible that two, so one,
Should not have lov'd the same. When he departed,
He took no leave; and that confirm'd my thoughts.

VENTIDIUS: It argues that he lov'd you more than her,
Else he had staid; but he perceiv'd you jealous,
And would not grieve his friend: I know he loves you. 110

ANTONY: I should have seen him then ere now.

VENTIDIUS:    Perhaps
He has thus long been lab'ring for your peace.

ANTONY: Would he were here.

VENTIDIUS:    Would you believe he lov'd you?
I read your answer in your eyes; you would.
Not to conceal it longer, he has sent
A messenger from *Cæsar*'s Camp, with Letters.

ANTONY: Let him appear.

VENTIDIUS:     I'll bring him instantly.
            (*Exit* VENTIDIUS *and re-enters immediately*
                                    *with* DOLLABELLA]
ANTONY: 'Tis he himself, himself, by holy Friendship!
                            (*Runs to embrace him*)
    Art thou return'd at last, my better half?
    Come, give me all my self. Let me not live,                    120
    If the young Bridegroom, longing for his night,
    Was ever half so fond.
DOLLABELLA: I must be silent; for my Soul is busie
    About a nobler work: she's new come home,
    Like a long-absent man, and wanders o'er
    Each room, a stranger to her own, to look
    If all be safe.
ANTONY:     Thou hast what's left of me.
    For I am now so sunk from what I was,
    Thou find'st me at my lowest water-mark.
    The Rivers that ran in, and rais'd my fortunes,                130
    Are all dry'd up, or take another course:
    What I have left is from my native Spring;
    I've still a heart that swells, in scorn of fate,
    And lifts me to my banks.
DOLLABELLA: Still you are Lord of all the World to me.
ANTONY: Why, then I yet am so; for thou art all.
    If I had any joy when thou wert absent,
    I grudg'd it to my self; methought I robb'd
    Thee of thy part. But, Oh my *Dollabella*!
    Thou hast beheld me other than I am.                          140
    Hast thou not seen my morning Chambers fill'd
    With Scepter'd Slaves, who waited to salute me:
    With Eastern Monarchs, who forgot the Sun,
    To Worship my uprising? Menial Kings
    Ran coursing* up and down my Palace-yard,
    Stood silent in my presence, watch'd my eyes,
    And, at my least command, all started out
    Like Racers to the Goal.
DOLLABELLA: Slaves to your fortune.
ANTONY: Fortune is *Cæsar*'s now; and what am I?

VENTIDIUS: What you have made your self; I will not
    flatter.                                                    150
ANTONY: Is this friendly done?
DOLLABELLA: Yes, when his end is so. I must join with
    him;
  Indeed I must, and yet you must not chide:
  Why am I else your friend?
ANTONY:    Take heed, young man,
  How thou upbraid'st my love: the Queen has eyes,
  And thou too hast a Soul. Canst thou remember
  When, swell'd with hatred, thou beheld'st her first
  As accessary to thy Brothers death?
DOLLABELLA: Spare my remembrance; 'twas a guilty day,
  And still the blush hangs here.                           160
ANTONY:    To clear her self,
  For sending him no aid, she came from *Ægypt*.
  Her Gally down the Silver *Cydnos* row'd,
  The Tackling Silk, the Streamers wav'd with Gold,
  The gentle Winds were lodg'd in Purple sails:
  Her Nymphs, like *Nereids**, round her Couch, were
    plac'd;
  Where she, another Sea-born *Venus*, lay.
DOLLABELLA: No more: I would not hear it.
ANTONY:    O, you must!
  She lay, and leant her cheek upon her hand,
  And cast a look so languishingly sweet,
  As if, secure of all beholders hearts,                     170
  Neglecting she could take 'em: Boys, like *Cupids*,
  Stood fanning, with their painted wings, the winds
  That plaid about her face: but if she smil'd,
  A darting glory seem'd to blaze abroad:
  That mens desiring eyes were never weary'd;
  But hung upon the object: to soft Flutes
  The Silver Oars kept time; and while they plaid,
  The hearing gave new pleasure to the sight;
  And both to thought: 'twas Heav'n, or somewhat more;
  For she so charm'd all hearts, that gazing crowds          180
  Stood panting on the shore, and wanted* breath

To give their welcome voice.
Then, *Dollabella*, where was then thy Soul?[7]
Was not thy fury quite disarm'd with wonder?
Didst thou not shrink behind me from those eyes,
And whisper in my ear. *Oh tell her not*
*That I accus'd her of my Brothers death?*

DOLLABELLA: And should my weakness be a plea for
    yours?
Mine was an age when love might be excus'd,
When kindly warmth, and when my springing youth          190
Made it a debt to Nature, Yours—

VENTIDIUS:       Speak boldly.
Yours, he would say, in your declining age,
When no more heat was left but what you forc'd,
When all the sap was needful for the Trunk,
When it went down, then you constrain'd the course,
And robb'd from Nature, to supply desire;
In you (I would not use so harsh a word)
But 'tis plain dotage.

ANTONY:     Ha!

DOLLABELLA:         'Twas urg'd too home.
But yet the loss was private that I made;
'Twas but my self I lost: I lost no Legions;               200
I had no World to lose, no peoples love.

ANTONY: This from a friend?

DOLLABELLA:     Yes, *Antony*, a true one;
A friend so tender, that each word I speak
Stabs my own heart, before it reach your ear.
O, judge me not less kind because I chide:
To *Cæsar* I excuse you.

ANTONY:     O ye Gods!
Have I then liv'd to be excus'd to *Cæsar*?

DOLLABELLA: As to your equal.

ANTONY:     Well, he's but my equal:
While I wear this,* he never shall be more.

DOLLABELLA: I bring Conditions from him.                  210

---

[7] 161–83. Based on *Antony and Cleopatra*, II.ii.200–28.

ANTONY:     Are they Noble?
  Methinks thou shouldst not bring 'em else; yet he
  Is full of deep dissembling; knows no Honour,
  Divided from his Int'rest. Fate mistook him;
  For Nature meant him for an Usurer:
  He's fit indeed to buy, not conquer Kingdoms.

VENTIDIUS: Then, granting this,
  What pow'r was theirs who wrought so hard a temper
  To honourable Terms!

ANTONY: It was my *Dollabella*, or some God.

DOLLABELLA: Nor I; nor yet *Mæcenas*, nor *Agrippa*;        220
  They were your Enemies; and I a Friend
  Too weak alone; yet 'twas a *Roman*'s deed.

ANTONY: 'Twas like a *Roman* done: show me that man
  Who has preserv'd my life, my love, my honour;
  Let me but see his face.

VENTIDIUS:     That task is mine,
  And, Heav'n, thou know'st how pleasing. [*Exit* VENTIDIUS]

DOLLABELLA:     You'll remember
  To whom you stand oblig'd?

ANTONY:     When I forget it,
  Be thou unkind, and that's my greatest curse.
  My Queen shall thank him too.

DOLLABELLA:     I fear she will not.

ANTONY: But she shall do't: the Queen, my *Dollabella*!        230
  Hast thou not still some grudgings* of thy Fever?

DOLLABELLA: I would not see her lost.

ANTONY:     When I forsake her,
  Leave me, my better Stars; for she has truth
  Beyond her beauty. *Caesar* tempted her,
  At no less price than Kingdoms, to betray me;
  But she resisted all: and yet thou chid'st me
  For loving her too well. Could I so do?

DOLLABELLA: Yes, there's my reason.

  *Re-enter* VENTIDIUS, *with* OCTAVIA, *leading* ANTONY's
               *two little Daughters*

ANTONY:     Where—*Octavia* there! (*Starting back*)

VENTIDIUS: What, is she poyson to you? a Disease?

Look on her, view her well; and those she brings:                240
Are they all strangers to your eyes? has Nature
No secret call, no whisper they are yours?

DOLLABELLA: For shame, my Lord, if not for love, receive
   'em
With kinder eyes. If you confess* a man,
Meet 'em, embrace 'em, bid 'em welcome to you.
Your arms should open, ev'n without your knowledge,
To clasp 'em in; your feet should turn to wings,
To bear you to 'em; and your eyes dart out,
And aim a kiss ere you could reach the lips.

ANTONY: I stood amaz'd to think how they came hither.   250

VENTIDIUS: I sent for 'em; I brought 'em in, unknown
To *Cleopatra's* Guards.

DOLLABELLA:     Yet are you cold?

OCTAVIA: Thus long I have attended for my welcome;
Which, as a stranger, sure I might expect.
Who am I?

ANTONY:     *Cæsar's* Sister.

OCTAVIA:          That's unkind!
Had I been nothing more than *Cæsar's* Sister,
Know, I had still remain'd in *Cæsar's* Camp;
But your *Octavia*, your much injur'd Wife,
Tho' banish'd from your Bed, driv'n from your House,
In spight of *Cæsar's* Sister, still is yours.        260
'Tis true, I have a heart disdains your coldness,
And prompts me not to seek what you should offer;
But a Wife's Virtue still surmounts that pride:
I come to claim you as my own; to show
My duty first, to ask, nay beg, your kindness:
Your hand, my Lord; 'tis mine, and I will have it.

                        *(Taking his hand)*

VENTIDIUS: Do, take it, thou deserv'st it.

DOLLABELLA:     On my Soul,
And so she does: she's neither too submissive,
Nor yet too haughty; but so just a mean,*
Shows, as it ought, a Wife and *Roman* too.        270

ANTONY: I fear, *Octavia*, you have begg'd my life.

OCTAVIA: Begg'd it, my Lord?

ANTONY:    Yes, begg'd it, my Ambassadress,
Poorly and basely begg'd it of your Brother.

OCTAVIA: Poorly and basely I could never beg;
Nor could my Brother grant.

ANTONY: Shall I, who, to my kneeling Slave, could say,
*Rise up, and be a King*; shall I fall down
And cry, *Forgive me*, Cæsar? shall I set
A Man, my Equal, in the place of *Jove*,
As he could give me being? No; that word,                   280
*Forgive*, would choke me up,
And die upon my tongue.

DOLLABELLA:    You shall not need it.

ANTONY: I will not need it. Come, you've all betray'd me:
My Friend too! To receive some vile conditions.
My Wife has bought me, with her prayers and tears;
And now I must become her branded Slave:
In every peevish mood she will upbraid
The life she gave: if I but look awry,
She cries, *I'll tell my Brother*.

OCTAVIA:    My hard fortune
Subjects me still to your unkind mistakes.                   290
But the Conditions I have brought are such
You need not blush to take: I love your Honour,
Because 'tis mine; it never shall be said
*Octavia*'s Husband was her Brothers Slave.
Sir, you are free; free, ev'n from her you loath;
For, tho' my Brother bargains for your love,
Makes me the price and cement of your peace,
I have a Soul like yours; I cannot take
Your love as alms, nor beg what I deserve.
I'll tell my Brother we are reconcil'd;                      300
He shall draw back his Troops, and you shall march
To rule the East: I may be dropt at *Athens*;
No matter where, I never will complain,
But only keep the barren Name of Wife,
And rid you of the trouble.

VENTIDIUS: Was ever such a strife of sullen* Honour!

Both scorn to be oblig'd.

DOLLABELLA: O, she has toucht him in the tender'st part;
　　See how he reddens with despight and shame
　　To be out-done in Generosity!　　　　　　　　　　　310

VENTIDIUS: See how he winks! how he dries up a tear,
　　That fain would fall!

ANTONY: *Octavia*, I have heard you, and must praise
　　The greatness of your Soul;
　　But cannot yield to what you have propos'd:
　　For I can ne'er be conquer'd but by love;
　　And you do all for duty. You would free me,
　　And would be dropt at *Athens*; was't not so?

OCTAVIA: It was, my Lord.

ANTONY:　　Then I must be oblig'd
　　To one who loves me not, who, to her self,　　　　　320
　　May call me thankless and ungrateful Man:
　　I'll not endure it, no.

VENTIDIUS: (*aside*)　　I'm glad it pinches there.

OCTAVIA: Would you triumph o'er poor *Octavia*'s Virtue?
　　That pride was all I had to bear me up;
　　That you might think you ow'd me for your life,
　　And ow'd it to my duty, not my love.
　　I have been injur'd, and my haughty Soul
　　Could brook but ill the Man who slights my Bed.

ANTONY: Therefore you love me not.

OCTAVIA:　　Therefore, my Lord,
　　I should not love you.　　　　　　　　　　　　　330

ANTONY:　　Therefore you wou'd leave me?

OCTAVIA: And therefore I should leave you—if I could.

DOLLABELLA: Her Souls too great, after such injuries,
　　To say she loves; yet she lets you see it.
　　Her modesty and silence plead her cause.

ANTONY: O, *Dollabella*, which way shall I turn?
　　I find a secret yielding in my Soul;
　　But *Cleopatra*, who would die with me,
　　Must she be left? Pity pleads for *Octavia*;
　　But does it not plead more for *Cleopatra*?

VENTIDIUS: Justice and Pity both plead for *Octavia*;　　340

For *Cleopatra*, neither.
One would be ruin'd with you; but she first
Had ruin'd you: the other, you have ruin'd,
And yet she would preserve you.
In every thing their merits are unequal.

ANTONY: O, my distracted* Soul!

OCTAVIA: Sweet Heav'n compose it.
Come, come, my Lord, if I can pardon you,
Methinks you should accept it. Look on these;
Are they not yours? Or stand they thus neglected
As they are mine? Go to him, Children, go; 350
Kneel to him, take him by the hand, speak to him;
For you may speak, and he may own you too,
Without a blush; and so he cannot all
His Children: go, I say, and pull him to me,
And pull him to your selves, from that bad Woman.
You, *Agrippina*, hang upon his arms;
And you, *Antonia*, clasp about his waste:
If he will shake you off, if he will dash you
Against the Pavement, you must bear it, Children;
For you are mine, and I was born to suffer. 360

(*Here the Children go to him, &c*)

VENTIDIUS: Was ever sight so moving! Emperor!

DOLLABELLA: Friend!

OCTAVIA: Husband!

BOTH CHILDREN: Father!

ANTONY: I am vanquish'd: take me,
*Octavia*; take me, Children; share me all. (*Embracing them*)
I've been a thriftless Debtor to your loves,
And run out much, in riot, from your stock;
But all shall be amended.

OCTAVIA: O blest hour!

DOLLABELLA: O happy change!

VENTIDIUS: My joy stops at my tongue;
But it has found two chanels here for one,
And bubbles out above.

ANTONY: (*to Octavia*) This is thy Triumph; lead me where 370
thou wilt;

Ev'n to thy Brothers Camp.

OCTAVIA:     All there are yours.

*Enter* ALEXAS *hastily*

ALEXAS: The Queen, my Mistress, Sir, and yours—

ANTONY:       'Tis past.
  *Octavia*, you shall stay this night; To morrow,
  *Cæsar* and we are one.

                    [*Exit leading* OCTAVIA; DOLLABELLA *and*
                                        *the Children follow*]

VENTIDIUS: There's news for you; run, my officious
      Eunuch,
  Be sure to be the first; haste foreward:
  Haste, my dear Eunuch, haste.                    [*Exit*]

ALEXAS: This downright fighting Fool, this thick-scull'd
      Hero,
  This blunt unthinking Instrument of death,
  With plain dull Virtue, has out-gone my Wit:                    380
  Pleasure forsook my early'st Infancy,
  The luxury of others robb'd my Cradle,
  And ravish'd thence the promise of a Man:
  Cast out from Nature, disinherited
  Of what her meanest Children claim by kind;
  Yet, greatness kept me from contempt: that's gone.
  Had *Cleopatra* follow'd my advice,
  Then he had been betray'd, who now forsakes.
  She dies for love; but she has known its joys:
  Gods, is this just, that I, who know no joys,                    390
  Must die, because she loves?

          *Enter* CLEOPATRA, CHARMION, IRAS, *Train*
  Oh, Madam, I have seen what blasts my eyes!
  *Octavia's* here!

CLEOPATRA:     Peace with that Raven's note.
  I know it too; and now am in
  The pangs of death.

ALEXAS:     You are no more a Queen;
  Ægypt is lost.

CLEOPATRA:     What tell'st thou me of Ægypt!
  My Life, my Soul is lost! *Octavia* has him!

O fatal name to *Cleopatra*'s love!
My kisses, my embraces now are hers;
While I—But thou hast seen my Rival; speak,                    400
Does she deserve this blessing? Is she fair,
Bright as a Goddess? and is all perfection
Confin'd to her? It is. Poor I was made
Of that course matter which, when she was finish'd,
The Gods threw by, for rubbish.

ALEXAS: She's indeed a very Miracle.

CLEOPATRA: Death to my hopes, a Miracle!

ALEXAS: (*bowing*)   A Miracle;
I mean of Goodness; for in Beauty, Madam,
You make all wonders cease.

CLEOPATRA:     I was too rash:
Take this in part of recompence. But, Oh, (*giving a Ring*)   410
I fear thou flatter'st me.

CHARMION:     She comes! she's here!

IRAS: Flie, Madam, *Cæsar*'s Sister!

CLEOPATRA: Were she the Sister of the Thund'rer *Jove*,
And bore her Brothers Lightning in her eyes,
Thus would I face my Rival.

(*Meets* OCTAVIA *with* VENTIDIUS. OCTAVIA *bears up to her.*
                    *Their Trains come up on either side*)

OCTAVIA: I need not ask if you are *Cleopatra*,
Your haughty carriage—

CLEOPATRA:     Shows I am a Queen:
Nor need I ask you who you are.

OCTAVIA:     A *Roman*:
A name that makes, and can unmake a Queen.

CLEOPATRA: Your Lord, the Man who serves me, is a
*Roman*.                    420

OCTAVIA: He was a *Roman*, till he lost that name
To be a Slave in *Ægypt*; but I come
To free him thence.

CLEOPATRA:     Peace, peace, my Lover's *Juno*.
When he grew weary of that Houshold-Clog,
He chose my easier bonds.

OCTAVIA:     I wonder not

Your bonds are easie; you have long been practis'd
In that lascivious art: he's not the first
For whom you spread your snares: let *Cæsar* witness.

CLEOPATRA: I lov'd not *Cæsar*; 'twas but gratitude
I paid his love: the worst your malice can,                          430
Is but to say the greatest of Mankind
Has been my Slave. The next, but far above him,
In my esteem, is he whom Law calls yours,
But whom his love made mine.

OCTAVIA: (*coming up close to her*) I would view nearer
That face, which has so long usurp'd my right,
To find th' inevitable* charms, that catch
Mankind so sure, that ruin'd my dear Lord.

CLEOPATRA: O, you do well to search; for had you known
But half these charms, you had not lost his heart.

OCTAVIA: Far be their knowledge from a *Roman* Lady,          440
Far from a modest Wife. Shame of our Sex,
Dost thou not blush, to own those black endearments
That make sin pleasing?

CLEOPATRA:          You may blush, who want 'em.
If bounteous Nature, if indulgent Heav'n
Have giv'n me charms to please the bravest Man;
Should I not thank 'em? should I be asham'd,
And not be proud? I am, that he has lov'd me;
And, when I love not him, Heav'n change this Face
For one like that.

OCTAVIA:          Thou lov'st him not so well.

CLEOPATRA: I love him better, and deserve him more.          450

OCTAVIA: You do not; cannot: you have been his ruine.
Who made him cheap at *Rome*, but *Cleopatra*?
Who made him scorn'd abroad, but *Cleopatra*?
At *Actium*, who betray'd him? *Cleopatra*.
Who made his Children Orphans? and poor me
A wretched Widow? only *Cleopatra*.

CLEOPATRA: Yet she who loves him best is *Cleopatra*.
If you have suffer'd, I have suffer'd more.
You bear the specious Title of a Wife,
To guild your Cause, and draw the pitying World          460

To favour it: the World contemns poor me;
For I have lost my Honour, lost my Fame,
And stain'd the glory of my Royal House,
And all to bear the branded Name of Mistress.
There wants but life, and that too I would lose
For him I love.

OCTAVIA:    Be't so then; take thy wish. [*Exit cum suis*]*
CLEOPATRA: And 'tis my wish,
Now he is lost for whom alone I liv'd.
My sight grows dim, and every object dances,
And swims before me, in the maze of death.                    470
My spirits, while they were oppos'd, kept up;
They could not sink beneath a Rivals scorn:
But now she's gone they faint.

ALEXAS:    Mine have had leisure
To recollect their strength, and furnish counsel,
To ruine her; who else must ruine you.

CLEOPATRA: Vain Promiser!
Lead me, my *Charmion*; nay, your hand too, *Iras*:
My grief has weight enough to sink you both.
Conduct me to some solitary Chamber,
And draw the Curtains round;                                   480
Then leave me to my self, to take alone
My fill of grief:
There I till death will his unkindness weep:
As harmless Infants moan themselves asleep.    [*Exeunt*]

# ACT IV

## Scene i

*Enter* ANTONY, DOLLABELLA

DOLLABELLA: Why would you shift it from your self, on
    me?

    Can you not tell her you must part?

ANTONY:    I cannot.

    I could pull out an eye, and bid it go,

    And t'other should not weep. Oh, *Dollabella*,

    How many deaths are in this word *Depart*!

    I dare not trust my tongue to tell her so:

    One look of hers, would thaw me into tears

    And I should melt till I were lost agen.

DOLLABELLA: Then let *Ventidius*;

    He's rough by nature.                   10

ANTONY:    Oh, he'll speak too harshly;

    He'll kill her with the news: Thou, only thou.

DOLLABELLA: Nature has cast me in so soft a mould,

    That but to hear a story feign'd for pleasure

    Of some sad Lovers death, moistens my eyes,

    And robs me of my Manhood—I should speak

    So faintly; with such fear to grieve her heart,

    She'd not believe it earnest.

ANTONY:    Therefore, therefore

    Thou only, thou art fit: think thy self me,

    And when thou speak'st (but let it first be long)

    Take off the edge from every sharper sound,     20

    And let our parting be as gently made

    As other Loves begin: wilt thou do this?

DOLLABELLA: What you have said, so sinks into my Soul,

    That, if I must speak, I shall speak just so.

ANTONY: I leave you then to your sad task: Farewel.

I sent her word to meet you.

(*Goes to the door, and comes back*)

   I forgot;

Let her be told, I'll make her peace with mine:

Her Crown and Dignity shall be preserv'd,

If I have pow'r with *Cæsar*. —O, be sure

To think on that.                                      30

DOLLABELLA:   Fear not, I will remember.

(ANTONY *goes again to the door, and comes back*)

ANTONY: And tell her, too, how much I was constrain'd;

I did not this, but with extreamest force:

Desire her not to hate my memory,

For I still cherish hers;—insist on that.

DOLLABELLA: Trust me, I'll not forget it.

ANTONY:   Then that's all. (*Goes out, and returns again*)

Wilt thou forgive my fondness this once more?

Tell her, tho' we shall never meet again,

If I should hear she took another Love,

The news would break my heart. —Now I must go;

For every time I have return'd, I feel                 40

My Soul more tender; and my next command

Would be to bid her stay, and ruine both.        [*Exit*]

DOLLABELLA: Men are but Children of a larger growth,

Our appetites are apt to change as theirs,

And full as craving too, and full as vain;

And yet the Soul, shut up in her dark room,

Viewing so clear abroad, at home sees nothing;

But, like a Mole in Earth, busie and blind,

Works all her folly up, and casts it outward

To the Worlds open view: thus I discover'd,          50

And blam'd the love of ruin'd *Antony*;

Yet wish that I were he, to be so ruin'd.

      *Enter* VENTIDIUS *above*

VENTIDIUS: Alone? and talking to himself? concern'd too?

Perhaps my ghess is right; he lov'd her once,

And may pursue it still.

DOLLABELLA:   O Friendship! Friendship!

Ill canst thou answer this; and Reason, worse:

Unfaithful in th' attempt; hopeless to win;
And, if I win, undone: meer madness all.
And yet th' occasion's fair. What injury,
To him, to wear the Robe which he throws by?                    60
VENTIDIUS: None, none at all. This happens as I wish,
To ruine her yet more with *Antony*.
*Enter* CLEOPATRA, *talking with* ALEXAS; CHARMION,
                    IRAS *on the other side*
DOLLABELLA: She comes! What charms have sorrow on
    that face!
Sorrow seems pleas'd to dwell with so much sweetness;
Yet, now and then, a melancholy smile
Breaks loose, like Lightning, in a Winter's night,
And shows a moments day.
VENTIDIUS: If she should love him too! Her Eunuch there!
That *Porcpisce*\* bodes ill weather. Draw, draw nearer,
Sweet Devil, that I may hear.                                    70
ALEXAS:      Believe me; try
                    (DOLLABELLA *goes over to* CHARMION *and*
                            IRAS; *seems to talk with them*)
To make him jealous; jealousie is like
A polisht Glass held to the lips when life's in doubt:
If there be breath, 'twill catch the damp and show it.
CLEOPATRA: I grant you jealousie's a proof of love,
But 'tis a weak and unavailing Med'cine;
It puts out\* the disease, and makes it show,
But has no pow'r to cure.
ALEXAS: 'Tis your last remedy, and strongest too:
And then this *Dollabella*, who so fit
To practice on? He's handsom, valiant, young,             80
And looks as he were laid for Nature's bait
To catch weak Womens eyes.
He stands already more than half suspected
Of loving you: the least kind word, or glance,
You give this Youth, will kindle him with love:
Then, like a burning Vessel set adrift,
You'll send him down amain\* before the wind,
To fire the heart of jealous *Antony*.

CLEOPATRA: Can I do this? Ah no; my love's so true,
  That I can neither hide it where it is,                        90
  Nor show it where it is not. Nature meant me
  A Wife, a silly harmless houshold Dove,
  Fond without art; and kind without deceit;
  But Fortune, that has made made a Mistress of me,
  Has thrust me out to the wide World, unfurnish'd
  Of falshood to be happy.

ALEXAS:    Force your self.
  Th' event* will be, your Lover will return
  Doubly desirous to possess the good
  Which once he fear'd to lose.

CLEOPATRA:    I must attempt it;
  But Oh with what regret!                                       100
        [*Exit* ALEXAS (*She comes up to* DOLLABELLA)]

VENTIDIUS: So, now the Scene draws near; they're in my
  reach.

CLEOPATRA: (*to Dollabella*) Discoursing with my
  Women! Might not I
  Share in your entertainment?

CHARMION:    You have been
  The Subject of it, Madam.

CLEOPATRA:    How; and how?

IRAS: Such praises of your beauty!

CLEOPATRA:    Meer Poetry.
  Your *Roman* Wits, your *Gallus* and *Tibullus*,*
  Have taught you this from *Citheris* and *Delia*.

DOLLABELLA: Those *Roman* Wits have never been in
  *Ægypt*,
  *Citheris* and *Delia* else had been unsung:
  I, who have seen—had I been born a Poet,              110
  Should chuse a nobler name.

CLEOPATRA:    You flatter me.
  But, 'tis your Nation's vice: all of your Country
  Are flatterers, and all false. Your Friend's like you.
  I'm sure he sent you not to speak these words.

DOLLABELLA: No, Madam; yet he sent me—

CLEOPATRA:    Well, he sent you—

DOLLABELLA: Of a less pleasing errand.

CLEOPATRA:     How less pleasing?
Less to your self, or me?

DOLLABELLA:     Madam, to both;
For you must mourn, and I must grieve to cause it.

CLEOPATRA: You, *Charmion*, and your Fellow, stand at
distance.
(*Aside*) Hold up, my Spirits. —Well, now your mournful   120
matter;
For I'm prepar'd, perhaps can ghess it too.

DOLLABELLA: I wish you would; for 'tis a thankless office
To tell ill news: and I, of all your Sex,
Most fear displeasing you.

CLEOPATRA:     Of all your Sex,
I soonest could forgive you, if you should.

VENTIDIUS: Most delicate advances! Woman! Woman!
Dear damn'd, inconstant Sex!

CLEOPATRA:     In the first place,
I am to be forsaken; is't not so?

DOLLABELLA: I wish I could not answer to that question.

CLEOPATRA: Then pass it o'er, because it troubles you:   130
I should have been more griev'd another time.
Next, I'm to lose my Kingdom. —Farewel, *Ægypt*.
Yet, is there any more?

DOLLABELLA:     Madam, I fear
Your too deep sense of grief has turn'd your reason.

CLEOPATRA: No, no, I'm not run mad; I can bear Fortune:
And Love may be expell'd by other Love,
As Poysons are by Poysons.

DOLLABELLA:     You o'erjoy me, Madam,
To find your griefs so moderately born.
You've heard the worst; all are not false, like him.

CLEOPATRA: No; Heav'n forbid they should.             140

DOLLABELLA:     Some men are constant.

CLEOPATRA: And constancy deserves reward, that's
certain.

DOLLABELLA: Deserves it not; but give it leave to hope.

VENTIDIUS: I'll swear thou hast my leave. I have enough:

But how to manage this! Well, I'll consider.          [*Exit*]

DOLLABELLA: I came prepar'd,
To tell you heavy news; news, which I thought,
Would fright the blood from your pale cheeks to hear:
But you have met it with a cheerfulness
That makes my task more easie; and my tongue,
Which on anothers message was employ'd,          150
Would gladly speak its own.

CLEOPATRA:     Hold, *Dollabella*.
First tell me, were you chosen by my Lord?
Or sought you this employment?

DOLLABELLA: He pick'd me out; and, as his bosom-friend,
He charg'd me with his words.

CLEOPATRA:     The message then
I know was tender, and each accent smooth,
To mollifie that rugged word *Depart*.

DOLLABELLA: Oh, you mistake: he chose the harshest
     words,
With fiery eyes, and with contracted brows,
He coyn'd his face in the severest stamp:          160
And fury, shook his Fabrick like an Earthquake;
He heav'd for vent,* and burst like bellowing *Ætna*,
In sounds scarce humane, *Hence, away for ever:*
*Let her begone, the blot of my renown,*
*And bane of all my hopes:*

(*All the time of this speech,* CLEOPATRA *seems more and*
                    *more concern'd, till she sinks quite down*)
*Let her be driv'n as far as men can think*
*From Mans commerce: She'll poyson to the Center.**

CLEOPATRA: Oh, I can bear no more!

DOLLABELLA: Help, help! Oh Wretch! Oh cursed, cursed
     Wretch!
What have I done!          170

CHARMION:     Help, chafe her Temples, *Iras*.

IRAS: Bend, bend her forward quickly.

CHARMION:     Heav'n be prais'd,
She comes again.

CLEOPATRA:     Oh, let him not approach me.

Why have you brought me back to this loath'd Being,
Th' abode of Falshood, violated Vows,
And injur'd Love? For pity, let me go;
For, if there be a place of long repose,
I'm sure I want it. My disdainful Lord
Can never break that quiet; nor awake
The sleeping Soul, with hollowing* in my Tomb
Such words as fright her hence. Unkind, unkind.                180

DOLLABELLA: (*kneeling*) Believe me, 'tis against my self I
    speak;
That sure deserves belief. I injur'd him:
My Friend ne'er spoke those words. Oh, had you seen
How often he came back, and every time
With something more obliging and more kind,
To add to what he said; what dear Farewels;
How almost vanquisht by his love he parted,
And lean'd to what unwillingly he left:
I, Traitor as I was, for love of you,
(But what can you not do, who made me false!)                 190
I forg'd that lye; for whose forgiveness kneels
This self-accus'd, self-punish'd Criminal.

CLEOPATRA: With how much ease believe we what we
    wish!
Rise, *Dollabella*; if you have been guilty,
I have contributed, and too much love
Has made me guilty too.
Th' advance of kindness which I made, was feign'd,
To call back fleeting love by jealousie;
But 'twould not last. Oh, rather let me lose
Than so ignobly trifle with his heart.                        200

DOLLABELLA: I find your breast fenc'd round from
    humane reach,
Transparent as a Rock of solid Crystal;
Seen through, but never pierc'd. My Friend, my Friend!
What endless treasure hast thou thrown away,
And scatter'd, like an Infant, in the Ocean,
Vain sums of Wealth which none can gather thence.

CLEOPATRA: Could you not beg

An hours admittance to his private ear?
Like one who wanders through long barren Wilds,
And yet foreknows no hospitable Inn                         210
Is near to succour hunger,
Eats his fill, before his painful march:
So would I feed a while my famish'd eyes
Before we part; for I have far to go,
If death be far, and never must return.

    *Enter* VENTIDIUS, *with* OCTAVIA, *behind*

VENTIDIUS: From hence you may discover—Oh, sweet,
    sweet!
Would you indeed? the pretty hand in earnest?
DOLLABELLA: (*takes her hand*) I will, for this reward.—
Draw it not back,
'Tis all I e'er will beg.
VENTIDIUS: They turn upon us.                               220
OCTAVIA:    What quick eyes has guilt!
VENTIDIUS: Seem not to have observ'd 'em, and go on.
    (*They come forward*)
DOLLABELLA: Saw you the Emperor, *Ventidius*?
VENTIDIUS:    No.
I sought him; but I heard that he was private,
None with him, but *Hipparchus* his Freedman.
DOLLABELLA: Know you his bus'ness?
VENTIDIUS:    Giving him Instructions,
And Letters, to his Brother *Cæsar*.
DOLLABELLA:    Well,
He must be found. [*Exeunt* DOLLABELLA *and* CLEOPATRA]
OCTAVIA:    Most glorious impudence!
VENTIDIUS: She look'd methought.
As she would say, *Take your old man*, Octavia;
*Thank you, I'm better here*. Well, but what use             230
Make we of this discovery?
OCTAVIA:    Let it die.
VENTIDIUS: I pity *Dollabella*; but she's dangerous:
Her eyes have pow'r beyond *Thessalian** charms
To draw the Moon from Heav'n; for Eloquence,
The Sea-green Syrens taught her voice their flatt'ry;

And, while she speaks, Night steals upon the Day,
Unmark'd of those that hear: Then she's so charming,
Age buds at sight of her, and swells to youth:
The holy Priests gaze on her when she smiles;
And with heav'd hands forgetting gravity,                          240
They bless her wanton eyes: Even I who hate her,[8]
With a malignant joy behold such beauty;
And, while I curse, desire it. *Antony*
Must needs have some remains of passion still,
Which may ferment into a worse relapse,
If now not fully cur'd. I know, this minute,
With *Caesar* he's endeavouring her peace.

OCTAVIA: You have prevail'd: – but for a farther purpose
                                                        (*Walks off*)
I'll prove how he will relish this discovery.
What, make a Strumpet's peace! it swells my heart:               250
It must not, sha' not be.

VENTIDIUS:     His Guards appear.
Let me begin, and you shall second me.

                    *Enter* ANTONY

ANTONY: *Octavia*, I was looking* you, my love:
What, are your Letters ready? I have giv'n
My last Instructions.

OCTAVIA:     Mine, my Lord, are written.

ANTONY: *Ventidius!*                    (*Drawing him aside*)

VENTIDIUS:     My Lord?

ANTONY:        A word in private.
When saw you *Dollabella*?

VENTIDIUS:   Now, my Lord,
He parted hence; and *Cleopatra* with him.

ANTONY: Speak softly. 'Twas by my command he went,
To bear my last farewel.                                         260

VENTIDIUS: (*aloud*)   It look'd indeed
Like your farewel.

ANTONY:     More softly. —My farewel?
What secret meaning have you in those words
Of my Farewel? He did it by my Order.

---

[8] 237-41. Based on *Antony and Cleopatra*, II.ii.245-50.

VENTIDIUS: *(aloud)* Then he obey'd your Order. I suppose
  You bid him to do it with all gentleness.
  All kindness, and all—love.

ANTONY: How she mourn'd, the poor forsaken Creature!

VENTIDIUS: She took it as she ought; she bore your parting
  As she did *Cæsar*'s, as she would anothers,
  Were a new Love to come.                 270

ANTONY: *(aloud)* Thou dost belye her;
  Most basely, and maliciously belye her.

VENTIDIUS: I thought not to displease you; I have done.

OCTAVIA: *(coming up)* You seem disturb'd, my Lord.

ANTONY:   A very trifle.
  Retire, my Love.

VENTIDIUS:   It was indeed a trifle.
  He sent—

ANTONY: *(angrily)* No more. Look how thou disobey'st
  me;
  Thy life shall answer it.

OCTAVIA:   Then 'tis no trifle.

VENTIDIUS: *(to* OCTAVIA*)* 'Tis less; a very nothing: you
  too saw it,
  As well as I, and therefore 'tis no secret.

ANTONY: She saw it!

VENTIDIUS:   Yes: she saw young *Dollabella*—

ANTONY: Young *Dollabella*!                  280

VENTIDIUS:   Young, I think him young,
  And handsom too; and so do others think him.
  But what of that? He went by your command,
  Indeed 'tis probable, with some kind message;
  For she receiv'd it graciously; she smil'd:
  And then he grew familiar with her hand,
  Squeez'd it, and worry'd it with ravenous kisses;
  She blush'd, and sigh'd, and smil'd, and blush'd again;
  At last she took occasion to talk softly,
  And brought her cheek up close, and lean'd on his:
  At which, he whisper'd kisses back on hers;      290
  And then she cry'd aloud, That constancy
  Should be rewarded.

OCTAVIA:    This I saw and heard.

ANTONY: What Woman was it, whom you heard and saw
So playful with my Friend! Not *Cleopatra*?

VENTIDIUS: Even she, my Lord!

ANTONY:    My *Cleopatra*?

VENTIDIUS: Your *Cleopatra*;
*Dollabella's Cleopatra*:
Every Man's *Cleopatra*.

ANTONY:    Thou ly'st.

VENTIDIUS: I do not lye, my Lord.
Is this so strange? Should Mistresses be left,                300
And not provide against a time of change?
You know she's not much us'd to lonely nights.

ANTONY: I'll think no more on't.
I know 'tis false, and see the plot betwixt you.
You needed not have gone this way, *Octavia*.
What harms it you that *Cleopatra's* just?
She's mine no more. I see; and I forgive:
Urge it no farther, Love.

OCTAVIA:    Are you concern'd
That she's found false?

ANTONY:    I should be, were it so;
For, tho 'tis past, I would not that the World                310
Should tax my former choice: That I lov'd one
Of so light note; but I forgive you both.

VENTIDIUS: What has my age deserv'd, that you should
think
I would abuse your ears with perjury?
If Heav'n be true, she's false.

ANTONY:    Tho Heav'n and Earth
Should witness it, I'll not believe her tainted.

VENTIDIUS: I'll bring you then a Witness
From Hell to prove her so. Nay, go not back;
            (*Seeing* ALEXAS *just entering, and starting back*)
For stay you must and shall.

ALEXAS:    What means my Lord?

VENTIDIUS: To make you do what most you hate; speak
truth.                                                        320

You are of *Cleopatra*'s private Counsel,
Of her Bed-Counsel, her lascivious hours;
Are conscious of each nightly change she makes,
And watch her, as *Chaldeans** do the Moon,
Can tell what Signs she passes through, what day.

ALEXAS: My Noble Lord.

VENTIDIUS:     My most Illustrious Pandar.
No fine set Speech, no Cadence, no turn'd Periods,*
But a plain home-spun Truth, is what I ask:
I did, my self, o'erhear your Queen make love
To *Dollabella*. Speak; for I will know,                    330
By your confession, what more past betwixt 'em;
How near the bus'ness draws to your employment;
And when the happy hour.

ANTONY: Speak truth, *Alexas*, whether it offend
Or please *Ventidius*, care not: justifie
Thy injur'd Queen from malice: dare his worst.

OCTAVIA: *(aside)* See, how he gives him courage! how he fears
To find her false! and shuts his eyes to truth,
Willing to be misled!

ALEXAS: As far as love may plead for Woman's frailty,     340
Urg'd by desert and greatness of the Lover;
So far (Divine *Octavia*!) may my Queen
Stand ev'n excus'd to you, for loving him,
Who is your Lord: so far, from brave *Ventidius*,
May her past actions hope a fair report.

ANTONY: 'Tis well, and truly spoken: mark, *Ventidius*.

ALEXAS: To you, most Noble Emperor, her strong passion
Stands not excus'd but wholly justifi'd.
Her Beauty's charms alone, without her Crown,
From *Ind* and *Meroe** drew the distant Vows              350
Of sighing Kings; and at her feet were laid
The Scepters of the Earth, expos'd on heaps,
To choose where she would Reign:
She thought a *Roman* only could deserve her;
And, of all *Romans*, only *Antony*.
And, to be less than Wife to you, disdain'd

Their lawful passion.

ANTONY: 'Tis but truth.

ALEXAS: And yet, tho love, and your unmatch'd desert,
   Have drawn her from the due regard of Honor,      360
   At last, Heav'n open'd her unwilling eyes
   To see the wrongs she offer'd fair *Octavia*,
   Whose holy Bed she lawlesly usurpt;
   The sad effects of this improsperous War,
   Confirm'd those pious thoughts.

VENTIDIUS: (*aside*) O, wheel* you there?
   Observe him now; the Man begins to mend,
   And talk substantial reason. Fear not, Eunuch,
   The Emperor has giv'n thee leave to speak.

ALEXAS: Else had I never dar'd t' offend his ears
   With what the last necessity has urg'd      370
   On my forsaken Mistress; yet I must not
   Presume to say her heart is wholly alter'd.

ANTONY: No, dare not for thy life, I charge thee dare not,
   Pronounce that fatal word.

OCTAVIA: (*aside*) Must I bear this? good Heav'n, afford me
   patience.

VENTIDIUS: On, sweet Eunuch; my dear half man, proceed.

ALEXAS: Yet *Dollabella*
   Has lov'd her long: he, next my God-like Lord,
   Deserves her best; and should she meet his passion,
   Rejected, as she is, by him she lov'd—      380

ANTONY: Hence, from my sight; for I can bear no more:
   Let Furies drag thee quick to Hell; let all
   The longer damn'd have rest; each torturing hand
   Do thou employ, till *Cleopatra* comes,
   Then joyn thou too, and help to torture her.

          [*Exit* ALEXAS, *thrust out by* ANTONY]

OCTAVIA: 'Tis not well,
   Indeed, my Lord, 'tis much unkind to me,
   To show this passion, this extream concernment
   For an abandon'd, faithless Prostitute.

ANTONY: *Octavia*, leave me: I am much disorder'd.      390

Leave me, I say.

OCTAVIA:    My Lord?

ANTONY:        I bid you leave me.

VENTIDIUS: Obey him, Madam: best withdraw a while,
And see how this will work.

OCTAVIA: Wherein have I offended you, my Lord,
That I am bid to leave you? Am I false,
Or infamous? Am I a *Cleopatra*?
Were I she,
Base as she is, you would not bid me leave you;
But hang upon my neck, take slight excuses,
And fawn upon my falsehood.                                    400

ANTONY:      'Tis too much,
Too much, *Octavia*; I am prest with sorrows
Too heavy to be born; and you add more:
I would retire, and recollect what's left
Of Man within, to aid me.

OCTAVIA:      You would mourn
In private, for your Love, who has betray'd you;
You did but half return to me: your kindness
Linger'd behind with her. I hear, my Lord,
You make Conditions for her,
And would include her Treaty. Wondrous proofs
Of love to me!                                                   410

ANTONY:    Are you my Friend, *Ventidius*?
Or are you turn'd a *Dollabella* too,
And let this Fury loose?

VENTIDIUS:      Oh, be advis'd,
Sweet Madam, and retire.

OCTAVIA: Yes, I wil go; but never to return.
You shall no more be haunted with this Fury.
My Lord, my Lord, love will not always last,
When urg'd with long unkindness, and disdain;
Take her again whom you prefer to me;
She stays but to be call'd. Poor cozen'd Man!
Let a feign'd parting give her back your heart,               420
Which a feign'd love first got; for injur'd me,
Tho' my just sense of wrongs forbid my stay,

My duty shall be yours.
To the dear pledges of our former love,
My tenderness and care shall be transferr'd,
And they shall cheer, by turns, my Widow'd Nights:
So, take my last farewel; for I despair
To have you whole, and scorn to take you half.   [*Exit*]

VENTIDIUS: I combat Heav'n, which blasts my best
    designs:
My last attempt must be to win her back;                        430
But Oh, I fear in vain.                         [*Exit*]

ANTONY: Why was I fram'd with this plain honest heart,
Which knows not to disguise its griefs and weakness,
But bears its workings outward to the World?
I should have kept the mighty anguish in,
And forc'd a smile at *Cleopatra*'s falshood:
*Octavia* had believ'd it, and had staid;
But I am made a shallow-forded Stream,
Seen to the bottom: all my clearness scorn'd,
And all my faults expos'd! —See, where he comes               440

*Enter* DOLLABELLA

Who has prophan'd the Sacred Name of Friend,
And worn it into vileness!
With how secure a brow, and specious form
He guilds the secret Villain! Sure that face
Was meant for honesty; but Heav'n mis-match'd it,
And furnish'd Treason out with Natures pomp,
To make its work more easie.

DOLLABELLA:     O, my friend!

ANTONY: Well, *Dollabella*, you perform'd my message?

DOLLABELLA: I did, unwillingly.

ANTONY:     Unwillingly?
Was it so hard for you to bear our parting?                    450
You should have wisht it.

DOLLABELLA:     Why?

ANTONY:     Because you love me.
And she receiv'd my message, with as true,
With as unfeign'd a sorrow, as you brought it?

DOLLABELLA: She loves you, ev'n to madness.

ANTONY:     Oh, I know it.
You, *Dollabella*, do not better know
How much she loves me. And should I
Forsake this Beauty? This all-perfect Creature?

DOLLABELLA: I could not, were she mine.

ANTONY:     And yet you first
Perswaded me: how come you alter'd since?

DOLLABELLA: I said at first I was not fit to go;        460
I could not hear her sighs, and see her tears,
But pity must prevail: and so, perhaps,
It may again with you; for I have promis'd
That she should take her last farewel: and, see,
She comes to claim my word.

*Enter* CLEOPATRA

ANTONY:     False *Dollabella*!

DOLLABELLA: What's false, my Lord?

ANTONY:     Why, *Dollabella*'s false,
And *Cleopatra*'s false; both false and faithless.
Draw near, you well-join'd wickedness, you Serpents,
Whom I have, in my kindly bosom, warm'd
Till I am stung to death.                               470

DOLLABELLA:     My Lord, have I
Deserv'd to be thus us'd?

CLEOPATRA:     Can Heav'n prepare
A newer Torment? Can it find a Curse
Beyond our separation?

ANTONY:     Yes, if Fate
Be just, much greater: Heav'n should be ingenious
In punishing such crimes. The rowling Stone,
And gnawing Vulture,* were slight pains, invented
When *Jove* was young, and no examples known
Of mighty ills; but you have ripen'd sin
To such a monstrous growth, 'twill pose* the Gods
To find an equal Torture. Two, two such,          480
Oh, there's no farther name, two such—to me,
To me, who lock'd my Soul within your breasts,
Had no desires, no joys, no life, but you,
When half the Globe was mine, I gave it you

In Dowry with my heart; I had no use,
No fruit of all, but you: a Friend and Mistress
Was what the World could give. Oh, *Cleopatra*!
Oh, *Dollabella*! how could you betray
This tender heart, which with an Infant-fondness
Lay lull'd betwixt your bosoms, and there slept          490
Secure* of injur'd Faith?

DOLLABELLA:    If she has wrong'd you,
  Heav'n, Hell, and You revenge it.

ANTONY:    If she wrong'd me,
  Thou wouldst evade thy part of guilt; but swear
  Thou lov'st not her.

DOLLABELLA:    Not so as I love you.

ANTONY: Not so! Swear, swear, I say, thou dost not love
  her.

DOLLABELLA: No more than Friendship will allow.

ANTONY:    No more?
  Friendship allows thee nothing: thou art perjur'd.—
  And yet thou didst not swear thou lov'dst her not;
  But not so much, no more. Oh trifling Hypocrite,
  Who dar'st not own to her thou dost not love,          500
  Nor own to me thou dost! *Ventidius* heard it;
  *Octavia* saw it.

CLEOPATRA:    They are enemies.

ANTONY: *Alexas* is not so; he, he confest it;
  He, who, next Hell, best knew it, he avow'd it.
  (*To* DOLLABELLA) Why do I seek a proof beyond your
    self?
  You whom I sent to bear my last Farewel,
  Return'd to plead her stay.

DOLLABELLA:    What shall I answer?
  If to have lov'd be guilt, then I have sinn'd;
  But if to have repented of that love
  Can wash away my crime, I have repented.              510
  Yet, if I have offended past forgiveness,
  Let not her suffer: she is innocent.

CLEOPATRA: Ah, what will not a Woman do who loves!
  What means will she refuse, to keep that heart

Where all her joys are plac'd! 'Twas I encourag'd,
'Twas I blew up the fire that scorch'd his Soul,
To make you jealous; and by that regain you.
But all in vain; I could not counterfeit:
In spight of all the damms, my love broke o'er,
And drown'd my heart again: Fate took th' occasion;          520
And thus one minutes feigning has destroy'd
My whole life's truth.

ANTONY:     Thin Cobweb Arts of Falshood;
Seen, and broke through at first.

DOLLABELLA:     Forgive your Mistress.

CLEOPATRA: Forgive your Friend.

ANTONY:     You have convinc'd* your selves,
You plead each others Cause: What Witness have you,
That you but meant to raise my jealousie?

CLEOPATRA: Our selves, and Heav'n.

ANTONY: Guilt witnesses for guilt. Hence, Love and
   Friendship;
You have no longer place in humane breasts,
These two have driv'n you out: avoid my sight;          530
I would not kill the Man whom I have lov'd;
And cannot hurt the Woman; but avoid me,
I do not know how long I can be tame;
For, if I stay one minute more to think
How I am wrong'd, my Justice and Revenge
Will cry so loud within me, that my pity
Will not be heard for either.

DOLLABELLA:     Heav'n has but
Our sorrow for our sins; and then delights
To pardon erring Man: sweet Mercy seems
Its darling Attribute, which limits Justice;          540
As if there were degrees in Infinite;
And Infinite would rather want perfection
Than punish to extent.*

ANTONY:     I can forgive
A Foe; but not a Mistress, and a Friend:
Treason is there in its most horrid shape,
Where trust is greatest: and the Soul resign'd

Is stabb'd by its own Guards: I'll hear no more;
Hence from my sight, for ever.

CLEOPATRA:    How? for ever!
I cannot go one moment from your sight,
And must I go for ever?                                          550
My joys, my only joys are center'd here:
What place have I to go to? my own Kingdom?
That I have lost for you. Or to the *Romans*?
They hate me for your sake. Or must I wander
The wide World o'er, a helpless, banish'd Woman,
Banish'd for love of you; banish'd from you?
I, there's the Banishment! Oh hear me, hear me,
With strictest Justice: for I beg no favour:
And if I have offended you, then kill me,
But do not banish me.                                          560

ANTONY:    I must not hear you.
I have a Fool within me takes your part;
But Honour stops my ears.

CLEOPATRA:    For pity hear me!
Wou'd you cast off a Slave who follow'd you,
Who crouch'd beneath your Spurn?* —He has no pity!
See, if he gives one tear to my departure;
One look, one kind farewel. Oh Iron heart!
Let all the Gods look down, and judge betwixt us,
If he did ever love!

ANTONY:    No more.—*Alexas!*

DOLLABELLA: A perjur'd Villain!

ANTONY: (*to* CLEOPATRA)   Your *Alexas;* yours.

CLEOPATRA: O 'twas his plot: his ruinous design         570
T' ingage you in my love by jealousie.
Hear him; confront him with me; let him speak.

ANTONY: I have; I have.

CLEOPATRA:    And if he clear me not—

ANTONY:  Your Creature! one who hangs upon your smiles!
Watches your eye to say or to unsay
Whate'er you please! I am not to be mov'd.

CLEOPATRA: Then must we part? Farewel, my cruel Lord,
Th' appearance is against me; and I go

Unjustifi'd, for ever from your sight.
How I have lov'd, you know; how yet I love,                 580
My only comfort is, I know my self:
I love you more, ev'n now you are unkind,
Than when you lov'd me most; so well, so truly,
I'll never strive against it; but die pleas'd
To think you once were mine.
ANTONY: Good Heav'n, they weep at parting.
Must I weep too? that calls 'em innocent.
I must not weep; and yet I must, to think
That I must not forgive.—
Live; but live wretched, 'tis but just you shou'd,          590
Who made me so: Live from each others sight:
Let me not hear you meet: Set all the Earth,
And all the Seas, betwixt your sunder'd Loves:
View nothing common but the Sun and Skys:
Now, all take several ways;
And each your own sad fate with mine deplore;
That you were false, and I could trust no more.

                                   [*Exeunt severally*]

# ACT V

## Scene i

*Enter* CLEOPATRA, CHARMION, IRAS

CHARMION: Be juster, Heav'n: such virtue punish'd thus,
  Will make us think that Chance rules all above,
  And shuffles, with a random hand, the Lots
  Which Man is forc'd to draw.

CLEOPATRA: I cou'd tear out these eyes, that gain'd his heart,
  And had not pow'r to keep it. O the curse
  Of doting on, ev'n when I find it Dotage!
  Bear witness, Gods, you heard him bid me go;
  You whom he mock'd with imprecating Vows
  Of promis'd Faith.—I'll die, I will not bear it.          10
  You may hold me—
        (*She pulls out her Dagger, and they hold her*)
  But I can keep my breath; I can die inward,
  And choak this Love.

                *Enter* ALEXAS

IRAS:   Help, O *Alexas*, help!
  The Queen grows desperate, her Soul struggles in her,
  With all the Agonies of Love and Rage,
  And strives to force its passage.

CLEOPATRA:    Let me go.
  Art thou there, Traitor!—O,
  O, for a little breath, to vent my rage!
  Give, give me way, and let me loose upon him.

ALEXAS: Yes, I deserve it, for my ill-tim'd truth.          20
  Was it for me to prop
  The Ruins of a falling Majesty?
  To place my self beneath the mighty flaw,
  Thus to be crush'd, and pounded into Atomes,

By its o'erwhelming weight? 'Tis too presuming
For Subjects, to preserve that wilful pow'r
Which courts its own destruction.

CLEOPATRA:     I wou'd reason
More calmly with you. Did not you o'er-rule,
And force my plain, direct, and open love
Into these crooked paths of jealousie?                          30
Now, what's th' event? *Octavia* is remov'd;
But *Cleopatra*'s banish'd. Thou, thou, Villain,
Hast push'd my Boat, to open Sea; to prove,
At my sad cost, if thou canst steer it back.
It cannot be; I'm lost too far; I'm ruin'd:
Hence, thou Impostor, Traitor, Devil—
I can no more: thou, and my griefs, have sunk
Me down so low, that I want voice to curse thee.

ALEXAS: Suppose some shipwrack'd Seaman near the
    shore,
Dropping and faint, with climbing up the Cliff,                40
If, from above, some charitable hand
Pull him to safety, hazarding himself
To draw the others weight; wou'd he look back
And curse him for his pains? The case is yours;
But one step more, and you have gain'd the heighth.

CLEOPATRA: Sunk, never more to rise.

ALEXAS: *Octavia*'s gone, and *Dollabella* banish'd.
Believe me, Madam, *Antony* is yours.
His heart was never lost; but started off
To Jealousie, Love's last retreat and covert:                  50
Where it lies hid in Shades, watchful in silence,
And list'ning for the sound that calls it back.
Some other, any man, ('tis so advanc'd)
May perfect this unfinish'd work, which I
(Unhappy only to my self) have left
So easie to his hand.

CLEOPATRA:     Look well thou do't; else—

ALEXAS: Else, what your silence threatens.—*Antony*
Is mounted up the *Pharos*;* from whose Turret,
He stands surveying our *Ægyptian* Gallies,

Engag'd with *Cæsar*'s Fleet: now Death, or Conquest.      60
If the first happen, Fate acquits my promise:
If we o'ercome, the Conqueror is yours.

                              (*A distant Shout within*)

CHARMION: Have comfort, Madam: did you mark that
   Shout?

                              (*Second Shout nearer*)

IRAS: Hark; they redouble it.

ALEXAS:      'Tis from the Port.
   The loudness shows it near: good news, kind Heavens.

CLEOPATRA: *Osiris* make it so.

                 *Enter* SERAPION

SERAPION:      Where, where's the Queen?

ALEXAS: How frightfully the holy Coward stares!
   As if not yet recover'd of th' assault,
   When all his Gods, and what's more dear to him,
   His Offerings were at stake.                           70

SERAPION:      O horror, horror!
   *Ægypt* has been; our latest hour is come:
   The Queen of Nations from her ancient seat,
   Is sunk for ever in the dark Abyss:
   Time has unrowl'd her Glories to the last,
   And now clos'd up the Volume.

CLEOPATRA:      Be more plain:
   Say, whence thou com'st, (though Fate is in thy face,
   Which from thy haggard eyes looks wildly out,
   And threatens ere thou speak'st.)

SERAPION:      I came from *Pharos*;
   From viewing (spare me and imagine it)
   Our Lands last hope, your Navy—                        80

CLEOPATRA:      Vanquish'd?

SERAPION:           No.
   They fought not.

CLEOPATRA:      Then they fled.

SERAPION:           Nor that. I saw,
   With *Antony*, your well-appointed Fleet
   Row out; and thrice he wav'd his hand on high,
   And thrice with cheerful cries they shouted back:

'Twas then, false Fortune, like a fawning Strumpet,
About to leave the Bankrupt Prodigal,
With a dissembled smile wou'd kiss at parting,
And flatter to the last; the well-tim'd Oars
Now dipt from every bank, now smoothly run
To meet the Foe; and soon indeed they met,                    90
But not as Foes. In few, we saw their Caps
On either side thrown up; th' *Ægyptian* Gallies[9]
(Receiv'd like Friends) past through, and fell behind
The *Roman* rear: and now, they all come forward,
And ride within the Port.

CLEOPATRA:    Enough, *Serapion*:
I've heard my doom. This needed not, you Gods:
When I lost *Antony*, your work was done;
'Tis but superfluous malice. Where's my Lord?
How bears he this last blow?

SERAPION: His fury cannot be express'd by words:             100
Thrice he attempted headlong to have faln
Full on his foes, and aim'd at *Cæsar*'s Galley:
With-held, he raves on you; cries, He's betray'd.
Should he now find you—

ALEXAS:    Shun him, seek your safety,
Till you can clear your innocence.

CLEOPATRA:    I'll stay.

ALEXAS: You must not, haste you to your Monument,
While I make speed to *Cæsar*.

CLEOPATRA:    *Cæsar!* No,
I have no business with him.

ALEXAS:    I can work him
To spare your life, and let this madman perish.

CLEOPATRA: Base fawning Wretch! wouldst thou betray
him too?                                                      110
Hence from my sight, I will not hear a Traytor;
'Twas thy design brought all this ruine on us.
*Serapion*, thou art honest; counsel me:
But haste, each moment's precious.

[9] 91–2. Based on *Antony and Cleopatra*, IV.xii.11–13.

SERAPION: Retire; you must not yet see *Antony*.
  He who began this mischief,
  'Tis just he tempt the danger: let him clear you;
  And, since he offer'd you his servile tongue,
  To gain a poor precarious life from *Cæsar*,
  Let him expose that fawning eloquence,       120
  And speak to *Antony*.
ALEXAS:    O Heavens! I dare not,
  I meet my certain death.
CLEOPATRA:    Slave, thou deserv'st it.
  Not that I fear my Lord, will I avoid him;
  I know him noble: when he banish'd me,
  And thought me false, he scorn'd to take my life;
  But I'll be justifi'd, and then die with him.
ALEXAS: O pity me, and let me follow you.
CLEOPATRA: To death, if thou stir hence. Speak, if thou
  cánst,
  Now for thy life, which basely thou wou'dst save;
  While mine I prize at this. Come, good *Serapion*.    130
      [*Exeunt* CLEOPATRA, SERAPION, CHARMION, IRAS]
ALEXAS: O that I less cou'd fear to lose this being,
  Which, like a Snow-ball, in my coward hand,
  The more 'tis grasp'd, the faster melts away.
  Poor Reason! what a wretched aid art thou!
  For still, in spight of thee,
  These two long Lovers, Soul and Body, dread
  Their final separation. Let me think:
  What can I say, to save my self from death?
  No matter what becomes of *Cleopatra*.
ANTONY: (*within*) Which way? where?    140
VENTIDIUS: (*within*)  This leads to the Monument.
ALEXAS: Ah me! I hear him; yet I'm unprepar'd:
  My gift of lying's gone;
  And this Court-Devil, which I so oft have rais'd,
  Forsakes me at my need. I dare not stay;
  Yet cannot far go hence.    [*Exit*]
      *Enter* ANTONY *and* VENTIDIUS
ANTONY: O happy *Cæsar*! Thou hast men to lead:

Think not 'tis thou hast conquer'd *Antony*;
But *Rome* has conquer'd *Ægypt*. I'm betray'd.
VENTIDIUS: Curse on this treach'rous Train!
Their Soil and Heav'n infect 'em all with baseness:    150
And their young Souls come tainted to the World
With the first breath they draw.
ANTONY: Th' original Villain sure no God created;
He was a Bastard of the Sun, by *Nile*,*
Ap'd* into Man; with all his Mother's Mud
Crusted about his Soul.
VENTIDIUS:    The Nation is
One Universal Traitor; and their Queen
The very Spirit and Extract of 'em all.
ANTONY: Is there yet left
A possibility of aid from Valor?    160
Is there one God unsworn to my Destruction?
The least unmortgag'd hope? for, if there be,
Methinks I cannot fall beneath the Fate
Of such a Boy as *Cæsar*.
The World's one half is yet in *Antony*;
And, from each limb of it that's hew'd away,
The Soul comes back to me.
VENTIDIUS:    There yet remain
Three Legions in the Town. The last assault
Lopt off the rest: if death be your design,
(As I must wish it now) these are sufficient    170
To make a heap about us of dead Foes,
An honest pile for burial.
ANTONY:    They're enough.
We'll not divide our Stars; but side by side
Fight emulous:* and with malicious eyes
Survey each other's acts: so every death
Thou giv'st, I'll take on me, as a just debt,
And pay thee back a Soul.
VENTIDIUS: Now you shall see I love you. Not a word
Of chiding more. By my few hours of life,
I am so pleas'd with this brave *Roman* Fate,    180
That I wou'd not be *Cæsar*, to out-live you.

When we put off this flesh, and mount together,
I shall be shown to all th' Etherial crowd;
*Lo, this is he who dy'd with* Antony.

ANTONY: Who knows but we may pierce through all their
    Troops,
And reach my Veterans yet? 'Tis worth the tempting,
T' o'er-leap this Gulph of Fate,
And leave our wond'ring Destinies behind.

                    *Enter* ALEXAS, *trembling*

VENTIDIUS: See, see, that Villain:
See *Cleopatra* stampt upon that face,                    190
With all her cunning, all her arts of falshood!
How she looks out through those dissembling eyes!
How he has set his count'nance for deceit;
And promises a lye, before he speaks!
Let me dispatch him first.                    (*Drawing*)

ALEXAS:    O, spare me, spare me.

ANTONY: Hold; he's not worth your killing. On thy life,
(Which thou mayst keep, because I scorn to take it)
No syllable to justifie thy Queen;
Save thy base tongue its office.

ALEXAS:    Sir, she's gone,
Where she shall never be molested more                    200
By Love, or you.

ANTONY:    Fled to her *Dollabella*!
Die, Traitor, I revoke my promise, die. (*Going to kill him*)

ALEXAS: O hold, she is not fled.

ANTONY:    She is: my eyes
Are open to her falshood; my whole life
Has been a golden dream, of Love and Friendship.
But, now I wake, I'm like a Merchant, rows'd
From soft repose, to see his Vessel sinking,
And all his Wealth cast o'er. Ingrateful Woman!
Who follow'd me, but as the Swallow Summer,
Hatching her young ones in my kindly Beams,                    210
Singing her flatt'ries to my morning wake;
But, now my Winter comes, she spreads her wings,
And seeks the Spring of *Cæsar*.

ALEXAS:     Think not so:
Her Fortunes have, in all things, mixt with yours.
Had she betray'd her Naval force to *Rome*,
How easily might she have gone to *Cæsar*,
Secure by such a bribe!

VENTIDIUS:     She sent it first,
To be more welcome after.

ANTONY:     'Tis too plain;
Else wou'd she have appear'd, to clear her self.

ALEXAS: Too fatally she has; she could not bear          220
To be accus'd by you; but shut her self
Within her Monument: look'd down, and sigh'd;
While, from her unchang'd face, the silent tears
Dropt, as they had not leave, but stole their parting.
Some undistinguish'd words she inly murmur'd;
At last, she rais'd her eyes; and, with such looks
As dying *Lucrece*\* cast,—

ANTONY:     My heart forebodes.—

VENTIDIUS: All for the best: go on.

ALEXAS:     She snatch'd her Ponyard,
And, ere we cou'd prevent the fatal blow,
Plung'd it within her breast: then turn'd to me,          230
*Go, bear my Lord* (said she) *my last Farewel;*
*And ask him if he yet suspect my Faith.*
More she was saying, but death rush'd betwixt.
She half pronounc'd your Name with her last breath,
And bury'd half within her.[10]

VENTIDIUS:     Heav'n be prais'd.

ANTONY: Then art thou innocent, my poor dear Love?
And art thou dead?
O those two words! their sound shou'd be divided:
Hadst thou been false, and dy'd: or hadst thou liv'd,
And hadst been true—But Innocence and Death!          240
This shows not well above. Then what am I,
The Murderer of this Truth, this Innocence!
Thoughts cannot form themselves in words so horrid
As can express my guilt!

[10] 234-5. Based on *Antony and Cleopatra*, IV.xiv.29–33.

VENTIDIUS: Is't come to this? The Gods have been too
    gracious:
And thus you thank 'em for't.
ANTONY: (*to* ALEXAS)  Why stay'st thou here?
Is it for thee to spy upon my Soul,
And see its inward mourning? Get thee hence;
Thou art not worthy to behold, what now
Becomes a *Roman* Emperor to perform.      250
ALEXAS: (*aside*) He loves her still:
His grief betrays it. Good! The joy to find
She's yet alive, compleats the reconcilement.
I've sav'd my self, and her. But, Oh! the *Romans*!
Fate comes too fast upon my Wit,
Hunts me too hard, and meets me at each double.*    [*Exit*]
VENTIDIUS: Wou'd she had dy'd a little sooner tho,
Before *Octavia* went; you might have treated:
Now 'twill look tame, and wou'd not be receiv'd.
Come, rouze your self, and lets die warm together.    260
ANTONY: I will not fight: there's no more work for War.
The bus'ness of my angry hours is done.
VENTIDIUS: *Cæsar* is at your Gates.
ANTONY:    Why, let him enter;
He's welcom now.
VENTIDIUS: What Lethargy has crept into your Soul?
ANTONY: 'Tis but a scorn of life, and just desire
To free my self from bondage.
VENTIDIUS:    Do it bravely.
ANTONY: I will; but not by fighting. O, *Ventidius*!
What shou'd I fight for now? My Queen is dead.
I was but great for her; my Pow'r, my Empire,    270
Were but my Merchandise to buy her love;
And conquer'd Kings, my Factors. Now she's dead,
Let *Cæsar* take the World,—
An Empty Circle, since the Jewel's gone
Which made it worth my strife: my being's nauseous;
For all bribes of life are gone away.
VENTIDIUS: Wou'd you be taken?
ANTONY:    Yes, I wou'd be taken;

But, as a *Roman* ought, dead, my *Ventidius*:
For I'll convey my Soul from *Cæsar*'s reach,
And lay down life my self. 'Tis time the World          280
Shou'd have a Lord, and know whom to obey.
We two have kept its homage in suspence,
And bent the Globe on whose each side we trod,
Till it was dinted inwards: Let him walk
Alone upon't; I'm weary of my part.
My Torch is out; and the World stands before me
Like a black Desart, at th' approach of night:
I'll lay me down, and stray no farther on.

VENTIDIUS: I cou'd be griev'd,
But that I'll not out-live you: choose your death;          290
For, I have seen him in such various shapes,
I care not which I take: I'm only troubled
The life I bear, is worn to such a rag,
'Tis scarce worth giving. I cou'd wish indeed
We threw it from us with a better grace;
That, like two Lyons taken in the Toils,
We might at least thrust out our paws, and wound
The Hunters that inclose us.

ANTONY:      I have thought on't.
*Ventidius*, you must live.

VENTIDIUS:      I must not, Sir.

ANTONY: Wilt thou not live, to speak some good of me?      300
To stand by my fair Fame, and guard th' approaches
From the ill Tongues of Men?

VENTIDIUS:      Who shall guard mine,
For living after you?

ANTONY:      Say, I command it.

VENTIDIUS: If we die well, our deaths will speak themselves,
And need no living witness.

ANTONY:      Thou hast lov'd me,
And fain I wou'd reward thee: I must die;
Kill me, and take the merit of my death
To make thee Friends with *Cæsar*.

VENTIDIUS:      Thank your kindness.

You said I lov'd you; and, in recompence,
You bid me turn a Traitor: did I think                    310
You wou'd have us'd me thus? that I shou'd die
With a hard thought of you?
ANTONY:     Forgive me, *Roman*.
Since I have heard of *Cleopatra*'s death,
My reason bears no rule upon my tongue,
But lets my thoughts break all at random out:
I've thought better; do not deny me twice.
VENTIDIUS: By Heav'n, I will not.
Let it not be t' out-live you.
ANTONY:     Kill me first,
And then die thou: for 'tis but just thou serve
Thy Friend, before thy self.                              320
VENTIDIUS:     Give me your hand.
We soon shall meet again. Now, Farewel, Emperor.
                                        (*Embrace*)
Methinks that word's too cold to be my last:
Since Death sweeps* all distinctions, Farewel, Friend.
That's all.—
I will not make a bus'ness of a trifle:
And yet I cannot look on you, and kill you;
Pray turn your face.
ANTONY:     I do: strike home, be sure.
VENTIDIUS: Home, as my Sword will reach.
                                        (*Kills himself*)
ANTONY:     O, thou mistak'st;
That wound was none of thine: give it me back:
Thou robb'st me of my death.                              330
VENTIDIUS:     I do indeed;
But, think 'tis the first time I e'er deceiv'd you;
If that may plead my pardon. And you, Gods,
Forgive me, if you will; for I die perjur'd,
Rather than kill my Friend.                       (*Dies*)
ANTONY: Farewel. Ever my Leader, ev'n in death!
My Queen and thou have got the start of me,
And I'm the lag of Honour. – Gone so soon?[11]

[11] 336–7. Based on *Antony and Cleopatra*, IV.xiv.98–100.

Is death no more? He us'd him carelessly,
With a familiar kindness: ere he knock'd,
Ran to the door, and took him in his arms,          340
As who shou'd say, *Y'are welcome at all hours*,
*A Friend need give no warning*. Books had spoil'd him;
For all the Learn'd are Cowards by profession.
'Tis not worth
My farther thought; for death, for ought I know,
Is but to think no more. Here's to be satisfi'd.

> (*Falls on his Sword*)

I've mist my heart. O unperforming hand!
Thou never cou'dst have err'd in a worse time.
My Fortune jades* me to the last; and death,
Like a great Man, takes state, and makes me wait          350
For my admittance.—              (*Trampling within*)
   Some perhaps from *Cæsar*:
If he shou'd find me living, and suspect
That I plaid booty* with my life! I'll mend
My work, ere they can reach me.(*Rises upon his knees*)

    *Enter* CLEOPATRA, CHARMION, IRAS

CLEOPATRA: Where is my Lord? where is he?
CHARMION:    There he lies,
And dead *Ventidius* by him.
CLEOPATRA: My fears were Prophets; I am come too late.
O that accurs'd *Alexas*!              (*Runs to him*)
ANTONY:    Art thou living?
Or am I dead before I knew? and thou
The first kind Ghost that meets me?          360
CLEOPATRA:    Help me seat him.
Send quickly, send for help.

> (*They place him in a Chair*)

ANTONY:    I am answer'd.
We live both. Sit thee down, my *Cleopatra*:
I'll make the most I can of life, to stay
A moment more with thee.
CLEOPATRA: How is it with you?
ANTONY:    'Tis as with a man
Removing in a hurry, all pack'd up,

But one dear Jewel that his haste forgot;
And he, for that, returns upon the spur:
So I come back, for thee.

CLEOPATRA: Too long, you Heav'ns, you have been cruel
  to me;                 370
Now show your mended Faith, and give me back
His fleeting life.

ANTONY: It will not be, my Love.
I keep my Soul by force.
Say but thou art not false.

CLEOPATRA: 'Tis now too late
To say I'm true: I'll prove it, and die with you.
Unknown to me, *Alexas* feign'd my death:
Which, when I knew, I hasted, to prevent
This fatal consequence. My Fleet betray'd
Both you and me.

ANTONY: And *Dollabella*—
CLEOPATRA:   Scarce
Esteem'd before he lov'd; but hated now.     380

ANTONY: Enough: my life's not long enough for more.
Thou sayst thou wilt come after: I believe thee;
For I can now believe whate'er thou sayst,
That we may part more kindly.

CLEOPATRA: I will come:
Doubt not, my life, I'll come, and quickly too:
*Cæsar* shall triumph o'er no part of thee.

ANTONY: But grieve not, while thou stay'st
My last disastrous times:
Think we have had a clear and glorious day;
And Heav'n did kindly to delay the storm    390
Just till our close of ev'ning. Ten years love,
And not a moment lost, but all improv'd
To th' utmost joys: What Ages have we liv'd!
And now to die each others; and, so dying,
While hand in hand we walk in Groves below,
Whole Troops of Lovers Ghosts shall flock about us,
And all the Train be ours.[12]

---

[12] 395-7. Based on *Antony and Cleopatra*, IV.xiv.52-5.

CLEOPATRA: Your words are like the Notes of dying
    Swans,
  Too sweet to last. Were there so many hours
  For your unkindness, and not one for love?                    400
ANTONY: No, not a minute.—This one kiss—more worth
  Than all I leave to *Cæsar*.                    (*Dies*)
CLEOPATRA: O, tell me so again,
  And take ten thousand kisses, for that word.
  My Lord, my Lord: speak, if you yet have being;
  Sigh to me, if you cannot speak; or cast
  One look: Do any thing that shows you live.
IRAS: He's gone too far, to hear you;
  And this you see, a lump of sensless Clay,
  The leavings of a Soul.                    410
CHARMION:    Remember, Madam,
  He charg'd you not to grieve.
CLEOPATRA:    And I'll obey him.
  I have not lov'd a *Roman* not to know
  What should become his Wife; his Wife, my *Charmion*;
  For 'tis that high Title I aspire,
  And now I'll not die less. Let dull *Octavia*
  Survive, to mourn him dead: my Nobler Fate
  Shall knit our Spousals with a tie too strong
  For *Roman* Laws to break.
IRAS:    Will you then die?
CLEOPATRA: Why shou'dst thou make that question?
IRAS: *Cæsar* is merciful.                    420
CLEOPATRA:    Let him be so
  To those that want his mercy: my poor Lord
  Made no such Cov'nant with him, to spare me
  When he was dead. Yield me to *Cæsar*'s pride?
  What, to be led in triumph through the Streets,
  A spectacle to base *Plebeian* eyes;
  While some dejected Friend of *Antony*'s,
  Close in a corner, shakes his head, and mutters
  A secret curse on her who ruin'd him?
  I'll none of that.
CHARMION:    Whatever you resolve,

I'll follow ev'n to death.                                          430
IRAS:     I only fear'd
  For you; but more shou'd fear to live without you.
CLEOPATRA: Why, now 'tis as it shou'd be. Quick, my
    Friends,
  Dispatch; ere this, the Town's in *Cæsar*'s hands:
  My Lord looks down concern'd, and fears my stay,
  Lest I shou'd be surpriz'd;
  Keep him not waiting for his love too long.
  You, *Charmion*, bring my Crown and richest Jewels,
  With 'em, the Wreath of Victory I made
  (Vain Augury!) for him who now lies dead.
  You, *Iras*, bring the cure of all our ills.                      440
IRAS: The Aspicks, Madam?
CLEOPATRA:     Must I bid you twice?
                    [*Exeunt* CHARMION *and* IRAS]
  'Tis sweet to die, when they wou'd force life on me,[13]
  To rush into the dark aboad of death,
  And seize him first; if he be like my Love,
  He is not frightful sure.
  We're now alone, in secresie and silence;
  And is not this like Lovers? I may kiss
  These pale, cold lips; *Octavia* does not see me;
  And, Oh! 'tis better far to have him thus,
  Than see him in her arms.—O welcome, welcome.                     450
                    *Enter* CHARMION, IRAS
CHARMION: What must be done?
CLEOPATRA:     Short Ceremony, Friends;
  But yet it must be decent. First, this Laurel
  Shall crown my Hero's Head: he fell not basely,
  Nor left his Shield behind him. Only thou
  Cou'dst triumph o'er thy self; and thou alone
  Wert worthy so to triumph.
CHARMION:     To what end
  These Ensigns* of your Pomp and Royalty?
CLEOPATRA: Dull, that thou art! why, 'tis to meet my
    Love;

---

[13] 441-3. Based on *Antony and Cleopatra*, IV.xv.84-6.

As when I saw him first, on *Cydnos* bank,
All sparkling, like a Goddess; so adorn'd,                    460
I'll find him once again: my second Spousals
Shall match my first, in Glory. Haste, haste, both,
And dress the Bride of *Antony*.

CHARMION:   'Tis done.

CLEOPATRA: Now seat me by my Lord. I claim this place;
For I must conquer *Cæsar* too, like him,
And win my share o'th' World. Hail, you dear Relicks
Of my Immortal Love!
O let no Impious hand remove you hence;
But rest for ever here. Let *Ægypt* give
His death that peace, which it deny'd his life.               470
Reach me the Casket.

IRAS: Underneath the fruit the Aspick lies.

CLEOPATRA: (*putting aside the leaves*) Welcom, thou kind
   Deceiver!
Thou best of Thieves; who, with an easie key,
Dost open life, and, unperceiv'd by us,
Ev'n steal us from our selves: discharging so
Death's dreadful office, better than himself,
Touching our limbs so gently into slumber,
That Death stands by, deceiv'd by his own Image,
And thinks himself but Sleep.                                480

SERAPION: (*within*)   The Queen, where is she?
The Town is yielded, *Cæsar*'s at the Gates.

CLEOPATRA: He comes too late t' invade the Rights of
   Death.
Haste, bare my Arm, and rouze the Serpent's fury.
               (*Holds out her Arm, and draws it back*)
Coward Flesh—
Wou'dst thou conspire with *Cæsar*, to betray me,
As thou wert none of mine? I'll force thee to't,
And not be sent by him,
But bring my self my Soul to *Antony*.
               (*Turns aside, and then shows her Arm bloody*)
Take hence; the work is done.

SERAPION: (*within*)   Break ope the door,

And guard the Traitor well.                                    490
CHARMION:    The next is ours.
IRAS: Now, *Charmion*, to be worthy
  Of our great Queen and Mistress. (*They apply the Aspicks*)
CLEOPATRA: Already, Death, I feel thee in my Veins;
  I go with such a will to find my Lord,
  That we shall quickly meet.
  A heavy numness creeps through every limb,
  And now 'tis at my head: my eye-lids fall,
  And my dear Love is vanish'd in a mist.
  Where shall I find him, where? O turn me to him,
  And lay me on his breast.—*Cæsar*, thy worst;            500
  Now part us, if thou canst.                  (*Dies*)
(IRAS *sinks down at her feet, and dies;* CHARMION *stands
                  behind her Chair, as dressing her head*)
           *Enter* SERAPION, *two Priests,* ALEXAS *bound,*
                                            *Ægyptians*

TWO PRIESTS: Behold, *Serapion*, what havock Death has
  made!
SERAPION: 'Twas what I fear'd. *Charmion*, is this well
  done?
CHARMION: Yes, 'tis well done, and like a Queen, the last
  Of her great Race: I follow her.      (*Sinks down; Dies*)
ALEXAS:      'Tis true,
  She has done well: much better thus to die,[14]
  Than live to make a Holy-day in *Rome*.
SERAPION: See, see how the Lovers sit in State together,
  As they were giving Laws to half Mankind.
  Th' impression of a smile left in her face,               510
  Shows she dy'd pleas'd with him for whom she liv'd,
  And went to charm him in another World.
  *Cæsar*'s just entring; grief has now no leisure.
  Secure that Villain, as our pledge of safety
  To grace th' Imperial Triumph. Sleep, blest Pair,
  Secure from humane chance, long Ages out,
  While all the Storms of Fate fly o'er your Tomb;

---

[14] 504–6. Based on *Antony and Cleopatra*, V.ii.324–6.

And Fame, to late Posterity, shall tell,
No Lovers liv'd so great, or dy'd so well.

[*Exeunt*]

# EPILOGUE

Poets, like Disputants, when Reasons fail,
Have one sure Refuge left; and that's to rail.
Fop, Coxcomb, Fool, *are thunder'd through the Pit;*
And this is all their Equipage of Wit.
We wonder how the Devil this diff'rence grows,
Betwixt our Fools in Verse, and yours in Prose:
For, 'Faith, the quarrel rightly understood,
'Tis Civil War *with their own Flesh and Blood.*
The thread-bare Author hates the gawdy Coat;
And swears at the Guilt Coach, but swears a-foot:*
For 'tis observ'd of every Scribling Man,
He grows a Fop as fast as e'er he can;
Prunes up, and asks his Oracle the Glass,
If Pink or Purple best become his face.
For our poor Wretch, he neither rails nor prays; ⎫
Nor likes your Wit just as you like his Plays; ⎬
He has not yet so much of Mr Bays.* ⎭
He does his best; and, if he cannot please,
Wou'd quietly sue out his Writ of Ease.*
Yet, if he might his own Grand Jury call,
By the Fair Sex he begs to stand or fall.
Let Cæsar's Pow'r the Mens ambition move,
But grace You him who lost the World for Love.
Yet if some antiquated Lady say,
The last Age is not Copy'd in his Play;
Heav'n help the Man who for that face must drudge,
Which only has the wrinkles of a Judge.
Let not the Young and Beauteous join with those;
For shou'd you raise such numerous Hosts of Foes,
Young Wits and Sparks he to his aid must call;
'Tis more than one Man's work to please you all.

FINIS

# KING LEAR

---

## BY NAHUM TATE

# THE

# HISTORY

OF

# KING

# LEAR.

Acted at the

## Duke's Theatre.

---

Reviv'd with Alterations.

---

By *N. TATE*.

---

*LONDON*,
Printed for *E. Flesher*, and are to be sold by *R. Bentley*, and *M. Magnes* in *Ruſſel-ſtreet* near *Covent-Garden*, 1681.

# My Esteemed FRIEND
## Thomas Boteler, Esq,*

SIR,

*You have a natural Right to this Piece, since by your Advice, I attempted the Revival of it with Alterations. Nothing but the Power of your Perswasion, and my Zeal for all the Remains of* Shakespear,* *cou'd have wrought me to so bold an Undertaking. I found that the Newmodelling of this Story, wou'd force me sometimes on the difficult Task of making the chiefest Persons speak something like their Character, on Matter whereof I had no Ground in my Author.* Lear's *real, and* Edgar's *pretended madness have so much of extravagant Nature (I know not how else to express it) as cou'd never have started but from our* Shakespear's *Creating Fancy. The Images and Language are so odd and surprizing, and yet so agreeable and proper, that whilst we grant that none but* Shakespear *cou'd have form'd such Conceptions, yet we are satisfied that they were the only Things in the World that ought to be said on those Occasions. I found the whole to answer your Account of it, a Heap of Jewels, unstrung and unpolisht; yet so dazling in their Disorder, that I soon perceiv'd I had seiz'd a Treasure. 'Twas my good Fortune to light on one Expedient to rectifie what was wanting in the Regularity and Probability of the Tale, which was to run through the whole, A Love betwixt* Edgar *and* Cordelia, *that never chang'd word with each other in the Original. This renders* Cordelia's *Indifference and her Father's Passion in the first Scene probable. It likewise gives Countenance to* Edgar's *Disguise, making that a generous Design that was before a poor Shift to save his Life. The Distress of the Story is evidently heightned by it; and it particularly gave Occasion of a New Scene or Two, of more Success (perhaps) than Merit. This Method necessarily threw me on making the Tale conclude in a*

*Success to the innocent distrest Persons: Otherwise I must have incumbred the Stage with dead Bodies, which Conduct makes many Tragedies conclude with unseasonable Jests. Yet was I Rackt with no small Fears for so bold a Change, till I found it well receiv'd by my Audience; and if this will not satisfie the Reader, I can produce an Authority that questionless will.*[1] Neither is it of so Trivial an Undertaking to make a Tragedy end happily, for 'tis more difficult to Save than 'tis to Kill: The Dagger and Cup of Poyson are alwaies in Readiness; but to bring the Action to the last Extremity, and then by probable Means to recover all, will require the Art and Judgment of a Writer, and cost him many a Pang in the Performance.

*I have one thing more to Apologize for, which is, that I have us'd less Quaintness of Expression even in the newest Parts of this Play. I confess 'twas Design in me, partly to comply with my Author's Style to make the Scenes of a Piece, and partly to give it some Resemblance of the Time and Persons here Represented. This, Sir, I submit wholly to you, who are both a Judge and Master of Style. Nature had exempted you before you went Abroad from the Morose Saturnine Humour of our Country, and you brought home the Refinedness of Travel without the Affectation. Many Faults I see in the following Pages, and question not but you will discover more; yet I will presume so far on your Friendship, as to make the Whole a Present to you, and Subscribe my self*

Your obliged Friend
and humble Servant,
N. Tate.

---

[1] Mr. Dryd. *Pref. to the Span. Fryar.*\*

# PROLOGUE

Since by Mistakes your best Delights are made,
(For ev'n your Wives can please in Masquerade)
'Twere worth our While t' have drawn you in this day
By a new Name to our old honest Play;
But he that did this Evenings Treat prepare
Bluntly resolv'd before-hand to declare
Your Entertainment should be most old Fare.
Yet hopes, since in rich Shakespear's soil it grew,
'Twill relish yet with those whose Tasts are True,
And his Ambition is to please a Few.          10
If then this Heap of Flow'rs shall chance to wear
Fresh Beauty in the Order they now bear,
Ev'n this Shakespear's Praise; each Rustick knows
'Mongst plenteous Flow'rs a Garland to Compose,
Which strung by his course Hand may fairer Show,
But 'twas a Pow'r Divine first made 'em Grow.
Why shou'd these Scenes lie hid, in which we find
What may at Once divert and teach the Mind?
Morals were alwaies proper for the Stage,
But are ev'n necessary in this Age.          20
Poets must take the Churches Teaching Trade,
Since Priests their Province of Intrigue invade;
But We the worst in this Exchange have got,
In vain our Poets Preach, whilst Church-men Plot.*

## THE PERSONS

KING LEAR Mr *Betterton*
GLOSTER, Mr *Gillo*
KENT, Mr *Wiltshire*
EDGAR, Mr *Smith*
BASTARD, Mr Jo. *Williams*
CORNWALL, Mr *Norris*
ALBANY, Mr *Bowman*
[Burgundy,]
GENTLEMAN-USHER, Mr *Jevon*
[An Old Man,]
[Physician,]
GONERILL, Mrs *Shadwell*
REGAN, Lady *Slingsby*
CORDELIA, Mrs *Barry*
[Arante,]
GUARDS, OFFICERS, MESSENGERS, [Two Ruffians,]
  ATTENDANTS

# ACT I

## Scene i

### Enter BASTARD *solus*

BASTARD: Thou Nature art my Goddess, to thy Law
My Services are bound, why am I then
Depriv'd of a Son's Right because I came not
In the dull Road that custom has prescrib'd?
Why Bastard, wherefore Base, when I can boast
A Mind as gen'rous and a Shape as true
As honest Madam's Issue? why are we
Held Base, who in the lusty stealth of Nature
Take fiercer Qualities than what compound
The scanted Births of the stale Marriage-bed?          10
Well then, legitimate *Edgar*, to thy right
Of Law I will oppose a Bastard's Cunning.
Our Father's Love is to the Bastard *Edmund*
As to Legitimate *Edgar*: with success[2]
I've practis'd yet on both their easie Natures:
Here comes the old Man chaf't with th' Information
Which last I forg'd against my Brother *Edgar*,
A Tale so plausible, so boldly utter'd
And heightned by such lucky Accidents,
That now the slightest circumstance confirms him,     20
And Base-born *Edmund* spight of Law inherits.

### Enter KENT *and* GLOSTER

GLOSTER: Nay, good my Lord, your Charity
O'reshoots it self to plead in his behalf;
You are your self a Father, and may feel
The sting of disobedience from a Son
First born and best Belov'd: Oh Villain *Edgar*!

---

[2] 1-14. Based on *King Lear*, I.ii.1-18: 'Thou, Nature ... to th' legitimate.'

KENT: Be not too rash, all may be forgery,
  And time yet clear the Duty of your Son.
GLOSTER: Plead with the Seas, and reason down the
    Winds,
  Yet shalt thou ne're convince me, I have seen        30
  His foul Designs through all a Father's fondness:
  But be this Light and Thou my Witnesses
  That I discard from here my Possessions,
  Divorce him from my Heart, my Blood and Name.
BASTARD: It works as I cou'd wish; I'll shew my self.
GLOSTER: Ha *Edmund*! welcome Boy; O *Kent* see here
  Inverted Nature, *Gloster*'s Shame and Glory,
  This By-Born,* the wild sally of my Youth,
  Pursues me with all filial Offices,
  Whilst *Edgar*, begg'd of Heaven and born in Honour,  40
  Draws plagues on my white head that urge me still
  To curse in Age the pleasure of my Youth.
  Nay weep not, *Edmund*, for thy Brother's crimes;
  O gen'rous Boy, thou shar'st but half his blood,
  Yet lov'st beyond the kindness of a Brother.
  But I'll reward thy Vertue. Follow me.
  My Lord, you wait the King who comes resolv'd
  To quit the Toils of Empire, and divide
  His Realms amongst his Daughters, Heaven succeed it,*
  But much I fear the Change.
KENT:    I grieve to see him        50
  With such wild starts of passion hourly seiz'd,
  As renders Majesty beneath it self.
GLOSTER: Alas! 'tis the Infirmity of his Age,
  Yet has his Temper ever been unfixt,
  Chol'rick and suddain; hark, They approach.
                  [*Exeunt* GLOSTER *and* BASTARD]
*Flourish. Enter* LEAR, CORNWALL, ALBANY, BURGUNDY,
EDGAR, GONERILL, REGAN, CORDELIA, EDGAR *speaking*
        *to* CORDELIA *at Entrance*
EDGAR: *Cordelia*, royal Fair, turn yet once more,[3]

  [3] 54–6: I.i.292–3.

And e're successfull *Burgundy* receive
The treasure of thy Beauties from the King,
E're happy *Burgundy* for ever fold Thee,
Cast back one pitying Look on wretched *Edgar*.                    60

CORDELIA: Alas what wou'd the wretched *Edgar* with
The more Unfortunate *Cordelia*;
Who in obedience to a Father's will
Flys from her *Edgar*'s Arms to *Burgundy*'s?

LEAR: Attend my Lords of *Albany and Cornwall*
With Princely *Burgundy*.

ALBANY:      We do, my Liege.

LEAR: Give me the Mapp – know, Lords, We have divided
In Three our Kingdom, having now resolved
To disengage from Our long Toil of State,
Conferring All upon your younger years;                           70
You, *Burgundy*, *Cornwall* and *Albany*,
Long in Our Court have made your amorous sojourn
And now are to be answer'd – tell me my Daughters
Which of you Loves Us most, that We may place
Our largest Bounty with the largest Merit.
*Gonerill*, Our Eldest-born, speak first.

GONERILL: Sir, I do love You more than words can utter,
Beyond what can be valu'd, Rich or Rare,
Nor Liberty, nor Sight, Health, Fame, or Beauty
Are half so dear, my Life for you were vile,*                     80
As much as Child can love the best of Fathers.

LEAR: Of all these Bounds, ev'n from this Line to this
With shady Forests and wide-skirted Meads,
We make Thee Lady, to thine and *Albany*'s Issue
Be this perpetual – What says Our Second Daughter?

REGAN: My Sister, Sir, in part exprest my Love,
For such as Hers, is mine, though more extended;
Sense has no other Joy that I can relish,
I have my All in my dear Lieges Love!

LEAR: Therefore to thee and thine Hereditary                      90
Remain this ample Third of our fair Kingdom.[4]

---

[4] 67–91. Based on *King Lear*, I.i.36–79: 'Give me the map ... our fair kingdom.'

CORDELIA: Now comes my Trial, how am I distrest,  (*Aside*)
  That must with cold speech tempt the chol'rick King
  Rather to leave me Dowerless, than condemn me
  To loath'd Embraces!
LEAR: Speak now Our last, not least in Our dear Love,
  So ends my Task of State, – *Cordelia* speak,
  What canst Thou say to win a richer Third
  Than what thy Sisters gain'd?[5]
CORDELIA: Now must my Love in words fall short of
    theirs                                                        100
  As much as it exceeds in Truth – Nothing my Lord.
LEAR: Nothing can come of Nothing, speak agen.
CORDELIA: Unhappy am I that I can't dissemble,
  Sir, as I ought, I love your Majesty,
  No more nor less.
LEAR:     Take heed *Cordelia*,
  Thy Fortunes are at stake, think better on't
  And mend thy Speech a little.
CORDELIA:     O my Liege,
  You gave me Being, Bred me, dearly Love me,
  And I return my Duty as I ought,
  Obey you, Love you, and most Honour you!                        110
  Why have my Sisters Husbands, if they love you All?
  Happ'ly when I shall Wed, the Lord whose Hand
  Shall take my Plight,* will carry half my Love,
  For I shall never marry, like my Sisters,
  To Love my Father All.
LEAR: And goes thy Heart with this?[6]
  'Tis said that I am Chol'rick, judge me Gods,
  Is there not cause? now Minion I perceive
  The Truth of what has been suggested to Us,
  Thy Fondness for the Rebel Son of *Gloster*,                    120
  False to his Father, as Thou art to my Hopes:
  And oh take heed, rash Girl, lest We comply
  With thy fond* wishes, which thou wilt too late
  Repent, for know Our nature cannot brook

---

[5] 96–9. Based on *King Lear*, I.i.81–5: 'Now, our joy ... than your sisters.'
[6] 102–16. Based on *King Lear*, I.i.89–104: 'Nothing will come ... heart with this?'

A Child so young and so Ungentle.

CORDELIA: So young my Lord and True.

LEAR: Thy Truth then be thy Dow'r,
   For by the sacred Sun and solemn Night
   I here disclaim all my paternal Care,
   And from this minute hold thee as a Stranger     130
   Both to my Blood and Favour.[7]

KENT:    This is Frenzy.
   Consider, good my Liege –

LEAR:    Peace *Kent*.
   Come not between a Dragon and his Rage.
   I lov'd her most, and in her tender Trust
   Design'd to have bestow'd my Age at Ease!
   So be my Grave my Peace as here I give
   My Heart from her, and with it all my Wealth:
   My Lords of *Cornwall* and of *Albany*,
   I do invest you jointly with full Right
   In this fair Third, *Cordelia*'s forfeit Dow'r.    140
   Mark me, My Lords, observe Our last Resolve,
   Our Self attended with an hundred Knights
   Will make Aboad with you in monthly Course,
   The Name alone of King remain with me,
   Yours be the Execution and Revenues,
   This is Our final Will, and to confirm it
   This Coronet part between you.

KENT:    Royal *Lear*,
   Whom I have ever honour'd as my King,
   Lov'd as my Father, as my Master follow'd,
   And as my Patron thought on in my Pray'rs—    150

LEAR: Away, the Bow is bent, make from the Shaft.

KENT: No, let it fall and drench* within my Heart,
   Be *Kent* unmannerly when *Lear* is mad:
   Thy youngest Daughter –

LEAR:    On thy Life no more.

KENT: What wilt thou doe, old Man?

LEAR:    Out of my sight!

KENT: See better first.

[7] 126–31. Based on *King Lear*, I.i.106–15: 'So young ... this for ever?'

LEAR:     Now by the gods –

KENT:  Now by the gods, rash King, thou swear'st in vain.

LEAR: Ha Traytour –

KENT:     Do, kill thy Physician, *Lear*,
  Strike through my Throat, yet with my latest Breath
  I'll Thunder in thine Ear my just Complaint,                  160
  And tell Thee to thy Face that Thou dost ill.

LEAR: Hear me rash Man, on thy Allegiance hear me;
  Since thou hast striv'n to make Us break our Vow
  And prest between our Sentence and our Pow'r,
  Which nor our Nature nor our Place can bear,
  We banish thee for ever from our Sight
  And Kingdom, if when Three days are expir'd
  Thy hated Trunk be found in our Dominions
  That moment is thy Death; Away.[8]

KENT:  Why fare thee well, King, since thou art resolv'd,   170
  I take thee at thy word, and will not stay
  To see thy Fall: the gods protect the Maid
  That truly thinks, and has most justly said.
  Thus to new Climates my old Truth I bear,
  Friendship lives Hence, and Banishment is Here.[9] [*Exit*]

LEAR: Now *Burgundy*, you see her Price is faln,
  Yet if the fondness of your Passion still
  Affects her as she stands, Dow'rless, and lost
  In our Esteem, she's yours, take her or leave her.

BURGUNDY: Pardon me, Royal *Lear*, I but demand          180
  The Dow'r your Self propos'd, and here I take
  *Cordelia* by the Hand Dutchess of *Burgundy*.

LEAR: Then leave her Sir, for by a Father's rage
  I tell you all her Wealth. Away.

BURGUNDY: Then Sir be pleas'd to charge the breach
  Of our Alliance on your own Will
  Not my Inconstancy.

                    [*Exeunt. Manent* EDGAR *and* CORDELIA]

EDGAR: Has Heaven then weigh'd the merit of my Love,
  Or is't the raving of my sickly Thought?

---

[8]  132–69. Based on *King Lear* I.i.119–77: 'Good my Liege . . . is my death.'
[9]  170–5. Based on *King Lear*, I.i.179–82: 'Fare thee well . . . most rightly said.'

Cou'd *Burgundy* forgoe so rich a Prize                      190
And leave her to despairing *Edgar*'s Arms?
Have I thy Hand *Cordelia*, do I clasp it,
The Hand that was this minute to have join'd
My hated Rivals? do I kneel before thee
And offer at thy feet my panting Heart?
Smile, Princess, and convince me, for as yet
I doubt, and dare not trust the dazling joy.

CORDELIA: Some Comfort yet that 'twas no vicious Blot
That has depriv'd me of a Father's Grace,
But meerly want of that that makes me rich            200
In wanting it, a smooth professing Tongue:
O Sisters, I am loth to call your fault
As it deserves; but use our Father well,
And wrong'd *Cordelia* never shall repine.

EDGAR: O heav'nly Maid that are thy self thy Dow'r,
Richer in Vertue than the Stars in Light,
If *Edgar*'s humble fortunes may be grac't
With thy Acceptance, at thy feet he lays 'em.
Ha my *Cordelia*! dost thou turn away?
What have I done t'offend Thee?

CORDELIA:   Talk't of Love.                               210

EDGAR: Then I've offended oft, *Cordelia* too
Has oft permitted me so to offend.

CORDELIA: When, *Edgar*, I permitted your Addresses,
I was the darling Daughter of a King,
Nor can I now forget my royal Birth,
And live dependent on my Lover's Fortune.
I cannot to so low a fate submit,
And therefore study to forget your Passion,
And trouble me upon this Theam no more.

EDGAR: Thus Majesty takes most State in Distress!         220
How are we tost on Fortune's fickle flood!
The Wave that with surprising kindness brought
The dear Wreck to my Arms, has snatcht it back,
And left me mourning on the barren Shore.

CORDELIA: This Baseness of th' ignoble *Burgundy* (Aside)
Draws just suspicion on the Race of Men,

His Love was In'trest,* so may *Edgar's* be
And He but with more Complement dissemble;
If so, I shall oblige him by Denying:
But if his Love be fixt, such Constant flame                    230
As warms our Breasts, if such I find his Passion,
My Heart as grateful to his Truth shall be,
And cold *Cordelia* prove as Kind as He.          [*Exit*]
                  *Enter* BASTARD *hastily*

BASTARD: Brother, I've found you in a lucky minute,
    Fly and be safe, some Villain has incens'd
    Our Father against your Life.

EDGAR: Distrest *Cordelia*! but oh! more Cruel!

BASTARD: Hear me Sir, your Life, your Life's in Danger.

EDGAR: A Resolve so sudden
    And of such black Importance!

BASTARD: 'Twas not sudden,                                      240
    Some Villain has of long time laid the Train.

EDGAR: And yet perhaps 'twas but pretended Coldness,
    To try how far my passion would pursue.

BASTARD: He hears me not; wake, wake Sir.

EDGAR: Say ye Brother? –
    No Tears good *Edmund*, if thou bringst me tidings
    To strike me dead, for Charity delay not,
    That present will befit so kind a Hand.

BASTARD: Your danger Sir comes on so fast
    That I want time t'inform you, but retire                   250
    Whilst I take care to turn the pressing Stream.
    O gods! for Heav'ns sake Sir.

EDGAR: Pardon me Sir, a serious Thought
    Had seiz'd me, but I think you talkt of danger
    And wisht me to Retire; must all our Vows
    End thus! – Friend I obey you – O *Cordelia*!     [*Exit*]

BASTARD: Ha! ha! fond Man, such credulous Honesty
    Lessens the Glory of my Artifice,
    His Nature is so far from doing wrongs
    That he suspects none: if this Letter speed[10]            260
    And pass for *Edgar's*, as himself wou'd own

---

[10] 259–60. Based on *King Lear*, I.ii.177–8: 'Whose nature is . . . suspects none.'

The Counterfeit but for the foul Contents,
Then my designs are perfect – here comes *Gloster*.

*Enter* GLOSTER

GLOSTER: Stay *Edmund*, turn, what paper were you read-
    ing?

BASTARD: A Trifle Sir.

GLOSTER: What needed then that terrible dispatch of it
    Into your Pocket, come produce it Sir.

BASTARD: A Letter from my Brother Sir, I had
    Just broke the Seal but knew not the Contents,
    Yet fearing they might prove to blame          270
    Endeavour'd to conceal it from your sight.

GLOSTER: 'Tis *Edgar*'s Character.* (*Reads*)
    *This Policy of Fathers is intollerable that keeps our*
    *Fortunes from us till Age will not suffer us to enjoy 'em; I*
    *am weary of the Tyranny: Come to me that of this I may*
    *speak more: if our Father would sleep till I wak'd him,*
    *you shou'd enjoy half his Possessions, and live beloved of*
    *your Brother*

Edgar

    Slept till I wake him, you shou'd enjoy
    Half his possessions – *Edgar* to write this[11]
    'Gainst his indulgent Father! Death and Hell!    280
    Fly, *Edmund*, seek him out, wind me into him*
    That I may bite the Traytor's heart, and fold
    His bleeding Entrals on my vengefull Arm.

BASTARD: Perhaps 'twas writ, my Lord, to prove my
    Vertue.

GLOSTER: These late Eclipses of the Sun and Moon
    Can bode no less; Love cools, and friendship fails,
    In Cities mutiny, in Countrys discord,
    The bond of Nature crack't 'twixt Son and Father:
    Find out the Villain, do it carefully
    And it shall lose thee nothing.         [*Exit*]

BASTARD: So, now my project's firm, but to make sure    291
    I'll throw in one proof more and that a bold one;
    I'll place old *Gloster* where he shall o're-hear us

---

[11] 264–79. Based on *King Lear*, I.ii.30–54: 'What paper . . . half his revenue.'

Confer of this design, whilst to his thinking,
Deluded *Edgar* shall accuse himself.
Be Honesty my Int'rest* and I can
Be honest too, and what Saint so Divine
That will successfull Villany decline!                    [*Exit*]

## Scene ii*

### Enter KENT *disguis'd*

KENT: Now banisht *Kent*, if thou canst pay thy duty
In this disguise where thou dost stand condemn'd,
Thy Master *Lear* shall find thee full of Labours.

### Enter LEAR *attended*

LEAR: In there, and tell our Daughter we are here
Now; What are Thou?

KENT:    A Man, Sir.

LEAR: What dost thou profess, or wou'dst with us?

KENT: I do profess to be no less then I seem, to serve him
truly that puts me in Trust, to love him that's Honest, to
converse with him that's wise and speaks little, to fight
when I can't choose; and to eat no Fish.*                      10

LEAR: I say, what are Thou?

KENT: A very honest-hearted fellow, and as poor as the
King.

LEAR: Then art thou poor indeed – What can'st thou do?

KENT: I can keep honest Counsel, marr a curious Tale in
the telling, deliver a plain Message bluntly, that which
ordinary Men are fit for I am qualify'd in, and the best of
me is Diligence.

LEAR: Follow me, thou shalt serve me.

### Enter one of GONERILL's *Gentlemen*

Now Sir?

GENTLEMAN: Sir—[*Exit*; KENT [*and* SERVANT] *run after him*]

LEAR: What says the fellow? Call the Clatpole* back.

ATTENDANT: My Lord, I know not, but methinks your
Highness is entertain'd with slender Ceremony.                  20

### Enter SERVANT

SERVANT: He says, my Lord, your Daughter is not well.

LEAR: Why came not the Slave back when I call'd him?

SERVANT: My Lord, he answer'd me i'th' surliest manner,
That he wou'd not.

*Re-enter Gentleman brought in by* KENT

LEAR: I hope our Daughter did not so instruct him:
Now, who am I Sir?

GENTLEMAN:     My Ladies Father.

LEAR: My Lord's Knave –                        (*Strikes him*)
        (GONERILL *at the Entrance*)
I'll not be struck my Lord.

KENT: Nor tript neither, thou vile Civet-box.*[12]

                                        (*Strikes up his heels*)

GONERILL: By Day and Night this is insufferable,          30
I will not bear it.

LEAR: Now, Daughter, why that frontlet on?
Speak, do's that Frown become our Presence?[13]

GONERILL: Sir, this licentious Insolence of your Servants
Is most unseemly, hourly they break out
In quarrels bred by their unbounded Riots,
I had fair hope by making this known to you
T'have had a quick Redress, but find too late
That you protect and countenance their out-rage;
And therefore, Sir, I take this freedom, which           40
Necessity makes Discreet.

LEAR:     Are you our Daughter?

GONERILL: Come, Sir, let me entreat you to make use
Of your discretion, and put off betimes
This Disposition that of late transforms you
From what you rightly are.

LEAR: Do's any here know me? why this is not *Lear*.
Do's *Lear* walk thus? speak thus? where are his Eyes?
Who is it that can tell me who I am?

GONERILL: Come, Sir, this Admiration's* much o'th'
savour

[12] 1–29. Based on *King Lear*: I.iv.4–83 with cuts: 'Now, banisht Kent ... base football player.'
[13] 32–3: I.iv.186–7: 'How now, daughter ... i' th' frown!'

Of other your new humours, I beseech you                    50
To understand my purposes aright;
As you are old, you shou'd be staid and wise,
Here do you keep an hundred Knights and Squires,
Men so debaucht and bold that this our Palace
Shews like a riotous Inn, a Tavern, Brothel;
Be then advised by her that else will take
That she beggs, to lessen your Attendance,
Take half away, and see that the remainder
Be such as may befit your Age, and know
Themselves and you.

LEAR:      Darkness and Devils!                              60
Saddle my Horses, call my Train together;
Degenerate Viper, I'll not stay with Thee;
I yet have left a Daughter – Serpent, Monster,
Lessen my Train, and call 'em riotous?
All men approv'd of choice and rarest Parts,
That each particular of duty know –
How small, *Cordelia*, was thy Fault? O *Lear*,
Beat at this Gate that let thy Folly in,
And thy dear Judgment out; Go, go, my People.
                  (*Going off meets* ALBANY *entring*)
Ingratefull Duke, was this your will?

ALBANY:      What Sir?                                       70

LEAR: Death! fifty of my Followers at a clap!

ALBANY: The matter Madam?

GONERILL: Never afflict your self to know the Cause,
But give his Dotage way.

LEAR:      Blasts upon thee,
Th' untented* woundings of a Father's Curse
Pierce ev'ry Sense about Thee; old fond Eyes
Lament this Cause again, I'll pluck ye out
And cast ye with the Waters that ye lose
To temper Clay – No, *Gorgon*, thou shalt find
That I'll resume the Shape which thou dost think        80
I have cast off for ever.

GONERILL:      Mark ye that.

LEAR: Hear Nature!

Dear Goddess hear, and if thou dost intend
To make that Creature fruitfull, change thy purpose;
Pronounce upon her Womb the barren Curse,
That from her blasted Body never spring
A Babe to honour her – but if she must bring forth,
Defeat her Joy with some distorted Birth,
Or monstrous Form, the Prodigy o'th' Time,
And so perverse of spirit, that it may Live            90
Her Torment as 'twas Born, to fret* her Cheeks
With constant Tears, and wrinkle her young Brow.
Turn all her Mother's Pains to Shame and Scorn,
That she may curse her Crime too late, and feel
How sharper than a Serpent's Tooth it is
To have a Thankless Child! Away, away.[14]

> [*Exit cum suis*]

GONERILL: Presuming thus upon his numerous Train
He thinks to play the Tyrant here, and hold
Our Lives at will.

ALBANY:    Well, you may bear too far.          [*Exeunt*]

---

[14] 34–96. Based on *King Lear*, I.iv.198–287, with cuts. 'Not only, Sir . . . away, away.'

# ACT II

## Scene i

*Scene,* GLOSTER's *House*

*Enter* BASTARD

BASTARD: The Duke comes here to night, I'll take advant-
    age
  Of his Arrival to compleat my project,
  Brother a Word, come forth, 'tis I your Friend,
              *Enter* EDGAR
  My Father watches for you, fly this place,
  Intelligence is giv'n where you are hid,
  Take the advantage of the Night, bethink ye
  Have you not spoke against the Duke of *Cornwall*
  Something might shew you a favourer of
  Duke *Albany*'s Party?
EDGAR:     Nothing, why ask you?
BASTARD: Because he's coming here to Night in haste      10
  And *Regan* with him – heark! the Guards, Away.
EDGAR: Let 'em come on, I'll stay and clear my self.
BASTARD: Your Innocence at leisure may be heard,
  But *Gloster*'s storming Rage as yet is deaf,
  And you may perish e're allow'd the hearing. [*Exit* EDGAR]
  *Gloster* comes yonder: now to my feign'd scuffle –
  Yield, come before my Father! Lights here, Lights!
  Some Blood drawn on me wou'd beget opinion
                      (*Stabs his Arm*)
  Of our more fierce Encounter – I have seen
  Drunkards do more than this in sport.           20
        *Enter* GLOSTER *and Servants*
GLOSTER: Now, *Edmund*, where's the Traytour?
BASTARD:     That Name, Sir,

Strikes Horrour through me, but my Brother, Sir,
Stood here i'th' Dark.
GLOSTER: Thou bleed'st, pursue the Villain
And bring him piece-meal to me.
BASTARD:       Sir, he's fled.
GLOSTER: Let him fly far, this Kingdom shall not hide him:
The noble Duke, my Patron, comes to Night,
By his Authority I will proclaim
Rewards for him that brings him to the Stake,
And Death for the Concealer.                          30
Then of my Lands, loyal and natural Boy,
I'll work the means to make thee capable.[15]      *[Exeunt]*


## Scene ii

*Enter* KENT *(disguis'd still) and* GONERILL's *Gentleman,*
*severally*

GENTLEMAN: Good morrow Friend, belong'st thou to this
    House?
KENT: Ask them will answer thee.
GENTLEMAN: Where may we set our Horses?
KENT: I'th' Mire.
GENTLEMAN: I am in haste, prethee an' thou lov'st me, tell
    me.
KENT: I love thee not.
GENTLEMAN: Why then I care not for Thee.
KENT: An' I had thee in *Lipsbury* Pinfold,* I'd make thee
    care for me.
GENTLEMAN: What dost thou mean? I know thee not.    10
KENT: But, Minion, I know Thee.
GENTLEMAN: What dost thou know me for?
KENT: For a base, proud, beggarly, white-liver'd, Glass-
    gazing,* superserviceable* finical* Rogue; one that wou'd
    be a Pimp in way of good Service, and art nothing but a
    composition of Knave, Beggar, Coward, Pandar –

[15] 4–32. Based on *King Lear*, II.i.20–84 with cuts. 'My father watches ... make thee
capable.'

GENTLEMAN: What a monstrous Fellow art thou to rail at
    one that is neither known of thee nor knows thee?

KENT: Impudent Slave, not know me, who but two days
    since tript up thy heels before the King: draw, Miscreant,      20
    or I'll make the Moon shine through thee.

GENTLEMAN: What means the Fellow? – Why prethee,
    prethee; I tell thee I have nothing to do with thee.

KENT: I know your Rogueship's Office, you come with
    Letters against the King, taking my young Lady *Vanity*'s
    part against her royal Father; draw Rascal.

GENTLEMAN: Murther, murther, help Ho!

KENT: Dost thou scream Peacock, strike Puppet, stand
    dappar* Slave.

GENTLEMAN: Help Hea'! Murther, help.

[*Exit.* KENT *after him*]

*Flourish. Enter Duke of* CORNWAL, REGAN, *attended,*
                    GLOSTER, BASTARD

GLOSTER: All Welcome to your Graces, you do me honour.     31

DUKE: *Gloster* w'ave heard with sorrow that your Life
    Has been attempted by your impious Son,
    But *Edmund* here has paid you strictest Duty.

GLOSTER: He did betray his Practice, and receiv'd
    The Hurt you see, striving to apprehend him.

DUKE: Is He pursu'd?

GLOSTER:     He is, my Lord.

REGAN: Use our Authority to apprehend
    The Traytour and do Justice on his Head;
    For you, *Edmund*, that have so signaliz'd
    Your Vertue, you from henceforth shall be ours;            40
    Natures of such firm Trust we much shall need.
    A charming Youth and worth my further Thought. (*Aside*)

DUKE: Lay comforts, noble *Gloster*, to your Breast,
    As we to ours, This Night be spent in Revels,
    We choose you, *Gloster*, for our Host to Night,
    A troublesome expression of our Love.
    On, to the Sports before us – who are These?

*Enter the Gentleman pursu'd by* KENT

GLOSTER: Now, what's the matter?

DUKE: Keep peace upon your Lives, he dies that strikes.    50
  Whence and what are ye?
ATTENDANT: Sir, they are Messengers, the one from your
    Sister,
  The other from the King.
DUKE: Your Difference? speak.
GENTLEMAN:    I'm scarce in breath, my Lord.
KENT: No marvel, you have so bestirr'd your Valour.
  Nature disclaims the Dastard, a Taylor made him.
DUKE: Speak yet, how grew your Quarrel?
GENTLEMAN: Sir this old Ruffian here, whose Life I spar'd
  In pity to his Beard –
KENT:    Thou Essence Bottle!
  In pity to my Beard? – Your leave, my Lord,    60
  And I will tread the Muss-cat* into Mortar.
DUKE: Know'st thou our Presence?
KENT: Yes, Sir, but Anger has a Privilege.
DUKE: Why art thou angry?
KENT: That such a Slave as this shou'd wear a Sword
  And have no Courage, Office and no Honesty.
  Not Frost and Fire hold more Antipathy
  Than I and such a Knave.
GLOSTER: Why dost thou call him Knave?
KENT: His Countenance likes me not.    70
DUKE: No more perhaps does Mine, nor His or Hers.
KENT: Plain-dealing is my Trade, and to be plain, Sir,
  I have seen better Faces in my time
  Than stands on any Shoulders now before me.
REGAN: This is some Fellow that having once been prais'd,
  For Bluntness, since affects a sawcy Rudeness,
  But I have known one of these surly Knaves
  That in his Plainness harbour'd more Design
  Than twenty cringing complementing Minions.
DUKE: What's the offence you gave him?    80
GENTLEMAN: Never any, Sir.
  It pleas'd the King his Master lately
  To strike me on a slender misconstruction,
  Whilst watching his Advantage this old Lurcher*

Tript me behind, for which the King extold* him;
And, flusht with th' honour of this bold exploit,
Drew on me here agen.

DUKE: Bring forth the Stocks, we'll teach you.

KENT: Sir I'm too old to learn;
Call not the Stocks for me, I serve the King,                       90
On whose Employment I was sent to you,
You'll shew too small Respect, and too bold Malice
Against the Person of my royal Master,
Stocking his Messenger.

DUKE: Bring forth the Stocks, as I have Life and Honour,
There shall he sit till Noon.

REGAN: Till Noon, my Lord? till Night, and all Night too.

KENT: Why, Madam, if I were your Father's Dog
You wou'd not use me so.

REGAN: Sir, being his Knave I will.                                 100

GLOSTER: Let me beseech your Graces to forbear him,
His fault is much, and the good King his Master
Will check him for't, but needs must take it ill
To be thus slighted in his Messenger.

DUKE: Wee'l answer that;
Our Sister may receive it worse to have
Her Gentleman assaulted: to our business lead.    [Exit]

GLOSTER: I am sorry for thee, Friend, 'tis the Duke's
pleasure
Whose Disposition will not be controll'd,
But I'll entreat for thee.

KENT:      Pray do not, Sir –                                       110
I have watcht and travell'd hard,
Some time I shall sleep out, the rest I'll whistle:
Fare-well t'ye, Sir.                           [Exit GLOSTER]
All weary and o're-watcht,
I feel the drowsy Guest steal on me; take
Advantage heavy Eyes of this kind Slumber,
Not to behold this vile and shameful Lodging.[16] (Sleeps)
                        Enter EDGAR

[16] 1–117. Based on King Lear, II.ii.1–169, with cuts.

EDGAR: I heard my self proclaim'd,
   And by the friendly Hollow of a Tree
   Escapt the Hunt, no Port is free, no place          120
   Where Guards and most unusual Vigilance
   Do not attend to take me – how easie now
   'Twere to defeat the malice of my Trale,
   And leave my Griefs on my Sword's reeking point;
   But Love detains me from Death's peaceful Cell,
   Still whispering me *Cordelia*'s in distress;
   Unkinde as she is I cannot see her wretched,
   But must be neer to wait upon her Fortune.
   Who knows but the white minute* yet may come
   When *Edgar* may do service to *Cordelia*,          130
   That charming Hope still ties me to the Oar
   Of painfull Life, and makes me too, submit
   To th' humblest shifts to keep that Life a foot;
   My Face I will besmear and knit my Locks,
   The Country gives me proof and president
   Of Bedlam Beggars, who with roaring Voices
   Strike in their numm'd and mortify'd bare Arms
   Pins, Iron-spikes, Thorns, sprigs of Rosemary,
   And thus from Sheep-coats Villages and Mills,
   Sometimes with Prayers, sometimes with Lunatick Banns 140
   Enforce their Charity, poor *Tyrligod*, poor *Tom*
   That's something yet, *Edgar* I am no more.[17]     [*Exit*]
      KENT *in the Stocks still; Enter* LEAR *attended*
LEAR: 'Tis strange that they shou'd so depart from home
   And not send back our Messenger.
KENT: Hail, noble Master.
LEAR: How? mak'st thou this Shame thy Pastime?
   What's he that has so much mistook thy Place
   To set thee here?
KENT: It is both He and She, Sir, your Son and Daughter.
LEAR: No.
KENT:   Yes.
LEAR:     No I say.

[17] 118–142. Based on *King Lear*, II.iii.1–21, with additions.

KENT:          I say yea.                                              150
LEAR: By *Jupiter* I swear no.
KENT: By *Juno* I swear, I swear I.
LEAR:      They durst not do't
　They cou'd not, wou'd not do't, 'tis worse then Murder
　To doe upon Respect such violent out-rage.
　Resolve me with all modest haste which way
　Thou mayst deserve, or they impose this usage?
KENT: My Lord, when at their Home
　I did commend your Highness Letters to them,
　E'er I was Ris'n, arriv'd another Post
　Steer'd* in his haste, breathless and panting forth          160
　From *Gonerill* his Mistress Salutations,
　Whose Message being deliver'd, they took Horse,
　Commanding me to follow and attend
　The leisure of their Answer; which I did,
　But meeting that other Messenger
　Whose welcome I perceiv'd had poison'd mine,
　Being the very Fellow that of late
　Had shew'n such rudeness to Your Highness, I
　Having more Man than Wit about me, Drew,
　On which he rais'd the House with Coward cries:            170
　This was the Trespass which your Son and Daughter
　Thought worth the shame you see it suffer here.
LEAR: Oh! how this Spleen swells upward to my Heart
　And heaves for passage – down thou climing Rage
　Thy Element's below; where is this Daughter?
KENT: Within, Sir, at a Masque.
                    *Enter* GLOSTER
LEAR: Now Gloster?—ha!
　Deny to speak with me? th'are sick, th'are weary,
　They have travell'd hard to Night – meer fetches;*
　Bring me a better Answer.
GLOSTER:      My dear Lord,                                       180
　You know the fiery Quality of the Duke –
LEAR: Vengeance! Death, Plague, Confusion,
　Fiery? what Quality – why *Gloster*, *Gloster*,
　I'd speak with the Duke of *Cornwal* and his Wife.

GLOSTER: I have inform'd 'em so.

LEAR: Inform'd 'em! dost thou understand me, Man,
I tell thee *Gloster* –

GLOSTER:    I, my good Lord.

LEAR: The King wou'd speak with *Cornwal*, the dear Father
Wou'd with his Daughter speak, commands her Service.
Are they inform'd of this? my Breath and Blood!          190
Fiery! the fiery Duke! tell the hot Duke –
No, but not yet, may be he is not well:
Infirmity do's still neglect all Office;
I beg his Pardon, and I'll chide my Rashness
That took the indispos'd and sickly Fit
For the sound Man – but wherefore sits he there?
Death on my State, this Act convinces me
That this Retiredness of the Duke and her
Is plain Contempt; give me my Servant forth,
Go tell the Duke and's Wife I'd speak with 'em.          200
Now, instantly, bid 'em come forth and hear me,
Or at their Chamber door I'll beat the Drum
Till it cry sleep to Death –

*Enter* CORNWALL *and* REGAN
Oh! are ye come?

DUKE: Health to the King.

REGAN: I am glad to see your Highness.

LEAR: *Regan*, I think you are, I know what cause
I have to think so; shoud'st thou not be glad
I wou'd divorce me from thy Mother's Tomb.
Beloved *Regan*, thou wilt shake to hear
What I shall utter: Thou coud'st ne'er ha' thought it,     210
Thy Sister's naught, O *Regan*, she has ty'd
(KENT *here set at liberty*)
Ingratitude like a keen Vulture here,
I scarce can speak to thee.

REGAN: I pray you, Sir, take patience; I have hope
That you know less to value her Desert,
Then she to slack her Duty.

LEAR:    Ha! how's that?

REGAN: I cannot think my Sister in the least
  Would fail in her respects, but if perchance
  She has restrain'd the Riots of your Followers
  'Tis on such Grounds, and to such wholsome Ends    220
  As clears her from all Blame.
LEAR:    My Curses on her.
REGAN: O Sir, you are old
  And shou'd content you to be rul'd and led
  By some discretion that discerns your State
  Better than you yourself, therefore, Sir,
  Return to our Sister, and say you have wrong'd her.
LEAR: Ha! ask her Forgiveness?
  No, no, 'twas my mistake thou didst not mean so,
  Dear Daughter, I confess that I am old;
  Age is unnecessary, but thou art good,    230
  And wilt dispense* with my Infirmity.
REGAN: Good Sir, no more of these unsightly passions,
  Return back to our Sister.
LEAR:    Never, *Regan*,
  She has abated me of half of my Train,
  Lookt black upon me, stabb'd me with her Tongue;
  All the stor'd Vengeances of Heav'n fall
  On her Ingratefull Head; strike her young Bones
  Ye taking Ayrs with Lameness.
REGAN: O the blest Gods! Thus will you wish on me
  When the rash mood –    240
LEAR: No, *Regan*, Thou shalt never have my Curse,
  Thy tender Nature cannot give thee o're
  To such Impiety; Thou better know'st
  The Offices of Nature, bond of Child-hood,
  And dues of Gratitude: Thou bear'st in mind
  The half o'th' Kingdom which our love conferr'd
  On thee and thine.
REGAN:    Good Sir, toth' purpose.
LEAR: Who put my Man i'th' Stocks?
DUKE: What Trumpet's that?
REGAN: I know't, my Sister's, this confirms her Letters.    250
  Sir, is your Lady come?

*Enter* GONERILL's *Gentleman*

LEAR:    More Torture still?
This is a Slave whose easie borrow'd pride
Dwells in the fickle Grace of her he follows;
A Fashion-fop that spends the day in Dressing,
And all to bear his Ladie's flatt'ring Message,
That can deliver with a Grace her Lie,
And with as bold a face bring back a greater.
Out Varlet from my sight.

DUKE:    What means your Grace?

LEAR: Who stockt my Servant? *Regan*, I have hope
Thou didst not know it.

*Enter* GONERILL

                            Who comes here! oh Heavens!  260
If you do love Old men, if your sweet sway
Allow Obedience; if your selves are Old,
Make it your Cause, send down and take my part;
Why, *Gorgon*, dost thou come to haunt me here?
Art not asham'd to look upon this Beard?
Darkness upon my Eyes they play me false,
O *Regan*, wilt thou take her by the Hand?

GONERILL: Why not by th' Hand, Sir, how have I
    offended?
All's not Offence that indiscretion finds,
And Dotage terms so.

LEAR:    Heart thou art too tough.                      270

REGAN: I pray you, Sir, being old confess you are so,
If till the expiration of your Month
You will return and sojourn with our Sister,
Dismissing half your Train, come then to me,
I am now from Home, and out of that Provision
That shall be needfull for your Entertainment.

LEAR: Return with her and fifty Knights dismist?
No, rather I'll forswear all Roofs, and chuse
To be Companion to the Midnight Wolf,
My naked Head expos'd to th' merciless Air             280
Then have my smallest wants suppli'd by her.

GONERILL: At your choice, Sir.

LEAR: Now I prithee Daughter do not make me mad;
  I will not trouble thee, my Child, farewell,
  Wee'l meet no more, no more see one another;
  Let shame come when it will, I do not call it,
  I do not bid the Thunder-bearer* strike,
  Nor tell Tales of thee to avenging Heav'n;
  Mend when thou canst, be better at thy leisure,
  I can be patient, I can stay with *Regan*,                    290
  I, and my hundred Knights.
REGAN:    Your Pardon, Sir.
  I lookt not for you yet, nor am provided
  For your fit welcome.
LEAR:    Is this well spoken now?
REGAN: My Sister treats you fair; what! fifty Followers;
  Is it not well? what shou'd you need of more?
GONERILL: Why might not you, my Lord, receive Attend-
      ance
  From those whom she calls Servants, or from mine?
REGAN: Why not, my Lord? if then they chance to slack
      you
  We cou'd controll 'em – if you come to me,
  For now I see the Danger, I entreat you                       300
  To bring but Five and Twenty; to no more
  Will I give place.
LEAR: Hold now my Temper, stand this bolt unmov'd
  And I am Thunder-proof;
  The wicked when compar'd with the more wicked
  Seem beautifull, and not to be the worst,
  Stands in some rank of Praise; now, *Gonerill*,
  Thou art innocent agen, I'll go with thee;
  Thy Fifty yet, do's double Five and Twenty,
  And thou art twice her Love.
GONERILL:    Hear me, my Lord,                                  310
  What need you Five and Twenty, Ten, or Five,
  To follow in a House where twice so many
  Have a Command t'attend you?
REGAN:    What need one?
LEAR: Blood, Fire! hear – Leaprosies and bluest Plagues!

Room, room for Hell to belch her Horrors up
And drench the *Circes* in a stream of Fire;
Heark how th' Infernals* eccho to my Rage
Their Whips and Snakes –
REGAN:     How lewd a thing is Passion!
GONERILL: So old and stomachfull.*

(Lightning and Thunder)

LEAR: Heav'ns drop your Patience down;                    320
You see me here, ye Gods, a poor old Man
As full of Griefs as Age, wretched in both –
I'll bear no more: no, you unnatural Haggs,
I will have such Revenges on you both,
That all the world shall – I will do such things
What they are yet I know not, but they shall be
The Terrors of the Earth; you think I'll weep,

(Thunder again)

This Heart shall break into a thousand pieces
Before I'll weep – O Gods! I shall go mad.          [*Exit*]
DUKE: 'Tis a wild Night, come out o'th' Storm.[18]

[Exeunt]

---

[18]  143–330 (end) Based on *King Lear*, II.iv.1–367 (whole scene).

## ACT III

## Scene i

*Scene, A Desert Heath*

*Enter* LEAR *and* KENT *in the Storm*

LEAR: Blow Winds and burst your Cheeks, rage louder yet,
Fantastick Lightning singe, singe my white Head;
Spout Cataracts, and Hurricanos fall
Till you have drown'd the Towns and Palaces
Of proud ingratefull Man.[19]

KENT: Not all my best intreaties can perswade him
Into some needfull shelter, or to 'bide
This poor slight Cov'ring on his aged Head
Expos'd to this wild war of Earth and Heav'n.

LEAR: Rumble thy fill, fight Whirlwind, Rain and Fire:          10
Not Fire, Wind, Rain or Thunder are my Daughters:
I tax not you ye Elements with unkindness;
I never gave you Kingdoms, call'd you Children,
You owe me no Obedience, then let fall
Your horrible pleasure, here I stand your Slave,
A poor, infirm, weak and despis'd old man;
Yet I will call you servile Ministers,
That have with two pernicious Daughters join'd
Their high-engendred* Battle against a Head
So Old and White as mine, Oh! oh! 'tis Foul.[20]          20

KENT: Hard by, Sir, is a Hovel that will lend
Some shelter from this Tempest.

LEAR: I will forget my Nature, what? so kind a Father,
I, there's the point.

KENT: Consider, good my Liege, Things that love Night

---

[19] 1-5. Based on *King Lear*, III.ii.1-9: 'Blow, winds ... ingrateful man.'
[20] 10-20. Based on *King Lear*, III.ii.16-24: 'Rumble thy bellyful ... 'tis foul.'

Love not such Nights as this; these wrathful Skies
Frighten the very wanderers o'th' Dark,
And make 'em keep their Caves; such drenching Rain,
Such Sheets of Fire, such Claps of horrid Thunder,
Such Groans of roaring Winds have ne're been known.    30
LEAR: Let the Great Gods,
That keep this dreadfull pudder* o're our Heads
Find out their Enemies now, tremble thou Wretch
That hast within thee undiscover'd Crimes.
Hide, thou bloody Hand,
Thou perjur'd Villain, holy, holy Hypocrite,
That drinkst the Widows Tears, sigh now and cry
These dreadful Summoners Grace, I am a Man
More sin'd against than sinning.
KENT: Good Sir, to th' Hovell.
LEAR:    My wit begins to burn,*                           40
Come on my Boy, how dost my Boy? art Cold?
I'm cold my self; shew me this Straw, my Fellow,
The Art of our Necessity is strange,
And can make vile things precious; my poor Knave,
Cold as I am at Heart, I've one place There    (*Loud Storm*)
That's sorry yet for Thee.[21]                  [*Exeunt*]


## Scene ii

### GLOSTER's *Palace*

#### *Enter* BASTARD

BASTARD: The Storm is in our louder Rev'lings drown'd.
Thus wou'd I Reign cou'd I but mount a Throne.
The Riots of these proud imperial Sisters
Already have impos'd the galling Yoke
Of Taxes, and hard Impositions on
The drudging Peasants Neck, who bellow out
Their loud Complaints in Vain – Triumphant Queens!
With what Assurance do they tread the Crowd.

[21] 25–46. Based on *King Lear*, III.ii.42–73: 'Alas! Sir ... sorry yet for thee.'

O for a Tast of such Majestick Beauty,
Which none but my hot Veins are fit t' engage;                    10
Nor are my Wishes desp'rate, for ev'n now
During the Banquet I observed their Glances
Shot thick at me, and as they left the Room
Each cast by stealth a kind inviting Smile,
The happy Earnest* – ha!

*Two Servants from several Entrances deliver him each a
Letter, and Exeunt*

*Where merit is so Transparent, not to behold it* (Reads)
*Were Blindness, and not to reward it Ingratitude.*
    Gonerill.
Enough! Blind, and Ingratefull should I be
Not to Obey the Summons of This Oracle.                          19
Now for a Second Letter.              (*Opens the other*)
*If Modesty be not your Enemy, doubt not to*     (Reads)
*Find me your Friend.*
    Regan.
Excellent *Sybill*! O my glowing Blood!
I am already sick of expectation,
And pant for the Possession – here *Gloster* comes
With Bus'ness on his Brow; be husht my Joys.

*Enter* GLOSTER

GLOSTER: I come to seek thee, *Edmund*, to impart
    A business of Importance; I knew thy loyal Heart
    Is toucht to see the Cruelty of these
    Ingratefull Daughters against our royal Master.            30
BASTARD: Most Savage and Unnatural.[22]
GLOSTER: This change in the State sits uneasie. The
    Commons
    Repine aloud at their female Tyrants,
    Already they Cry out for the re-installment
    Of their good old King, whose Injuries
    I fear will inflame 'em into Mutiny.
BASTARD: 'Tis to be hopt, not fear'd.
GLOSTER: Thou hast it Boy, 'tis to be hopt indeed,

---

[22] 31: III.iii.6: 'Most savage and unnatural.'

On me they cast their Eyes, and hourly Court me
To lead 'em on, and whilst this Head is Mine                40
I am Theirs, a little covert Craft, my Boy,
And then for open Action, 'twill be Employment
Worthy such honest daring Souls as Thine.
Thou, *Edmund*, art my trusty Emissary,
Haste on the Spur at the first break of day
                              (*Gives him Letters*)
With these Dispatches to the Duke of *Combray*;
You know what mortal Feuds have alwaies flam'd
Between this Duke of *Cornwall*'s Family, and his;
Full Twenty thousand Mountaners
Th' invetrate* Prince will send to our Assistance.          50
Dispatch; Commend us to his Grace, and Prosper.
BASTARD: Yes, credulous old Man,            (*Aside*)
I will commend you to his Grace,
His Grace the Duke of *Cornwall* – instantly
To shew him these Contents in thy own Character,
And Seal'd with thy own Signet; then forthwith
The Chol'rick Duke gives Sentence on thy Life;
And to my hand thy vast Revenues fall
To glut my Pleasure that till now has starv'd.
GLOSTER *going off is met by* CORDELIA *entring* [*with*
        ARANTE], BASTARD *observing at a Distance*
CORDELIA: Turn, *Gloster*, Turn, by all the sacred Pow'rs  60
I do conjure you give my Griefs a Hearing,
You must, you shall, nay I am sure you will,
For you were always stil'd the Just and Good.
GLOSTER: What wou'dst thou, Princess? rise and speak thy
        Griefs.
CORDELIA: Nay, you shall promise to redress 'em too,
Or here I'll kneel for ever; I intreat
Thy succour for a Father and a King,
An injur'd Father and an injur'd King.
BASTARD: O charming Sorrow! how her Tears adorn her
Like Dew on Flow'rs, but she is Virtuous,                  70
And I must quench this hopeless Fire i'th' Kindling.
GLOSTER: Consider, Princess,

For whom thou begg'st, 'tis for the King that wrong'd
    Thee.

CORDELIA: O name not that; he did not, cou'd not wrong
    me.

Nay muse not, *Gloster*, for it is too likely
This injur'd King e're this is past your Aid,
And gone Distracted with his savage Wrongs.

BASTARD: I'll gaze no more – and yet my Eyes are
    Charm'd.

CORDELIA: Or what if it be Worse? can there be Worse?

As 'tis too probable this furious Night                    80
Has pierc'd his tender Body, the bleak Winds
And cold Rain chill'd, or Lightning struck him Dead,
If it be so your Promise is discharg'd,
And I have only one poor Boon to beg,
That you'd Convey me to his breathless Trunk,
With my torn Robes to wrap his hoary Head,
With my torn Hair to bind his Hands and Feet,
Then with a show'r of Tears
To wash his Clay-smear'd Cheeks, and Die beside him.

GLOSTER: Rise, fair *Cordelia*, thou has Piety                    90
Enough t' attone for both thy Sisters Crimes.
I have already plotted to restore
My injur'd Master, and thy Vertue tells me
We shall succeed and suddenly.                    [*Exit*]

CORDELIA: Dispatch, *Arante*,
Provide me a Disguise, we'll instantly
Go seek the King, and bring him some Relief.

ARANTE: How, Madam? are you Ignorant
Of what your impious Sisters have decreed?
Immediate Death for any that relieve him.                    100

CORDELIA: I cannot dread the Furies in this case.

ARANTE: In such a Night as This? Consider, Madam,
For many Miles about there's a scarce a Bush
To shelter in.

CORDELIA: Therefore no shelter for the King,
And more our Charity to find him out:
What have not Women dar'd for vicious Love,

And we'll be shining Proofs that they can dare
For Piety as much; blow Winds, and Lightnings fall,
Bold in my Virgin Innocence, I'll flie                    110
My Royal Father to Relieve, or Die. [*Exit (with* ARANTE)]
BASTARD: Provide me a Disguise, we'll instantly
    Go seek the King:—ha! ha! a lucky change,
    That Vertue which I fear'd would be my hindrance
    Has prov'd the Bond to my Design;
    I'll bribe two Ruffians that shall at a distance follow,
    And seise 'em in some desert Place, and there
    Whilst one retains her t'other shall return
    T' inform me where she's Lodg'd; I'll be disguis'd too.
    Whilst they are poching* for me I'll to the Duke          120
    With these Dispatches, then to th' Field
    Where like the vig'rous *Jove* I will enjoy
    This *Semele** in a Storm, 'twill deaf her Cries
    Like Drums in Battle, lest her Groans shou'd pierce
    My pittying Ear, and make the amorous Fight less fierce.
                                                    [*Exit*]


# Scene iii

## *Storm Still. The Field Scene*

### Enter LEAR *and* KENT

KENT: Here is the place, my Lord; good my Lord enter;
    The Tyranny of this open Night's too rough
    For Nature to endure.
LEAR:    Let me alone.
KENT: Good my Lord, enter.
LEAR:       Wilt break my Heart?
KENT: Beseech you, Sir.
LEAR: Thou think'st 'tis much that this contentious Storm
    Invades us to the Skin; so 'tis to thee
    But where the greater Malady is fixt
    The lesser is scarce felt: the Tempest in my Mind
    Do's from my Senses take all feeling else          10

Save what beats there. Filial Ingratitude!
Is it not as this Mouth shou'd tear this Hand
For lifting Food to't – but I'll punish home.
No, I will weep no more; in such a Night
To shut me out – pour on, I will endure
In such a Night as this: O *Regan*, *Gonerill*,
Your old kind Father whose frank heart gave All,
O that way madness lies, let me shun that,
No more of that.

KENT: See, my Lord, here's the Entrance.                          20

LEAR: Well, I'll go in
And pass it all, I'll pray and then I'll sleep:
Poor naked Wretches wheresoe're you are,
That 'bide the pelting of this pittiless Storm,
How shall your houseless Heads and unfed Sides
Sustain this Shock? your raggedness defend you
From Seasons such as These. O I have ta'ne
Too little Care of this, take Physick, Pomp,
Expose thy self to feel what Wretches feel,
That thou may'st cast the superflux* to them,                    30
And shew the Heav'ns more Just.

EDGAR: (*in the Hovell*) Five Fathom and a half, poor *Tom*.

KENT: What art thou that dost grumble there i'th' Straw?
Come forth.

                 *Enter* EDGAR *disguis'd as a madman*

EDGAR: Away! The foul Fiend follows me – through the
sharp Haw-thorn blows the cold Wind – Mum, Go to thy
Bed and warm Thee. –
Ha! what do I see?
By all my Griefs the poor old King bareheaded, (*Aside*)
And drencht in this fow Storm, professing *Syren*,           40
Are all your Protestations come to this?

LEAR: Tell me, Fellow, didst thou give all to thy Daughters?

EDGAR: Who gives any thing to poor *Tom*, whom the foul
Fiend has led through Fire and through Flame, through
Bushes and Boggs, that has laid Knives under his Pillow,
and Halters in his Pue,* that has made him proud of
Heart to ride on a Bay-trotting Horse over four inch'd

Bridges, to course* his own Shadow for a Traytor. – bless
thy five Wits, *Tom*'s a cold (*Shivers*) Bless thee from
Whirlwinds, Star-blasting and Taking:* do poor *Tom*
some Charity, whom the foul Fiend vexes – Sa, sa, there
I could have him now, and there, and there    50
agen.

LEAR: Have his Daughters brought him to this pass?
Coud'st thou save Nothing? didst thou give 'em All?

KENT: He has no Daughters, Sir.

LEAR: Death, Traytor, nothing cou'd have subdu'd Nature
To such a Lowness but his unkind Daughters.

EDGAR: Pillicock sat upon Pillicock Hill; Hallo, hallo,
hallo.

LEAR: Is it the fashion that discarded Fathers
Should have such little Mercy on their Flesh?
Judicious punishment, 'twas this Flesh begot    60
Those Pelican* Daughters.

EDGAR: Take heed of the fow* Fiend, obey thy Parents,
keep thy Word justly, Swear not, commit not with Man's
sworn Spouse, set not thy sweet Heart on proud Array:
*Tom*'s a Cold.

LEAR: What hast thou been?

EDGAR: A Serving-man proud of Heart, that curl'd my
Hair, us'd Perfume and Washes,* that serv'd the Lust of
my Mistresses Heart, and did the Act of Darkness with
her. Swore as many Oaths as I spoke Words, and broke
'em all in the sweet Face of Heaven: Let not the Paint, nor
the Patch, nor the rushing of Silks betray thy poor Heart
to Woman, keep thy Foot out of Brothels, thy Hand out
of Plackets, thy Pen from Creditors Books, and defie the
foul Fiend – still through the Hawthorn blows the cold
Wind – Sess, Suum, Mun, Nonny, Dolphin my Boy – hist!
the Boy, Sesey! soft let him Trot by.

LEAR: Death, thou wert better in thy Grave, than thus to
answer with thy uncover'd Body this Extremity of the
Sky. And yet consider him well, and Man's no more than
This; Thou art indebted to the Worm for no Silk, to the

Beast for no Hide, to the Cat for no Perfume – ha! here's
Two of us are Sophisticated; Thou art the Thing     80
it self, unaccommodated Man is no more than such a
poor bare forkt Animal as thou art. Off, Off, ye vain
Disguises, empty Lendings, I'll be my Original Self, quick,
quick, Uncase me.

KENT: Defend his Wits, good Heaven!

LEAR: One point I had forgot; what's your Name?

EDGAR: Poor *Tom* that eats the swimming Frog, the Wall-
nut, and the Water-nut;* that in the fury of his Heart
when the foul Fiend rages eats Cow-dung for Sallets,
swallows the old Rat and the Ditch-dog, that drinks the
green Mantle of the standing Pool, that's whipt from     90
Tithing* to Tithing; that has Three Suits to his Back, Six
Shirts to his Body,

 Horse to Ride, and Weapon to wear,
 But Rats and Mice, and such small Deer
 Have been *Tom*'s Food for Seven long Year.

Beware, my Follower; Peace, Smulkin; Peace, thou foul
Fiend.

LEAR: One word more, but be sure true Councel; tell me, is
a Madman a Gentleman, or a Yeoman?

KENT: I fear'd 't wou'd come to This, his Wits are gone.

EDGAR: *Fraterreto* calls me, and tells me, *Nero* is an Angler     100
in the Lake of Darkness. Pray, Innocent, and beware the
foul Fiend.

LEAR: Right, ha! ha! was it not pleasant to have a
Thousand with red hot Spits come hizzing in upon 'em?

EDGAR: My Tears begin to take his part so much
They marr my Counterfeiting.

LEAR: The little Dogs and all, Trey, Blanch and Sweet-
heart, see they Bark at me.

EDGAR: *Tom* will throw his Head at 'em; Avaunt ye Curs.
 Be thy Mouth or black or white,
 Tooth that poysons if it bite,     110
 Mastiff, Grey-hound, Mungrill, Grim,
 Hound or Spanniel, Brach* or Hym,*
 Bob-tail, Tight, or Trundle-tail,

  *Tom* will make 'em weep and wail,
  For with throwing thus my Head
  Dogs leap the Hatch, and All are fled.
Ud, de de, de. Se, se, se. Come march to Wakes, and Fairs,
and Market-Towns, – poor *Tom*, thy Horn is dry.

LEAR: You Sir, I entertain you for One of my Hundred,
 only I do not like the fashion of your Garments, you'll say
 they're *Persian*, but no matter, let 'em be chang'd.  120

     *Enter* GLOSTER

EDGAR: This is the foul *Flibertigibet*, he begins at Curfew
 and walks at first Cock, he gives the Web and the Pin,*
 knits the Elflock,* squints the Eye, and makes the Hair-
 lip, mildews the white Wheat, and hurts the poor
 Creature of the Earth;
  *Swithin* footed Thrice the Cold,
 He met the Night-mare and her Nine-fold,
  'Twas there he did appoint her;
 He bid her alight and her Troth plight,
  And arroynt* the Witch arroynt her.  130

GLOSTER: What, has your Grace no better Company?

EDGAR: The Prince of Darkness is a Gentleman; *Modo* he is
 call'd, and *Mahu*.

GLOSTER: Go with me, Sir, hard by I have a Tenant.
 My Duty cannot suffer me to obey
 In all your Daughters hard Commands,
 Who have enjoyn'd me to make fast my Doors,
 And let this Tyrannous Night take hold upon you.
 Yet have I ventur'd to come seek you out,
 And bring you where both Fire and Food is ready.  140

KENT: Good my Lord, take his offer.

LEAR: First let me talk with this Philosopher,
 Say, *Stagirite*,* what is the Cause of Thunder.

GLOSTER: Beseech you, Sir, go with me.

LEAR: I'll talk a Word with this same Learned *Theban*.
 What is your Study?

EDGAR: How to prevent the Fiend, and to kill Vermin.

LEAR: Let me ask you a Word in private.

KENT: His Wits are quite unsetled; Good Sir, let's force him
hence.                                                                         150
GLOSTER: Canst blame him? his Daughters seek his Death;
This Bedlam
But disturbs him the more. Fellow, be gone.
EDGAR: Child *Rowland* to the dark Tow'r came,[23]
His Word was still Fie, Fo, and Fum,
I smell the Bloud of a British Man.* – Oh Torture!    [*Exit*]
GLOSTER: Now, I prethee Friend, let's take him in our
Arms,
And carry him where he shall meet both Welcome,
And Protection. Good Sir, along with us.[24]
LEAR: You say right, let 'em Anatomize *Regan*, see what
breeds about her Heart; is there any Cause in Nature for
these hard Hearts?[25]                                                        160
KENT: Beseech your Grace.
LEAR: Hist! – Make no Noise, make no Noise – so so;
we'll to Supper i' th' Morning.[26]                              [*Exeunt*]


# Scene iv

### *Enter* CORDELIA *and* ARANTE


ARANTE: Dear Madam, rest ye here, our search is Vain,
Look here's a shed, beseech ye, enter here.
CORDELIA: Prethee go in thy self, seek thy own Ease,
Where the Mind's free, the Body's Delicate:
This Tempest but diverts me from the Thought
Of what wou'd hurt me more.
### *Enter Two Ruffians*
I. RUFFIAN: We have dog'd 'em far enough, this Place is
private,
I'll keep 'em Prisoners here within this Hovell,

---

[23] 1–154. Based on *King Lear*, III.iv.1–181 (whole scene).
[24] 156–8: III.vi.85–90: 'Good friend, I prithee ... welcome and protection.'
[25] 159–60: III.vi.74–5: 'Then let them ... about her heart.'
[26] 163–4: III.vi.81–2: 'Make no noise ... supper i' th' morning.'

Whilst you return and bring Lord *Edmund* Hither;
But help me first to House 'em.                                    10
2. RUFFIAN: Nothing but this dear Devil   (*Shows Gold*)
    Shou'd have drawn me through all this Tempest;
    But to our Work.
        (*They seize* CORDELIA *and* ARANTE, *who Shriek out*)
    Soft, Madam, we are Friends, dispatch, I say.
CORDELIA: Help, Murder, help! Gods! some kind
    Thunderbolt
To strike me Dead.
                        *Enter* EDGAR
EDGAR: What Cry was That? – ha, Women seiz'd by
    Ruffians?
Is this a Place and Time for Villany?
Avaunt ye Bloud-hounds.
                        (*Drives 'em with his Quarter-staff*)*
BOTH: The Devil, the Devil!                     (*Run off*)
EDGAR: O speak, what are ye that appear to be          21
    O' th' tender Sex, and yet unguarded Wander
    Through the dead Mazes of this dreadfull Night,
    Where (tho' at full) the Clouded Moon scarce darts
    Imperfect Glimmerings.
CORDELIA: First say what art thou
    Our Guardian Angel, that wer't pleas'd t' assume
    That horrid shape to fright the Ravishers?
    We'll kneel to Thee.
EDGAR: O my tumultuous Bloud!
    By all my trembling Veins *Cordelia*'s Voice!          30
    'Tis she her self! – My Senses sure conform
    To my wild Garb, and I am Mad indeed.
CORDELIA: Whate're thou art, befriend a wretched Virgin,
    And if thou canst direct our weary search.
EDGAR: Who relieves poor *Tom*, that sleeps on the Nettle,
    with the Hedge-pig* for his Pillow.
    Whilst Smug ply'd the Bellows
    She truckt* with her Fellows,
        The Freckle fac't Mab
        Was a Blouze* and a Drab,*                         40

Yet *Swithin* made *Oberon* jealous – Oh! Torture.

ARANTE: Alack, Madam, a poor wandring Lunatick.

CORDELIA: And yet his Language seem'd but now well
    temper'd.

  Speak, Friend, to one more wretched than thy self,

  And if thou hast one Interval of sense,

  Inform us if thou canst where we may find

  A poor old Man, who through this Heath has stray'd

  The tedious Night – Speak, sawest thou such a One?

EDGAR: The King, her Father, whom she's come to seek
                                        (*Aside*)

  Through all the Terrors of this Night. O Gods!        50

  That such amazing Piety, such Tenderness

  Shou'd yet to me be Cruel—

  Yes, Fair One, such a One was lately here,

  And is convey'd by some that came to seek him,

  T' a Neighb'ring Cottage; but distinctly where,

  I know not.

CORDELIA: Blessings on 'em,

  Let's find him out, *Arante*, for thou seest

  We are in Heavens Protection.        (*Going off*)

EDGAR: O *Cordelia*!

CORDELIA:    Ha! – Thou knowst my Name.

EDGAR: As you did once know *Edgar*'s.

CORDELIA:    *Edgar*!                        60

EDGAR: The poor Remains of *Edgar*, what your Scorn
  Has left him.

CORDELIA:    Do we wake, *Arante*?

EDGAR: My Father seeks my Life, which I preserv'd

  In hopes of some blest Minute to oblidge

  Distrest *Cordelia*, and the Gods have giv'n it;

  That Thought alone prevail'd with me to take

  This Frantick Dress, to make the Earth my Bed,

  With these bare Limbs all change of Seasons bide,

  Noons scorching Heat, and Midnights piercing Cold,

  To feed on Offals, and to drink with Herds,*       70

  To Combat with the Winds, and be the Sport

  Of Clowns,* or what's more wretched yet, their Pity.

ARANTE: Was ever Tale so full of Misery!
EDGAR: But such a Fall as this I grant was due
  To my aspiring Love, for 'twas presumptuous,
  Though not presumptuously persu'd;
  For well you know I wore my Flames conceal'd,
  And silent as the Lamps that Burn in Tombs,
  'Till you perceiv'd my Grief, with modest Grace
  Drew forth the Secret, and then seal'd my Pardon.          80
CORDELIA: You had your Pardon, nor can you Challenge
      more.
EDGAR: What do I Challenge more?
  Such Vanity agrees not with these Rags;
  When in my prosp'rous State rich *Gloster*'s Heir,
  You silenc'd my Pretences,* and enjoyn'd me
  To trouble you upon that Theam no more;
  Then what Reception must Love's Language find
  From these bare Limbs and Beggers humble Weeds?
CORDELIA: Such as the Voice of Pardon to a Wretch
      Condemn'd; such as the Shouts of succ'ring Forces      90
  To a Town besieg'd.
EDGAR: Ah! what new Method now of Cruelty?
CORDELIA: Come to my Arms, thou dearest, best of Men,
  And take the kindest Vows that e're were spoke
  By a protesting* Maid.
EDGAR:   Is't possible?
CORDELIA: By the dear Vital Stream that baths my Heart,
  These hallow'd Rags of Thine, and naked Vertue,
  These abject Tassels, these fantastick Shreds,
  (Ridiculous ev'n to the meanest Clown)
  To me are dearer than the richest Pomp                     100
  Of purple Monarchs.
EDGAR:   Generous charming Maid,
  The Gods alone that made, can rate thy Worth!
  This most amazing Excellence shall be
  Fame's Triumph, in succeeding Ages, when
  Thy bright Example shall adorn the Scene,*
  And teach the World Perfection.
CORDELIA:   Cold and weary,

We'll rest a while, *Arante*, on that Straw,
Then forward to find out the poor old King.
EDGAR: Look I have Flint and Steel, the Implements
Of wandring Lunaticks, I'll strike a Light,                              110
And make a Fire beneath this Shed, to dry
Thy Storm-drencht Garments, e're thou Lie to rest thee;
Then Fierce and Wakefull as th' *Hesperian* Dragon,*
I'll watch beside thee to protect thy Sleep;
Mean while, the Stars shall dart their kindest Beams,
And Angels Visit my *Cordelia*'s Dreams.          [*Exeunt*]


## Scene v

*Scene, The Palace*
Enter CORNWALL, REGAN, BASTARD, *Servants.* CORNWALL
*with* GLOSTER's *Letters*


DUKE: I will have my Revenge e're I depart his house.
   *Regan*, see here, a Plot upon our State,
   'Tis *Gloster*'s Character, that has betray'd
   His double Trust of Subject, and of Ost.*
REGAN: Then double be our Vengeance, this confirms
   Th' Intelligence that we now receiv'd,
   That he has been this Night to seek the King;
   But who, Sir, was the kind Discoverer?
DUKE: Our Eagle, quick to spy, and fierce to seize,
   Our trusty *Edmund*.
REGAN:     'Twas a noble Service;                              10
   O *Cornwall*, take him to thy deepest Trust,
   And wear him as a Jewel at thy Heart.
BASTARD: Think, Sir, how hard a Fortune I sustain,
   That makes me thus repent of serving you!     (*Weeps*)
   O that this Treason had not been, or I
   Not the Discoverer.
DUKE: *Edmund*, Thou shalt find
   A Father in our Love, and from this Minute
   We call thee Earl of *Gloster*; but there yet

Remains another Justice to be done,                    20
And that's to punish this discarded Traytor;
But least thy tender Nature shou'd relent
At his just Sufferings, nor brooke the Sight,
We wish thee to withdraw.

REGAN: The *Grotto*, Sir, within the lower Grove,
                     (*To* EDMUND *aside*)
  Has Privacy to suit a Mourner's Thought.

BASTARD: And there I may expect a Comforter,
  Ha, Madam?

REGAN: What may happen, Sir, I know not,
  But 'twas a Friends Advice.       [*Exit* BASTARD]

DUKE:   Bring in the Traytour.
             GLOSTER *brought in*
  Bind fast his Arms.

GLOSTER:   What mean your Graces?                    30
  You are my Guests, pray do me no foul Play.

DUKE: Bind him, I say, hard, harder yet.

REGAN: Now, Traytor, thou shalt find—

DUKE: Speak, Rebel, where hast thou sent the King?
  Whom spight of our Decree thou saw'st last Night.

GLOSTER: I'm tide to th' Stake, and I must stand the
  Course.

REGAN: Say where, and why thou hast conceal'd him.

GLOSTER: Because I wou'd not see thy cruel Hands
  Tear out his poor old Eyes, nor thy fierce Sister
  Carve his anointed Flesh; but I shall see                    40
  The swift wing'd Vengeance overtake such Children.

DUKE: See't shalt thou never, Slaves perform your Work,
  Out with those treacherous Eyes, dispatch, I say,
  If thou seest Vengeance—

GLOSTER: He that will think to live 'till he be old,
  Give me some help – O cruel! oh! ye Gods.
                   (*They put out his Eyes*)

SERVANT: Hold, hold, my Lord, I bar your Cruelty,
  I cannot love your safety and give way
  To such a barbarous Practise.

DUKE:   Ha, my Villain.

SERVANT: I have been your Servant from my Infancy,               50
    But better Service have I never done you
    Then with this Boldness—

DUKE:    Take thy Death, Slave.

SERVANT: Nay, then Revenge whilst yet my Bloud is
    Warm.                                          (*Fight*)

REGAN: Help here – are you not hurt, my Lord?

GLOSTER: *Edmund*, enkindle all the sparks of Nature
    To quit this horrid Act.

REGAN: Out, treacherous Villain,
    Thou call'st on him that Hates thee, it was He
    That broacht thy Treason, shew'd us thy Dispatches;
    There – read, and save the *Cambrian*\* Prince a Labour,   60
    If thy Eyes fail thee call for Spectacles.

GLOSTER: O my Folly!
    Then *Edgar* was abus'd, kind Gods forgive me that.

REGAN: How is't, my Lord?

DUKE: Turn out that Eye-less Villain, let him smell
    His way to *Cambray*,\* throw this Slave upon a Dunghill.
    *Regan*, I Bleed apace, give me your Arm.          [*Exeunt*]

GLOSTER: All Dark and Comfortless![27]
    Where are those various Objects that but now
    Employ'd my busie Eyes? where those Eyes?          70
    Dead are their piercing Rays that lately shot
    O're flowry Vales to distant Sunny Hills,
    And drew with Joy the vast Horizon in.
    These groping Hands are now my only Guids,\*
    And Feeling all my Sight.
    O Misery! what words can sound\* my Grief?
    Shut from the Living whilst among the Living;
    Dark as the Grave amidst the bustling World.
    At once from Business and from Pleasure bar'd;
    No more to view the Beauty of the Spring,          80
    Nor see the Face of Kindred, or of Friend.
    Yet still one way th' extreamest Fate affords,

[27] 29–68. Based on *King Lear*, III.vii.27–83 with cuts. 'Who's there? ... dark and comfortless.'

And ev'n the Blind can find the Way to Death.
Must I then tamely Die, and unreveng'd?
So *Lear* may fall: No, with these bleeding Rings
I will present me to the pittying Crowd,
And with the Rhetorick of these dropping Veins
Enflame 'em to Revenge their King and me;
Then when the Glorious Mischief is on Wing,
This Lumber* from some Precipice I'll throw,                    90
And dash it on the ragged Flint below;
Whence my freed Soul to her bright Sphear shall fly,
Through boundless Orbs, eternal Regions spy,
And like the Sun, be All one glorious Eye.          [*Exit*]

# ACT IV

## Scene i

### A Grotto.

EDMUND *and* REGAN *amorously Seated, Listning to Musick*

BASTARD: Why were those Beauties made Another's Right
  Which None can prize like Me? charming Queen
  Take all my blooming Youth, for ever fold me
  In those soft Arms, Lull me in endless Sleep
  That I may dream of pleasures too transporting
  For Life to bear.
REGAN:   Live, live, my *Gloster*,
  And feel no Death but that of swooning joy,
  I yield thee Blisses on no harder Terms
  Than that thou continue to be Happy.
BASTARD: This Jealousie is yet more kind, is't possible     10
  That I should wander from a Paradise
  To feed on sickly Weeds? such Sweets live here
  That Constancy will no Vertue in me,
  And yet must I forthwith go meet her Sister,    (*Aside*)
  To whom I must protest as much—
  Suppose it be the same; why best of all,
  And I have then my Lesson ready conn'd.
REGAN: Wear this Remembrance of me – I dare now
                    (*Gives him a Ring*)
  Absent my self no longer from the Duke
  Whose Wound grows Dangerous – I hope Mortal.    20
BASTARD: And let this happy Image of your *Gloster*,
          (*Pulling out a Picture drops a Note*)
  Lodge in that Breast where all his Treasure lies.   (*Exit*]
REGAN: To this brave Youth a Womans blooming beauties

Are due: my Fool usurps my Bed – What's here?[28]
Confusion on my Eyes.                                    (*Reads*)
*Where Merit is so Transparent, not to behold it were*
*Blindness, and not to reward it, Ingratitude.*
    Gonerill.
Vexatious Accident! yet Fortunate too,
My Jealousie's confirm'd, and I am taught
To cast* for my Defence—
                    *Enter an Officer*
Now, what mean those Shouts? and what thy hasty
    Entrance?                                                        31
OFFICER: A most surprizing and a sudden Change,
The peasants are all up in Mutiny,
And only want a Chief to lead 'em on
To Storm your Palace.
REGAN:    On what Provocation?
OFFICER: At last day's* publick Festival, to which
The Yeomen from all Quarters had repair'd,
Old *Gloster*, whom you late depriv'd of Sight,
(His Veins yet Streaming fresh) presents himself,
Proclaims your Cruelty, and their Oppression                40
With the King's Injuries; which so enrag'd em,
That now that Mutiny which long had crept
Takes Wing, and threatens your Best Pow'rs.
REGAN: White-liver'd Slave!
Our Forces rais'd and led by Valiant *Edmund*,
Shall drive this Monster of Rebellion back
To her dark Cell; young *Gloster*'s Arm allays
The Storm, his Father's feeble Breath did Raise.    [*Exeunt*]


# Scene ii

### *The Field Scene*

#### *Enter* EDGAR

EDGAR: The lowest and most abject Thing of Fortune

---

[28] 23–4: IV.ii. 27–8: 'To thee ... usurps my bed.'

Stands still in Hope, and is secure from Fear,
The lamentable Change is from the Best,
The Worst returns to Better – who comes here?

*Enter* GLOSTER, *led by an old Man*

My Father poorly led? depriv'd of Sight,[29]
The precious Stones torn from their bleeding Rings!
Some-thing I heard of this inhumane Deed
But disbeliev'd it, as an Act too horrid
For the hot Hell of a curst Woman's fury,
When will the measure of my woes be full?                    10

GLOSTER: Revenge, thou art afoot, Success attend Thee.
Well have I sold my Eyes, if the Event*
Prove happy for the injur'd King.

OLD MAN: O, my good Lord, I have been your Tenant, and
your Father's Tenant these Fourscore years.

GLOSTER: Away, get thee Away, good Friend, be gone,
Thy Comforts can do me no good at All,
Thee they may hurt.

OLD MAN:      You cannot see your Way.

GLOSTER: I have no Way, and therefore want no Eyes,
I stumbled when I saw: O dear Son *Edgar*,                   20
The Food of thy abused Father's Wrath,
Might I but live to see thee in my Touch
I'd say, I had Eyes agen.[30]

EDGAR: Alas, he's sensible that I was wrong'd,
And shou'd I own my Self, his tender Heart
Would break betwixt th' extreams of Grief and Joy.

OLD MAN: How, now, who's There?

EDGAR: A Charity for poor *Tom*. Play fair, and defie the
foul Fiend.
O Gods! and must I still persue this Trade,        (*Aside*)
Trifling beneath such Loads of Misery?                       30

OLD MAN: 'Tis poor mad *Tom*.

GLOSTER: In the late Storm I such a Fellow saw,
Which made me think a Man a Worm,
Where is the Lunatick?

---

[29] 1–5. Based on *King Lear*, IV.i.3–10: 'The lowest ... poorly led.'
[30] 14–23: IV.i.12–24: 'O my Lord ... eyes again.'

OLD MAN:    Here, my Lord.

GLOSTER: Get thee now away, if for my sake
Thou wilt o're-take us hence a Mile or Two
I' th' way tow'rd *Dover*, do't for ancient* Love,
And bring some cov'ring for this naked Wretch
Whom I'll intreat to lead me.

OLD MAN: Alack, my Lord, He's Mad.                    40

GLOSTER: 'Tis the Time's Plague when Mad-men lead the
Blind.
Do as I bid thee.

OLD MAN: I'll bring him the best 'Parrel that I have
Come on't what will.                          [*Exit*]

GLOSTER:    Sirrah, naked Fellow.

EDGAR: Poor *Tom*'s a cold;—I cannot fool it longer,
And yet I must – bless thy sweet Eyes they Bleed,
Believe't poor *Tom* ev'n weeps his Blind to see 'em.

GLOSTER: Know'st thou the way to *Dover*?

EDGAR: Both Stile and Gate, Horse-way and Foot-path,
poor *Tom* has been scar'd out of his good Wits; bless
every true Man's Son from the foul Fiend.            50

GLOSTER: Here, take this Purse, that I am wretched
Makes thee the Happier, Heav'n deal so still.
Thus let the griping Userers Hoard be Scatter'd,
So Distribution shall undo Excess,
And each Man have enough. Dost thou know *Dover*?

EDGAR: I, Master.

GLOSTER: There is a Cliff, whose high and bending Head
Looks dreadfully down on the roaring Deep.
Bring me but to the very Brink of it,                 60
And I'll repair the Poverty thou bearst
With something Rich about me, from that Place
I shall no leading need.

EDGAR: Give me thy Arm: poor *Tom* shall guid thee.[31]

GLOSTER: Soft, for I hear the Tread of Passengers.*

*Enter* KENT *and* CORDELIA

CORDELIA: Ah me! your Fear's too true, it was the King;

[31] 31–64. Based on *King Lear*; IV.i.26–77: "Tis poor mad Tom . . . no leading need.'

I spoke but now with some that met him
As Mad as the vext Sea, Singing aloud,
Crown'd with rank Femiter* and furrow Weeds,
With Berries, Burdocks, Violets, Dazies, Poppies,                    70
And all the idle Flow'rs that grow
In our sustaining Corn, conduct me to him[32]
To prove my last Endeavours to restore him,
And Heav'n so prosper thee.
KENT :     I will, good Lady.
    Ha, *Gloster* here!—turn, poor dark Man, and hear
    A Friend's Condolement, who at Sight of thine
    Forgets his own Distress, thy old true *Kent*.
GLOSTER: How, *Kent*? from whence return'd?
KENT: I have not since my Banishment been absent,
    But in Disguise follow'd the abandon'd King;                    80
    'Twas me thou saw'st with him in the late Storm.
GLOSTER: Let me embrace thee, had I Eyes I now
    Should weep for Joy, but let this trickling Blood
    Suffice instead of Tears.
CORDELIA:     O misery!
    To whom shall I complain, or in what Language?
    Forgive, O wretched Man, the Piety
    That brought thee to this pass, 'twas I that caus'd it,
    I cast me at thy Feet, and beg of thee
    To crush these weeping Eyes to equal Darkness,
    If that will give thee any Recompence.                         90
EDGAR: Was ever Season so distrest as This?        (*Aside*)
GLOSTER: I think *Cordelia*'s Voice! rise, pious Princess,
    And take a dark Man's Blessing.
CORDELIA:     O, my *Edgar*,
    My Vertue's now grown Guilty, works the Bane
    Of those that do befriend me, Heav'n forsakes me,
    And when you look that Way, it is but Just
    That you shou'd hate me too.
EDGAR: O wave* this cutting Speech, and spare to wound
    A Heart that's on the Rack.
GLOSTER: No longer cloud thee, *Kent*, in that Disguise,   100

[32] 68-72. *King Lear*, IV.iv.2-6: 'as mad ... sustaining corn.'

There's business for thee and of noblest weight;
Our injur'd Country is at length in Arms,
Urg'd by the King's inhumane Wrongs and Mine,
And only want a Chief to lead 'em on.
That Task be Thine.

EDGAR: Brave *Britains* then there's Life in't yet.   [*Aside*]

KENT : Then have we one cast* for our Fortune yet.
Come, Princess, I'll bestow you with the King,
Then on the Spur to Head these Forces.
Farewell, good *Gloster*, to our Conduct trust.                110

GLOSTER: And be your Cause as Prosp'rous as tis Just.

[*Exeunt*]


## Scene iii

### GONERILL's *Palace*

#### Enter GONERILL, *Attendants*


GONERILL: It was great Ignorance *Gloster*'s Eyes being out
To let him live, where he arrives he moves
All Hearts against us, *Edmund* I think is gone
In pity to his Misery to dispatch him.[33]

GENTLEMAN: No, Madam, he's return'd on speedy
Summons
Back to your Sister.

GONERILL:      Ha! I like not That,
Such speed must have the Wings of Love; where's
*Albany*?

GENTLEMAN: Madam, within, but never Man so chang'd;
I told him of the uproar of the Peasants,
He smil'd at it, when I inform'd him                              10
Of *Gloster*'s Treason –

GONERILL:      Trouble him no further,[34]
It is his coward Spirit, back to our Sister,

---

[33] 1–4: IV.v.8–13: 'It was great ... his nighted life.'
[34] 7–12. Based on *King Lear*, IV.ii.2–12: 'Now, where's your master ... terror of his spirit.'

Hasten her Musters, and let her know I have giv'n
The Distaff into my Husband's Hands. That done,
With special Care deliver these Dispatches
In private to young *Gloster*.

*Enter a Messenger*

MESSENGER: O Madam, most unseasonable News,
The Duke of *Cornwall*'s Dead of his late Wound,
Whose loss your Sister has in part supply'd,
Making brave *Edmund* General of her Forces.                    20

GONERILL: One way I like this well;
But being Widow and my *Gloster* with her
May blast the promis'd Harvest of our Love.[35]
A word more, Sir, – add Speed to your Journey,
And if you chance to meet with that blind Traytor,
Preferment falls on him that cuts him off.        [*Exeunt*]


# Scene iv

### *Field Scene*

#### [*Enter*] GLOSTER *and* EDGAR

GLOSTER: When shall we come to th' Top of that same
     Hill?

EDGAR: We climb it now, mark how we Labour.

GLOSTER: Methinks the Ground is even.

EDGAR: Horrible Steep; heark, do you hear the Sea?

GLOSTER: No truly.

EDGAR: Why then your other Senses grow imperfect,
By your Eyes Anguish.

GLOSTER:     So may it be indeed.
Methinks thy Voice is alter'd, and thou speak'st
In better Phrase and Matter than thou did'st.

EDGAR: You are much deceiv'd, in nothing am I Alter'd     10
But in my Garments.

GLOSTER:     Methinks y'are better Spoken.

EDGAR: Come on, Sir, here's the Place, how fearfull

---

[35] 21–23. Based on *King Lear*, IV.ii.83–6: 'One way ... hateful life.'

And dizy 'tis to cast one's Eyes so Low.
The Crows and Choughs* that wing the Mid-way Air
Shew scarce so big as Beetles, half way down
Hangs one that gathers Sampire,* dreadfull Trade!
The Fisher-men that walk upon the Beach
Appear like Mice, and yon tall Anch'ring Barque
Seems lessen'd to her Cock*, her Cock a Buoy
Almost too small for Sight; the murmuring Surge          20
Cannot be heard so high, I'll look no more
Lest my Brain turn, and the disorder make me
Tumble down head long.

GLOSTER: Set me where you stand.

EDGAR: You are now within a Foot of th' extream Verge.
For all beneath the Moon I wou'd not now
Leap forward.

GLOSTER:     Let go my Hand,
Here, Friend, is another Purse, in it a Jewel
Well worth a poor Man's taking; get thee further,
Bid me Farewell, and let me hear thee going.          30

EDGAR: Fare you well, Sir – that I do Trifle thus
With this his Despair is with Design to cure it.

GLOSTER: Thus, mighty Gods, this World I do renounce,
And in your Sight shake my Afflictions off;
If I cou'd bear 'em longer and not fall
To quarrel with your great opposeless Wills,
My Snuff* and feebler Part of Nature shou'd
Burn it self out; if *Edgar* Live, O Bless him.
Now, Fellow, fare thee well.

EDGAR:     Gone, Sir! Farewell.
And yet I know not how Conceit* may rob          40
The Treasury of Life, had he been where
He thought, by this had Thought been past – Alive,
Or Dead? Hoa Sir, Friend; hear you, Sir, speak –
Thus might he pass indeed – yet he revives.
What are you, Sir?

GLOSTER: Away, and let me Die.

EDGAR: Hadst thou been ought but Gosmore,* Feathers,
    Air,

Falling so many Fathom down thou hadst Shiver'd like an
    Egg;
But thou dost breath, hast heavy Substance, bleedst not,
Speak'st, art sound; Thy Live's a Miracle.

GLOSTER: But have I faln or no?                              50

EDGAR: From the dread Summet of this chalky Bourn:*
Look up an Height, the Shrill-tun'd Lark so high
Cannot be seen, or heard; do but look up.

GLOSTER: Alack, I have no Eyes.
Is wretchedness depriv'd that Benefit
To End it self by Death?

EDGAR:     Give me your Arm.
Up, so, how is't? feel you your Legs? you stand.

GLOSTER: Too well, too well.

EDGAR: Upon the Crown o'th' Cliff, what Thing was that
Which parted from you?

GLOSTER:     A poor unfortunate Begger.                     60

EDGAR: As I stood here below, me-thought his Eyes
Were two Full Moons, wide Nostrils breathing Fire.
It was some Fiend, therefore thou happy Father,
Think that th'all-powerfull Gods who make them
    Honours
Of Mens Impossibilities have preserv'd thee.

GLOSTER: 'Tis wonderfull; henceforth I'll bear Affliction
Till it expire; the Goblin which you speak of,
I took it for a Man; oft-times 'twould say,
The Fiend, the Fiend: He led me to that Place.

EDGAR: Bear free and patient Thoughts: but who comes
here?                                                       70

*Enter* LEAR, *a Coronet of Flowers on his Head. Wreaths
                and Garlands about him*

LEAR: No, no, they cannot touch me for Coyning, I am the
King Himself.

EDGAR: O piercing Sight.

LEAR: Nature's above Art in that Respect; There's your
press-money:* that Fellow handles his Bow like a Cow-
keeper,—draw me a Clothier's yard.* A mouse, a Mouse;
peace hoa: there's my Gauntlet, I'll prove it on a Giant:

bring up the brown Bills:* O well flown Bird; i'th' White,
i'th' White* – Hewgh! give the Word.

EDGAR: Sweet *Marjorum*.                                    80

LEAR: Pass.

GLOSTER: I know that Voice.

LEAR: Ha! *Gonerill* with a white Beard! they flatter'd me
like a Dog, and told me I had white Hairs on my Chin,
before the Black ones were there; to say I and No to every
thing that I said, I and No too was no good Divinity.
When the Rain came once to wet me, and the Winds to
make me Chatter; when the Thunder wou'd not Peace at
my Bidding. There I found 'em, there I smelt 'em out; go
too, they are not men of their words, They told me I was a
King, 'tis a Lie, I am not Ague proof.                     90

GLOSTER: That Voice I well remember, is't not the King's?

LEAR: I, every Inch a King, when I do Stare
See how the Subject quakes.
I pardon that Man's Life, what was the Cause?*
Adultery? Thou shalt not Die. Die for Adultery!
The Wren goes to't, and the small gilded Flie
Engenders in my Sight: Let Copulation thrive,
For *Gloster*'s Bastard Son was kinder to his Father
Than were my Daughters got i'th'lawfull Bed.
To't Luxury, pell mell, for I lack Souldiers.             100

GLOSTER: Not all my Sorrows past so deep have toucht
me,
As the sad Accents: Sight were now a Torment –

LEAR: Behold that simp'ring Lady, she that starts
At Pleasure's Name, and thinks her Ear profan'd
With the least wanton Word, wou'd you believe it,
The Fitcher* nor the pamper'd Steed goes to't
With such a riotous Appetite: down from the Wast they
are Centaurs, tho Women all Above; but to the Girdle do
the Gods inherit, beneath is all the Fiends; There's Hell,
there's Darkness, the Sulphurous unfathom'd – Fie! fie!
pah! – an Ounce of Civet,* good Apothecary, to         110
sweeten my Imagination – There's Money for thee.

GLOSTER: Let me kiss that Hand.

LEAR: Let me wipe it first; it smells of Mortality.

GLOSTER: Speak, Sir; do you know me?

LEAR: I remember thy Eyes well enough: Nay, do thy worst, blind *Cupid*, I'll not Love – read me this Challenge, mark but the penning of it.

GLOSTER: Were all the Letters Suns I cou'd not see.

EDGAR: I wou'd not take this from Report: wretched *Cordelia*,                                                      120
What will thy Vertue do when thou shalt find
This fresh Affliction added to the Tale
Of thy unparrallel'd Griefs.

LEAR: Read.

GLOSTER: What! with this Case of Eyes?

LEAR: O ho! are you there with me? no Eyes in your Head, and no money in your Purse? yet you see how this World goes.

GLOSTER: I see it Feelingly.

LEAR: What? art Mad? a Man may see how this World goes with no Eyes. Look with thy Ears, see how yon Justice rails on that simple Thief; shake 'em together,  130
and the first that drops, be it Thief or Justice, is a Villain.–Thou hast seen a Farmer's Dog bark at a Beggar.

GLOSTER: I, Sir.

LEAR: And the Man ran from the Curr; there thou mightst behold the great Image of Authority, a Dog's obey'd in Office. Thou Rascal, Beadle, hold thy bloody Hand, why dost thou Lash that Strumpet? thou hotly Lust'st to enjoy her in that kind for which thou whipst her, do, do, the Judge that sentenc'd her has been before-hand with thee.  140

GLOSTER: How stiff* is my vile Sense that yields not yet?

LEAR: I tell thee the Usurer hangs the Couz'ner, through tatter'd Robes small Vices do appear, Robes and Fur-gowns hide All: Place Sins with Gold, why there 'tis for thee, my Friend, make much of it, it has the Pow'r to seal the Accuser's Lips. Get thee glass Eyes, and like a scurvy Politician,* seem to see the Things thou dost not. Pull, pull off my Boots, hard, harder, so, so.

GLOSTER: O Matter and Impertinency mixt!

Reason in Madness.

LEAR: If thou wilt weep my Fortunes take my Eyes,                    150
I know thee well enough, thy Name is *Gloster*.
Thou must be patient, we came Crying hither
Thou knowst, the first time that We tast the Air
We Wail and Cry – I'll preach to thee, Mark.

EDGAR: Break lab'ring Heart.

LEAR: When we are Born we Cry that we are come
To this great Stage of Fools.—

*Enter Two or Three Gentlemen*

GENTLEMAN: O here he is, lay hand upon him, Sir,
Your dearest Daughter sends—

LEAR: No Rescue? what, a Prisoner? I am even the natural   160
Fool of Fortune: Use me well, you shall have Ransome
– let me have Surgeons, Oh I am cut to th' Brains.

GENTLEMAN: You shall have any Thing.

LEAR: No Second's? all my Self? I will Die bravely like a
smug Bridegroom, flusht and pamper'd as a Priest's
Whore. I am a King, my Masters, know ye that?

GENTLEMAN: You are a Royal one, and we Obey you.

LEAR: It were an excellent Stratagem to Shoe a Troop of
Horse with Felt, I'll put in proof* – no Noise, no Noise –
now will we steal upon these Sons in Law, and then –
Kill, kill, kill, kill!                    170

[*Exit Running*]

GLOSTER: A Sight most moving in the meanest Wretch,
Past speaking in a King. Now, good Sir, what are you?

EDGAR: A most poor Man made tame to Fortune's strokes,
And prone to Pity by experienc'd Sorrows; give me your
Hand.

GLOSTER: You ever gentle Gods take my Breath from me,
And let not my ill Genius tempt me more
To Die before you please.

*Enter* GONERILL's *Gentleman-Usher*

GENTLEMAN: A proclaim'd Prize, O most happily met,
That Eye-less Head of thine was first fram'd Flesh
To raise my Fortunes; Thou old unhappy Traytor,                    180
The Sword is out that must Destroy thee.

GLOSTER: Now let thy friendly Hand put Strength enough
to't.

GENTLEMAN: Wherefore, bold Peasant,
Darst thou support a publisht Traytor, hence,
Lest I destroy Thee too. Let go his Arm.

EDGAR: 'Chill* not Let go Zir, without 'vurther 'Casion.

GENTLEMAN: Let go Slave, or thou Dyest.

EDGAR: Good Gentleman go your Gate, and let poor Volk
pass, and 'Chu'd* ha' bin Zwagger'd out of my Life it
wou'd not a bin zo long as 'tis by a Vort-night – Nay, an'
thou com'st near th' old Man, I'ce try whether your     190
Costard* or my Ballow* be th' harder.

GENTLEMAN: Out, Dunghill.

EDGAR: 'Chill pick your Teeth, Zir; Come, no matter vor
your Voines.*                                      [They fight]

GENTLEMAN: Slave, thou hast Slain me; oh untimely
Death.

EDGAR: I know thee well, a serviceable Villain,
As duteous to the Vices of thy Mistress
As Lust cou'd wish.

GLOSTER: What, is he Dead?

EDGAR:     Sit you, Sir, and rest you.
This is a letter Carrier, and may have                      200
Some Papers of Intelligence that may stand
Our Party in good stead, to know—what's here?
     [Takes a Letter out of his Pocket, opens, and reads]
To Edmund Earl of Gloster.
     Let our Mutual Loves be remembered, you have many
     opportunities to Cut him off, if he return the Con-
     queror then I am still a Prisoner, and his Bed my Goal,
     from the loath'd Warmth of which deliver me, and
     supply the Place for your Labour.
                         Gonerill.
A Plot upon her Husband's Life,
And the Exchange my Brother – here i'th' Sands           210
I'll rake thee up thou Messenger of Lust,
Griev'd only that thou hadst no other Deaths-man.
In Time and Place convenient I'll produce

These Letters to the Sight of th' injur'd Duke
As best shall serve our Purpose; Come, your Hand.
Far off methinks I hear the beaten Drum,
Come, Sir, I will bestow you with a Friend.[36]    [*Exeunt*]


## Scene v

*A Chamber.* LEAR *a Sleep on a Couch;* CORDELIA,
[*Physician,*] *and Attendants standing by him*

CORDELIA: His Sleep is sound, and may have good Effect
  To Cure his jarring Senses, and repair
  This Breach of Nature.[37]
PHYSICIAN: We have employ'd the utmost Pow'r of Art,
  And this deep Rest will perfect our Design.
CORDELIA: O *Regan, Gonerill,* inhumane Sisters,
  Had he not been your Father, these white Hairs
  Had challeng'd sure some pity, was this a Face
  To be expos'd against the jarring Winds?
  My Enemy's Dog though he had bit me shou'd              10
  Have stood that Night against my Fire—he wakes,
  Speak to him.
GENTLEMAN:     Madam, do you, 'tis fittest.
CORDELIA: How do's my royal Lord? how fares your
    Majesty?
LEAR: You do me wrong to take me out o'th'Grave.
  Ha! is this too a World of Cruelty?
  I know my Priviledge, think not that I will
  Be us'd still like a wretched Mortal, no,
  No more of That.
CORDELIA:     Speak to me, Sir, who am I?
LEAR: You are a Soul in Bliss, but I am bound
  Upon a wheel of Fire, which my own Tears                20
  Do scald like Molten Lead.
CORDELIA:     Sir, do you know me?

[36] 1–217 (whole scene). Based on *King Lear,* IV.vi.1–283 (Whole scene).
[37] 1–3: IV.vii.15–16: 'Cure this great breach ... jarring senses.'

LEAR: You are a Spirit, I know, where did you Die?

CORDELIA: Still, still, far wide.

PHYSICIAN: Madam, he's scarce awake; he'll soon grow
    more compos'd.

LEAR: Where have I been? where am I? fair Day-light!
  I am mightily abus'd.* I shou'd ev'n Die with pity
  To see Another thus. I will not swear
  These are my Hands.

CORDELIA:    O look upon me Sir,
  And hold your Hands in Blessing o're me, nay,
  You must not kneel.

LEAR:    Pray do not mock me.                        30
  I am a very foolish fond Old Man,
  Fourscore and upward, and to deal plainly
  With you, I fear I am not in my perfect Mind.

CORDELIA: Nay, then farewell to patience; witness for me
  Ye mighty Pow'rs, I ne're complain'd till now!

LEAR: Methinks I shou'd know you, and know this Man,
  Yet I am Doubtfull, for I am mainly Ignorant
  What Place this is, and all the skill I have
  Remembers not these Garments, nor do I know
  Where I did Sleep last Night – pray do not mock me –   40
  For, as I am a Man, I think that Lady
  To be my Child *Cordelia*.

CORDELIA: O my dear, dear Father!

LEAR: Be your Tears wet? yes faith; pray do not weep,
  I know I have giv'n thee Cause, and am so humbled
  With Crosses since, that I cou'd ask
  Forgiveness of thee were it possible
  That thou cou'dst grant it, but I'm well assur'd
  Thou canst not; therefore I do stand thy Justice,*
  If thou hast Poyson for me I will Drink it,            50
  Bless thee and Die.

CORDELIA: O pity, Sir, a bleeding Heart, and cease
  This killing Language.

LEAR:    Tell me, Friends, where am I?

GENTLEMAN: In your own Kingdom, Sir.

LEAR:    Do not Abuse me.

GENTLEMAN: Be comforted, good Madam, for the Violence
  Of his Distemper's past; we'll lead him in
  Nor trouble him, till he is better Setled.
  Wilt please you, Sir, walk into freer Air.
LEAR: You must bear with me, I am Old and Foolish.[38]
                              [*They lead him off*]
CORDELIA: The Gods restore you –                    60
  Heark, I hear afar the beaten Drum,
  Old *Kent*'s a Man of's Word. O for an Arm
  Like the fierce Thunderer's, when th' earth-born Sons
  Storm'd Heav'n,* to fight this injur'd Father's Battle.
  That I cou'd shift my Sex, and die me deep
  In his Opposer's Blood, but as I may
  With Womens Weapons, Piety and Pray'rs,
  I'll aid his Cause – You never-erring Gods
  Fight on his side, and Thunder on his Foes
  Such Tempest as his poor ag'd Head sustain'd;    70
  Your Image suffers when a Monarch bleeds.
  'Tis your own Cause, for that your Succours bring,
  Revenge your Selves, and right an injur'd King.    [*Exeunt*]

---

[38] 7–59. Based on *King Lear*, IV.vii.30–84: 'Had you not been ... old and foolish.'

# ACT V

## Scene i

*Scene, A Camp*
*Enter* GONERILL *and Attendants*

GONERILL: Our Sisters Pow'rs already are arriv'd,
  And She her self has promis'd to prevent*
  The Night with her Approach: have you provided
  The Banquet I bespoke for her Reception
  At my Tent?
ATTENDANT:  So, please your Grace, we have.
GONERILL: But thou, my Poysner, must prepare the Bowl
  That Crowns this Banquet, when our Mirth is high,
  The Trumpets sounding and the Flutes replying,
  Then is the Time to give this fatal Draught
  To this imperious Sister; if then our Arms succeed,       10
  *Edmund* more dear than Victory is mine.
  But if Defeat or Death it self attend me,
  'Twill charm my Ghost to think I've left behind me
                                                    [*Trumpet*]
  No happy Rival: heark, she comes.         [*Exeunt*]

## Scene ii

*Enter* BASTARD *in his Tent*

BASTARD: To both these Sisters have I sworn my Love,
  Each jealous* of the other, as the Stung
  Are of the Adder; neither can be held
  If both remain Alive; where shall I fix?[39]
  *Cornwall* is Dead, and *Regan*'s empty Bed

---

[39] 1–4 V.i.55–9: 'To both . . . both remain alive.'

Seems cast by Fortune for me, but already
I have enjoy'd her, and bright *Gonerill*
With equal Charms brings dear variety,
And yet untasted Beauty: I will use
Her Husband's Countenance* for the Battail, then          10
Usurp at once his Bed and Throne.
                    *Enter Officers*
My trusty Scouts y'are well return'd, have ye descry'd
The Strength and Posture* of the Enemy?
OFFICER: We have, and were surpriz'd to find
    The banisht *Kent* return'd, and at their Head;
    Your Brother *Edgar* on the Rear; Old *Gloster*
    (A moving Spectacle) led through their Ranks,
    Whose pow'rfull Tongue, and more prevailing Wrongs,
    Have so enrag'd their rustick Spirits, that with
    Th'approaching Dawn we must expect their Battle.         20
BASTARD: You bring a welcome Hearing;* Each to his
    Charge.
    Line well your Ranks and stand on your Award,*
    To Night repose you, and i'th'Morn we'll give
    The Sun a Sight that shall be worth his Rising.    [*Exeunt*]


## Scene iii

*Scene, A Valley near the Camp*
*Enter* EDGAR *and* GLOSTER

EDGAR: Here, Sir, take you the shadow of this Tree
    For your good Host, pray that the Right may thrive:
    If ever I return to you again
    I'll bring you Comfort.[40]                      [*Exit*]
GLOSTER:     Thanks, friendly Sir;
    The Fortune your good Cause deserves betide you.
            *An Alarum, after which* GLOSTER *speaks*
    The Fight grows hot; the whole War's now at Work,
    And the goar'd Battle bleeds in every Vein,
    Whilst Drums and Trumpets drown loud

---

[40] 1–4: V.ii.1–4: 'Here, father ... bring you comfort.'

Slaughter's Roar:
Where's *Gloster* now that us'd to head the Fray,
And scour the Ranks where deadliest Danger lay?          10
Here like a Shepherd in a lonely Shade,
Idle, unarm'd, and listning to the Fight.
Yet the disabled Courser,* Maim'd and Blind,
When to his Stall he hears the ratling War,
Foaming with Rage tears up the batter'd Ground,
And tugs for Liberty.
No more of Shelter, thou blind Worm, but forth
To th' open Field; the War may come this way
And crush thee into Rest. – Here lay thee down
And tear the Earth, that work befits a Mole.            20
O dark Despair! when, *Edgar*, wilt thou come
To pardon and dismiss me to the Grave!

                      (*A Retreat sounded*)

Heark! a Retreat, the King has Lost or Won.

             *Re-enter* EDGAR, *bloody*

EDGAR: Away, old Man, give me your Hand, away!
   King *Lear* has lost, He and his Daughter tane,
   And this, ye Gods, is all that I can save
   Of this most precious Wreck: give me your Hand.
GLOSTER: No farther, Sir, a Man may Rot even here.
EDGAR: What? in ill Thoughts again? Men must endure
   Their going hence ev'n as their coming hither.          30
GLOSTER: And that's true too.[41]                    [*Exeunt*]


# Scene iv

*Flourish. Enter in Conquest,* ALBANY, GONERILL, REGAN,
BASTARD, –
LEAR, KENT, CORDELIA *Prisoners*


ALBANY: It is enough to have Conquer'd, Cruelty
   Shou'd ne're survive the Fight, Captain o'th'Guards
   Treat well your royal Prisoners till you have

---

[41] 24–31: V.ii.5–11: 'Away, old man ... true too.'

Our further Orders, as you hold our Pleasure.

GONERILL: Heark, Sir, not as you hold our Husbands
    pleasure                        (*To the Captain aside*)
But as you hold your Life, dispatch your Pris'ners.
Our Empire can have no sure Settlement
But in their Death, the Earth that covers them
Binds fast our Throne. Let me hear they are Dead.

CAPTAIN: I shall obey your Orders.              10

BASTARD: Sir, I approve it safest to pronounce
Sentence of Death upon this wretched King,
Whose Age has Charms in it, his Title more,
To draw the Commons once more to his Side,
'Twere best prevent—

ALBANY:    Sir, by your Favour,
I hold you but a Subject of this War,
Not as a Brother.

REGAN:    That's as we list to Grace him.
Have you forgot that He did lead our Pow'rs?
Bore the Commission of our Place and Person?
And that Authority may well stand up      20
And call it self your Brother.

GONERILL:    Not so hot,
In his own Merits he exalts himself
More than in your Addition. [42]

*Enter* EDGAR, *disguised*

ALBANY: What art thou?

EDGAR: Pardon me, Sir, that I presume to stop
A Prince and Conquerour, yet e'er you Triumph,
Give Ear to what a Stranger can deliver
Of what concerns you more than Triumph can.
I do impeach your General there of Treason,
Lord *Edmund*, that usurps the Name of *Gloster*,    30
Of fowlest Practice 'gainst your Life and Honour;
This Charge is True, and wretched though I seem
I can produce a Champion that will prove
In single Combat what I do avouch,*
If *Edmund* dares but trust his Cause and Sword.

[42] 11–23. Based on *King Lear*, V.iii.46–69: 'Sir, I thought it . . . your addition.'

BASTARD: What will not *Edmund* dare, my Lord, I beg
  The favour that you'd instantly appoint
  The Place where I may meet this Challenger,
  Whom I will sacrifice to my wrong'd Fame,*
  Remember, Sir, that injur'd Honour's nice*        40
  And cannot brook delay.

ALBANY: Anon, before our Tent, i'th' Army's view,
  There let the Herald cry.

EDGAR: I thank your Highness in my Champion's Name,
  He'll wait your Trumpet's call.

ALBANY:    Lead.                       [*Exeunt*]
      (*Manent* LEAR, KENT, CORDELIA, *guarded*)

LEAR: O *Kent, Cordelia*!
  You are the onely Pair that I e'er wrong'd,
  And the just Gods have made you Witnesses
  Of my Disgrace, the very shame of Fortune,
  To see me chain'd and shackled at these years!      50
  Yet were you but Spectatours of my Woes,
  Not fellow-sufferers, all were well!

CORDELIA: This language, Sir, adds yet to our Affliction.

LEAR: Thou, *Kent*, didst head the Troops that fought my
    Battel,
  Expos'd thy Life and Fortunes for a Master
  That had (as I remember) banisht Thee.

KENT: Pardon me, Sir, that once I broke your Orders,
  Banisht by you, I kept me here disguis'd
  To watch your Fortunes, and protect your Person,
  You know you entertain'd a rough blunt Fellow,    60
  One *Cajus*, and you thought he did you Service.

LEAR: My trusty *Cajus*, I have lost him too!    (*Weeps*)
  'Twas a rough Honesty.

KENT:    I was that *Cajus*,
  Disguis'd in that course Dress to follow you.

LEAR: My *Cajus* too! wer't thou my trusty *Cajus*,
  Enough, enough! –

CORDELIA: Ah me, he faints! his Blood forsakes his Cheek,
  Help, *Kent* –

LEAR:    No, no, they shall not see us weep,

We'll see them rot first, – Guards lead away
To Prison, come, *Kent*, *Cordelia* come,                    70
We Two will sit alone, like Birds i'th' Cage,
When Thou dost ask me Blessing, I'll kneel down
And ask of Thee Forgiveness; Thus we'll live,
And Pray, and Sing, and tell old Tales, and Laugh
At gilded Butter-flies, hear Sycophants
Talk of Court News, and we'll talk with them too,
Who loses, and who wins, who's in, who's out,
And take upon us the Mystery of Things
As if we were Heav'ns Spies.
CORDELIA: Upon such Sacrifices                    80
The Gods themselves throw Incense.
LEAR:     Have I caught ye?[43]
He that parts us must bring a Brand from Heav'n.
Together we'll out-toil* the spight of Hell,
And Die the Wonders of the World; Away.

                              [*Exeunt, guarded*]


# Scene v

*Flourish: Enter before the Tents,* ALBANY, GONERILL,
REGAN, *Guards and Attendants;* GONERILL *speaking apart to
the Captain of the Guards entring*


GONERILL: Here's Gold for Thee, Thou knowst our late
    Command
Upon your Pris'ners Lives, about it streight, and at
Our Ev'ning Banquet let it raise our Mirth
To hear that They are Dead.
CAPTAIN: I shall not fail your Orders.             [*Exit*]
        (ALBANY, GONERILL, REGAN *take their Seats*)
ALBANY: Now, *Gloster*, trust to thy single Vertue,*
For thy Soldiers, all levied in my Name,
Have in my Name took their Discharge; now let
Our Trumpets speak, and Herald read out This.

---

[43] 70–82: V.iii.8–23: 'Let's away to prison ... hence like foxes.'

*(Herald Reads)*
> *If any Man of Quality, within the Lists of the Army,*   10
> *will maintain upon* Edmund, *suppos'd Earl of* Gloster,
> *that he is a manifold Traytour, let him appear by the*
> *third sound of the Trumpet; He is bold in his*
> *Defence.—Agen, Agen.*[44]

                *(Trumpet Answers from within)*
             *Enter* EDGAR, *Arm'd*

ALBANY: Lord *Edgar*!

BASTARD:    Ha! my Brother!
This is the onely Combatant that I cou'd fear;
For in my Breast Guilt Duels on his side,
But, Conscience, what have I to do with Thee?
Awe Thou thy dull Legitimate Slaves, but I
Was born a Libertine, and so I keep me.

EDGAR: My noble Prince, a word – e'er we engage     20
Into your Highness's Hands I give this Paper,
It will the truth of my Impeachment prove
Whatever be my fortune in the Fight.

ALBANY: We shall peruse it.

EDGAR: Now, *Edmund*, draw thy Sword,
That if my Speech has wrong'd a noble Heart,
Thy Arm may doe thee Justice: here i'th' presence
Of this high Prince, these Queens, and this crown'd List,
I brand thee with the spotted name of Traytour,
False to thy Gods, thy Father and thy Brother,[45]     30
And what is more, thy Friend; false to this Prince:
If then Thou shar'st a spark of *Gloster*'s Vertue,
Acquit thy self, or if Thou shar'st his Courage,
Meet this Defiance bravely.

BASTARD:    And dares *Edgar*,
The beaten routed *Edgar*, brave his Conquerour?
From all thy Troops and Thee, I forc't the Field,
Thou has lost the gen'ral Stake, and art Thou now
Come with thy petty single Stock* to play
This after-Game?*

---

[44] 6–13: V.iii.103–15: 'Trust to thy single ... again! again!'
[45] 30: V.iii.133: 'False ... Brother.'

EDGAR: Half-blooded Man,*
  Thy Father's Sin first, then his Punishment,                    40
  The dark and vicious Place where he begot thee
  Cost him his Eyes: from thy licentious Mother[46]
  Thou draw'st thy Villany; but for thy part
  Of *Gloster*'s Blood, I hold thee worth my Sword.

BASTARD: Thou bear'st thee* on thy Mother's Piety,
  Which I despise; thy Mother being chaste
  Thou art assur'd Thou art but *Gloster*'s Son,
  But mine, disdaining Constancy, leaves me
  To hope that I am sprung from nobler Blood,
  And possibly a King might be my Sire:                              50
  But be my Birth's uncertain Chance as 'twill,
  Who 'twas that had the hit to Father me
  I know not; 'tis enough that I am I:
  Of this one thing I'm certain—that I have
  A daring Soul, and so have at thy Heart.
  Sound Trumpet.                            (*Fight,* BASTARD *falls*)

GONERILL, AND REGAN: Save him, save him.

GONERILL: This was Practice,* *Gloster*,
  Thou won'st the Field, and wast not bound to Fight
  A vanquisht Enemy, Thou art not Conquer'd                          60
  But couz'ned and betray'd.

ALBANY: Shut your Mouth, Lady,
  Or with this Paper I shall stop it—hold, Sir,
  Thou worse than any Name, reade thy own evil,
  No Tearing, Lady, I perceive you know it.

GONERILL: Say if I do, who shall arraign me for't?
  The Laws are Mine, not Thine.

ALBANY: Most monstrous! ha, Thou know'st it too?

BASTARD: Ask me not what I know,[47]
  I have not Breath to Answer idle Questions.

ALBANY: I have resolv'd – your Right, brave Sir, has
    conquer'd,

                                (*To* EDGAR)

  Along with me, I must consult your Father.

[46] 41–42: V.iii.171–2: 'The dark and vicious . . . his eyes.'
[47] 57–69: V.iii.149–59: 'Save him . . . what I know.'

[*Exeunt* ALBANY *and* EDGAR]

REGAN: Help every Hand to save a noble Life;
  My half o'th' Kingdom for a Man of Skill
  To stop this precious stream.

BASTARD:    Away ye Empericks,*
  Torment me not with your vain Offices:
  The Sword has pierc'd too far; *Legitimacy*
  At last has got it.

REGAN:    The Pride of Nature Dies.

GONERILL: Away, the minutes are too precious,
  Disturb us not with thy impertinent Sorrow.                    80

REGAN: Art Thou my Rival then profest?

GONERILL: Why, was our Love a Secret? cou'd there be
  Beauty like Mine, and Gallantry like His
  And not a mutual Love? just Nature then
  Had err'd: behold that Copy of Perfection,
  That Youth whose Story will have no foul Page
  But where it says he stoopt to *Regan*'s Arms:
  Which yet was but Compliance, not Affection;
  A Charity to begging, ruin'd Beauty!

REGAN: Who begg'd when *Gonerill* writ That? expose it        90
                              (*Throws her a Letter*)
  And let it be your Army's mirth, as 'twas
  This charming Youth's and mine, when in the Bow'r
  He breath'd the warmest ecstasies of Love,
  Then panting on my Breast, cry'd matchless *Regan*
  That *Gonerill* and Thou shou'd e'er be Kin!

GONERILL: Die, *Circe*,* for thy Charms are at an End,
  Expire before my Face, and let me see
  How well that boasted Beauty will become
  Congealing Blood and Death's convulsive Pangs.
  Die and be husht, for at my Tent last Night              100
  Thou drank'st thy Bane, amidst thy rev'ling Bowls:
  Ha! dost thou Smile? is then thy Death thy Sport
  Or has the trusty Potion made thee Mad?

REGAN: Thou com'st as short of me in thy Revenge
  As in my *Gloster*'s Love, my Jealousie
  Inspir'd me to prevent thy feeble Malice

And Poison Thee at thy own Banquet.

GONERILL:    Ha!

BASTARD: No more, my Queens, of this untimely Strife,
You both deserv'd my Love and both possest it.
Come, Souldiers, bear me in; and let                    110
Your royal Presence grace my last minutes:
Now, *Edgar*, thy proud Conquest I forgive;
Who wou'd not choose, like me, to yield his Breath
T'have Rival Queens contend for him in Death?    [*Exeunt*]


## Scene vi

*Scene, A Prison*
LEAR *asleep, with his Head on* CORDELIA'S *Lap*


CORDELIA: What Toils, thou wretched King, has Thou
    endur'd
To make thee draw, in Chains, a Sleep so sound?
Thy better Angel charm thy ravisht Mind
With fancy'd Freedom; Peace is us'd to lodge
On Cottage Straw, Thou hast the Begger's Bed,
Therefore shou'dst have the Begger's careless Thought.
And now, my *Edgar*, I remember Thee,
What Fate has seiz'd Thee in this general Wreck
I know not, but I know thou must be wretched
Because *Cordelia* holds Thee Dear. O Gods!                    10
A suddain Gloom o'er-whelms me, and the Image
Of Death o'er-spreads the Place. – ha! who are These?
    *Enter* CAPTAIN *and* OFFICERS *with Cords*

CAPTAIN: Now Sirs, dispatch, already you are paid
In part, the best of your Reward's to come.

LEAR: Charge, charge upon their Flank, their last Wing
    haults;
Push, push the Battel, and the Day's our own.
Their Ranks are broke, down, down with *Albany*.
Who holds my Hands? – O thou deceiving Sleep,
I was this very Minute on the Chace;

And now a Prisoner here – What mean the Slaves?          20
You will not Murder me?

CORDELIA:    Help Earth and Heaven!
For your Souls sake's, dear Sirs, and for the Gods.

OFFICER: No Tears, good Lady, no pleading against
Gold
And Preferment; Come, Sirs, make ready your Cords.

CORDELIA: You, Sir, I'll seize,
You have a humane Form, and if no Pray'rs
Can touch your Soul to spare a poor King's Life,
If there be any Thing that you hold dear,
By That I beg you to dispatch me First.

CAPTAIN: Comply with her Request, dispatch her first.          30

LEAR:  Off Hell-hounds, by the Gods I charge you spare her;
'Tis my *Cordelia*, my true pious Daughter:
No Pity? – Nay then take an old Man's Vengeance.
*Snatches a Partizan*, and strikes down two of them;
the rest quit* CORDELIA, *and turn upon him. Enter*
EDGAR *and* ALBANY

EDGAR: Death! Hell! Ye Vultures hold your impious
Hands,
Or take a speedier Death than you wou'd give.

CAPTAIN: By whose Command?

EDGAR:      Behold the Duke your Lord.

ALBANY: Guards, seize those Instruments of Cruelty.

CORDELIA: My Edgar, Oh!

EDGAR: My dear *Cordelia*, Lucky was the Minute
Of our Approach, the Gods have weigh'd our Suffrings;          40
W'are past the Fire, and now must shine to Ages.

GENTLEMAN: Look here, my Lord, see where the
generous* King
Has slain Two of 'em.

LEAR:     Did I not, Fellow?
I've seen the Day, with my good biting Faulchion*
I cou'd have made 'em skip; I am Old now,
And these vile Crosses* spoil me; Out of Breath!48

---

48 44–7: V.iii.275–7: 'I have seen ... spoil me.'

Fie, Oh! quite out of Breath and spent.

ALBANY: Bring in old *Kent*, and, *Edgar*, guide you hither
Your Father, whom you said was near,   [*Exit* EDGAR]
He may be an Ear-witness at the least                           50
Of our Proceedings.

KENT *brought in here*

LEAR: Who are you?
My Eyes are none o'th' best, I'll tell you streight;[49]
Oh *Albany*! Well, Sir, we are your Captives,
And you are come to see Death pass upon us.
Why this Delay? – or is't your Highness pleasure
To give us first the Torture? Say ye so?
Why here's old *Kent* and I, as tough a Pair
As e'er bore Tyrant's Stroke; – but my *Cordelia*,
My poor *Cordelia* here, O pitty!—                              60

ALBANY: Take off their Chains – Thou injur'd Majesty,
The Wheel of Fortune now has made her Circle,
And Blessings yet stand 'twixt thy Grave and Thee.

LEAR: Com'st Thou, inhumane Lord, to sooth us back
To a Fool's Paradise of Hope, to make
Our Doom more wretched? go too, we are too well
Acquainted with Misfortune to be gull'd
With Lying Hope; No, we will hope no more.

ALBANY: I have a Tale t' unfold so full of Wonder
As cannot meet an easy Faith;                                  70
But by that Royal injur'd Head 'tis True.

KENT: What wou'd your Highness?

ALBANY:    Know the noble *Edgar*
Impeacht Lord *Edmund* since the Fight, of Treason,
And dar'd him for the Proof to single Combat,
In which the Gods confirm'd his Charge by Conquest;
I left ev'n now the Traytor wounded Mortally.

LEAR: And whither tends this Story?

ALBANY:    E'er they fought
Lord *Edgar* gave into my Hands this Paper,
A blacker Scrowl* of Treason, and of Lust

---

[49] 52–3: V.iii.277–8: 'Who are you … you straight.'

Than can be found in the Records of Hell;                    80
There, Sacred Sir, behold the Character
Of *Gonerill* the worst of Daughters, but
More Vicious Wife.

CORDELIA: Cou'd there be yet Addition to their Guilt?
What will not They that wrong a Father doe?

ALBANY: Since then my Injuries, *Lear*, fall in with* Thine:
I have resolv'd the same Redress for Both.

KENT: What says my Lord?

CORDELIA:     Speak, for me thought I heard
The charming Voice of a descending God.

ALBANY: The Troops by *Edmund* rais'd, I have disbanded;    90
Those that remain are under my Command.
What Comfort may be brought to cheer your Age
And heal your savage Wrongs, shall be apply'd;
For to your Majesty we do Resign
Your Kingdom, save what Part your Self conferr'd
On Us in Marriage.

KENT:     Hear you that, my Liege?

CORDELIA: Then there are Gods, and Vertue is their Care.

LEAR: Is't Possible?
Let the Spheres stop their Course, the Sun make Hault,
The Winds be husht, the Seas and Fountains Rest;           100
All Nature pause, and listen to the Change.
Where is my *Kent*, my *Cajus*?

KENT:     Here, my Liege.

LEAR: Why I have News that will recall thy Youth;
Ha! Didst Thou hear't, or did th'inspiring Gods
Whisper to me Alone? Old *Lear* shall be
A King again.

KENT: The Prince, that like a God has Pow'r, has said it.

LEAR: *Cordelia* then shall be a Queen, mark that:
*Cordelia* shall be Queen; Winds catch the Sound
And bear it on your rosie Wings to Heav'n.                 110
*Cordelia* is a Queen.

            *Re-enter* EDGAR *with* GLOSTER

ALBANY: Look, Sir, where pious *Edgar* comes
Leading his Eye-less Father: O my Liege!

His wondrous Story will deserve your Leisure:
What He has done and suffer'd for your Sake,
What for the Fair *Cordelia*'s.

GLOSTER: Where is my Liege? Conduct me to his Knees to
    hail
His second Birth of Empire; my dear *Edgar*
Has, with himself, reveal'd the King's blest Restauration.

LEAR: My poor dark *Gloster*.                    120

GLOSTER: O let me kiss that once more sceptred Hand!

LEAR: Hold, Thou mistak'st the Majesty, kneel here;
*Cordelia* has our Pow'r, *Cordelia*'s Queen.
Speak, is not that the noble Suff'ring *Edgar*?

GLOSTER: My pious Son, more dear than my lost Eyes.

LEAR: I wrong'd Him too, but here's the fair Amends.

EDGAR: Your leave, my Liege, for an unwelcome Message.
*Edmund* (but that's a Trifle) is expir'd;
What more will touch you, your imperious Daughters
*Gonerill* and haughty *Regan*, both are Dead,                    130
Each by the other poison'd at a Banquet;
This, Dying, they confest.

CORDELIA: O fatal Period* of ill-govern'd Life!

LEAR: Ingratefull as they were, my Heart feels yet
A Pang of Nature for their wretched Fall;—
But, *Edgar*, I defer thy Joys too long:
Thou serv'dst distrest *Cordelia*; take her Crown'd:
Th'imperial Grace fresh Blooming on her Brow;
Nay, *Gloster*, Thou hast here a Father's Right;
Thy helping Hand t'heap Blessings on their Heads.                    140

KENT: Old *Kent* throws in his hearty Wishes too.

EDGAR: The Gods and You too largely recompence
What I have done; the Gift strikes Merit Dumb.

CORDELIA: Nor do I blush to own my Self o'er-paid
For all my Suffrings past.

GLOSTER: Now, gentle Gods, give *Gloster* his Discharge.

LEAR: No, *Gloster*, Thou hast Business yet for Life;
Thou, *Kent* and I, retir'd to some cool Cell
Will gently pass our short reserves of Time
In calm Reflections on our Fortunes past,                    150

Cheer'd with relation of the prosperous Reign
Of this celestial Pair; Thus our Remains*
Shall in an even Course of Thought be past,
Enjoy the present Hour, nor fear the Last.
EDGAR: Our drooping Country now erects her Head,
Peace spreads her balmy Wings, and Plenty Blooms.
Divine *Cordelia*, all the Gods can witness
How much thy Love to Empire I prefer!
Thy bright Example shall convince the World
(Whatever Storms of Fortune are decreed)                    160
That Truth and Vertue shall at last succeed.

                                        [*Exeunt Omnes*]

## Spoken by Mrs. *Barry*.

*Inconstancy, the reigning Sin o'th' Age,*
*Will scarce endure true Lovers on the Stage;*
*You hardly ev'n in Plays with such dispense,*
*And Poets kill 'em in their own Defence.*
*Yet One bold Proof I was resolv'd to give,*
*That I cou'd three Hours Constancy Out-live.*
*You fear, perhaps, whilst on the Stage w'are made*
*Such Saints, we shall indeed take up the Trade;*
*Sometimes we Threaten – but our Vertue may*
*For Truth I fear with your Pit-Valour weigh:*      10
*For (not to flatter either) I much doubt*
*When We are off the Stage, and You are out,*       }
*We are not quite so Coy, nor You so Stout.*
*We talk of Nunn'ries – but to be sincere*
*Whoever lives to see us Cloyster'd There,*         }
*May hope to meet our Critiques at* Tangier*
*For shame give over this inglorious Trade*
*Of worrying Poets, and go maule th'* Alcade*
*Well – since y'are All for blustring in the Pit,*   }
*This Play's Reviver humbly do's admit*             20
*Your abs'lute Pow'r to damn his Part of it;*
*But still so many Master-Touches shine*
*Of that vast Hand that first laid this Design,*
*That in great* Shakespear's *Right, He's bold to say*  }
*If you like nothing you have seen to Day*
*The Play your Judgment damns, not you the Play.*

# RICHARD III

BY COLLEY CIBBER

# THE
# Tragical History
## OF
# King Richard III.

### As it is Acted at the

# THEATRE ROYAL.

---

## By C. Cibber.

---

——— *Domestica Facta.*

---

## LONDON,

Printed for B. *Lintott* at the Middle *Temple-Gate*, in *Fleet-street*, and
A. *Bettesworth* at the *Red-Lyon* on *London*-Bridge.

---

# THE PREFACE

This Play came upon the Stage with a very Unusual disadvantage, the whole first Act being Intirely left out in the Presentation;* and tho' it had been read by several persons of the first Rank and Integrity, some of which were pleas'd to honour me with an offer of giving it under their hands that the whole was an Inoffensive piece, and free from any bold Paralel, or ill manner'd reflection, yet this was no satisfaction to him, who had the Relentless power of licensing it for the Stage. I did not spare for intreaties; but all the reason I could get for its being refus'd was, that *Henry* the Sixth being a Character Unfortunate and Pitied, wou'd put the Audience in mind of the late *King James*: Now, I confess, I never thought of him in the Writing it, which possibly might proceed from there not being any likeness between 'em. But however, there was no hazard of offending the Government, though the whole Play had been refus'd, and a man is not obliged to be Just, when he can get as much by doing an Injury. I am only sorry it hapned to be the best Act in the Whole, and leave it to the Impartial Reader how far it is offensive, and whether its being Acted would have been as injurious to good Manners, as the omission of it was to the rest of the Play.

Tho' there was no great danger of the Readers mistaking any of my lines for *Shakespear's*; yet, to satisfie the curious, and unwilling to assume more praise than is really my due, I have caus'd those that are intirely *Shakespear's* to be Printed in this *Italick Character*; and those lines with this mark (') before 'em, are generally his thoughts, in the best dress I could afford 'em: What is not so mark'd, or in a different Character is intirely my own.* I have done my best to imitate his Style, and manner of thinking: If I have fail'd, I have still this comfort, that our best living Author* in his imitation of *Shakespear's* Style only writ Great and Masterly.

# THE PERSONS

---

KING HENRY THE SIXTH, Mr *Wilks*
  designed for
EDWARD Prince of *Wales*,     Mrs *Allison*
RICHARD DUKE OF YORK,     Miss *Chock*
  the young Sons of
  *Edward* the Fourth
RICHARD DUKE OF GLOUCESTER, afterwards King of *England*,
Mr *Cibber**
DUKE OF BUCKINGHAM, Mr *Powel*
LORD STANLEY, Mr *Mills*
DUKE OF NORFOLK, Mr *Simpson*
RATCLIFF, Mr *Kent*
CATESBY, Mr *Thomas*
HENRY EARL OF RICHMOND, afterwards King of *England*, Mr
*Evans*
OXFORD, Mr *Fairbank*
BLUNT
[TRESSELL
[LIEUTENANT OF THE TOWER
[LORD MAYOR
[TIRREL
[FORREST
[DIGHTON
[RIVERS]
[DORSET]
[LOVEL]
ELIZABETH, Relict of *Edward* the Fourth, Mrs *Knight*
ANN, Relict of *Edward* Prince of *Wales*, Son to *Henry* the
Sixth, afterwards married to *Richard* the Third, Mrs *Rogers*

CICELY, Dutchess of York, Mother to *Richard* the Third, Mrs *Powel*

[GENTLEMEN, LADIES, GUARDS and ATTENDANTS]

# ACT I

## Scene i

*The Scene, A Garden within the* Tower

*Enter the* LIEUTENANT *with a* SERVANT

LIEUTENANT: Has King *Henry* walk'd forth this Morning?

SERVANT: No, Sir, but 'tis near his Hour.

LIEUTENANT: At any time when you see him here,
Let no Stranger into the Garden:
I wou'd not have him star'd at – See! Who's that
Now entring at the Gate?
     (*Knocking without*)

SERVANT:      Sir, the Lord *Stanley.*

LIEUTENANT: Leave me.—    [*Exit* SERVANT]
   *Enter Lord* STANLEY
My Noble Lord you're welcome to the Tower,
I heard last Night you late arriv'd with News
Of *Edward*'s Victory to his joyful Queen.    10

STANLEY: Yes, Sir; and I am proud to be the Man
That first brought home the last of Civil Broils,
The Houses now of *York,* and *Lancaster,*
Like Bloody Brothers fighting for Birth-right,
No more shall wound the Parent that wou'd part 'em.
*Edward* now sits secure on *England*'s Throne.

LIEUTENANT: Near *Tewskesbury,* my Lord I think they fought:
Has the Enemy lost any Men of Note?

STANLEY: Sir, I was Posted Home
E're an Account was taken of the Slain,    20
But as I left the Field, a Proclamation
From the King was made in Search of *Edward,*
Son to your Prisoner, King *Henry* the Sixth,

Which gave Reward to those Discover'd him,
And him his Life, if he'd surrender.

LIEUTENANT: That Brave Young Prince, I fear's unlike his
    Father,
Too high of Heart to brook* submissive Life:
This will be heavy News to *Henry*'s Ear:
For on this Battles cast his All was set.

STANLEY: King *Henry*, and ill Fortune are familiar:                    30
He ever threw with an indifferent Hand,
But never yet was known to lose his Patience:
How does he pass the Time in his Confinement?

LIEUTENANT: As one whose Wishes never reacht a Crown,
The King seems Dead in him: But as a Man
He sighs sometimes in want of Liberty.
Sometimes he Reads, and Walks, and wishes
That Fate had blest him with an humbler Birth,
Not to have felt the falling from a Throne.

STANLEY: Were it not possible to see this King?                         40
They say he'll freely talk with *Edward*'s Friends,
And ever treats them with Respect, and Honour.

LIEUTENANT: This is his usual Time of walking forth,
(For he's allow'd the freedom of the Garden;)
After his Morning-Prayer; he seldom fails:
Behind this Arbor we unseen may stand
A while t'observe him.                              (*They retire*)
    *Enter King* HENRY *the Sixth in Mourning*

HENRY: By this time the Decisive Blow is struck,
Either my Queen and Son are blest with Victory,
Or I'm the cause no more of Civil Broils.                               50
*Wou'd I were Dead if Heavens good Will were so,*
'For what is in this World but Grief and Care?'[1]
What Noise, and Bustle do Kings make to find it?
When Life's but a short Chace, our Game content
Which most pursued is most compell'd to fly;
And he that mounts him on the swiftest Hope,
Shall often Run his Courser* to a stand,

[1] 51-2. *Henry VI*, Part 3, II.v.19-20: 'Would I were ... grief and woe.'

While the poor Peasant from some distant Hill
Undanger'd, and at Ease views all the Sport,
And sees Content take shelter in his Cottage.                60
STANLEY: He seems Extreamly mov'd.
LIEUTENANT:                              Does he know you?
                                         (Aside)
STANLEY: No! nor wou'd I have him.
LIEUTENANT:                              We'll show our selves.
                                         (They come forward)
HENRY: Why, there's another Check to Proud Ambition.
    That Man receiv'd his Charge from me, and now
    I'm his Prisoner, he lock's me to my Rest:
    Such an unlook'd for Change who cou'd suppose,
    That saw him kneel to Kiss the Hand that rais'd him?
    But that I shou'd not now complain off,
    Since I to that, 'tis possible, may owe
    His Civil Treatment of me,—'Morrow Lieutenant,           70
    Is any News arriv'd?—Who's that with you?
LIEUTENANT: A Gentleman that came last Night Express
    From *Tewkesbury*. We've had a Battle.
HENRY: Comes he to me with Letters or Advice?
LIEUTENANT: Sir, he's King *Edward*'s Officer, your Foe.
HENRY: Then he won't flatter me, you're welcome, Sir;
    Not less because you are King *Edward*'s Friend;
    For I have almost learn'd my self to be so:
    Cou'd I but once forget I was a King,
    I might be truly Happy, and his Subject.                 80
    You've gain'd a Battle? Is't not so?
STANLEY: We have, Sir; How, will reach your Ear too
    soon.
HENRY: If my Loss, it can't too soon – Pray speak,
    For Fear makes Mischief greater than it is:
    My Queen! my Son! say, Sir! are they living!
STANLEY: Since my Arrival, Sir, another Post
    Came in, which brought us word your Queen, and Son
    Were Prisoners now at *Tewkesbury*.
HENRY: Heav'ns Will be done! the Hunters have 'em now –
    And I have only Sighs, and Prayers to help 'em!          90

STANLEY: King *Edward*, Sir, depends upon his Sword,
 Yet prays heartily, when the Battle's won:
 And Soldiers love a Bold and Active Leader,
 Fortune like Women will be close pursu'd;
 The *English* are high Mettl'd, Sir, and 'tis
 No easie part to Sit 'em well. King *Edward*
 Feels their Temper, and 'twill be hard to throw him.
HENRY: Alas, I thought 'em Men, and rather hop'd
 To win their Hearts by Mildness, than Severity.
 My Soul was never form'd for Cruelty,     100
 In my Eye Justice has seem'd bloody,
 When on the City Gates I have beheld
 A Traytor's Quarters parching in the Sun,
 My Blood has turn'd with Horror at the Sight,
 I took 'em down, and Buried with his Limbs
 The Memory of the Dead Man's Deeds: Perhaps
 That Pity made me look less Terrible,
 Giving the mind of weak Rebellion Spirit:
 For King's are put in Trust for all Mankind,
 And when themselves take Injuries, who is safe?  110
 If so I have deserv'd these frowns of Fortune.
    *Enter a* SERVANT *to the* LIEUTENANT
SERVANT: Sir, here's a Gentleman brings a Warrant
 For his Access to King *Henry*'s Presence.
LIEUTENANT: I come to him.
STANLEY: His Business may require your Privacy,
 I'll leave you, Sir, wishing you all the Good
 That can be wish'd, not wronging him I serve. [*Exeunt*]
HENRY: Farewell: Who can this be? A sudden Coldness
 Like the Damp Hand of Death has seiz'd my Limbs:
 I fear some heavy News!—         120
     *Enter* LIEUTENANT
 Who is it, good Lieutenant?
LIEUTENANT: A gentleman, Sir, from *Tewkesbury*, he
  seems
 A melancholly Messenger: For when I ask'd
 What News? His Answer was a deep faught Sigh:
 I wou'd not urge him, but I fear 'tis fatal.   [*Exit*]

*Enter* TRESSELL *in Mourning*

HENRY: *Fatal indeed! His Brows the Title Page*
  *That speaks the Nature of a Tragick Volume;*
  'Say, Friend, how does my Queen, my Son!
  *Thou tremblest, and the whiteness of thy Cheek*
  *Is apter than thy Tongue to tell the Errand,*         130
  *Ev'n such a Man, so Faint, so Spiritless,*
  *So Dull, so Dead in Look, so Woe be gone,*
  *Drew* Priam's *Curtain in the Dead of Night,* *
  *And wou'd have told him half his* Troy *was burn'd,*
  *But* Priam *found the Fire, e're he his Tongue,*
  *And I my poor Son's Death e're thou relatest it;*
  *Now wou'd'st thou say: Your Son did thus and thus,*
  'And thus your Queen; So fought the Valiant *Oxford,*
  *Stopping my greedy Ear with their bold Deeds,*
  *But in the End (to stop my Ear indeed,)*         140
  *Thou hast a Sigh to blow away this Praise,*
  'Ending with Queen and Son, and all are Dead.
TRESSELL: 'Your Queen yet Lives, and many of your
    Friends,
  'But for my Lord your Son—
HENRY: Why, he is Dead:—yet speak, I Charge thee!
  'Tell thou thy Master his Suspicion lies,
  *And I will take it as a kind Disgrace,*
  'And thank thee well, for doing me such wrong.
TRESSELL: Wou'd it were wrong to say, but, Sir, your Fears
    are true.
HENRY: Yet for all this, say not my Son is Dead.[2]      150
TRESSELL: Sir, I am sorry I must force you to
  Believe, what wou'd to Heav'n I had not seen!
  But in this last Battle, near *Tewkesbury,*
  'Your Son, whose Active Spirit lent a Fire
  'Ev'n to the dullest Peasant in our Camp,[3]
  Still made his way, where Danger stood t'oppose him,
  A braver Youth of more Couragious Heat,

[2] 126–50. Substantially based on *Henry IV, Part 2,* I.i.60–104: 'Yea, this man's
brow . . . son is dead.'
[3] 154–5. *Henry IV, Part 2,* I.i.112–13: 'In few . . . in his camp.'

'Ne'er spurr'd his Courser at the Trumpets sound:
But who can Rule th' uncertain Chance of War,
In Fine, King *Edward* won the Bloody Field,                    160
Where both your Queen, and Son were made his
Prisoners.

HENRY: 'Yet, hold! for oh! this Prologue lets me in
'To a most fatal Tragedy to come.—[4]
Dy'd he Prisoner, say'st thou? How? By Grief,
Or by the bloody Hands of those, that caught him?

TRESSELL: After the Fight, *Edward* in Triumph ask'd
To see the Captive Prince; the Prince was brought,
Whom *Edward* roughly Chid for bearing Arms,
Asking what Reparation he cou'd make
For having stirr'd his Subjects to Rebellion?                    170
Your Son impatient of such Taunts, reply'd,
'Bow like a Subject, Proud Ambitious *York*!
'While I now speaking with my Father's Mouth,
'Propose the self same Rebel Words to thee,
'Which, Traytor, thou wou'dst have me answer to:[5]
From these, more Words arose, till in the End
King *Edward* swell'd with what th'unhappy Prince
At such a time too freely spoke, his Gauntlet
In his young Face with Indignation struck:
At which Crook'd *Richard*, *Clarence*, and the rest           180
Buried their fatal Daggers in his Heart:
*In Bloody State I saw him on the Earth,*
*From whence with Life he never more sprung up.*[6]

HENRY: 'O had'st thou stabb'd at every Words deliverance,
'Sharp Ponyards in my Flesh, while this was told
'Thy Wounds had giv'n less Anguish than thy Words.—[7]
O Heav'ns! methinks I see my tender Lamb
Gasping beneath the Ravenous Wolves fell gripe!
But say, did all? Did they all strike him, say'st thou?

---

[4] 162–3. Possibly *Henry VI*, Part 2, III.i.151–3: 'But mine is made . . . plotted tragedy.'

[5] 172–5. *Henry VI*, Part 3, V.v.17–21: 'Speak like . . . answer to.'

[6] 182–3. Possibly *Henry IV*, Part 2, I.i.105–7: 'I am sorry . . . bloody state.'

[7] 184–6. *Henry VI*, Part 3, II.i.96–9: 'Great Lord . . . than the wounds.'

TRESSELL: All, sir: But the first Wound Duke *Richard* gave. 190
HENRY: There let him stop! be that his last of Ills!
O barbarous Act; Unhospitable Men!
Against the rigid Laws of Arms to kill him!
Was't not enough, his hope of Birth-right gone,
But must your Hate be levell'd at his Life?
Nor cou'd his Father's Wrongs content you?
Nor cou'd a Father's Grief disswade the Deed?
'You have no Children, (Butchers if you had)
'The thought of them wou'd sure have stirr'd Remorse.[8]
TRESSELL: Take Comfort, Sir; and hope a better Day. 200
HENRY: *O! who can hold a Fire in his Hand,*
*By thinking on the Frosty* Caucasus?*
*Or wallow Naked in* December's *Snow,*
'By bare remembrance of the Summer's Heat?[9]
Away! by Heav'n, I shall abhor his Sight,
Whoever bids me be of Comfort more:
If thou wilt sooth my Sorrows, then I'll thank thee:
Ay! now thou'rt kind indeed! these Tears oblige me.
TRESSELL: Alas, my Lord! I fear more Evils toward you.
HENRY: Why, let it come! I scarce shall feel it now, 210
My present Woes have beat me to the Ground,
And my hard Fate can make me fall no lower:
What can it be? Give it its ugliest Shape,—O my poor
Boy!—
TRESSELL: A word does that; it comes in *Gloucester*'s
Form.
HENRY: Frightful indeed! give me the worst that threatens.
TRESSELL: After the Murther of your Son, stern *Richard*,
As if unsated with the Wounds he had giv'n,
With unwash'd Hands went from his Friends in hast,
And being ask'd by *Clarence* of the Cause,
He low'ring cry'd, Brother, I must to the *Tower*! 220
I've Business there, excuse me to the King,
Before you reach the Town, expect some News:
This said, he vanish'd, and I hear's arriv'd.

[8] 198-9. *Henry VI*, Part 3, V.v.61-2: 'You have no ... stirred up remorse.'
[9] 201-4. *Richard II*, I.iii.201-4: 'O who can ... Summer's heat.'

HENRY: Why, then the Period\* of my Woes is set;
  For Ills but thought by him are half perform'd.
           *Enter* LIEUTENANT *with an Order*
LIEUTENANT: Forgive me, Sir; what I'm compell'd t'obey
  An Order for your close Confinement.
HENRY: Whence comes it, good Lieutenant?
LIEUTENANT: Sir, from the Duke of *Gloucester.*
HENRY: Good Night to all then: I obey it –                    230
  And now good Friend suppose me on my Death-bed,
  And take of me, thy last, short, Living leave:—
  Nay, keep thy Tears till thou hast seen me Dead:
  *And when in tedious Winter Nights, with Good*
  *Old Folks, thou sit'st up late*
  *To hear 'em tell thee Dismal Tales*
  'Of times long past, even now with Woe remember'd;
  *Before thou bidst good night, to quit their Grief,*
  *Tell thou the lamentable fall of me,*
  *And send thy hearers weeping to their Beds.*[10]  [*Exeunt*]


# Scene ii

### *Enter* RICHARD *Duke of* Gloucester. *Solus*


RICHARD: *Now are our Brows bound with Victorious*
      *wreaths,*
  *Our stern allarms are changed to Merry-meetings,*
  *Our dreadfull marches to delightful measures.*
  *Grim visaged War has smoothed his wrinkled Front,*
  *And now instead of mounting Barbed\* Steeds*
  *To fright the Souls of fearful Adversaries*
  *He Capers nimbly in a Ladies Chamber*
  *To the Lascivious Pleasing of a Lute;*
  *But I that am not shaped for sportive tricks,*
  *I that am curtailed of Man's fair proportion,*                    10
  *Deform'd, Unfinish'd, sent before my time*
  *Into this breathing World scarce half made up,*

[10] 234–40. *Richard II*, V.i.40–5: 'In winter's tedious . . . to their beds.'

*And that so lamely and unfashionable*
*That Dogs bark at me as I halt by 'em;*
*Why I, in this weak, this piping time of Peace,* *
*Have no delight to pass away my hours,*
*Unless to see my shadow in the Sun,*
*And descant* on my own deformity:*[11]
*—Then since this Earth affords no joy to me,*
*But to Command, to Check, and to Orebear such,*                    20
*'As are of Happier Person than my self,*
*'Why then to me this restless World's but Hell,*
*Till this mishapen trunks aspiring head*
*'Be circled in a glorious Diadem—*[12]
But then 'tis fixt on such an heighth, O! I
Must stretch the utmost reaching of my Soul.
    I'll climb betimes without Remorse or Dread,
    And my first step shall be on *Henry*'s Head.    [*Exit*]


## Scene iii

*Scene, a Chamber in the* Tower: KING HENRY *sleeping*

### *Enter* LIEUTENANT

LIEUTENANT: Asleep so soon! But sorrow minds no sea-
   sons,
  The Morning, Noon, and Night with her's the same,
  She's fond of any hour that yields Repose.
HENRY: Who's there? Lieutenant! is it you? Come hither.
                           (*Rising*)
LIEUTENANT: You shake, my Lord, and look affrighted.
HENRY: O! I have had the fearfull'st Dream; such sights,
  That, as I live—
  I would not pass another hour so dreadful
  Though 'twere to buy a world of happy days.[13]
  Reach me a Book – I'll try if reading can                    10

[11] 1–18. *Richard III*, I.i.5–17: 'Now are our brows ... my own deformity.'
[12] 19–24. *Henry VI*, Part 3, III.ii.165–71: 'Then since ... glorious diadem.'
[13] 6–9. *Richard III*, I.iv.2–6: 'I have passed ... happy days.'

Divert these melancholy thoughts.

*Enter* RICHARD

RICHARD: *Good day, my Lord; what, at your Book so hard?*

I disturb you.

HENRY: You do indeed—                              (*Sighing*)

RICHARD: Go, Friend, leave us to our selves; we must confer.                              [*Exit* LIEUTENANT]

HENRY: What Bloody Scene has *Roscius** now to Act?

RICHARD: *Suspicion always haunts the guilty mind,*
*The Thief does fear each bush an Officer.*

HENRY: Where Thieves without Controulment rob and kill,
The Traveller does fear each bush a Thief:
*The poor bird that has been already lim'd*                    20
*With trembling Wings misdoubts of every Bush,*
*And I, the hapless Male** to one sweet Bird,*
*Have now the fatal object in my Eye,*
'By whom my young one bled, was caught and kill'd.

RICHARD: *Why, what a peevish Fool was that of* Creet,
*That taught his Son the office of a Fowl?*
*And yet for all his Wings the fool was drown'd:**
Thou should'st have taught thy Boy his Prayers alone,
And then he had not broke his neck with Climbing.*

HENRY: *Ah, kill me with thy weapon, not with words,*          30
*My breast can better brook thy Daggers point,*
'Than can my ears that piercing story.
*But wherefore dost thou come, is't for my life?*

RICHARD: *Thinkest thou I am an Executioner?*

HENRY: *If Murthering Innocents be Executing*
'Then thou'rt the worst of Executioners.

RICHARD: *Thy Son I kill'd for his Presumption.*

HENRY: *Hadst thou been kill'd when first thou didst Presume,*
*Thou hadst not liv'd to kill a Son of mine.*
But thou wert born to Massacre Mankind.                        40
'How many Old Mens sighs, and Widows moans,
'How many Orphans Water standing eyes,
*Men, for their Sons, Wives for their Husbands Fate,*

*And Children, for their Parents timeless death,*
*Will rue the hour that ever thou wert born?*
*The Owl shriek'd at thy Birth: An Evil sign.*
*The night Crow cry'd, foreboding luckless time,*
*Dogs howl'd, and hideous Tempests shook down Trees;*
*The Raven rook'd\* her on the Chimneys top,*
*And chattering Pies\* in dismal discords sung.*          50
*Thy Mother felt more than a Mothers Pain,*
*And yet brought forth less than a Mother's Hope:*
*Teeth hadst thou in thy head when thou wert born,*
*Which plainly said, Thou cam'st to bite Mankind,*
*And, if the rest be true which I have heard,*
*Thou cam'st—*
RICHARD: *I'll hear no more: Dye, Prophet, in thy speech.*
                                      *(Stabs him)*

*For this, amongst the rest was I ordain'd.*
HENRY: *O! and for much more slaughter after this.*
*Just Heaven forgive my sins, and pardon thee.*    *(Dies)*   60
RICHARD: *What, will the aspiring blood of* Lancaster
*Sink in the ground? – I thought it would have mounted.*
*See how my Sword weeps for the poor King's death;*
*—O, may such purple tears be always shed*
*From those that wish the Downfall of our House.*
*If any spark of Life be yet remaining,*
*Down, down to Hell! and say, I sent thee thither.*
*I that have neither Pity, Love nor Fear:*
*Indeed 'tis true, what* Henry *told me of,*
*For I have often heard my Mother say,*                        70
*I came into the World with my Legs forward:*
*The Midwife wonder'd, and the Women cry'd,*
*Good Heaven bless us, he is born with Teeth;*
*And so I was, which plainly signified,*
*That I should snarl and bite, and play the Dog.*
*Then since the Heavens have shap'd my body so,*
*Let Hell make crooked my mind to answer it—*
*I have no Brother, am like no Brother,*
*And this word Love, which Gray beards call Divine,*
*Be resident in Men, like one another,*                        80

*And not in me – I am – my self alone.*
Clarence, *beware, thou keep'st me from the Light,*
*But if I fail not in my deep intent,*[14]
*Thou'st not another day to live, which done,*
*Heaven take the weak King* Edward *to his Mercy,*
*And leave the World for me to bustle in:*
But soft – I'm sharing spoil before the Field is won,[15]
   Clarence still Breaths, *Edward* still Lives and Reigns,
   When they are gone, then I must count my gains.[16]

                              [*Exit*]

---

[14] 12–83. Substantially *Henry VI*, Part 3, V.vi.1–85: 'Good day ... from the light.'
[15] 84–7. *Richard III*, I.i.149–52: 'And if I fail ... bustle in.'
[16] 88–9. *Richard III*, I.i.160–2: 'But yet ... count my gains.'

# ACT II

## Scene i

*The Scene, St* Pauls
*Enter* TRESSELL *meeting Lord* STANLEY

TRESSELL: My Lord, your Servant, pray what brought you
    to *Paul*'s?
STANLEY: I came amongst the Crowd to see the Corps
    Of poor King *Henry*. 'Tis a dismal sight,
    But yesterday I saw him in the Tower;
    His talk is still so fresh within my memory:
    That I could weep to think how Fate has us'd him.
    I wonder where's Duke *Richard*'s policy
    In suffering him to lie exposed to view?
    Can he believe that Men will love him for't?
TRESSELL: O yes, Sir, love him, as he loves his Brothers: 10
    When was you with King *Edward*, pray, my Lord?
    I hear he leaves his Food, is Melancholy,
    And his Physicians fear him* mightily.
STANLEY: 'Tis thought he'll scarce recover:
    Shall we to Court, and hear more News of him?
TRESSELL: I am oblig'd to pay Attendance here,
    The Lady *Ann* has license to remove
    King *Henry*'s Corps to be Interr'd at *Chertsey*,
    And I am engag'd to follow her.
STANLEY: Mean you King *Henry*'s Daughter-in-Law? 20
TRESSELL: The same, Sir, Widow to the late Prince
    *Edward*,
    Whom *Gloucester* kill'd at *Tewkesbury*.
STANLEY: Alas, poor Lady, she's severely used.
    And yet I hear *Richard* attempts her Love:
    Methinks the wrongs he's done her should

discourage him.

TRESSELL: Neither those wrongs nor his own shape can
    fright him;

He sent for leave to visit her this morning,

And she was forc'd to keep her Bed to avoid him.

But see, she is arriv'd: Will you along

To see this doleful Ceremony?

STANLEY: I'll wait on you.                  [*Exeunt*]  30

*Enter* RICHARD *Solus*

RICHARD: 'Twas her excuse t' avoid me – Alas!

She keeps no Bed –

She has health enough to progress far as *Chertsey*,

Tho' not to bear the sight of me;

– I cannot blame her—

*Why Love forswore\* me in my Mothers Womb,*

*And for I should not deal in his soft Laws,*

*He did corrupt frail Nature with some Bribe*

*To shrink my Arm up like a wither'd Shrub,*

*To make an envious\* Mountain on my back,*      40

*Where sits Deformity to mock my Body,*

*To shape my Legs of an unequal size,*

*To disproportion me in every part:*

And am I then a man to be belov'd?[17]

O monstrous Thought! more vain my Ambition.

*Enter* LIEUTENANT *hastily*

LIEUTENANT: My Lord, I beg your Grace—

RICHARD: Be gone, Fellow—I'm not at leisure—

LIEUTENANT: My Lord, the King your Brother's taken ill.

RICHARD: I'll wait on him, leave me, Friend—

[*Exit* LIEUTENANT]

Ha! *Edward* ta'en ill!—                    50

*Wou'd he were wasted, Marrow, Bones and all,*

'That from his loins no more young Brats may rise

'To cross me in the golden time I look for—[18]

*Scene draws and discovers Lady* ANN *in Mourning, Lord*

    STANLEY, TRESSELL, Guards *and* Bearers, *with King*

---

[17] 36–44. *Henry VI, Part 3*, III.ii.153–64: 'Why, Love ... harbour such a thought.'

[18] 51–3. *Henry VI, Part 3*, III.ii.125–7: 'Would he were ... I look for.'

HENRY's *Body*

But see, my Love appears: Look where she shines,
Darting pale Lustre, like the Silver Moon
Through her dark Veil of Rainy sorrow:
So mourn'd the Dame of *Ephesus* her Love,
And thus the Soldier arm'd with Resolution
Told his soft tale, and was a thriving Woer.*
'Tis true, my Form perhaps, will little move her,                    60
But I've a Tongue shall wheadle with the Devil.
Yet hold; She mourns the Man whom I have kill'd:
First, let her sorrows take some vent – Stand here;
I'll take her passion in its wain, and turn
This storm of grief to gentle drops of pity
For his Repentant Murderer.—                    (*He retires*)

ANN: 'Hung be the Heavens with black, yield day to night,
  'Comets importing* change of Times and States,
  'Brandish your fiery Tresses in the Sky,
  'And with 'em scourge the bad revolting Stars                    70
  'That have consented to* King *Henry*'s death:'[19]
  *O be Accurst the Hand that shed this Blood;*
  *Accurst the Head that had the Heart to do it,*
  *More direful hap betide that hated Wretch*
  *Than I can wish to Wolves, to Spiders, Toads,*
  *Or any creeping venom'd thing that lives:*
  *If ever he have Wife, let her be made*
  'More miserable by the Life of him,
  'Than I am now by *Edward*'s death and thine.

RICHARD: Poor Girl! What pains she takes to curse her
    self?                                    (*Aside*)  80

ANN: *If ever he have Child Abortive* be it,*
  *Prodigious and Untimely brought to Light,*
  'Whose hideous Form, whose most unnatural Aspect
  *May fright the hopeful Mother at her view,*
  *And that be Heir to his unhappiness.*
  'Now on, to *Chertsey** with your sacred Load.
        (RICHARD *comes forward*)

RICHARD: *Stay, you that bear the Coarse, and set it down.*

---

[19] 67–71. *Henry VI*, Part 1, I.i.1–5: 'Hung be . . . Henry's death.'

ANN: *What black Magician Conjures up this Fiend*
    *To stop devoted charitable deeds?*

RICHARD: *Villains, set down the Coarse, or, by St* Paul,   90
    *I'll make a Coarse of him that disobeys.*

GUARD: *My Lord, stand back, and let the Coffin pass.*

RICHARD: *'Unmanner'd Slave! Stand thou, when I command:*
    *Advance thy Halbert\* higher than my Breast,*
    *Or, by St* Paul, *I'll strike thee to my foot,*
    *And spurn thee, beggar, for this boldness.*

ANN: Why dost thou haunt him thus, unsated Fiend?
    *Thou hadst but power over his mortal Body,*
    *His Soul thou canst not reach; therefore be gone.*

RICHARD: *Sweet Saint, be not so* hard *for Charity.*   100

ANN: *If thou delight to view thy heinous deeds,*
    *Behold this pattern of thy Butcheries.*
    Why didst thou do this deed? Cou'd not the Laws
    Of Man, of Nature, nor of Heavan disswade thee?
    *No Beast so fierce, but knows some touch of pity.*

RICHARD: If want of pity be a Crime so hateful,
    Whence is it thou, fair Excellence, art guilty?

ANN: What means the slanderer?

RICHARD: *Vouchsafe, Divine Perfection of a Woman,*
    *Of these my Crimes suppos'd to give me leave*   110
    *By Circumstance, but to acquit my self.*

ANN: Then take that Sword, whose bloody point still reeks
    With *Henry*'s Life, with my lov'd Lord's young *Edwards*,
    And here let out thy own t' appease their Ghosts.

RICHARD: *By such despair I shou'd accuse my self.*

ANN: *Why by despairing only canst thou stand excused?*
    *Didst thou not kill this King?*

RICHARD:           *I grant ye.*

ANN: *O! he was Gentle, Loving, Mild and Vertuous:*
    But he's in Heaven, where thou canst never come.

RICHARD: Was I not kind to send him thither then?   120
    *He was much fitter for that place than Earth.*

ANN: *And thou unfit for any place but Hell.*

RICHARD: *Yes, one place else, if you will hear me name it.*

ANN: *Some Dungeon.*

RICHARD:    *Your Bed Chamber.*

ANN: *Ill rest betide the Chamber where thou liest.*

RICHARD: *So it will, Madam, till I lie in yours.*

ANN: *I hope so.*

RICHARD: *I know so. But gentle Lady* Ann,
  'To leave this keen encounter of our Tongues,
  'And fall to something a more serious method.    130
  *Is not the causer of th' untimely deaths*
  *Of these* Plantagenets, Henry *and* Edward,
  *As blameful as the Executioner?*

ANN: *Thou wert the cause, and most accurst effect.*

RICHARD: *Your Beauty was the cause of that effect:*
  *Your Beauty that did haunt me in my sleep,*
  *To undertake the Death of all the World,*
  *So I might live one hour in that soft Bosom.*

ANN: *If I thought that, I tell thee, Homicide,*
  'These Hands shou'd rend that Beauty from my Cheeks. 140

RICHARD: *These Eyes cou'd not endure that Beauties rack,*
  *You shou'd not blemish it, if I stood by.*
  'As all the World is nourish'd by the Sun,
  *So I by that: It is my Day, my Life.*

ANN: *I wou'd it were to be reveng'd on thee.*

RICHARD: *It is a Quarrel most Unnatural*
  *To wish revenge on him that loves thee.*

ANN: Say rather 'tis my duty,
  'To seek revenge on him that kill'd my Husband.

RICHARD: Fair Creature, he that kill'd thy Husband    150
  'Did it to – help thee to a better Husband.

ANN: *His better does not breath upon the Earth.*

RICHARD: *He lives that lov'd thee better, than he could.*

ANN: *Name him.*

RICHARD:      *Plantagenet.*

ANN:             *Why, that was he.*

RICHARD: *The self same Name, but one of softer Nature.*

ANN: *Where is he?*

RICHARD: Ah! take more pity in thy Eyes, and see him –
  here.

ANN: *Wou'd they were Basilisks\* to strike thee dead.*

RICHARD: *I wou'd they were, that I might die at once,*
   *For now they kill me with a living death,*        160
   Darting with cruel aim Despair and Love;
   *I never sued to Friend or Enemy,*
   *My Tongue could never learn sweet smoothing Words,*
   *But now thy Beauty is propos'd my Fee\**
   *My proud Heart sues, and prompts my Tongue to speak.*

ANN: Is there a Tongue on Earth can speak for thee?
   Why dost thou Court my hate?

TRESSELL: Where will this end? she frowns upon
    him yet.
STANLEY: But yet she hears him in her frowns; I    }   (*Aside*)
    fear him.

RICHARD: 'O! teach not thy soft lip such cold contempt— 170
   *If thy Relentless Heart cannot forgive,*
   *Lo, here I lend thee this sharp pointed Sword,*
   *Which if thou please to hide in this true Breast,*
   *And let the honest Soul out, that adores thee,*
   *I lay it naked to the deadly stroke,*
   *And humbly beg that Death upon my knee.*

ANN: What shall I say or do? Direct me Heaven;
   When stones weep sure the tears are natural,   }
   And Heaven it self instructs us to forgive,        (*Aside*)
   When they do flow from a sincere Repentance.  }   180

RICHARD: *Nay, do not pause: For I did kill King* Henry,
   *But 'twas thy wondrous Beauty did provoke me;*
   *Nay now dispatch: 'Twas I that stab'd young* Edward,
   *But 'twas thy Heavenly face that set me on,*
   *And I might still persist (so stubborn is*
   *My Temper) to rejoice at what I've done,*
   *But that thy powerful Eyes (as roaring Seas*
   *Obey the changes of the Moon) have turn'd*
   *My Heart, and made it flow with Penitence.*
                        (*She lets fall the Sword*)
   *Take up the Sword agen, or take up me.*      190

ANN: *No, tho' I wish thy Death,*
   *I will not be thy Executioner.*

RICHARD: *Then bid me kill my self, and I will do it.*

ANN: *I have already.*

RICHARD: *That was in thy rage:*
  *Say it again, and even with thy word*
  'This guilty hand that rob'd thee of thy Love
  'Shall for thy Love revenge thee on thy Lover;
  *To both their deaths shalt thou be Accessary.*

TRESSELL: By Heaven she wants the heart to
  bid him do't.

STANLEY: What think you now, Sir?                    200

TRESSELL: I'm struck! I scarce can credit what
  I see.

STANLEY: Why, you see – A Woman.                    *(Aside)*

TRESSELL: When future Chronicles shall speak
  of this
  They will be thought Romance, not History.

RICHARD: What, not a word to pardon or condemn me?
  But thou art wise – and canst with silence kill me;
  Yet even in death my fleeting Soul pursues thee:
  Dash not the tears of Penitence away.
  I ask but leave t' indulge my cold despair:
  By Heaven, there's Joy in this extravagance                    210
  Of Woe; 'tis Melting, Soft, 'tis pleasing Ruin.
  Oh! 'tis too much, too much for Life to bear
  This aching tenderness of thought.

ANN: *Wou'dst thou not blame me to forgive thy Crimes?*

RICHARD: They are not to be forgiven: No, not even
  Penitence can atone 'em. O misery
  Of Thought! that strikes me with at once Repentance
  And Despair; tho' unpardon'd, yield me pity.

ANN: *Wou'd I knew thy heart.*

RICHARD: *'Tis figur'd in my Tongue.*                    220

ANN: *I fear me both are false.*

RICHARD: *Then never Man was true.*

ANN: *Put up thy Sword.*

RICHARD: *Say then, my Peace is made.*

ANN: *That shalt thou know hereafter.*

RICHARD: *But shall I live in hope?*

ANN: *All Men, I hope, live so.*

RICHARD: I swear, bright Saint, I am not what I was:
Those Eyes have turn'd my stubborn heart to Woman,
Thy goodness makes me soft in Penitence,                          230
And my harsh thoughts are tun'd to Peace and Love.
*O! if thy poor devoted Servant might*
*But beg one favour at thy gracious hand,*
*Thou wouldst confirm his Happiness for ever.*

ANN: *What is it?*

RICHARD: *That it may please thee, leave these sad designs*
*To him that has most cause to be a Mourner,*
*And presently repair to* Crosby House,*
*Where, after I have solemnly Interr'd*
*At Chertsey Monastery, this Injur'd King,*                        240
*And wet his Grave with my repentant Tears,*
*I will with all expedient duty see you:*
*For divers unknown reasons I beseech you*
'Grant me this favour.

ANN: *I do my Lord, and much it joys me too*
*To see you are become so Penitent.*
Tressel *and* Berkley *go along with me.*

RICHARD: *Bid me Farewell.*

ANN: *'Tis more than you deserve;*
*But since you teach me how to flatter you,*
*Imagine I have said Farewell already.*                            250

              [*Exit with* TRESSELL *and* BERKLEY]

GUARD: *Towards* Chertsey, *my Lord?*

RICHARD: No, to White-Fryars,* there attend my coming.

              [*Exeunt Guards with the Body*]

           (RICHARD *Solus*)

RICHARD: (*smiling*) *Was ever Woman in this humour*
    *wooed?*
*Was ever Woman in this humour won?*
*I'll have her: But I will not keep her long.*
*What! I that kill'd her Husband and his Father,*
*To take her in her Hearts extreamest hate,*
*With Curses in her mouth, Tears in her Eyes,*
*The bleeding witness of my hatred by,*

Having Heaven, her Conscience, and these Bars against
    me,                                                                          260
And I no Friends to back my suit withal,
But the plain Devil, and dissembling looks?
And yet to win her! All the world to nothing.
Can she abase her Beauteous eyes on me?
Whose all not equals Edward's moiety?
On me! that halt and am mishapen Thus!
'My Dukedom to a Widows Chastity
I do mistake my Person all this while!
Upon my life! she finds, altho I cannot,
My self to be a marvellous proper Man,                                          270
'I'll have my Chambers lin'd with Looking-glass
And entertain a score or two of Taylors
To study fashions to adorn my body.
Since I am crept in favour with my self,
I will maintain it with some little cost.
'But first, I'll turn St Harry to his grave,
And then return lamenting to my Love.
'Shine out fair Sun till I salute my Glass,
That I may see my shadow as I pass.[20]                          [Exit]


## Scene ii

*Scene, the Presence: Enter the Duke of* BUCKINGHAM
*hastily, Lord* STANLEY *meeting him*


BUCKINGHAM: Did you see the Duke?
STANLEY:                                               What Duke my
    Lord?
BUCKINGHAM: His Grace of *Gloucester*, did you see him?
STANLEY: Not lately, my Lord – I hope no ill news.
BUCKINGHAM: The worst that heart e're bore, or tongue
    can utter.
*Edward* the King! his Royal Brother's Dead.

[20] 72-279. Substantially *Richard III*, I.ii.14-268, with cuts and additions. The inter-
ventions of Tressell and Stanley are Cibber's inventions.

STANLEY: 'Tis sad indeed—I wish by your impatience
  To acquaint him tho you think it so to him.      (*Aside*)
  Did the King, my Lord, make any mention
  Of a Protector for his Crown and Children?
BUCKINGHAM: He did, Duke *Richard* has the care of both.      10
STANLEY: That sad news you are afraid to tell him too.
                                              (*Aside*)
BUCKINGHAM: He'll spare no toile, I'm sure to fill his
  Place!
STANLEY: Pray Heav'n he's not too diligent!      (*Aside*)
  My Lord, is not that the Dutchess of *York*,
  The King's Mother? coming I fear to visit him.
BUCKINGHAM: 'Tis she! little thinking what has befallen
  us.
            *Enter* DUTCHESS OF YORK
DUTCHESS OF YORK: Good day, my Lords! How takes the
  King his Rest.
BUCKINGHAM: Alas! Madam, too well! he sleeps for ever.
DUTCHESS OF YORK: Dead! – Good Heav'n support me!
BUCKINGHAM: Madam, 'twas my unhappy lot to hear      20
  His last Departing Groans, and close his eyes.
DUTCHESS OF YORK: Another taken from me too! why
  just Heav'n
  Am I still left the last in life and woe?
  'First I bemoan'd a noble Husbands death,
  'Yet liv'd with looking on his Images.*
  'But now my last support is gone, First *Clarence*,[21]
  Now *Edward* is forever taken from me.
  Both Crutches now the unrelenting hand
  Of Death has striken from my feeble Arms
  And I must now of force sink down with sorrow.      30
BUCKINGHAM: Your youngest Son, the Noble *Richard*
  lives.
  His love I know will feel his Mothers Cares,
  And bring new comfort to your latter days.
DUTCHESS OF YORK: 'Twere new indeed! for yet of him
  I've none,

---

[21] 24–6. *Richard III*, II.ii.49–50: 'I have bewept . . . his images.'

Unless a churlish disobedience may
Be counted from a Child a Mothers Comfort:
'From his malicious grudge I know my Son,
'His brother *Clarence* death was first contriv'd,[22]
But may his Penitence find Heav'n's mercy.
Where is the Queen, my Lord?                                    40

BUCKINGHAM: I left her with her kinsmen deep in Sorrow,
Who have with much adoe perswaded her
To leave the Body – Madam they are here.
*Enter the* QUEEN *attended with* RIVERS *and* DORSET,
*and others*

QUEEN: Why do you thus oppose my grief, unless
To make me Rave, and Weep the faster? Ha!
My Mother too in Tears! Fresh Sorrow strikes
My heart, at sight of every Friend, that lov'd
My *Edward* living – O Mother!* He's Dead!
*Edward*, my Lord, thy Son, our King is Dead.
O that my eyes cou'd weep away my Soul!                         50
Then I might follow worthy of his Hearse.

STANLEY: Your Duty, Madam, of a Wife is Dead,
And now the Mother's only claims your care.
Think on the Prince your Son: send for him strait,
And let his Coronation clear your eyes.
Bury your griefs in the dead *Edward*'s Grave,
Revive your Joys on living *Edward*'s Throne.

QUEEN: Alas! That thought, but adds to my Afflictions.
New Tears for *Edward* gone, and fears for *Edward* living,
'An helpless Child, and his Minority*                           60
'Is in the Trust of his stern Uncle *Gloucester*,[23]
A man that frowns on me, and all of mine.      (*Weeps*)

BUCKINGHAM: Judge not so hardly, Madam, of his love,
Your Son will find in him a Father's Care.
*Enter* RICHARD *behind*

RICHARD: Why ay! – These tears look well! sorrow's the
mode,
And every one at Court must wear it now –

---

[22] 37-8. Possibly *Richard III*, II.ii.29-30: 'He is my son … deceit.'
[23] 60-1. *Richard III*, I.iii.11-12: 'Ah, he is young … Richard Gloucester.'

With all my heart, I'll not be out of Fashion.     (*Aside*)

QUEEN: My Lord, just Heav'n knows I never hated
    *Richard*,

But wou'd on any terms embrace his friendship.

BUCKINGHAM: These words would make him weep, – I
    know him yours.                                                                  70

See where he comes in sorrow for our loss.

RICHARD: My Lords, – good morrow – Cousin of *Bucking-
    ham*,

I am yours—                                                   (*Weeping*)

BUCKINGHAM: Good-morning to your Grace.

RICHARD: Methinks—

We meet, like men, that had forgot to speak.

BUCKINGHAM: We may remember: But our argument
Is now too mournful to admit much talk.[24]

RICHARD: It is indeed! Peace be with him has made it so.
'Sister! Take Comfort – Tis true we've all cause
'To mourn the dimming of our shining Star:[25]                     80
But sorrow never cou'd revive the dead –
– And if it cou'd, hope wou'd prevent our fears,
So we must weep, because we weep in vain.
'Madam, my Mother – I do cry you mercy:
'My grief was blind – I did not see your Grace,
*Most humbly on my knee I crave your Blessing.*

DUTCHESS OF YORK: Thou hast it, and may thy charitable
Heart, and Tongue love one another, may Heaven
Indow thy breast with meekness, and obedience.

RICHARD: *Amen, and make me die a good old man,*                    90
*That's the old Butt-end of a Mother's Blessing;*
*I marvel that her Grace did leave it out.*[26]     (*Aside*)

BUCKINGHAM: *My Lords, I think 'twere fit, that now*
    *Prince Edward*
*Forthwith from* Ludlow *shou'd be sent for home,*
*In order to his Coronation.*[27]

---

[24] 75–7. *Henry IV*, Part 2, V.ii.23–5: 'we meet . . . admit such talk.'
[25] 79–80. *Richard III*, II.ii.101–2: 'Sister, have comfort . . . shining star.'
[26] 85–92. *Richard III*, II.ii.104–11: 'Madam my mother . . . leave it out.'
[27] 93–5. *Richard III*, II.ii.120–2: 'Meseemeth good . . . crown'd our King.'

RICHARD: By all means, my Lords, come let's in to
    Counsel,
And appoint who shall be the messengers.
*Madam, and you my Sister, please you go*
'To give your sentiments on this occasion?[28]

QUEEN: My Lord, your Wisdom needs no help from me,  100
My glad consent you have in all that's just:
Or for the peoples good, tho I suffer by't.

RICHARD: Please you to retire, Madam, we shall propose
What you'd not think the peoples wrong, nor yours.

QUEEN: May Heav'n prosper all your good intent.

    [*Exit with all but* BUCKINGHAM *and* RICHARD]

RICHARD: Amen, with all my Heart. For mine's the
    Crown.
And is not that a good one? ha! Pray'd she not well,
    Cousin?

BUCKINGHAM: I hope she prophesied – You now stand
    Fair.

RICHARD: Now by St *Paul*, I feel it here! Methinks
The massy weight on't galls my laden Brow.  110
What think'st thou, Cousin, wer't not an easie matter
To get Lord *Stanley*'s hand to help it on.

BUCKINGHAM: 'My Lord, I doubt that for his Fathers sake,
'He loves the Prince to well, he'll scarce be won
'To any thing against him.[29]

RICHARD: Poverty the reward of Honest Fools
O'retake him for't! what thinkst thou then of *Hastings*?

RICHARD: He shall be tri'd my Lord: I'll find out *Catesby*,
Who shall at subtle distance sound his thoughts,
But we must still suppose the worst may happen,  120
What if we find him cold in our design?

RICHARD: *Chop of his head.—Something we'll soon deter-*
    *mine.*

[28] 98–9. *Richard III*, II.ii.143–4: 'Madam . . . business.'
[29] 113–15. *Richard III*, III.i.165–6: 'He for his father's . . . against him.'

But haste, and find out *Catesby*,[30]
That done, follow me to the Counsel Chamber;
We'll not be seen together much, nor have
It known that we confer in Private – Therefore
Away good Cousin.

BUCKINGHAM:           I am gone, My Lord.

                                    [*Exit* BUCKINGHAM]

RICHARD: Thus far we run before the wind;
My Fortune smiles, and gives me all that I dare ask.
The conquer'd Lady *Ann* is bound in vows,                    130
Fast as the priest can make us, we are one.
The King my Brother, sleeps without his Pillow,
And I am left the Guardian of his Infant Heir.
Let me see—
The Prince will soon be here – let him – the Crown!
O yes! he shall have twenty, Globes, and Scepters too,
New ones made to play withall – But no Coronation!
No! nor no Court flies about him, no Kinsmen –
– Hold ye! – Where shall he keep his Court!
– Ay! – the *Tower*.                                        [*Exit*]

[30] 122. *Richard III*, III.i.193: 'Chop off ... will we do.' Cibber's line here follows the
Folio reading. It became one of Richard's best-known 'points', or moments for which an
audience especially looked out. The Quarto version is 'Chop off his head,
man; somewhat will we do.'

# ACT III

## Scene i

*Enter Prince* EDWARD, *with the Dukes of* GLOUCESTER,
BUCKINGHAM, *Lord* STANLEY, TRESSELL, *and Attendants*

RICHARD: 'Now, my Royal Cousin, welcome to *London*,
'Welcome to all those honour'd Dignities
'Which by your Father's Will, and by your Birth,
'You stand the undoubted Heir Possess'd of;[31]
And, if my plain simplicity of Heart
May take the liberty to shew it self,
You're farther welcome to your Uncles Care
And Love: Why do you sigh, my Lord?
*The weary way has made you melancholy.*

PRINCE EDWARD: *No, Uncle, but our crosses\* on the way*    10
*Have made it Tedious, Wearisome and Heavy,*
*I want more Uncles here to welcome me.*[32]

TRESSELL: More Uncles! What means his Highness?

STANLEY: Why Sir, the careful Duke of *Gloucester*
    has
Secur'd his Kinsmen on the way: Lord *Rivers*,
    *Gray*,
Sir *Thomas Vaughan*, and others of his Friends,    (Aside)
Are Prisoners now in *Pomfret* Castle;
On what pretence it boots not: There they are;
Let the Devil and the Duke alone to accuse 'em.

RICHARD: *My Lord, the Mayor of* London *comes to greet
    you.*[33]    20

*Enter* LORD MAYOR, *and Citizens*

---

[31] 1–4. Possibly an expanded version of *Richard III*, III.i.1.
[32] 9–12. *Richard III*, III.i.3–6: 'The weary way . . . welcome me.'
[33] 20. *Richard III*, III.i.17: 'My Lord . . . greet you.'

LORD MAYOR: Vouchsafe, most Gracious Sovereign to accept

The general Homage of your Loyal City;
We farther beg your Royal leave to speak
In deep Condolement of your Father's loss:
And, far as our true sorrow will permit
To gratulate* your Accession to the Throne.

PRINCE EDWARD: *I thank you, good my Lord, and thank you all.*

Alas, my youth is yet unfit to govern,[34]
Therefore the Sword of Justice is in abler hands:
But be assur'd of this, so much already                              30
I perceive I love you, that tho' I know not yet
To do you offices of good, yet this I know,
I'll sooner die, than basely do you wrong.

RICHARD: *So wise, so young, they say do never live long.*[35]
                                                      (*Aside*)

PRINCE EDWARD: *My Lords,*
*I thought my Mother and my Brother York*
*Wou'd long e're this have met us on the way:*[36]
*Say, Uncle Gloucester, if our Brother come,*
*Where shall we sojourn till our Coronation?*

RICHARD: *Where it shall seem best to your Royal self,*       40
*May I advise you, Sir, some day or two*
*Your Highness shall repose you at the* Tower,*
*Then where you please, and shall be thought most fit*
*For your best Health and Recreation.*[37]

PRINCE EDWARD: Why at the *Tower?* But be it as you please.

BUCKINGHAM: My Lord, your Brother's Grace of *York.*
              *Enter* DUKE *and* DUTCHESS OF YORK

PRINCE EDWARD: Richard *of* York! *How fares our dearest Brother?*                                          (*Embracing*)

DUKE OF YORK: 'O! my dear Lord! So I must call you now.

PRINCE EDWARD: *I, Brother, to our grief, as it is yours:*

---

[34]  28. *Richard III*, III.i.19: 'I thank you ... thank you all.'
[35]  34. *Richard III*, III.i.79: 'So wise ... live long.'
[36]  36–7. *Richard III*, III.i.20–1: 'I thought ... the way.'
[37]  38–44. *Richard III*, III.i.61–7: 'Say, Uncle ... recreation.'

'Too soon he dy'd who might have better worn                     50
'That Title, which in me will loose its Majesty.

RICHARD: *How fares our Cousin, Noble Lord of* York?

DUKE OF YORK: *Thank you kindly, dear Uncle. O my Lord,*
*You said that Idle Weeds were fast in growth,*
*The King my Brother has out grown me far.*

RICHARD: *He has my Lord.*

DUKE OF YORK:          *And therefore is he Idle?*

RICHARD: O *pretty Cousin, I must not say so.*[38]

DUKE OF YORK: Nay, Uncle, I don't believe the sayings true,
For if it were, you'd be an Idle Weed.

RICHARD: *How so, Cousin?*                     60

DUKE OF YORK: *Because I've heard Folks say you grew so fast*
*Your Teeth wou'd gnaw a Crust at two hours old,*
*Now 'twas two years e'er I cou'd get a Tooth.*[39]

RICHARD: Indeed – I find the Brat is taught this lesson.

                                                (*Aside*)

Who told thee this, my pretty merry Cousin?

DUKE OF YORK: *Why, your Nurse, Uncle.*[40]

RICHARD: *My Nurse, Child, she was dead before thou wert born.*

DUKE OF YORK: *If 'twas not she, I can't tell who told me.*

RICHARD: *So subtle too; 'tis pity thou art short liv'd.*

                                                (*Aside*)

PRINCE EDWARD: *My Brother, Uncle, will be cross\* in talk.*                     70

RICHARD: O, *fear not, my Lord, we shall never Quarrel.*

PRINCE EDWARD: *I hope your Grace knows how to bear with him?*

DUKE OF YORK: *You mean to bear me; not to bear With me,*
*Uncle, my Brother mocks both you and me,*

---

[38] 47–57. *Richard III*, III.i.96–106: 'Richard . . . say so.'
[39] 60–3. *Richard III*, III.iv.26–9: 'How, my young . . . get a tooth.'
[40] 65–9. *Richard III*, II.iv.31–5: 'I prithee . . . too shrewd.'

*Because that I am little, like an Ape,*
*He thinks that you should bear me on your shoulders.*
PRINCE EDWARD: *Fie, Brother, I have no such meaning.*
STANLEY: *With what a sharp, provided\* Wit he*
   *reasons,*
*To mitigate the scorn he gives his Uncle:* } (Aside)
*He prettily and aptly taunts himself.*
TRESSELL: *So cunning, and so young, is wonderful.* }                80
RICHARD: *My Lord, wilt please you pass along?*
*My self, and my good Cousin* Buckingham
*Will to your Mother to entreat of her*
*To meet and bid you welcome at the* Tower.
DUKE OF YORK: *What! will you go to the* Tower, *my dear*
   *Lord?*
PRINCE EDWARD: *My Lord Protector will have it so.*
DUKE OF YORK: *I sha'n't sleep in quiet at the* Tower.
RICHARD: I'll warrant you. King *Henry* lay there,
And he sleeps in quiet.                    (Aside)  90
PRINCE EDWARD: *What shou'd you fear, Brother?*
DUKE OF YORK: *My Uncle* Clarence *Ghost, my Lord.*
*My Grandmother told me he was kill'd there.*
PRINCE EDWARD: *I fear no Uncles dead.*
RICHARD: 'Nor any, Sir, that live, I hope.
PRINCE EDWARD: 'I hope so too. But come, my Lords,
'To the *Tower*, since it must be so.
      [*Exeunt all but* RICHARD *and* BUCKINGHAM]
BUCKINGHAM: *Think you, my Lord, this little prating*
   York
*Was not instructed by his subtle Mother*
*To taunt and scorn you thus Opprobriously?\**               100
RICHARD: 'No doubt, no doubt. O! 'tis a shrewd young
   Master:
*Stubborn, Bold, Quick, Forward and Capable;*
*He is all the Mothers from the Top to the Toe.*
*But let them rest: now what says* Catesby? [41]
BUCKINGHAM: My Lord, 'tis much as I suspected, and
   He's here himself to inform you.

[41] 70, 72–104. *Richard III*, III.i.126–56: 'My lord of York ... let them rest.'

*Enter* CATESBY

RICHARD: So, *Catesby*, hast thou been tampering? What News?

CATESBY: My Lord, according to the instruction given me,
With words at distance dropt I sounded *Hastings*,
Piercing how far he did affect your purpose,                110
To which indeed I found him Cold, Unwilling.
The sum is this, he seem'd a while to understand me not.
At length from plainer speaking urg'd to answer,
He said in heat, rather than wrong the Head
To whom the Crown was due, he'd lose his own.

RICHARD: Indeed, his own then answer for that saying,
He shall be taken care of: Mean while *Catesby*,
Be thou near me: *Cousin of* Buckingham
*Lets lose no time: The Mayor and Citizens*
*Are now buisie meeting in Guild-Hall,**                    120
'Thither I'd have you haste immediately,
'And at your meetest 'vantage of the time
'Improve those Hints I gave you late to speak of:
*But above all, infer the Bastardy*
*Of Edward's Children;*
*Nay, for a need, thus far come near my Person,*
*Tell 'em, when my Mother went with Child of him,*
*My Princely Father then had Wars in* France,
*And by true Computation of the time*
*Found, that the issue was not his begot,*                 130
*Which in his lineaments too plain appear'd,*
*Being nothing like the Noble* York *my Father:*
*Yet touch this sparingly, as 'twere far of,*
*Because, my Lord, you know my Mother lives.*

BUCKINGHAM: 'Doubt not, my Lord, I'll play the Orator
'As if my self might wear the Golden Fee,
'For which I Plead.

RICHARD: *If you thrive well, bring 'em to see me here,*
'Where you shall find me seriously employ'd
'With the most Learned Fathers of the Church.[42]          140

BUCKINGHAM: I fly, my Lord, to serve you.

---

[42] 118–40. *Richard III*, III.v.71–99: 'Go after ... well-learned bishops.'

RICHARD: To serve thy self, my Cousin;
 *For look, when I am King, claim thou of me*
 *The Earldom of Hereford, and all those Moveables,*\*
 *Whereof the King my Brother stood possest.*[43]

BUCKINGHAM: *I shall remember that your Grace was*
 *Bountiful.*

RICHARD: Cousin, I have said it.

BUCKINGHAM: I am gone, my Lord.

         *[Exit* BUCKINGHAM]

RICHARD: So – I've secur'd my Cousin here: These Move-
 ables
 Will never let his Brains have rest till I am King:  150
 Catesby, *go thou with speed to Doctor* Shaw, *and thence*
 'To Fryar *Beuker*: Haste, and bid 'em both
 'Attend me here, within an hour at Farthest:[44]

           *[Exit* CATESBY]

 Mean while my private orders shall be given
 To lock out all admittance to the Princes.
 Now, by St *Paul*, the work goes bravely on—
 How many frightful stops wou'd Conscience make
 In some soft heads to undertake like me:
 – Come; this Conscience is a convenient Scarecrow,
 It Guards the fruit which Priests and Wisemen tast,  160
 Who never set it up to fright themselves:
 They know 'tis rags, and gather in the face on't,
 While half-starv'd shallow Daws\* thro Fear are honest.
 Why were Laws made, but that we're Rogues by Nature?
 Conscience! 'tis our Coin, we live by parting with it,
 And he thrives best that has the most to spare:
 The protesting Lover buys hope with it,
 And the deluded Virgin short liv'd pleasure.
 Old gray beards cram their Avarice with it,
 Your Lank-jaw'd hungry Judge will dine upon't,  170
 And hang the Guiltless rather than eat his Mutton cold.
 The Crown'd Head quits it for Despotick sway,
 The stubborn People for unaw'd Rebellion:

---

[43] 142–5. *Richard III*, III.i.194–7: 'And look . . . your Grace's hand.'
[44] 151–3. *Richard III*, III.v.102–4: 'Go, Lovell . . . Bayard's Castle.'

There's not a Slave but has his share of Villain;
Why then shall after Ages think my deeds
Inhumane? Since my worst are but Ambition:
   Ev'n all Mankind to some lov'd Ills incline,
   Great Men chuse Greater Sins – Ambition's mine.  [*Exit*]


## Scene ii

*Enter Lady* ANN, *Sola*

ANN: When, when shall I have rest? Was Marriage made
   To be the Scourge of our Offences here?
   Oh no! 'Twas meant a Blessing to the Vertuous,
   It once was so to me, tho' now my Curse:
   The fruit of *Edward*'s Love was sweet and pleasing:
   But oh! Untimely cropt by cruel *Richard*,
   Who rudely having grafted on his stock
   Now makes my Life yield only sorrow.
   Let me have Musick to compose my thoughts.

           (*Soft Musick*)

   It will not be: Nought but the grave can close my Eyes.  10
   —How many labouring Wretches take their rest,
   While I, night after night, with cares lie waking,
   As if the gentle Nurse of Nature, Sleep,
   Had vow'd to rock my peevish* sense no more.
   'O partial sleep! Canst thou in smoaky Cottages
   'Stretch out the Peasants Limbs on Beds of Straw,
   'And lay him fast, cram'd with distressful* Bread?
   Yet in the softest breeze of Peaceful Night
   'Under the Canopies of costly State,
   'Tho' lull'd with sounds of sweetest melody,       20
   Refuse one moments slumber to a Princess?
   O mockery of Greatness! But see,[45]
   He comes! The rude disturber of my Pillow.
         *Enter* RICHARD, *Aloof*

---

[45] 11–22. A version of *Henry IV*, Part 2, III.i.4–17: 'How many thousand ...
common 'larum bell.'

RICHARD: Ha! still in tears; let 'em flow on;
  they're signs
  Of a substantial grief – Why don't she die?
  She must: My Interest will not let her live.
  The fair *Elizabeth* hath caught my Eye,
  My Heart's vacant; and she shall fill her place –    (*Aside*)
  They say that Women have but tender hearts,
  'Tis a mistake, I doubt; I've found 'em tough:    30
  They'll bend, indeed: But he must strain that
    cracks 'em.
  All I can hope's to throw her into sickness:
  Then I may send her a Physicians help.
  So, Madam: What, you still take care, I see
  To let the World believe I love you not,
  This outward Mourning now has malice in't,
  So have these sullen disobedient tears:
  I'll have you tell the World I doat on you.

ANN: I wish I could, but 'twill not be believ'd:
  Have I deserv'd this usage?    40

RICHARD: You have: You do not please me as at first.

ANN: What have I done? What horrid Crime committed?

RICHARD: To me the worst of Crimes, out-liv'd my liking.

ANN: If that be Criminal, Just Heaven be kind,
  And take me while my Penitence is warm:
  O Sir, forgive, and kill me.

RICHARD: Umh! No,—The medling World will call it
  murder,
  And I wou'd have 'em think me pitifull:
  Now wert thou not afraid of self-Destruction,
  Thou hast a fair excuse for't.    50

ANN: How fain wou'd I be Friends with Death? O name it.

RICHARD: Thy Husband's hate: Nor do I hate thee only
  From the dull'd edge of sated Appetite
  But from the eager Love I bear another:
  Some call me Hypocrite: What think'st thou now,
  Do I dissemble?

ANN: Thy Vows of Love to me were all dissembled.

RICHARD: Not one: For when I told thee so, I lov'd:

Thou art the only Soul I never yet deceiv'd:
And 'tis my honesty that tells thee now                    60
With all my heart, I hate thee –
If this have no Effect, she is immortal.          (*Aside*)

ANN: Forgive me Heaven, that I forgave this Man.
O may my story told in after Ages,
Give warning to our easie Sexes ears:
May it Unveil the hearts of Men, and strike
Them deaf to their dissimulated Love.

*Enter* CATESBY

CATESBY: My Lord, his Grace of *Buckingham* attends
Your Highness Pleasure.

RICHARD: Wait on him; I'll expect him here.          70

[*Exit* CATESBY]

Your Absence, Madam, will be necessary.

ANN: Wou'd my death were so.          [*Exit*]

RICHARD:                    It may be shortly.

*Enter* BUCKINGHAM

*So, my Cousin, What say the Citizens?*

BUCKINGHAM: 'Now, by our hopes, my Lord, they're
senseless stones,
'Their hesitating fear has struck 'em dumb.

RICHARD: *Touch'd you the Bastardy of* Edward's
*Children?*

BUCKINGHAM: *I did, with his Contract to Lady* Lucy.
*Nay, his own Bastardy and Tyranny for Trifles;*
*—Laid open all your Victories in* Scotland,
*Your Discipline in War, Wisdom in Peace:*          80
*Your Bounty, Justice, fair Humility.*
*Indeed left nothing that might gild our Cause*
*Untouch'd, or slightly handled in my talk,*
*And when my Oration drew towards an end,*
*I urg'd of them that lov'd their Countries good*
*To do you right, and cry, Long live King* Richard.

RICHARD: *And did they so?*

BUCKINGHAM: 'Not one, by Heaven: But each like Statues
fix'd
'Speechless and Pale, star'd in his fellows Face,
*Which when I saw, I reprehended them,*          90

*And ask'd the Mayor what meant this wilfull silence?*
*His answer was, the people were not us'd*
*To be spoken to but by the Recorder,*
'Who then took on him to repeat my words.
*Thus saith the Duke, thus hath the Duke inferr'd:*
*But nothing urg'd in Warrant from himself.*
*When he had done, some Followers of my own*
*At lower end of th' Hall, hurl'd up their Caps,*
*And some ten voices cry'd, God save King* Richard,
*At which I took the 'vantage of those few,*                    100
*And cry'd, Thanks gentle Citizens and Friends,*
*This general applause and chearful shout*
*Argues your Wisdom, and your Love to* Richard,
*And even here broke of, and came away.*
RICHARD: O *Tongueless Blocks! Wou'd they not speak?*
*Will not the Mayor then and his Brethren come?*
BUCKINGHAM: *The Mayor is here at hand: Feign you some*
    *fear,*
*And be not spoke with, but by mighty suit:*
'A *Prayer-Book in your hand, my Lord, were well,*
*Standing between two Churchmen of Repute,*                     110
*For on that ground I'll make an holy descant:*
*Yet be not easily won to our Requests,*
'Seem, like the Virgin, fearful of your wishes.
RICHARD: 'My other self! My Counsel's Consistory![46]
'My Oracle! my Prophet! My dear Cousin!        (*Embracing*)
'I, as a Child, will go by thy direction.[47]
BUCKINGHAM: Hark! the Lord Mayor's at hand: Away,
    my Lord;
No doubt, but yet we reach our point propos'd.
RICHARD: We cannot fail, my Lord, while you are Pilot.
A little flattery sometimes does well.              (*Aside*) 120
                                        [*Exit* RICHARD]
          Enter LORD MAYOR *and Citizens*
BUCKINGHAM: *Welcome, my Lord, I dance attendance*
    *here;*

[46] 73–114. *Richard III*, III.vii.1–51: 'How now ... and take it', with some changes.
[47] 114–16. *Richard III*, II.ii.151–4: 'My other self ... by thy direction.'

*I'm afraid the Duke will not be spoke withal.*
                    *Enter* CATESBY
*Now,* Catesby, *what says your Lord to my request?*
CATESBY: My Lord, he humbly does entreat your Grace
To visit him to morrow, or next day.
He's now retir'd with two Right Reverend Fathers
Divinely bent to Meditation,
And in no worldly suits wou'd be he mov'd,
To interrupt his Holy Exercise.
BUCKINGHAM: *Return, good* Catesby, *to the gracious
    Duke;*                                              130
*Tell him, my Self, the Mayor, and Citizens,*
*In deep designs, in matters of great moment,*
*No less importing than our general good,*
*Are come to have some Conference with his Grace.*
CATESBY: My Lord, I'll instantly inform his Highness.
BUCKINGHAM: *Ah! my good Lord! This Prince is not an
    Edward,*
*He is not lolling on a lewd Love-bed;*
*But on his knees at Meditation:*
*Not dallying with a brace of Curtizans,*
*But with two deep Divines in secret praying.*      140
*Happy were* England *wou'd this Vertuous Prince
Take on himself the toil of Sovereignty.*[48]
LORD MAYOR: Happy indeed, my Lord.
He will not sure refuse our proffer'd Love?
BUCKINGHAM: Alas my Lord, you know him not, his
    mind's
Above this World; he's for a Crown Immortal!
Look there! His door opens: Now where's our hope?
LORD MAYOR: *See where his Grace stands 'tween two
    Clergymen?* [49]
BUCKINGHAM: Ay, ay; 'tis there he's caught: There's his
Ambition.
LORD MAYOR: How low he bows to thank 'em for their
    care!                                               150

[48] 121–42. *Richard III*, III.vii.54–78: 'Welcome ... sovereignty thereof.'
[49] 148. *Richard III*, III.vii.94: 'See where ... two clergymen.'

And, see, a Prayer-Book in his hand!

BUCKINGHAM: Wou'd he were King, we'd give him leave
 to pray.

Methinks I wish it for the love he bears the City.

How have I heard him vow he thought it Hard

The Mayor should lose his Title with his Office?

Well! who knows? he may be won?

LORD MAYOR: Ah! my Lord!

BUCKINGHAM: See! He comes forth: my Friends be
 resolute,

I know he's cautious to a fault but do not

Leave him till our honest suit be granted.    160

    *Enter* RICHARD *with a Book*

RICHARD: *Cousin of Buckingham!*

*I do beseech your Grace to pardon me,*

*Who, earnest in my Zealous Meditation,*

*So long deferr'd the service of my Friends:*

*Now do I fear I've done some strange offence,*

*That looks disgracious\* in the City's Eye;*

*If so, 'tis Just you shou'd reprove my Ignorance.*

BUCKINGHAM: *You have, my Lord: We wish your Grace*

*On our entreaties wou'd amend your fault.*

RICHARD: *Else wherefore breath I in a Christian Land?* 170

BUCKINGHAM: *Know then it is your fault, that you resign*

*The Sceptred Office of your Ancestors,*

*Fair England's Throne, your own due right of Birth,*

*To the Corruption of a blemisht stock,*

*While in the Mildness of your sleeping thoughts,*

*(Which here we waken to our Country's good)*

*This wounded Isle does want her proper Limbs,*

*'Which to recure,\* joyn'd with these Loyal Men,*

*'Your very Worshipful and Loving Friends,*

*And by their zealous Instigation,*      180

*In this Just Cause, I come to move your Highness,*

*That on your gracious self you'd take the Charge*

*And Kingly Government of this your Land,*

*Not as Protector, Steward, Substitute,*

*Or lowly Factor\* for another's Gains:*

*But as successively from Blood to Blood,*
*Your own, by right of Birth, and lineal Glory.*
RICHARD: *I cannot tell, if to depart in silence,*
    *Or bitterly to speak in your reproof,*
    *Fits best with my Degree or your Condition:*                    190
    'Therefore to speak in just refusal of your suit,
    *And then in speaking not to check my Friends.*
    *Definitively thus I answer you;*
    *Your Love deserves my Thanks, but my desert*
    *Unmeritable shuns your fond Request:*
    *For, Heaven be thanked, there is no need of me;*
    *The Royal stock has left us Royal fruit,*
    *Which mellow'd by the stealing hours of time,*
    *Will well become the seat of Majesty,*
    *And make us (no doubt) happy by his Reign.*                    200
    *On him I lay what you wou'd lay on me,*
    *The Right and Fortune of his happier Stars,*
    'Which Heaven forbid my thoughts shou'd rob him of.
BUCKINGHAM: *My Lord, this argues Conscience in your*
    *Grace,*
    *But Circumstances well consider'd:*
    *The weak respects thereof are nice\* and trivial.*
    *You say that* Edward *was your Brothers Son*
    *So say we too, but not by* Edward's *Wife:*
    'If solemn Contracts are of any force,
    'That Title Justice gave to Lady *Lucy*:                         210
    'Even of his Birth cou'd I severely speak;
    *Save that for reverence to some alive,*
    *I give a spairing limit to my Tongue.*
LORD MAYOR: Upon our knees, my Lord, we beg your
    Grace[50]
To wear this precious Robe of Dignity,
Which on a Child must sit too loose and heavy.
'Tis yours; befitting both your Wisdom and your Birth.
CATESBY: My Lord, this coldness is unkind,
    Nor suits it with such ardent Loyalty.

[50] 162–214. *Richard III,* III.vii.104–93: 'I do beseech . . . to my tongue.'

BUCKINGHAM: *O make 'em happy: Grant their Lawful*
  *Suit.*                                                      220
RICHARD: *Alas! Why wou'd you heap this care on me?*
  *I am unfit for State and Majesty.*
  *I thank you for your Loves, but must declare*
  *(I do beseech you take it not amiss)*
  *I will not! dare not! must not yield to you.*
BUCKINGHAM: *If you refuse us through a soft remorse,*
  *Loth to depose the Child, your Brother's Son:*
  *(As well we know your tenderness of Heart)*
  *Yet know, tho' you deny us to the last,*
  *Your Brother's Son shall never Reign our King:*         230
  *But we will plant some other in the Throne,*
  *To the disgrace and downfall of your House.*
  *'And thus resolv'd I bid you, Sir, Farewell.*[51]
  *My Lord, and Gentlemen, I crave your pardon*
  *For this vain trouble: M' intent was good,*
  *I wou'd have serv'd my Country and my King;*
  *But 'twill not be: Farewell! When next we meet—*
LORD MAYOR: *Be not too rash, my Lord, his Grace relents.*
BUCKINGHAM: *Away, you but deceive your selves—*
                              [*Exit* BUCKINGHAM]
CATESBY: *Sweet Prince accept their suit.*                   240
LORD MAYOR: *If you deny us, all the Land will rue it.*
RICHARD: *Call him again – You will enforce me to*
  *A World of cares; I am not made of stone,*
  *But penetrable to your kind entreaties:*
  *Tho' Heaven knows against my own Inclining.*
                    *Re-enter* BUCKINGHAM
  *Cousin of* Buckingham, *and sage grave Men.*
  *Since you will buckle Fortune on my Back*
  *To bear her burthen whether I will or no,*
  *I must have patience to endure the load:*
  *But if black Scandal or foul-fac'd Reproach*            250
  *Attend the sequel of your Imposition,*
  *Your meer Enforcement shall Acquittance* me:*

---

[51] 220–33. *Richard III*, III.vii.202–16: 'O make them . . . of your House.'

*For Heaven knows, as you may all partly see,*
*How far I am from the desire of this.*
LORD MAYOR: *Heaven guard your Grace: We see it, and*
    *will say it.*
RICHARD: You will but say the truth, my Lord.[52]
BUCKINGHAM: My heart's so full it scarce has vent for
    words;
    My knee will better speak my duty now.        (*Kneels*)
    Long live our Soveraign, *Richard* King of *England.*
RICHARD: Indeed your words have touch'd me nearly
    Cousin:                                                      260
    Pray rise. I wish you cou'd recall 'em.
BUCKINGHAM: It wou'd be Treason now, my Lord: To
    morrow,
    'If it so please your Majesty, from Counsel
    'Orders shall be given for your Coronation.
RICHARD: *Even when you please: for you will have it so.*
BUCKINGHAM: *To morrow then we will attend your*
    *Majesty:*
    And now we take our leaves with joy.
RICHARD: *Cousin Adieu! my loving Friends farewel:*
    *I must to my Holy Work again.*[53]
                    [*Exeunt* BUCKINGHAM *and Citizens*]
                    (RICHARD. *Solus*)
Why now my golden dream is out –                            270
Ambition like an early Friend throws back
My Curtains with an eager Hand, o'rejoy'd
To tell me what I dreamt is true – A Crown!
Thou bright reward of ever daring minds,
O! How thy awful Glory fills my Soul!
Nor can the means that got thee dim thy lustre;
For, not mens Love, Fear pays thee Adoration:
And Fame not more survives from Good than Evil deeds.
Th' aspiring youth that fir'd th' *Ephesian* Dome
Out-lived in Fame the pious Fool that rais'd it:*          280

---

[52] 240–56. *Richard III*, III.vii.220–37: 'Call him again ... say the truth.'
[53] 262–9. *Richard III*, III.vii.241–4: 'Tomorrow ... work again.'

Conscience, lie still – More lives must yet be drain'd,
Crowns got with Blood must be with Blood maintain'd.

                                                    [*Exit*]

# ACT IV

## Scene i

*The Scene, the* Tower

*Enter the two Princes with the* QUEEN, *the* DUTCHESS
OF YORK, *and Lady* ANN *in tears*

PRINCE EDWARD: Pray, Madam, do not leave me yet,
  For I have many more complaints to tell you.
QUEEN: And I unable to redress the least:
  What wou'dst thou say, my Child?
PRINCE EDWARD: O Mother! Since I first have lain i'th'
  *Tower*
  My rest has still been broke with frightful Dreams,
  Or shocking News has wak'd me into tears.
  I'm scarce allow'd a Friend to visit me:
  All my old honest Servants are turn'd off,
  And in their rooms are strange ill-natur'd fellows,   10
  Who look so bold, as they were all my Masters;
  And, I'm afraid, they'll shortly take you from me.
DUTCHESS OF YORK: O mournful hearing!
ANN:                            O unhappy
  Prince!
DUKE OF YORK: Dear Brother, why do you weep so?
  You make me cry too.
QUEEN: Alas, poor Innocence!
PRINCE EDWARD: Wou'd I but knew at what my Uncle
  aims;
  If 'twere my Crown, I'd freely give it him,
  So he'd but let me 'joy my life in quiet.
DUKE OF YORK: Why! will my Uncle kill us, Brother?   20
PRINCE EDWARD: I hope he wo'n't: We never injur'd him.

QUEEN: I cannot bear to see 'em thus. –          (*Weeping*)
    *Enter to them, Lord* STANLEY
STANLEY: Madam, I hope your Majesty will pardon
 What I am griev'd to tell, Unwelcome News.
QUEEN: Ah me! more sorrow yet! My Lord; we've long
 Despair'd of happy Tydings, pray what is't?
STANLEY: On *Tuesday* last, your noble Kinsmen *Rivers*,
 *Grey*, and Sir *Thomas Vaughan* at *Pomfret*,
 Were Executed on a publick Scaffold.
DUTCHESS OF YORK: O dismal Tydings.                                    30
PRINCE EDWARD: O poor Uncles! I doubt my turn is next.
ANN: Nor mine, I fear, far off.
QUEEN: Why, then let's welcome Blood and Massacre,
 Yield all our Throats to the fierce Tygers rage,
 And die lamenting one another's wrongs.
 O! I foresaw this ruin of our House.          (*Weeps*)
    *Enter* CATESBY *to Lady* ANN
CATESBY: Madam, the King
 Has sent me to inform your Majesty
 That you prepare (as is advis'd from Counsel)
 To morrow for your Royal Coronation.                              40
QUEEN: What do I hear? Support me, Heaven!
ANN: Despightful* Tydings! O unpleasing News!
 Alas, I heard of this before, but cou'd not
 For my soul take heart to tell you of it.
CATESBY: The King does further wish your Majesty
 Wou'd less employ your visits at the *Tower*.
 He gives me leave t' attend you to the Court,
 And is impatient, Madam, till he sees you.
ANN: Farewel to all, and thou, poor injur'd Queen:
 Forgive the unfriendly duty I must pay.                           50
QUEEN: Alas, kind Soul, I envy not thy Glory,
 Nor think I'm pleas'd thou'rt partner in our sorrow.
CATESBY: Madam. –
ANN:  I come––
QUEEN: *Farewel, thou woeful welcomer of Glory.*[54]

---

[54] 54. *Richard III*, IV.i.89: 'Farewell ... glory.'

CATESBY: Shall I attend your Majesty?

ANN: Attend me! Whither, to be Crown'd?
*Let me with deadly Venome be Anointed,*
*And die e'er Men can say, Long live the Queen.*

QUEEN: *Poor grieving heart, I pity thy complaining.*[55]

ANN: *No more than with my Soul I mourn for yours:*          60
A long farewel to all.— [*Exit Lady* ANN *and* CATESBY]

STANLEY:               Take comfort, Madam.

QUEEN: Alas, where is it to be found?
Death and Destruction follow us so close,
They shortly must o'retake us.

STANLEY: In *Brittany*
My Son-in-Law the Earl of *Richmond* still
Resides, who with a jealous* Eye observes
The lawless actions of aspiring *Richard*:
To him, (wou'd I advise you) Madam, fly
Forthwith for Aid, Protection, and Redress.
He will I'm sure with open arms receive you.          70

DUTCHESS OF YORK: Delay not Madam,
For 'tis the only hope that Heaven has left us.

QUEEN: Do with me what you please: For any Change
Must surely better our Condition.

STANLEY: I farther wou'd advise you, Madam, this
Instant to remove Princes to some
Remote Abode, where you your self are Mistress.

PRINCE EDWARD: Dear Madam take me hence: For I shall
ne'er
Enjoy a moments quiet here.

DUKE OF YORK: Nor I: Pray Mother let me go too?          80

QUEEN: Come then, my pretty young ones, lets away:
For here you lie within the Falcon's reach,
Who watches but th' unguarded hour to seize you.
*Enter the* LIEUTENANT *with an Order*

LIEUTENANT: I beg your Majesty will pardon me:
But the young Princes must, on no account,
Have Egress from the *Tower*,

[55] 57–9. *Richard III*, IV.i.61–3: 'Anointed let me . . . thy glory.'

Nor must, without the King's especial License,
Of what degree soever, any Person
Have admittance to 'em. – All must retire.

QUEEN: 'I am their Mother, Sir, who else commands 'em?     90
'If I pass freely, they shall follow me.
'For you – I'll take the peril of your fault upon my self.[56]

LIEUTENANT: My Inclination, Madam, wou'd oblige you,
'But I am bound by Oath, and must obey.
Nor, Madam, can I now with safety answer
For this continued Visit.
Please you my Lord to read these Orders.

                              (*Gives 'em Lord* STANLEY)

QUEEN: O Heavenly powers! Shall I not stay with 'em?

LIEUTENANT: Such are the Kings Commands, Madam.

QUEEN: My Lord!

STANLEY: 'Tis too true, and it were vain t' oppose 'em.     100

QUEEN: Support me Heaven!
For life can never bear the pangs of such a parting.
O my poor Children! O distracting thought!
I dare not bid 'em (as I shou'd) farewel,
And then to part in silence stabs my Soul.

PRINCE EDWARD: What, must you leave us, Mother?

QUEEN:                              What shall I say?
                              (*Aside*)

But for a time, my Loves – we shall meet again,
At least in Heaven.           (*To her self*)

DUKE OF YORK: Won't you take me with you, Mother?
I shall be so 'fraid to stay when you are gone.     110

QUEEN: I cannot speak to 'em, and yet we must
Be parted – Then let these kisses say farewel. (*Kissing 'em*)
Why! O why just Heaven, must these be our last?

DUTCHESS OF YORK: Give not your grief such way: be
sudden when you part.

QUEEN: I will – since it must be, to Heaven I leave 'em.
Hear me, you Guardian powers of Innocence!
Awake or sleeping: O! protect 'em still,
Still may their helpless youth attract mens pity;

---

[56] 90–2. *Richard III*, IV.i.21: 'I am ... from them.'

That when the arm of Cruelty is rais'd,
Their looks may drop the lifted Dagger down          120
From the stern murderers relenting hand,
And throw him on his knees in penitence.

BOTH PRINCES: O Mother! Mother!

QUEEN:                                O my poor Children!
                              [*Exeunt parted severally*]


## Scene ii

*The Scene changes to the Presence, discovering* RICHARD
*seated with* BUCKINGHAM, CATESBY, RATCLIFF, LOVEL,
*other Lords and Attendants*

RICHARD: *Stand all apart: Cousin of* Buckingham.

BUCKINGHAM: *My gracious Sovereign.*

RICHARD:                          *Give me thy hand:*
  *At length by thy advice and thy assistance*
  *Is* Richard *seated on the* English *Throne.*
  *But say, my Cousin, what,*
  *Shall we wear these Glories for a day?*
  *Or shall they last, and we rejoyce in 'em?*

BUCKINGHAM: I hope for Ages, Sir, Long may they Grace
  you.

RICHARD: O Buckingham! *now do I play the touch-stone,*
  'To try if thou be current Friend indeed.          10
  'Young *Edward* lives: So does his Brother *York.*
  'Now think what I wou'd speak!

BUCKINGHAM: 'Say on, my gracious Lord.[57]

RICHARD: I tell thee, Cuz, I've lately had two Spiders
  Crawling upon my startled hopes: Now tho'
  Thy friendly hand has brush'd 'em from me,
  Yet still they Crawl offensive to my Eyes,
  I wou'd have some Friend to tread upon 'em.
  *I wou'd be King, my Cousin—*

BUCKINGHAM: *Why so I think you are, my Royal Lord.*    20

---

[57] 1–13. *Richard III*, IV.ii.1–11: 'Stand all apart ... my loving lord.'

RICHARD: *Ha, am I King? 'Tis so – But – Edward lives!*
BUCKINGHAM: Most true, my Lord.
RICHARD: *Cousin, thou wert not wont to be so dull –*
*Shall I be plain? I wish the Bastards dead.*
*And I wou'd have it suddenly perform'd –*
'Now Cousin, canst thou answer me?
BUCKINGHAM: *None dare dispute your Highness Pleasure.*
RICHARD: 'Indeed, methinks thy kindness freezes Cousin;
'Thou dost refuse me then! – They shall not die?
BUCKINGHAM: 'My Lord, since 'tis an action cannot be            30
'Recall'd, allow me but some pause to think,
'Ill instantly resolve your Highness.          [*Exit* BUCKINGHAM]
CATESBY: *The King seems angry; see he gnaws his lip.*
RICHARD: *I'll henceforth deal with shorter sighted Fools,*
*None are for me that look into my Deeds,*
'With thinking Eyes –
*High reaching* Buckingham *grows Circumspect.*[58]
The best on't is it may be done without him,
Tho' not so well perhaps – had he consented,
Why, then the murther had been his, not mine.—        40
– We'll make a shift as 'tis – Come hither, *Catesby.*
Where's that same *Tirrel* whom thou toldst me of?
Hast thou given him those sums of Gold I order'd?
CATESBY: I have, my Liege.
RICHARD: Where is he?
CATESBY: He waits your Highness pleasure.
RICHARD: Give him this Ring, and say my self
Will bring him farther Orders instantly.        [*Exit* CATESBY]
'The deep revolving Duke of *Buckingham*
*No more shall be the Neighbour to my Counsels:*
*Has he so long held out with me untir'd,*        50
*And stops he now for Breath? Well, be it so. –*
                    *Enter Lord* STANLEY
*How now, Lord* Stanley? *What's the News?*
STANLEY: *I hear, my Liege, the Lord Marquess of* Dorset
*Is fled to* Richmond, *now in* Brittany.[59]

---

[58]  19–37. *Richard III*, IV.ii.12–31: 'Why, Buckingham ... circumspect.'
[59]  48–54. *Richard III*, IV.ii.42–9: 'The deep-revolving ... where he abides.'

RICHARD: Why let him go, my Lord, he may be spar'd.
Hark thee, *Ratcliff*, when saw'st thou *Ann*, my Queen?
Is she still weak? Has my Physician seen her?

RATCLIFF: He has, my Lord, and fears her mightily.

RICHARD: But he's excelling skillful, she'll mend shortly.

RATCLIFF: I hope she will, my Lord.                    60

RICHARD: And, if she does, I have mistook my man. (*Aside*)
*I must be married to my Brother's Daughter,*
At whom I know the *Brittain\* Richmond* aims;
*And by that knot looks proudly on the Crown.*
*But then to stain me with her Brother's Blood:*
*Is that the way to wooe the Sisters Love?*
' – No matter what's the way – For while they live[60]
'My goodly Kingdom's on a weak Foundation.
'Tis done: My daring heart's resolv'd – they're dead.
            *Re-enter Duke of* BUCKINGHAM

BUCKINGHAM: *My Lord, I have consider'd in my mind,*    70
*The late Request that you did sound me in.*

RICHARD: *Well, let that rest:* Dorset *is fled to* Richmond.

BUCKINGHAM: *I have heard the News, my Lord.*

RICHARD: Stanley, *he's your near Kinsman – Well, look to*
*him.*

BUCKINGHAM: *My Lord, I claim that gift, my due by*
*promise,*
'For which your Honour and your Faith's engag'd;
'The Earldom of *Hereford*, and those Moveables,
'Which you have promis'd I shall possess.

RICHARD: Stanley, *look to your Wife; if she conveys*
Letters *to* Richmond, *you shall answer it.*        80

BUCKINGHAM: 'What says your Highness to my Just
request?

RICHARD: *I do remember me,* Harry *the Sixth*
*Did Prophecy that* Richmond *should be King,*
*When* Richmond *was a peevish\* Boy!*
''Tis odd – A King perhaps.[61]

[60] 62–6. A version of *Richard III*, IV.ii.60–5: 'I must be . . . in this eye.'
[61] 70–85. *Richard III*, IV.ii.82–97: My lord, I have . . . perhaps.'

*Enter* CATESBY

CATESBY: My Lord, I have obey'd your Highness Orders.

BUCKINGHAM: May it please you to resolve me in my Suit?

RICHARD: Lead *Tirrel* to my Closet, I'll meet him.

BUCKINGHAM: I beg your Highness ear my Lord – [62]

RICHARD: *I'm busie: Thou troubl'st me – I'm not i'th' vein.*   90

[*Exit* RICHARD]

BUCKINGHAM: O patience, Heaven! Is't thus he pays my
   service?

  Was it for this I rais'd him to the Throne?[63]

  O! if the peaceful dead have any sence

  Of those vile injuries they bore, while living:

  Then sure the joyful Souls of Blood-suck'd *Edward*,

  *Henry*, *Clarence*, *Hastings*, and All that through

  His foul corrupted dealings have miscarried,

  Will from the Walls of Heav'n in smiles look down

  To see this Tyrant tumbling from his Throne,

  His Fall unmourn'd, and Bloody as their own.

[*Exit*]

## Scene iii

### *Scene the* Tower

*Enter* TIRREL, DIGHTON, *and* FOREST

TIRREL: Come, Gentlemen:

  Have you concluded on the means?

FORREST: Smothering will make no noise, Sir.

TIRREL: Let it be done i'th' dark: For shou'd you see

  Their young faces, who knows how far their looks

  Of Innocence may tempt you into pity.

FORREST: 'Tis ease and living well makes Innocence:

  I hate a face less guilty than my own:

  Were all that now seem Honest deep as we

  In trouble and in want they'd all be Rogues.   10

---

[62] 87–9. *Richard III*, IV.ii.117–18: 'May it please ... in the vein.'
[63] 91–2. *Richard III*, IV.ii.119–20: 'And is it ... for this?'

TIRREL: Stand back – Lieutenant, have you brought the
    Keys?

*Enter* LIEUTENANT

LIEUTENANT: I have 'em, Sir.

TIRREL: Then here's your warrant to deliver 'em
                                    (*Gives a Ring*)

LIEUTENANT: Your Servant, Sir.—
    What can this mean? Why, at this dead of night
    To give 'em too? – 'Tis not for me t' enquire.
                                    [*Exit* LIEUTENANT]

TIRREL: There, Gentlemen:        (*Giving them the Keys*)
    That way! You have no farther need of me.
                                    [*Exeunt severally*]

*Enter* RICHARD*

RICHARD: Wou'd it were done: There is a busie something
    here,
    That foolish Custom has made terrible,                    20
    To the intent of evil Deeds; And Nature too,
    As if she knew me Womanish, and Weak,
    Tugs at my Heart-Strings with complaining Cries,
    To talk me from my Purpose –
    And then the thought of what Mens Tongues will say,
    Of what their Hearts must think; To have no Creature
    Love me Living, nor my Memory when Dead.
    Shall future Ages, when these Childrens Tale
    Is told, drop Tears in pity of their hapless Fate,
    And read with Detestation the Misdeeds of *Richard*,      30
    The crook-back Tyrant, Cruel, Barbarous,
    And Bloody—will they not say too,
    That to possess the Crown, nor Laws Divine
    Nor Human stopt my way – Why let 'em say it;
    They can't but say I had the Crown;
    I was not Fool as well as Villain.
    Hark! the Murder's doing; Princes farewel,
    To me there's Musick in your Passing-Bell.       [*Exit*]

*Enter* TIRREL. *Solus*

TIRREL: "Tis done: The barbarous bloody act is done.
    Ha! the King: His coming hither at this                   40

Late hour, speaks him impatient for the welcome News.
*Enter* RICHARD

RICHARD: Now my *Tirrel*, how are the Brats dispos'd?
Say; am I happy? Hast thou dealt upon 'em?

TIRREL: 'If to have done the thing you gave in charge
'Beget your happiness, then, Sir, be happy;
For it is done.[64]

RICHARD: *But didst thou see 'em dead?*

TIRREL: *I did, my Lord.*

RICHARD:                 *And buried, my good* Tirrel?

TIRREL: In that I thought to ask your Grace's Pleasure.

RICHARD: I have't – I'll have 'em sure – Get me a Coffin
Full of holes, let 'em be both cram'd into't;                    50
And, hark thee, in the night-tide throw 'em down
The *Thames*; once in, they'll find the way to th' bottom,
*Mean time but think how I may do thee good,*
*And be Inheritor of thy desire.*[65]

TIRREL: I humbly thank your Highness.

RICHARD: About it strait, good *Tirrel*.

TIRREL: Conclude it done, my Lord.        [*Exit* TIRREL]

RICHARD: Why then my lowdest fears are husht.
'The Sons of *Edward* have Eternal Rest,
'And *Ann*, my Wife, has bid this World good night,[66]      60
While fair *Elizabeth* my beauteous Neice
Like a New Morn lights onward to my wishes.
*Enter* CATESBY

CATESBY: My Lord!

RICHARD: *Good News, or bad, that thou comest in so*
*bluntly?*

CATESBY: Bad News, my Lord, *Morton* is fled to *Rich-*
*mond,*
*And Buckingham, back'd with the hardy* Welshmen,
*Is in the Field, and still his Power increases.*

RICHARD: Morton *with* Richmond, *touches me more near*
*Than* Buckingham *and his rash levied numbers.*

---

[64] 44–6. *Richard III*, IV.iii.25–8: 'If to have done ... gentle Tyrell.'
[65] 53–4. *Richard III*, IV.iii.33–4: Meantime, but think ... thy desire.'
[66] 60. *Richard III*, IV.iii.39: 'And Anne ... good night.'

'But come, dangers retreat when boldly they're
    confronted,                                                    70
'And dull delays lead impotence and fear.
'Then fiery Expedition raise my Arm,
And fatal may it fall on crush'd Rebellion.
    *Let's muster Men, my Councel is my Shield,*
    *We must be brief when Traytors brave the Field.*[67]

                                        [*Exeunt*]


# Scene iv

### *Enter the* QUEEN *and* DUTCHESS OF YORK

QUEEN: O my poor Children! O my tender Babes!
  My unblown flowers pluck'd by untimely hands:
  'If yet your gentle Souls fly in the Air,
  'And be not fix'd in doom perpetual;
  'Hover about me with your Airy wings,
  'And hear your Mothers Lamentation:
  Why slept their Guardian Angels, when this deed was
    done?
DUTCHESS OF YORK: 'So many miseries have drain'd my
    Eyes,
  'That my woe-wearied Tongue is still and mute.[68]
  'Why should Calamity be full of Words?[69]                      10
QUEEN: Let's give 'em scope, for tho' they can't remove,
  'Yet they do ease Affliction.[70]
DUTCHESS OF YORK: Why then let us be loud in Exclama-
    tions
  To *Richard*! Haste, and pierce him with our cries!
  That from henceforth his Conscience may out-Tongue
  The close whispers of his relentless heart.
  Hark! His Trumpet sounds! This way he must pass.
                *(Trumpet sounds a march)*

---

[67] 63–75. *Richard III*, IV.iii.44–57: 'My lord . . . brave the field.'
[68] 1–9. *Richard III*, IV.iv.9–18: 'Ah, my poor . . . still and mute.'
[69] 10. *Richard III*, IV.iv.126: 'Why should calamity . . . full of words.'
[70] 11–12. *Richard III*, IV.iv.131–2: 'Let them have . . . ease the heart.'

QUEEN: Alas, I've not the Daring to confront him.

DUTCHESS OF YORK: I have a Mothers right, I'll force him
  hear me.

 *Enter* RICHARD *with his Powers, the* DUTCHESS *meets*
     *and stops him, &c.*

RICHARD: *Who intercepts me in my Expedition?* ⃰      20

DUTCHESS OF YORK: *Dost thou not know me? Art thou
  not my Son?*

RICHARD: *I cry you mercy, Madam, is it you?*

DUTCHESS OF YORK: 'Art thou my Son?

RICHARD: *I, I thank Heaven, my Father and your Self.*

DUTCHESS OF YORK: 'Then I command thee, hear me.

RICHARD: *Madam, I have a touch of your condition,*
  *That I cannot brook the accent of Reproof.*

DUTCHESS OF YORK: *Stay, I'll be mild and gentle in my
  Words.*

RICHARD: *And brief, good Mother, for I am in haste.*

DUTCHESS OF YORK: *Why, I have staid for thee (just
  Heaven knows)*            30
 *In Torment and Agony.*

RICHARD: *And came I not at last to comfort you?*

DUTCHESS OF YORK: *No, on my Soul, too well thou
  know'st it.*
 *A grievous burthen was thy Birth to me;*
 *Tetchy and way-ward was thy Infancy,*
 *Thy prime of Manhood daring, bold and stubborn:*
 *Thy Age confirm'd most subtle, proud and bloody.*

RICHARD: *If I am so disgracious in your eye,*
 *Let me march on, and not offend you, Madam.*
 *Strike up the Drum.*

DUTCHESS OF YORK: Yet stay, I charge thee hear me.   40

QUEEN: If not, hear me; for I have wrongs will speak
 Without a Tongue: methinks the very sight
 Of me shou'd turn thee into stone.
 'Where are my Children, *Richard*?

DUTCHESS OF YORK: 'Where is thy Brother *Clarence*?

QUEEN:            Where *Hastings*?

DUTCHESS OF YORK: 'Rivers?

QUEEN:                              *'Vaughan?*
DUTCHESS OF YORK:           *'Grey?*
RICHARD: *A Flourish, Trumpets: Strike Allarum, Drums.*
*Let not the Heavens hear these Tell-tale Women*
*Rail on the Heavens Anointed. Strike, I say.*
         *(Allarum of Drums and Trumpets)*
*Either be patient and intreat me fair,*                        50
*Or with the Clamorous report of War*
*Thus will I drown your Exclamations.*
DUTCHESS OF YORK: Then hear me Heaven, and Heaven
   at his latest hour[71]
Be Deaf to Him as he is now to me:
'E'er from this War he turn a Conqueror,
Ye Pow'rs, cut off his dangerous thread of Life,
Least his black sins rise higher in Account,
Than Hell has pains to punish—
Mischance and sorrow wait thee to the Field:
Hearts Discontent, languid and lean Despair                    60
With all the Hells of Guilt pursue thy steps for ever.
                              [*Exit* DUTCHESS OF YORK]
QUEEN: Tho' far more cause, yet much less power to curse
   Abides in me: I say *Amen* to her.
RICHARD: *Stay, Madam, I wou'd beg some words with*
   *you?*
QUEEN: 'What canst thou ask, that I have now to grant?
'Is't another Son? *Richard* I have none.
RICHARD: *You have a Beauteous Daughter call'd* Eliza-
   beth.
QUEEN: 'Must she die too?
RICHARD: *For whose fair sake I'll bring more Good to*
   *you,*
*Than ever You or Yours from me had Harm;*                     70
*So in the* Lethe* *of thy angry Soul*
*Thou'lt drown the sad remembrance of those wrongs*
'Which thou supposest me the cruel cause of.
QUEEN: *Be brief, least that the process of thy Kindness*

---

[71] 20–53. Based on *Richard III*, IV.iv.136–54: 'Who intercepts me ... drown your exclamations', with changes and some re-arrangement.

*Last longer telling than thy kindness Date.*

RICHARD: 'Know then, that from my Soul I love the fair
'*Elizabeth*, and will, with your permission,
'Seat her on the Throne of *England*.

QUEEN: 'Alas, vain man, how canst thou wooe her?

RICHARD: *That would I learn of you,*                    80
*As one being best acquainted with her humour.*

QUEEN: *If thou wilt learn of me, then wooe her thus,*
*Send to her, by the man that kill'd her Brothers,*
'A pair of bleeding Hearts; thereon Engrave
'*Edward* and *York*: Then haply will she weep.
'On this present her with an Handkerchief
'Stain'd in their Blood, to wipe her woeful Eyes.
*If this Inducement move her not to Love,*
*Read o'er the History of thy Noble Deeds;*
'Tell her, thy Policy took off her Uncle                    90
*Clarence, Rivers, Grey*; nay, and for her sake,
*Made quick conveyance with her dear Aunt* Ann.

RICHARD: *You mock me, Madam; this is not the way*
*To win your Daughter.*

QUEEN: *There is no other way,*
*Unless thou couldst put on some other form,*
*And not be* Richard *that has done all this.*[72]

RICHARD: *As I intend to prosper and Repent,*
*So thrive I in my dangerous Affairs*
*Of Hostile Arms: My self, my self confound,*
*Heaven and Fortune bar me happy hours:*                    100
*Day yield me not thy light, nor Night thy Rest;*
*Be opposite all Planets of good luck,*
*To my Proceedings, if with dear Hearts Love,*
*Immaculate Devotion, Holy Thoughts,*
*I tender\* not the fair* Elizabeth,
*In her consists thy happiness and mine:*
*Without her follows to my self and thee,*
*Her self, the Land, and many a Christian Soul,*
*Death, Desolation, Ruin and Decay.*

[72] 62–96. Based on *Richard III*, IV.iv.197–287: 'Though far more ... done all this',
with considerable cuts.

'It cannot, will not be avoided, but by this.[73]                110
QUEEN: What shall I say? still to affront his love,
  I fear will but incense him to Revenge.
  And to consent I shou'd abhor my self,
  Yet I may seemingly comply, and thus                    *(Aside)*
  By sending *Richmond* Word of his Intent,
  Shall gain some time to let my Child escape him.
  It shall be so,
  I have consider'd, Sir, of your important wishes,
  And cou'd I but believe you real –
RICHARD: Now by the sacred Hosts of Saints above –           120
QUEEN: O do not swear, my Lord, I ask no Oath;
  Unless my Daughter doubts you more than I.
RICHARD: *O my kind Mother (I must call you so)*
  *Be thou to her my loves soft Orator;*
  *Plead what I Will be, not what I Have been;*
  *Not my deserts, but what I Will deserve:*[74]
  'And when this Warlike arm shall have chastis'd
  'Th' audacious Rebel hot-brain'd *Buckingham*:
  *Bound with Triumphant Garlands will I come,*
  *And lead thy Daughter to a Conqueror's Bed.*[75]          130
QUEEN: My Lord, farewel: in some few days expect
  To hear how fair a progress I have made.
  Till when be Happy, as you're Penitent.
RICHARD: My heart goes with you to my Love, farewel.
                                    *[Exit* QUEEN]
  'Relenting, Shallow-thoughted Woman.
               *Enter* RATCLIFF
  How now! the News?
RATCLIFF: *Most gracious Sovereign, on the Western*
    *Coasts*
  *Rides a most powerful Navy and our fears*
  *Inform us* Richmond *is their Admiral,*
  *There do they Hull* expecting but the aid,*              140
  *Of* Buckingham *to welcome them a shore.*     *[Exit]*

---

[73] 97–110. *Richard III*, IV.iv.397–411: 'As I intend . . . but by this.'
[74] 123–6. *Richard III*, IV.iv.412–15: 'Therefore, dear mother . . . I will deserve.'
[75] 127–30. *Richard III*, IV.iv.331–4: 'And when this . . . conqueror's bed.'

RICHARD: 'We must prevent him then. Come hither
    *Catesby.*

CATESBY: 'My Lord, your pleasure?

RICHARD: *Post to the Duke of* Norfolk *instantly;*
*Bid him strait levy all the strength and power*
*That he can make, and meet me suddenly*
*At* Salisbury: Commend me to his Grace: away!

                              *[Exit* CATESBY]

              *Enter Lord* STANLEY

Well my Lord, What News have you gather'd?

STANLEY: Richmond *is on the Seas, my Lord.*

RICHARD: *There let him sink, and be the Seas on Him:*   150
*White Liver'd Runnagade,\* what does he there?*

STANLEY: *I know not, mighty Sovereign, but by guess.*

RICHARD: *Well, as you guess?*

STANLEY: *Stir'd up by* Dorset, Buckingham, *and* Morton,
*He makes for* England *here to claim the Crown.*

RICHARD: Traytor, the Crown: Where is thy power then
To beat him back?
*Where be thy Tenants, and thy Followers?*
'The Foe upon our Coast, and thou no Friends to meet
    'em?
*Or hast thou marched 'em to the Western shore,*   160
*To give the Rebels Conduct from their Ships?*

STANLEY: *My Lord, my Friends are ready all, i'th' North.*

RICHARD: *The North! Why, what do they do in the North,*
*When they shou'd serve their Sovereign in the West?*

STANLEY: They yet have had no Orders, Sir, to move:
If 'tis your Royal Pleasure they should march,
'I'll lead 'em on with utmost haste to joyn you,
'Where, and what Time your Majesty shall please.

RICHARD: *What, thou wou'dst be gone, to joyn with*
    Richmond?

STANLEY: 'Sir, you've no Cause to doubt my Loyalty;   170
'I ne'er yet was, nor ever will be false.

RICHARD: Away then, to thy Friends, and lead 'em on
'To meet me – Hold! Come back! I will not trust thee,
I've thought a way to make thee sure: Your Son

George Stanley, *Sir, I'll have him left behind;*
*And look your Heart be Firm,*
*Or else his heads Assurance is but Frail.*
STANLEY: *As I prove true, my Lord, so deal with him.*[76]

[*Exit* STANLEY]

*Enter* RATCLIFF

RATCLIFF: *My Lord, the Army of Great* Buckingham
*By sudden Floods, and fall of Waters,*                    180
*Is half lost and scatter'd,*
*And he himself wander'd away alone;*
*No man knows whither.*
RICHARD: 'Has any careful Officer proclaim'd
*Reward to him that brings the Traytor in?*
RATCLIFF: *Such Proclamation has been made, my Lord.*

*Enter* CATESBY

CATESBY: *My Liege, the Duke of* Buckingham *is taken.*
RICHARD: *Off with his head. So much for* Buckingham.*
CATESBY: *My Lord, I'm sorry I must tell more News.*
RICHARD: Out with it.                    190
CATESBY: *The Earl of* Richmond *with a mighty power*
*Is Landed, sir, at* Milford:[77]
*And, to confirm the News, Lord Marquess* Dorset,
*And Sir* Thomas Lovewel *are up in* Yorkshire.[78]
RICHARD: Why ay, this looks Rebellion. Ho! my Horse!
By Heaven the News allarms my stirring Soul.
'And as the Wretch, whose fever-weakned joynts,
'Like strengthless hinges buckle under Life;
'Impatient of his fit, breaks like a fire
'From his fond Keeper's Arms, and starts away:                    200
'Even so these War-worn Limbs grown weak
'From Wars disuse, being now inrag'd with War,
'Feel a new Fury, and are thrice themselves.[79]
Come forth my Honest Sword, which here I vow,

---

[76] 135–78. Based on *Richard III*, IV.iv.431–97: 'Relenting fool ... true to you', with cuts and changes.
[77] 179–92. *Richard III*, IV.iv.509–33: 'Buckingham's army ... landed at Milford.'
[78] 193–4. *Richard III*, IV.iv.518–19: 'Sir Thomas Lovel ... are in arms.'
[79] 197–203. *Henry IV*, *Part 2*, I.i.140–5: 'And as the wretch ... thrice themselves.'

By my Souls hope, shall ne'er again be sheath'd,
Ne'er shall these watching Eyes have needful rest,
Till Death has clos'd 'em in a glorious Grave,
Or Fortune given me Measure of Revenge.     [*Exeunt*]

# ACT V

## Scene i

*Scene, The Field*
*Enter* RICHMOND, OXFORD, BLUNT, HERBERT, *and others,*
*marching*

RICHMOND: *Thus far into the bowels of the Land*
*Have we march'd on without Impediment.*
'*Richard*, the bloody and devouring Boar,
'Whose Ravenous Appetite has spoil'd your Fields;
'Laid this rich Country waste, and rudely crop'd
'Its ripned hopes of fair Posterity,
*Is now ev'n in the center of the Isle,*
*As we're inform'd, near to the Town of* Leicester:
*From* Tamworth *thither, is but one days march,*
*And, here receive we from our Father* Stanley,　　　　10
*Lines of fair Comfort and Encouragement,*
Such as will help and animate our cause,
On which lets Cheerly on, Couragious Friends,
To reap the harvest of a lasting Peace;
Or Fame more lasting from a well fought War.
OXFORD: Your words have fire, my Lord, and warm our
　　men,
Who look'd methought but cold before, disheartned
With the unequal numbers of the Foe.
RICHMOND: Why, double 'em still, our Cause wou'd
　　Conquer 'em.
*Thrice is he arm'd that has his Quarrel Just,*　　　　20
*And he but naked, tho' lock'd up in Steel,*
*Whose Conscience with Injustice is Corrupted:*
The very weight of *Richard*'s guilt shall crush him.
BLUNT: His best of Friends, no doubt will soon be ours.
OXFORD: He has no Friends but what are such thro' fear.

RICHMOND: And we no Foes but what are such to Heaven;
　　Then doubt not, Heaven's for us. Let's on, my Friends:
　　*True hope ne'er tires, but mounts with Eagles wings,*
　　*Kings it makes Gods, and meaner Creatures Kings.*[80]
　　　　　　　　　　　　　　　　　　　　　　*[Exeunt]*

## Scene ii

*The Scene,* Bosworth *Field: Enter* RICHARD *in Arms, with*
NORFOLK, RATCLIFF, SURREY, *&c.*

RICHARD: *Here pitch our Tent, ev'n in* Bosworth *Field:*[81]
　　My good Lord of *Norfolk,* the cheerful speed
　　Of your supply, has merited my thanks.
NORFOLK: I am rewarded, Sir, in having power
　　To serve your Majesty.
RICHARD: You have our thanks, my Lord. *Up with my*
　　　*Tent:*
　　*Here will I lie to night – But where to morrow? Well,*
　　*No matter where – Has any careful Friend*
　　*Discover'd yet the number of the Rebels?*
NORFOLK: 'My Lord, as I from certain Spies am well　　10
　　'Inform'd, six or seven thousand is their
　　'Utmost Power.
RICHARD: *Why, our Battalions treble that account:*
　　*Beside, the Kings name is a Tower of strength,*
　　*Which they upon the adverse Faction want.*[82]
NORFOLK: Their wants are greater yet, my Lord: Those
　　ev'n
　　Of Motion, Life, and Spirit – Did you but know
　　How wretchedly their Men disgrace the Field.
　　O! such a tatter'd Host of mounted Scare-crows,
　　'So poor, so famish'd; their Executors,　　　　20
　　'The greedy Crows, fly hovering o'er their heads,

[80] 1–29. Based closely on *Richard III,* V.ii.3–24: 'Thus far ... meaner creatures kings.'
[81] 1. *Richard III,* V.iii.1: 'Here pitch ... Bosworth field.'
[82] 6–15. *Richard III,* V.iii.7–13: 'Up with my tent ... faction want.'

Impatient for their lean Inheritance.

RICHARD: 'Now, by St *Paul*, we'll send 'em Dinners and
    Apparel;
'Nay, give their fasting Horses Provender,
'And after fight 'em. How long must we stay,[83]
My Lords, before these desp'rate Fools will give
Us time to lay 'em with their Faces upwards?

NORFOLK: Unless their Famine saves our Swords that
    labour,
To morrows Sun will light 'em to their ruin,
So soon, I hear, they mean to give us Battle.                    30

RICHARD: The sooner still the better. – *Come, my Lords,*
    *Now let's survey, the 'vantage of the Ground:*
    *Call me some men of sound direction.*[84]

NORFOLK: My Gracious Lord.—

RICHARD: What say'st thou, *Norfolk*?

NORFOLK: Might I advise your Majesty, you yet
Shall save the blood that may be shed to morrow.

RICHARD: How so, my Lord?

NORFOLK: The poor Condition of the Rebels tells me,
That on a Pardon offer'd to the lives
Of those who instantly shall quit their Arms,                    40
Young *Richmond*, e'er to morrows dawn, were Friend-
    less.

RICHARD: Why, that indeed was our Sixth *Harry*'s way,
Which made his Reign one Scene of rude Commotion.
I'll be in mens despite a Monarch: No,
Let Kings that Fear, Forgive; Blows and Revenge for me.
                                            [*Exeunt*]

# Scene iii

*Enter* RICHMOND, OXFORD, BLUNT, *Sir* WILLIAM
                    BRANDON, *&c.*

[83] 20–5. *Henry* V, IV.ii.51–2, 57–9: 'And their executors ... for their hour', 'Shall
we go send ... after fight with them.'
[84] 31–3. *Richard III*, V.iii.14–16: 'Come, noble gentlemen ... sound direction.'

RICHMOND: *The weary Sun has made a Golden set,*
*And by yon ruddy brightness of the Clouds,*
*Gives token of a goodly Day to morrow;*
*Sir* William Brandon, *you shall bear my Standard.*
'Here have I drawn the model* of our Battle,
'Which parts in just proportion our small Power.
*Here may each Leader know his several Charge:*
*My Lord of* Oxford, *you Sir* Walter Herbert,
And Sir *William Brandon*, stay with me:
*The Earl of* Pembroke *keeps his Regiment.*[85]          10
           *Enter a* SOLDIER
SOLDIER: Sir, a Gentleman that calls himself *Stanley*,
Desires admittance to the Earl of *Richmond*.
RICHMOND: Now by our hopes, my Noble Father-in-Law,
Addmit him – My good Friends, your leave a while.
                         (*They retire*)
        *Enter Lord* STANLEY *in a Cloak*
My Honour'd Father! On my Soul
The joy of seeing you this night is more,
Than my most knowing hopes presag'd – What News?
STANLEY: *I, by Commission bless thee from thy Mother,*
*Who prays continually for* Richmond's *good:*
'The Queen too, has with tears of joy consented,          20
'Thou should'st espouse *Elizabeth* her Daughter,
*At whom the Tyrant* Richard *closely aims:*
'In brief (for now the shortest moment of
'My stay is bought with hazard of my Life)
*Prepare thy Battle early in the morning,*
(*For so the season of Affairs requires*)
'And this be sure of, I, upon the first
*Occasion offer'd, will deceive some Eyes,*
*And aid thee in this doubtful shock of Arms;*
'In which I had more forward been e'er this,          30
'But that the Life of thy young Brother *George*
(Whom for my pawn of Faith stern *Richard* keeps)

---

[85] 1–10. *Richard III*, V.iii.19–25: 'The weary sun . . . keeps his regiment.'

'Wou'd then be forfeit to his wild Revenge.
*Farewel: The rude enforcement of the time*
'Denies me to revive those Vows of Love –
*Which so long sunder'd Friends shou'd dwell upon.*

RICHMOND: We may meet again, my Lord –
STANLEY: Till then, once more farewel: Be resolute, and
     Conquer.
RICHMOND: *Give him safe Conduct to his Regiment.*[86]
                         [*Exit Lord* STANLEY]

Well, Sirs, to morrow proves a busie day:                    40
But come, the night's far spent – Let's in to Counsel.
Captain, an hour before the Sun gets up
*Let me be wak'd; I will in Person walk*
*From Tent to Tent, and early chear the Soldiers.*[87]
                         [*Exeunt*]


## Scene iv

*The Scene, before* RICHARD*'s Tent:* RICHARD, RATCLIFF,
                    NORFOLK *and* CATESBY

RICHARD: Catesby!
CATESBY: *Here, my Lord.*
RICHARD: *Send out a Pursuivant at Arms**
     *To Stanley's Regiment: Bid him 'fore Sun-rise,*
     *Meet me with his Power, or young George's Head*[88]
     *Shall pay the forfeit of his cold delay.*
     *What, is my Beaver easier than it was?*
     *And all my Armour laid into my Tent?*
CATESBY: It is, my Liege: All is in readiness.
RICHARD: *Good Norfolk, hye thee to thy Charge;*
     *Use careful Watch: Chuse trusty Centinals.*           10
NORFOLK: *Doubt not, my Lord.*
RICHARD: *Be stirring with the Lark, good Norfolk.*
NORFOLK: I shall, my Lord.[89]  [*Exit Duke of* NORFOLK]

[86]  18–39. *Richard III,* V.iii.84–104: 'I by attorney . . . to his regiment', with changes.
[87]  43–4. Perhaps a reminiscence of *Henry V,* IV. Chorus 29–32.
[88]  1–5. *Richard III,* V.iii.58–64: 'Catesby . . . of eternal night.'
[89]  6–13. *Richard III,* V.iii.51–7: 'What, is my beaver . . . my lord.'

RICHARD: *Saddle White* Surrey *for the Field to morrow.*[90]
   *Is Ink and Paper ready?*
CATESBY: *It is, my Lord.*
RICHARD: *An hour after Midnight, come to my Tent,*[91]
   *And help to Arm me. A good night, my Friends.* [*Exit*]
CATESBY: Methinks the King has not that pleas'd
     Alacrity[92]
   Nor Cheer of Mind that he was wont to have.
RATCLIFF: The meer effect of business—                              20
   You'll find him, Sir, another Man i'th' Field,
   When you shall see him with his Beavour up,
   Ready to mount his Neighing Steed, with whom
   He smiling, seems to have some wanton talk,
   Clapping his pamper'd sides to hold him still;
   Then, with a motion swift, and light as Air,
   Like fiery *Mars* he Vaults him to the saddle;[93]
   Looks Terror to the Foe, and Courage to his Soldiers.
CATESBY: Good night to *Richmond* then; for, as I hear,
   His numbers are so few, and those so sick                     30
   And famish'd in their march, if he dares fight us –
   He jumps into the Sea to cool his Feaver.
   But come, 'tis late: Now let's to our Tents,
   We've few hours good before the Trumpet wakes us.
                                    [*Exeunt*]

# Scene v

### *Enter* RICHARD *from his Tent. Solus*

RICHARD: 'Tis now the dead of Night, and half the World
   Is with a lonely solemn darkness hung;
   Yet I (so coy a dame is sleep to me)
   With all the weary Courtship of

---

[90] 14. *Richard III*, V.iii.65: 'Saddle White Surrey.'
[91] 15–17. *Richard III*, V.iii.76–9: 'Is ink ... arm me.'
[92] 18–19. *Richard III*, V.iii.74–5: 'I have not ... wont to have.'
[93] 22–7. Perhaps a reminiscence of *Henry IV*, Part 1, IV.ii.105–8: 'I saw young Harry ... into his seat.'

My Care-tir'd thoughts can't win her to my Bed;
Tho' ev'n the Stars do wink as 'twere, with over
    watching –
I'll forth, and walk a while – The Air's refreshing,
And the ripe Harvest of the new-mown Hay
Gives it a sweet and wholesome Odour:
'How awful is this gloom – and hark from Camp to
    Camp                                                    10
'The humm of either Army stilly sounds:
*That the fixt Centinels almost receive*
*The secret whispers of each other's watch.*
'Steed threatens Steed in high and boastful neighings,
'Piercing the nights dull Ear. Hark from the Tents,
*The Armourers accomplishing.\* the Knights,*
'With clink of hammers closing rivets up
*Give Dreadful note of Preparation; while some*
'Like sacrifices by their fires of watch,
'With patience sit, and inly ruminate                      20
'The mornings danger. By yon Heav'n my stern
'Impatience chides this tardy-gated night,
'Who, like a foul and ugly Witch, does limp
So tediously away: I'll to my Couch,[94]
And once more try to sleep her into morning.
                              (*Lies down; a groan is heard*)
Ha! What means that dismal voice? Sure 'tis
The Eccho of some yawning Grave,
That teems with an untimely Ghost. – 'Tis gone!
'Twas but my Fancy, or perhaps the Wind
Forcing his entrance thro' some hollow Cavern;            30
No matter what – I feel my eyes grow heavy.   (*Sleeps*)
*King* HENRY*'s Ghost, Lady* ANN*'s Ghost, and the Ghosts*
             *of the young Princes rise*
HENRY'S GHOST: O thou, whose unrelenting thoughts, not
    all
The hideous Terrours of thy Guilt can shake,
Whose Conscience with thy Body ever sleeps:

[94] 10-24. *Henry V*, IV. Chorus 4-22: 'From camp to camp ... tediously away.'

Sleep on, while I by Heavens high Ordinance
In dreams of horror wake thy frighted Soul:
Now give thy thoughts to me, let 'em behold
These gaping Wounds, which thy Death-dealing hand
Within the *Tower* gave my Anointed Body,
Now shall thy own devouring Conscience gnaw                    40
Thy heart, and terribly revenge my Murder.

PRINCES' GHOSTS: *Richard*, dream on; and see the
    wandring spirits
Of thy young Nephews, murder'd in the *Tower*:
Cou'd not our Youth, our Innocence perswade
Thy cruel heart to spare our harmless lives?
Who, but for thee, alas, might have enjoy'd
Our many promis'd years of Happiness.
No Soul, save thine, but pitties our misusage:
O! 'twas a cruel deed! therefore alone,
Unpittying, unpittied shalt thou fall.                         50

ANN'S GHOST: Think on the wrongs of wretched *Ann* thy
    Wife,
*Ev'n in the Battles heat remember me,*
*And edgeless fall thy Sword – Despair, and Die.*[95]

HENRY'S GHOST: The mornings dawn has summon'd me
    away:
Now *Richard* wake in all the Hells of Guilt,
And let that wild despair which now does prey
Upon thy mangled thoughts, allarm the World.
Awake *Richard*, awake! To guilty minds
A terrible Example. –
      (*All ghosts sink.* RICHARD *starts out of his sleep*)

RICHARD: *Give me a Horse: Bind up my wounds!*              60
'Have mercy, Heaven. Ha! – soft! – 'Twas but a dream:
But then so terrible, it shakes my Soul.
Cold drops of sweat hang on my trembling Flesh,
My blood grows chilly, and I freze with horror.[96]
O Tyrant Conscience! how dost thou aflict me!
When I look back, 'tis terrible Retreating:

[95] 52–3. *Richard III*, V.iii.163–4: 'Tomorrow in the battle . . . die.'
[96] 60–4. *Richard III*, V.iii.178–82: 'Give me a horse . . . trembling flesh.'

I cannot bear the thought, nor dare repent:
I am but Man, and Fate, do thou dispose me.
Who's there?

*Enter* CATESBY

CATESBY: *'Tis I, my Lord; the Village Cock*                    70
*Has thrice done salutation to the morn:*
*Your Friends are up, and buckle on their Armour.*

RICHARD: 'O *Catesby*! I have had such horrid dreams. –

CATESBY: 'Shadows, my Lord, below the Soldier's heeding.

RICHARD: Now, by my this days hopes, shadows to night
*Have struck more terror to the Soul of* Richard,
*Than can the substance of Ten Thousand Soldiers*
*Arm'd all in Proof, and led by shallow Richmond.*[97]

CATESBY: 'Be more your self, my Lord: Consider, Sir;
'Were it but known a dream had frighted you,                    80
'How wou'd your animated* Foes presume on't.[98]

RICHARD: Perish that thought: No, never be it said,
That Fate it self could awe the Soul of *Richard*.
Hence, Babling dreams, you threaten here in vain:
Conscience avant; *Richard*'s himself again.
    Hark! the shrill Trumpet sounds, to Horse: Away!
    My Soul's in Arms, and eager for the Fray. [*Exeunt*]


# Scene vi

*Enter* RICHMOND, OXFORD, *Soldiers, &c. Marching*

RICHMOND: Halt. –

SOLDIERS:          Halt, halt!

RICHMOND: *How far is it into the morning, Friends?*[99]

OXFORD: *Near four, my Lord.*

RICHMOND: 'Tis well: I'm glad to find we are such early
    stirers.

OXFORD: Methinks the Foe's less forward than we thought
    'em.

---

[97] 70–8. *Richard III*, V.iii.210–20: 'Ratcliffe, my lord . . . shallow Richmond.'
[98] 79–81. No obvious source.
[99] 2–3. *Richard III*, V.iii.235–6: 'How far . . . stroke of four.'

Worn as we are, we brave the Field before 'em.

RICHMOND: Come, there looks life in such a cheerful
   haste:
 'If dreams should animate a Soul resolv'd,
 'I'm more than pleas'd with those I've had to night.
 'Methought that all the Ghosts of them, whose Bodies    10
 '*Richard* murther'd, came mourning to my Tent,
 'And rous'd me to revenge 'em.[100]

OXFORD: A good Omen, Sir: Hark! the Trumpet of
The Enemy. It speaks them on the march.

RICHMOND: 'Why, then let's on, my Friends, to face 'em:
 'In Peace there's nothing so becomes a Man
 'As mild behaviour and humility:
 'But when the blast of War blows in our ears,
 'Let us be Tygers in our fierce deportment.[101]
 *For me, the ransome of my bold attempt.*    20
 'Shall be this Body, on the Earth's cold Face:
 *But, if we thrive, the Glory of the Action*
 *The meanest here shall share his part of.*
 'Advance your Standards, draw your willing Swords:
 'Sound, Drums and Trumpets, boldly and cheerfully.
 The Word's Saint *George*, *Richmond*, and *Victory*.[102]

                               [*Exeunt*]


## Scene vii

### *Enter* RICHARD, CATESBY, *marching*

RICHARD: *Who saw the Sun to day?*

CATESBY: He has not yet broke forth, my Lord.

RICHARD: *Then he disdains to shine; For, by the Clock,*
 *He should have brav'd the East an hour ago.*
 *Not shine to day? – Why, what is that to me,*
 'More than to *Richmond*? For the self-same Heaven
 'That frowns on me, looks lowring upon him.

---

[100] 8–12. *Richard III*, V.iii.228–32: 'The sweetest ... cried on victory.'
[101] 15–19. *Henry V*, III.i.2–6: 'In peace ... of the tiger.'
[102] 20–6. *Richard III*, V.iii.266–71: 'For me ... Richmond and victory.'

*Enter* NORFOLK *with a Paper*

NORFOLK: *Prepare, my Lord, the Foe's in the Field.*

RICHARD: *Come, bustle, bustle; Caparison my Horse:*
   *Call forth Lord Stanley; bid him bring his Power.*       10
   *My self will lead the Soldiers to the Plain.*[103]

                                     *[Exit CATESBY]*

   Well, *Norfolk*, what thinkst thou now?

NORFOLK: *That we shall Conquer; but on my Tent*
   *This morning early was this Paper found.*

RICHARD: *(Reads)* Jockey *of Norfolk be not too bold,*
              For Dickon *thy Master is bought and sold.*
   'A weak invention of the Enemy.[104]

   'Come, Gentlemen, now each man to his Charge.
   And e're we do bestride our foaming Steeds,
   *Remember whom you are to Cope withal,*           20
   *A scum of* Britains, *Rascals, Run-aways;*
   *Whom their o'er cloy'd Country vomits forth*
   *To desperate adventures and assur'd destruction.*[105]
   *If we be Conquer'd, let Men Conquer us,*
   *And not these Bastard* Britains, *whom our Fathers*
   'Have in their own Land, beaten, spurn'd, and trod on,
   And left 'em on Record, the Heirs of shame;
   Are these Men fit to be the Heirs of England?[106]

                *Enter* CATESBY

   What says Lord *Stanley: Will he bring his Power?*

CATESBY: *He does refuse, my Lord: He will not, Sir.*      30

RICHARD: *Off with his Son* Georges *head.*

              *(Trumpet sounds)*

NORFOLK: My Lord, the Foe's already past the Marsh:
   After the Battle let young *Stanley* die.

RICHARD: Why, after be it then –
   A thousand hearts are swelling in my bosom.
   'Draw Archers, draw your Arrows to the head,
   'Spur your proud Horses hard, and ride in blood:

---

[103] 1–11. *Richard III,* V.iii.278–92: 'Who saw the sun . . . to the plain', with changes.
[104] 12–17. *Richard III,* V.iii.302–8: 'What think'st thou . . . unto his charge.'
[105] 20–3. *Richard III,* V.iii.316–20: 'Remember whom . . . assur'd destruction.'
[106] 24–8. *Richard III,* V.iii.333–7: 'If we be conquered . . . ravish our daughters.'

And thou, our Warlike Champion, thrice Renown'd
St *George* inspire me with the Rage of Lyons –
Upon 'em! Charge! – Follow me –[107]                    [*Exeunt*]


## Scene viii

*Several Excursions, Soldiers drove across the Stage by*
RICHARD

*Re-enter* RICHARD

RICHARD: What, ho! young *Richmond*, ho! 'tis *Richard*
   calls.
   I hate thee, *Harry*, for thy blood of *Lancaster*;
   'Now if thou dost not hide thee from my Sword,
   'Now while the angry Trumpet sounds Allarms,
   'And dying groans transpierce* the wounded Air.
   '*Richmond*, I say, come forth, and single face me:
   '*Richard* is Hoarse with Daring thee to Arms.[108]   [*Exit*]
        *The Allarm continues: Enter* CATESBY, *and the*
               *Duke of* NORFOLK *in disorder*
CATESBY: Rescue! rescue! my Lord of *Norfolk*, haste.
   *The King Enacts more wonders than a Man,*
   *Daring an opposite to every danger:**                    10
   *His Horse is slain, and all on foot he fights,*
   *Seeking for* Richmond *in the throat of Death.*
   'Nay, haste, my Lord: the day's against us.[109]   [*Exeunt*]
        *Enter* RICHARD *and* RATCLIFF *in disorder*
RICHARD: *A Horse! a Horse! my Kingdom for a Horse!*
RATCLIFF: 'This way, this way, my Lord; below yon
   thicket
   'Stands a swift Horse. Away, ruin pursues us.
   'Withdraw, my Lord, for only flight can save you.
RICHARD: *Slave, I have set my Life upon a Cast,**

---

[107] 29–40. *Richard III*, V.iii.343–52: 'What says ... sits on our helms.'
[108] 3–7. *Henry VI*, Part 2, V.viii.3–7: 'Now, when ... thee to arms.'
[109] 8–13. *Richard III*, V.iv.1–13: 'Rescue, my lord ... for a horse', with minor
changes.

*And I will stand the hazard of the Dye.*
*I think there be six* Richmonds *in the Field;*                    20
*Five have I slain to day, instead of him.*
*A Horse! a Horse! my Kingdom for a Horse.* [*Exeunt*]


# Scene ix

*Re-enter* RICHARD, *and* RICHMOND *meeting*

RICHARD: 'Of one, or both of us the time is come.[110]

RICHMOND: Kind Heaven I thank thee, for my Cause is thine;

If *Richard*'s fit to live let *Richmond* fall.

RICHARD: Thy Gallant bearing, *Harry*, I cou'd plaud,

But that the spotted Rebel stains the Soldier.

RICHMOND: Nor shou'd thy Prowess, *Richard*, want my praise,

But that thy cruel deeds have stampt thee Tyrant.

So thrive my Sword as Heaven's high Vengeance draws it.

RICHARD: 'My Soul and Body on the Action both.[111]

RICHMOND: A dreadful lay: Here's to decide it.                    10

(*Allarm, fight*)

RICHARD: Perdition catch thy Arm. The chance is thine:[112]

(RICHARD *is wounded*)

But oh! the vast Renown thou hast acquired

In Conquering *Richard*, does afflict him more

Than even his Bodies parting with its Soul:

'Now let the World no longer be a Stage

'To feed contention in a lingring Act:

'But let one spirit of the First-born *Cain**

'Reign in all bosoms, that each heart being set

'On bloody Actions, the rude Scene may end,

'And darkness be the Burier of the Dead.[113]                    (*Dies*) 20

RICHMOND: Farewel, *Richard*, and from thy dreadful end

---

[110]  1. *Henry VI*, Part 2, V.ii.13: 'Of one or both ...'

[111]  9. *Henry VI*, Part 2, V.ii.26: 'My soul and body ...'

[112]  11. A recollection of *Othello*, III.iii.91: 'Perdition catch my soul'?

[113]  15–20. *Henry IV*, Part 2, I.i.155–60: 'And let this world ... burier of the dead.'

May future Kings from Tyranny be warn'd;
Had thy aspiring Soul but stir'd in Vertue
With half the Spirit it has dar'd in Evil,
How might thy Fame have grac'd our *English* Annals:
But as thou art, how fair a Page thou'st blotted.
Hark! the glad Trumpets speak the Field our own.

*Enter* OXFORD *and Lord* STANLEY: *Soldiers follow with*
RICHMOND's *Crown*

O welcome, Friends: My Noble Father welcome.
*Heaven and our Arms be prais'd the day is ours.*
See there, my Lords, stern *Richard* is no more.                    30
STANLEY: *Victorious* Richmond *well hast thou acquitted*
    *thee:*
– And see, the just reward that Heaven has sent thee.
'Among the Glorious spoils of *Bosworth* Field,
'We've found the Crown, which now in right is thine:
'Tis doubly thine by Conquest, and by Choice.
'Long Live *Henry* the Seventh, King of *England.*[114]

(*Shouts here*)

RICHMOND:  Next to Just Heaven, my Noble Countrymen,
    I owe my thanks to you, whose love I'm proud of,
    And Ruling well shall speak my Gratitude.
    *But now, my Lords, what Friends of us are missing?*      40
    *Pray tell me; Is young* George Stanley *living?*
STANLEY: *He is, my Liege, and safe in* Leicester *Town,*
    *Whither, if you please, we may withdraw us.*[115]

*Enter* BLUNT

BLUNT: My Lord, the Queen and fair *Elizabeth*,
    Her beauteous Daughter, some few miles of, are
    On their way to Gratulate* your Victory.
RICHMOND: Aye, there indeed, my toil's rewarded
    Let us prepare to meet 'em, Lords, and then,
    *As we're already bound by solemn Vows;*
    'We'll twine the Roses red and white together,         50
    'And both from one kind stalk shall flourish:

[114] 29–36. *Richard III*, V.v.1–7: 'God, and your arms ... make much of it', with changes.
[115] 41–3. *Richard III*, V.v.9–11: 'But tell me ... withdraw us.'

England *has long been mad, and scarr'd her self.*
'The Brother blindly shed the Brother's blood:
'The Father rashly slaughter'd his own Son:
'The bloody Son compell'd, has kill'd his Sire.
'O! Now let *Henry* and *Elizabeth*,
*The true Successors of each Royal House*
'Conjoyn'd together, heal those deadly wounds:
'And be that wretch of all mankind abhor'd,
'That wou'd reduce those bloody days again:                    60
  'Ne'er let him live to taste our Joys encrease,
  'That wou'd with Treason wound fair *England's*
    Peace.[116]                                    [*Exeunt*]

---

[116] 49–62. *Richard III*, V.v.18–39: 'And then, as we . . . fair land's peace', with cuts.

*Scene: a Chamber, the Princes in Bed. The Stage darkned*

PRINCE EDWARD: Why do you startle, Brother?

DUKE OF YORK: O! I have been so frighted in my sleep!
Pray turn this way?

PRINCE EDWARD: Alas, I fain wou'd sleep, but cannot
Tho' 'tis the stillest night I ever knew.
Not the least breath has stir'd these four hours[.]
Sure all the World's asleep but we.

DUKE OF YORK: Hark! Pray Brother count the Clock!

*[Clock strikes]*

—But two! O tedious night: I've slept an Age.
Wou'd it were day, I am so melancholy.                    10

PRINCE EDWARD: Hark! What noise is that?
I thought I heard some one upon the stairs!
Hark! Again!

DUKE OF YORK: O dear, I hear 'em too! Who is it,
Brother?

PRINCE EDWARD: Bless me! a light too thro' the door! look
there!

DUKE OF YORK: Who is it? Hark! it unlocks! O! I am so
afraid!

Enter DIGHTON *and* FORREST *with dark lanthorns*

PRINCE EDWARD: Bless me! What frightful men are these?

BOTH: Who's there?

PRINCE EDWARD: Who's there?

DIGHTON: Hist, we've wak'd 'em! What shall we say?

FORREST: Nothing. We come to do.                          20

DIGHTON: I'll see their Faces—

DUKE OF YORK: Won't they speak to us?

[DIGHTON *looks in with his Lanthorn*]

O save me! Hide me! Save me, Brother!

PRINCE EDWARD: O mercy Heaven! Who are you, Sirs,
That look so ghastly pale and terrible?

DIGHTON: I am a Fool. – I cannot answer 'em.

FORREST: You must die, my Lord, so must your Brother.

PRINCE EDWARD: O stay, for pity sake! What is our
Crime, Sir?
Why must we die?

DIGHTON: The King, your Uncle, loves you not.

PRINCE EDWARD: O Cruel man!                                30
Tell him we'll live in Prison all our days,
And, when we give occasion of offence,
Then let us die: H'as yet no cause to kill us.

FORREST: Pray.

PRINCE EDWARD: We do, Sir, to you. O spare us Gentle-
men!
I was some time your King, and might have shown
You mercy: For your dear Souls sake pity us.

FORREST: We'll hear no more.

BOTH PRINCES: O Mercy, Mercy!

FORREST: Down, down with 'em.

(*They smother them, and the Scene shuts on them*)

# APPENDIX

## Extracts from Thomas Otway, *Caius Marius*

This appendix contains extracts from Thomas Otway's adaptation of *Romeo and Juliet, Caius Marius*, written in 1679 and printed the next year. This play has been chosen for various reasons, but particularly to illustrate an important method of adapting Shakespeare not shown in the five complete plays in this volume; that is, setting the play in a different time and place in order to give it topical significance. One of a group of Shakespearean adaptations written between 1679 and 1681, which includes Tate's *King Lear, Caius Marius* is a response to the Popish Plot and the Exclusion Crisis, though its message is much less politically well-defined than that of Tate's play. Otway, then only twenty-seven, an actor turned playwright, had already scored a theatrical success with his second play *Don Carlos* (1676), and he was starting to gain a reputation at the time he wrote *Caius Marius*; the play did well in the theatre, and remained influential long after it had ceased to be topical. According to the eighteenth-century commentator Thomas Davies in *Dramatic Miscellanies* (1785), the play's success initially was due in large part to the performances of the famous comic actor James Nokes in the drag role of the Nurse (he subsequently became known as 'Nurse Nokes'), and Cave Underhill, often Nokes's partner in comedy, as Sulpitius. But the play held the stage in preference to *Romeo and Juliet* until the revivals of Shakespeare's play (still with adaptations) by Theophilus Cibber in 1744 and David Garrick in 1748.

In *Caius Marius*, Otway sets the Romeo and Juliet story in republican Rome of the first century BC, during the period of rivalry and violent civil war between Caius Marius, a self-made man of the people, and Lucius Cornelius Sulla, an aristocratic soldier who was to become Dictator. In the play, Caius Marius and his sons, the eldest of which is Marius Junior, represent the

house of Montague, and Metellus, a former consul and once
Marius's commander, with his daughter Lavinia represent the
Capulets. The setting is chosen to highlight the theme of the
horrors of civil war. In 1679 Parliament was debating the
Exclusion bill, sponsored by the Earl of Shaftesbury and his
supporters, which would prevent Charles's brother, the Catholic
James, Duke of York, from succeeding to the throne. Opponents
of the bill, including the King and the Tories, argued that if
James were forced into banishment, his supporters in France and
Scotland might be prepared to go to war on his behalf, and the
fear of civil war was intense at the time Otway was writing his
play. But although he was a known Tory and had dedicated
*Don Carlos* to James, the play is not unequivocally Tory in its
stance. Sympathy switches between the factions, and neither side
emerges as morally preferable. The setting in republican Rome
serves to distance this state from the English monarchy and
suggests that Otway was aiming for something more than
topicality in his reworking of Shakespeare.[1]

The play's opening lines raise important questions about
government, which must have struck home in the troubled
London of 1679, rife with fears of Catholic plots and the unrest
caused by the knowledge of rival claimants for the succession to
Charles, whose recent serious illness is referred to ('Caesar's
absence') in Otway's prologue:

> When will the Tut'lar Gods of Rome awake,
> To fix the Order of our wayward State,
> That we may once more know each other; know
> Th'extent of Laws, Prerogatives and Dues;
> The Bounds of Rules and Magistracy; who
> Ought first to govern, and who must obey?

But the play ends without suggesting any answers to these
challenging questions; its last moments offer a glimpse of
imminent anarchy as Marius, having watched Lavinia stab
herself, calls down chaos: 'Be Nature's Light extinguisht; let the
Sun/Withdraw his Beams, and put the world in Darkness.' In
such a context Otway's lovers appear even more helpless than
Shakespeare's; Marius Junior contributes less than does Romeo
to his own downfall. Lavinia has a larger part than Juliet,
including a strange scene when she escapes from imprisonment
in her bedroom to join her husband and father-in-law in

pastoral exile, and to enjoy a Cordelia-like reunion with the misogynistic Caius Marius, bringing him restorative food and drink. The old man remembers this scene when he finds Lavinia in the tomb with his dead son at the end of the play, and speaks what is probably the play's motto as he is led away to political defeat:

> Be warn'd by me, ye Great ones, how y'embroil
> Your Country's Peace, and dip your Hands in Slaughter:
> Ambition is a Lust that's never quencht,
> Grows more inflam'd and madder by Enjoyment.

Instead of the reconciliations achieved by the Prince that round off *Romeo and Juliet* with such finality, Otway's play concludes more ominously with an announcement of new uproar in Rome and the curses of the angry and dying Sulpitius. Though Otway, in the defeat of the old and embittered Caius Marius, in some sense figured what he might have hoped to be the fate of the Whig Shaftesbury, his play offers little positive encouragement to the Royalist cause. But Michael Dobson's suggestion that 'in resorting to Shakespeare, Otway is searching like many readers after him for an antidote to politics'[2] seems off the mark; there is no doubt that the play responds powerfully to the violence and uncertainty of the times in which it was written.

As an adaptation of Shakespeare, *Caius Marius* is respectful but also eclectic. In the prologue Otway presents himself as a thief, who has 'rifled' Shakespeare of 'half a play': 'Amidst this baser Dross you'll see it shine/Most beautiful, amazing and Divine.' The implication of something unassimilated is apt. Despite the changes made to the *Romeo and Juliet* material to fit it for a place in a play about war and government in ancient Rome, *Caius Marius* falls to a disturbing extent into two halves; and it is probably true to say that, paradoxically, the Shakespearean influence is more 'formative and emancipatory'[3] in the political sections, where *Coriolanus* and to a lesser extent *Julius Caesar* and *King Lear* shadow the action, than in the romantic plot where the more consistent presence of the parent play seems to create a series of challenges for Otway which he never quite manages to meet. Where he is verbally closest to Shakespeare is, significantly, not in the lyrical sections, but in the more gothic style of Lavinia/Juliet's speeches of foreboding about the effects of the Priest/Friar's potion and Marius Junior/Romeo's description of the apothecary.[4] With some exceptions ('O Marius, Marius! wherefore art thou Marius?'), he avoids the wholesale lifting of scenes and speeches that one finds in Tate or Cibber, aiming rather to capture 'the spirit, mode of expression, and sense of drama of Shakespeare's work'.[5] The play is perhaps more of a curiosity than any other represented in this selection, but it does represent a response to a range of Shakespeare's work, not just to a single text, and a distinctive way of reworking a body of material to speak to a particular historical moment.

[1] John M. Wallace discusses the effects of Otway's moral ambivalence in 'Otway's *Caius Marius* and the Exclusion Crisis', *Modern Philology*, 85 (1988), pp. 363–72.

[2] Michael Dobson, *The Making of the National Poet. Shakespeare, Adaptation, and Authorship, 1660–1769* (Oxford: Clarendon Press, 1992), p. 80.

[3] See Hazel M. Batzer, 'Shakespeare's Influence on Thomas Otway's *Caius Marius*', *Revue de L'Université d'Ottawa*, 39 (1969), 533–61, p. 560.

[4] Compare *Romeo and Juliet*, IV. I. 77–88, IV. iii. 13–58, and V. i. 35–56 with *Caius Marius*, IV. 505–16, 526–48, V. 273–91. The line references for Caius Marius are to the edition of J. C. Ghosh, *The Works of Thomas Otway*, 2 vols. (Oxford: Clarendon Press, 1932).

[5] Batzer, p. 543.

# THE
# HISTORY and FALL
OF
# Caius Marius.
# A
# TRAGEDY.

As it is Acted at the
# Duke's Theatre.

---

By *Thomas Otway*.

---

*Qui color Albus erat nunc est contrarius Albo.*

---

*LONDON*,
Printed for *Tho. Flesher*, at the *Angel and Crown*
in S. *Paul's Church-yard*. 1680.

# ACT II

## Scene i*

*Enter* METELLUS *and* NURSE

METELLUS: I cannot rest to night: Ill-boding Thoughts
Have chas'd soft Sleep from my unsettled Brains.
This seems *Lavinia*'s Chamber, and she up.
Rest too to night has bin a stranger here.
*Lavinia*! my Daughter, hoa! where art thou?
NURSE: Now by my Maidenhead, (at twelve years old I had
one)
Come: what, Lamb? what, Lady-bird? Gods forbid.
Where's this Girl *Lavinia*?[1]

*Enter* LAVINIA

LAVINIA:     How now? who calls?
NURSE: Your Father, Child.
LAVINIA:     I'm here. Your Lordship's
pleasure?
METELLUS: Why up at this unlucky time of Night,   10
When nought but loathsome Vermin are abroad,
Or Witches gathering pois'nous Herbs for Spells
By the pale light of the cold waning Moon?
LAVINIA: Alas! I could not sleep: in a sad Dream,
Methought I saw one standing by my Bed,
To warn me I should have a care of Sleep,
For 'twould be banefull—
METELLUS:    Dreams give Children Fears.
LAVINIA: At which I rose from my uneasy Pillows,
And to my Closet went, to pray the Gods
T' avert th' unlucky Omen.
METELLUS:     'Twas well done.   20
Nurse, give us leave a while: I must impart

---

[1] 5-9. Based on *Romeo and Juliet*, I.iii.1-8.

Something to my *Lavinia*. Yet stay,
And hear it too. Thou know'st *Lavinia*'s Age.

NURSE: 'Faith, I know her Age to an hour.

METELLUS: She's bare Sixteen.*

NURSE: I'll lay Sixteen of my Teeth of it; and yet no Disparagement, I have but Six: she's not Sixteen. How long is't now since *Marius* triumph'd last?

METELLUS: No matter, Woman, what is that to thee?

NURSE: Even or odd, of all days in the year, since *Marius*    30
enter'd *Rome* in Triumph,* 'tis now even Thirteen years. Young *Marius* then too was but a Boy. My *Lais* and she were both of an Age. Well, *Lais* is in Happiness: she was too good for me. But as I was saying, a month hence she'll be Sixteen. 'Tis since *Marius* triumph'd now full Thirteen years, and then she was weaned. Sure I shall never forget it of all days. . . . Upon that day, (for I had then laid Wormseed to my Breast, sitting in the Sun under the Dove-house-Wall) my lady and you were at the Show. Nay, I do bear a Brain! but, as I said before, when it did    40
tast the Wormseed on my Nipple, and felt it bitter, pretty Fool! to see it teachy and fall out with the Nipple. Shout quo' the people in the streets. 'Twas no need, I trow, to bid me trudge. And since that time it is Thirteen years; and then she cou'd stand alone, nay, she cou'd run and waddle all about: for just the day before, she broke her Forehead, and then my Husband (Peace be with him, he was a merry man) took up the Baggage. Ay, quoth he, dost thou fall upon thy Face? thou wilt fall backward when thou hast more wit; wilt thou not, *Vinny*? and by    50
my fackings, the pretty Chit left Crying, and said, Ay. . . . I warrant and I should live a Thousand years, I never should forget it. Wilt thou not, *Vinny*? quoth he; and, pretty Fool, it stopt, and said, Ay.

METELLUS: Enough of this; stop thy impertinent Chat.

NURSE: Yes, my Lord: yet I cannot chuse but laugh, to think it should leave Crying, and say, Ay. . . . And yet in sadness it had a Bump on its Brow as big as a Cockrill's stone, a parlous Knock, and it cry'd bitterly. Ay, quo' my

Husband, fall'st upon thy Face? thou wilt fall backward   60
when thou com'st to Age, wilt thou not, *Vinny?* Look
you now, it stinted, and said, Ay. . . .

METELLUS: Intolerable trifling Gossip, peace.

NURSE: Well; thou wast the pretty'st Babe that e're I nurst.
Might I but live to see thee marry'd once, I should be
happy. It stinted, and said, Ay.

METELLUS: What think you then of Marriage, my *Lavinia?*
It was the subject that I came to treat of.

LAVINIA: It is a thing I have not dreamt of yet.

NURSE: Thing? the thing of Marriage? were I not thy   70
Nurse, I would swear thou hadst suckt thy Wisedome
from thy Teat. The thing?

METELLUS: Think of it now then, for I come to make
Proposals may be worthy of your Wishes.
They are for *Sylla,* the young, the gay, the handsome,
Noble in Birth and Mind, the valiant *Sylla.**

NURSE: A man, young Lady, Lady, such a man as all the
world . . . why, he's a man of Wax.[2]

METELLUS: Consider, Child, my Hopes are all in Thee.
And now Old age gains ground so fast upon me,   80
'Mongst all its sad Infirmities, my Fears
For Thee are not the smallest.
Therefore I've made Alliance with this *Sylla,*
A high-born Lord, and of the noblest Hopes
That *Rome* can boast, to give thee to his Arms;
So in the Winter of my Age to find
Rest from all worldly Cares, and kind rejoycing
In the warm Sun-shine of thy Happiness.

LAVINIA: If Happiness be seated in Content,
Or that my being blest can make you so,   90
Let me implore it on my Knees. I am
Your onely Child, and still, through all the Course
Of my past Life, have bin obedient too:
And as y' have ever bin a loving Parent,
And bred me up with watchfull tender'st Care,
Which never cost me hitherto a Tear;

---

[2] 19–78. Based on *Romeo and Juliet,* I.iii.9–80.

    Name not that *Sylla* any more: indeed
    I cannot love him.
METELLUS:         Why?
LAVINIA:             In deed I cannot.
METELLUS: Oh early Disobedience! by the Gods,
    Debaucht already to her Sexe's Folly,          100
    Perverseness, and untoward headstrong Will!
LAVINIA: Think me not so; I gladly shall submit
    To any thing; nay, must submit to all:
    Yet think a little, or you sell my Peace.
    The Rites of Marriage are of mighty moment:
    And should you violate a thing so Sacred
    Into a lawful Rape, and load my Soul
    With hatefull Bonds, which never can grow easy,
    How miserable am I like to be?
METELLUS: Has then some other taken up your Heart?   110
    And banisht Duty as an Exile thence?
    What sensual lewd Companion of the Night
    Have you bin holding Conversation with,
    From open Windows at a midnight-hour,
    When your loose Wishes would not let you sleep?[3]
LAVINIA: If I should love, is that a fault in one
    So young as I? I cannot guess the Cause,
    But when you first nam'd *Sylla* for my Love,
    My Heart shrunk back as if you'd done it wrong.
    If I did love, I'd tell you ... if I durst.        120
    Oh *Marius*!
METELLUS: Hah!
LAVINIA:       'Twas *Marius*, Sir, I nam'd
    That Enemy to you and all your House.
    'Twas an unlucky Omen that he first
    Demanded me in Marriage for his Son.
    Yet, Sir, believe me, I as soon cou'd wed
    That *Marius*, whom I've cause to hate, as *Sylla*.[4]
METELLUS: No more: by all the Gods, 'twill make me mad,
    That daily, nightly, hourly, every way

---

[3] 112-15. Reminiscent of *Much Ado About Nothing* IV.i.89-95.
[4] 125-6. Based on *Romeo and Juliet*, III.v.126-8.

My care has bin to make thy Fortune high;
And having now provided thee a Lord       130
Of noblest Parentage, of fair Demeans,
Early in Fame, Youthful, and well ally'd,
In every thing as thought cou'd wish a man,
To have at last a wretched puling Fool,
A whining Suckling, ignorant of her Good,
To answer, *I'll not wed, I cannot love.*
If thou art mine, resolve upon Compliance,
Or think no more to rest beneath my Roofs.
Go, try thy Risk in Fortune's barren Field,
Graze where thou wilt, but think no more of Me,[5]    140
Till thy Obedience welcome thy Return.
LAVINIA: Will you then quite cast off your poor *Lavinia*?
And turn me like a Vagrant out of Doors,
To wander up and down the streets of *Rome*,
And beg my bread with sorrow? Can I bear
The proud and hard Revilings of a Slave,
Fat with his Master's plenty, when I ask
A little Pity for my pinching Wants?
Shall I endure the cold, wet, windy Night,
To seek a shelter under dropping Eves,      150
A Porch my Bed, a Threshold for my Pillow,
Shiv'ring and starv'd for want of warmth and food,
Swell'd with my Sighs, and almost choak'd with Tears?
Must I at the uncharitable Gates
Of proud great men implore Relief in vain?
Must I, your poor *Lavinia*, bear all this,
Because I am not Mistriss of my Heart,
Or cannot love according to your liking?
METELLUS: Art thou not Mistriss of thy Heart then?
LAVINIA: No.
'Tis giv'n away.
METELLUS: To whom?
LAVINIA: I dare not tell.      160
But I'll endeavour strangely to forget him,
If you'll forget but *Sylla*.

[5] 127-40. Based on *Romeo and Juliet*, III.v.186-200.

METELLUS: Thou dost well.
  Conceal his Name if thou'dst preserve his Life.
  For if there be a Death in *Rome* that might
  Be bought, it should not miss him. From this hour
  Curst be thy Purposes, most curst thy Love.
  And if thou marry'st in thy Wedding-night
  May all the Curses of an injur'd Parent
  Fall thick, and blast the Blessings of thy Bed.[6]

LAVINIA: What have you done? alas! Sir, as you spoke,   170
  Methought the Fury of your words took place,
  And struck my Heart, like Lightning, dead within me.
  Gone too?                       [*Exit* METELLUS]
  Is there no Pity sitting in the Clouds
  That sees into the bottom of my Grief?[7]
  Alas! that ever Heav'n should practise Stratagems
  Upon so soft a Subject as my self!
  What say'st Thou? hast not thou a word of Joy?
  Some Comfort, Nurse, in this Extremity.

NURSE: Marry, and there's but need on't: 'ods my life, this  180
Dad of ours was an arrant Wag in his young days for all
this. Well, and what then? *Marius* is a Man, and so's
*Sylla.* Oh! but *Marius*'s Lip! and then *Sylla*'s Nose and
Forehead! But then *Marius*'s Eye agen! how 'twill sparkle,
and twinckle, and rowl, and sleer? But to see *Sylla* a
horseback! But to see *Marius* walk, or dance! such a Leg,
such a Foot, such a Shape, such a Motion. Ah h h . . .
Well, *Marius* is the man, must be the man, and shall be
the man.[8]

LAVINIA: He's by his Father's Nature rough and fierce,
  And knows not yet the follies of my Love:   190
  And when he does, perhaps may scorn and hate me.

NURSE: Yes, yes, he's a rude, unmannerly, ill-bred Fellow.
He is not the Flow'r of Curtesy; but I'll warrant him, as
gentle as a Lamb. Go thy ways, Child, serve God. What?
a Father's an Old man, and old man they say will take

---

[6]  167-9. Reminiscent of *King Lear,* I.iv.250-5.
[7]  174-5. *Romeo and Juliet,* III.v.208-9.
[8]  178-88. Based on *Romeo and Juliet,* III.v.224-33.

care. But a Young man! Girl, ah! a Young man! There's a
great deal in a Young man, and thou shalt have a Young
man. What? I have bin thy Nurse these Sixteen years, and
I should know what's good for thee surely. Oh! ay . . . a
Young man!                                                      200
LAVINIA: Now prithee leave me to my self a while.

                                                [*Exit* NURSE]

'Tis hardly yet within two hours of Day.
Sad Nights seem long. . . . I'll down into the Garden.
The Queen of Night.
Shines fair with all her Virgin-stars about her.
Nor one amongst 'em all a Friend to me:
Yet by their Light a while I'll guide my steps,
And think what course my wretched state must take.
Oh *Marius*!                                    [*Exit* LAVINIA]


## Scene ii

### A walled Garden belonging to METELLUS house

#### Enter MARIUS JUNIOR

MARIUS JUNIOR: How vainly have I spent this idle Night!
Ev'n Wine can't heal the ragings of my Love.
This sure should be the Mansion of *Lavinia*;
For in such Groves the Deities first dwelt.
Can I go forward when my Heart is here?
Turn back, dull Earth, and find thy Center out. . .

                                          [*Enters the Garden*]
            *Enter* GRANIUS *and* SULPITIUS*

GRANIUS: This way . . . he went . . . Why, *Marius*! Brother
    *Marius*!
SULPITIUS: Perhaps he's wise, and gravely gone to bed.
    There's not so weak a Drunkard as a Lover;
    One Bottle to his lady's health quite addles him.      10
GRANIUS: He ran this way, and leapt this Orchard-Wall.
    Call, good *Sulpitius*.[9]

---

[9] 11-12. *Romeo and Juliet*, II.i.6-7.

SULPITIUS: Nay, I'll conjure too.
  Why, *Marius*! Humours! Passion! mad-man Lover!
  Appear thou in the likeness of a Sigh.
  Speak but one word, and I am satisfy'd.
  He hears not, neither stirs he yet. Nay then
  I conjure thee by bright *Lavinia*'s Eyes,
  By her high Forehead, and her scarlet Lip,
  By her fine Foot, straight Leg, and quivering Thigh,
  And the Demeans that there adjacent ly,                          20
  That in thy likeness thou appear to us.
GRANIUS: Hold, good *Sulpitius*, this will anger him. . . .
SULPITIUS: This cannot anger him. 'Twould anger him
  To raise a Spirit in his Lady's Arms,
  Till she had laid and charm'd it down agen.
GRANIUS: Let's go: h' has hid himself among these Trees,
  To dy his melancholick Mind in Night.
  Blind is his Love, and best befits the Dark.[10]
SULPITIUS: Pox o' this Love, this little Scarcrow Love,
  That frights Fools with his painted Bow of Lath              30
  Out of their feeble sense.
GRANIUS: Stop there . . . let's leave the Subject and its
    Slave;
  Or burn *Metellus* House about his ears.
SULPITIUS: This morning *Sylla* means to enter *Rome*:
  Your Father too demands the Consulship.
  Yet now when he shou'd think of cutting Throats,
  Your Brother's lost; lost in a maze of Love,
  The idle Truantry of Callow Boys.
  I'd rather trust my Fortunes with a Daw,
  That hops at every Butterfly he sees,                         40
  Then have to doe in honour with a man
  That sells his Vertue for a Woman's Smiles. . . [*Exeunt*]
            Enter MARIUS JUNIOR *in the Garden*
MARIUS JUNIOR: He laughs at Wounds that never felt their
    smart.
  What Light is that which breaks through yonder Shade?

[10] 12–28. Based on *Romeo and Juliet*, II.i.7–34 (with cuts).

(LAVINIA *in the Balcony*)

Oh! 'tis my Love.
She seems to hang upon the cheek of Night,
Fairer then Snow upon the Raven's back,
Or a rich Jewel in an *Æthiop*'s ear.
Were she in yonder Sphear, she'd shine so bright,
That Birds would sing, and think the Day were breaking.   50

LAVINIA: Ah me!

MARIUS JUNIOR: She speaks.

Oh! speak agen, bright Angel: for thou art
As glorious to this Night, as Sun at Noon
To the admiring eyes of gazing Mortals,
When he bestrides the lazy puffing Clouds,
And fails* upon the bosom of the Air.

LAVINIA: O *Marius, Marius*! wherefore art thou *Marius*?
Deny thy Family, renounce thy Name:
Or if thou wilt not, be but sworn my Love,                60
And I'll no longer call *Metellus* Parent.

MARIUS JUNIOR: Shall I hear this, and yet keep silence?

LAVINIA: No.
'Tis but thy Name that is my Enemy.
Thou would'st be still thy self, though not a *Marius*,
Belov'd of me, and charming as thou art.
What's in a Name? that which we call a Rose,
By any other name wou'd smell as sweet.
So *Marius*, were he not *Marius* call'd,
Be still as dear to my desiring Eyes,
Without that Title. *Marius*, lose thy Name,              70
And for that Name, which is no part of Thee,
Take all *Lavinia*.

MARIUS JUNIOR: At thy word I take thee.
Call me but Thine, and Joys will so transport me,
I shall forget my self, and quite be chang'd.

LAVINIA: Who art Thou, that thus hid and veil'd in Night
Hast overheard my Follies?

MARIUS JUNIOR: By a Name
I know not how to tell thee who I am.
My Name, dear Creature, 's hatefull to my self,

Because it is an Enemy to Thee.

LAVINIA: *Marius*? how cam'st thou hither? tell, and why? 80
The Orchard-walls are high, and hard to climb,
And the place Death, consid'ring who thou art,
If any of our Family here find thee.[11]
By whose Directions didst thou find this place?

MARIUS JUNIOR: By Love, that first did prompt me to enquire.
He lent me Counsell, and I lent him Eyes.
I am no Pilot; yet wert thou as far
As the vast Shoar washt by the farthest Sea,
I'd hazard Ruine for a Prize so dear.—

LAVINIA: Oh *Marius*! vain are all such Hopes and Wishes. 90
The hand of Heav'n has thrown a Bar between us,
Our Houses Hatred and the Fate of *Rome*,
Where none but *Sylla* must be happy now.
All bring him Sacrifices of some sort,
And I must be a Victim to his Bed.
To night my Father broke the dreadfull news;
And when I urg'd him for the Right of Love,
He threaten'd me to banish me his House,
Naked and shiftless to the World. Would'st thou,
*Marius*, receive a Beggar to thy Bosom? 100

MARIUS JUNIOR: Oh! were my Joys but fixt upon that point,
I'd then shake hands with Fortune and be friends;
Thus grasp my Happiness, embrace it thus,
And bless th 'ill turn that gave thee to my Arms.

LAVINIA: Thou know'st the mask of Night is on my Face,
Else should I blush for what th' hast heard me speak.
Fain would I dwell on Form; fain, fain deny
The things I've said: but farewell all such Follies.
Dost thou then love? I know thou'lt say thou dost;
And I must take thy word, though thou prove false.[12]

MARIUS JUNIOR: By yon bright *Cynthia*'s beams that shines above. 110

---

[11] 43–83. Based on *Romeo and Juliet*, II.ii.1–69.
[12] 105–10. *Romeo and Juliet*, II.ii.90–7.

LAVINIA: Oh! swear not by the Moon, th' inconstant
   Moon,
  That changes Monthly, and shines but by seasons,
  Lest that thy Love prove variable too.

MARIUS JUNIOR: What shall I swear by?

LAVINIA:                  Do not swear at
  all.
  Or, if thou wilt, swear by thy gracious Self,
  Who art the God of my Idolatry,
  And I'll believe thee.

MARIUS JUNIOR: Witness, all ye Powr's.

LAVINIA: Nay, do not swear: although my Joy be great,
  I'm hardly satisfy'd with this night's Contract:
  It seems too rash, too unadvis'd and sudden,
  Too like the Lightning, which does cease to be
  E're one can say it is. Therefore this time
  Good night, my *Marius*: may a happier hour
  Bring us to crown our Wishes.

MARIUS JUNIOR: Why wilt thou leave me so unsatisfy'd?

LAVINIA: What wouldst thou have?

MARIUS JUNIOR:             Th' Exchange of Love
  for mine.

LAVINIA: I gave thee mine before thou didst request it;
  And yet I wish I could retrieve it back.

MARIUS JUNIOR: Why?

LAVINIA:             But to be frank, and give it thee
  agen.
  My Bounty is as boundless as the Sea,
  My Love as deep: the more I give to Thee,
  The more I have: for both are Infinite.
  I hear a Noise within. Farewell, my *Marius*;
  Or stay a little, and I'll come agen.

MARIUS JUNIOR: Stay? sure for ever.

LAVINIA: Three words, and, *Marius*, then good night
  indeed.
  If that thy Love be honourably meant,
  Thy Purpose Marriage, send me word tomorrow,
  And all my Fortunes at thy feet I'll lay.

120

130

140

NURSE: (*within*) Madam!

LAVINIA: I come anon. But if thou mean'st not well,
I do beseech thee,

NURSE: (*within*) Madam! Madam! . . .

LAVINIA: By and by, I come.
To cease thy Suit, and leave me to my Griefs.
To morrow I will send. . . .                         [*Exit*]

MARIUS JUNIOR: So thrive my Soul. Is not all this a
Dream,
Too lovely, sweet and flatt'ring, to be true?

                    *Re-enter* LAVINIA

LAVINIA: Hist, *Marius*, hist. Oh for a Falkner's voice,
To Lure this Tassell-gentle back agen.                  150
Restraint has Fears, and may not speak aloud:
Else would I tear the Cave where Echo lies,
With repetition of my *Marius*.—

MARIUS JUNIOR: It is my Love that calls me back agen.
How sweetly Lovers voices sound by night!
Like softest Musick to attending ears.

LAVINIA: *Marius*.

MARIUS JUNIOR: My dear.

LAVINIA: What a clock tomorrow?

MARIUS JUNIOR:                          At the hour of nine.

LAVINIA: I will not fail: 'Tis twenty years till then.
Why did I call thee back?                                160

MARIUS JUNIOR: Let me here stay till thou remember'st
why.

LAVINIA: The Morning's breaking, I wou'd have thee gone,
And yet no farther than a Wanton's Bird,
That lets it hop a little from his hand,
To pull it by its Fetters back agen.

MARIUS JUNIOR: Would I were thine.

LAVINIA: Indeed and so would I.
Yet I should kill thee sure with too much cherishing.
No more . . . Good night.

MARIUS JUNIOR: There's such sweet Pain in parting,
That I could hang for ever on thy Arms,

And look away my life into thy Eyes.[13]                    170
LAVINIA: Tomorrow will come.
MARIUS JUNIOR: So it will. Good night.
    Heav'n be thy Guard; and all its Blessings wait thee . . .
                               [*Exit* LAVINIA]
    Tomorrow! 'tis no longer: but Desires
    Are swift, and longing Love wou'd lavish time.
    Tomorrow! oh tomorrow till that come,
    The tedious Hours move heavily away,
    And each long Minute seems a lazy Day.
    Already Light is mounted in the Air,
    Striking it self through every Element.
    Our Party will by this time be abroad,                   180
    To try the Fate of *Marius* and *Rome*.
    Love and Renown sure court me thus together.
    Smile, smile, ye Gods, and give Success to both.   [*Exit*]

## Scene iii*

### The Forum

### Enter Four Citizens

3 CITIZEN: Well, Neighbours, now we are here, what must
    we doe?
1 CITIZEN: Why you must give your Vote for *Caius Marius*
    to be Consul: and if any body speaks against you, knock
    'em down.
2 CITIZEN: The truth on't is, there's nothing like a Civil
    Government, where good Subjects may have leave to
    knock Brains out to maintain Privileges.
3 CITIZEN: Look you . . . but what's this *Sylla*? this *Sylla*?
    I've heard great talk of him. . . . He's a damnable fighting   10
    fellow they say; but hang him . . . he's a Lord.
1 CITIZEN: Ay, so he is, Neighbours: and I know not why
    any one should be a Lord more then another. I care not
    for a Lord: what good do they doe? nothing but run in

---

[13] III-70. Based on *Romeo and Juliet*, II.ii.112–201.

our debts, and ly with our Wives.—

4 CITIZEN: Why, there's a Grievance now. I have three
Boys at home, no more mine than *Rome*'s mine. They are
all fair curl'd-hair *Cupids*; and I am an honest black
tawny Kettle-fac'd Fellow. . . . I'll ha' no Lords. . . .[14]

[*Drum and Trumpets*]

\*     \*     \*

# ACT III

# Scene ii\*

METELLUS *house*
*Enter* LAVINIA

LAVINIA: Gallop apace, ye firy-footed Steeds,
Tow'rds *Phœbus* Lodging. Such a Charioteer
As *Phaeton* would lash you to the West,
And bring in cloudy Night immediately.
Spread thy close Curtains Love-performing Night
To sober-suited Matron all in black;
That jealous eyes may wink, and *Marius*
Leap to these Arms untalkt-of and unseen.
Oh! give me *Marius*; and when he shall dy,
Take him, and cut him out in little Stars;                    10
And he will make the Face of Heav'n so fine,
That all the world shall grow in love with Night,
And pay no worship to the gaudy Sun.
Oh! I have bought the Mansion of a Love,
But not possest it. . . . Tedious is this Day,
As is the Night before some Festival
To an impatient Child that has new Robes,

---

[14] 1–19. Reminiscent of *Coriolanus*, II.ii.

*Enter* NURSE *and* CLODIUS

And may not wear 'em. Welcome, Nurse: what news?
How fares the Lord of all my Joys, my *Marius*?[15]

NURSE: Oh! a Chair! a Chair! no Questions, but a Chair!   20
So.

LAVINIA: Nay, prithee Nurse, why dost thou look so sad?
Oh! do not spoil the Musick of good Tidings
With such a melancholick wretched Face.

NURSE: Oh! I am weary, very weary. *Clodius*, my
Cordial-bottle. Fy! how my bones ake! what a Jaunt
have I had!

LAVINIA: Do not delay me thus, but quickly tell me,
Will *Marius* come to night? speak, will he come?

NURSE: Alas! alas! what haste? oh! cannot you stay a   30
little? oh! do not you see that I'm out of breath? oh this
Ptisick! *Clodius*, the Cordial.

LAVINIA: Th' Excuse thou mak'st for this unkind Delay
Is longer then the Tale thou hast to tell.
Is thy News good or bad? answer to that.
Say either, and I'll stay the Circumstance.

NURSE: Well, you have made a simple Choice: you know
not how to chuse a man. Yet his Leg excells all mens.
And for a Hand and a Foot and a Shape, though they are
not to be talkt of . . . yet they are past compare. What,   40
have you Din'd within?

LAVINIA: No, no: what foolish Questions dost thou ask?
What says he of his Coming? what of that?

NURSE: Oh! how my Head akes! what a Head have I!
It beats as it would fall in twenty pieces.
My Back o' tother side! ah! my Back! my Back!
Beshrew your heart for sending me about
To catch my Death. . . . This Back of mine will break.
                                       *[Drinks]*

LAVINIA: Indeed I'm sorry if thou art not well.
But prithee tell me, Nurse, what says my Love?   50

NURSE: Why, your Love says like an honest Gentleman,

---

[15] 1–19. *Based on* Romeo and Juliet, *III.ii.1–33.*

and a kind Gentleman, and a handsome ... and I'll
warrant a vertuous Gentleman. [*Drinks.*] Well ... what?
where's your Father?

LAVINIA: Where's my Father? why, he's at the Senate.
How odly thou reply'st?
Your Love says like an honest Gentleman,
Where's your Father?

NURSE: Oh good Lady dear!
Are you so hot? marry come up, I trow.
Is this a Poultice for my aking Bones?                    60
Henceforward do your Messages your self.[16]

LAVINIA: Nay, prithee be not angry, Nurse; I meant
No ill. Speak kindly, will my *Marius* come?

NURSE: Will he? will a Duck swim?

LAVINIA: Then he will come.

NURSE: Come? why, he will come upon all four, but he'll
come. Go, get you in, and say your Prayers: go.

LAVINIA: For Blessings on my *Marius* and Thee.

NURSE: Well, it would be a sad thing though. ...

LAVINIA: What?                                            70

NURSE: If *Marius* should not come now ... for there's old
doings at the Gates, they are at it ding-dong. Tantarara go
the Trumpets; Shout, cry the Souldiers; Clatter go The
Swords. I'll warrant ... I made no small haste. ...

LAVINIA: And is my *Marius* there? alas my Fears!

[*Trumpets*]

The Noise comes this way. Guard my Love, ye Gods,
Or strike me with your Thunder when he falls.

[*Exeunt*]

\*        \*        \*

---

[16] 20–61. Based on *Romeo and Juliet*, II.v.26–66.

# ACT V

## Scene iv*

### A Church-yard

*Enter* MARIUS JUNIOR

MARIUS JUNIOR: As I have wander'd musing to and fro,
 Still am I brought to this unlucky place,
 As I had business with the horrid Dead:
 Though could I trust the flattery of Sleep,
 My Dreams presage some joyfull news at hand.
 My Bosome's Lord sits lightly on his Throne,
 And all this day an unaccustom'd Spirit
 Lifts me above the ground with chearfull thoughts.
 I dream'd *Lavinia* came and found me dead,
 And breath'd such Life with Kisses on my Lips,　　　10
 That I reviv'd, and was an Emperour.[17]

          *Enter* CATULUS

CATULUS: My Lord already here?

MARIUS JUNIOR:　　　　　　　My trusty *Catulus*,
 What News from my *Lavinia*? speak, and bless me.

CATULUS: She's very well. . . .

MARIUS JUNIOR:　　　　　Then nothing can be ill.
 Something thou seem'st to know that's terrible.
 Out with it boldly, man, What canst thou say
 Of my *Lavinia*?

CATULUS:　　　　　But one sad word. She's dead.*
 Here in her Kindreds Vault I've seen her laid,
 And have bin searching you to tell the News.

MARIUS JUNIOR: Dead? is it so? then I deny you, Stars.　　20
 Go, hasten quickly, get me Ink and Paper.
 'Tis done: I'll hence to night.

[17] 4–11. Based on *Romeo and Juliet*, V.i.1–9.

Hast thou no Letters to me from the Priest?

CATULUS: No, my good Lord.

MARIUS JUNIOR: No matter, get thee gone. . . .

[*Exit* CATULUS]

*Lavinia*! yet I'll ly with thee to night;
But, for the means. Oh Mischief! thou art swift
To catch the straggling Thoughts of Desp'rate men.
I do remember an Apothecary,
That dwelt about this Rendezvous of Death:
Meager and very rufull were his Looks;                          30
Sharp Misery had worn him to the Bones;
And in his needy Shop a Tortoise hung,
An Allegator stufft, and other Skins
Of ill-shap'd Fishes: and about his Shelves
A beggarly account of empty Boxes,
Green earthen Pots, Bladders, and musty Seeds,
Remnants of Packthread, and old Cakes of Roses,
Were thinly scatter'd, to make up a Show.
Oh for a Poison now! his Need will sell it,
Though it be present Death by *Roman* Law.                     40
As I remember this should be the House.
His Shop is shut: with Beggars all are Holydays.
Holla! Apothecary; hoa!

*Enter* APOTHECARY

APOTHECARY: Who's there?

MARIUS JUNIOR: Come hither, man. I see thou 'rt very
poor;
Thou mayst doe any thing: there's fifty *Drachma's*,
Get me a Draught of that will soonest free
A Wretch from all his Cares: thou understand'st me.

APOTHECARY: Such mortal Drugs I have; but *Roman* Law
Speaks Death to any he that utters 'em.

MARIUS JUNIOR: Art thou so base and full of Wretched-
ness,                                                          50
Yet fear'st to dy? Famine is in thy Cheeks,
Need and Oppression stareth in thy Eyes,
Contempt and Beggary hang on thy Back;
The World is not thy Friend, nor the World's Law;

The World affords no Law to make thee rich:
Then be not poor, but break it, and take this.

APOTHECARY: My Poverty, but not my Will consents. . . .
              [*Goes in, fetches a Vial of Poison*]
Take this and drink it off, the Work is done.

MARIUS JUNIOR: There is thy Gold, worse Poison to mens
    Souls,
  Doing more Murthers in this loathsome world                60
  Then these poor Compounds thou 'rt forbid to sell.
  I sell thee Poison, thou hast sold me none.[18]
  Farewell . . . buy Food . . . and get thy self in flesh.
  Now for the Monument of the *Metelli*. . . .    [*Exit*]
(*Scene draws off, and shews the Temple and Monument*)
                  *Re-enters*
  It should be here: the door is open too.
  Th' insatiate mouth of Fate gapes wide for more.
  Enter PRIEST,* *and Boy with a Mattock and Iron Crow*

PRIEST: Give me the Mattock and the wrenching Iron:[19]
  Now take this Letter, with what haste thou canst
  Find out young *Marius*, and deliver it.     [*Exit Boy*]
  Now must I to the Monument alone.[20]                      70
  What Wretch is he that's entring into th' Tomb?
  Some Villain come to rob and spoil the Dead.
  Whoe're thou art, stop thy unhallowed purpose.

MARIUS JUNIOR: Whoe're thou art, I warn thee to be gone,
  And do not interrupt my horrid purpose.
  For else, by Heav'n, I'll tear thee joint by joint,
  And strew this hungry Church-yard with thy Lims.
  My Mind and its Intents are savage wild,
  More fierce and more inexorable far
  Then empty Tigers or the roaring Sea.                      80

PRIEST: Then as a sacrilegious Slave I charge thee,
  Obey and go with me, or thou must dy.

MARIUS JUNIOR: I know I must, and therefore I came
    hither.

---

[18] 13–63. Based on *Romeo and Juliet*, V.i.12–87.
[19] 67–8. *Romeo and Juliet*, V.iii.22–3.
[20] 70. *Romeo and Juliet*, V.ii.24.

Good Reverence, do not tempt a desp'rate man.
By Heav'n, I love thee better than my self:
For I against my self come hither arm'd.
Stay not, be gone. . . . Live, and hereafter say,
A Mad-man's Mercy gave thee honest Counsell.

PRIEST: I do defy thy mercy and thy Counsell,
And here will seize thee as a Thief and Robber.                90

MARIUS JUNIOR: Wilt thou provoke me? then here, take
thy Wages.                                           [Kills him]

PRIEST: I'm kill'd. Oh *Marius*! now too late I know thee.
Thou'st slain the onely man could doe thee good.
*Lavinia* . . . oh! . . .                                [Dies]

MARIUS JUNIOR: Let me peruse this Face.
It is the honest Priest that joyn'd our hands,*
In a Disguize conceal'd. Give me thy Hand,
Since in ill Fate's black Roll with me thou'rt writ,
I'll bury thee in a triumphant Grave.[21]
Thou detestable Maw, thou Womb of Death,
Gorg'd with the dearest Morsell of the Earth,
Thus will I force thy rotten Jaws to open, . . .              100
                (*Pulls down the side of the Tomb*)
And spite of thee yet cram thee with more Food.
Oh gorgeous Palace! oh my Love! my Wife!
Death has had yet no pow'r upon thy Beauty;
That is not conquer'd. Beauty's Ensign yet
Is Crimson in thy Lips and in thy Cheeks;
And the pale Flag is not advanc'd yet there.
Why art thou still so fair? shall I believe
That the lean Monster Death is amorous,
And keeps thee here in Darkness for his Paramour?            110
For fear of that, I'll stay with thee for ever.
Come, bitter Conduct, thou unsavoury Guide:
Here's to my Love. . . .                      [Drinks the Poison]
And now Eyes look your last.[22]
Arms take your last Embrace, whilst on these Lips
I fix the Seal of an eternall Contract. . . .

---

[21] 74–98. Based on *Romeo and Juliet*, V.iii.32–83.
[22] 103–14. Based on *Romeo and Juliet*, V.iii.91–113.

She breaths and stirs. . . .                    [LAVINIA *wakes**]

LAVINIA: (*in the Tomb*) Where am I? bless me, Heav'n!
'Tis very cold; and yet here's something warm. . . .

MARIUS JUNIOR: She lives, and we shall both be made
    immortall.

Speak, my *Lavinia*, speak some heav'nly news,
And tell me how the Gods design to treat us.                    120

LAVINIA: Oh! I have slept a long Ten thousand years.
What have they done with me? I'll not be us'd thus;
I'll not wed *Sylla*. *Marius* is my Husband.
Is he not, Sir? Methinks you're very like him.
Be good as he is, and protect me.

MARIUS JUNIOR: Hah!
Wilt thou not own me? am I then but like him?
Much, much indeed I'm chang'd from what I was;
And ne'r shall be my self, if thou art lost.

LAVINIA: The Gods have heard my Vows; it is my *Marius*.
Once more they have restor'd him to my Eyes.                    130
Hadst thou not come, sure I had slept for ever.
But there's a soveraign Charm in thy Embraces,
That might doe Wonders, and revive the Dead.

MARIUS JUNIOR: Ill Fate no more, *Lavinia*, now shall part
    us,
Nor cruel Parents, nor oppressing Laws.
Did not Heav'n's Pow'rs all wonder at our Loves?
And when thou toldst the tale of thy Disasters,
Was there not Sadness and a Gloom amongst 'em?
I know there was; and they in pity send thee,
Thus to redeem me from this vale of Torments,                    140
And bear me with thee to those Hills of Joys.
This World's gross air grows burthensome already.
I'm all a God: such heav'nly Joys transport me,
That mortal Sense grows sick and faints with lasting.

                                 [*Dies*]

LAVINIA: Oh! to recount my Happiness to thee,
To open all the Treasure of my Soul,
And shew thee how 'tis fill'd, would waste more time
Then so impatient Love as mine can spare.

He's gone; he's dead; breathless: alas! my *Marius*.
A Vial too: here, here has bin his Bane.                    150
Oh Churl! drink all? not leave one friendly Drop
For poor *Lavinia*? Yet I'll drain thy Lips.
Perhaps some welcom Poison may hang there,[23]
To help me to o'retake thee on thy Journy.
Clammy and damp as Earth. Hah! stains of Bloud?
And a man murther'd? 'Tis th'unhappy *Flamen*.
Who fix their Joys on any thing that's Mortall,
Let 'em behold my Portion, and despair.
What shall I doe? how will the Gods dispose me?           160
Oh! I could rend these Walls with Lamentation,
Tear up the Dead from their corrupted Graves,
And dawb the face of Earth with her own Bowels.

*Enter* MARIUS SENIOR, *and Guards driving in* METELLUS

MARIUS SENIOR: Pursue the Slave; let not his Gods protect
    him.
LAVINIA: More Mischiefs? hah! my Father?
METELLUS: Oh! I am slain.

                                      [*Falls down and dies*]

LAVINIA: And murther'd too. When will my Woes have
    end?
    Come, cruel Tyrant.
MARIUS SENIOR: Sure I have known that Face.
LAVINIA: And canst thou think of any one good Turn
    That I have done thee, and not kill me for't?
MARIUS SENIOR: Art thou not call'd *Lavinia*?
LAVINIA: Once I was:                                          170
    But by my Woes may now be better known.
MARIUS SENIOR: I cannot see thy Face. . . .
LAVINIA: You must, and hear me.
    By this, you must: nay, I will hold you fast. . . .

                                      [*Seizes his Sword*]

MARIUS SENIOR: What wouldst thou say? where's all my
    Rage gone now?
LAVINIA: I am *Lavinia*, born of Noble race.

---

[23] 151–3. *Romeo and Juliet*, V.iii.168–70.

My blooming Beauty conquer'd many Hearts,
But prov'd the greatest Torment of my own:
Though my Vows prosper'd, and my Love was answer'd
By *Marius*, the noblest, goodliest Youth
That Man e're envy'd at, or Virgin sigh'd for.                    180
He was the Son of an unhappy Parent,
And banish'd with him when our Joys were young;
Scarce a night old.

MARIUS SENIOR: I do remember't well,
And thou art She, that Wonder of thy kind,
That couldst be true to exil'd Misery,
And to and fro through barren Desarts range,
To find th'unhappy Wretch thy Soul was fond of.*

LAVINIA: Do you remember't well?

MARIUS SENIOR: In every point.

LAVINIA: You then were gentle, took me in your Arms,
Embrac'd me, blest me, us'd me like a Father.                    190
And sure I was not thankless for the Bounty.

MARIUS SENIOR: No; thou wert next the Gods my onely
    Comfort.
When I lay fainting on the dry parcht Earth,
Beneath the scorching heat of burning Noon,
Hungry and dry, no Food nor Friend to chear me:
Then Thou, as by the Gods some Angel sent,
Cam'st by, and in Compassion didst relieve me.

LAVINIA: Did I all this?

MARIUS SENIOR: Thou didst, thou sav'dst my Life.
Else I had sunk beneath the weight of Want,
And bin a Prey to my remorseless Foes.                    200

LAVINIA: And see how well I am at last rewarded.
All could not balance for the short-term'd Life
Of one Old man: You have my Father butcher'd,
The onely Comfort I had left on Earth.
The Gods have taken too my Husband from me.
See where he lies, your and my onely Joy.
This Sword yet reeking with my Father's Gore,
Plunge it into my Breast: plunge, plunge it thus.
And now let Rage, Distraction and Despair

Seize all Mankind, till they grow mad as I am.                210

[*Stabs her self with his Sword*]

MARIUS SENIOR: Nay, now thou hast outdone me much in
    Cruelty.

Be Nature's Light extinguisht; let the Sun
Withdraw his Beams, and put the world in Darkness,
Whilst here I howl away my Life in Sorrows.
Oh! let me bury Me and all my Sins
Here with this good Old man. Thus let me kiss
Thy pale sunk Cheeks, embalm thee with my Tears.
My Son, how cam'st thou by this wretched End?
We might have all bin Friends, and in one House
Enjoy'd the Blessings of eternal Peace.                      220
But oh! my cruel Nature has undone me.

*Enter* MESSENGER

MESSENGER: My Lord, I bring you most disastrous News.
*Sylla*'s return'd: his Army's on their march
From *Capua*, and to morrow will reach *Rome*.
At which the Rabble are in new Rebellion,
And your *Sulpitius* mortally is wounded.

*Enter* SULPITIUS (*led in by two of the Guards*) *and*
GRANIUS

MARIUS SENIOR: Oh! then I'm ruin'd from this very
    moment.

Has my good Genius left me? Hope forsakes me.
The Name of *Sylla*'s banefull to my Fortune.
Be warn'd by me, ye Great ones, how y' embroil        230
Your Country's Peace, and dip your Hands in Slaughter.
Ambition is a Lust that's never quencht,[24]
Grows more inflam'd and madder by Enjoyment.
Bear me away, and lay me on my Bed,
A hopelesse Vessel bound for the dark Land
Of loathsome Death, and loaded deep with Sorrows.

[*He is led off*]

SULPITIUS: A Curse on all Repentance! how I hate it!
I'd rather hear a Dog howl than a Man whine.

[24] 230–3. Compare *Romeo and Juliet*, V.iii.305–8.

GRANIUS: You're wounded, Sir: I hope it is not much.

SULPITIUS: No; 'tis not so deep as a Well, nor so wide as a 240
Church-door. But 'tis enough; 'twill serve; I am pep-
per'd[25] I warrant, I warrant for this world. A Pox on all
Mad-men hereafter. If I get a Monument, let this be my
Epitaph:
*Sulpitius lies here, that troublesome Slave,*
*That sent many honester men to the Grave,*
*And dy'd like a Fool when h' had liv'd like a Knave.*

[*Exeunt omnes*]

FINIS

---

[25] 239–41. *Romeo and Juliet*, III.i.95–7.

Tilley: refers throughout to M. P. Tilley, *A Dictionary of Proverbs in England in the Sixteenth and Seventeenth Centuries* (Michigan: Ann Arbor, 1950) which is the standard reference work.

## *John Lacy,* Sauny the Scot

**p.7 Fondness:** Foolish affection.

**p.7 Rough-casts:** Fashions roughly.

**p.8 Trammel's:** Hobbles, shackles.

**p.8 Stale:** Bait.

**p.8 Mates:** Fellows.

**p.9 Muckinders:** Handkerchiefs.

**p.9 Neats-Leather:** Leather from an ox., i.e., rough, weather-beaten.

**p.9 Froward:** Refractory, perverse.

**p.9 live:** (lief) Willingly.

**p.9 *Chairing-cross*:** Charing Cross, where malefactors were publicly punished, and sometimes executed.

**p.9 there's small choice in rotten *Apples*:** Proverbial. See Tilley C358.

**p.9 he that can win her, wear her:** Proverbial. See Tilley W408 ('Win it and wear it').

**p.9 Woe her, Wed her, and Bed her:** Proverbial. See Tilley W731 ('Woo, wed, and bed her').

**p.9 hold your tack:** Be a match for you.

**p.10 mew'd her up:** Confined her.

p.10 **Salve:** Solution.

p.10 **uncase:** Undress.

p.12 **Muckle:** (or muccle) Great (Scots).

p.12 **Mowing:** Jesting (Scots).

p.13 **gar:** Make (Scots).

p.13 **I may not beat yea o' yee'r e'ne Dunghill:** Cf. Tilley C486 ('A cock is bold on his own dunghill').

p.14 **That shall break no Squares:** Cf. Tilley 154 ('An inch breaks no square', i.e., a small fault is of no import).

p.14 **Cragg:** Neck (Scots).

p.16 **Country:** Native.

p.16 **muckle:** Much (Scots).

p.16 **brave:** Finely dressed.

p.18 **Whisk:** Neckerchief.

p.18 **Clouts:** Pieces.

p.19 **lead Apes in Hell:** Proverbial. See Tilley M37 ('Old maids lead apes in hell'; a traditional fate of unmarried women).

p.20 **Whim–whum:** Whimsically(?); perhaps simply suggesting a lively rhythm.

p.20 **Ligby:** (lig = lie, + by) Bedfellow, mistress.

p.21 **Portion:** Dowry.

p.21 **Jointure:** Estate settled upon a wife to make provision for her widowhood.

p.21 **Lutes:** Play on 'lute', a kind of cement.

p.21 **break her to thy Lute:** Teach her to play the lute, with a pun on 'breaking' in a horse.

p.22 **Luggs:** Ears (Scots).

p.22 **faw:** Fall, or fell (Scots).

p.22 **Rubbers at Cuffs:** Fisticuffs.

p.22 **Ragmanners:** Slang for someone of bad manners.

p.22 *Moveable*: Portable item of furniture, or changeable person.

p.23 **tea:** Too.

p.23 **grand Paw:** *Grand pas* (French), a dance step.

p.23 *Mad Couple well match'd*: A successful comedy by Richard Brome (pub. 1653).

p.23 **wamble:** Churn.

p.23 **faw:** Foul.

p.23 **Logger heads:** Blockheads.

p.24 **loose your Armes:** Forfeit your coat-of-arms (signifying a gentleman).

p.24 **Blazon:** Describe, embellish (in heraldic terms).

p.24 **Scotch wutch:** Scottish witches may have been particularly associated with the supposed power to summon up winds; some of those executed for treason against King James VI in 1590/1 were accused of this.

p.24 **weeme:** (wame) Belly, womb (Scots).

p.24 **Whupster:** (whipster) Various meanings, including a person who is lively or violent, wanton or lascivious, or slight and contemptible (the usual Shakespearean sense), may be appropriate here.

p.24 **pump:** Labour.

p.24 **Jack a Lent:** A figure set up to be pelted, in a custom practised during Lent; hence, a contemptible person.

p.24 **Clutter:** Turmoil.

p.25 **Grizel:** Patient Griselda, model of wifely patience and obedience, heroine of Chaucer's *Clerk's Tale*.

p.26 *De clara*: Probably means clear, manifest.

p.27 **nip't:** Checked.

p.27 **Cavel:** (cavil) Quibbling objection.

p.27 **set footing:** Take up a new position.

**p.27 the Case must be alter'd:** Proverbial. See Tilley C111 ('The case is altered').

**p.28 Prickt:** With music set down by 'pricks' or notes.

**p.30 kikshaw:** Trifle.

**p.30 Woo'd in hast, and means to Wed at Leisure:** Proverbial, alluding to Tilley H196 ('Marry in haste, repent at leisure').

**p.31 Chape:** Scabbard.

**p.31 Spavin'd:** Suffering from swellings on the leg-joints.

**p.31 Glander'd:** Affected with the glanders, a disease of horses characterised by swellings beneath the jaw and mucous discharge.

**p.32 Scotch Directory:** The Presbyterian service book, ratified in 1645.

**p.32 Knight of the Post:** Professional perjurer, who made a living by giving false evidence.

**p.33 Chous'd:** Duped.

**p.34 you may be jogging while your boots be green:** Proverbial expression for hastening someone's departure. See Tilley B536 ('Be jogging while your boots are green').

**p.35 big:** Haughty.

**p.35 my proper goods and Chattells, my House, my Ox, my Ass:** Parodying the Tenth Commandment.

**p.35 smoak:** Smart.

**p.35 Dudgeon Dagger:** A dagger with a hilt made of dudgeon, a kind of wood used specially for this purpose.

**p.35 Buckler:** Shield.

**p.36 Bears me fair in hand:** Gives me fair assurances.

**p.36 Attractive:** Having influence over others.

**p.37 *No point*:** Not a bit, i.e., nothing.

**p.37 Jack-pudding:** Buffoon.

**p.37 Willow garland:** Symbol of unrequited love.

**p.38 to a hair:** To a nicety.

p.39 **look to your Eares, if you have any**: Cutting off the ears was a punishment for perjury.

p.39 **Scaud**: Scold.

p.39 **draw bit**: Stop or slacken (a horse is stopped by drawing on the reins and hence the bit).

p.41 **faw**: Perhaps 'foul' (as above), meaning 'catch'.

p.42 **Chollar**: Bile, supposed to engender irascibility.

p.43 **Boyes**: Probably 'Bodyes' is intended.

p.43 **blathers**: Bladders.

p.43 **Dinger**: Danger.

p.43 **swatch**: Unknown. Perhaps switch (or whip), or passage, route (to the gallows).

p.43 **head-peice**: Helmet.

p.44 **March Beer**: Strong beer brewed in March.

p.44 **Hackny Horse**: Horse of middling size and quality, an ordinary horse, also one kept for hire; used figuratively here for a common person, perhaps a prostitute.

p.46 **Braw**: Fine (Scots).

p.46 **Bull's puzzle**: The penis of a bull, often used as a whip.

p.46 **Liquor'd bute**: Boot dressed with oil or grease.

p.47 *Scotch* **Pudding**: Presumably a frugal dish of meal and water, brose.

p.47 **Fou**: Foul.

p.47 **Whinyard**: Short sword.

p.47 *Gilderoy*: A Scottish robber said to have been hanged higher than other criminals on account of the severity of his crimes.

p.47 **lath**: Loath.

p.48 **for a Race**: For a while.

p.48 **a Nag with a Weam, but a Mare with Nean**: Proverbial. See Tilley N3 ('A nag with a weamb [womb] and a mare with nean [none]').

**p.48 Demmy cannon:** (demi-cannon) A kind of large gun.

**p.49 Queen Margaret:** No such portrait is known. There were various Scottish Queen Margarets, most recently Margaret Tudor, mother of James V of Scotland. Two portraits of her exist, neither in Edinburgh Castle.

**p.49 Antickly:** Grotesquely.

**p.49 a cruppen:** Has crept.

**p.50 Lands end:** Presumably the end of his estate.

**p.51 Yet:** Then.

**p.51 Rogue Paramount:** As in 'lord paramount', a feudal lord superior or overlord.

**p.51 lay the Dragon asleep while my Master steals the Pippins:** Alluding to one of the labours of Hercules, which was to steal the golden apples of the Hesperides which were guarded by a dragon; this he achieved by putting the dragon to sleep.

**p.51 Peece:** Coin.

**p.53 Pitchers have Eares:** Proverbial. See Tilley P363 ('Small pitchers have wide ears').

**p.53 *Obadiah*:** Perhaps a Puritan name.

**p.54 *Matrimony*:** The marriage service.

**p.54 Grub:** An insult, probably with additional meaning of 'money-grubber'.

**p.54 Privity:** Cognisance.

**p.55 Sheat:** Perhaps made notorious on a broadsheet, or else just 'a shit'.

**p.55 save you harmless:** Keep you from harm.

**p.56 the Bowl runs with a Right Byas:** Metaphor from bowling, where the bias is the eccentric weight which causes the ball to follow a curving path.

**p.56 March Hare:** Proverbial type of madness.

**p.57 Trundle Taile Tike:** Curly-tailed (i.e., low-bred) dog.

p.58 **mattle:** (mettle) Disposition.

p.58 **put me in a Heat:** Aroused me.

p.58 **Thrumming of Caps:** Literally covering caps with thrums, which are odds and ends of thread (tassels); proverbial for wasting time.

p.60 **Frivelous circumstances:** Trivial details.

p.60 **Counter-Name:** Name used instead of a real or proper name, hence a false identity.

p.60 **seen the Church on their Back:** i.e., seen them married.

p.60 **Crack Hemp:** One likely to crack or strain the hangman's rope.

p.61 **below stayres:** In the servants' quarters.

p.61 **Clootes:** (clouts) Rags, pieces.

p.61 **Good Husband:** Thrifty manager.

p.61 **to anger:** To trouble you.

p.61 **Hemp-dresser:** One who hackles, or prepares, hemp.

p.61 *Partha*: Unknown.

p.61 **fow:** (fou) Full (Scots).

p.62 **forth-coming:** Available for trial.

p.62 **take the *Covenant*:** Enter into a formal agreement, probably alluding to the Covenant maintaining the principles of the Scottish Presbyterian church.

p.63 **te Vous la menes:** False French. Perhaps Winlove intends something like '*je vous l'amene*', I'm bringing her to you.

p.63 **breath a Vein:** Let blood.

p.64 **Patching with a Mistriss:** Joining or uniting with a lover.

p.64 **forgat and forgive:** Proverbial. See Tilley 597 ('Forgive and forget'), with a characteristic amendment by Sauny.

p.66 **within his verge:** Under his jurisdiction (the verge was originally an area surrounding the royal court and coming under its jurisdiction).

p.66 **freaks:** Caprices.

p.66 Trust him and hang him: Probably proverbial, though no specific proverb fits.

p.67 active: diligent.

p.67 the case is alter'd: Proverbial. See Tilley C111.

p.67 another gaits: Of a different sort.

p.67 *Grantham Steple*: Proverbially tall. See Tilley H396 ('It is height makes Grantham steeple stand awry').

p.67 Scauden Queen: Scolding queen (i.e. a harlot).

p.68 bra: (braw) Fine (Scots).

p.69 Curry: Comb a horse.

p.69 *man of Clouts*: Doll in the garb of a man.

p.69 smoakes: Fumes.

p.69 his own Dunghill: Alluding to Tilley C486 ('Every cock is proud on his own dunghill').

p.69 brangle: Dispute.

p.70 Stool of Repantance: A seat for an offender.

p.70 Laugh and be Hang'd: Perhaps a variant of Tilley L91 ('Laugh and be fat').

p.72 Coalepit: Coalmine.

p.72 Deel's arse o' Peake: The Deel's (or Devil's) arse on the Peak was a well-known hill on the north side of the road from Buxton to Castleton in Derbyshire. See Defoe, *A Tour Thro' the Whole Island of Great Britain* (1725), vol. 3, letter 8.

p.73 long home: Grave, or future state.

p.74 change: Exchange.

p.76 be your halves: Pay half the stake (and take half the winnings).

p.76 Durke: (dirk) A Highlander's dagger.

p.76 daft: Mild, meek, humble (though the *Oxford English Dictionary* gives no example of this sense after 1200); simple.

p.76 steake: (steek) Imprison (Scots; the *Oxford English Dictionary* v.1.1) or cling tenaciously to (the *Oxford English Dictionary* v.2.11); the sense is 'take hold of'.

**p.77 streake:** ('stroke' or 'streek') Lay prostrate (perhaps with a bawdy sense).

**p.78 the *Tamer Tam'd*:** A play by John Fletcher, otherwise known as *The Woman's Prize* (*c.* 1611), also based on *The Taming of the Shrew*, and performed in tandem with *Sauny the Scot* in the Restoration.

## John Dryden and William Davenant, The Tempest

**p.83 *Sir* William D'avenant ... *alteration of it*:** Davenant died on 7 April 1668, five months after the play's first performance on 7 November 1667. Dryden's preface was published in 1670. The two writers may have formed a friendship after the publication of Dryden's first long poem, *Annus Mirabilis*, in 1666, in which he imitated the stanza form of Davenant's epic, *Gondibert* (1651).

**p.83 *excellent* Fletcher ... *his* Sea-Voyage:** Fletcher's *The Sea-Voyage* (*c.* 1622), probably a collaboration with Massinger, had been revived by the King's Company on 25 September 1667, less than a fortnight before the opening of the Dryden-Davenant *Tempest*, to which it continued to run as a rival. It was far from being a 'copy of Shakespeare's *Tempest*'.

**p.83 John Suckling ... *his* Goblins ... *copied from* Ariel:** Sir John Suckling's *The Goblins* (*c.* 1637) was revived by the King's Company in January, May, and November 1667. The heroine's name is actually Reginella.

**p.84 a Man who had never seen a Woman:** Davenant had already experimented with such a character in Gridonell in *The Platonick Lovers* (1636), who has never seen a woman until adulthood and consequently is aroused at the sight of even the ugliest.

**p.84 *the old* Latine *Proverb*:** Cicero, *Philippics*, XII.ii.5: 'Posteriores enim cogitationes, ut aiunt, sapientores solent esse.' (Translated in the Loeb edition (transl. Walter A. C. Kerr, Loeb Classical Library, London: Heinemann, New York: G. P. Putnam's Sons, 1926) as 'For the later thoughts, as the saying is, are usually the wiser.')

**p.87 *(taught by none)*:** The idea of Shakespeare as an untaught genius seems to stem from Jonson himself, in his tribute to the poet in the First Folio (1623). It was later fostered by Milton, among many others.

**p.87** *One of our Women to present a Boy*: Hippolyto's role was played by a woman, commonly now supposed to have been Mary (known as Moll) Davis, famed for her legs, and for a liaison with Charles II which began soon after the premiere of *The Tempest*.

**p.91** hoaming: Tempestuous.

**p.91** Scud: Light clouds.

**p.92** reef: meaning to gather up the top part of the square sail with small ropes and tie it to the yardarm. Both Davenant and Dryden had knowledge of nautical terminology, and used a good deal of it in this scene, including 'jeere-capstorm', 'capstorm-bar', 'nippers', 'viall', 'vial-block', 'the anchor's a peek', 'cat', 'misen-tack', 'mackrel-gale', 'fore-boling', etc. All these and more are elucidated in the notes to *The Tempest*, ed. M. E. Novak and G. R. Guffey, in *The Works of John Dryden* (Berkeley, Los Angeles, and London: University of California Press, 1970), vol. 10.

**p.96** Fifteen Years since: Twelve in Shakespeare. Dryden and Davenant's Miranda is more sophisticated.

**p.97** over-toping: Cut down from growing too high.

**p.97** *Savoy's*: The change from Naples to Savoy may be made in the interests of geography or of topical significance. See Introduction, p.vii.

**p.97** *Nissa's*: Nice, under the control of Savoy at the time.

**p.99** coil: Confusion.

**p.100** Glasses: Hours.

**p.100** *Argier*: Algiers

**p.103** Abhor'd Slave!: In Shakespeare this speech is made by Miranda. The first Shakespearean editor to give it to Prospero was Lewis Theobald in his seven-volume *The Works of Shakespeare* (1733), who argued that Shakespeare originally intended it for Prospero.

**p.107** *Portugal*: The Moors were actually driven from Portugal in the thirteenth century, and from Spain in 1492. Davenant had earlier explored Christian/Moslem conflict in *The Siege of Rhodes* (1656).

**p.107 I pull'd a Tree . . . my hand:** A motif with a long ancestry, going back to Virgil, *Aeneid*, III, 328–48.

**p.107 [song] *Where does proud* Ambition *dwell* ?:** A good brief account of the music in the Restoration *Tempest*, and the scholarship concerning it, is given in C. Spencer (ed.) *Five Restoration Adaptations of Shakespeare* (University of Illinois Press: Urbana, 1965), pp.409–10.

**p.109 peid:** Pecked.

**p.110 Burthen:** A continuous chorus playing behind the main melody.

**p.111 Runlet:** Cask.

**p.111 soop:** A sip, or small quantity of liquid.

**p.111 steal Custom:** Cheat the custom-house.

**p.112 marry agen:** Topical reference. A law passed in 1666 permitted remarriage after the absence of a spouse for seven years.

**p.112 dry:** i.e. thirsty. This proverbial expression applies to widows or widowers to excuse their drinking for consolation (Tilley, S656).

**p.112 the next that catches his fellow may eat him:** Cannibalism is also proposed in Fletcher's *The Sea-Voyage*. The subject contributes to the contemporary debate about primitivism and natural man. See Susan Staves, *Players' Sceptres. Fictions of Authority in the Restoration* (University of Nebraska Press: Lincoln and London, 1979), esp. ch. 5.

**p.114 Old *Simon* the King:** The title of a popular song recommending drink as a panacea, but given new words with topical significance after the Restoration, and entitled 'Rebellion given over to House-Keeping: or, A General Sale of Rebellious Household Stuff'.

**p.115 Urchin shows:** Tricks of elves or goblins.

**p.121 Form:** Nest or burrow.

**p.129 purvey'd:** Provided food.

**p.132 forth-rights and Meanders:** Straight paths and winding ones.

**p.133 *eight fat Spirits*:** In the farce, *The Rehearsal*, by George Villiers, Duke of Buckingham, Mr Bayes (a caricature of Dryden), says to some soldiers, 'Udsookers, you dance worse than the Angels in *Harry* the Eight, or the fat Spirits in *The Tempest*, Igad' (II.v).

**p.133 Burgo-Masters:** Pun on burgomaster as mayor of a Dutch town (traditionally fat) and burgomasquer (or bergamesquer), dancer in a burgomasque or comic anti-masque.

p.135 **Plashes**: Marshy pools.

p.135 **flipant**: Sexually playful.

p.136 old *Simon* the King: See note to 'Old Simon the King', p.505.

p.138 **freshes**: Fresh streams.

p.139 **Cornute**: Cuckold.

p.140 *(He sings)* . . .: This echo song was much admired by Pepys who took pains to get both words and music copied down as soon as he had seen the production for the first time, on 7 May 1668.

p.151 **wants your conversation**: Lacks your social skills.

p.155 **One is enough for you, but not for me**: Polygamy also features in the contemporary debate about natural man; in 1668 was published *The Isle of Pines, or, A Late Discovery of a forth Island near Terra Australis, Incognita* by Henry Neville, a utopian fiction in which a man settles on a remote island with four women, and sleeps with each in turn. See Staves, op. cit., ch. 5.

p.159 **behaviour**: Good behaviour.

p.160 **skink about**: Pour out drink.

p.160 *Haunse in Kelder*: Hans-in-Kelder, then slang for a child in the womb.

p.161 **Brindis**: A health or toast.

p.161 *Up se Dutch*: In the manner of the Dutch.

p.162 **Monsour *De-Viles***: 'Mounsor' probably means 'Mounseer', a slang form of 'monsieur', and 'De-Viles' is of course a pun on devils.

p.162 **Tory, Rory, and Ranthum, Scantum**: Rhyming nonsense suggesting copulation.

p.162 **O Jew! make love in her own Tribe?**: Perhaps a reference to the Old Testament story of Lot's daughters who copulated with their father when drunk (Genesis, XIX, 30–6).

p.163 **Haws**: Hawthorn berries.

p.163 **Wildings**: Crab-apples.

p.163 **Hackney-Devil**: Devil, used as a hackney coach or carriage, to take them through the air.

p.163 **Pigs-nye**: Darling.

p.166 **Mount *Hecla***: A volcanic mountain in Iceland.

p.171 **long of you**: Your fault.

p.174 **Moly ... trickling Balm ... purple Panacea**: Moly was the herb used by Ulysses for protection against the charms of Circe (*Odyssey*, X.302–6): trickling balm was probably Smith's Balm or Jews' Allheal; purple panacea may have been Clown's Wound-wort or All-heal, a herb common in England. Matthew Wikander speculates that this 'densely allegorical speech' (cut in the 1674 operatic *Tempest*) has strong royalist connotations, implying the 'semi-divine nature of kingship', especially in the 'purple panacea', and that it draws on royalist images used by Jonson in *The Masque of Blackness* (1606). (' "The Duke my fathers wrack": The Innocence of the Restoration *Tempest*', *Shakespeare Survey* 43, 1991, p.93.)

p.174 **Simples**: Single ingredients.

p.175 **vulnerary**: Capable of healing wounds.

p.175 **Weapon-Salve**: There was a belief that the touch of a weapon, anointed with a particular substance, could heal any wounds it had made.

p.183 **Dy-dapper**: Didapper or dive-dapper, a small diving bird.

p.184 ***Saraband***: A slow and stately Spanish dance.

## *John Dryden,* All For Love

p.191 **a Subject which has been treated by the greatest Wits of our Nation**: The most recent stage version of the story was Sir Charles Sedley's *Antony and Cleopatra* (1671). Previously there had been Mary, Countess of Pembroke's *Antonius* (1592); Samuel Daniel, *The Tragedy of Cleopatra* (c. 1593); Thomas May, *The Tragedie of Cleopatra* (acted 1626); and Fletcher and Massinger, *The False One* (c. 1620).

p.191 **Bowe of *Ulysses***: The bow with which Odysseus (Ulysses), on his return to Ithaca, proved his identity by shooting an arrow through twelve axe-rings. None of the suitors for his wife, Penelope, could even string the bow. See Homer, *Odyssey*, XXI–XXII.

**p.191** *Plutarch, Appian,* **and** *Dion*: Plutarch (*c.* AD 46 – *c.* 127) was a Greek biographer and essayist); Appian (*fl. c.* AD 140) and Dio Cassius (*c.* AD 159 – *c.* 229) were Greek historians. All wrote Roman history. Plutarch's *Life of Antony* was Dryden's main source.

**p.191** **turn:** Change of fortune.

**p.192** **Machine:** Contrivance, i.e. the bringing of Octavia to Alexandria, where the whole play is set and which she never in reality visited.

**p.193** *Montaigne . . .*: 'We are nought but ceremonie; ceremonie doth transport us, and wee leave the substance of things; wee hold-fast by the boughs, and leave the trunk or body. Wee have taught ladies to blush, onely by hearing named, which they nothing feare to doe. Wee dare not call our members by their proper names, feare not to employ them in all kind of dissoluteness. Ceremonie forbids us by words to expresse lawfull and naturall things; and we beleeve it. Reason willeth us to doe no bad or unlawfull things, and no man giveth credit unto it' (*The Essays of Michael, Lord of Montaigne*, Book II, ch. xvii, 'Of Presumption', in Florio's translation of 1603).

**p.193** **sucking:** Immature.

**p.193** **pall'd:** Stale.

**p.193** *Hippolitus*: Son of Theseus. The tragedy of his step-mother Phaedra and her love for him was dramatised first by Euripides; Dryden here refers to Racine's *Phedre* (1677), originally called *Phèdre et Hippolyte*.

**p.194** *Chedreux*: Fashionable, modish. Chedreux was famous as a maker of fashionable wigs.

**p.194** **draws his own stake:** Withdraws his own bet.

**p.194** **witty men:** Dryden probably means the Earl of Rochester, formerly a friend, but at this time no longer so.

**p.195** *Rarus . . . Fortunâ*: 'For common sense is rare in that station of life' (Juvenal, *Satire* VIII, 73–4).

**p.196** *Dionysius and Nero*: Dionysius, tyrant of Syracuse, who wrote plays; Nero (AD 37–65), Roman emperor and dilettante, who wrote tragedies.

p.196 *Lucan*: Roman epic poet (AD 39–65), who was forced to commit suicide after becoming involved in a conspiracy against Nero.

p.197 grinning honour: Dryden here quotes the phrase 'grinning honour' from Shakespeare, *Henry IV*, Part 1, V.iii.62.

p.197 *Mæcenas*: Roman patron of the arts in the reign of the Emperor Augustus (*d.* 8 BC); his protégés included Virgil and Horace.

p.197 *Seneca*: Probably Seneca the Elder, Roman rhetorician (55 BC – AD 40?).

p.197 *Virgil and Horace*: Virgil (70–19 BC), supreme Roman poet and author of the *Aeneid*; Horace (65–8 BC), Roman lyric poet and satirist.

p.197 *Zanies* ... imitations of him: A zany is a mimic or imitator, especially an incompetent one. Dryden here refers again to Rochester, and his poem 'An allusion to Horace'.

p.197 *Holy Way*: Horace, in *Satires*, (I.i.120) describes meeting a bore, usually identified as Crispinus, on the Via Sacra (Holy Way) in Rome.

p.197 *Demetri* ... *Cathedras*: 'Demetrius, and you, Tigellus, go and whine in the seats of your pupils' (Horace, *Satires*, I.x.90–1).

p.198 *Saxum* ... *arvis*: 'An antique stone he saw: the common Bound/ Of neighb'ring Fields; and barrier of the Ground (*Aeneid*, XII, 897–8; in Dryden's translation ll. 1300–1).

p.198 *Genua* ... *ictum*: 'His knocking Knees are bent beneath the Load;/ And shiv'ring Cold congeals his vital Blood./ The Stone drops from his arms; and falling short,/ For want of Vigor, mocks his vain Effort' (*Aeneid*, XII, 905–7; in Dryden's translation, ll. 1308–11).

p.198 Twelvepenny Gallery: A seat in the upper gallery of theatres (the cheapest part) at this period cost 12 pence.

p.198 *Sternhold*: Thomas Sternhold (1500–49), part-author (with John Hopkins) of a metrical version of the Psalms, and by-word for a bad poet.

p.198 Lyons Skin: Reference to Aesop's fable in which an ass, disguised in a lion's skin, was detected by his braying.

p.198 they whom he praises ... Magistrates whom he has elected: Rochester in 'An allusion to Horace' names critics of whom he approves, including Sedley, Shadwell, and Wycherley.

p.198 *Vellum ... honestum*: 'I wish that we might blunder thus in friendship, and that good sense had put an honourable name on errors such as these' (Horace, *Satires*, I.iii.41–2).

p.198 *Canibus ... violentius*: 'Lazy dogs, bare from long-standing mange, who lick the edges of a dry lamp [for oil], will be called Panther, Tiger, Lion, or whatever fierce beast roars in the world' (Juvenal, *Satires*, vii, 34–7).

p.199 *Nigra ...&c.*: 'The Sallow Skin is for the Swarthy put,/ And Love can make a Slattern of a Slut .../ She stammers, Oh what grace in lisping lies,/ If she says nothing, to be sure she's wise' (*De Rerum Natura*, IV, 1160, 1164; in Dryden's translation, 145–6, 151–2).

p.199 *ad Æthiopem Cygnum*: Complex allusion. The phrase is from Juvenal, *Satires*, viii, 33, 'so far as to call an Ethiopian a swan'. Dryden attacks Rochester as a nobleman without nobility, and alludes to the Black Swan tavern on Tower Hill, where Rochester masqueraded in public as an astrologer.

p.199 Mr. *Rymer*: Thomas Rymer, contemporary neoclassical critic, most famous for his attack on *Othello* in *A Short View of Tragedy*.

p.199 *Vos exemplaria ...diurnâ*: Study your Greek models night and day (Horace, *Ars Poetica*, 268–9).

p.199 reserve it for a more fit occasion ... hereafter: Dryden wrote a version of this play in collaboration with Nathaniel Lee in 1678.

p.199 *Ben Johnson* tells us, without Learning: In his ode 'To the Memory of my beloved, the author, Master William Shakespeare', published in the First Folio of Shakespeare's plays, 1623.

p.201 *As sad as* Dido's: The story of Dido, Queen of Carthage, and her tragic love for Aeneas, told by Virgil in the *Aeneid*, is often compared with that of Antony and Cleopatra.

p.201 *Bates of his mettle*: Lowers his spirit.

p.201 Tonyes: Fools, with a pun on Antony.

p.201 Hectors: Bullies, braggarts.

p.202 Rasher: Of bacon.

p.202 rivell'd: Shrivelled.

p.205 *Phocæ*: Seals.

**p.205 Sea-Horses:** Hippopotami.

**p.205 Boy-King:** Ptolemy, Cleopatra's half-brother and second husband, whom she probably had killed.

**p.206 intranc'd:** Overcome.

**p.206 *Actium*:** The battle of Actium, 31 BC, which Shakespeare dramatises, was the decisive defeat of Antony by Octavius.

**p.207 Prognosticks:** Prognostications.

**p.207 erected look:** Uplifted, dignified.

**p.209 The Boy *Octavius*:** 'Boy' is used as an insult; Octavius was in fact thirty-three to Antony's fifty-three.

**p.209 present:** At once.

**p.211 Engin:** Instrument or tool.

**p.211 Timbrels:** Hand-held percussion instrument such as a tambourine.

**p.212 sooth:** Support or encourage.

**p.212 Commoner:** A citizen of nature, as opposed to someone who lives in society.

**p.214 Hag that rides my Dreams:** Nightmare.

**p.215 officious:** Obliging or attentive.

**p.215 *Tully*:** Cicero, whom in 43 BC Antony ordered to be executed; when overtaken in flight from Rome he thrust his head out of the litter to be killed.

**p.216 *Parthian* Marches:** Frontier territories.

**p.216 chopt:** Chapped.

**p.216 trim Bands:** Presumably referring to Octavius's troops, in better physical condition than Antony's.

**p.216 us'd:** Accustomed.

**p.217 rank:** Excessively luxuriant.

**p.218 hindred:** Hindered, created an obstacle.

p.220 **taste fate to 'em**: i.e. act like tasters of the king's food, who prove its goodness (or otherwise) before the king does.

p.224 **Intrest**: Self-interest, personal concerns.

p.224 **Virtue**: In the sense of Latin *virtus*, manly honour.

p.224 **deliberate**: Calculating.

p.224 **close**: Secret.

p.225 **Wren**: Allusion to the fable of the wren who hid in the eagle's feathers and then soared above it.

p.227 **blewest**: Most livid.

p.227 **Aconite**: Poisonous plant.

p.228 **washed an Æthiope**: Proverbial expression, meaning to labour in vain. See note to *ad Æthiopem Cygnum* p.172 and Tilley, E186.

p.229 *Cæsar*: Julius Caesar.

p.233 **second place in Murder**: Antony refers to the part played by Octavius as leader of the triumvirate in drawing up a list of enemies to die after the assassination of Julius Caesar (dramatised by Shakespeare in *Julius Caesar*, IV.i).

p.235 **Gu-gau**: Juju (from French *jou-jou*, a plaything), trivial, insignificant.

p.236 *Phlegræan*: In Macedonia, where the gods were victorious over the Titans in battle.

p.236 **par'd off**: Parried.

p.236 *Vulcan*: Husband of Venus, who used a net to trap her with her lover Mars.

p.237 **awful**: Awe-inspiring.

p.237 **my Father *Hercules***: Antony was supposedly descended from the god Hercules.

p.240 **coursing**: Chasing.

p.241 *Nereids*: Sea-nymphs.

p.241 **wanted**: Lacked.

p.242 this: i.e. his head, or perhaps his sword.

p.243 grudgings: Slight symptoms, remaining traces.

p.244 confess: Acknowledge yourself to be.

p.244 so just a mean: So true a medium, of such temperate behaviour.

p.245 sullen: Stubborn.

p.247 distracted: Divided.

p.250 inevitable: Inescapable.

p.251 *Exit cum Suis*: Exit with her own, i.e. her children.

p.254 *Porcpisce*: Porpoise, thought to be a herald of tempests.

p.254 puts out: Brings out.

p.254 amain: At full speed.

p.255 event: Result.

p.255 *Gallus* and *Tibullus*: Gallus (*c.* 69–26 BC) and Tibullus (?48–19 BC) were Roman lyric poets who wrote in praise of Citheris and Delia respectively.

p.257 vent: Release of strong emotion.

p.257 the Center: Centre of the earth, i.e. Cleopatra will corrupt Antony to the heart of his being.

p.258 hollowing: Hallooing, calling out to attract attention.

p.259 *Thessalian*: Thessaly was traditionally the home of witchcraft.

p.260 looking: Looking for.

p.263 *Chaldeans*: Astrologers. Astrology was central to the religious practices of the Chaldeans.

p.263 turn'd Periods: Rhetorical or formal language.

p.263 *Meroe*: Supposedly an island in the Nile.

p.264 wheel: Make a sudden change of direction.

p.267 rowling Stone . . . gnawing Vulture: The punishments in Hades of Sisyphus and Tityrus respectively.

p.267 pose: Baffle, puzzle.

p.268 Secure: Safe from.

p.269 convinc'd: Convicted.

p.269 sweet Mercy ... punish to extent: The operations of mercy counteract those of justice, and hence God prefers to limit his infinite justice rather than exert punishment to the fullest extent.

p.270 Spurn: Kick.

p.273 *Pharos*: The lighthouse at Alexandria, one of the seven wonders of the ancient world.

p.277 *Nile*: The mud of the Nile was thought to be so fertile that creatures could be bred out of it.

p.277 Ap'd: Counterfeited.

p.277 emulous: As rivals (for glory).

p.279 *Lucrece*: Having been raped by Tarquin, Lucrece killed herself.

p.280 double: Doubling back.

p.282 sweeps: Sweeps aside.

p.283 jades: Acts like a jade, makes a fool of.

p.283 plaid booty: Lose deliberately, for some future advantage.

p.286 Ensigns: Symbols.

p.290 *swears a-foot*: i.e. swears when he is on foot.

p.290 *Mr.* Bays: The poet in Buckingham's satirical play *The Rehearsal* who represents Dryden.

p.290 Writ of Ease: Certificate of discharge from employment.

## *Nahum Tate,* King Lear

p.295 **Thomas Boteler, Esq:** A cousin of the playwright Sir Aston Cockaigne, whose play *Trappolin Suppos'd a Prince* Tate adapted for his very successful farce *A Duke and No Duke* (1684), and perhaps the 'Mr Butler' who contributed, along with Tate, to Dryden's *Ovid's Epistles, Translated by Several Hands* (1680).

p.295 *my Zeal for all the Remains of* Shakespear: Apart from *King Lear*, Tate adapted two other Shakespeare plays, *Richard II* as *The*

*Sicilian Usurper* (1681), and *Coriolanus* as *The Ingratitude of a Common-Wealth* (1682).

**p.296n Span. Fryar:** Dryden's tragicomedy *The Spanish Friar* was first produced around November 1680. In his preface he says that the audience has wearied of 'continued melancholy scenes'.

**p.297 Poets must ... whilst Church-men Plot:** These lines refer to current political events, the disclosure of the Popish Plot in 1678, and the Exclusion Crisis in 1680. A number of Shakespeare adaptations were produced at this period, which comment, usually from a Tory standpoint, on these events. See Michael Dobson, *The Making of the National Poet. Shakespeare, Adaptation, and Authorship, 1660–1769* (Clarendon Press; Oxford, 1992), pp.72–90.

**p.300 By-Born:** By-blow, or illegitimate child.

**p.300 succeed it:** Prosper.

**p.301 my Life for you were vile:** My life without you would be worthless. Goneril's words here appear garbled, perhaps deliberately to suggest the extravagance of her claim.

**p.302 Plight:** Troth-plight.

**p.302 fond:** Foolish.

**p.303 drench:** Drown.

**p.306 Int'rest:** Regard for his own profit.

**p.307 Character:** Handwriting.

**p.307 wind me into him:** Let me get close to him.

**p.308 Int'rest:** Pun on 'interest' in the senses of both concern and profit.

**p.308 Scene ii:** In the early texts the acts are not divided into scenes, and 'scenes', or opening stage-directions indicating the location of the action, are not consistently supplied. This text follows that of Christopher Spencer in *Five Restoration Adaptations of Shakespeare*.

**p.308 eat no Fish:** Observe the Protestant faith.

**p.308 Clatpole:** Blockhead.

**p.309 Civet-box:** perfume-box, an insult to the gentleman's masculinity.

**p.309 Admiration's:** Pretended amazement.

p.310 **untented:** Unprotected.

p.311 **fret:** Wear away.

p.313 *Lipsbury* **Pinfold:** Somewhere private. A pinfold is a cattle-pen, but Lipsbury has not been identified. In Shakespeare, it is possibly a punning expression; other words beginning with 'lip', such as 'lipland', and 'lipsius' are used in this way in the period.

p.313 **Glass-gazing:** Vain.

p.313 **superserviceable:** Over-zealous.

p.313 **finical:** Finicky, over-fastidious.

p.314 **dappar:** Dapper.

p.315 **Muss-cat:** Musk-cat, an insult suggesting foppishness and effeminacy.

p.315 **Lurcher:** Rogue, swindler.

p.316 **extold:** Extolled, praised.

p.317 **white minute:** Precious minute, opportunity.

p.318 **Steer'd:** Dialect form of 'stirred', or agitated. Shakespeare has 'stewed'.

p.318 **fetches:** Excuses.

p.320 **dispense:** Excuse.

p.322 **Thunder-bearer:** Jupiter.

p.323 **Infernals:** Furies.

p.323 **stomachfull:** Full of pride, obstinate.

p.324 **high-engendred:** Engendered in the heavens.

p.325 **pudder:** Uproar.

p.325 **burn:** Shakespeare has 'turn' which makes more sense.

p.326 **Earnest:** Pledge.

p.327 **invetrate:** Full of hatred.

p.329 **poching:** Poaching, looking out for.

p.329 *Semele*: Jove came to Semele in the form of a thunderbolt, which destroyed her.

p.330 cast the superflux: Bestow what is super-abundant.

p.330 Pue: Pew (to tempt him to suicide).

p.331 course: Chase.

p.331 Taking: Bewitching.

p.331 Pelican: Young pelicans were traditionally believed to feed on their parents' blood.

p.331 fow: Foul.

p.331 Washes: Liquid cosmetics, or hair preparations.

p.332 Water-nut: Water-chestnut.

p.332 Tithing: Rural district, parish.

p.332 Brach: Female hound.

p.332 Hym: Lym, a species of bloodhound.

p.333 the Web and the Pin: Cataract of the eye.

p.333 Elflock: Tangle in a horse's mane, made by elves.

p.333 arroynt: Avoid.

p.333 Stagirite: Aristotle, who was born at Stagira in Macedonia.

p.334 Child *Rowland* ... the Bloud of a British Man: Child Roland probably comes from a lost ballad, but his words from the story of Jack the Giant-Killer.

p.335 *Quarter-staff*: Long club.

p.335 Hedge-pig: Hedgehog.

p.335 truckt: Had sex with.

p.335 Blouze: Ruddy-faced woman.

p.335 Drab: Slut.

p.336 Herds: Shepherds.

p.336 Clowns: Peasants.

p.337 **Pretences:** Protestations of love.

p.337 **protesting:** Protesting love.

p.337 **adorn the Scene:** Adorn the stage.

p.338 *Hesperian* **Dragon:** The dragon Ladon, which guarded the golden apples on the trees in the gardens of the Hesperides, daughters of the evening.

p.338 **Ost:** Host.

p.340 *Cambrian*: Welsh.

p.340 *Cambray*: Wales.

p.340 **Guids:** Guides.

p.340 **Sound:** Measure the depth of.

p.341 **Lumber:** Worthless body

p.343 **cast:** Plot

p.343 **last day's:** Yesterday's.

p.344 **Event:** Outcome.

p.345 **ancient:** Long established.

p.345 **Passengers:** Passers-by.

p.346 **Femiter:** Fumitor, weed of the genus fumaria.

p.346 **wave:** Waive, set aside.

p.347 **cast:** Throw of the dice, chance.

p.349 **Choughs:** Jackdaws.

p.349 **Sampire:** Rock-herb that grows on cliffs, often used in pickling.

p.349 **Cock:** Cock-boat, dinghy.

p.349 **Snuff:** Used up, as in snuff, meaning a burnt-out candle wick.

p.349 **Conceit:** Imagination.

p.349 **Gosmore:** Gossamer.

p.350 **Bourn:** Boundary, meaning here cliff.

p.350 **press-money:** Money paid to a soldier when he was recruited, or impressed, to the army.

p.350 **a Clothier's yard:** A cloth-yard, or three feet, the length of a standard English arrow.

p.351 **Bills:** Halberds, long handled weapons ending in a head that combines spearhead and battleaxe.

p.351 **White:** The inner part of an archer's target.

p.351 **Cause:** Charge.

p.351 **Fitcher:** Fitchew, polecat.

p.351 **Civet:** Musky perfume, obtained from the anal glands of the civet-cat.

p.352 **stiff:** Sturdy.

p.352 **Politician:** Schemer or intriguer.

p.353 **put in proof:** Try it out.

p.354 **'Chill:** Dialect for 'I will'. Edgar adopts West country rural speech here.

p.354 **'Chu'd:** If I could.

p.354 **Costard:** Head.

p.354 **Ballow:** Cudgel.

p.354 **Voines:** Foins, or sword thrusts.

p.356 **abus'd:** Deluded.

p.356 **stand thy Justice:** Accept your judgement.

p.357 **Like the fierce Thunderer's .. Heav'n:** This refers to Jupiter's power in repressing the rebellion of the Titans.

p.358 **prevent:** Anticipate.

p.358 **jealous:** Suspicious.

p.359 **Countenance:** Authority.

p.359 **Posture:** Strategic disposition.

p.359 **Hearing:** Report.

**p.359 stand on your Award:** Stand your guard.

**p.360 Courser:** War-horse.

**p.361 avouch:** Maintain.

**p.362 Fame:** Reputation.

**p.362 nice:** Fastidious.

**p.363 out-toil:** Wear out.

**p.363 single Vertue:** Individual valour.

**p.364 Stock:** Stake, as in gambling.

**p.364 after-Game:** A second game, played to improve upon, or reverse, the results of the first.

**p.365 Half-blooded Man:** Bastard.

**p.365 bear'st thee:** Gloat about.

**p.365 Practice:** Treacherous contrivance.

**p.366 Empericks:** Quacks.

**p.366 *Circe*:** A witch with power to turn men into animals.

**p.368 *Partizan*:** Long-handled spear.

**p.368 generous:** Courageous.

**p.368 Faulchion:** Broad curved sword with its cutting edge on the convex side.

**p.368 Crosses:** Disappointments, misfortunes.

**p.369 Scrowl:** Scroll, list.

**p.370 fall in with:** Match.

**p.371 Period:** Appointed end.

**p.372 Remains:** Remaining days.

**p.373 Tangier:** Topical reference to the fighting then taking place between the English forces, who had controlled Tangier since 1662, and the Moors, who besieged it from 1679 to 1681. It was abandoned by the English in 1684. The lines mean that actresses are as likely to enter nunneries as gallants from the pit to fight in Tangier.

p.373 Alcade: Spanish for the governor of a fortress.

## Colley Cibber, Richard III

p.379 the whole first Act being Intirely left out in the Presentation: The Lord Chamberlain, Charles Killigrew, demanded the omission of Cibber's Act I on political grounds; the former James II was living in exile in France at this time, but had supporters in England. Cibber refers again to this censorship, with some bitterness, in *An Apology for the Life of Colley Cibber*, ed. B.R.S. Fore (Ann Arbor: University of Michigan Press, 1968), p.152.

p.379 What is not so mark'd ... intirely my own: Cibber is sometimes careless about his indications, which were given only in the first edition of the play. Examples are given elsewhere in the footnotes.

p.379 best living Author: Dryden, who died in May 1700, shortly after the publication of Cibber's play.

p.381 *Richard ... Cibber*: In his *Apology*, Cibber says that he wanted Samuel Sandford, who specialised in villain roles and had played Richard in Shakespeare's play for the King's Company, to play the part; but as he was contracted to the King's Company Cibber decided to take the part himself, imitating Sandford's manner as far as he could (see pp.81–2). His performance did not meet with universal approbation, especially in the battle scenes. See Christopher Spencer, *Five Restoration Adaptations of Shakespeare*, pp.417, 420–1.

p.384 brook: Tolerate.

p.384 Courser: Warhorse.

p.387 *Ev'n such a Man ... Night*: This episode does not occur in versions of the Troy story in the *Iliad* or the *Aeneid*. A. R. Humphreys in his edition of *Henry IV*, Part 2 (Arden Shakespeare, Methuen: London, 1966) suggests it is an echo of Kyd, *The Spanish Tragedy*, Act III, fourth additional passage, ll. 156–8, which seems likely.

p.389 Caucasus: Mountainous region between the Black and Caspian seas.

p.390 Period: Limit, fullest extent.

p.390 Barbed: Covered with armour over the breast and flanks.

p.391 *piping time of Peace*: The pipe is the music of shepherds and pastoral peace (as opposed to the warlike drum).

p.391 *descant*: Enlarge upon a theme.

p.392 *Roscius*: Quintus Roscius Gallus (d. 62 BC), the most famous Roman actor.

p.392 Male: Parent (to a single offspring). Henry (in *Henry VI, Part 3*) is referring to his son Edward, killed by Richard and his brothers.

p.392 *for all his Wings the fool was drown'd*: Reference to the story of Daedalus, the legendary Athenian craftsman, who constructed waxen wings for himself and his son Icarus to enable them to escape from imprisonment on the island of Crete. Icarus flew too near the sun, his wings melted, and he was drowned in the sea.

p.392 Climbing: Aspiring too high.

p.393 rook'd: Cowered, hid away.

p.393 Pies: Magpies, also birds of ill omen.

p.395 fear him: Fear for his health.

p.396 *forswore*: Abjured, abandoned.

p.396 *envious*: Spiteful

p.397 So mourn'd the Dame of *Ephesus* . . . Woer: The story of the widow of Ephesus comes from Petronius, *Satyricon*, 111–12, though there are many other versions of it. The widow is so devoted to her late husband that she spends all her time in mourning at his tomb, refusing to sleep or eat. But she is eventually persuaded to eat by a young soldier who is guarding the corpses of some thieves which have been placed near the husband's body. He then seduces her, and when one of the corpses is stolen away while they are making love, she allows him to put her husband's body in its place, so that he won't be executed for dereliction of duty.

p.397 importing: Bringing in.

p.397 consented to: Conspired in.

p.397 *Abortive*: Misshapen, like the offspring of an untimely birth.

p.397 *Chertsey*: Then, the site of a famous abbey by the river Thames.

p.398 *Halbert*: Long-handled weapon ending in a head that combines spearhead and battleaxe.

p.400 *Basilisks*: Legendary serpent that can kill at a glance.

p.400 *Fee*: Prize or reward. The language is legalistic.

p.402 Crosby *House*: Fifteenth-century house in Bishopsgate.

p.402 White-Fryars: Formerly a monastery in the Whitefriars district, but no longer extant in Shakespeare's time.

p.404 his Images: i.e. his children.

p.405 Mother: i.e. mother-in-law.

p.405 An helpless Child ... Minority: Still a minor, not legally an adult.

p.409 *crosses*: Vexations.

p.410 gratulate: Congratulate.

p.410 Tower: The Tower of London, notorious in Shakespeare's time as, among other things, a prison of state; Henry VI and Clarence were murdered in it.

p.411 cross: Argumentative.

p.412 provided: Penetrating and thoughtful.

p.412 *Opprobriously*: So as to cause opprobrium or disgrace.

p.413 *Guild-Hall*: Fifteenth-century building in the City of London still used for formal civic occasions.

p.414 *Moveables*: Moveable as opposed to heritable property.

p.414 Daws: Simpletons.

p.415 peevish: Fretful.

p.415 distressful: Gained by hard effort.

p.420 *disgracious*: Disgraceful, displeasing.

p.420 recure: Restore, remedy.

p.420 Factor: Agent.

p.421 nice: Unimportant.

p.422 *Acquittance*: Acquit.

p.423 the pious Fool that rais'd it: Herostratus, who, in 356 BC, the year of the birth of Alexander the Great, burnt the temple of Artemis at Ephesus, in his wild desire to achieve fame at any cost.

p.426 Despightful: Cruel.

p.427 jealous: Watchful.

p.431 *Brittain*: Breton, referring to the fact that Richmond was in exile in Brittany.

p.431 *peevish*: Childish and fretful.

p.433 *Enter* Richard: In the first edition of Cibber's play a 38-line scene depicting the murder of the princes onstage (reprinted on pp.458–9) was printed in place of ll. 19–38. It does not appear in any other edition of the play printed during Cibber's lifetime. Spencer, *Five Restoration Adaptations of Shakespeare*, suggests that the scene was thought to be in bad taste after the death in July 1700 of William, the only son of Princess Anne, at the age of 10 (p.420).

p.436 *Expedition*: Setting forth, with military intentions.

p.437 Lethe: Literally, one of the seven rivers of Hades whose water caused its drinkers to forget the past; here, forgetfulness.

p.438 tender: Act tenderly towards, cherish.

p.439 *Hull*: Drift on the current, or float with sails furled.

p.440 *White Liver'd Runnagade*: Cowardly renegade or rebel.

p.441 *Off with his head. So much for* Buckingham: This line, one of Cibber's most famous additions, was incorporated into Olivier's script for his film of the play (1954).

p.446 drawn the model: Made a sketch-plan.

p.447 *Pursuivant at Arms*: Heraldic officer.

p.449 *accomplishing*: Completing the arming of.

p.451 animated: Emboldened.

p.454 transpierce: Penetrate.

p.454 *Daring an opposite to every danger*: Challenging an enemy to the death.

p.454 *a Cast*: Throw of the dice, i.e. a single chance.

p.455 First-born *Cain*: Son of Adam and Eve who murdered his brother Abel.

**p.456 Gratulate:** Congratulate.

**p.458–9 Original version of Act iv, Scene iii, ll. 19–38:** The first version of IV.iii.19–38, printed only in the first edition of the play, and thereafter replaced by the lines which appear as given in the main text. See note to *Enter* Richard p.386.

## *Thomas Otway,* Caius Marius

**p.467 Scene i:** This is the first complete scene in the play based on Shakespeare. Act 1 is largely concerned with the play's political setting in republican Rome at the time of civil wars between Caius Marius (whose faction represents the Montagues) and Sylla (the analogue for Paris in Otway's play). Metellus is Old Capulet; in this scene he replaces Lady Capulet in the equivalent scene in *Romeo and Juliet*, I.iii.

**p.468 Sixteen:** As in Dryden and Davenant's *The Tempest*, the age of the female lead is raised. Shakespeare's Juliet is two years younger than Otway's.

**p.468 enter'd** *Rome* **in Triumph:** Historically this would have been around 107 BC, when Caius Marius returned from North Africa, having subdued Jugurtha, King of Numidia. The Nurse's insistence on the date of Marius's triumph would have been tactless in Metellus's company, since the two men were enemies, and Marius succeeded in Africa at Metellus's expense. Otway's main historical source is Plutarch, 'The life of Caius Marius' from *The Lives of the Noble Grecians and Romans*.

**p.469** *Sylla***:** L. Cornelius Sulla – Sylla – was originally a supporter of Marius, but turned against him in 88 BC, and the so-called 'Social War' of 88–82 BC was a bloody civil war between the factions of the two, eventually won by Sylla.

**p.473 GRANIUS** *and* **SULPITIUS:** Sons to Caius Marius. Sulpitius = Mercutio.

**p.475 fails:** The copy-text quite clearly misreads the long 's' in the 1680 quarto of the play for 'f'. Shakespeare has 'sails' at this point, which makes much more sense.

**p.479 Scene iii:** This brief extract from II.iii. illustrates the very different style of the more overtly political and 'Roman' scenes in *Caius Marius*. As in Shakespeare's *Coriolanus*, which must have been in Otway's mind here, the citizens are fickle, and having initially supported Marius for the consulship, they change sides when Metellus speaks in the forum against him.

**p.480 Act III Scene ii:** In the previous scene Marius Junior tells the Nurse that he and Lavinia have been secretly married. The wedding is not staged. At the end of Act II Sulpitius (Mercutio) kills Young Pompeius (Tybalt) in a scuffle in the Forum (whereas in Shakespeare Tybalt kills Mercutio, and is killed in turn by Romeo).

**p.483 Act V Scene iv:** At the start of Act IV the balance has tilted against Caius Marius and his supporters who have been in exile in the countryside. In a scene which draws on Shakespeare's *King Lear*, Lavinia, having escaped from her father's house, joins up with Caius Marius and is received by him as his daughter. But then the tide of fortune turns, Marius is recalled to Rome to form an alliance with Cinna against Metellus, and Lavinia is recaptured and taken back to her father's house in Rome.

**p.483 She's dead:** Lavinia has taken the sleeping potion, given her by a priest in IV.iii.

**p.485 *Enter* PRIEST:** There is a change of plot at this point in Otway. The historical role of Sylla (Paris) makes it impossible for him to meet Marius Junior in the tomb, and for the two rivals to fight; so his place is taken by the Priest (a figure for Shakespeare's Friar Lawrence), who is killed by Marius.

**p.486 Let me . . . that joyn'd our hands:** In Shakespeare the body is of course that of Paris.

**p.487 LAVINIA *wakes*:** Another change of plot. This innovation, the awakening of Lavinia (Juliet) before the death of Marius (Romeo), was retained by both Theophilus Cibber and David Garrick when they revived *Romeo and Juliet* in 1744 and 1748 respectively.

**p.489 couldst be true . . . To find th'unhappy Wretch thy Soul was fond of:** Caius Marius recalls his reunion with Lavinia in exile in IV.ii.

# SUGGESTIONS FOR FURTHER READING

## *Useful Editions of the Texts*

*Five Restoration Adaptations of Shakespeare*, ed. Christopher Spencer (Urbana, Illinois: University of Illinois Press, 1965). Contains Davenant's *Macbeth*, Shadwell's operatic version of the Davenant/Dryden *Tempest*, Tate's *King Lear*, Cibber's *Richard III*, and Granville's *The Jew of Venice*, plus notes and a useful, unprejudiced introduction.

*Shakespeare Adaptations*, ed. Montague Summers (London: Cape, 1922). Contains the Davenant/Dryden *Tempest*, Duffet's amusing travesty of it, *The Mock-Tempest*, and Tate's *King Lear*, with an introduction on theatre-history of the period.

Dryden, John, *The Works of John Dryden*, 20 vols, E. N. Hooker and H. T. Swedenberg, general editors (Berkeley, Los Angeles and London: University of California Press, 1956–89); *All for Love* is in vol. 13 and *The Tempest* in vol. 10. These are the most up-to-date editions of the plays, with full and informative notes drawing on recent scholarship.

Lacy, John, *The Dramatic Works of John Lacy, Comedian*, ed. James Maidment and W. H. Logan (Edinburgh: William Paterson and London: H. Sotheran and Co., 1875; New York: B. Blom, 1967). The only edition of Lacy's four plays, *The Old Troop, or Monsieur Ragoû, The Dumb Lady, or The Farrier made Physician, Sir Hercules Buffoon, or The Poetical Squire and Sauny the Scot*, in mildly bowdlerised Victorian texts with little annotation.

Otway, Thomas, *The Works of Thomas Otway*, ed. J. C. Ghosh, 2 vols (Oxford: Clarendon Press, 1932). *Caius Marius* is in volume 1 of this edition, which contains a useful brief introduction on Otway's life and works.

Shakespeare, *King Lear*, ed. J. S. Bratton, Plays in Performance (Bristol: Bristol Classical Press, 1987). Contains annotated text of Shakespeare's play, with emphasis on stage-history to the present day. Includes appendices on Tate's *King Lear*, with annotated extracts from the text, discussing the effects of the modifications made to this version in the eighteenth and nineteenth centuries.

Shakespeare, *Richard III*, ed. Julie Hankey, Plays in Performance (London: Junction Books, 1981). Very fully annotated text of Shakespeare's play, with emphasis on stage-history to the present day, and useful details about Cibber's version.

Tate, Nahum, *The History of King Lear*, ed. James Black, Regents Restoration Drama Series (London: Edward Arnold, 1975). The most fully annotated text available, with useful introduction.

## Criticism

Adler, Doris, 'The Half-Life of Tate in *King Lear*', *Kenyon Review*, 3rd series, 7 (1985), pp.52–6. Describes how vestiges of Tate's version have survived in productions of Shakespeare's play up to the present day.

Ashley, L. R. N., *Colley Cibber* (New York: Twayne Publishers, 1989). Up-to-date account of Cibber's life and works.

Batzer, Hazel M., 'Shakespeare's Influence on Thomas Otway's *Caius Marius*', *Revue de l'Université d'Ottawa* 39 (1969), pp.533–61. Helpful account of Otway's debt to Shakespeare, and evaluation of his achievement in *Caius Marius*.

Black, James, 'An Augustan Stage-History: Nahum Tate's King Lear', *Restoration and Eighteenth-Century Theatre Research* 6 (1967), pp.36–54. Traces stage-history of the play from 1681 to the 1960s, with some account of the restoration context.

Brown, J. R., 'Three Adaptations', *Shakespeare Survey* XIII (1960), pp.137–45. Discusses a production of the Davenant/Dryden *Tempest* in 1959, with some stage-history.

Cibber, Colley, *An Apology for the Life of Colley Cibber*, ed. B. R. S. Fone (Ann Arbor: University of Michigan Press, 1968). Gossipy autobiography, with invaluable information about early eighteenth-century theatrical practice.

Colley, Scott, *Richard's Himself Again. A Stage History of Richard III* (New York and London: Greenwood Press, 1992). Stage history from Cibber to the 1990s, with a sympathetic and detailed account of Cibber's version.

Dennis, John, *Critical Works*, 2 vols, ed. E. N. Hooker (Baltimore: Johns Hopkins Press, 1939–43). Volume 2 contains interesting comment on *All for Love* and on Cibber's acting; the extensive annotations also contain material on Tate's *King Lear*.

Dobson, Michael, *The Making of the National Poet: Shakespeare, Adaptation and Authorship, 1660–1769* (Oxford: Clarendon Press, 1992). An invaluable account of Shakespeare's reputation in this period, which explores the interests, political and otherwise, served by the process of adaptation.

Freehafer, J., 'The Formation of the London Patent Companies in 1660', *Theatre Notebook* 20 (1965), pp.6–30. Closely documented article on the early years of the theatrical companies in Restoration London, with information about legislation, repertories, etc.

Guffey, George, 'Politics, Weather and the Contemporary Reception of the Dryden-Davenant *Tempest*', *Restoration* 8 (1984), pp.1–9. On the topicality of the play.

Holland, Peter, *The Ornament of Action: Text and Performance in Restoration Comedy* (Cambridge: Cambridge University Press, 1979). Detailed account of all aspects of the relationship between text and staging in comedy of the period.

Hume, Robert D., *The Development of English Drama in the Late Seventeenth Century* (Oxford: Clarendon Press, 1979). Chronological survey of over five hundred plays, discussing the emergence and decline of numerous genres and sub-genres, aiming to update Nicholl's work.

Maguire, Nancy Klein, 'Nahum Tate's *King Lear*. "The King's Blest Restoration" ', in *The Appropriation of Shakespeare: Post-Renaissance Reconstructions of the Works and the Myth*, ed. Jean Marsden (Hemel Hempstead: Harvester-Wheatsheaf, 1991). On the political significance of Tate's alterations.

Maus, Katherine Eisamen, 'Arcadia Lost: Politics and Revision in the Restoration *Tempest*', *Renaissance Drama*, new series 13 (1982), pp.189–209. Important article on the politics of the play, contrasting its lack of Arcadian vision with Shakespeare's play.

Merchant, W. Moelwyn, 'Shakespeare Made Fit', in *Restoration Theatre*, Stratford-upon-Avon Studies (London: Edward Arnold, 1965). pp.195–219. Generally sympathetic and informative discussion of *All for Love* and Tate's *King Lear*, among other adaptations.

Nicoll, Allardyce, *A History of Restoration Drama 1660–1700* (Cambridge: Cambridge University Press, 1923). Contains much useful documentation, particularly in the appendices.

Odell, G. C., *Shakespeare from Betterton to Irving*, 2 vols (London and New York: Constable and Co., 1920–21). Standard history of the adaptations, but dated in its attitudes.

Raddadi, Mongi, *Davenant's Adaptations of Shakespeare* (Uppsala: Almquist and Wiksell International, 1979). Detailed descriptive account of Davenant's four adaptations, with discussion of verbal alterations.

Sorelius, Gunnar, 'The Rights of the Restoration Theatre Companies in the Older Drama', *Studia Neophilologica* 37 (1965), pp.174–89. Seminal account of the legislation surrounding the formation of the companies.

Spencer, Christopher, *Nahum Tate* (New York: Twayne Publishers, 1972). Basic account of Tate's life and works.

Spencer, Hazelton, *Shakespeare Improved: The Restoration Versions in Quarto and on the Stage* (Cambridge, Mass.: Harvard University Press, 1927). Detailed descriptive account, with attention to verbal alterations. Dated in its attitudes.

Staves, Susan, *Players' Sceptres: Fictions of Authority in the Restoration* (Lincoln, Nebraska: University of Nebraska Press, 1979). Sets the drama in the context of an account of the crisis of authority in the period.

Wallace, John M., 'Otway's *Caius Marius* and the Exclusion Crisis', *Modern Philology* 85 (1988), pp.363–72. Highlights themes in *Romeo and Juliet* that Otway found appropriate to this political crisis.

Wikander, Matthew, ' "The King my Father's Wrack": the Innocence of the Restoration *Tempest*', *Shakespeare Survey* 43 (1991), pp.91–8. Takes issue with Maus on some aspects of the play's politics; discusses the subplot in more detail.

Wikander, Matthew, 'The Spitted Infant: Scenic Emblem and Exclusionist Politics in Restoration Adaptations of Shakespeare', *Shakespeare Quarterly* 37 (1986), pp.340–58. Discussion of the adaptations produced in the years of the Exclusion Crisis, including Tate's *King Lear*.

Wood, Alice, *The Stage History of Shakespeare's King Richard the Third* (New York: Cambridge University Press, 1909). Contains plenty of detail about Cibber's version, and its modifications by Garrick, Kemble and others.

## *John Lacy,* Sauny the Scot

### Act I
#### Scene i
Winlove (Lucentio) and Tranio come up to London from the country looking for the excitements of city life. They witness Beaufoy (Baptista) refusing to allow his younger daughter Biancha to be wooed by her suitors Woodall (Gremio) and Geraldo (Hortensio) before he finds a suitor for his shrewish elder daughter Margaret. Winlove falls in love at first sight with Biancha and exchanges identities with Tranio, so as to present himself as a French tutor to her. Jamy (Biondello) is amazed at the transformations of the two.

### Act II
#### Scene i
Petruchio arrives with his man Sauny (Grumio) at Geraldo's lodgings. He has come to London in search of a wife. Geraldo tells him of Margaret, and he resolves to woo her. Woodall comes in with Winlove in his French tutor's disguise, and is delighted to hear of Petruchio's decision. Tranio enters disguised, also claiming to be a suitor for Biancha. All the men go off to drink together before venturing on their courtships.

#### Scene ii
Margaret treats Biancha abusively, and is reproved by Beaufoy. Woodall presents the disguised Winlove to Beaufoy as a tutor, and Tranio introduces himself as a suitor. Geraldo also offers himself as a music tutor. Sauny presents Petruchio to Beaufoy, who assures him about the size of Margaret's dowry. Geraldo is violently dismissed by Margaret, whom Petruchio then proceeds to court. Beaufoy, somewhat surprised at the speed of the courtship, agrees to prepare for the wedding. Tranio and Woodall then bargain for Biancha, and Beaufoy

offers her to Tranio, if he can produce the amount of money he has promised.

## Act III
### Scene i

Winlove and Geraldo attempt to tutor Biancha. Each sends her a secret message, and she makes clear her preference for Winlove. Beaufoy, his daughters, and company then enter awaiting the arrival of Petruchio to marry Margaret. He comes late, in bizarre attire, and all except Winlove and Tranio go off to the church for the wedding. Winlove and Tranio plan their next move, which involves finding an old man to impersonate Winlove's father. The company then returns from the church, and Petruchio insists on taking Margaret back to his house before the bridal dinner. Woodall and Geraldo witness Winlove courting Biancha, and both agree not to press their claims further. Jamy brings in Snatchpenny who is to act as Winlove's father so that he can marry Biancha at once.

### Scene ii

Petruchio's servants prepare for his arrival; Sauny is delighted to get home. Petruchio and Margaret enter; he abuses the servants, rejects the food, and insists on Margaret going fasting to bed.

### Scene iii

In the bedroom Petruchio declares that the bed is damp and dirty, and that they must sit up for the night. He also makes her drink beer and smoke tobacco.

## Act IV
### Scene i

Sauny, assisting Petruchio in his taming process, teases Margaret, who is desperate with hunger. Petruchio brings food, but won't allow her to eat. He rejects the gown that the tailor has made for her, and then insists that they return at once to her father's house.

### Scene ii

Tranio and Jamy prepare Snatchpenny for his part in the deception of Beaufoy. Beaufoy easily believes that he is Sir Lyonel Winlove, and prepares to marry Biancha to the disguised Tranio. Jamy meanwhile has found a parson ready to marry Biancha to Winlove. Woodall bribes the disguised Winlove to let him steal Biancha away from Tranio.

### Scene iii

Petruchio and Margaret are on their way back to London, and he tests how far she is tamed. When they meet Sir Lyonell Winlove she convinces him of her change of heart by joining in with his games of pretence.

### Scene iv
Winlove and Biancha go off to the priest to be married. Woodall, in accordance with the plot he thinks he has made with Winlove, prepares to kidnap Biancha. Meanwhile Petruchio, Margaret and their company arrive. Snatchpenny, disguised as Winlove's father, confronts the real Sir Lyonell Winlove. Sir Lyonell beats Jamy, whom he recognises as a trickster, and confusion breaks out. Beaufoy and Tranio, still disguised as Winlove, come on the scene, and Tranio attempts to brazen it out with Sir Lyonell, who recognises him too. Beaufoy is confused and attempts to have Sir Lyonell sent to jail. Into the confusion enter Winlove and Biancha, now married. They ask their fathers' pardon. Sir Lyonell and Beaufoy are reconciled, and all adjourn to Beaufoy's house. Woodall realises he has been tricked, but goes along to join in the celebrations.

### *Act V*
### Scene i
Margaret tells Biancha, now that she is back in town, that she still intends to have her revenge on Petruchio for his treatment of her. She then proceeds to challenge him in public, and after refusing his command to return to the country and striking him, falls totally silent. Petruchio in response claims that she is suffering from toothache, and sends for the barber; but she strikes him so that he leaves in haste, and Petruchio is forced to think of another trick. He now asserts that she has suddenly died, though neither Beaufoy nor Biancha is convinced. He sends Sauny for a bier and coffin bearers, and prepares to have Margaret's body taken away, despite the bearers' insistence that she is still alive. Finally she calls his bluff, and speaks out, but Petruchio claims that it is the voice of a devil, until Margaret promises to behave as a humble wife in future. Geraldo enters to announce that he too has got married, and, the women absent from the stage, Petruchio proposes a wager on the obedience of the three wives. Neither Biancha nor Geraldo's wife will come when summoned, but Margaret obediently appears, winning the bet for Petruchio. She briefly reproves the other women for neglecting their duties as wives, and the play ends with a dance.

# *John Dryden and William Davenant,* The Tempest

## Act I

### Scene i

Storm at sea. The ship containing Alonzo, Antonio, Gonzalo and mariners is wrecked.

### Scene ii

Prospero tells Miranda of their past lives in Italy; he questions Ariel about the safety of the ship, and when Ariel demands his liberty reminds him of his sufferings at the hands of the witch Sycorax, from which Prospero rescued him. Miranda's sister Dorinda is introduced and the two wish vehemently to see the men they have heard are on the ship.

## Act II

### Scene i

Alonzo and other courtiers, exploring the island, hear a song sung by spirits about guilt and damnation; the spirits, representing the sins of which they are guilty, Pride, Fraud, Rapine and Ambition, appear and torment them. Alonzo and Antonio promptly repent.

### Scene ii

Ariel, invisible, leads Ferdinand on with his singing.

### Scene iii

Stephano, Mustacho and Ventoso, mariners, drink brandy and discuss how they will govern the island; Trincalo, the boatswain, challenges Stephano's plan to be duke of the island, and Stephano declares him a rebel; Trincalo then forges an alliance with Caliban, who offers to introduce him to his sister.

### Scene iv

Prospero encounters his ward, Hippolito, Duke of Mantua, whom he has kept on the island unknown to Miranda and Dorinda because of a prophecy that Hippolito will die if he sees a woman; he warns Hippolito of this danger. He then instructs Miranda and Dorinda to avoid men, but they plan to be on the look-out for them none the less.

### Scene v

Hippolito meets Miranda and Dorinda; Miranda is fearful and runs off to tell her father, but Hippolito and Dorinda are immediately attracted to each other.

## Act III

### Scene i

Prospero chides Miranda for not looking after Dorinda better, but reveals to her that Hippolito, as a man, is in fact designed by nature to protect and comfort women; he warns Dorinda against Hippolito but she refuses to be discouraged. He asks Ariel for news of the courtiers, and, hearing that they are penitent, plans to forgive them.

## Scene ii
The courtiers are tired and discouraged, but cheer up when Ariel sings to them and spirits present them with a magical banquet.

## Scene iii
Caliban introduces Trincalo to his sister Sycorax, who is eager to marry him. Ariel, invisible, sets Trincalo and Caliban at odds. The other mariners ask Trincalo for a truce, since they are without food or drink, but he is now in a position of power and refuses them hospitality.

## Scene iv
Ferdinand is led further into the island by the music of the invisible Ariel.

## Scene v
Ferdinand sees Miranda for the first time and falls in love with her, just as Prospero has planned. Prospero pretends anger, and imprisons Ferdinand in his cave, where he will encounter Hippolito. He then questions Hippolito about his response to his first sight of women. In soliloquy, he expresses surprise that Hippolito has seen a woman but lives, contrary to the prophecy, and wonders about the extent of human free will.

## Scene vi
Ferdinand gives Hippolito some instruction about women and sexual conduct, but Hippolito, discovering that more women than one exist, hopes to have as many as he can.

## Act IV
## Scene i
Miranda visits Ferdinand in the cave, and they admit their love; but when she urges him to love Hippolito also, he becomes jealous. Prospero questions Miranda as to her feelings for Ferdinand; she pretends not to like him, but Prospero sees through her pose. Hippolito questions Dorinda about her sister, and she becomes jealous. Ferdinand, fearing that Hippolito will try to attract Miranda, tries to dissuade him but to no avail; the two then prepare to fight over Miranda.

## Scene ii
Stephano and his supporters come to make peace with Trincalo and

Caliban, agreeing that Trincalo shall rule the island; but they get drunk, and dissension breaks out when Stephano makes overtures to Sycorax. Trincalo decides to divorce her.

## Scene iii

Ferdinand and Hippolito have a brief sword-fight, which Ferdinand easily wins, apparently and unintentionally killing Hippolito. Prospero is horrified, and summons Ariel's help. Dorinda tries to revive him, by lighting a fire, but without success. At this point Alonzo and the courtiers enter, and Alonzo is united with Ferdinand. But Prospero condemns Ferdinand to death for killing Hippolito and will not change his mind, despite entreaties from Miranda and Alonzo. Miranda and Dorinda then quarrel and the act ends with a mournful soliloquy from Ariel on the spirit of discord which has infected everyone, and he curses the power of magic which he holds responsible.

## Act V
### Scene i

Miranda begs Prospero to pardon Ferdinand, but he refuses and prepares to send for Caliban to act as executioner. Ariel then brings news that Hippolito is not actually dead, but has been restored by magic herbs, which he himself has procured.

## Scene ii

Dorinda sits at the side of the convalescent Hippolito, whose promiscuous desires for many women have vanished with his loss of blood. Miranda enters to dress his wound, and when Ferdinand comes in with Dorinda it seems as if discord between the two couples is about to break out, but Ferdinand prevents this. Prospero enters with Alonzo and the others, now all in amity; he gives his two daughters to their respective lovers. Ariel drives in the rebellious mariners, with Caliban and Sycorax, and they resign their claims to power. Ariel bids farewell to Prospero, but before he departs for his freedom he is joined by his love, Milcha, who has waited fourteen years for this moment.

# John Dryden, All for Love

## Act I

Opens in Egypt with a speech of Serapion, priest of Isis, on the many recent portents of disaster to come for Egypt. Alexas, Cleopatra's eunuch, regrets her passion for Antony, now a defeated man. Ventidius,

Antony's general, bemoans Antony's enslavement to Cleopatra; eventually he persuades the despairing Antony to return to military duty.

## Act II

Cleopatra's first appearance. She is partly genuinely distraught at the news of Antony's defection, but also partly cunning, plotting with Charmion, Iras and Alexas to get him back. Antony reports to Ventidius that Octavius has rejected his proposal of single combat, and they prepare to march against him. But Alexas then enters with greetings and gifts for Antony from Cleopatra, and he is persuaded to give her a final interview. She overcomes his initial resistance to her by various ploys, finally proving that she has rejected a secret offer of alliance from Octavius. They are reunited.

## Act III

In a ceremonial scene, Cleopatra crowns Antony with laurel. Ventidius begs Antony to take his military position seriously, and urges him to use Dollabella as emissary between the two camps. Dollabella, formerly Antony's friend but now of Octavius's party, is reconciled with Antony, and then claims to have procured good terms from Octavius for Antony, with the assistance of a third party. The third party turns out to be Antony's wife, Octavia, who comes in with their two daughters. Antony, torn between the rival claims of wife and lover, is won back to the former. But Cleopatra, alerted by Alexas, arrives to confront Octavia. She departs grief-stricken.

## Act IV

Antony, in a state of emotional turmoil, sends Dollabella to bring to Cleopatra the news that he must leave her. Alexas takes advantage of this to persuade Cleopatra to use Dollabella, who has long loved her, to arouse Antony's jealousy. This she does, and Ventidius, overhearing, tells Antony that both Dollabella and Cleopatra are unfaithful to him. Antony is outraged at this double betrayal; he first vents his anger on Octavia, who, recognising the continuing strength of his passion for Cleopatra, leaves him permanently. He then violently rejects both Dollabella and Cleopatra.

## Act V

Cleopatra is furious with Alexas at the failure of his scheme, especially when Serapion brings news that Antony and Cleopatra's combined naval fleet has joined forces with Octavius. Antony enters with Ventidius, planning a last-ditch suicidal assault on Octavius. Alexas, desperate to save his skin, tells Antony that Cleopatra has killed herself.

Antony and Ventidius then make a suicide pact, and Ventidius dies first. Antony stabs himself, and Cleopatra enters to find him dying. They are reconciled in the last moments of his life. Cleopatra sends Iras for the asps; she dies, followed by Charmion and Iras. They are found by Serapion and Alexas.

## *Nahum Tate,* King Lear

### Act I
#### Scene i
Opens with the Bastard (Edmund) describing the plot he has already forged against his brother Edgar. Kent pleads with Gloster on Edgar's behalf, but the old man is already persuaded of his elder son's treachery. King Lear then stages the love-test between his daughters. Gonerill and Regan answer predictably and are rewarded with large portions of land, but Cordelia answers abruptly because she does not wish to marry the Duke of Burgundy, her father's candidate for her hand; she loves Edgar. Lear disinherits her, and Burgundy refuses to marry her without her dowry. Kent goes into exile, disgusted with Lear's behaviour. Edgar protests his love for Cordelia, but she, now suspicious of all men, decides that she must test him. Edmund urges Edgar to flee from Gloster's anger; he cements his plot against his brother by showing Gloster the forged letter, supposedly from Edgar.

#### Scene ii
Kent returns in disguise to attend on Lear, who is insulted by Gonerill's gentleman. Gonerill defends her servant's insolence, and Lear in a rage curses her, and leaves her household.

### Act II
#### Scene i
Edmund stages a further scene against his brother, pretending Edgar has wounded him, and Gloster plans to have Edgar executed so that Edmund may inherit.

#### Scene ii
Kent repays Gonerill's servant for his insult to Lear. Kent is put in the stocks by the Duke of Cornwall, husband of Regan, who encourages him. Edgar on the heath decides to assume a disguise as a beggar to escape capture. Lear finds Kent in the stocks, and realises that Regan and her husband are unlikely to treat him any better than Gonerill. This is confirmed when Gonerill arrives and joins forces with her sister. The

sisters refuse to entertain their father in their homes unless he dismisses all his followers. He refuses, and goes off to the heath with Kent. The sounds of a storm are heard.

*Act III*
Scene i

Lear and Kent are on the heath in the storm. Lear, feeling the onset of madness, is led into a hovel by Kent.

Scene ii

The Bastard, revelling at a feast held by Gonerill and Regan as queens, receives simultaneous love-letters from them. Gloster, disturbed at the sisters' ungrateful treatment of their father, gives Edmund secret letters for the Duke of Cambrai to enlist help against them, but Edmund plans to reveal this to Cornwall at once. Cordelia arrives, and tearfully begs Gloster to help her father. She plans to disguise herself in order to find and help Lear. Edmund observes all this unseen, and plots to waylay and rape her.

Scene iii

Lear and Kent enter the hovel, and are joined by Edgar in his disguise as poor Tom. Lear has now gone mad. Gloster finds them, and prepares to take Lear to a place of safety.

Scene iv

Cordelia and her woman Arante are about to be attacked on the heath by Edmund's hired ruffians, when Edgar, still as Poor Tom, intervenes. He reveals his identity to the women, and Cordelia recognises his love as true.

Scene v

Gloster is captured by Cornwall and Regan, and blinded. He realises that he has mistaken the true natures of his sons. Cornwall is mortally wounded by a servant.

*Act IV*
Scene i

Edmund, wooing Regan in a grotto, by accident lets drop a love-letter from Gonerill. News comes of a peasants' rebellion against the rule of Gonerill and Regan; this has been exacerbated by the presence of the blinded Gloster.

Scene ii

Edgar meets up with his blinded father, who wishes to be led to the cliffs of Dover. Kent arrives with Cordelia, and Gloster urges him to lead the country against the oppression of Gonerill and Regan.

Scene iii
Gonerill hears that her husband, the Duke of Albany, has turned against her, and also that Cornwall has died of his wound.

Scene iv
Gloster and Edgar reach Dover cliff, and Gloster is deceived into believing that he has been saved from death by suicide. The mad Lear joins them, but runs away when gentlemen sent by Cordelia attempt to take him. Gonerill's gentleman comes to arrest Gloster, and is killed by Edgar, who finds her love-letter to Edmund.

Scene v
The sleeping Lear is attended by Cordelia and a doctor. He wakes and is reunited with her. She hears in the distance sounds of Kent's approaching army.

Act V
Scene i
Gonerill plans to poison Regan in order to secure Edmund for herself.

Scene ii
Edmund is in a dilemma, having promised himself to both sisters. He hears news of the approach of Kent's army.

Scene iii
An interval during the battle, when Gloster, unable to fight, sits under a tree and wishes for death; Edgar brings news that Lear's troops have lost and he and Cordelia have been captured.

Scene iv
While Albany orders his royal captives to be well treated, Gonerill and Edmund command their deaths. Edgar in disguise accuses Edmund of treason, and promises to produce a champion who will meet him in single combat. Lear, Cordelia, and the still disguised Kent enter in chains; Kent reveals himself to Lear.

Scene v
Edgar, no longer disguised, meets Edmund in combat and mortally wounds him. Albany now joins forces with Edgar. Gonerill and Regan discover their mutual rivalry over the body of the dying Edmund.

Scene vi
Cordelia and Lear in prison are about to be taken for execution when
Edgar enters to save them. Albany releases them from chains, and tells
the story of Edmund's end. He resigns his rights in the kingdom to Lear.
Edgar brings Gloster to be reunited with Lear. Lear, with Gloster and
Kent, plans to end his days in retirement, leaving Edgar and Cordelia to
rule the kingdom.

## *Colley Cibber,* Richard III

*Act I*
Scene i
The scene opens in the garden of the Tower of London. Lord Stanley
announces to the Lieutenant of the Tower that the Wars of the Roses
are over, and Edward IV established as King. King Henry VI enters, a
prisoner; he is informed that his wife and son have been taken prisoner,
but Tressell comes with the latest news from the battlefield at
Tewkesbury that Henry's son, Prince Edward, has been murdered by
Edward IV's brothers, Richard Duke of Gloucester (soon to become
Richard III) and the Duke of Clarence.

Scene ii
Richard in soliloquy rejoices at the turn of events, longs to become king,
and as a first step plans to murder Henry.

Scene iii
Richard enters Henry's chamber in the Tower and murders him. In a
soliloquy at the end of the scene, he plans next to murder Clarence, and
looks forward to the death of King Edward.

*Act II*
Scene i
Tressell meets Lord Stanley at St Pauls, where they have come to view
King Henry's corpse. They talk of King Edward's illness, and of
Richard's interest in Ann, widow of Prince Edward. She enters in
mourning, and Richard wooes her. Tressell and Stanley comment with
amazement on his success, and Richard joyfully soliloquises.

Scene ii
Courtiers meet in the Royal presence chamber to discuss King Edward's
death. The Duchess of York, mother to Edward, is full of foreboding
about the future, Clarence also having recently died. Edward's widow

laments and Richard pretends to share her grief, but remains behind at the end of the scene with the Duke of Buckingham to plan for his takeover.

## Act III

### Scene i

Richard welcomes his nephews, first young Prince Edward (heir to the throne), and then his little brother (the Duke of York) to London; the children are suspicious of their uncle. Richard then plans his next moves with his supporters Catesby and Buckingham. In soliloquy he scorns the idea of conscience.

### Scene ii

Ann regrets her marriage to Richard. Richard plans her death, having now become interested in his niece Elizabeth. Buckingham reports that the citizens have not responded favourably to his campaign for Richard's kingship. The two then stage a show for the Lord Mayor of London and the citizens to convince them of Richard's piety, and of the benefits of an adult rather than a child king. The Lord Mayor is convinced, and the coronation planned for the next day.

## Act IV

### Scene i

The two princes in the Tower with their mother and other women are filled with foreboding, especially when they hear that several of the Queen's relatives have been executed. Catesby informs them of the imminent coronation of Richard. Lord Stanley urges the Queen to take sanctuary with her sons with the Earl of Richmond in Brittany, but an order comes from Richard forbidding the princes to leave the Tower.

### Scene ii

Richard, now crowned king, asks Buckingham to rid him of the princes, but Buckingham is hesitant. Catesby offers to procure Tyrrell. Stanley brings news that the Queen's brother Dorset has fled to Richmond, and Richard recalls a prophecy that Richmond will be king. Richard prepares to entertain Tyrrell. Buckingham realises his folly in serving Richard.

### Scene iii

Tyrrell sends in his assassins to kill the princes, and while the murder takes place offstage Richard in soliloquy expresses his unease. Tyrrell returns to report the murder, and Richard makes further plans. Catesby brings news of another desertion to Richmond's side, and also that Buckingham is levying troops against Richard.

Scene iv
The Queen and the Duchess of York lament Richard's murderous activities. Richard mocks his mother, but then seeks to persuade the Queen to woo her daughter Elizabeth for him. She pretends to comply, and he is taken in. Ratcliff and Stanley bring news of Richmond's progress to England with a large navy. Ratcliff also reports that Buckingham's rebellion has failed, and Richard orders his execution. Finally Catesby announces that Richmond has landed at Milford Haven.

Act V
Scene i
Richmond appears with his followers.

Scene ii
Richard pitches his tent at Bosworth Field.

Scene iii
Richmond makes his final preparations for battle. He is informed by Stanley that the Queen has given her consent for him to marry Elizabeth.

Scene iv
Richard in his tent sends a messenger to Stanley to say that unless Stanley surrenders to him he will kill his son George.

Scene v
Richard, sleepless, soliloquises in his tent. He sees the ghosts of King Henry, Ann and the princes, who prophesy his fall. He wakes in terror. Catesby announces that dawn has risen.

Scene vi
Richmond rises, confident and cheerful.

Scene vii
Richard, preparing to fight, receives a paper brought by Norfolk foretelling his defeat. He urges on his troops. Catesby brings news that Stanley refuses to surrender.

Scene viii
Richard on the battlefield calls out Richmond. His troops are in disorder and Ratcliff urges flight but he refuses.

Scene ix
Richmond and Richard meet in battle at last, and Richmond wins the

fight. After Richard's death Stanley hands the crown to Richmond as Henry VII. Richmond, as uniter of the houses of York and Lancaster by his marriage to Elizabeth, looks forward to establishing peace.

# ACKNOWLEDGEMENTS

I want to acknowledge, as so many times before, the invaluable assistance of David Atkinson, who worked hard from an awkward facsimile edition of *Sauny the Scot* to render the text intelligible, and also supplied most of the annotations. I am also grateful for financial support from the Research Priority Fund of Birkbeck College.